AN EXPLORER'S GUIDE

Iowa

AN EXPLORER'S GUIDE

Iowa

Lauren R. Rice

with photographs by the author

FIRST EDITION

The Countryman Press ✷ Woodstock, Vermont

ISBN: 978-0-88150-833-8

Interior photographs by the author unless otherwise specified
Maps by Mapping Specialists, © The Countryman Press
Book design by Bodenweber Design
Composition by PerfecType, Nashville, TN

Published by The Countryman Press, P.O. Box 748, Woodstock, VT 05091

Distributed by W. W. Norton & Company, Inc., 500 Fifth Avenue, New York, NY 10110

Printed in the United States of America

10 9 8 7 6 5 4 3 2 1

For my mother, who brought me here and got me here.

EXPLORE WITH US!

Welcome to the first edition of *Iowa: An Explorer's Guide,* the state's most comprehensive travel companion. All attractions, inns, restaurants, and shops are chosen based on merit, not paid advertising. The layout of the book is simple, making it easy to read and use. Here are some pointers to help you get started.

WHAT'S WHERE

In the beginning of the book you'll find an alphabetical listing of special highlights, important information, and items unique to Iowa. You'll find advice on everything from where to swim in summer to where to find the best tenderloins.

LODGING

Places included in this book have been selected on merit alone. This is the only travel guide that tries to personally check every place of lodging to assure quality accommodations. It is also one of the few that doesn't charge for inclusion. It is recommended that you make lodging reservations well in advance, especially during the peak tourist season.

RATES

Please don't hold the author or innkeepers responsible for the rates listed as of press time. Rate changes are often inevitable. Note that the prices quoted do not include state and local taxes.

SMOKING

Virtually all Iowa inns, restaurants, and other establishments are smoke free—with the exception of casinos.

RESTAURANTS

Note the distinction between "dining out" and "eating out." Restaurants listed under Eating Out are generally more casual and less expensive than those listed under Dining Out.

KEY TO SYMBOLS

✪ **Essential Must See.** Not-to-be-missed sites and attractions.

Special Value. The special-value icon appears next to lodging, restaurants, and attractions that offer a particularly good deal.

Child and Family Friendly. The crayon icon appears next to lodging, restaurants, and activities that appeal to families with young children.

♿ The wheelchair symbol appears next to listings that are partially or fully handicap accessible.

🐾 **Pet Friendly.** The dog paw symbol appears next to lodgings and other establishments that are accommodating to pets. Not all establishments advertise the fact that they do accept pets, so be sure to inquire when making reservations if you are bringing Fido or Fifi with you. Some establishments may charge a rather nominal fee, while others may charge quite a bit to accommodate your four-legged companion.

🍸 **Nightlife.** This icon appears in front of restaurants and other establishments with good bars—or just good bars in and of themselves.

Keep in mind that as of press time, all information was current and accurate. However, as with anything in life, change is inevitable. Some new businesses will open, while others may close or change ownership. Stores and restaurants may change their hours. Please be sure to call ahead if you are traveling any distance to a particular establishment to avoid disappointment. If you happen to discover a business or attraction not reviewed in this book that you feel should be included, please let the publisher know so that it can be considered for inclusion in future editions. I would appreciate comments and corrections. Please write to me in care of The Countryman Press, PO Box 748, Woodstock VT 05091, or e-mail countrymanpress@wwwnorton.com.

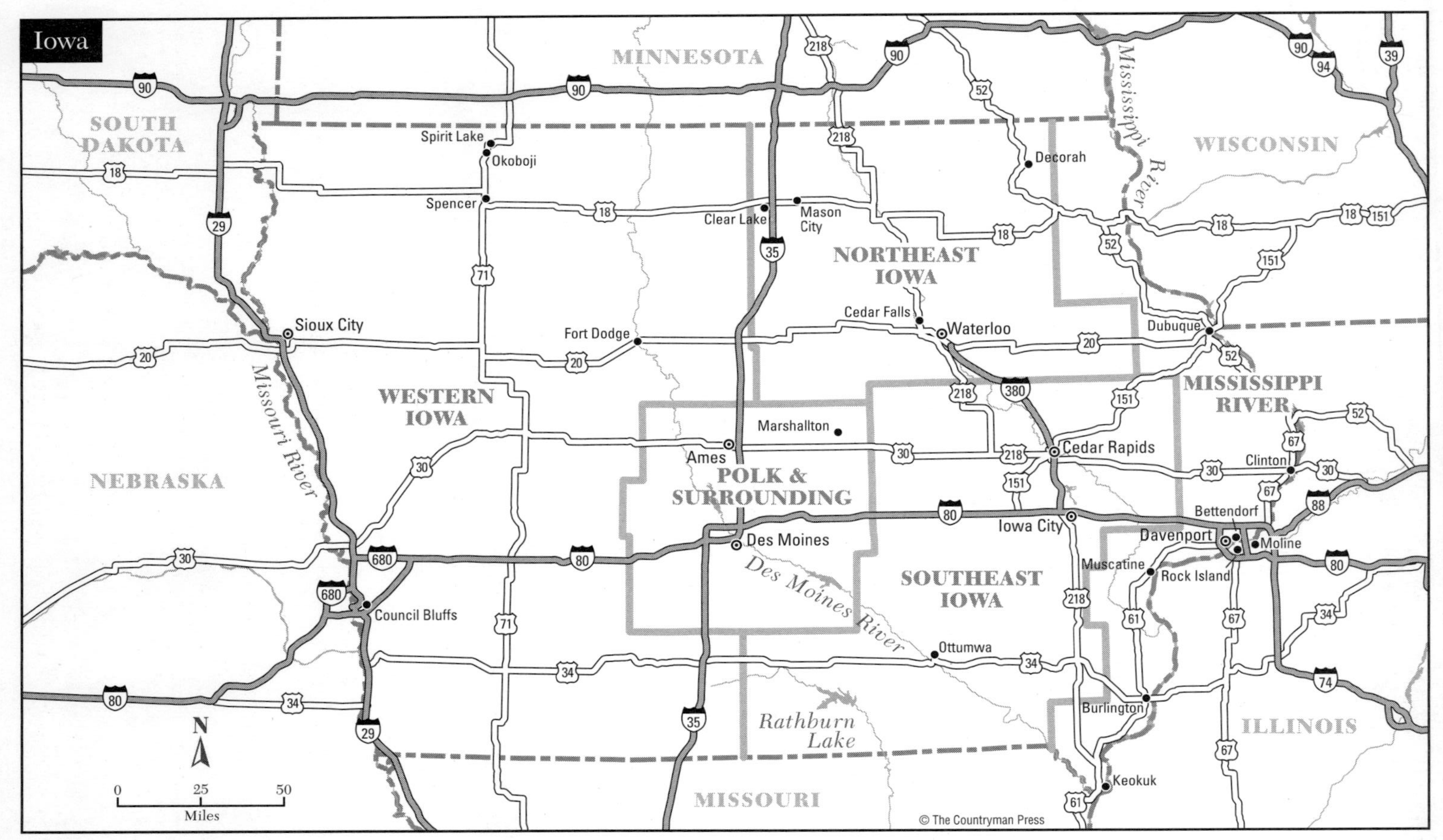

Iowa
MINNESOTA
SOUTH DAKOTA
WISCONSIN
NEBRASKA
ILLINOIS
MISSOURI
NORTHEAST IOWA
WESTERN IOWA
POLK & SURROUNDING
SOUTHEAST IOWA
MISSISSIPPI RIVER
Mississippi River
Missouri River
Des Moines River
Rathburn Lake
Spirit Lake
Okoboji
Spencer
Clear Lake
Mason City
Decorah
Cedar Falls
Waterloo
Dubuque
Sioux City
Fort Dodge
Marshallton
Ames
Cedar Rapids
Clinton
Bettendorf
Iowa City
Davenport
Moline
Des Moines
Muscatine
Rock Island
Council Bluffs
Ottumwa
Burlington
Keokuk
N
0
25
50
Miles
© The Countryman Press

CONTENTS

11 ACKNOWLEDGMENTS
12 INTRODUCTION
15 IOWA HISTORY: A BRIEF OVERVIEW
18 WHAT'S WHERE IN IOWA

1 Des Moines and Environs / 29

33 DES MOINES AND POLK COUNTY
55 STORY COUNTY
63 MARSHALL AND JASPER COUNTIES
74 MARION COUNTY
82 MADISON AND WARREN COUNTIES
87 DALLAS COUNTY
92 BOONE COUNTY

2 The Great River Road / 99

103 ALLAMAKEE COUNTY
110 CLAYTON COUNTY
121 DUBUQUE COUNTY
135 JACKSON AND CLINTON COUNTIES
143 SCOTT COUNTY
151 MUSCATINE COUNTY
155 LOUISA AND DES MOINES COUNTIES
160 LEE COUNTY

3 Northeast Iowa / 169

172 CLEAR LAKE AND THE MASON CITY AREA
181 MITCHELL, FLOYD, AND CHICKASAW COUNTIES
191 WINNESHIEK, HOWARD, AND FAYETTE COUNTIES
209 CEDAR FALLS AND THE WATERLOO AREA
224 FRANKLIN, HARDIN, BUTLER, AND GRUNDY COUNTIES

4 Southeast Iowa / 231

235 CEDAR RAPIDS AREA
256 IOWA AND POWESHIEK COUNTIES
266 IOWA CITY AREA
281 FAIRFIELD, MOUNT PLEASANT, AND THE VILLAGES OF VAN BUREN COUNTY
292 OTTUMWA AND THE LAKE RATHBUN AREA

5 Western Iowa / 307
311 IOWA'S GREAT LAKES: OKOBOJI AND ENVIRONS
320 NORTHWEST
Including Sioux City, Orange City, Storm Lake, Cherokee, Sac City, and Lake View
340 FORT DODGE AND ENVIRONS
348 WEST CENTRAL
Including Monona, Harrison, Crawford, Shelby, Audubon, Carroll, Greene and Guthrie Counties
365 SOUTH AND WEST
Including Council Bluffs, Red Oak, Stanton, Villisca, Clarinda, Shenandoah, Walnut, Atlantic, Greenfield, and Environs

385 INDEX

ACKNOWLEDGMENTS

Iowans are the most helpful people in the world, and I am ever so grateful for the copious and unending help Iowans offered me. My gratitude to Keri Jacobson is unending. She is the most dedicated, hardworking, unpaid intern a girl could hope for. My dear friend Frank Swoboda took on the arduous task of copyediting my manuscript with care and what seemed like delirious joy. I learned everything I know about photography from Lexi Wornson, and she and my other "research assistants"—Jason Boehme, Jessica Hicks, and Bill Morefield—turned my travels into adventures. Thanks to my aunt Sue for doing her homework. Many others offered their love and support in ways too many to mention: my parents, Deb and Dale Thelen; Jamie and Diana Wornson; Diane Hicks, who kept sending me helpful books; Michael "Miggs" Hubbard at DMACC; and all my friends at Back Country Outfitters, where great adventures begin.

I also could not have produced this work without the help of two great editors. Kim Grant, of Countryman Press, has been both an inspiration and a mentor. Nicole McClelland, of *Mother Jones* magazine, manages to both constantly believe in my writing and administer tough love, grammatical and otherwise. Thank you also to all of the editors and staff at Countryman Press for giving me the opportunity to explore this great state. Special thanks are in order for the tireless patience and hard work of my project editor Dale Evva Gelfand—I owe you way more than a tenderloin lunch. Thank you so to all the innkeepers, restaurateurs, chamber members, and characters I met along the way and on whose unending hospitality I depended. And, finally, I would be loath not to thank my mentors at the University of New Orleans, Dr. Randolph Bates and Dr. Carol Gelderman, from whom I learned that everything must have a point and that point should be expressed with grace and with care.

INTRODUCTION

So you've purchased *Iowa: An Explorer's Guide.* That means you already have the two qualities necessary to make the most of your travels in Iowa: curiosity and an open mind. Iowa is not known as a hot destination for travelers and has few of the features that normally attract tourists. There are no mountains, no shorelines, no large cosmopolitan cities, so it has often been overlooked as a destination. But don't be mistaken: Iowa is great place to explore.

I grew up in Des Moines, and I couldn't wait to move away. I fantasized about living somewhere urbane and glamorous. After college I moved to New Orleans and lived there for several years. Then I came back. Now I find myself defending my choice of home to my friends and family who live elsewhere, even native Iowans.

Many people only see Iowa as they are passing through on their way to California or New York. They don't know that much about Iowa, and what they do know—corn, pork, caucuses—is not all that alluring. Most people don't think about Iowa at all, much less as a destination.

But most people spend their vacations trying to avoid crowds, trying to eat at hidden-away local joints, trying to find that perfect landscape unspoiled by fellow travelers. They are looking for the authentic experience of a place. To those people, I offer Iowa. Every experience in Iowa is an authentic experience. There is no tourist industry to speak of, and so there are no tourist traps. While that fact presents some unique challenges for the traveler, it does mean that you will be seeing and experiencing Iowa as Iowans do. The attractions, lodgings, and restaurants I recommend in this book are patronized and beloved by the Iowans—this author included—who live with them.

Because Iowa has not established itself as a tourist destination, Iowans aren't really accustomed to tourists. You might surprise them with travel-related questions. Don't worry. Iowans are known for being helpful—sometimes too helpful. A small request in Iowa can lead to a landslide of assistance. An Iowan may not know how to get to your hotel, but he or she will be happy to track down a map, plot a route, point out any hazards, and then walk with you to make sure you get along all right.

Iowans are wonderful ambassadors for their state. I can't count how many times I had to throw my schedule out the window because of some spellbinding storyteller. The best piece of advice I can offer is to talk to the locals. Strike up a conversation with the guy on the next barstool or the lady sitting behind the counter at a shop. If you travel deep enough into rural Iowa, you won't be able to help talking to the locals. In small towns, where everyone knows everyone, folks are curious about outsiders, and the locals aren't shy about talking to strangers. Tell them you're traveling around, and they can reveal the best-kept secrets.

Let me offer as an example the elusive 2-pound hamburger. I first heard about this hamburger while enjoying a beer in a bar in Pleasantville. The couple sitting next to me, not recognizing me, politely inquired what I was doing in that corner of the world. When I mentioned I was writing a travel guide, their eyes lit up, and out came the colorful local customs and recommendations.

Not only did I learn about the wacky annual springtime ritual where Pleasantville High School alumni force the seniors to dress up in wild costumes and perform ridiculous stunts in the public square and the local custom of neighborhood barflies driving riding lawn mowers and horse-drawn buggies to the bar, but they told me about the "world's biggest hamburger, somewhere near Chariton." Intrigued with any meats of large size, I made a note of it in my journal. When I found my way to that corner of the state, I started asking questions. It wasn't necessarily the world's biggest hamburger, though at 2 pounds—with a matching bun—it was certainly a contender. "Oh, yeah," I heard from one local, "that place is owned by my husband's ex-wife's brother." I learned that it was in Williamson, in the only joint in town, that it had closed, and also that it was still open. Open it was, and, for a mere $7, I enjoyed a cheeseburger the size of my face—well, half of it at least. (The cheeseburger, not my face.) It is a great little secret, but you won't find it on Google.

This book exists because in Iowa there still are places to explore. Everywhere I went, every time I talked with the natives, I learned something new—some fascinating tidbit about local history, some quirky little restaurant serving up great homemade food, some tucked-away place I had to see. Even with as much as I learned for this book, I am convinced there are still countless treasures waiting to be unearthed. Don't think of this book as definitive. Think of it as a mustering point for your own expedition.

Iowa is a constantly surprising place. Take the Loess Hills in western Iowa. A landscape created from windblown silt thousands of years ago, it exists in only two places in the world: Iowa and China. And the one in Iowa is gorgeous. Rolling hills of woods and fields hide hollows and canyons that have the feel of being miles from civilization. It is also a virtually unknown landscape to hike, camp, and explore.

Or think about coffee. Most metropolitan cities are chock-a-block with Starbucks, one on every corner. Des Moines may seem like a provincial capital—the first Starbucks only opened in 2003—but Des Moines has a vibrant, homegrown, local coffee shop scene. Iowa, because it is sleepy and forgotten, has avoided the homogenization of mass-consumer culture.

Consider that because of shifts in the Missouri River, the Iowa town of Carter Lake is actually inside the city limits of Omaha, Nebraska.

Of course, the stereotypes about Iowa are based in truth. Iowa *is* corn and pork and insurance and the home of the Iowa Test of Basic Skills, but it is a whole lot more. In Iowa, I have relatives that serve elaborate Jell-O salads without a hint of irony, but I can also eat raw oysters flown in daily from both coasts. Iowa is home to the real Boondocks, USA, and also UNESCO's literary capital of the world, Iowa City. Amish farmers still use horses to cultivate their fields, but Iowa is also central to the green revolution through wind energy and ethanol fuels. Iowa is a land in transition. It's growing, but it grows slowly, and while it does, it maintains its wholesome charm.

This book is organized first into five regions, then by county or groups of counties, and then cities and their surrounding areas. Iowa is a big state, and to see it properly requires a lot of driving, but the highways and back roads are laid out in a grid so it's easy to navigate. A dedicated driver can cross the state in less than a day, which makes it perfect for day and weekend trips. Many of the attractions mentioned in this book are accessible from the main interstates and highways, so if you are driving through, slow down, pull over, and spend a little time exploring Iowa. But whether you are passing through, visiting for business or pleasure, or a resident hoping to discover more about your home, I know that you will find this book useful and fun.

—Lauren R. Rice, Des Moines, IA

IOWA HISTORY: A BRIEF OVERVIEW

The history of the state of Iowa reflects the history of the United States as a whole. It's believed that the first Europeans to explore Iowa were Louis Joliet and Jacques Marquette in 1673. They canoed down the Wisconsin River and into the Mississippi to the mouth of the Arkansas River. Supposedly they met with Native Americans at the mouth of a river—perhaps the Iowa—but the record is unclear. Further French exploration came with René-Robert Cavelier de La Salle who in 1682 traveled to the mouth of the Mississippi and claimed the lands around the river for the king of France.

In 1762 Louis XV, then the French monarch, transferred the vast tract of land known as Louisiana to Spain during the French and Indian War. Julien Dubuque, a Frenchman and trapper, became the first white settler in the state when he went to work on silver mines along the bluffs of the Mississippi River. The Spanish colonial government condoned Dubuque's claim.

In 1802 France under Napoleon reclaimed Louisiana from the Spanish and planned to make it the economic base for their colonial empire, shipping goods through the port of New Orleans to the Caribbean. The young United States saw French control of the port as a threat, so President Thomas Jefferson sent American diplomats to Paris to attempt to purchase New Orleans. To everyone's surprise, Napoleon sold not only New Orleans but the entire Louisiana Territory to the U.S. for a mere $15 million.

Jefferson, eager to explore the purchase, mustered the skills of Meriwether Lewis and William Clark to launch an expedition to the Pacific Ocean. In 1804, with a small crew, Lewis and Clark began traveling up the Missouri River from St. Louis, camping at several points along what would become Iowa's western border. Remarkably, only one crewman died on the trip. Sergeant Charles Floyd suffered a ruptured appendix; the crew buried him at the junction of two rivers near Sioux City.

In 1805 Lieutenant Zebulon Pike explored the Upper Mississippi River, encountering Native Americans, French and American trappers and traders, and visiting the camp of Julien Dubuque, still hard at work on his silver mines. Throughout the period of exploration, Iowa was redistributed numerous times, becoming part of the District of Louisiana, the Territory of Louisiana, the Territory of Missouri, having no government jurisdiction from 1821 to 1834, then being folded into the territories of Michigan and Wisconsin, before finally being designated "Iowa."

In 1808 the U.S. Army built Fort Madison, but it was so besieged by local Native American tribes that the soldiers absconded in the middle of the night, abandoning the fort as they burned it to the ground. Dragoons—lightly armed cavalry soldiers—explored the state, as did Nathan Boone, son of Daniel Boone.

During the early part of the 19th century, the state's history was marked with negotiations with the Native American peoples—some upstanding, others not so much. Fort Atkinson, near present day Decorah, was established to protect the Winnebago from the Sioux and the Sauk and to keep them from returning to Wisconsin. The Missouri Compromise ensured that Iowa would be a nonslave territory, and settlers started to move into the state. In 1838 Iowa received territorial status, and a constitutional convention and statehood followed in 1846.

In the same year, Mormons—in a mass exodus from their settlement in Nauvoo, Illinois, after the assassination of Joseph Smith—began the arduous trek across southern Iowa toward Salt Lake City. In 1847 Dutch settlers, under the leadership of Dominine Hendrik Peter Scholte, establish the community that is now Pella. Many other European immigrants followed, including the Irish, the Scandinavians, and the Czechs. The influence of their rich cultural heritage can be seen throughout the state.

Steamboats were the first major form of transportation into the state, traveling up the Mississippi and Des Moines Rivers. In 1856 huge land grants were made to railroad lines, which changed the landscape and the layout of the state. Before the railroads, towns and settlements hovered close to waterways. After railroads were established, towns sprung up in the countryside to service the trains. Legislators moved the capital of the state from Iowa City to Des Moines in 1857. The gold-domed baroque capitol building in use today was built in 1884.

Pioneer life was extremely difficult. The prairies were a sea of densely rooted tall grasses, with trees and woodlands not as readily available for timber as in eastern states like Illinois and Ohio. In areas where wood was sparse, settlers tended to live in straw or sod houses. Beneath the prairie sod was rich, black soil; but the grasses, tall as a horse, were held in place by a thick mat of roots, so the land wasn't tilled, it was busted—thanks in large part to John Deere's sharper and stronger steel plow. Blizzards, tornadoes, floods, and prairie fires were constant threats.

The violence of the Civil War barely brushed the state—though the tiny town of Croton in southeast Iowa received some damage from wayward shells in Missouri. The state did send an outpouring to recruits, finances, and food to the Union Army. All across Iowa slaves who were escaping the south on the Underground Railroad hid in cupboards and secret rooms in private homes.

The turn of the 20th century brought significant changes for the life in the state. In Froelich, a gasoline-powered tractor was invented, and with it came vast improvements in farm productivity. Automobiles ended the isolation of rural farms but also led to the decline of small towns as people drove to cities to do their selling, shopping, and working. The invention of the radio in 1919 brought news of the world to faraway places, including the boonies of Iowa.

The state is built on industry, especially the industry of farming. Companies like Pioneer Hybrids and John Deere got their starts in Iowa, and such thinkers as Henry Wallace, Bob Garst, and Dr. Norman Borlaug reinvented the way Americans thought about feeding the world. Small-town Main Street, which so many politicians speak about, still exists in Iowa today, along with 21st-century industries in aeronautics, engineering, finance, and computing; Microsoft and Google are among the companies that have most recently expanded into the state. Iowa is one of the nation's leaders in green energy, and massive wind farms are popping up in the corn and soybean fields first settled by our great-grandparents.

And today's descendants of the Native Americans, Germans, Irish, Czechs, and Scandinavians open their communities to new arrivals from Guatemala, Bosnia, Sudan, Somalia, Vietnam, Laos, and even Palau. All across the state, small communities are reinventing themselves for the global economy; farmers host trade delegations from China and Russia, and Iowa's universities draw cutting-edge international researchers working in areas from biotechnology to medical science to legal reform.

WHAT'S WHERE IN IOWA

AIRPORTS AND AIRLINES Three major airports service the state of Iowa: the **Des Moines International Airport** (515-256-5050; www.dsmairport.com), **Eastern Iowa Airport** (319-362-8336; www.eiairport.org) in Cedar Rapids, and the **Sioux Gateway Airport** (712-279-6165; www.flysux.com) in Sioux City.

Many locals use airports out-of-state for lower airfares. The **Quad Cities International Airport** (309-764-9621; www.qcairport.com) in Moline is just across the Mississippi from Davenport. **Eppley Airfield** (402-661-8017; www.eppleyairfield.com) in Omaha serves the Council Bluffs area. Kansas City is just 200 miles from central Iowa, and Minneapolis is 250 miles from Des Moines on major interstates.

Several of Iowa's smaller cities are serviced by regional airports, but most traveling within the state is done by car.

AQUARIUMS The only major aquarium in the state is the fabulous **National River Museum & Aquarium** (563-557-9545; www.rivermuseum.com) in Dubuque.

ART MUSEUMS The **Art Center** in Des Moines and the **Figge Art Museum** in Davenport are the premier museums in the state, though the **Cedar Rapids Museum of Art** is also exceptional. Many minor cities have small but outstanding galleries, as well.

ATTIRE For the most part, Iowans are casual dressers. With the exception of businesspeople and politicians, almost no one wears a suit. Jeans and T-shirts are perfectly acceptable, and polo shirts and khakis will get you through most "dress up" situations.

AREA CODE From west to east the area codes are 712, 515, 541, 319, and 563.

🍸 **BARS** Look for this symbol adjacent to restaurants and entertainment venues that are comfortable places to enjoy a drink or that offer a special menu of cocktails and beer. You'll find a friendly neighborhood bar in every

community, typically, on Main Street, and they run from full-service cafés to dive bars. Iowa City has the highest concentration and best variety of fun bars in the downtown area.

BICYCLING Iowa has a great bicycling culture. The state publishes a transportation map specifically for cyclists at www.iowadot.gov/iowabike, and cyclists should visit www.bikeiowa.com before a trip to learn about special-event rides. Only a few shops offer bike rentals, but the ones that do are indicated in the text. The yearly **RAGBRAI** (Register's Annual Great Bike Ride Across Iowa) attracts thousands of pedal pushers to make a cross-country trek from river to river.

BOAT EXCURSIONS Iowa is a landlocked state, but plenty of excursion boats traverse the rivers and lakes of Iowa. On the Missisippi River, Captain Jack and his crew at **Mississippi Explorer Cruises** (1-877- 647-7397; www.mississippiexplorer.com), with ports in Dubuque and Lansing, La Crosse and Prairie du Chien, Wisconsin, and Galena, Illinois, lead informative ecotours through the backwaters of the **Upper Mississippi National Wildlife Refuge** on small boats. In the Quad Cities try **River Cruises** in Le Claire (815-777-1660; www.riverboattwilight.com) for overnight trips up the river to Dubuque and back. In Okoboji the **Queen Mary II Excursions** (712-332-2183; www.arnoldspark.com) is a replica of the steamboats that once served as the major form of transportation on the lakes. The **Lady of the Lake** (641-357-2243; www.cruiseclearlake.com) cruises Clear Lake all summer. In Iowa Falls the **Scenic City Empress** (641-648-9517; www.iafalls.com) runs tours of the Iowa River.

BOAT RENTAL From two-story pontoon boats to Jet-skis, boat rental is available on most major lakes and rivers. For Clear Lake call **Clear Lake Boat Rentals** (641-357-5571; www.clearlakeboats.com) at the PM Park Marina. All kinds of boats are available to rent in Okoboji. Call **Okoboji Boat Works** (712-332-9904; www.parksmarina.com) for a great variety. In Lansing try **S&S Houseboat Rentals** (563-538-4454; www.ssboatrentals.com).

BOTANICAL GARDENS The **Botanical Center** (515-323-6290; www.botanicalcenter.org), in Des Moines is the largest all-season garden in the state. A glass dome protects it from both weather and foraging wildlife. The cities of Clinton and Cedar Falls have large and well-kept public gardens, too.

CAMPING Iowans love to camp in tents and in RVs. All summer long the state parks are filled with locals and travelers alike, sitting around campfires, drinking beer, and listening to music. The state park system offers the best camping. All state campgrounds have both reserveable sites and first-come sites; many have cabins for rent, as well. Campsites range in cost from around $10 per night for primitive

camping to $20 for RV sites with full hookups (electric, water, sewer). Many state, county, and city parks also have campgrounds. Some are listed in this book under "Camping," others are listed in *Green Space* with a cross reference.

CANOEING AND KAYAKING Iowa has a great network of water trails linking wetlands, streams, rivers, and lakes. Learn more about the public water-trails system through the **Iowa Department of Natural Resources** Web site www.iowadnr.com/watertrails. An excellent guide to these trails is *Paddling Iowa: 96 Great Trips by Canoe and Kayak*, by Nate Hoogeveen.

The best river for canoeing and kayaking is the **Upper Iowa River,** which runs through Decorah. Countless outfitters rent canoes and kayaks and can offer trip-planning assistance.

CAR RENTAL Commercial car rental companies serve all major cities and airports in the state.

CAUCUSES Every four years the political spotlight shines on Iowa. The state holds the first electoral caucuses, which usually offer early indications of which nominee each party will chose for its presidential candidate. Caucuses are held in 1,784 precincts to chose representatives for the 99 county conventions. County-level conventions send delegates on to the congressional district and state conventions, where delegates are then selected to attend the national conventions.

Caucuses are a unique form of politicking. Citizens stand together for the candidate of their choosing, and the number of delegates each candidate receives is based on the percentage of people standing for that candidate. Members of each candidate's party try to convince others to join groups. Alliances are formed and broken; the debate is spirited.

CHILDREN, ESPECIALLY FOR Look for the indicating attractions and activities geared specifically toward children, especially water and amusement parks. **The Science Center of Iowa** in Des Moines, the **Iowa Children's Museum** (319-625-6255; www.theicm.org) in Iowa City, and the **Family Museum** (563-344-4106; www.familymuseum.org) in the Quad Cities are museums that combine learning with play.

COCKTAILS See *Bars*.

COFFEE SHOPS Two kinds of coffee shops are found in Iowa. Espresso bars, in the spirit of Starbucks, serve gourmet coffee, lattes, and cappuccinos along with pastries and light fare. Most offer free wireless Internet access and are quiet places to relax and refuel. These types of coffee shops can be found in cities large and small throughout the state. Des Moines has an excellent coffee shop culture, but the best cup of coffee in the state is brewed at the **Java House** (319-341-0012; www.thejavahouse.com) in Iowa City, which brews each cup one at a time.

The other kind of coffee shop is the type found in every small town. Look for where the pickup trucks are lined up midmorning. In rural Iowa it is customary for locals to gather at these coffee shops to visit with friends and neighbors. Some are local businessmen, some are retired people. Sometimes the talk is just gossip, other times important civic decisions are made over a cup. These coffee shops are typically cafés that serve home cooking all day and offer free or very cheap refills of basic brew.

COSTS Iowa is a relatively inexpensive place to travel. In the *Where to Eat* sections, the cost of an average meal is indicated in $. For breakfast and lunch, $ is less than $5, $$ is $5 to $10, and $$$ is $10+. For dinner, $ is less than $10, $$ is $10 to $20, and $$$ is $20+.

COUNTIES Iowa has 99 counties. They were designed to be small enough so that any county resident could reach the county seat in a day's buggy ride. In most counties, the seat is still the largest city, and many have gorgeous courthouses in the town square.

COUNTY MUSEUMS Every county in Iowa has a county museum and historical society. They range from well organized and intriguing to repositories for the junk found in Grandpa's barn after he passed. Each offers greater insight into local and state history. Most are run by volunteers and have limited and seasonal hours.

DINING OUT The *Dining Out* sections include a range of restaurants from high-end white-linen-tablecloth and tuxedoed-waiters places to classic meat-and-potato steakhouse supper clubs. The definition loosely applies to restaurants where one would sit down, have a cocktail, and enjoy a high-quality meal.

EATING OUT The *Eating Out* sections are for casual dining and include hole-in-the-wall BBQ joints, bars that serve good food, and neighborhood cafés. As a whole they are more informal and less expensive than Dining Out restaurants.

EMERGENCIES For all medical emergencies call **911**. I've included some regional hospitals with emergency rooms, but for travelers in rural areas, the best way to get connected to medical attention is through emergency services.

ENTERTAINMENT Near the end of each chapter, you'll find listings for theaters, music halls, and bars that double as music venues. In general they are listed in order from "high-culture" events such as symphony and opera down to venues that specialize in rock and indie music.

ETHNIC RESTAURANTS You'll find the best assortment of ethnic restaurants in the state in **Iowa City** and

Fairfield. Most small towns have at least one Chinese restaurant and one Mexican restaurant. In general, the Chinese restaurants are not so good and the Mexican restaurants are excellent. It is my experience that chefs dedicated to preserving the art of 3,000 years of Chinese cuisine don't find their ways to small towns in Iowa. On the other hand, the migrants from Latin American countries have brought delicious, inexpensive Mexican cuisine to Iowa.

FAMILIES See *Children, Especially For.*

FESTIVALS Most small towns have a summer festival, and many have fall festivals. At the end of each part I have included a partial list of these festivals under the *Special Events* sections. These festivals always include a parade, food, music, and various competitions such as scavenger hunts and 5K races. The festivals I've included are some of the best representations of a traditional Iowa summer festival or are especially large or unique.

FAIRS The **Iowa State Fair** held every August in Des Moines is the biggest and longest-running cultural event in the state. But before the state fair can take place, every county in the state holds a fair. Traditionally, agricultural competitors win a county fair competition before moving on to the state fair. Some county fairs are small, mainly agricultural events while others, like the **Clay County State Fair** in Spencer, rival the state fair in size and scope. Most county fairs take place in July and early August.

FISHING The state requires sportsmen to carry fishing licenses, which can be obtained through the **Iowa Department of Natural Resources.** Call 515-281-5918 or visit their Web site (www.iowadnr.com/fish/regulations/licenses) for more information and to buy annual licenses online.

FOOD Iowa's signature dishes have to be sweet corn, "Iowa Chops" (massive pork chops), and the pork tenderloin. Sweet corn is best bought at a farmer's market or from a roadside stand the day it was picked. The best is prepared at home, either lightly boiled or grilled in the husk. Visit in August for the Adel **Sweet Corn Festival** (515-993-5472; www.partners.adeliowa.org/sweetcorn.page) or the **Iowa State Fair** in Des Moines to sample this treat. The Iowa Chop is so good, friends of mine who moved out of state asked me to bring some when I visit. (I flew with them in a cooler.) Look for my survey of the state's biggest and best tenderloins in Section 2: The Great River Road.

In rural areas, restaurant cuisine is going to be hearty home cooking (burgers, sandwiches, meat loaf—you get the picture). Every small town has a café and a local bar, so it's easy to get a bite to eat. Most small towns are laid out in a pretty typical way; just look for the "business district" sign off the highway, and follow it to the main street. In larger cities like Des Moines, Iowa City, and the Quad Cities, there are better selections for fine dining and ethnic cuisine.

GOLF Iowa has more golf courses per capita than any other state. They range from 9-hole municipal courses to elaborate, professional 18-hole and larger masterpieces. Try the **Brooks National Golf Club** (712-332-5011; www.brooksgolfclub.com), Okoboji. It offers a gorgeous 27-hole course built in cooperation with the Audubon Cooperative Sanctuary System.

GUIDANCE At the beginnings of many chapters in this book, look for a *Guidance* section with contact information for helpful, local organizations. Most of these organizations are run by area chambers of commerce. They often include an office open during normal business hours and a rack or two of brochures. Sometimes they are run by volunteers. Their Web sites vary from excellent to wanting, but if you are looking for more in-depth information on a topic or you are completely lost, these can be helpful guides. For even more information about what is going on in the state, visit the **Iowa Tourism** office at 200 East Grand Avenue, Des Moines. Call 515-242-4705, e-mail tourism@iowalifechanging.com, or visit www.iowatravel.com.

GREEN SPACE Most parts include a *Green Space* section, with listings for state, county, and city parks. Many of these parks include campgrounds.

HIKING Iowa is not known for great hiking. The many state parks and preserves don't have enough land for long-distance trekking. There are many trails, but most are paved for biking.

HISTORIC HOUSES AND MUSEUMS Iowa is packed with historic homes and museums and historic homes that have been converted into museums and historic homes inside museums. Log cabins must have been especially well built because many are still standing. And there are whole neighborhoods of elaborate turn-of-the-20th-century homes that serve as museums, restaurants, bed & breakfasts, or just residential homes.

HOURS In rural Iowa lots of establishments—especially bars—don't have set hours, have hours that change seasonally, or have hours that change capriciously. Some stay open as long as there are customers. Some entries in this book will say "Open to Close" or "Open to ?" to indicate joints that don't have set closing hours. Legally bars can sell alcohol until 2 AM, but in rural Iowa, lots of places close around 10 or 11 at night. On the other

hand, many are open during the day. When specific restaurant hours are available and fairly reliable, they are included here. Because many places, especially in rural areas, close when business is dead or change their hours often, only the type of meals served are stated. It's always best to call ahead. In general park hours are from sunrise to sunset, year-round, with some exceptions for hunters and fishermen. Campgrounds typically close at 10 PM to outside visitors.

HUNTING Hunting is an extremely popular activity for locals and visitors. Whitetail deer, pheasant, and wild turkey are common quarry. Licenses are required for all types of hunting in the state. Most can be purchased online through www.iowadnr.com, by calling 1-800-367-1188, or at one of the 900 license vendors across the state.

INFORMATION See *Guidance*.

MAPS The state of Iowa provides free maps in all visitors centers and rest stops along highways. The state also publishes a transportation map just for bicyclists, available at www.iowadot.gov/iowabike. My favorite map is DeLorme's *Iowa Atlas & Gazetteer*, which has 64 pages of maps done in excruciating detail. All the tiny dirt roads and hidden-away green spaces are listed along with topographical information.

HISTORY MUSEUMS For the most comprehensive museum on Iowa history, the **State Historical Museum** (515-281-5111; www.iowahistory.org) in Des Moines is absolutely essential. Otherwise, the best way to learn about Iowa history is through the various county and specialty museums throughout the state. See *County Museums*.

✪ **MUST SEE** Look for this symbol next to attractions that are totally awesome or the essential "thing to see" in an area.

NEWSPAPERS The *Des Moines Register* is the newspaper of record throughout the state, but most small cities have newspapers, as well.

POPULATION According to the 2006 U.S. Census, Iowa has nearly 3 million residents—and, yes, there really are more pigs than people, with nearly 17 million hogs growing fat in the state.

RECOMMENDED READING—FICTION Iowa has been the setting for quite a few best-sellers. *Shoeless Joe,* by W. P. Kinsella, a novel of ghostly ballplayers and an Iowa cornfield, inspired the hit film *Field of Dreams. Gilead,* by Marilyn Robinson, takes place in 1956; a minister contemplating life and spirituality writes a letter to his young son in this novel by the acclaimed Iowa Writer's Workshop professor. The epic novel *Ten Thousand Acres,* by Jane Smiley, is a reinterpretation of Shakespeare's King Lear played out on a family farm. In *The Bridges of Madison County,* by Robert James Waller, an Iowa housewife learns about passion and love in rural Warren County—an inspiration for the movie of the same name. *State Fair,* by Phil Strong, describes the adventures of the Frake family at the Iowa State Fair in the 1920s.

RECOMMENDED READING—NONFICTION Reading a few books about Iowa will give you a better understanding of the place and its people. *The Life and Times of the Thunderbolt Kid: A Memoir* is Bill Bryson's funny and poignant memoir of growing up in Des Moines in the 1950s and 1960s. *Little Heathens: Hard Times and High*

Spirits on an Iowa Farm During the Great Depression, by Mildred Armstrong Kalish, describes life in Iowa during those difficult years. *Iowa: The Middle Land,* by Dorothy Schwieder, is a comprehensive contemporary history of the state. Stephen G. Bloom's *Postville: A Clash of Cultures in the American Heartland* is an investigation into the conservative Jewish group that runs a kosher meat-packing plant in a small Iowa town. *American Dreamer: A Life of Henry A. Wallace,* by John C. Culver and John Hyde, describes the life of one of Iowa's—and agriculture's—greatest men. *Oddball Iowa* is Jerome Pohlen's exceptionally well-researched and funny guide to the quirkiest places in the state. In *Denison, Iowa: Searching for the Soul of America Through the Secrets of a Midwest Town,* by Dale Maharidge and Michael Williamson, an outsider describes life and the complex social issues at work in this controversial portrait.

SCENIC DRIVES The **Grant Woods Scenic Byway** (see the essay in Part 4: Southeast Iowa) runs through hills and fields from Anamosa to Bellevue. The **Great River Road Scenic Byway** travels down the length of the Mississippi from New Albin to Keokuk and showcases all the cities along the way. The **Loess Hills Scenic Byway** travels through the hills along the Missouri River from Akron to Hamburg and travels through Sioux City and Council Bluffs.

SHOPPING At the end of each part are listings for *Selective Shopping.* Shops were selected for this section based on their uniqueness or for being especially "Iowa." Entries are listed according to preference. Des Moines has more malls than the rest of the state, but for an eclectic shopping experience, visit downtown Iowa City.

SMOKING In 2008 the state passed a smoking ban, outlawing smoking in all public places. A few exceptions include the **Meskwaki Resort and Casino** (641-484-2108; www.meskwaki.com) in Tama and the **Iowa Veteran's Home** in Marshalltown.

SPAS **The Raj** (641-472-9580; www.theraj.com) in Vedic City provides clients with a holistic spa experience, including treatments, accommodations, and spiritual guidance.

SPECIAL EVENTS Lists of special events appear at the end of each part and are organized by month. I've included the best, most popular, and most unique events and festivals in the state. The state publishes an annual guide to all the events in Iowa. Visit the **Iowa Tourism** Web site at www.traveliowa.com for more information.

SPELUNKING The best place to explore caves is **Maquoketa Caves State Park** (563-652-5833; www.iowadnr.gov), which features several caves and limestone bluffs near the town of

Maquoketa. **Wapsipinicon State Park** (319-462-2761; www.iowadnr.com/parks) near the town of Anamosa also features two caves. **Spook Cave** (563-873-2144; www.spookcave.com) near McGregor is one of two cave tours done by boat.

STATE PARKS The **Department of Natural Resources** runs an excellent network of state parks. To learn more about all of the parks, visit www.iowadnr.com/parks. Most state parks include multiuse trails, playground equipment, picnic areas and shelters, and primitive and RV camping, and many have cabins for rent. Visitors can reserve campsites or cabins by calling 1-877-427-2757 or visiting www.reserveiaparks.com.

TAXES Iowa sales tax is 6 percent statewide. The hotel and motel tax is 5 percent. Some innkeepers include tax in their quoted prices, others do not.

TENNIS Most city parks and some campgrounds have free tennis courts, but for a real Wimbledon experience, visit the **All Iowa Lawn Tennis Club** (www.alliowalawntennisclub.com) in Charles City.

TIME ZONE Iowa is in the Central Time Zone and follows Daylight Savings Time.

TO SEE AND TO DO In the *To See* sections, you will find attractions such as museums, art galleries, and historical sites. The *To Do* section is for more active pursuits, from interactive museums to boat and bicycle outfitters to golf courses—anything that gets you up and moving.

TRAFFIC Most cities have rush hour; Iowa cities have rush 20 minutes. Traffic jams are rarely an issue, though there is seemingly constant road construction. For up-to-date information on construction on Iowa roads visit the **Department of Transportation** at www.iowadot.gov/roadcon.

VALUE Look for the symbol, which indicates an exceptional value at attractions and restaurants.

WEATHER Late spring and early summer in Iowa are mild. Summers are hot, humid, and punctuated with sudden thunderstorms. Autumn is generally cool and drier. Winter is cold with lots of snow and ice. Plan for sudden changes. A frigid winter night can turn into a 50-degree day.

WHEN TO COME There is plenty to do in Iowa year-round, but the best time to visit is summer. Iowans embrace kind weather when they can get it, and summers in Iowa feel like one long backyard cookout. Every small town has a summer festival (though most have fall festivals, too), and throughout the summer each county holds a fair as a prelude to the state fair in August. There is no tourist season, and only parts of a city get busy during special events. Most attractions are open only seasonally, generally from Memorial Day weekend to Labor Day weekend or October. Volunteers staff many historical attractions, and many have limited hours. Generally they are open on weekends. To get the most out of a visit, come during the summer, and stay for a Saturday.

WINERIES Iowa has a burgeoning wine industry. New vineyards and wineries are popping up across the state, and older wineries are enjoying increased popularity. Contact the Iowa **Wine and Beer Promotion Board** at www.iowawineandbeer.com for descriptions, contact information, and maps of most of the wineries and some of the breweries in the state. Touring wineries and sampling wines is lots of fun, and a selection of excellent wineries is listed in the To Do sections.

Des Moines and Environs

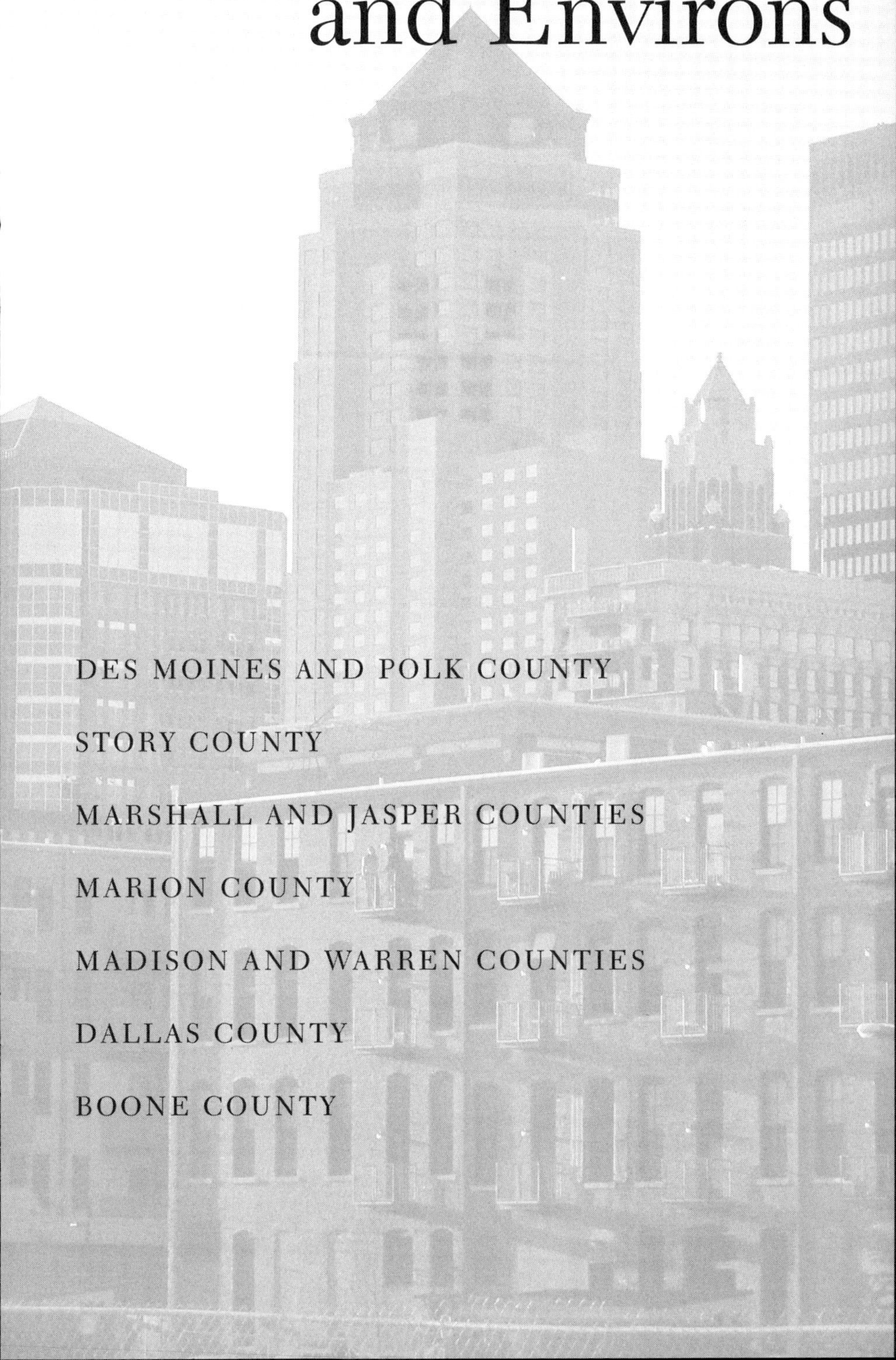

1

DES MOINES AND POLK COUNTY

STORY COUNTY

MARSHALL AND JASPER COUNTIES

MARION COUNTY

MADISON AND WARREN COUNTIES

DALLAS COUNTY

BOONE COUNTY

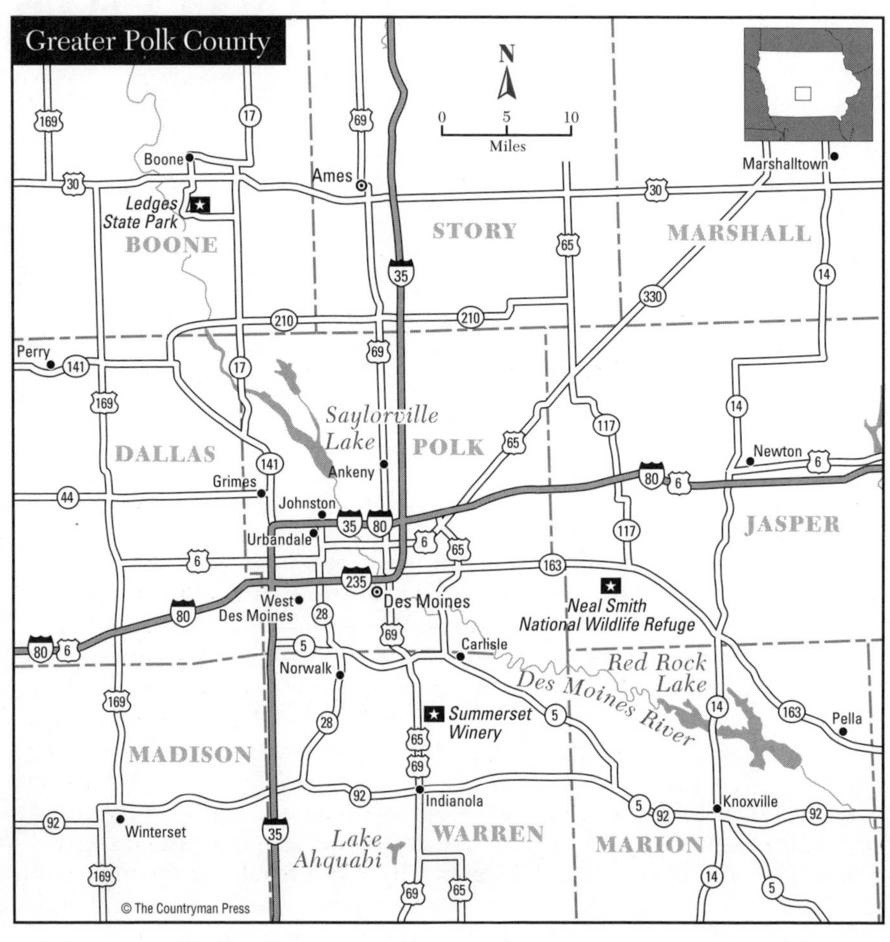

Greater Polk County
N
0 5 10
Miles
Boone
Ames
Marshalltown
Ledges State Park
BOONE
STORY
MARSHALL
Perry
Saylorville Lake
DALLAS
POLK
Newton
Grimes
Ankeny
Johnston
Urbandale
JASPER
West Des Moines
Des Moines
Neal Smith National Wildlife Refuge
Carlisle
Red Rock Lake
Norwalk
Des Moines River
Summerset Winery
Pella
MADISON
Indianola
Knoxville
Winterset
Lake Ahquabi
WARREN
MARION
© The Countryman Press

DES MOINES AND ENVIRONS: A BRIEF OVERVIEW

Nestled between the Des Moines and the Raccoon Rivers and radiating out from the crossing of Interstates 80 and 35, the capital and largest city in the state, Des Moines, is the heart of Iowa. The metro area extends beyond Polk County and is home to around 500,000 people. Des Moines has big-city attractions, restaurants, and entertainment but retains its small-town convenience and ease. Because the Des Moines area has so much to offer travelers, the scope of this chapter is limited to Polk County and the eight surrounding counties: Story, Marshall and Jasper, Marion, Madison and Warren, Dallas, and Boone.

The Des Moines and Raccoon River valleys were treasured by the Sac and Fox Indian tribes as hunting and fishing grounds. This geographically important spot was too good for the U.S. military not to claim, and in 1843 Fort Des Moines No. 2 was established. Initially it was a small outpost on the northern frontier, but by 1851 Fort Des Moines was incorporated as a city, and the name was changed to simply Des Moines in 1857, the same year it took over as state capital from Iowa City.

Because of its location at the hub of railway and interstate lines, Des Moines has long held a place of preeminence in the state. Business—especially the business of insurance—developed the city from Civil War–era shacks to the modern downtown. Today, greater Des Moines expands westward into the suburbs of Polk and Dallas Counties, while urban revitalization in the past decade has encouraged a dramatic rebirth of downtown. Remarkably, Des Moines grows without many of the problems like crime, traffic, and high prices that afflict other metropolitan areas.

The original city of Fort Des Moines was on the west side of the Des Moines River and the town of Demoin on the east side of the river. Residents on both banks joined together to win the site of the capital in 1857, but some shady dealings secured the site for the capital on the east. The separatist "Lee Township against the world" attitude of today's east-side residents is an echo of that historic rivalry.

Many of the cities and towns that surround Des Moines today—such as Ames, Ankeny, and Valley Junction—began as stops on the railroad lines that brought extensive growth to Polk County in the later half of the 19th century. Those railroad stops grew in turn, becoming centers of rural life.

Story County to the north of Des Moines is home to Iowa State University in Ames. Iowa State was one of the first land-grant institutions, and it is also one of the most lovely college campuses in the country. Ames itself is still a small town, but its large population of young people gives it a cosmopolitan vibrancy.

Marshalltown, the county seat of Marshall County, has a great old downtown, but don't miss the Big Treehouse just south and east of the city in a historic Lincoln Highway campground. The city of Newton, once known for building Maytag washing machines, is turning its factories over to windmill production and welcomes race fans to its state-of-the-art NASCAR track.

For more racing action, visitors can travel south to Knoxville in Marion County, the sprint car capital of the world. Lake Red Rock, Iowa's largest lake, covers much of Marion County and attracts both outdoor enthusiasts and a population of bald eagles that spend the winter nesting below the dam. To the north of the lake is the city of Pella. Famous for its Dutch population, it is a delight of historical museums, an authentic Dutch windmill and canal, and the tens of thousands of tulips that bloom there each spring.

Madison County, made famous by the book and movie celebrating its covered bridges, is an easy drive southwest of Des Moines on I-35. Both Warren and Madison Counties are pictures of pastoral splendor, with rolling hills, sleepy rivers, and cozy towns. Their location, soil, and climate make them the birthplace of Iowa's reemerging winemaking culture.

In Dallas County, travel the Raccoon River in a canoe, wander the brick streets of Adel, and dine on sweet corn before retiring to one of the many lovely bed & breakfasts or the historic Hotel Patee. To the north is Boone County, famous for its scenic railroad tours and the sandstone bluffs of Ledges State Park.

Each county is an easy drive from the center of Des Moines, making them perfect for day excursions or weekend adventures, and each has a distinct beauty and charm. Whether you explore one or visit them all, the counties at the center of the state are a great place to start exploring all that Iowa has to offer.

DES MOINES AND POLK COUNTY

The long, balmy days of summer fill the city of Des Moines with a festive spirit. Downtown office workers unwind with live music in Nollen Plaza. Dining and drinking move out to the sidewalks and patios of restaurants and bars. On Saturday mornings the Downtown Farmer's Market fills Court Avenue with the flavors of locally grown produce, meat, wine, and flowers. Every weekend, it seems, brings a festival celebrating food, music, and the arts. Each August the east side brims with the bounty of summer at the Iowa State Fair, a tribute to all aspects of life in Iowa, from 4-H awards to fine arts.

Iowa's longstanding policy of welcoming refugees and immigrants brought diverse populations to Des Moines. The south side is home to the Italian population, who settled there in the early part of the 20th century much as the same area later welcomed Hispanic immigrants. After the conflicts in Southeast Asia in the 1960s and '70s, numerous Asians—mainly Vietnamese, Hmong, Laotians, and Tai Dam—settled along the rivers. In the '90s, Des Moines and its suburbs welcomed Bosnians and other groups from the Balkans, and today Sudanese and other East Africans continue to settle around the Drake University neighborhood. For the traveler, the diverse populations of Des Moines offer a variety of delicious ethnic restaurants.

The growth of the suburbs west of the city makes them enticing places to explore. West Des Moines is the home of Jordan Creek, the metro's largest shopping mall, but many of the restaurants and businesses in the area are chains and big-box stores. Still, the countryside is never far from Des Moines. Johnston and Ankeny on the northwest side offer access to Saylorville Lake, with many opportunities for outdoor activities. Despite the growth of the area, it rarely takes more than 20 minutes to drive anywhere in the metro.

The many historic neighborhoods of Des Moines, such as Sherman Hill, Ingersoll Avenue, and the East Village as well as downtown, are the sites of the city's rebirth. What was once a sleepy (and, let's face it, dull) insurance town, now sees residents moving back to the city center. With them comes a host of new excellent restaurants, shops, festivals, and cultural events that make Des Moines an exciting place to explore.

GUIDANCE **Greater Des Moines Convention and Visitors Bureau** (1-800-451-2625; www.seedesmoines.com), 400 Locust Street, Suite 265, Des Moines. Open weekdays 8:30–5. Call or stop by for information, maps, and brochures.

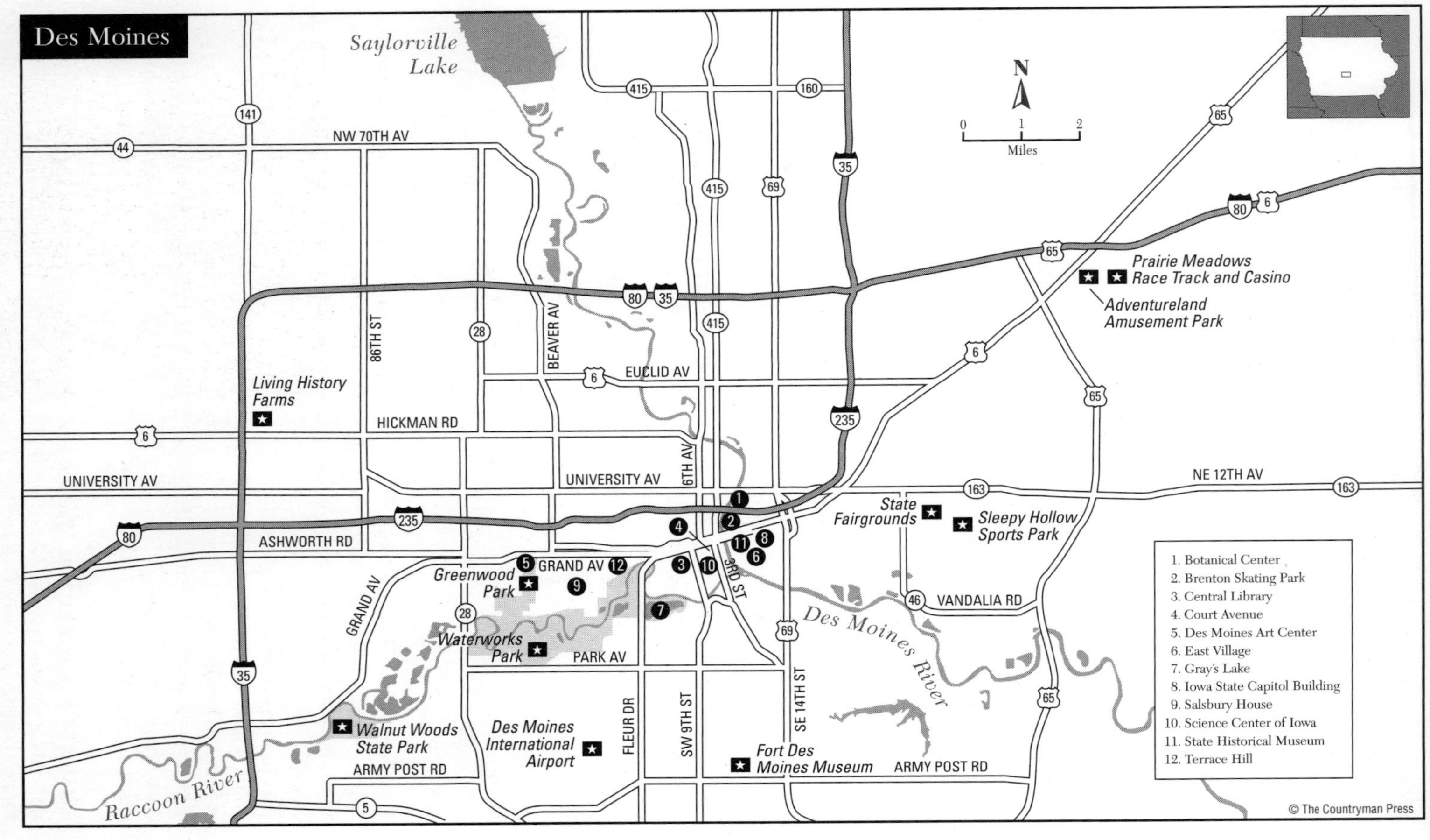
Des Moines
Saylorville Lake
NW 70TH AV
86TH ST
BEAVER AV
EUCLID AV
HICKMAN RD
UNIVERSITY AV
UNIVERSITY AV
6TH AV
ASHWORTH RD
GRAND AV
GRAND AV
3RD ST
PARK AV
FLEUR DR
SW 9TH ST
SE 14TH ST
ARMY POST RD
ARMY POST RD
VANDALIA RD
NE 12TH AV
Living History Farms
Greenwood Park
Waterworks Park
Walnut Woods State Park
Des Moines International Airport
Fort Des Moines Museum
State Fairgrounds
Sleepy Hollow Sports Park
Prairie Meadows Race Track and Casino
Adventureland Amusement Park
Des Moines River
Raccoon River
N
0 1 2
Miles
1. Botanical Center
2. Brenton Skating Park
3. Central Library
4. Court Avenue
5. Des Moines Art Center
6. East Village
7. Gray's Lake
8. Iowa State Capitol Building
9. Salsbury House
10. Science Center of Iowa
11. State Historical Museum
12. Terrace Hill
© The Countryman Press

GETTING THERE *By car:* All roads lead to Des Moines; you'll find Iowa's capital city at the intersection of **I-80** and **I-35**.

By air: **Des Moines International Airport** (515-256-5050; www.dsmairport.com), 5800 Fleur Drive, Des Moines. Most major airlines offer connecting flights into Des Moines.

GETTING AROUND Many neighborhoods are great for walking, but you'll want a car to get from one to the next. Des Moines has few traffic congestion problems and is easily navigated using the interstate system.

DART, the Des Moines Area Regional Transit Authority (515-283-8100; www.dmmta.com), offers service around the metro. Call or check their Web site for a schedule and routes.

MEDICAL EMERGENCY Call **911.**

Mercy Medical Center (515-643-4160; www.mercydesmoines.org), 1111 Sixth Avenue, Des Moines, is located just north of downtown.

MEDIA ***The Des Moines Register*** (1-800-247-5346; www.desmoinesregister.com) is the paper of record in Iowa. Its "Datebook," published on Thursdays, is the weekly entertainment guide.

Cityview (515-953-4822; www.dmcityview.com) is the weekly alternative paper, offering both news and entertainment information.

INTERNET ACCESS/PUBLIC LIBRARY **Central Library** (515-283-4152; www.desmoineslibrary.com), 1000 Grand Avenue, Des Moines. Open 9–8 Mon.–Thurs., 9–6 Fri., 9–5 Sat., and 1–5 Sun. The Central Library is the largest of the six branches of the Des Moines Public Libraries. All branches offer free wireless Internet access and public computers, but by all means visit the modern, copper-colored Central Library, which was featured in *Architectural Digest.* Author readings and programs for both children and adults are a constant.

Most coffee shops and hotels also offer free wireless Internet.

✷ To See

Des Moines Art Center (515-277-4405; www.desmoinesartcenter.org), 4700 Grand Avenue, Des Moines. Open 11–4 Tues., Wed., Fri.; 11–9 Thurs.; 10–4 Sat.; 12–4 Sun., closed Mon. Admission: free, but donations are welcomed. For a city the size of Des Moines, the Art Center is exceptional. Visitors can stare down Edouard and Marie-Louise Pailleron in John Singer Sargent's portrait and admire the works of Edward Hopper, Henri Matisse, Georgia O'Keeffe, and Francis Bacon. The building itself is a

ART INSIDE AND OUT AT THE ART CENTER IN DES MOINES

THE GILDED DOME OF THE IOWA STATE CAPITOL

work of world-class architecture, and the grounds are studded with an impressive sculpture collection. In June the formal rose garden on the south side of the building blossoms in a vast array of colors and variety of flowers. Don't miss lunch beside the reflecting pool at the Art Center Restaurant, open Tue.–Sat. 11–2. The museum's gift shop offers unique gifts.

Iowa State Capitol (515-281-5591; www.legis.state.ia.us), East 12th Street and Grand Avenue, Des Moines. Tours last 80 minutes and are available weekdays 8–3:30, Sat. hourly 9:30–2:30. Admission: free. The gold dome of the Iowa State Capitol, dating to 1886, is one of the most impressive and prominent features of the Des Moines skyline. Up close, the scale and magnificence of the structure is even more awe inspiring. The dome is 275 feet high and 80 feet in diameter and gilded with 23-karat gold. The building houses the state's governing bodies as well as a collection of historical artifacts and art. The law library, with its distinctive spiral staircases, is open for public use.

State Historical Museum (515-281-5111; www.iowahistory.org), 600 East Locust Street, Des Moines. Open 9–4:30 Mon.–Sat., 12–4:30 Sun. Admission: free. The State Historical Museum showcases Iowa's history from the Ice Age glaciers that deposited the rich topsoil to an exhibit on Iowa's first-in-the-nation caucus system. Browse the library and archives for genealogical information, and possibly discover that your great-uncle Sven was an early Iowa settler. Visitors view the museum on their own; guided tours are given on the third Saturday of every month, but tickets sell out quickly, so reserve a spot in advance. The State Historical Museum also offers café dining and a museum shop.

A FAMILY OF BISON MAKES THE STATE HISTORICAL MUSEUM HOME

Living History Farms (515-278-5286; www.lhf.org), 2600 111th Street, Urbandale. Open May 1–Sept. 3 daily 9–5, Sept. 5–October 21 Wed.–Sun. 9–5. Admission: $11 adults, $10 seniors, $6 children 4–12. Living History Farms is a series of working farms, complete with crops, livestock, and volunteers in period costumes giving visitors an up-close experience with Iowa life through the ages, from Native American farms to the 1875 town of Walnut Hill. Cabinetmakers build authentic furniture using tools from the period. Housewives cook on wood-burning stoves and tend kitchen gardens. In the general store, visitors can purchase rock candy, bullwhips, or a mouth harp, among other items.

✐ **Science Center of Iowa** (515-274-6868; www.sciowa.org), 401 West Martin Luther King Jr. Parkway, Des Moines. Hours and admission vary, depending on activity; call ahead, or check their Web site. This bright, modern facility lets amateur scientists explore caves, travel through space in the Planetarium, and become mesmerized watching Foucault's pendulum. Exhibits change often, with a focus on hands-on learning that's fun and educational. The IMAX theater screens both documentary films and first-run movies. Snacks and ice cream are available in the Food Chain Café and the A-ha! gift shop. Visit their Web site to register for classes, camps, and special events.

✐ **Botanical Center** (515-323-6290; www.botanicalcenter.com), 909 Robert D. Ray Drive, Des Moines. Open daily 10–5. Admission: $4 adults, $2 students and seniors. Under a glass dome, diverse ecosystems thrive at the Botanical Center, with a koi pond, a running stream, cacti, greenhouses, and landscaped gardens along the river. Kids can enjoy a scavenger hunt or pick up a backpack to use during their visit. Guided tours are available, and music and programs occur throughout the year.

✐ **Blank Park Zoo** (515-323-8383; www.blankparkzoo.com), 7401 Southwest Ninth Street, Des Moines. Open May–Sept. daily 10–5, Oct.–Apr. Wed.–Sun. 10–4. Admission: $8 adults, $5 children 3–14. Blank Park is a relatively small zoo, but that scope makes it less intimidating than larger facilities. Ancient Aldabra tortoises reside near the entrance. The zoo also features an African savanna, big cats, a sea lion exhibit, a crawl-through prairie dog exhibit, and camel rides. There is also a fantastic petting zoo with a llama and some very demanding domestic goats. The zoo sponsors several events, such as Friday Family Night and Zoo Brew. Check their Web site for more information.

Terrace Hill (515-281-3604; www.terracehill.org), 2300 Grand Avenue, Des Moines. Open Mar.–Dec. Tues.–Sat. 10–1:30. Admission: free. Tours last 45 minutes to an hour and begin each hour on the half hour. Built by Iowa's first millionaire, Benjamin Franklin Allen, and completed in 1869, the governor's mansion sits high above the Raccoon River Valley. The building is filled with stained glass, period furniture, and a one-person elevator. Guides explain the role each room played historically. The governor and his family live on the third floor of this ornate mansion. The grounds are

TERRACE HILL, THE GOVERNOR'S MANSION

exceptional, and Terrace Hill is in the center of the beautiful "South of Grand" neighborhood that overlooks the Raccoon River.

Salisbury House and Gardens (515-274-1777; www.salisburyhouse.org), 4025 Tonawanda Drive, Des Moines. Public tours available Mar. 1–Dec. 31 Tues.–Fri. and Sun. at 1:00 and 2:30. Admission: $7 adults, $6 seniors, $3 children. Built as a dream home by Carl Weeks and his wife, the Salisbury House is one of the most impressive mansions in Des Moines. Constructed between 1923 and 1928 and modeled after "Kings House," a 15th-century English manor house, this 42-room mansion contains 16th-century English oak, English flint work, and rafters as old as Shakespeare. The richly furnished and well-preserved home is open to a marvelous tour, but hours and schedules are notoriously fussy, so call ahead.

Fort Des Moines Museum (1-888-828- 3678; www.fortdesmoines.org), 75 East Army Post Road, Des Moines. Tours available Mon.–Fri. 10–4. Admission: $5 adults, $4 children. Technically the third Fort Des Moines in Iowa history—following a military fort downriver and the initial site of the city itself—Fort Des Moines was the location of major strides toward equality in U.S. military history. The fort was home to two companies of the all-black U.S. Army 25th Infantry during World War I. The army's first officer-candidate class of African Americans graduated from Fort Des Moines. Then during World War II, the first and largest Women's Army Auxiliary Corps was formed in the same spot. Today it is home to a U.S. Army Reserve recruitment center, and visitors can see artifacts and learn more about these events.

✷ To Do

Downtown Farmer's Market (515-286-4943; www.downtowndesmoines.com) stretches the length of Court Avenue from the Polk County Courthouse to the Des Moines River Saturday mornings 7–12 from Mother's Day weekend to Halloween. Start early; bring cash and an appetite. With way more than fruits and vegetables, this farmer's market is a weekly extravaganza of food, drinks, music, and people watching. Shop for everything from locally raised elk meat to fine Iowa wine to Hmong-grown herbs and vegetables. Start with a cup of coffee from **Java Joes** (see *Eating Out: Coffee and Treats*) on Fourth Street, and then get a sticky pecan roll from the stand on the corner of Fourth Street and Court. It will change everything you know about breakfast pastry.

FRESH-PICKED HEIRLOOM TOMATOES AT THE FARMER'S MARKET IN DOWNTOWN DES MOINES

Brenton Skating Plaza (515-284-1000; www.brentonplaza.com), 520 Robert D. Ray Drive, Des Moines. Open winter months daily 10 AM–11 PM. Admission: $3 adults, $2 children, $2.50 skate rental. This permanent open-air ice-skating rink can stay frozen up to 50 degrees, which makes for a long season. The rink is downtown next to the river and is extremely popular and very busy. Be ready to dodge careening children, hand-in-

SPORTS AROUND DES MOINES

Iowa grows more than corn; it grows professional athletes. The **Iowa Cubs** are the AAA team that feeds the Chicago Cubs. On balmy summer evenings, watch up-and-coming Cubbies step up to the plate at **Principal Park** (515-243-6111; www.iowacubs.com), 1 Line Drive, Des Moines. The **Des Moines Buccaneers** (515-278-2827; www.bucshockey.com) play at the **95KGGO Arena** at 7201 Hickman Road in Urbandale. "Bucs" games get a little rowdy, with lots of beer drinking, on-ice brawls, and bawdy chants from the crowd. **Iowa Chops** (515-564-8700; www.iowachops.com) play at the **Wells Fargo Arena, 833 Fifth Avenue,** downtown. The hockey is of a higher caliber, and the games are more family friendly but less exciting. Another local favorite for all types of sports enthusiasts are the events of the **Drake University Athletics** (515-271-3647; www.godrakebulldogs.com). The Bulldogs play fantastic basketball, among other sports, but they are famous for hosting the **Drake Relays,** a world-class track meet held every April. Call or visit their Web site for more information.

hand teenage lovebirds, and former high-school hockey stars. Daytime hours are much quieter. The snack bar offers hot chocolate and other treats. Bike rental is available during the summer.

✐ **Sleepy Hollow Sports Park** (515-262-4100; www.sleepyhollowsportspark.com), 4051 Dean Avenue, Des Moines. Hours and pricing depend on activity. Sleepy Hollow is a multiuse sports complex. In winter there is tubing and skiing. In summer there are batting cages, miniature golf, a driving range and nine-hole golf course, a climbing wall, sand-volleyball courts, and go-karts. Sleepy Hollow is also home to the **Renaissance Festival** on weekends in September, so bring your battle ax and Elizabethan gown. Also enjoy a pretty serious haunted forest during October and music events throughout the year.

Prairie Meadows Race Track and Casino (1-800-325-9015; www.prairiemeadows.com), 1 Prairie Meadows Drive, Altoona. Open 24 hours daily. Prairie Meadows tempts gamblers with both on-track and off-track horse racing and casino games, but the restaurants are nothing to write home about—especially after you've dropped your mortgage payment betting on the ponies.

✐ **Adventureland** (1-800-532-1286; www.adventureland-usa.com), 305 34th Avenue Northwest, Altoona. Open late Apr.–Sept. daily 10–10. Admission: $31 adults, $27 children under 10 and seniors, $5 parking. This locally owned amusement park is neither big nor showy, but in its down-homeyness, it's quaint. Cool off in the unnatural teal water of the log ride, watch a corny song-and-dance show, and scream your way through the Twister, one of the park's wooden roller coasters. On one ride, thrill seekers are spun in a centrifuge; the floor drops out beneath them as they stick to the walls. There is also the usual assortment of carnival food: corn dogs, pizza, and ice cream from the future. Plan for steamy sidewalks, crying children, and high prices, but embrace Adventureland for what it is: a pretty good time.

Jasper Winery (515-282-9463; www.jasperwinery.com), 2400 George Flagg Parkway, Des Moines. Open daily for tours and tasting. This urban winery began operation in Newton in a turn-of-the-20th-century farmhouse. Their wines handcrafted from French-American grapes proved so popular and successful that Jasper Winery relocated to a larger facility in Des Moines Water Works Park in the summer of 2008. The tasting room offers a view of the production area and barrel room, giving visitors a close-up peek at winemaking. Enjoy a glass of wine either in the café or outside on the large patio. Call or check their Web site for more information.

✷ Green Space

Gray's Lake (515-237-1386; www.ci.des-moines.ia.us/departments/pr/grayslake.htm), Fleur Drive and George Flagg Parkway, just south of downtown Des Moines. Join locals on warm, sunny days as they jog, rollerblade, and walk dogs around the 2-mile paved trail at Gray's Lake. The bridge over the lake is illuminated with multicolored lights at night. If you're inclined toward water-borne activities, rent a paddleboat, swim, or fish in permitted areas. Paddleboat, canoe, and kayak rentals are available for $4 per half hour. Rental hours are 10–8 daily through the summer, and then weekends, weather permitting. The Gray's Lake path connects to trails that lead to **Principal Park,** downtown, and **Water Works Park.** Gray's Lake is also the site for the annual **Hy-Vee Triathlon,** which was the qualifying event for the 2008 Olympics.

Ashworth and Greenwood Parks (515-237-1386; www.dmgov.org/departments/pr/parks/Greenwood.htm) 4500 Grand Avenue in Des Moines. These parks extend behind the Des Moines Art Center and have formal gardens, a prairie-and-pond learning facility, and an amphitheater.

Union Park (515-237-1386; www.dmgov.org), 1801 Pennsylvania Avenue, Des Moines. Overlooking the Des Moines River and **Birdland Marina**, the park's best attraction is the **Heritage Carousel** (515-323-8200; www.heritagecarousel.org), a

A RUNNER ENJOYS THE QUIET TRAIL AROUND GRAY'S LAKE

A PEACEFUL AFTERNOON IN ASHWORTH PARK

classic wooden carousel with a menagerie of animals and scenes from around Des Moines. It's only 50 cents for kids to ride, $1 for adults. Open Memorial Day–Labor Day and some weekends in May and Sept., Tues.–Thurs. 12–7, Fri.–Sun. 11–8. Union Park's playground offers an excellent rocket slide, which towers over the park. The park also has walking paths, picnic tables, and a wading pool.

🐾 **Raccoon River Park** (515-222-3444; www.wdm-ia.com) 2500 Grand Avenue, West Des Moines. This 600-acre park on the Raccoon River has a fishing lake, a beach, hiking trails, and soccer and softball fields. There is also an off-leash dog park. Permit required.

Brown's Woods (515-285-7612), Southwest 63rd Street and Brown's Woods Drive, West Des Moines. Tucked into an urban setting, the trails at Brown's Woods offer hikers an easy 10-minute loop or a longer 1-hour loop through Iowa's largest forest preserve.

Saylorville Reservoir Area (515-964-0672; www.corpslakes.us/saylorville) north of Des Moines. The Saylorville Lake area offers a variety of outdoor activities from boating, camping, and disk golfing to bike trails, swimming, and hunting.

BIKE IOWA

Iowans take biking very seriously. All year, road warriors cruise the back roads and highways and travel up and down the many bike trails around the city. Pedal the **Neal Smith Trail,** a 24-mile multiuse trail that travels from the Botanical Center in Des Moines to the Saylorville Lake reservoir (see *Green Space*). Bring your own bike as there are few rental facilities in the Des Moines area. For more information on cycling and trails in Des Moines and throughout the state, contact **Bike Iowa** (www.bikeiowa.com).

Jester Park (515-323-5366; www.conservationboard.org/Pages/jp.aspx), 11407 Northwest Jester Park Drive, Granger. Located a half hour from downtown, Jester Park, on the western shore of Saylorville Lake, offers 8 miles of hiking trails, picnicking, boating, an 18-hole golf course, an equestrian center, and elk and buffalo herds.

Big Creek State Park (515-984-6473; www.iowadnr.gov/parks) IA 415, Polk City. On the north side of the Saylorville Lake project, Big Creek is a favorite park for locals to swim, picnic, fish, and boat in the clear waters. There are an abundance of playgrounds plus sports fields for disk golf, volleyball, and softball. Big Creek is at the end of the Neal Smith Trail and is also connected to the **Central State Park Bike Route,** a 91-mile trail that connects the park with **Ledges State Park** in Boone County and, farther on, **Springbrook State Park** in Guthrie County (see Section 5: Western Iowa). Boats and bikes can be rented from the **Big Creek Marina** (515-984-6083; www.bigcreekmarina.com), 12397 Northwest 89th Court, Polk City. The marina also offers sailing lessons.

✷ Where to Stay

Fair warning: While an abundance of franchise hotels pepper the interstate exits and suburbia, and there are countless run-down motels within the city proper, Des Moines has a deficiency of quality, inexpensive, independent establishments. Many of the cheap motels that are not chains are downright sketchy.

HOTELS AND MOTELS **Hotel Fort Des Moines** (1-800-532-1466; www.hotelfortdesmoines.com), 1000 Walnut Street, Des Moines. Listed on the National Registry of Historic Places, the Hotel Fort Des Moines has been a landmark—physically and politically—of the Des Moines landscape for 80 years. The well-appointed rooms welcomed Mae West and Jack Kennedy. Standard suites include a mini-fridge, a sofa, high-speed Internet, and use of the penthouse spa. The Hotel Fort Des Moines is also home to two excellent restaurants that transcend both the typical hotel restaurant food and scene. The **Raccoon River Brewing Company** (515-362-5222; www.raccoonbrew.com) brews several types of delicious beers on site and serves upscale pub food; lunch and dinner $$. **Django** (515-288-0268; www.djangodesmoines.com) offers fine French dining in a friendly environment; dinner $$–$$$. Rooms from $69–$130.

The Suites at Locust (515-288-5800; www.800locust.com), 800 Locust, Des Moines. Opened in 2000, this beautifully renovated downtown building began life as the original Des Moines Club and later became the home of the Za-Ga-Zig Shriners temple. After being abandoned for 11 years, the building was reborn as a hotel that combines Old-World elegance and modern convenience. There are 51 guest rooms, 31 fireplace suites, and 11 whirlpool suites. Amenities include in-room dining, valet parking, high-speed Internet, coffeemakers, and refrigerators. Guests have access to the business center, health club, and spa, as well as dining privileges at the **Embassy Club** (515-244-2582; embassyclub.com), the hallowed private dining club located at the top of 801 Grand (the tallest building in Iowa); lunch and dinner $$–$$$. Rates includes a full breakfast of omelets, eggs to order, waffles, and more in the **Cosmopolitan Lounge,** the bar in the lobby. Rooms from $179–$450.

Heartland Inn (515-967-2400, 1-800-334-3277; www.heartlandinns.com) Interstate 80 Exit 141, 300 Northwest 34th Avenue, Altoona. This Iowa-based chain of motels is, without fail, clean, friendly, and serviceable. The Heartland Inn also has a location near the airport; see the Web site for more information. Rooms usually include two queen beds, Internet access, and a continental breakfast in the morning. Rooms from $80–$165.

Adventureland Inn (515-265-7321; www.adventurelandpark.com) Interstate 80 at IA 65, Altoona. Adjacent to the amusement park, the hotel has a great indoor pool with a swim-up bar, hot tubs, and tropical courtyards; it's a good place to stay with children after a long day of roller coasters and funnel cakes. There is also a good Sunday brunch buffet in the restaurant. Rooms from $75–$195.

Village Inn Motel (515-265-1674; www.villageinnmotel.com), 1348 East Euclid Avenue, Des Moines. This basic motel offers 62 rooms, cable, and wireless Internet access. Rooms from $45–$160.

BED & BREAKFASTS **The Cottage** (515-277-7559; www.thecottagedsm.com), 1094 28th Street, Des Moines, is a 1929 brick home in the historic Kingman Avenue neighborhood near Drake University. Becky Brown and John Gatts welcome guests to their cozy four guest room bed & breakfast, with a pool table on the second floor and a hot tub on the patio. The Cottage is a favorite among visiting politicians during caucus season, including now-president Barack Obama. Rooms (including breakfast) from $99–$110; apartment-style accommodations also available.

The Butler House on Grand (515-255-4096; www.butlerhouseongrand.com), 4507 Grand Avenue, Des Moines. This award-winning bed & breakfast in a 1923 Tudor-style mansion continues to win honors. The well-appointed rooms and suites are full of light as well as little touches like feather mattresses, whirlpool tubs, and game tables that make the inn beautiful and romantic. Rooms from $105–$190.

♿ **Wells Bed & Breakfast** (515-251-4724; www.wellsbedandbreakfast.com) 4724 72nd Street, Urbandale. Built in 2005, this bed & breakfast is thoughtfully designed with a focus on comfort, with big fat chairs, a screening room, and an expansive front porch. All rooms have wireless Internet and private baths; the Bellagio Room features a bathroom big enough to host a disco (it's wheelchair accessible). Rooms (including evening dessert and breakfast) from $95–$225.

CAMPING **Saylorville Reservoir** (515-276-4656; www.corpslakes.us/saylorville.htm) has multiple campgrounds with tent and full hook-up sites. See *Green Space*.

Jester Park (515-323-5366; www.conservationboard.org/Pages/jp.aspx), 11407 Northwest Jester Park Drive, Granger. More than 200 campsites for tents, RVs, and equestrians in wooded hills along Saylorville Lake. From mid-Apr.–mid-Oct. Rates $17 for electric sites, $12 for nonelectric sites. See *Green Space*.

✱ Where to Eat

DINING OUT 🍸 **801 Steak and Chop House** (515-288-6000; www.801steakandchop.com), 801 Grand Avenue (the Principal Building), Des Moines. Open for dinner Mon.–Sat. 5–11, Sun. 5–9. In grand old-school steakhouse style, 801 indulges carnivores and is so serious about beef that it takes no responsibility for steaks cooked above medium-well. Chef Brian Dennis also offers live Nova Scotia lobster and fresh shellfish. Cigar-friendly 801 has its own humidor. The wine list has won *Wine Spectator*'s Award of Excellence for 13 years running and specializes in rare vintages. Reservations recommended. $$$

Centro (515-248-1780; www.centrodesmoines.com), 1007 Locust Street, Des Moines. Open for lunch Mon.–Fri. 11-2, Sat. 11–3; dinner Mon.–Thurs. 5–10, Fri.–Sat. 5–11, Sun. 4:30–9; pizza and cocktails Tues.–Sat. 2–5. Pronounced "chen-tro"—Italian for "city center"—and located in the restored Temple for the Performing Arts, Centro is a lively upscale downtown restaurant with an atmosphere that is casual and chic. Chef George Formaro creates Italian cuisine, wood-fired oven pizza, and pasta using fresh ingredients. He also teaches cooking classes. There is a great patio, too. $$

🍸 **Dos Rios** (515-282-2995; www.dosriosrestaurant.com), 316 Court Avenue, Des Moines, is a downtown hot spot. Open Tues.–Thurs. 11–10, Fri.–Sat. 11–11; bar open until 2 AM. The beautiful people come for the atmosphere. It's dim, lushly decorated, and hip, but the food is the real treasure. The rotating menu features locally sourced and sustainable foods in contemporary, upscale Guadalajaran dishes. The duck empanada with chorizo is stellar as are the other meat and fish dishes, but the simplest foods, like the fish tacos, are the best. Dos Rios also offers a thoughtful selection of high-end tequilas and local wines on the menu. Lunch $$, Dinner $$–$$$.

Sam and Gabes (515-271-9200; www.samandgabes.com), Des Moines. Open for dinner Mon.–Sat. Sam and Gabes is an elegant Italian restaurant with delicious, traditional dishes of pasta with homemade sausage, veal, and fantastic cuts of beef. The tenderloin with gorgonzola is to die for. The waitstaff is friendly and knowledgeable, and the restaurant is gorgeous to boot. $$–$$$

Café di Scala (515-244-1353; www.cafediscala.com) 644 18th Street, Des Moines. Open for dinner Thurs.–Sat. 5–10. Located in a 100-year-old Victorian mansion in Sherman Hill, Café di Scala is one of the most romantic restaurants in the Des Moines metro. Chef Tony Lemmo, who lives upstairs from the restaurant, is one of the bluebloods of Italian cuisine in Des Moines, and he takes time-honored Calabrese dishes and gives them a 21st-century spin. The menu follows the traditional style of Italian courses: antipasto, pasta, meat, and salad. Wine from $18–$180. $$–$$$

Waterfront Seafood Market (515-223-5106; www.waterfrontseafoodmarket.com), 2900 University Avenue, West Des Moines. Open for lunch Mon.–Thurs. 11–2:30, Fri.–Sat. 11–5; dinner Mon.–Thurs. 5–10, Fri.–Sat. 11–11. It's not on an actual waterfront, but the seafood doesn't get much fresher in landlocked Iowa. The fish is flown in daily, and diners can enjoy seafood in the dining room or purchase fish from the market to cook at home. The sushi is the best in Des Moines, and Saturdays bring half-price steamed shrimp and oysters so tasty, you'll believe you've left the sea of corn. Lunch $$, Dinner $$$.

Simo's Cafistro (515-274-2463) 227 Fifth Street. West Des Moines. Open for lunch Tues.–Sat. 11–2; dinner Tues.–Thurs. 5:30–9:30, Fri.–Sat. 5:30–10:30. This hybrid of a café and a bistro in Valley Junction is as comfortable and eclectic as the Big Easy itself. The Cajun cuisine somehow manages to be both upscale and stick-to-your ribs down home. An example: The escargot is not served in one of those fancy dishes with toast points. Instead it comes out on a huge hunk of amazing bread covered in what can only be described as gravy. The dish is epic and fantastic. $$–$$$

Tursi's Latin King (515-266-4466; www.tursislatinking.com), 2200 Hubbell Avenue, Des Moines. Open for lunch Tues.–Fri. 11–2; dinner Tues.–Thurs. 4–10, Fri.–Sat. 4–11. The Latin King is an east-side institution, serving fine Italian cuisine since 1947. The menu offers steaks, pastas, and chicken dishes like "Chicken Spiedini," marinated, breaded, and sauced to perfection. Lunch $$, Dinner $$–$$$.

Flying Mango (515-255-4111; www.flyingmango.com), 4345 Hickman Road, Des Moines. Open for dinner Tues.–Sat. 5–close. A fusion of BBQ, Caribbean, and New Orleans flavors, the Flying Mango is one of the best-kept secrets in Des Moines. Owners Michael Wedeking and Suzanne Van Englehoven make everybody feel like a friend; eating, drinking, and merry-making required. Meats are smoked out back daily, and the restaurant is cozy, eclectic, and funky. $$

Y **Christopher's** (515-274-3694; www.christophers-restaurant.com), 2816 Beaver Avenue, Des Moines. Open for dinner Mon.–Sat. 4–close. This Beaverdale neighborhood favorite serves a menu of classic Italian dishes. The cream-filled pastas are rich and delicious as are the steaks, chicken, and prime rib. Salads are served with an addicting, homemade creamy-Italian dressing. While the dining room is nice, locals hang out in the lounge for sandwiches, pizza, and drinks. $$

Bistro Montage (515-557-1924; www.bistromontage.com/bistro), 2724 Ingersoll Avenue, Des Moines. Open for dinner Tues.–Sat. 5–close. Truly fine bistro cuisine in a romantic little space. Entrées include such Frenchie delights as calf's liver and cassoulet—but don't worry; this is still Iowa, and you can get steak with pommes frites. $$–$$$

EATING OUT Y **El Bait Shop** (515-284-1970; www.baitshop.com), 200 Southwest Second Street, Des Moines. Open daily for lunch, dinner, and bar hours. El Bait Shop slow smokes ribs and serves killer fish tacos and Baja-style food. Wash it all down with 104 of America's finest crafted beers on tap. The service is knowledgeable and friendly, especially when it comes to beer, so don't be afraid to ask for a recommendation. Daily specials of both food and beverage are always worth a try. There's a working shower in the bar, too, just in case you need to clean up after a day of fishing, or for any other reason. $–$$

Y **High Life Lounge** (515-280-1965), 200 Southwest Second Street, Des Moines. Open daily for lunch and dinner. Imagine a 1970s rec room. Then add food, beer, and often the members of the Des Moines Rugby Club. The High Life recreates the good times of the '60s and '70s, from the vintage Miller High Life signs on the walls to the shag carpeting on the floor. You'll also find tasty, if not diet-friendly, delights like Spam sandwiches, broasted (a combination of basted and roasted but tastes like fried) chicken, and tater tots. They also serve Miller High Life on tap as well as other vintage brews like Hamm's and Schlitz in the can. $

A Dong (515-284-5632) 1511 High Street, Des Moines. Open daily for lunch, dinner, and late night. This Vietnamese restaurant is a favorite among the downtown lunch crowd, evening diners, and late-night grazers. The menu is lengthy and authentic, and it's hard to go wrong. There are several kinds of pho—traditional Vietnamese soup—but the one with meatballs is the best. The vegetarian egg rolls are so good, it's OK to order extra. $

Big Tomato (515-288-7227), 2613 Ingersoll Avenue, Des Moines. The neon sign at Big Tomato reads LOUSY SERVICE,—but the pizza is worth it. The crust is flakey and fresh, and there are lots of wacky toppings. Try the Big Tomato Special, with Alfredo sauce, fresh tomatoes, and basil. The real after hours in Des Moines starts here around 1:30 AM in the line waiting for slices. Regular takeout during the day and early evening; slices after 11 PM. Delivery available—but only at the capricious whim of the drivers. $–$$

Ban Thai (515-244-4749) 215 East Walnut Street, Des Moines. Open for lunch daily 11–2:30; dinner Mon.–Thurs. 5–9, Fri. 5–10, Sat. 1–10. This East Village restaurant does both classic Thai dishes like pad Thai and specialties like duck better than anyone in the city. The portions are large and full of fresh vegetables, but underestimate the level of spiciness you can handle: they don't hold back, thankfully, on the pepper. The dining room is cool and understated. The menu is the same for lunch and dinner, but the portions are larger in the evening. $$

Drake Diner (515-277-1111) 1111 25th Street, Des Moines. Open for breakfast, lunch, and dinner Mon.–Sat. 7–11, Sun. 7–10. This Drake neighborhood landmark is the most central of the three Diner locations, which all have the same menu. The Diner specializes in upscale burgers, milkshakes, meat loaf sandwiches, and brunch. With a full bar, the Diner is a great place for a casual meal any time of the day or for a bloody Mary on Sunday morning. $–$$

Tasty Tacos (www.tastytacos.com) four locations around the Des Moines metro: 8549 Hickman Road, Urbandale (331-2000), 5847 Southeast 14th Street, Des Moines (285-1946), 2900 East Euclid, Des Moines (262-1100), 3715 Douglas, Des Moines (274-0884), 1418 East Grand, Des Moines (266-4242). There are few things that Des Moinesians are fanatic about, and the flour tacos at this restaurant are on the list. The fried tortillas are puffy and chewy and filled with beef, steak, chicken, or beans. Two make a meal, though it's easy to overindulge. The enchiladas are also excellent and well loved. The menu is full of other Mexican favorites and fried side dishes. $

Smitty's Tenderloin Shop (515-287-4742; www.smittystenderloins.com), 1401 Southwest Army Post Road, Des Moines. Open for lunch and dinner Tues.–Sat. 10–9. The best place in the metro for those big, breaded, fried-to-perfection pieces of pork. They've been making tenderloins and handmade onion rings since 1952. $

Los Laureles (515-265-2200) 1518 East Grand Avenue. Open for lunch and dinner daily 10–10, though sometimes open later. Which is the best Mexican restaurant in Des Moines is hotly debated, but almost everyone can agree that Los Laureles is a serious contender. The menu is huge and varied, including red snapper, but stick with the classic, down-to-earth favorites. The burrito is so big it should probably just be called the "burro," and it is stuffed with fresh vegetables, well-seasoned meats, and generous amounts of sour cream. Lunch $, Dinner $–$$.

George the Chili King (515-277-9433) 5722 Hickman Road, Des Moines. Open for lunch and dinner daily 11–10, but they will close early if things are slow. George's drive-in has

"I COME FROM DES MOINES. SOMEBODY HAD TO." —BILL BRYSON

Bill Bryson, the author of many hilarious travel books and books on the English language, was born in Des Moines in 1951. "When you come from Des Moines," he writes in *The Lost Continent,* "you either accept the fact without question and settle down with a local girl named Bobbi and get a job at the Firestone factory and live there forever and ever, or you spend your adolescence moaning at length about what a dump it is and how you can't wait to get out, and then you settle down with a local girl named Bobbi and get a job in the Firestone factory and live there forever and ever."

Bryson did neither. The Roosevelt High alum and Drake graduate did manage to leave Des Moines. He backpacked around Europe, met his wife, settled in the United Kingdom, and became an international literary sensation. His works include *A Walk in the Woods, Notes on a Small Island, Made in America,* and many others.

Even though Bryson left Iowa, the experience of growing up in the state influences his work. In *The Lost Continent,* his book on travels in small-town America, Bryson describes the magnet power of Des Moines: "People who have nothing to do with Des Moines drive in off the interstate, looking for gas or hamburgers, and stay forever."

Jack Kerouac, they say, was standing outside of Lincoln High School, on the south side of Des Moines, when he said that the prettiest girls in the world live in Iowa, but Bryson is not as kind to the ladies of his home state. He writes, "Iowa women are almost always sensationally overweight—you see them at Merle Hay Mall in Des Moines on Saturdays, clammy and meaty in their shorts and halter tops, looking a little like elephants dressed in children's clothes, yelling at their kids, calling out names like Dwayne and Shauna."

His most recent work, a memoir about growing up in Des Moines called *The Life and Times of the Thunderbolt Kid,* describes with both affection and wry humor the experience of growing up in the middle of America in the 1950s and '60s. While many of Bryson's memories are of institutions now long gone, some—such as George the Chili King—are still around for travelers to explore, even if they don't stay forever.

been pleasing diners in need of chili dogs, pork tenderloins, and onion rings for five decades, but if you're not a fan of greasy stuff, consider going elsewhere. The place is a little rundown, but if you're not too picky about ambiance, eat at the counter inside. Otherwise, use the drive-in window, or call ahead for takeout. The only thing that costs more than $5 is the "Fatman," a pork tenderloin topped with ham, cheese, lettuce, and tomato. $

IN DES MOINES, STOP IN AT GEORGE THE CHILI KING FOR A FAT MAN TENDERLOIN

DMACC's Bistro (515-964-6369; www.dmacc.edu/ici), Building 7, DMACC Campus, Ankeny. Open for lunch daily during the school year. Students learn the art of food preparation and service in a hands-on classroom. Students, faculty, and neighbors can dine from a menu of gourmet salads and sandwiches, rich entrées, or an extensive buffet. Drinks and a choice of dessert are included for a very reasonable price. Though, as in any learning institution, there are some teaching moments when the food or the waitstaff slips. $$

COFFEE AND TREATS Des Moines didn't get its first Starbucks until 2003, but that doesn't mean its citizens were without a liquid buzz. The city supports a vibrant coffee culture of local shops, many of which roast in house and serve only organic and fair-trade coffee. There's a jolt for every mood, so skip the mass marketing, and check out what's roasting locally.

Java Joes (515-288-5282; www.javajoescoffeehouse.com), 214 Fourth Street (in the Court Avenue District), Des Moines. Open Mon.–Thurs. 7 AM–11 PM, Fri.–Sat. 7 AM–12 AM, Sun. 9 AM–10 PM. Java Joes roasts and brews distinctive, high-quality coffee in a funky, high-ceilinged building downtown. Sunday mornings read the paper and listen to live jazz; then take a pound of beans home. (This author has a longstanding relationship with the French roast.) Espresso drinks, light lunches, pastries, beer, and wine are also served. $

Zanzibar's Coffee Adventure (515-244-7694; www.zanzibarscoffee.com), 2723 Ingersoll Avenue, Des Moines. Open Mon.–Thurs. 7 AM–9 PM, Fri.–Sat. 7 AM–11 PM, Sun. 8 AM–6 PM. The coffee is roasted daily next to the counter, so it's fresh and well brewed. Espresso drinks and breakfasts are also well done. Order the "egg-spress," an egg steamed in an espresso machine, toast from the bakery around the corner, fresh squeezed juice, and a cup of coffee. $

Mars Café (515-369-6277; www.marscafe.net), 2318 University Avenue, Des Moines (Earth). Open Mon.–Thurs. 7 AM–11 PM, Fri.–Sat. 7 AM–12 PM, and Sun. 8 AM–11 PM. Catering to the Drake University crowd in the surrounding neighborhood of Dogtown, the Mars offers organic and fair-trade coffee and tea, a rotating gallery of art from young local artists, and a spacey cosmonaut theme. Beer, wine, light breakfasts, and lunches also served. If you're brave, sample the Skylab: mocha blended with Tang. $

Gong Fu Tea (515-288-3388; www.gongfu-tea.com) 414 East Sixth Avenue, Des Moines. Open Mon.–Sat. 7–6. The selection of loose top-end leaf teas at this East Village shop could make even the most dedicated java lover rethink her drink. Big silver jars line the cool green walls, and the smart staff guides you through the world of exotic and refreshing black, white, green, and herbal teas. Buy tea sold in bulk to drink at home, or enjoy a cup brewed at the counter. Snacks and tea accessories also available. $

Black Cat Café (515-255-9895; www.blackcatcafebar.com), 3701 Ingersoll Avenue, Des Moines. Open Mon.–Thurs. 10–10, Fri.–Sat. 10–midnight. A European-style coffee bar with wine and imported beer as well as both savory and sweet crepes, the Black Cat is great for quiet time during the day or live jazz in the evenings. An otherwise-blah Tuesday night can be classed up with their free foreign-film screenings. $$

Classic Frozen Custard (515-287-1194) 4000 Southeast 14th Street, Des Moines. Open daily 10–5:30; hours vary with season. Thick frozen custard is richer and tastier than ice cream, and there are plenty of classic favorites like butter pecan as well as fresh seasonal flavors. $

Chocolaterie Stam (515-282-9575; www.stamchocolate.com) 2814 Ingersoll Avenue, Des Moines. Open Mon.–Fri. 9–7, Sat. 9–5, Sun. 12–5. It's easy to get overwhelmed confronting the rows of gleaming, heavenly bonbons, made in the traditional Dutch style with lots of care and fresh cream. Don't fret. The staff will help you choose—but be sure to get at least one chocolate hedgehog. They're the best. $

MARKETS **Gateway Market** (515-243-1754; www.gatewaymarket.com), 2002 Woodland Avenue, Des Moines. Open daily 8–9. The Gateway is a foodie's market, with specialty and organic meats, cheese, wines, and groceries. The prepared foods are outstanding, the service is both intelligent and friendly, and the adjoining café is a popular place to eat lunch during the week, serving omelets, sandwiches, gourmet ramen, pastries, and coffee.

Graziano's Brothers Grocery (515-244-7103), 1601 South Union Street, Des Moines. Graziano's is at the core of the Italian neighborhood on the near-south side. Their Italian sausage is legendary; local chefs use nothing else. With bread, olives, cheese, and meats, Graziano's is both a grocery store and a pillar of the city's Italian American community.

Double Dragon (515-284-0527), 1537 Second Avenue, Des Moines. The length of Second Avenue north of University is peppered with Asian markets, video, and specialty stores, but the best grocery is the Double Dragon. The floor-to-ceiling shelves, coolers, and a complete fish stand are bursting with imported Asian foods. The sights and smells of this grocery can be a little overwhelming, but it's the best place to find Asian provisions and fresh seafood.

✱ Drinking Establishments

The Lift (515-288-3777; www.dmlift.com), 222 Fourth Street, Des Moines. Open evenings daily. The Lift is a low-key martini bar with a showcase of local art and nightly specials. The bar is quiet and comfortable, with sofas and lots of nooks in which drinkers can relax.

The Continental (515-244-5845), 428 East Locust Street, Des Moines. Open for dinner Mon.–Thurs. Sample unique cocktails, martinis, and wine in this swanky East Village spot. Live jazz on the weekends and contemporary small-plate dining.

A. K. O'Connor's (515-277-2227), 4050 Urbandale Avenue, Des Moines. Open daily for lunch, dinner, and bar hours. On the weekends brunch is served until 2:30 PM, with the regular menu available later on. The Beaverdale neighborhood's go-to bar, this Irish pub is great for Friday-afternoon happy hour or hangover breakfast on Sundays. Keep your eyes out for members of Des Moines's own rock band, the Nadas, who frequent this pub. There are two other locations, one downtown on Court Avenue and one in West Des Moines.

Tonic (515-255-6755; www.toniciowa.com), 5535 George M. Mills Civic Parkway, West Des Moines. Open afternoons and evenings daily. Located in West Glen, Tonic is a chic upscale bar with outdoor seating on the street level and on a balcony upstairs. Despite the big-screen TVs and happy-hour specials, it reaches slightly above the typical bar scene.

Royal Mile and **Red Monk** (515-280-3771; www.royalmilebar.com), 210 Fourth Street, Des Moines. Open Mon.–Sat. 11–2, Sun. 12–2. Downstairs is an authentic English pub with an impressive selection of beer both on tap and in the bottle, 40 varieties of Scotch, and British pub food. Upstairs it's a dim and richly decorated Belgian-style bar with even more obscure imported brews and liquors. Both bars are great for those who take their drinks seriously.

Locust Avenue Tap (515-243-9399), 434 East Locust Street, Des Moines. Open daily. Renowned as Des Moines's best dive, the place looks a little like a cave, with graying walls covered in graffiti and a tile floor that slouches toward the bar with age, but it's a friendly place to get cheap drinks, and an unusual assortment of characters are always walking through the door.

✷ Entertainment

THEATERS AND MOVIES **Civic Center of Greater Des Moines** (515-246-2300; www.civiccenter.org), 221 Walnut Street, Des Moines. This not-for-profit arts center offers Broadway shows, symphony performances, ballet, and concerts. The Civic Center is a quick walk from downtown hotels, restaurants, and nightlife. Stroll over and spend a few minutes in Nollen Plaza with Claus Oldenburg's *Crusoe Umbrella.* Visit their Web site, or call for show and ticket information.

Stage West (515-309-0251; www.stagewestiowa.com), Stoner Theatre, Civic Center, 221 Walnut Street, Des Moines. This urbane, and often odd, community-theater troupe produces shows such as *Reefer Madness* and *Jerry Springer: The Opera.* In a theater tucked under the main stage at the Civic Center, the productions are more casual and intimate than their cohorts upstairs. Call or visit their Web site for schedule and ticket information.

Hoyt Sherman Theater (515-244-0507; www.hoytsherman.org), 1501 Woodland Avenue, Des Moines. Built as a manor home by businessman Hoyt Sherman in 1877, the Hoyt Sherman Theater was renovated in 1923 and serves as a venue for music, theatrical productions, and performing arts. The home also contains a gallery of 19th- and 20th-century art and 17th-century furniture and artifacts. Call or visit their Web site for event information.

Des Moines Playhouse (1-877-862-5621; www.dmplayhouse.com), 831 42nd Street, Des Moines. This is community theater at its very best, producing popular and debut plays and musicals and harnessing the many talents of locals. The Des Moines Playhouse stages several performances throughout the year. Consult their Web site or box office for schedule and ticket information.

Varsity Theatre (515-277-0404; www.varsitydesmoines.com), 25th and University Avenue, Des Moines. The city's only remaining single-screen theater, showing independent features and progressive cinema. In a metropolitan area awash in multiplexes and blockbuster hits, the recently refurbished Varsity is a neighborhood and community institution—and they have great popcorn. Call or check their Web site for features, show times, and ticket prices.

Fleur Cinema and Theater (515-287-4545; www.fleurcinema.com), 4545 Fleur Drive, Des Moines. Patrons can combine cinema with unconventional movie refreshments such as wine, beer, and espresso beverages. The Fleur also offers traditional movie snacks plus a unique selection of independent and documentary films. Arrive early to take advantage of the free wireless Internet and enjoy the mod lobby.

NIGHTLIFE **Blues on Grand** (515-244-3092; www.bluesongrand.com), 1501 Grand Avenue, Des Moines. Open Tues.–Sat. The home of the Iowa Blues Hall of Fame, this local joint is a great place to hear original music from local to national blues acts. The club itself is not much to look at—it's dingy, dark, and funky—but if the music's kicking, there's a guarantee that the waitresses will be dancing on the bar by the end of the night. Feel free to join them.

Val Air Ballroom (515-223-6152; www.valairballroom.com), 301 Ashworth Road, West Des Moines. This 8,000-square foot ballroom first opened its doors in 1939 as a traditional open-air dance hall for big bands. Since then, the Val Air—short for "Valley Junction open air"—has established itself as one of the premier locations for midsize acts and live music in central Iowa. Call for box-office information.

Vaudeville Mews (515-243-3270; www.vaudevillemews.com), 212 Fourth Street, Des Moines. Open evenings daily, but the Mews is more of a nightclub than hang out. Call or visit the Web site for show and ticket information. A den of exceedingly hip and progressive entertainment, the Mews is *the* venue to catch local and regional bands, independent films, dance parties, and occasionally independent theater. The crowd is mostly pierced and tattooed, so the place can't help but be happening.

People's Court (515-422-5128), 216 Court Avenue Suite 301, Des Moines. High above historic Court Avenue, national and regional musicians testify at the People's Court. There's a large open bar and a stage for music events as diverse as George Clinton and the Parliament Funkadelic to big-dreaming locals wailing at Rock Star Karaoke (played in front of a live band). Check local newspapers, or call for show information.

✷ Selective Shopping

CLOTHING **Smash** (515-288-1323; www.thesmashsite.com), 400 East Locust Street, Des Moines. Open Mon.–Sat. 11–7, closed Sun. except in Dec. You won't find apparel proclaiming MY FRIENDS WENT TO IOWA AND ALL I GOT WAS THIS T-SHIRT, but you can represent some Iowa pride with Iowa- and Des Moines-themed T-shirts and garb at this independent screen-printing shop.

Back Country (515-255-0031; www.theoriginalbackcountry.com), 2702 Beaver Avenue, Des Moines. Open Mon., Wed., Sat. 10–6; Tues. and Fri. 10–8; Sun. 12–4. It's a little hard to explain. For 30 years, Back Country has outfitted clients for every adventure, from first dates to first ascents. They sell high-end backpacking gear, tents, backpacks, sleeping bags, and climbing gear, but they also sell stylish and unique clothing, shoes, and jewelry.

Atomic Garage (515-274-8787), 127 Fifth Street, West Des Moines. Open Mon.–Fri. 11–6, Sat. 10:30–6, Sun. 12–4. Find the platforms, polyester shirts, and albums you've been missing since the '70s in this quirky Valley Junction vintage apparel shop.

SPECIALTY SHOPS **The Theatrical Shop** (1-800-383-7469; www.theatricalshop.com), 145 Fifth Street, West Des Moines. Open Mon.–Thurs. 8–9, Fri.–Sat. 9–5:30, Sun. 12–5. This is the place for costumes, theatrical make-up, wigs, and dance clothing. It's a fun place to poke around even when it's not Halloween.

Kitchen Collage (515-270-8202; www.kitchencollageofdesmoines.com) 430 East Locust Street, Des Moines. Open Mon.–Fri. 10–5:30, Sat. 9–5. Locally owned store specializing in gourmet cook- and bakeware, pottery, linens, books, specialty foods, and gadgets as well as offering demonstrations and classes.

A WALL OF MASKS AT THE THEATRICAL SHOP IN VALLEY JUNCTION (WEST DES MOINES)

BOOKS **Beaverdale Books** (515-279-5400; www.beaverdalebooks.com) 2629 Beaver Avenue. Suite 1, Des Moines. Open Mon.–Fri. 10–8, Sat. 10–5, Sun. 12-5. Beaverdale Books is more than just a bookstore, it's a community hub. Ladies out lunching, moms taking the kids for a walk, young people on their way to the watering hole, neighborhood writers

A PERFECT DAY IN DES MOINES

8:00 A cup of fresh-roasted coffee and the paper at Java Joes.

9:00 Hit the bike trail at Principal Park to ride through downtown, Gray's Lake, and Water Works Park to the Art Center.

10:00 Check out the paintings and sculptures at the Art Center and the roses in the surrounding gardens.

12:00 Grab lunch at the Gateway Market in historic Sherman Hill.

1:00 Visit the gold-domed state capitol building, and spend the afternoon browsing the shops in the East Village.

5:00 Check in at the Continental for a cocktail and some tapas.

7:00 Catch an Iowa Cubs game at Principal Park.

8:30 Eat fish tacos, drink beer, and enjoy live music with the locals at El Bait Shop.

SHOPPING VILLAGES

The retail scene in Des Moines is moving out of the malls and into shopping "villages" with a neighborhood feel, with restaurants, cafés, and condo living. Start with the up-and-coming **East Village** (www.eastvillagedesmoines.com) between the Des Moines River and East 14th Street, west of the capitol building. In the '90s, the area was made up of abandoned buildings, an Army-surplus store, and dive bars, but when several of the historic buildings were slated for demolition, a group of citizens got together to keep the East Village alive. Today, many of the historic buildings have been converted to boutiques, restaurants, and upscale bars. In West Des Moines, historic **Valley Junction** (www.valleyjunction.com) started life in 1892 as a repair depot for the Rock Island Railroad Line. The neighborhood is full of small boutiques of vintage apparel, upscale jewelry, fair-trade gifts, and a whole lot of antiques. **West Glen** (www.westglentowncenter.com), at 5525 Mills Civic Parkway, West Des Moines, is a planned community on the rapidly growing suburban west side. Although it's brand new, the West Glen community strives to strike a balance between convenience and a neighborhood sensibility.

THE STATE CAPITOL ABOVE THE EAST VILLAGE NEIGHBORHOOD OF DES MOINES

and bibliophiles—everyone finds his or her way into Alice's bookshop. They browse, they gossip, and they always find something new and exciting to read. The gals at Beaverdale Books are also happy to track down and special order any book your heart desires.

STORY COUNTY

Directly north of Des Moines is Story County, established in 1846 and named for Joseph Story, a U.S. Supreme Court Justice. Early settlers to the county came from east of the Mississippi, and they were followed by Europeans, primarily Norwegians, Germans, and Dutch. The population grew along with the rest of the state through the 1850s.

Nevada was named the county seat, but when the railroads came to Iowa, Ames and its busy depot gained both population and stature. Today, Ames is home to Iowa State University, which opened in 1869 as the first federal land-grant college in the country. Iowa State University—birthplace of both the Frostie ice-cream treat and the first digital computer—is one of the most beautiful campuses in the U.S. and is known globally for its agricultural and engineering programs.

Story City, a pretty little town just a few miles up the road from Ames, holds on to its Scandinavian roots and tempts visitors off Interstate 35 with an antique carousel.

GUIDANCE **Main Street Cultural District** (515-233-3472; www.mainstreetculturaldistrict.com), 312½ Main Street, Suite 201, Ames. Lobby is open with brochures; offices upstairs are open during normal business hours. A good place to start for information on Ames's unique main-street neighborhood.

Ames Convention & Visitors Bureau (515-232-4032; www.visitames.com), 1601 Golden Aspen Drive, Suite 100, Ames. Great information is available on their Web site.

Story City Greater Chamber of Commerce (515-733-4214; www.storycity.net), 602 Broad Street, Story City. Open Mon.–Fri. 9–5. Super helpful staff.

GETTING THERE *By car:* Ames is 40 miles north of Des Moines, just off **I-35.**

JACK TRICE STADIUM AT IOWA STATE UNIVERSITY

GETTING AROUND **CyRide** (515-292-1100; www.cyride.com), 1700 University Boulevard, Ames. The Ames bus system for both town and the ISU campus.

Ames Taxi (515-232-13434), 2006 East Lincoln Way, Building 2, Ames. Cabs available seven days a week. Des Moines airport trips can also be arranged.

MEDICAL EMERGENCY Call **911.**

INTERNET ACCESS Most coffee shops and hotels have free wireless available for laptop users, but if you need a computer, try the **Ames Public Library** (515-239-5656; www.ames.lib.ia.us), 515 Douglas Avenue, Ames. Open Mon–Thurs. 9–9, Fri.–Sat. 9–6, Sun. 1–5.

✳ To See

Iowa State University (515-294-4111, www.iastate.edu), Ames. The ISU campus is one of the most beautiful college campuses in America, with sprawling green lawns, an abundance of trees, and the much-beloved—and sometimes feared—campus swans. Any visit to Ames should include a stop at the **Stanton Memorial Carillon** in the Campanile, a 53-bell tower at the center of campus. The bells ring out the hours, and carillonneurs play 15-minute recitals at noon each weekday when classes are in session. The **Iowa State Memorial Union** (515-296-6848; www.mu.iastate.edu), 2229 Lincoln Way, is the epicenter of student life. There's a music venue in the basement, food, a hotel, and a lot of history. **Gold Star Hall** displays the names of Iowa State students killed in action from World War I to the conflicts in Iraq and Afghanistan; the stained-glass windows extol such virtues as learning, courage, and integrity. Students believe that stepping on the zodiac in the north entry will cause them to fail their next test, but the curse is removed by tossing a penny into the **Four Seasons Fountain.**

Iowa State University Museums (515-294-3342; www.museums.iastate.edu), Iowa State Center, 290 Scheman Building, Ames. ISU runs four unique museums

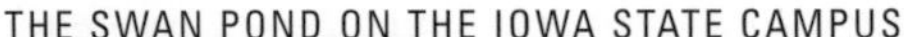

THE SWAN POND ON THE IOWA STATE CAMPUS

on campus. The **Brunnier Art Museum** at 295 Scheman Building, next to the performance space, emphasizes decorative arts. Open Tues.–Fri. 11–4, Sat.–Sun. 1–4. The **Christian Petersen Art Museum**, at Morrill Hall, is named for the first artist in residence, who created sculptures at ISU from 1934–1955. The exhibits focus on Petersen's art and contemporary exhibits. Open Mon.–Fri. 11–4. The **Farm House Museum**, on Farm House Lane, offers visitors, by appointment, a glimpse into rural life between 1860–1910 and is the oldest building on campus. The **Art on Campus** collection is one of the most extensive collections of public art in the nation, with over two thousand works. Sculpture and murals from nationally recognized artists such as Grant Wood are on display. The museums offer an art walk and self-guided tours. Visit their Web site or the Scheman Building office for more information.

STANTON MEMORIAL CARILLON AT IOWA STATE UNIVERSITY

✐ **Insect Zoo** (515-294-4537; www.ent.iastate.edu/zoo), Department of Entomology, Science II Building, Room 407, Ames. Tours by appointment only; e-mail insect zoo@iastate.edu, or call for an appointment. This zoo is filled exclusively with little creatures that creep: hissing cockroaches, millipedes, mosquitoes, ticks, and beetles of all shapes and sizes. The purpose of the zoo is to teach visitors about biodiversity and ecology and to cultivate an appreciation for our multiple-eyed and -legged friends rather than simply eliciting squeals of horror. If you are too squeamish to get up close and personal, visit the zoo's Web site for a live webcam of the insects in their habitats.

Octagon Center for the Arts (515-232-5331; www.octagonarts.org), 427 Douglas Avenue, Ames. Open Tues.–Fri. 10–5, Sat.–Sun. 1–5. The gallery features 175 local and regional artists and craftspeople. The Octagon also offers art classes and workshops for children and adults, sells gifts and art supplies in their store, and hosts an art festival in September.

Reiman Gardens (515-294-2710; www.reimangardens.iastate.edu), 1407 University Boulevard, Ames. Open Jan. 1–Apr. 4, 9–4:30, Butterfly Wing by appointment; Apr. 5–May 25, 9–4:30, including Butterfly Wing; May 26–Sept. 1, 9–6, Butterfly Wing 9–4:30; Sept. 2–Dec. 31, 9–4:30, including Butterfly Wing. Admission: $7 adults, $6 seniors, $3 children 4–17. One of the largest public gardens in Iowa, this 14-acre facility offers beautiful and educational rotating displays of plants and landscapes. The formal rose garden uses sustainable growing and design practices, and the Butterfly Wing is, as expected, an extensive indoor garden with a butterfly exhibit.

✐ **Antique Carousel** (515-733-4214; www.storycity.net), North Park on Broad Street, Story City, behind the city pool. Memorial Day–Labor Day, Mon.–Tues. 12–6, Wed.–Sun. 12–9; May and Sept., Sat.–Sun. 12–8. Tickets: $1 per ride.

RIDE A PIG ON THE HISTORIC STORY CITY CAROUSEL

Originally this 1913-built carousel traveled to county fairs and town celebrations, but when the owner decided to stop traveling in 1938, the citizens of Story City bought the carousel and installed it in the park. Exposed to the elements, it fell into disrepair until 1980, when the 20 wooden horses, 2 roosters, 2 pigs, 2 dogs, 2 chariots, and 1 whirling tub were restored to their present splendor. Today kids of all ages can enjoy riding their steeds (or other animal of choice) to the sound of the Wurlitzer Military Band organ in the covered pavilion.

Swinging Bridge, South Park, Story City. The bridge, spanning the Skunk River, was built in 1936 under Franklin D. Roosevelt's WPA program. Located in the center of South Park, the bridge is a great place for a picnic in the afternoon or for a stroll across the beautifully lit structure in the evening.

✷ To Do

WINERIES **Prairie Moon Winery** (515-232-2747; www.prairiemoonwinery.com), 3801 West 190th Street, Ames. Open Tues.–Sat. 12–7, Sun. 12–6. Prairie Moon stands out by specializing in organic grapes and by being home to Iowa's only ice wine, which is made from grapes that have been allowed to freeze on the vine. There is a beautiful tasting room as well as summer music events.

White Oak Vineyards (515-367-7777; www.whiteoakvineyards.com), 15065 Northeast White Oak Drive, Cambridge. Open Tues.–Sat. 10–6.

THE ROLLING VINEYARDS OF THE WHITE OAK WINERY IN ELKHART

Located in lush, rolling farmland in the south of Story County, just outside the town of Elkhart, White Oak Vineyards offers wine lovers a spacious wood-paneled tasting room, a big wraparound porch, acres of vines, and authentic Midwestern wine varieties.

✱ Green Space

Prairie Park, corner of Riverhills Drive and Broad Street, Story City. The park began as part of the Living Roadway Trust Fund Grant in 1996. Today it features a variety of native prairie plants, a wetlands area, and an oak savanna. The park has wide, mowed hiking trails and an abundance of native Iowa wildflowers and butterflies.

Iowa State University Campus See *To See.*

✱ Where to Stay

HOTELS AND MOTELS **Gateway Hotel** (515-292-8600; www.gatewayames.com), 2100 Green Hills Drive, Ames. A full-service, 187-room independent hotel and conference center complete with comfortable beds, artwork, and a pet goldfish. Rooms from $85–$200.

Hotel Memorial Union (515-296-6848; www.mu.iastate.edu), 2229 Lincoln Way, Ames. Stay right in the middle of the Iowa State campus in one of the 52 rooms on the upper floors of the Union. Free parking, high-speed wireless Internet, and laundry services. All rooms are nonsmoking. Rooms from $75–$85.

University Inn (515-232-0280), 229 South Duff Avenue, Ames. Forty-seven recently remodeled rooms include free wireless Internet, HBO, and a continental breakfast. Close to downtown and area restaurants. Rooms from $50–$125.

The Viking Motel (515-733-4306; www.vikinghotel.us), 1520 Broad Street, Story City. The Viking is a clean, inexpensive hotel off the interstate and close to the outlet mall. Don't worry about the name; they don't overdo it with the Scandinavian theme. Rooms from $45–$52.

BED & BREAKFASTS AND INNS **Iowa House Bed & Breakfast** (515-292-2474; www.iowahouseames.com), 405 Hayward Avenue, Ames. Tucked away in a quiet neighborhood, this recently remodeled residence was built in 1924 and is on the National Historic Registry. With 13 rooms—some with whirlpool baths, flat-screen TVs, and free wireless—the Iowa House combines modern convenience with small-town charm. Continental breakfast included. Rooms from $79–$169.

MonteBello Bed & Breakfast (515-296-2181; www.montebellobandbinn.com), 3535 South 530th Avenue, Ames. The brilliant gold paint of this hacienda stands out against the blue Iowa sky. Each of the four rooms is decorated with Mexican art, ceramic tile, and vibrant colors. The full breakfast is also authentic Mexican style. Rooms from $95–$125.

CAMPING **Whispering Oaks Campground** (515-733-4663; www.whisperingoakscampground.net), 1011 Timberland Drive, Story City. A shady campground with sites for both RVs and tents, offering electricity, showers, a Laundromat, and a store. Sites

$15–$20. Discounted rates Nov. 1–Mar. 31.

✷ Where to Eat

DINING OUT **Aunt Maude's** (515-233-4136; www.auntmaudesames.com), 547 Main Street, Ames. Open for lunch Mon.–Fri. 11–2, dinner Mon.–Sat. after 5; lounge opens at 4. Specializing in carefully prepared, locally sourced dishes for the sophisticated carnivore, Aunt Maude's offers diners a unique, evolving menu of elegant steaks, chicken, and fish entrées in a friendly atmosphere. Soups, sandwiches, and a small selection of vegetarian options are also available. $$–$$$

✪ **Hickory Park** (515-232-8940; www.hickorypark-bbq.com), 1404 South Duff Avenue, Ames. Open for lunch and dinner Sun.–Thurs. 10:30–9, Fri.–Sat. 10:30–10. Mention Hickory Park BBQ anywhere in central Iowa, and the response will be the same: a hungry *ooooh.* This Ames landmark is so beloved that it isn't rare to see prom dates with slabs of ribs (especially delicious) or to find their catered dishes miles away from the homestead. $$

DINE AL FRESCO AT THE COTTAGE ON BROAD IN STORY CITY

The Spice (515-232-0200; www.thespiceames.com), 402 Main Street, Ames. Open Mon–Fri. for lunch 11–2:30, dinner Mon.–Thurs. 5–9, Fri.–Sat. 5–10. An excellent Thai restaurant on Main Street, with traditional Thai noodles, soup, and appetizers as well as specials such as tamarind shrimp and the amusingly named "Salmon See Ew." $$

The Cottage on Broad (515-733-4376; www.cottageonbroad.com), 410 Broad Street, Story City. Open for lunch Tues.–Sat.11–2, dinner Tues.–Sat. after 5, closed Sun. and Mon. Chef Chris Hansen brings big-city dining to little Story City with a focus on seafood. Contemporary favorites such as butternut-squash ravioli and roasted summer vegetables come with, of course, corn. Small plates, wine, and cocktails are also available. The patio in the back is not to be missed on balmy summer nights. Lunch $$, Dinner $$–$$$.

EATING OUT **The Grove Café** (515-232-9784; grovecafeamesiowa.tripod.com), 124 Main Street, Ames. Open for breakfast and lunch Mon.–Fri. 5–2, Sat. 5–noon, Sun. 7–noon. One giant pancake and a pork product on the side at the Grove Café is all a hungry traveler needs. You may leave with that diner smell, but the home-style breakfast and lunch are worth it. $

Battle's Barbeque (515-292-1670), 218 Welch Avenue, Ames. Open for lunch and dinner Mon.–Thurs. 11–9, Fri.–Sat. 11–6. The sandwich that Cyclone alumni crave after they move away is the BBQ from Battle's, which is slow smoked, well sauced, and served with a pickle. Add a piece of sweet-potato pie for dessert, and you will be in BBQ heaven. Lunch $, Dinner $$.

✪ **Great Plains Sauce & Dough Company** (515-232-4263; www.greatplainspizza.com), 129 Main Street, Ames. Open for lunch and dinner Mon.–Fri. 11–2 and 4:30–12, Sat. 11 AM–midnight, and Sun. noon–11 PM. The best pizza, hands down, in Ames since 1979. It's the crust: handmade, full of delicious whole grains, and so thick you can eat it like a breadstick. Try dipping it in honey. (Browse the shops while you wait for your pie.) Eat in the restaurant on Main Street, or stay home—Great Plains delivers. $$

The Bistro (515-733-4620; www.bistroonbroad.com), 624 Broad Street, Story City. Open for lunch Mon.–Fri. 11:30–1:30. This lunch spot on the main thoroughfare in Story City offers a fresh alternative to the burgers travelers will find elsewhere on the road, with dainty salads, soups, and sandwiches served both hot and cold. $$.

Downtown Deli (515-232-3626), 328 Main Street, Ames. Open for lunch and dinner Mon.–Fri. 10–7, Sat 10–5. Sometimes you just need a sandwich. That sandwich might be turkey, or it might be bratwurst and Canadian bacon. Either way, this no-frills sandwich shop is the place to find it. $

COFFEE AND TREATS **Stomping Grounds Café** (515-292-5258), 303 Welch Avenue, Ames. Open for coffee and bakery treats Mon.–Fri. 7 AM–12 AM, Sat.–Sun. 8 AM–-12 AM. Kitchen open for breakfast, lunch, and dinner Mon.–Fri. 7 AM–10 PM, Sat. and Sun 8 AM–10 PM. This elegant, European-style café brews each coffee one cup at a time and serves cookies and other baked goods. Meal times find light breakfasts served in the morning, while filling sandwiches and crepes are the fare for lunch and dinner. Seasonal produce and products from local and organic farms are the rule of thumb. $$

Temptations on Main (515-232-6393; www.temptationsfinechocolates.com), 309 Main Street, Ames. Open Mon.–Sat. 10–6, Thurs. 10–8. Not a place for a well-balanced lunch—unless you consider dessert lunch—and don't have any delusions of your purchases making it home. With homemade chocolates, fudge, ice cream, and candy, Temptations is the place to indulge a sweet tooth.

MARKETS **Wheatsfield Co-op** (515-232-4094; www.wheatsfield.coop), 413 Douglas Avenue, Ames. Open daily 9–9. An organic and natural grocery store with local produce, meat, poultry, snacks, bulk foods, wine, beer, books, and natural health and beauty supplies. Open to the public.

Ames Farmers Market (www.amesfarmersmarket.com), Main Street Depot, Ames. Open Sat. 8–3, Thurs. 2–7, and North Grand Mall parking lot Wed. 3–6, Sat. 8–12. Shop outdoors for produce and local products all summer long.

✷ Drinking Establishments

Welch Avenue Station (515-292-2334; www.welchavestation.com), 207 Welch Avenue, Suite 101, Ames. Open Mon.–Thurs. 4–2, Fri. 1 PM–2 AM, and Sat.–Sun. 12 PM–2 AM. Every college town has a beloved college bar, and in Ames *this* is that bar. With Cyclone football on TV, darts, pool tables, a DJ booth, and a pizza joint upstairs, Welch Avenue Station has everything a college freshman—or someone who wants to relive college days with beer—could desire.

Olde Main Brewing Co. and Restaurant (515-232-0553; www.oldemainbrewing.com), 316 Main Street, Ames. Open Mon.–Sat. 11 AM–close, brunch Sun. 10:30 AM–2 PM. Home of the "Dinkey wheat," a brew named after the train that once ran through

QUAFF A HANDCRAFTED BREW AT OLD MAIN BREWING CO. IN AMES

Ames, and a favorite among the college crowd, Olde Main features unique, handcrafted brews and a menu with steaks, pasta dishes, sandwiches, and salads. Beer and root beer lovers can bring or purchase growlers home to take home. $$

✷ Entertainment

Iowa State Center (515-294-3347; www.center.iastate.edu), Scheman Building Suite 4, Ames. The Iowa State Center offers a range of venues for entertainment. For fine arts and theater, there are the **Scheman Center, Fisher Theater,** and **Stephens Auditorium.** For ISU athletics and stadium concerts, there's **Hilton Coliseum.** Call or consult their Web site for upcoming events and ticketing information at the four facilities.

The Maintenance Shop (515-294-2969; www.m-shop.com), 2229 Lincoln Way, west basement of the Union, Ames. Since 1974 the "M-Shop" has entertained locals and students alike with music, comedy, and community events. The M-Shop is a midsize music venue that attracts national and regional acts. The focus is on rock and alternative music, but in a typical week there is something for everyone. Check the schedule on the Web site for more information on shows and ticketing.

The Bali Satay House (515-292-7719; balisatayhouse.tripod.com), 2424 Lincoln Way, Ames. Open daily for dinner and bar time. If there is a really unique show going on in central Iowa, it's probably at the Bali Satay. With eccentric musicians, DJs spinning records, and Chinese and Indonesian food, the Bali is a fun place to hang out with the young and eclectic set.

✷ Selective Shopping

The Pumpkin Patch (515-232-6398), 302 Main Street, Ames. Open Mon.–Fri., Sat. 9:30–5:30, Thurs. 9:30–8, Sun. 1–4. Even grownups will love this cozy toy store offering unique books, toys, and clothing. No batteries required for the selection of vintage wind-up toys and marbles.

Skunk River Cycles (515-232-0322; www.skunkrivercycles.com), 308 Main Street, Ames. Open Mon.–Wed, Fri.–Sat. 10–6; Thurs. 10–8. This bike shop is staffed by the kind of dedicated cyclists who ride every day and really know their stuff. With bikes for commuters, joy riders, and road warriors, it is a friendly place to pick up a new ride or just talk shop.

Iowa State University Book Store (515-294-5684; www.isubookstore.com), ISU Memorial Union, 2229 Lincoln Way, Ames. Open Mon.–Thurs. 7:45–6, Fri. 7:45–5, Sat. 9–5, Sun. 12–4, shorter hours during breaks. All the scarlet-and-gold Cyclone apparel and gifts an ISU fan requires, plus books of all kinds, office supplies, and computer gear.

The Little Bookroom (515-233-2126), 328 Main Street, Ames. Open Mon.–Wed., Fri. 11–2; Thurs. 12–6; Sat. 11–3. This tiny bookstore secreted away in a building with shops, offices, and a deli offers a small but well-chosen selection of books, with an excellent Iowa and regional section, stationery, and a discount on special orders.

MARSHALL AND JASPER COUNTIES

Henry Anson chose the scenic Iowa River Valley as the spot for Marshalltown, the county seat of Marshall County, in 1851. Since that time Marshall County history has been based in both agriculture and coal mining. Marshalltown is known as "the BBQ Capital of Iowa" as it plays host to the annual Iowa State BBQ Championship in a weekend-long event of smoked meat, home cooking, and music. Just north of downtown, on a beautifully landscaped campus, is the Iowa Veterans Home, which cares for aging veterans, preserves military history, and is one of the only places exempt from Iowa's statewide smoking ban. To the east of the city is the Big Treehouse—one of the biggest in the world—in a campground on the historic Lincoln Memorial Highway.

Newton is Jasper County's seat and was home to the Maytag family with their appliances and blue cheese. When Maytag closed its manufacturing plant in Newton, the city faltered but did not struggle. Today it is quickly becoming the racing capital of the state. Famous NASCAR driver Rusty Wallace designed the Iowa Speedway as his first signature racetrack, and it plays host to national-level racing events. Jasper County is also home to the Neal Smith National Wildlife Reserve, an expanse of restored prairie with native plants and animals, including a herd of bison and elk that live on the grounds. Driving through the reserve gives visitors an idea of what the state looked like before settlement and farming.

GUIDANCE **Marshalltown Convention and Visitors Bureau** (1-800-697-3155; www.visitmarshalltown.com), 709 South Center Street, Marshalltown. Open during business hours. This organization produces a brochure with complete listings of restaurants, lodging, and attractions.

Newton Convention and Visitors Bureau (1-800-798-0299; www.visitnewton.com), 113 First Avenue West, Newton. Open during business hours. Brochures and guidance are available on the main square.

GETTING THERE *By car:* **IA 30** runs through Marshall County and connects with **IA 65** out of Des Moines or **I-35** to the west. **I-80** runs east-west through Jasper County.

STATE CENTER IN MARSHALL COUNTY IS THE "ROSE CAPITAL OF IOWA"

GETTING AROUND The cities of Marshalltown and Newton have lovely downtown areas and squares, but to see all the sights, a car is required.

MEDICAL EMERGENCY Call **911.**

Marshalltown Medical & Surgical Center (641-754-5151; www.everydaychampions.org), 3 South Fourth Avenue, Marshalltown. Full-service hospital with emergency medical care.

Skiff Medical Center (641-792-1273; www.skiffmed.com), 204 North Fourth Avenue East Newton. Full-service hospital with emergency medical care.

INTERNET ACCESS/PUBLIC LIBRARY Some cafés, restaurants, and hotels have wireless Internet access as do the I-80 rest stops.

Marshalltown Public Library (641-754-5738; www.marshalltownlibrary.org), 108 West Boone Street, Marshalltown. Open 9–8 Mon.–Thurs., 9–6 Fri., 9–5 Sat., closed Sun. Free wireless Internet access throughout the library and public computers are available.

SCULPTURE OUTSIDE AND IMPRESSIONIST ARTISTS INSIDE CAN BE FOUND AT THE FISHER COMMUNITY CENTER IN MARSHALLTOWN

✷ To See

Fisher Community Center (641-753-9013; www.centraliowaartassociation.com), 709 South Center Street, Marshalltown. Open Mon.–Fri. 11–5, and Sat.–Sun., Apr.–Oct. 1–5, and by request. Inside the Fisher Center, visitors will find a small but impressive collection of impressionist and post-impressionist work by artists such as Degas and Matisse in the **Fisher Impressionist Collection**. A collection of sculptures graces the grounds outside. *Dedication to the Future,* the final work of Iowa State University professor Christian Petersen, plays in the fountain in front of the building. The center also features the **Ceramic Study Collection** and a community art studio.

The Big Treehouse (641-752-2946; www.bigtreehouse.net) 2370 Shady Oaks Road, east of Marshalltown. The

THE LINCOLN HIGHWAY

Before the Lincoln Highway, America's roads were bumpy, rutted dirt tracks that were impossible to travel in bad weather and not linked together in any organized way. In 1913 the Lincoln Highway Association sold "highway memberships" to raise funds for this New York–to–San Francisco road, one of the earliest prototypes for a transcontinental automobile highway.

Completed in 1927, the Lincoln Highway opened America up for the kind of travel that is so common today and that Americans love: the open road. It also created other institutions we live with today, including roadside attractions and campgrounds, and it brought commerce, travelers, and economic development to small towns across the United States. The Lincoln Highway still exists, running through Iowa north of Interstate 80, today's main east-west thoroughfare, and passing through such cities as Marshalltown, State Center, and Ogden. To learn more about this historic roadway, visit the Lincoln Highway Association at www.lincolnhighwayassoc.org.

Big Treehouse has been Mike Jurgensen's hobby for over 25 years. It is the *Titanic* of tree houses, with 6 stories, 12 levels, 13 porch swings, a spiral staircase, music, electricity, and a microwave. But be warned: Tours of the Big Treehouse are by appointment only, and the tour guide is notoriously fickle. Make appointments in advance, give a follow-up call, and don't get your hopes up too high because you may be turned away from the gates of tree house nirvana for any number of reasons.

Marshall County Historical Society (641-752-6664;www.marshallhistory.org), 202 East Church Street, Marshalltown. Contact the historical society for the specific hours for each location as they vary. With four facilities in Marshalltown and Haverhill, the Marshall County Historical Society explores the history of the county from fossils to industrial development. The free **Marshall County Historical Museum**, at the address listed above, provides historical context for exploring the area, with displays on geology and archaeology as well as information on baseball celebrity "Cap" Anson. The **Glick-Sower House**, 201 East State Street, was the residence of George Sower, a German immigrant who established the local newspaper. The house is full of period furniture and art, and a garden project is in the

A HISTORIC BLACKSMITH SHOP IS PART OF THE MARSHALL COUNTY HISTORICAL SOCIETY IN HAVERHILL

works. The home may be toured by appointment through the historical society. The **Taylor #4 Country School**, 60 North Second Avenue, is a turn-of-the-20th-century one-room schoolhouse. Tours are by appointment. South of Marshalltown is the **Matthew Edel Blacksmith Shop**, CR E63, Haverhill, the shop and home of a German immigrant who operated the smithy from 1883–1940. The shop is full of tools and equipment from a life spent smithing. A volunteer on staff can answer any questions. Open daily Labor Day–Memorial Day 12–4. Free.

Watson's Grocery Store (641-483-2458), 106 West Main Street, State Center. Open Memorial Day–Labor Day, Sat.–Sun. 1–4 and by appointment. History buffs will want to swing through State Center to see this restored grocery store, complete with food and original fixtures and cabinetry.

✐ **Trainland U.S.A.** (515-674-3813; www.trainlandusa.com), 3135 IA 117 North, Colfax. Open daily Memorial Day–Labor Day 10–6. Admission: $5 adults, $4.50 seniors, $3 children. "Red" Atwood began collecting toy trains in 1964. Since then his hobby has chugged into an obsession and now fills a remodeled basement with over 4,000 feet of track re-creating scenes across the landscapes of America. Toy-train enthusiasts will appreciate the tour. On the property there is also an old train car-turned-toy train and a store with antiques.

Maytag Dairy Farms (1-800-247-2458; www.maytagblue.com), 2282 East Eighth Street North, Newton. Open Mon.–Fri. 8–5, Sat. 9–1. The birthplace of the award-winning Maytag blue cheese is a humble dairy farm on the north side of town. Visitors can watch the office workers, the ladies cutting and wrapping cheese, and a hilarious video from the 1980s that explains the cheese-making process. But a visit to the Maytag farm also offers a complimentary tasting and a retail shop with the fresh blue cheese that is made on site. Try a hunk of Maytag blue cheese with a cut of Iowa steak.

The Jasper County Historical Museum (641-792-9118; www.jaspercountymuseum.net), I-80 and IA 14, exit 164 in Newton. Open daily May 1–Sept. 30 1–5, other times by appointment. Admission: $5 adults, $2 children. The museum focuses on the agrarian and coal-mining history of Jasper County, with a 40-foot bas-relief sculpture by Newton artist Herman L. Deaton depicting the county's history. The grounds also feature different styles of barns, a "main street," and a furnished 1930s home. Another exhibit features Maytag washing machines starting from 1907.

L. J. Maasdam Wheel Art, South 48th Avenue East, Lynnville. Take IA 38 to the Lynnville exit, head south, turn west on South 48th Avenue East, and travel 0.5 mile west. Ninety iron wagon wheels welded into a massive sculpture loom over the cornfields of rural Jasper County. They were built by L. J. Maasdam in 1994 when he was 90 years old. It's just a pull off the highway. There's no information on the art, no interpretive center, no volunteer docent, and no fee, but the piece is surprising, impressive, and definitely well worth the visit.

Wagaman Mill (641-792-9780; www.iagenweb.org/jasper/history/wagamanmill/index.htm), located on the North Skunk River on the north side of Lynnville. Open Sun. 2–4 in summer. This historic mill, built in 1848 by John R. Sparks, is now listed on the National Register of Historic Places. Tours—all 12 hours a year that they are actually available—include interior restoration of the mill and wheelhouse and displays of local history. If you don't find yourself in Lynnville when the build-

SOME 90 WAGON WHEELS COMPRISE THE L. J. MAASDAM WHEEL ART DISPLAY AT THE CORNFIELDS OUTSIDE OF LYNNVILLE.

ing is open, the area is still a picturesque beauty spot with a little city park and canoe and kayak access on the river.

✷ To Do

✪ ✐ **Neal Smith National Wildlife Refuge** (515-994-3400; www.tallgrass.org), 9981 West 109th Street and IA 163, Prairie City. Open Mon.–Sat. 9–4, Sun. 12–5; auto-tour route and trails open during daylight hours. One of the best-kept secrets in central Iowa and just a 20-minute drive from the Des Moines metro are these 8,600 acres of restored prairie land. In the middle is the **Prairie Learning Center,** which is filled with entertaining information on the landscape that once dominated the Midwest. Hundreds of species of plants, animals, and insects inhabit the prairie, but none are as exciting as the herds of bison and elk that live on the preserve. Visitors can drive through their enclosure and are rewarded with up-close encounters with the animals.

THOUGH RARELY OPEN, THE HISTORIC WAGAMAN MILL, LYNNVILLE, IS A GREAT PLACE TO PICNIC

Grimes Farm and Conservation Center (www.grimesfarm.com), 2539 233rd Street, Marshalltown. Interpretive center open Mon.–Fri. 8:30–4, Sat. 9–12. The 160 acres of this nature preserve serve as an educational and recreational space on the many landscapes—as well as the history and future—of Iowa. The farm features woodlands, prairies, wetlands, progressive agricultural areas, Linn Creek, and rolling Iowa hills. Visitors are welcome to use the self-guided trail maps available at the trailheads when the educational center is not open.

✪ **Iowa Speedway** (641-791-8000; www.iowaspeedway.com), south of I-80, exit 168 in Newton. NASCAR, for those who don't know, stands for National Association for Stock Car Auto Racing, and like the Indianapolis 500, the races at this state-of-the-art track are world class. Rusty Wallace—one of the winningest drivers in the sport, with over $50 million in earnings—turned his attention to track design and produced this signature racetrack, which cost $70 million and includes seating for twenty-five thousand NASCAR racing fans. Each summer the speedway is home to the Iowa Corn 250, with the cars powered on Iowa's pride: ethanol. Call or visit their Web site for schedule and ticket information. There are concerts and other events, and RV camping is available on the compound.

Newton Kart Club (641-792-4266 or 641-792-8182; www.newtonkarting.com), 2801 East Fifth Street South, Newton. Go-kart races start Fridays at 5:30 and Saturdays at 4. When compared with the professional NASCAR racing just up the road, go-karts may seem like child's play, but these are tiny cars with serious drivers, and the races are more entertaining and competitive that you might imagine. Set back on 10 acres of land, the track is basically in a cow pasture, but fans are closer to the action.

Appleberry Farm (641-752-8443; www.appleberryfarm.com), 2402 West Main Street, Marshalltown. Open late summer and fall. Amateur farmers can pick their own apples and pumpkins in-season and shop for produce, cider, antiques, and crafts.

OUTDOOR ACTIVITIES **The Harvester Golf Club** (641-227-4653; www.harvestergolf.com), 833 Foster Drive, Rhodes. *Golf Digest* magazine ranks this club as the #1 golf course in Iowa—and that's saying something in the state with the most golf courses per capita. Designed by Keith Foster, the club also includes an attractive clubhouse with restaurant.

Chichaqua Valley Recreational Trail (641-792-9708), from east of Bondurant to Baxter. This favorite 20-mile rails-to-trails line travels through the forests and bottomlands of the Skunk River. Reward yourself for making it to Baxter with a steak and beer at O'Kelly's, just off the parking lot in Baxter.

Westwood Golf Course (641-792-3087; www.westwoodgolfcourse.com) 3387 IA F48 West, Newton. Open seasonally and according to the weather but usually daily and daylight hours; call for tee-times. This 18-hole municipal course offers golfers challenging rolling hills and a flat back with lots of water and sand.

✱ Green Space

State Center Memorial Rose Garden (641-483-2559; www.statecenteriowa.org), CR E41, on the south and east side of State Center. This rose garden displays the pride of State Center, the Rose Capital of Iowa. With hundreds of varieties laid out in a formal style, the park is a nice place to stop and, well, smell the roses. State Center, with a charming Main Street, is the geographic center of the state and is on the original Lincoln Highway.

Neal Smith National Wildlife Refuge See *To Do*

Grimes Farm and Conservation Center See *To Do*.

STATE CENTER'S MEMORIAL ROSE GARDEN BLOOMS IN TIME FOR THE ANNUAL ROSE FESTIVAL

Maytag Park (641-792-1470; www.newtongov.org), 301 South 11th Avenue West, Newton. This featured city park is home to the **Bowl Full of Blues Festival,** a fantastic city pool with two waterslides, and one of the most challenging Frisbee (aka "disk") golf courses in the United States.

✷ Where to Stay

HOTELS AND MOTELS **Executive Inn Motel** (641-752-3631), 2009 South Center Street, Marshalltown. Of the several inexpensive motels in Marshall County, this is probably the best. The rooms are clean and not terribly generic, and most are recently remodeled. One suite offers a whirlpool tub. Rooms from $45–$55.

Baxter Inn (641-227-3959), 102 North Main Street, Baxter. The Baxter Inn is a simple hotel built in the old People's Savings Bank, dating back to 1906. Each of the five rooms is basic but complete with a queen-size bed, television, and refrigerator; the bathroom of the Canfield Room is built in the old bank vault. Rooms from $40–$80.

Sully Suites Hotel (641-521-5107), 806 First Street, Sully. More like staying in a tidy little house than a hotel, with two rooms and a kitchen area. Rooms from $75. Weekly rates available.

BED & BREAKFASTS AND INNS **Historic Tremont Inn on Main** (641-752-1234; www.tremontonmain.com), 24 West Main Street, Marshalltown. Above the two restaurants sharing the same Tremont name, the Tremont Inn offers guests six uniquely furnished rooms, all with high ceilings and views of Main Street. Amenities include wireless Internet, bathrobes, and a billiard room. Rooms from $109–$149.

✪ **La Corsette Maison Inn** (641-792-6833; www.lacorsette.com), 629 First Avenue East, Newton. La Corsette is a nationally renowned inn with 4½-star gourmet cuisine. Located in a 1909 Arts and Crafts–style mansion, the inn boasts what seems like miles of sumptuous woodwork, stained glass, fireplaces, and fine furnishings. The French-style bedrooms include four-poster beds, fireplaces, and whirlpool tubs. Rooms from $100–$220. Call for dinner reservations.

Aerie Glen (641-792-9032; www.aerieglen.com), 2364 First Avenue West, Newton. Situated on 8 wooded acres just outside of Newton, this two-room, one-suite, one-private-cottage bed & breakfast offers a multilevel deck overlooking the pool, a hot tub, and a full breakfast. Rooms from $75–$225.

The Country Connection (515-994-2023; www.iowa-country-bed-breakfast.com), 9737 West 93rd Street, Prairie City, is a turn-of-the-20th-century Iowa farmhouse. In "Grandpa's Hideaway," guests sleep on the bed in which innkeeper Alice Foreman was born more than 80 years ago. A stay includes breakfast, snacks, and homemade ice cream. Open May through November (the proprietors spend the winter in Arizona). Reservations are appreciated, and evening meals can be arranged. Rooms from $50–$65.

The Old Mill Riverside Inn (641-527-2300; www.bbonline.com/ia/oldmill), 202 East Street, Lynnville. Located next to the Wagaman Mill dam, this new Old Mill with English country decor has four rooms with private baths and two bunkrooms. Rocking chairs on the wooden front porch look out over the Skunk River. Rooms from $50–$85.

Front Porch Bed & Breakfast (641-527-3620), 7843 IA 38 South, Lynnville. The two rooms in this contemporary farmhouse are neat and comfortable, and one room contains three twin beds, which is nice for families and separate-bed friends. The B&B also has a great front porch, private kitchen, and chickens in the yard. Rooms from $65–$125.

CAMPING **Shady Oaks Campground** (641-752-2946), 2370 Shady Oaks Road, Marshalltown. The campground, which is also home to the **Big Treehouse** (see *To See*), is a landmark on the historic Lincoln Highway. Opened in 1925, it was the first camp-

ENJOY THE VIEW OF THE NORTH SKUNK RIVER FROM THE FRONT PORCH OF THE OLD MILL RIVERSIDE INN IN LYNNVILLE

ground with cabins west of the Mississippi on this cross-country road. Visitors can bring their RVs or tents. Campsites from $20–$22

Rock Creek State Park (641-236-3722; www.iowadnr.gov/parks), 5627 Rock Creek East, Kellogg. A popular campground with 200 sites, half with electricity hook-ups for RVs. The park also offers hiking, biking, and a lake for boating, fishing, and swimming. Reservations available online through the Iowa Department of Natural Resources (DNR) Web site. Campsites from $11–$16.

✳ Where to Eat

DINING OUT 🍸 **Tremont on Main** (641-752-1234; www.tremontonmain.com), 22 West Main Street, Marshalltown. Open for dinner Mon.–Sat. 4–10. This elegant restaurant is a treasure tucked away in a historic building on Main Street. Start with the unique small-plate tapas menu before moving on to choice cuts of meat and seafood. The gorgeous bar was built from reclaimed wood. The restaurant is dim and chic but very comfortable. $$–$$$

Mexico Antiguo (641-752-6666), 25 West Main Street, Marshalltown. Open for lunch and dinner. Marshalltown has a reputation for delicious Mexican restaurants and Antiguo is one the best. The fajitas are well seasoned and sizzling, the burritos are huge, and the margaritas are handmade and just a bit dangerous. $$

EATING OUT ✪ **Taylor's Maid-Rite** (641-753-9684; www.maidrite.com), 106 South Third Avenue, Marshalltown. Open for breakfast, lunch, and dinner Mon.–Sat., lunch and dinner Sun. In 1928 the loose-meat sandwich was a born at this Taylor's Maid-Rite. A loose-meat sandwich is finely ground beef, cooked on a slanted grill to let the grease roll away, and served with mustard, pickles, and onions. For 70 years Taylor's did not serve ketchup because hobos would steal it to make tomato soup. The Maid-Rite concept expanded to a chain of shops across the state, and now ketchup is available to put on top of this Iowa-born sandwich. $

Tremont Grille (641-754-9082; www.tremontonmain.com), 26 West Main Street, Marshalltown. Open for breakfast, lunch, and dinner Mon.–Sat. 7 AM–9 PM. This is the kind of café diners can enjoy all day. There are hot breakfasts, freshly brewed coffee and espresso, unique sandwiches, and pasta dishes. The big front windows look out on Main Street, and it is bright and cheerful inside. The "Cap Anson" sandwich and others are tasty and very filling. Sweet-potato fries on the side are a nice change of pace. Breakfast $, Lunch $$, Dinner $$.

Sisters of the Heart (515-994-3139 www.pcsisters.com), 116 East Jefferson Street, Prairie City. Open for lunch Fri.–Sat. 10–4, Sun. 10–3. Two friends dreamed of opening a place where women could relive their girlhood memories of visiting tearooms with their mothers. The shop plays host to ladies' luncheons, little girls' tea parties, and other special events. The menu includes light soups and salads, great desserts, tea, and coffee. $

O'Kelly's Steak and Pub (641-227-3013; www.okellyssteakandpub.com), 108 Main Street, Baxter. Lounge open Mon.–Sat. 5–10, steakhouse open Fri.–Sat. 5–10. Located at the north end of the popular Chichaqua Valley Trail, O'Kelly's, in the center of Baxter, is a big comfortable bar to grab a beer and grill your own steak after a day of pedaling. People from all over Jasper County rave about "Bike Night" on Wednesdays, when motorcyclists and bicyclists meet at this watering hole. The beer garden out back is one of the largest in the state and often hosts live music. Food includes bar-standard sandwiches, fried appetizers, a salad bar, and steaks. $–$$

Coffee Cup Café (641-594-3765; www.coffeecupcafe.com), 616 Fourth Street, Sully. Open for breakfast, lunch, and dinner Mon. 6 AM–1:30 PM, Tues.–Thurs. 6 AM–8 PM, Fri. 6 AM–9 PM, Sat. 6 AM–1:30 PM and 5 PM–9 PM. For over 30 years, the Coffee Cup Café has been serving residents and travelers home cooking better than Grandma's, but it's really famous for the pie. Try their lemon-icebox pie if it's not sold out. Nightly specials like meat loaf and roasted chicken are served family style. $

Iowa's Best Burger Café (641-526-8535; www.iowasbestburgercafe.com), Phillips 66 Station, I-80 and IA 224 (exit 173), Kellogg. Grill open daily for lunch and dinner 11–9:30. Without trying every burger in Iowa—which would be a life's work—it's hard to choose a definitive best burger, but this gas station off the interstate—also known as the Kellduff 5 & 10—does a thoroughly commendable job. The beef is extremely tasty, the toppings (tomatoes, onions, lettuce, etc.) are plentiful, and the whole thing is cheap. Tenderloins are excellent, as well. $

Zeno's Pizza (641-752-3214), 109 East Main Street, Marshalltown. Open for dinner Mon.–Sat. 4:30–close. Marshalltown's favorite for old-school greasy pies. Carry out available. $$

COFFEE AND TREATS **Lillie Mae Chocolate** (641-752-6041; www.lilliemaechocolate.com), 23 West Main Street, Marshalltown. Open Tues.–Sat. 10–5:30. Lillie Mae's chocolate makers are so dedicated to the craft of handmade, hand-dipped chocolate and caramels that they attend chocolate conventions. What a job! Visit their store for a little sugar pick-me-up.

Remarkable Rose Floral & Gifts (641-483-3546; www.remarkablerose.com), 122 West Main Street, State Center. Open Mon.–Fri. 7–6, and Sat. 9–6. When in the Rose Capital of Iowa, it's only natural to visit a floral shop, especially when there are also coffee, fresh pastries, Iowa wine, chocolate, and gifts.

Uncle Nancy's Coffeehouse and Eatery (641-787-9709), 114 North Second Avenue West, Newton. Hours vary with the season but generally open from 7 AM to early evening. This funky little coffee shop on the square features coffee, of course, along with espresso beverages, smoothies, and light lunches.

✷ Drinking Establishments

13th Street Inn (641-752-9218), 229 North 13th Street, Marshalltown. Open Tues.–Sat. 7:30 AM–10 PM. Just across the street from the Iowa Veterans Home, this U-shaped bar is full of squishy booths and serves beer and cocktails along with breakfast, burgers, and fried food. Patio seating.

Stein's (641-792-5823), 219 North Second Avenue West, Newton. Open Mon.–Sat. 3–close. While there are several places to get a drink around Newton, Stein's is one of the most comfortable sports bars. With high ceilings and a long, wide bar, it has lots of televisions to catch up on the game. Live music on weekends.

✷ Entertainment

Valle Drive-In Theater (641-792-3558), 4074 CR F48, Newton. Open Apr.–mid-Oct. Call for show times. Built in 1949, the Valle Drive-In is one of only three drive-in theaters remaining in the state. The Valle features both digital sound and the in-car speakers used at drive-ins decades ago. Drive-in fans from across the state and the Midwest fill their cars with friends to experience this classic movie-watching experience.

✷ Selective Shopping

Willard's Fur and Fashions (641-753-3751; www.willardsfurs.com), 36 West Main Street, Marshalltown. Open Mon.–Sat. 9:30–5. Since 1864, five generations have sold and serviced furs and women's clothing in this family-owned local store. Fur is controversial today, but a walk through Willard's reminds shoppers of the glamorous bygone days. Vintage furs are available.

Kreativ, ent. (641-831-6010; www.KreativEntIowa.com), 306 First Avenue West, Newton. Open Mon.–Wed., Fri. 10–5:30; Thurs. 10–6; Sat. 10–4. This eclectic gallery just a block off the main square features paintings, sculpture, and photographs from area artists, along with arts and craft supplies.

The Farmer's Wife (641-787-1206), 124 North Second Avenue West, Newton. Open Mon.–Fri. 10–5:30 and Sat. 10–4. Home-and-garden accessories, furniture, gifts, and candles in a quaint shop on the square.

MARION COUNTY

Native Americans prized the land of the Des Moines River Valley in what is now Marion County for its fertility and plentiful wildlife. White trappers and settlers began arriving in the first half of the 19th century, and the county was founded in 1845. Today visitors can explore the three very distinct regions of Marion County.

Knoxville, the county seat, is famous as the "Sprint Car Capital of the World" and home to the Sprint Car Nationals and the Sprint Car Hall of Fame. To the north, outdoor enthusiasts can explore Iowa's largest body of water, Lake Red Rock, with an abundance of recreation, camping, and wildlife. Bald eagles winter below the dam where the water never freezes. Wild turkeys, river otters, and deer also roam the shores. North of the lake is the community of Pella, settled in 1847 by a group of Dutch immigrants seeking religious freedom. The community maintains its historic connection to the Netherlands with an authentic windmill, the delectable Dutch letter pastries, and thousands of tulips that bloom each spring. Pella is also home to Central College, a four-year liberal arts school.

While many businesses throughout the state close on Sundays, in Pella in particular almost every place observes the day of rest. Schedule visits during the week or on Saturdays to avoid spending a day in a quaint Dutch ghost town.

GUIDANCE **Knoxville Chamber of Commerce** (641-828-7555; www.discoverknoxville.org), 309 East Main Street, Knoxville. Open during business hours. Pamphlets and brochures on local businesses available.

Marion County Development Commission (641-828-2257; www.redrockarea.com), Courthouse, 214 East Main Street, Knoxville. Open during usual business hours. Pamphlets and brochures on local businesses available, but the best resource is their Web site.

Pella Convention & Visitors Bureau (1-888-746-3882; www.pella.org), 518 Franklin Street, Pella. Open during business hours, but the best resources are on the Web. Pella is one of Iowa's major tourist destinations, and their tourism office can help visitors find lodging.

Pleasantville Tourism Office (515-848-3903; www.therealpleasantville.com), 104 East Monroe Street, Pleasantville. Open during business hours. Pleasantville is a little town with a lot of treasures. Call or visit their Web site to learn more.

Army Corps of Engineers (641-828-7522; www.lakeredrock.org), Lake Red Rock Project, 1105 CR T15, Knoxville. Memorial Day–Labor Day open 9:30–6 daily, with shorter hours in summer. The Red Rock visitors center is a fun place to visit and works as a nerve center for information on the lake and surrounding area.

GETTING THERE *By car:* Marion County sits at the crossroads of **IA 5** and **CR 14** and is accessible from **I-80** by going south on **CR 14** or from Des Moines by going east on **IA 5.** Lake Red Rock divides the state, with Pella to the north and east and Knoxville to the south and west.

GETTING AROUND Pella is a lovely place to park the car and walk, but you will need a car to enjoy Marion County.

MEDICAL EMERGENCY Call **911**.

Pella Regional Health Center (641-628-3150; www.pellahealth.org), 404 Jefferson Street, Pella. Small local hospital that can handle minor emergencies.

✷ To See

'**Historical Village** and **Vermeer Mill** (641-628-2409; www.pellatuliptime.com), East First and Franklin Streets, Pella. Open Apr.–Dec., Mon.–Sat. 9–5; Jan.–Feb., call or visit Web site for hours; Mar., Mon.–Sat. 10–4. Admission: $8 adults, $2 children. This complex paints a vivid and complete picture of Pella's Dutch heritage. The courtyard village comprises over 20 buildings, some more than 150 years old. One is the boyhood home of Wyatt Earp. Each are furnished to re-create different periods in Pella's history, from the underground straw huts that settlers lived in during their first winter to the wooden shoe shop. Another exhibit shows visitors the history of the **Tulip Time Festival** (see *To Do*) and images of each Tulip Queen.

The **Vermeer Mill,** towering 124 feet over downtown Pella and completed in 2002, is an authentic windmill built in the Netherlands, by windmill maker Lucas Verbij and then assembled in Pella by two Dutch craftsmen. While it is a new mill, it is built in the style of the 1850s, and the flour it grinds can be purchased in the gift shop. The mill also contains a detailed miniature Dutch village built by Pella Historical Society volunteers.

MARION COUNTY IS HOME TO THE NATIONAL SPRINT CAR MUSEUM IN KNOXVILLE

Scholte House Museum (641-628-3684; www.scholtehouse.com), 728 Washington Street, Pella. Open Mar.–Dec. Mon.–Sat. 1–4, Jan.–Feb. by appointment. Admission: $5 adults but can be combined with admission to the **Historic Village** and **Vermeer Windmill**. Dominie Scholte, a Dutch

PELLA: LAND OF THE WOODEN SHOES

Dominie Scholte wasn't a religious radical; like many who immigrated to the United States, he simply wanted religious freedom. In 1847 he traveled with 800 Dutch settlers to Iowa. They found land between the Des Moines and Skunk Rivers—rich, fertile farming and hunting land—and purchased the area for $1.23 an acre. With little timber on the open prairie with which to build cabins, the Dutch pioneers spent their first winter in straw and sod huts, giving birth to the name Strawtown.

That Dutch heritage remains alive in today's Pella. It rings across the city in the sounds of the Klokkenspel. It spins in the blades of the authentic 1850s-style windmill built by Dutch craftsmen that catches the wind and grinds wheat for flour. It can be tasted in Dutch letters and Pella bologna. And it can be seen in the tens of thousands of tulips blooming each spring, and during Tulip Time, when locals dressed in traditional Dutch costumes scrub and parade the streets in their wooden shoes, called *klompen.* Pella embraces its Dutch heritage in daily life but without being tacky or over the top, which makes it a place travelers, rather than tourists, delight in.

minister and founder of the colony of Pella, lived with his family on the city's main square in a grand house that has been restored and furnished with original family artifacts. Tours are self-guided and a little confusing, but the docent in residence is happy to answer questions. The gardens behind the house, with over twenty-five thousand tulips, are especially lovely in spring and summer.

Klokkenspel (641-628-2626; www.pella.org), one-half block east of the square on Franklin Street, Pella. Klokkenspel plays: Mon.–Fri. 11, 1, 3, 5, and 9; Sat.–Sun. every hour from 11–9. The bells of the Klokkenspel ring out across Pella's square. Up close, this animated clock features eight 4-foot-tall mechanical figures performing to the sounds of a 147-bell, computer-driven carillon and telling the story of the settling of Pella. An automaton Mrs. Scholte cries over her broken plates, while another automaton creates wooden shoes.

The Molengracht (641-628-2246; www.molengracht.com), one-half block southeast of Pella's square. Amsterdam is known for its canals, and the Molengracht brings canal life to Iowa, with a plaza, drawbridge, hotel, restaurants, and shops. Open year-round, but it's much better in the summer because the canal is mostly drained and frozen in the winter.

Calvary Wayside Chapel (641-628-9193), Oskaloosa Street, Pella. With room for only eight churchgoers, the Calvary Wayside Chapel is one of the smallest churches in the world, featuring four two-seat benches. Built in 1965 by the Calvary Christian Reformed Church, the building is open to everyone as long as guests are respectful and close the door when they leave.

✷ To Do

Knoxville Raceway (641-842-5431; www.knoxvilleraceway.com),1000 North Lincoln Street, Knoxville. Open Oct.–Mar., Mon.–Fri. 10–6, Sat.–Sun. 12–5;

Apr.–Sept., Mon.–Fri. 10–6, Sat. 10–5, Sun. 12–5. Admission: $4 adults, $3 children. The heart of the "Sprint Car Capital of the World" is Knoxville's Raceway. The half-mile dirt track hosts races on Saturday nights from April through September. Speed demons can win big money, so the competition is fierce. Visit their Web site for racing schedule and ticketing. The raceway is also home to the **National Sprint Car Hall of Fame and Museum** (641-842-6176; www.sprintcarhof.com), where visitors can learn about the drivers that made history and see sprint cars up close. Open Oct.–Mar., Mon.–Fri. 10–6, Sat.–Sun. 12–5; Apr.–Sept., Mon.–Fri. 10–6, Sat. 10–5, Sun. 12–5. Admission: $4 adults, $3 children.

Grape Escape Vineyard and Winery (515-848-3094; www.grapeescapeiowa.com), 1185 40th Place, Pleasantville. Open Fri.–Sun. 12–7 or by appointment. The Grape Escape Winery is a great example of a retirement hobby getting out of hand. Ron and Karen Haworth started with just 22 grapevines; now they tend 8 acres and produce 6,000 gallons of wine a year. Essentially a residential garage dominated by state-of-the-art glycol-chilled vats and a German-made bottling line that fills 35 bottles per minute, this winery churns out tasty and not-too-sweet wines. Special events include "wine-in" movie on Saturday nights in the summer when visitors bring lawn chairs and picnic blankets and watch films al fresco.

Bos Landen Golf Course (1-800-916-7888; www.boslanden.com), 2411 Bos Landen Drive, Pella. One of Iowa's highest-ranked golf courses, this 18-hole championship golf course is laid out on 350 acres of rolling countryside. Restaurant and lounge in the clubhouse.

✷ Green Space

Lake Red Rock (641-828-7522; www.lakeredrock.org), 1105 CR T15, Knoxville. Lake Red Rock—named for the rose-colored bluffs that rise over its waters—offers outdoor enthusiasts all sorts of fun. Start at the **visitors center**, open daily Memorial Day–Labor Day 9:30–6, to learn about the history and ecology of the lake and shore. The center is full of informative displays, live reptiles, and plenty of taxidermy. There is also an observation deck with great views of the lake and dam.

BE GREETED BY A TORTOISE AT THE LAKE RED ROCK VISITORS CENTER, KNOXVILLE

The **Volksweg Trail** is a 10-mile paved multiuse trail that runs along the north side of the lake and to the city of Pella. Another long trail is the **Elk Rock Equestrian Trail,** a natural path that runs 13 miles around **Elk Rock State Park** (see *Where to Stay: Camping*). The area also offers several other, shorter trails. Bike rental is available at **Iowa Bike and Fitness** (see *Selective Shopping*).

Swimmers can use either the **North Overlook Beach** (1007 Highway T15, Pella, on the north side of the dam) or **Whitebreast Beach** (971 S71, Knoxville); $1 per person.

The **Red Rock Marina** (1-800-728-1301 or 641-627-5743), 1768 G28, Pella, offers a boat ramp, shelter, and trail access. Boat rental available.

Next cross the **Red Rock Dam** (641-828-7522; www.lakeredrock.org), 1105 CR T15, Knoxville. Built to control the Des Moines River, the dam forms Iowa's largest lake at 19,000 acres. The dam is more than a mile long and 110 feet tall. Short tours can be arranged to see inside the structure and learn about its history. In the winter bald eagles nest in the valley below the dam, where the water never freezes and fish are abundant. Just south of the dam is the **Gladys Black Bald Eagle Refuge** (515-281-4815) on Jewell Drive. This 38-acre refuge offers habitat for wintering bald eagles, migrating tropical birds, and other wildlife. Open Apr.–Nov. The best place to watch for eagles is the **Horn's Ferry Bridge** (641-828-2213), 198th Place near the **Howell Station Recreation Area.** Built in 1881, the Horn's Ferry Bridge was the first wagon bridge over the Des Moines River.

Sunken Gardens (641-628-4173; www.pellacity.com), Main Street, two blocks north of the square, Pella. The focal point of the sunken gardens is the pond in the shape of a wooden shoe, surrounded by formal tulip beds and a windmill. Ice skate in the winter, or enjoy the fifteen thousand tulips that bloom every spring.

THE CORDOVA PARK OBSERVATION TOWER OFFERS THE FINEST VIEWS OF LAKE RED ROCK

Cordova Park (641-627-5935; www.redrockarea.com), 1378 G28, Otley. Open year-round, 7 AM–8 PM. Admission: 50 cents per person. Cordova Park's observation tower, at the top of 170 steps, offers expansive views over the Des Moines River Valley and Lake Red Rock. The converted water tower is made of fiberglass that doesn't get hot to the touch, even on the warmest days. The park also offers a butterfly garden, plenty of picnicking, and cabins.

✱ Where to Stay

HOTELS AND MOTELS **The Inn at Strawtown** (641-621-9500; www.strawtown.com), 1111 Washington Street, Pella. The inn of choice for visiting royalty, Strawtown was originally the home of an early Dutch immigrant. The inn features 17 luxurious *kamers*, or rooms, with thoughtful, historical touches. The unique rooms and suites with unpronounceable Dutch names offer quaint details such as Dutch bunkbeds and claw-foot tubs in addition to modern amenities like Jacuzzi suites. Queen Wilhelmina slept in the suite bearing her name. Rooms (including breakfast) from $89–$140.

Royal Amsterdam Hotel (641-620-8400; www.royalamsterdam.com), 705 East First Street, Pella. The Royal Amsterdam has a regal name, but with just 38 rooms, it has a cozier scope. The rooms are clean and pleasant if a bit stark. It's built on the Molengracht, with boutique shopping and a cinema, just two blocks from Pella's main square. Rooms from $89–$129.

Dutch Mill Inn (641-628-1060; www.dutchmillinn.com), 205 Oskaloosa Street, Pella. Twenty-five wallet-friendly rooms with continental breakfast, cable television, and free wireless Internet. Rooms from $39–$50.

BED & BREAKFASTS AND INNS

De Boerderij Bed & Breakfast (641-628-1448; www.deboerderij-iowa.com), 420 Idaho Drive, Pella. Offering four supremely comfortable and well-decorated rooms with soaking tubs and robes, this B&B tends toward the romantic. Rooms (including gourmet breakfast) from $110–$140.

✐ **Spring Valley** (641-828-9021; www.springvalleybb.com), 1567 Rutledge Street, Knoxville. Lodging at Spring Valley ranges from cozy, country-themed rooms inside the bed & breakfast to more rustic cabin and bunkhouse accommodations. Guests are invited to help with sheepshearing and other farm chores. Breakfast serves up traditional country favorites. Rooms from $65–$85.

CAMPING **Lake Red Rock Campgrounds** (641-828-7522; www.lakeredrock.org). The Army Corps of Engineers operates five campgrounds on Lake Red Rock. The **North Overlook Recreation Area** (1007 CR T15) is on the Pella side of the dam with 55 sites for RVs and tents. Rates are $10 a night for a tent site and $16 for electric RV sites. The **Whitebreast Recreation Area** (971 CR S71, Knoxville) is even larger, with 125 sites at $16 a night. The **Howell Station Recreation Area** (1081 198th Place Street, Pella), below the dam on the Des Moines River, has over a hundred campsites and is the most expensive at $20 a night. **Wallashuk Recreation Area** (890 190th Avenue, Pella) has 80 sites at $16 a night. The campground at **Ivans Recreation Area** (1125 198th Place Street, Knoxville) is the smallest, with just 19 nonreservable sites at $16 a night.

Cordova Park Cabins (641-627-5935), 1378 CR G28, Otley. Modern cabins with views of Lake Red Rock. The cabins come complete with central heat and air-conditioning, a furnished kitchen, television, and a game room. Three cabins sleep 5 to 8; the others sleep between 10 and 12 and have Jacuzzi tubs. Guests need to bring linens and table service. Memorial Day–Labor Day, one-week minimum rental from $650–$900. In winter, two night minimum from $190–$260.

Elk Rock State Park (641-842-6008; www.exploreiowaparks.com), 811 146th Avenue, Knoxville. The park offers a boat ramp, picnicking, and 13 miles of trails. Campers will find sites for tent, RV, and equestrian camping, with modern shower buildings, horse stalls, and a riding arena. Rates depend on the type of campsite.

✱ Where to Eat

DINING OUT 🍸 **Monarchs Restaurant & Lounge** (641-628-1633; www.monarchsofpella.com), 705 East First Street, Pella. Open for lunch Mon.–Sat. 11–2, dinner Mon.–Fri. 4:30–9, Sat. 4:30–10. Located in the Royal Amsterdam Hotel, with outdoor seating along the Molengracht in the summer, Monarchs is a new favorite among locals and visitors. The menu is tasty but not adventurous, with lots of steaks, sandwiches, salads, and pastas. Appetizers are typical bar favorites: artichoke dip, chicken wings, onion rings. The full bar specializes in imported beer and wines. $$

🍸 **The Restaurant at Strawtown** and the **DeKalder** (641-621-9500; www.strawtown.com), 1111 Washington Street, Pella. Open for lunch and dinner Mon.–Sat. Upstairs, enjoy fine dining of homestyle meals, Greek food, steaks, and seafood as well as some traditional Dutch dishes. $$ Downstairs at the DeKalder, a cozy brick room is a casual restaurant with sandwiches, salads, and less-expensive dinners. $

EATING OUT **In't Veld Meat Market** (641-628-3440), 820 Main Street, Pella. Deli open Mon.–Sat. 9–2, meat market open until 5. This deli on the main square is a great place to dig into a sandwich of Pella bologna—which is spicier and meatier than Oscar Meyer. I ate mine with imported Gouda. The dried beef is another popular specialty. Most sandwiches are less than $5 and come with a pickle. $

Checkerboard Restaurant & Antiques (515-848-3742), 108 East Monroe Street, Pleasantville. Open for lunch and dinner Tues. 11–2, Wed.–Thurs. 11–9, Fri.–Sat. 11–10, Sun. 5–9. Diners come from all over for the onion rings and the antiques at this family-owned restaurant in little Pleasantville. Home-cooked pork fritters, cheeseburgers, and pies are the rule. Lunch $, Dinner $–$$.

The Original Kin Folks Barbeque (641-943-2362), 1731 High Street, Attica. Tues.–Thurs. 10:30–8:30, Fri.–Sat. 10:30–9, Sun. 10:30–3, closed Sunday. Located in "downtown Attica," just a bump on the road, Kin Folks is the center of the community and is worth the trip. In a state with a BBQ joint in every town, the Texas-style slow-smoked meats, homemade sides, and homemade ice cream at Kin Folks are truly exceptional. Lunch $, Dinner $–$$.

🍸 **Swamp Fox Pub & Grill** (641-842-5221), 116 North Second Street, Knoxville. Open for breakfast, lunch, and dinner Tues.–Thurs. 8–8, Fri.–Sat. 8–9. Serving hot breakfasts, salads and sandwiches, and fries and steaks, plus wine and a good bar. $–$$

COFFEE AND TREATS **Smokey Row** (641-621-0008), 639 Franklin Street, Pella. Open Mon.–Fri. 6:30 AM–11 PM, Sat. 7 AM–10 PM. A hip coffeehouse with just the right amount of warm lighting and music, serving not just coffee and espresso drinks but also ice cream and other soda-fountain specialties, soups, sandwiches, and a hot breakfast. The menu offers both pot pies and a selection for kids. A second **Smokey Row** (515-848-5959) is located at 111 East Monroe, Pleasantville. Open Mon.–Thurs. 7 AM–9 PM, Fri. 7 AM–10 PM, Sat. 7:30 AM–10 AM, Sun. 11 AM–9 AM. $–$$

Jaarsma Bakery (641-628-2940; www.jaarsmabakery.com), 727 Franklin Street, Pella. Open Mon.–Sat. 6–6, Thurs. 6–8. Dutch letters: S-shaped, light as air, warm as sunshine, and wrapped around a luscious ambrosia of almond filling. They are the distinctive taste of Pella, and the taste is transporting. Jaarsma bakes the best of these and many other Old-World pastry delights. Enjoy one while sitting on the bench out front and watching the people on the square—but don't go far because you'll probably want seconds.

The Coffee Connection (641-828-8141), 213 East Main Street, Suite 2, Knoxville. Open Mon.–Fri. 7–5, Sat. 7–2. Inexpensive breakfasts, sandwiches, and salads alongside freshly brewed coffee and espresso drinks. Meals $.

✷ Drinking Establishments

Back in the Day Lounge (515-848-3642), 107 South Jefferson Street, Pleasantville. Open Mon.–Fri. 11–11, Sat.–Sun. 11–2. The bartender himself built the wooden bar and welcomes a friendly crowd of neighbors, motorcyclists, and weary travelers to enjoy the comforts of inexpensive draft beer ($1.50 a glass) and delicious bar food. The tenderloin really hits the spot.

✷ Entertainment

Pella Opera House (1-800-720-6327; www.pellaoperahouse.org), 611 Franklin Street, Pella. Box office open Mon.–Sat. 10–4. The Pella Opera House opened in this elegantly appointed four-story building in 1900. Restored in the last decade, it is now a nonprofit theater featuring a wide range of performances, from comedy to musicals to children's theater. Admission varies by performance, but tickets rarely cost more than $30.

Pella Cinema (641-621-0329), on the Molengracht (see *To See*). Three-screen first-run movie theater with stadium seating.

✷ Selective Shopping

The Work of Our Hands International Crafts (641-628-8687; www.workofourhands.org), 602 Franklin Street, Pella. Open Mon.–Fri., Sat. 9–5; Tues. until 8:30. Run almost completely by volunteers from local churches, this small nonprofit shop offers imported fair-trade jewelry, clothing, instruments, and gifts made by workers in developing countries. Eliminating payroll expenses allows the profits to be returned to the artisans, who produce everything from soapstone carvings to dangly bone earrings.

Ulrich's Meat Market (641-628-2771; www.dutchmall.com), 715 Franklin Street, Pella. Ulrich's spicy aroma is overwhelming and delicious. Along with specialty meat and cheese, shoppers will find local wines, mustard, and other foodstuffs.

Iowa Bike & Fitness (641-628-1373), 814 Main Street, Pella. Open in winter Mon.–Wed. and Fri. 9–5:30, Thurs. 9–8, Sat. 9–5; in summer Mon.–Wed. 9–5:30, Thurs.–Fri. 9–8, Sat. 9–5, and Sun. 1–4. A top-notch bike shop specializing in Trek road, mountain, and comfort bikes. The staff is friendly and helpful, and bike rental is available: $15 for 4 hours, $20 for 24 hours.

The Cornerstone Boutique (641-628-8707; www.cornerstoneofpella.com), 617 Franklin Street, Pella. Open Mon.–Wed. and Fri. 9:30–5:30, Thurs. 9:30–8, and Sat. 9–5. This funky little boutique just off the square in downtown Pella sells unique clothing, shoes, and handbags as well as children's clothing.

MADISON AND WARREN COUNTIES

While historic covered bridges dot the countryside throughout the state, "the bridges of Madison County" are the most well known, thanks to the book and the film of that name. Because of the fame of its bridges, Madison County does an excellent job of maintaining them and making it easy for visitors to find and enjoy them.

Warren County has interesting diversions other than its covered bridges. Some of the highest-quality coal to be found in the state was removed from the area that is now **Summerset State Park.** And the two excellent wineries found in Warren County—**Summerset** and **La Vida Loca**—are both at the heart of revitalizing oenology and viticulture in the state of Iowa. Indianola, the county seat, is also home to the **National Balloon Museum** and holds the National Balloon Classic and surrounding festival every year.

GUIDANCE **Madison County Chamber of Commerce** (515-462-1185; www.madisoncounty.com), 73 Jefferson Street, Winterset. Madison County is prepared for bridge lovers. Open during business hours. Their Web site offers a detailed map of *The Bridges of Madison County* movie locations.

Indianola Chamber of Commerce (515-961-6269; www.indianolachamber.com), 515 North Jefferson Way, Suite D, Indianola. Office hours Mon.–Fri. 8:15–4:30. A helpful staff can answer questions about the county.

GETTING THERE *By car:* **I-35** runs north-south between Madison and Warren Counties, and the major cities are connected by **IA 92.**

MEDICAL EMERGENCY Call **911**.

Madison County Healthcare System (515-462-2373; www.madisonhealth.com), 300 Hutchings Street, Winterset. Emergency and inpatient care.

INTERNET ACCESS/PUBLIC LIBRARY **Indianola Public Library** (515-961-9418; www.indianola.lib.ia.us), 207 North B Street, Indianola. Open 10–8:30 Mon.–Thurs., 10–6 Fri., 10–5 Sat., 1–4 Sun. Wireless Internet and public computers are available for "patrons in good standing." Visitors should inquire at the desk for available computers.

✳ To See

✪ **The Bridges of Madison County** (515-462-1185; www.madisoncounty.com). The novel and film were enough to make the six bridges of Madison County collectively one of the most popular attractions in central Iowa. Beginning in 1870, 19 bridges—named for the nearest residents—were built with covers to protect the expensive wooden floorboards. Five of the original bridges remain, and most have been relocated. (A sixth, the Cedar Covered Bridge, was destroyed by arson but has been rebuilt.) The Cutler-Donahoe Covered Bridge is now at the entrance of the Winterset City Park. Visit the chamber of commerce Web site for more information and a map, which also outlines other famous spots from the film, including the now-closed Texaco Station and the "Blue Note Lounge"—really a bar called Pheasant Run.

Birthplace of John Wayne (515-462-1044; www.johnwaynebirthplace.org), 216 South Second Street, Winterset. Open year-round 10–4:30 except Thanksgiving Day, Christmas Day, New Year's Day, and Easter Sunday. Admission: $4 adults, $3 seniors, $1 children. Born Marion Morrison, Wayne only lived in Iowa for a few years after his 1907 birth before moving with his family to California and later finding fame, but the John Wayne Birthplace is determined to celebrate him. Visitors take a 20-minute guided tour through the house, which is designed to represent the period (although the furniture is not original; the family took it with them to California). Two of the rooms are filled with Wayne photos and memorabilia, and the organization hopes to raise $5 million to build a museum. The adjacent building houses the ticket office and a wide variety of John Wayne gifts.

Madison County Historical Complex (515-462-2134; www.madisoncounty historicalsociety.com), 815 South Second Avenue, Winterset. Open May 1–Oct. 31 Mon–Sat. 11–4, Sun. 1–5, or by appointment. Admission to both mansion and museum: $5 adults, children under 12 free. With a wide variety of period buildings from its early settlement, the Madison County Historical Complex is an educational and entertaining outdoor museum. Buildings include a stone barn and privy made with local limestone, a log post office and school, a blacksmith shop, and Winterset's original railroad depot. The 14 buildings are located on 18 acres on the south side of the city.

Madison County Courthouse, 112 North John Wayne Drive, Winterset. Open Mon.–Fri. 8–4:30. Built in 1876 of native limestone and black walnut, the courthouse stands 122 feet above the square. The graffiti left by prisoners who were kept on the third floor—which is open for viewing—has been preserved.

National Balloon Museum (515-961-3714; www.nationalballoonmuseum .com), 1601 North Jefferson Way, Indianola. Open May–Dec. 23 Mon.–Fri. 9–4, Sat. 10–4, Sun. 1–4; Dec. 27–Apr. Mon.–Sat. 10–2, Sun. 1–4. Free. Indianola was home to the National Balloon (hot air, that is) Championships, and is currently home of the National Balloon Classic. Rightly, then, it is also home to a museum dedicated to this American sport. Good for kids and rainy days.

✳ To Do

WINERIES ✪ **La Vida Loca Winery** (515-962-2236; www.lavidalocawinery .com), 7852 Jesup Street, Indianola. Open Tues.–Sat. 10–5, Sun. 12–5. When I visited La Vida Loca, the winemaker was out on the riding lawn mower, so needless to say, I had some skepticism. Iowa has a reputation for producing sticky sweet and mindlessly simple fruit wines, so I was surprised and delighted to find the wines at La Vida Loca complex, drinkable, and fun. Against my prejudice, my favorite turned out to be a delicious white made from pears and peaches called Autumn Harvest. Other vintages are made from fruits including gooseberries and cherries as well as classic grapes—all grown on site. Garlic and jalapeño wines, designed for cooking and marinating, will intrigue chefs.

Summerset Winery (515-961-3545; www.summersetwine.com), 15101 Fairfax Street, Indianola. Open Tues.–Sun. 10–5. This vineyard and winery is located above the Middle River, just south of Indianola. Sample popular Iowa wines in the tasting room, and enjoy live music on Friday nights and Sunday afternoons. In the fall the grapes are picked by volunteers who enjoy complimentary wine for their trouble.

✷ Green Space

Lake Ahquabi State Park (515-961-7101; www.iowadnr.gov/parks/state_park_list/lake_ahquabi.html), 1650 118th Avenue, Indianola. Park open during daylight hours year-round, boat rental concession open daily in summer. Canoe, kayak, or paddleboat around the lake. The park also offers fishing, swimming, and picnic shelters in addition to an 8-mile hiking trail that circles the lake.

Winterset City Park (515-462-3258; www.winterset.govoffice.com), 124 West Court Avenue, Winterset. This park is something special, with 76 acres of hilly countryside, an English hedge maze, the Cutler-Donahoe Covered Bridge, a stone bridge, and Clark Tower, a three-story limestone structure that overlooks the river valley. Visitors can lose themselves for a while on the long and winding paths, picnic, or camp at the adjoining campground.

Pammel Park (515-462-3636; www.madisoncountyparks.org). From Winterset, travel west on IA 92 for 1 mile, and then go south on IA 322 for 3 miles. Pammel Park is a gem on the Middle River that offers camping, canoeing, hiking, and many other activities. The park has many unique features, including a tunnel through the limestone bluff, a ford over the Middle River, and yurts available to rent year-round in the modern campground.

Banner Lakes at Summerset State Park (515-961-7101; www.iowadnr.gov/parks), north of Indianola on IA 65/69. Created from the Banner Pits, a coal mine in the 1930s, Banner Lakes is Iowa's newest state park, with picnicking, bicycling, mountain biking, and excellent fishing. The coal pilings created hills around the edges of the lake, making it feel secluded.

✷ Where to Stay

HOTELS AND MOTELS **Apple Tree Inn** (515-961-0551; www.appletreeindianola.com), 1215 North Jefferson Street, Indianola. An indoor motel with 60 rooms and suites offering wireless Internet, microwaves and refrigerators, cable television, and free continental breakfast. Rooms from $57–$85.

BED & BREAKFASTS **Garden and Galley B&B** (515-961-7749; www.gardenandgalley.com), 1321 South Jefferson Way, Indianola. Four rooms in a 1950s Frank Lloyd Wright–style home set among 9 acres of garden and orchard views above the South River Valley. Enjoy hors d'oeuvres and beverages when you arrive and gourmet breakfasts in the morning. Rooms from $100–$120.

The Fitch House Bed & Breakfast (641-396-2443; www.thefitchhouse .com), 2748 Woodland Avenue, St. Charles. The Fitch House began when a father-and-son team got a little too enthusiastic when building a garage. The building became a six-room, 1,200-square-foot B&B with all the amenities of home. Rick and Diane Fitch also have accommodations in a refurbished chicken coop with air-conditioning and heat. Antiques on display are for sale. The six-room suite $125, the chicken coop $75.

CAMPING **Winterset City Park Campgrounds** (515-462-3258; winter set.govoffice.com), 124 West Court Avenue, Winterset. Open Apr. 1–Nov. 15. Thirty-four sites with electric, water, and sewer hook-ups for RVs, a shower building, fire rings, and picnic tables. Campsites $10 for tent sites, $14–$16 for RV sites.

Pammel Park See *Green Space.*

Lake Ahquabi State Park See *Green Space.*

✷ Where to Eat

EATING OUT **Porky's Deli** (515-462-4037), 106 East Court Avenue, Winterset. Open 10:30–6. The motto at Porky's is "Where meat meets its maker," but that seems a little too grim for this fantastic deli. The meat and cheese (try the smoked Gouda) are fresh and delicious. But the best part about Porky's is the salad bar. Diners are invited to dress their own sandwiches with a rotating selection of fancy-pants toppings. The menu also features a bottomless root beer float for only $2.50. Cash or local checks only. No credit cards. $

Montrose Pharmacy (515-462-2282), 118–120 North First Avenue, Winterset. Open for breakfast and lunch. This full-service pharmacy is also the oldest family-owned restaurant in Madison County. Get a full breakfast at the counter, a cafeteria-style lunch, or a hand-dipped malt. $

The Corner Sundry (515-961-9029), 101 North Buxton, Indianola. Open Mon.–Sat. 8–5:30, Sun. 1–5:30. An old-fashioned soda fountain where ice-cream lovers can dive into root beer floats and Green Rivers, along with sundaes, Cokes, and other treats. $

✷ Drinking Establishments

Pheasant Run (515-462-4444), 103 South John Wayne Drive, Winterset. Open—well, it's a bar, so. . . . The Pheasant Run is the kind of joint where all heads turn and the music zips to silence when a stranger walks through the door, which is funny because it made its big-screen debut as the Blue Note Lounge in *The Bridges of Madison County.* It's a dive but a beloved dive. Cash only.

ENTERTAINMENT ✪ **Des Moines Metro Opera** (515-961-6221; www .desmoinesmetroopera.org), 106 West Boston Avenue, Indianola. Opera lovers in central Iowa welcome the coming of summer with Festival Season. Call or consult their Web site for more information on schedules and tickets.

✷ Selective Shopping

Blue Horse Enterprises (515-462-4308), 111 South John Wayne Drive, Winterset. Open Tues.–Wed., Fri. 10–6, Thurs. 10–7, Sat. 10–2, and by appointment. A crowded little art gallery and framing store. Owner Tom Koehler, originally from St. Louis, is well connected to regional and national artists and is a talented framer to boot. Much of the art on display in his shop is very reasonably priced.

The Roseman Covered Bridge Shop (1-888-999-2902; www.rosemanbridge.com), 2451 Elderberry Lane, Winterset, just north of the Roseman Covered Bridge. The store was opened by Wyman Wilson in 1994 when Hollywood came to Madison County. Some of the filming took place in Wilson's pasture next to the Roseman Bridge. The shop offers all the usual souvenirs, T-shirts, mugs, cards, and jewelry. Hours vary, so call ahead.

Court Avenue Books (515-462-1090), 116 East Court Avenue, Winterset. Open Mon.–Sat. 1–5, but if it's slow they close up at 4:30. This secondhand bookshop is packed with used books that people actually want to read. They also sell a small selection of new books and regional Iowa books.

Canoe Sport Outfitters (515-961-6117; www.canoesportoutfitters.com), 203 West Salem Avenue, Indianola. Open Mon.–Wed. and Fri.–Sat. 10–6, Thurs. 10–8, and Sun. 12–5. This top-notch shop just off the square is a paddler's delight. Offered are canoe and kayak rentals, instructions, and adventure trips, along with boats, paddles, and accessories. These guys also have a great salesroom with used boats and equipment.

The Garden Barn (515-962-0024; www.thegardenbarn.com), 11879 CR G24, just outside of Indianola. Open Apr.–Christmas Thurs.–Sat. 10–5 and 2–5 Sun. Florals, antiques, garden art, and unique gifts in a pretty turn-of-the-20th-century, post-and-beam-style barn just outside of Indianola.

DALLAS COUNTY

Dallas County, directly west of Polk County, has seen dramatic growth in the past decade as the Des Moines metro has spilled across the county line. In the eastern part of the county, visitors will find the suburban joys of the West Glen Shopping Village and Jordan Creek Mall, the newest and largest shopping center in the area. As visitors drive west, they find themselves in the fertile farmlands of the Raccoon River Valley. Adel is the county seat and is known for its brick streets and annual Sweet Corn Festival. In the northwest corner of the county is the city of Perry, home of the historic and luxurious Hotel Pattee.

GUIDANCE **Perry Chamber of Commerce** (515-465-4601; www.perryia.org), 1226 Second Street, Perry. City officials in Perry work very hard to keep their community alive and vibrant and are especially helpful and eager.

Adel City Hall (515-993-4525; www.adeliowa.org), 301 South 10th Street, Adel. Chamber of Commerce and other information available through the city's Web site.

GETTING THERE *By car:* **I-80** runs east-west along the bottom section of the county, and **IA 169** runs north–south through the center of the county.

MEDICAL EMERGENCY Call **911**.

Dallas County Hospital (515-465-3547; www.dallascohospital.org), 610 Tenth Street, Perry. Emergency and walk-in care available at this hospital in the northeast part of the county, but for emergencies in other areas, it is probably quicker to go to hospitals in Des Moines.

INTERNET ACCESS/PUBLIC LIBRARY **Adel Public Library** (515–993–3512; www.adelpl.org), 303 South Tenth Street, Adel. Open 10–8 Mon.–Thurs., 10–5:30 Fri., 10–1:30 Sat., 1–4 Sun. Public computers available for up to an hour at a time.

* To See

Bob Feller Museum (515-996-2806; www.bobfellermuseum.org), 310 Mill Street, Van Meter. Open Tues.–Sat. 10–3, Sun. 12–4. Admission: $5 adults, $3 children. On display is baseball memorabilia from this Hall of Fame pitcher's career. The "heater from Van Meter" grew up on a farm just north of this little town off I-80. Starting for the Cleveland Indians at age 17, Feller melted batters with his blazing 100-mile-an-hour fastball. Here fans can find signed baseballs, bats, and photos that tell the story of the baseball legend and Iowa native.

✷ To Do

Forest Park Museum and Arboretum (515-465-3577; www.co.dallas.ia.us/conservation), 14581 K Avenue, Perry. Open May 1–Oct. 31 Mon.–Fri. 8–4:30, Sat., Sun., and holidays 1–4:30; Nov. 1–Apr. 30 open by appointment. Free. The arboretum—true to Iowa's practical, farming heritage—was planted in straight lines by local historian and author Eugene Hastie to allow rows of crops between the trees. Enjoy 12 acres of restored prairie, a museum showcasing the history of Dallas County, and the Alton School, a one-room schoolhouse that closed in 1961.

Penoach Winery (515-993-4374; www.penoach.com), 26759 North Avenue, Adel. Open Fri. 12–6, Sat. 12–5, and Sun. 1–5. Pronounced "pen-oak," this small winery built on the site of the original 1900s farmstead is as delightful to see as its wines are to taste. Grapes are tended from start to finish on this picturesque vineyard just north of Adel.

Perry Bowl (515-465-3863), 1115 Warford Street, Perry. Open Mon.–Wed. 10–9, Thurs.–Sat. 10–10. Walking into this slightly rundown, six-lane bowling alley is like stepping back in time to a small-town hangout in the 1950s, complete with a popular lunch counter and cheeseburgers.

Sportsplex West (515-987-0806; www.sportsplexwest.com), 890 Southeast Olson Drive, Waukee. Open in summer Mon.–Sat. 8–9, Sun. 12–8; the rest of the year Mon.–Sat. 9–9, Sun. 12–9. A variety of sports and fitness activities under one roof—rock climbing, bouldering, football, soccer, basketball, golf, and ultimate Frisbee—to burn off some calories. Fees vary by activity, so call or visit their Web site for more information.

OUTDOOR ADVENTURES IN DALLAS COUNTY

Bicycle the **Raccoon River Valley Trail** (515-465-3577; www.raccoonrivervalleytrail.org). This 56-mile, multiuse trail is a converted railway that runs from Clive in Polk County to Jefferson in Greene County. A favorite ride is from Des Moines to the Dairy Stripe ice cream shop in Adel. There are trailheads along the entire route. Fee: $2 per day for adults or $10 annual pass.

Paddle the **Raccoon River,** which runs through Dallas County. **Raccoon River Valley Adventures** (515-422-6420; www.kayakiowa.com) outfits paddlers with canoes and kayaks at **Island Park** in Adel. They offer drop-offs, pickups, and overnight rental and can recommend the best stretches of river. They also rent bicycles. While walk-ins are accepted, it is better to schedule your trip ahead of time. Call or visit their Web site for rate information.

✷ Green Space

Hanging Rock County Park (515-465-3577; www.co.dallas.ia.us), 916 Redfield Street, Redfield. The park is named for the 45-foot sandstone ledges that hang over the Middle Raccoon River. Visitors can bring their own canoes and enjoy the river, hike, fish, or picnic among 440 acres of woodland, wetland, prairie, and river landscapes.

Voas Nature Area (515-465-3577), 19286 Lexington Road, Minburn. Open until 10 PM daily. This 372-acre park combines restored wetland, prairie, and woodland on a farm donated by brother and sister Dallas County residents Mae and Lyle Voas. Picnic and fire-ring facilities are available for visitors. A small museum displays the siblings' rock collection, but the building is only open during the summer—and hours vary, so call ahead.

Forest Park Museum and Arboretum See *To Do*.

✷ Where to Stay

HOTELS AND MOTELS **Hotel Pattee** (515-465-3511; www.hotelpattee.com), 1112 Willis Avenue, Perry. The Hotel Pattee originally opened to serve the railway in 1913 and was restored in 1997. The Arts and Crafts building is a gem on the prairie, with richly appointed—but never tacky—specialty rooms, from the Louis Armstrong Suite to the Woodworking Room to the Welsh Room. Rooms from $149–$229.

Edgetowner Motel (515-834-2641), 804 Guthrie Street, De Soto. A small-town motel with clean rooms and basic amenities, located close to I-80 between Madison and Dallas Counties. The manager lives in an on-site apartment and is very helpful. Rooms from $40–$50.

BED & BREAKFASTS

✪ **Timberpine Lodge** (515-993-3386; www.timberpinelodge.com), 23675 Sportsman Club Lane, Adel. Innkeepers Greg and Cheryl Arganbright and their three sons built this gorgeous timber-frame home with their own hands. Since the lodge opened their labor of love has been entertaining guests. Set on 6 acres of a former Christmas-tree farm, the inn is as beautiful inside as it is out. The Pinecone Suite offers a whirlpool tub, fireplace, and deck; the cozy Wildflower Room has a private bath. The innkeepers make guests feel like family. Breakfast on organic food outside on the deck while enjoying the birds. Suite $140–$150, room $105–$115.

Yellow Swan Bed & Breakfast (515-992-3118; www.yellowswanbb.com), 400 Hatton Avenue, Dallas Center. The two guest rooms at the Yellow Swan are named for relatives in Jan and Gary Busby's families and are full of antiques and charm. Enjoy evening dessert, a full breakfast, and a hot tub. Guests love spending time on the front porch in this quiet Dallas Center home. Rooms from $100–$125.

Purviance Farm (515-677-2619; www.purviancefarm.com), 21501 H Avenue, Minburn. The farm has been in innkeeper Nadine Weiser's family since 1915, and her goal is to preserve the beauty of rural Iowa life in this Arts and Crafts bed & breakfast. The five guest rooms are furnished with original items from the 1915 Sears Roebuck catalog, and they are warm and pretty without being fussy. The inn also offers a game room, conference room, hot tub, fire circle, and camping. Rooms from $70–$100.

✷ Where to Eat

EATING OUT **Waveland Café West** (515-987-1038), 3571 Ute Avenue, Booneville. Open for breakfast, lunch, and dinner. Mon.–Tues. 7–8, Wed.–Fri. 7–9, Sat. 6–9, and Sun. 8–7. If you can't get a table for breakfast at this beloved diner at their location on University Avenue in Des Moines, try the Dallas County version, just a short drive past the western suburbs. Waveland Café West serves up all the same eggs, skillets, and sandwiches as its sibling back east. Breakfast $–$$, Lunch and Dinner $$.

LT Organic Farm (515-987-3561), 3241 Ute Avenue, Waukee. Open daily 11–8. Outside the windows of the banquet-style dining room at this working organic farm, diners can watch the food grow while they enjoy it. The menu changes based on the season, with one three-course meal (for just $12!) offered per day based on what is ripe. The day I stopped in it was chicken Marsala and early-spring vegetables. The farm is open all day and can typically accommodate diners when they arrive. The farm also offers a health-food store, cooking classes, and a community-supported agriculture program. $$

Casa de Oro (515-465-8808), 1110 Second Street, Perry. Open for lunch and dinner Mon.–Thurs. and Sun. 11–9, Fri.–Sat. 11–10. Delicious, authentic, inexpensive Mexican cuisine. The portions are enormous, cheesy, and filling. $

Y **Harvest Moon** (515-992-3868; www.dcharvestmoon.com), 1405 Walnut Street, Dallas Center. Open for lunch Mon.–Sat. 11–2, dinner Mon.–Thurs. 5–8, Fri.–Sat. 5–9. This quirky little local-favorite restaurant with a fun bar offers steaks, burgers, sandwiches, and the occasional Italian dinner blowout. $$

The Master Griller's Homestead (515-758-2200; www.mastergriller.com), 142 South Chestnut Avenue, Earlham. Deli open Mon.–Fri. 6:30–2:30, dinner Thurs.–Sat. 5–10, Sun. brunch 9–2. Meat lovers can track down the master griller—known throughout the Midwest for superb and creative BBQ—at his restaurant in the sleepy town of Earlham. Dinner $$ with a killer prime-rib special.

COFFEE AND TREATS **Jackie's Kafe and Coffeebar** (515-993-3663), 820 Prairie Street, Adel. Open for lunch and dinner Tues.–Sat. 11–2 and 5–9. Tucked away on a quiet brick street, this Lincoln-era church (later the city library) is as lovely and historic a place to eat as the sandwiches and salads are flavorful. There is a beautiful garden patio for outside seating. $$

Thymes Remembered Tea Room (515-465-2631; www.thymesrememberedtearoom.com), 1020 Otley Street, Perry. Open for lunch Mon.–Sat. 10–4. The tinkling of china and laughter ring through rich displays of jewelry, clothing, and candles in the **Calico Shops** adjoining the tearoom. Ladies can shop after enjoying elegant salads, entrées, and desserts. Reservations recommended.$$

✷ Selective Shopping

Atherton House (515-993-2034), 202 South Ninth Street, Adel. Open Mon.–Sat. 9–5. This little shop is full of surprising handmade crafts and gifts from around the world and close to home. There are hand-blown glass marbles, artwork, paper products, and specialty foods. Nothing plastic or made in China.

Adel Quilting and Dry Goods (515-993-1170; www.adelquilting.blogspot.com), 909 Prairie Street, Adel. Open Mon.–Sat. 9–5, Thurs. 9–7. Quilters and quilt lovers will enjoy this bright and cozy quilting shop, just one block off the square in Adel.

The Cameo Rose Collection (515-993-4211; www.cameorosecollection.com), 107 North Ninth Street, Adel. Open Tues.–Sat. 9–5. The shop features unique gifts, home furnishings, and jewelry, but the best part of the store is the upstairs apartment-turned-retail space. The rich furnishings and splendid rooms may make you want to relocate to Adel.

Mary Rose (515-465-4222; www.maryrosecollection.com), 1215 Warford Street, Perry. Open Tues.–Fri. 10–5, Sat. 10–3. Part art gallery, part antiques store, part gift shop, Mary Rose sells linens and Polish pottery but specializes in local arts in a historic 1913 telephone-company building.

BOONE COUNTY

Named for Capt. Nathan Boone, the youngest son of Daniel Boone, Boone County's history began when Company H of the U.S. Dragoons (lightly armed cavalry officers) explored the region on a mapping expedition. The city of Boone, which is also the county seat, was born in 1865 when John I. Blair of New Jersey built a railroad across the country. That railroad history, along with coal mining, is still a part of Boone County today. The county is graced by the scenic Des Moines River Valley and offers visitors a charming look into the past, just a short drive from the Des Moines metro area. Boone has several chain hotels, but there really aren't any acceptable independent hotels or inns. Visitors might consider staying in Des Moines, Ames, or Dallas County.

GUIDANCE **Boone Area Convention and Visitors Bureau** (1-800-266-6312; www.booneiowa.com), 903 Story Street, Boone. Information on local businesses is available during normal business hours.

GETTING THERE *By car:* Access Boone County by taking the **US 30** exit from **I-35** just south of Ames in Story County. Boone sits just north and west of the crossroads of **IA 17** and **US 30**.

MEDICAL EMERGENCY Call **911**.

Boone County Hospital (515-432-3140; www.boonehospital.com), 1015 Union Street, Boone. Emergency medical services available in this county hospital.

INTERNET ACCESS/PUBLIC LIBRARY **Ericson Public Library** (515–432–3727; www.boone.lib.ia.us), 702 Greene Street, Boone. Open 9–8 Mon.–Tues., 9–6 Wed.–Fri., 9–3 Sat. Eight computers with Internet access are available, but you will need a library card.

✷ To See

✐ **Boone & Scenic Valley Railroad** (1-800-626-0319; www.scenic-valleyrr.com), 225 10th Street, Boone. Excursion trains operate daily Memorial Day–Oct. 31. Call for schedule and tickets. Boone County is known for its railroad, and the Boone & Scenic Valley offers visitors a 15-mile round-trip or 22-mile dinner train through the picturesque Des Moines River Valley. Excursion trains feature 1920s coach cars, two cabooses, and an open-air car. Or consider a dinner, dessert, or picnic train on the 1950s City of Los Angeles or City of San Francisco cars. The trip is especially lovely in autumn when the leaves are colorful. The special Thomas the Tank Engine 5, Pumpkin Express, and Santa Express trains are for children. The **East Side Electric Trolley Company** lets riders relive the experience of Iowa's interurban trolley system. Departs weekends at 225 10th Street Memorial Day–Oct. 31. While waiting for departure, train riders can explore the museum and train cars on the grounds.

Boone County Historical Center (515-432-1907; www.ameshistoricalsociety.org/attractions.htm), 602 Story Street, Boone. Open Sept.–May, Mon.–Fri. 1–5; June–Aug., Mon.–Sat. 1–5; or by appointment. Admission: $3 adults, children under 18 free. The Boone County Museum gives visitors a decade-by-decade tour of the area in the 20th century. Informative exhibits include birds and wildlife, a replica coal mine, and a diorama on the heroism of Kate Shelley. The center is also available for historical and genealogical research.

Mamie Doud Eisenhower Birthplace (515-432-1907; www.mamiebirthplace.homestead.com), 709 Carroll Street, Boone. Open Apr.–May Tues.–Sat. 1–5, June–Oct. Mon.–Sat. 10–5, or by appointment. Admission: $4 adults, $1 children. Carefully restored to Victorian elegance, this five-room house contains many furnishings donated by the 24th First Lady's family, including her 1962 Plymouth Valiant residing in the carriage house. Although Mrs. Eisenhower did not live in the house past the age of one, it is full of her possessions as well as the bed in which she was born.

Kate Shelley Railroad Museum and **Kate Shelley Memorial High Bridge** (515-432-1907; www.boonecountyhistory.org), 1198 232nd Street, Boone. Museum open June–Sept. 1–5 Sat. and Sun., other times by appointment. Free. When a storm destroyed the railroad bridge over Honey Creek on July 6, 1881, 15-year-old Kate Shelley crawled across the railroad trestle spanning the Des Moines River to alert Moingona station officials and stop the oncoming passenger train. Her heroics saved hundreds of lives. The museum, located in a 19th-century railroad station on the site of the original Moingona station, includes a video narrated by Kate's nephew and a walking trail to the site of the dramatic events. The grounds are open throughout the year, but make an appointment to see the museum. The Kate Shelly Memorial High Bridge is the longest and highest double-track railroad bridge in the United States, spanning the Des Moines River at a height of 185 feet.

Snus Hill Winery (515-795-3535; www.snushillwine.com), 2183 320th Street, Madrid. Open Thurs., Fri., Sun. 12–5; Sat. 10–5; and by appointment; call ahead for winter hours. Using American and French-American grapes, Snus Hill creates unique Iowa wines on a peaceful farm in rural Boone County with pastoral views of the Iowa landscape. Taste Iowa wines for every palate in a winery named after a beloved pet cat.

✷ To Do

Seven Oaks (515-432-9457; www.sevenoaksrec.com), 1086 222nd Drive, Boone. Outdoor adventures include day and overnight canoe and kayak trips, tubing, paintball, mountain biking, motocross and quad racing, skiing, and snowboarding.

Seven Oaks also offers rustic camping, a lodge for special events, and catered meals for the hungry adventurer. Hours and schedules vary based on activity, season, and weather, so call ahead, or visit their Web site for more information.

Honey Creek Golf Club (515-432-6162; www.golfhoneycreek.com), 1323 Noble Lynx Drive, Boone. This 18-hole golf course neighbors the scenery of **Ledges State Park** (see *Green Space*) and is appealing to golfers of all skill levels.

✷ Green Space

✪ **Ledges State Park** (515-432-1852; www.iowadnr.gov/parks), on E52 between IA 17 and the Des Moines River. One of Iowa's oldest and best-loved state parks, Ledges charms hikers and sightseers with impressive sandstone bluffs carved by the Des Moines River. The park also offers a pretty wooded campground for both RV and tent campers. Sites from $11-$16.

Iowa Arboretum (515-795-3216; www.iowaarboretum.org), 1875 Peach Avenue, Madrid. Open sunrise to sunset year-round; office hours 8:30–4:30; guided tours by appointment. Free. The 378-acre garden is nestled in scenic Boone County, with a living "library" of the plants that grow in Iowa. A helpful pamphlet guides visitors through a walking tour, and there are three hiking trails through restored prairie and woodlands. The facility also features a banquet room and garden store.

✷ Where to Stay

CAMPING **Don Williams Recreational Area** (515-353-4237; www.wccta.net/gallery/bccb), 610 H Avenue, Ogden. Modern camping with a well-stocked fishing lake, a nine-hole golf course, and luxury cabins. Two restaurants are open during the summer months. Campsites from $10–$13.

✷ Where to Eat

EATING OUT **Van Hemert's Dutch Oven Bakery and Koffie Huis** (515-432-9567; www.dutchovenbakeryiowa.com), 605 Story Street, Boone. Open for breakfast and lunch Mon.–Fri. 5 AM–6 PM, Sat. 5 AM–5:30 PM. There is just something magical about Dutch bakeries, and the Dutch Oven is no exception, with flakey Dutch letters, doughnuts, hot breakfasts, and soups, salads, and sandwiches for lunch. This little bakery on the central street in Boone is a nice place for a coffee or a light meal. Outside seating available. $–$$

Iris Tea Room (515-432-3459), 803 Story Street, Boone. Open for lunch; winter hours Oct.–May, Tues.–Sat. 11–4; summer hours June–Sept., Mon.–Fri. 11–3. Decorated with silk irises and antiques, and located on the lower level of an antiques mall, the Iris Tea Room offers salads, sandwiches, and a soup of the day for ladies who lunch, but the portions are big enough for skeptical husbands to come along. Reservations recommended, no credit cards. $$

Jimmy's Bar-b-Que Pit (515-433-1227), 717 Story Street, Boone. Open for lunch and dinner Mon.–Sat. 11–9. When Ames's favorite BBQ chef moved to Boone, mouths started watering, and people started driving in to eat smoked brisket, pork, ham, ribs, and chicken. Sizes of sandwiches and sides are proportioned geographically: Boone at ¼-pound, Iowa at ⅓-pound, and Texas at ½-pound. $

🏵 **La Carreta** (515-432-5100), 1215 South Story Street, Boone. Open

Mon.–Thurs. and Sat. 11–10, Fri. 11–11, and Sun. 11–9. Boone residents love La Carreta for the delicious Mexican food, the gigantic portions, and the low prices. Don't let the location in the slightly sketchy motel frighten you away from the delights of Chori Pollo and excellent margaritas. $

Y **Tic Toc Restaurant & Flame Lounge** (515-432-5979), 716 Keeler Street, Boone. Open for lunch and dinner Mon.–Thurs. 11–2 and 4:30–10, Fri. 11–2 and 4:30–11, Saturday 4:30–11. This local favorite has been serving steaks, seafood, chicken, pizza, and sandwiches for 35 years. Reservations accepted. $$

✱ Selective Shopping

Iron Horse Antique Mall (515-432-5577), 803 Story Street, Boone. Open Mon.–Sat. 10–5, Sun. 11–4. Iowa is awash with antiques stores, but the Iron Horse is more fun than most. More than 20 vendors fill the small, well-organized space, and with good prices on antiques from furniture to railroad memorabilia to linens and jewelry, even the most anti-antiques shopper can find a treasure.

The Farm Toy Store (515-846-6437) US 169 North, Boxholm. Open Mon.–Fri. 9–4:30, Sat. 9–3. If you make it as far north as the tiny town of Boxholm (population 200+), you might stop in at the Farm Toy Store and wonder at the collection of replica farm toys for both children and collectors.

✱ Special Events

April: **Drake Relays** (515-271-3647; www.godrakebulldogs.com), Drake Stadium, Forest Avenue, Des Moines. World-class athletes race for glory at this famous track meet. Don't miss the beautiful bull dog contest.

Iowa Book Festival (515-993-5472; www.adeliowa.org/iowabookfestival.page), throughout Adel. Guest authors, book art, workshops, and a book sale.

VEISHEA (515-294-1026; www.veishea.iastate.edu), Iowa State Campus, Ames. "VEISHEA" stands for the first letters of ISU's colleges at the birth of the festival in 1922: veterinary medicine, engineering, industrial science, home economics, and agriculture. Nowadays it's ISU's annual celebration of education and entertainment, though it has a reputation for getting a bit rowdy after dark.

May: **Tulip Time** (www.pellatuliptime.com), City Square, Pella. This popular three-day event is scheduled in May to coincide with the blooming of the thousands of tulips in Pella. Festivities include parades with citizens in traditional Dutch costumes, food, and the crowning of the Tulip Queen.

Asian American Festival (515-273-5101; www.iowaasianalliance.com), Water Works Park, Des Moines. A celebration of Asian heritage and culture, featuring exhibits, history, performance artists, sports, and family activities.

June: **Hy-Vee Triathlon** (515-267-2857; www.hy-veetriathlon.com), downtown Des Moines and Gray's Lake Park. The Hy-Vee Triathlon offers the largest purse in North America and served as a qualifying event for the Beijing Olympics in 2008.

Greek Food Festival (515-277-0780; stgeorge.ia.goarch.org), St. George Greek Orthodox Church, 1110 35th Street, Des Moines. The first weekend in June finds this celebration of Greek food, art, and dance.

Scandinavian Days (515-733-4214; www.storycity.net) North and South Parks, Story City. All the rides and food of a small-town carnival, plus

IOWA STATE FAIR: "OUR STATE FAIR IS A GREAT STATE FAIR. . . ." Many writers, including Rodgers and Hammerstein, have tried to impress upon visitors the cultural significance of the Iowa State Fair—but, seriously, you have to see it to believe it.

Once a year the state's best and brightest descend on the east side of Des Moines. Farm girls show their prized and polished steers. Artists construct elaborate sand castles and cows sculpted in butter. Salesmen hawk the newest innovations in hot tubs and log cabins. There is a llama competition. There are concerts, drag races, and rodeos. Tractors and farm equipment sit on display side by side with the Bengal tiger show. Fairgoers can enter the pig-calling contest, the mom-calling contest, or the beard-growing contest. There are carnival rides by the dozen.

And then there is the food. Tasty morsels of all kinds are skewered, breaded, and deep-fat fried: cheese, pork chops, candy bars, the classic corn dog. There are hot beef sundaes, mammoth smoked-turkey legs, and a deep-fried hot dog (not to be confused with a corn dog; it's a different thing, though equally delicious). Enjoy a tasty lamb burger, funnel cake, an ice cream cone made with milk pumped fresh out of the dairy barn, or watch saltwater taffy get pulled and stretched.

There are various schools of thought when it comes to seeing the fair. Some fairgoers form an agenda: corn dog, then art displays, then lemonade, then horse barn, followed by midway rides, and then the beer tent. Others arrive at the gate and let fancy lead them. Truly dedicated fairgoers spend the entire 10 days on site, from the opening parade to the closing fireworks; others get their fair fix in a single evening. However you decide to see the fair, three "rules" apply: wear comfortable clothes and shoes, bring cash and an open mind, and be prepared to be amazed.

theatrical performances, a Viking Age Village, and canoe rides on the Skunk River.

State Center Rose Festival (641-483-3002; www.statecenteriowa.org), State Center. Rides, food, and lots of roses—a small-town festival with a floral theme.

BBQ, Buggies & Tunes (1-800-697-3155; www.marshalltownbbq.com), Riverview Park, Marshalltown. Each year Iowa's BBQ champion is crowned at this weekend-long event of food and music.

Iowa Sculpture Festival (641-792-1391; www.iowasculpturefestival.org), Maytag Park, Newton. Over 30 artists gather each summer to celebrate sculpture in a beautiful outdoor space. Events include a cocktail reception and sale.

Iowa Corn Indy 250 (641-791-8000; www.iowaspeedway.com), Iowa Speedway, Newton. The Speedway's and Iowa's signature race. Like Iowa's economy, it's powered on ethanol.

Bowlful of Blues (641-792-1470), Maytag Park, Newton. Big-name blues

WORLD-CLASS ART AT THE DES MOINES ARTS FESTIVAL HELD IN LATE JUNE–EARLY JULY

artists play in the Fred Maytag Bowl every summer.

Macksburg Skillet Throw (641-768-2208), Macksburg. On the third Sunday in June, teams gather to vie for the title of Macksburg National Skillet Throwing Champion. Picnic and battle for points while trying to knock the head off a dummy with a heavy cast-iron skillet.

Late June–Early July: **Des Moines Arts Festival** (515-286-4950; www.desmoinesartsfestival.org), Western Gateway Park between 13th and 16th Streets, Des Moines. This three-day, nationally recognized arts festival showcases 135 national and Iowa artists accompanied by music and, of course, food.

July: **RAGBRAI** (515-474-3342; www.ragbrai.org), statewide. While not technically a Des Moines event, the Register's Annual Great Bike Ride Across Iowa is a treasured summer institution. Racers and recreational cyclists join this rolling party across the plains with an emphasis on beer drinking and pie eating. Nonriders will often join the party when RAGBRAI stops in their region.

Boone County Fair (515-432-5899; www.boonecountyfairia.com), Boone County Fairgrounds, Boone. Agricultural and commercial contests as well as music, food, and carnival rides.

Dallas County Fair (515-993-3728; www.dallascountyfair.com), Dallas County Fairgrounds, Adel. All the sheep-showing, tractor-pulling, and corn-dog eating of a great county fair.

Adel Paddlefest (515-277-3279), Kinnick-Feller Park, Adel. This party for paddlers is sponsored by the Raccoon River Watershed Association and includes a canoe and kayak show, races, and art.

Kermis Dutch Summer Festival (641-628-2409; www.pellatuliptime.com), Pella. A traditional summer festival with a Dutch twist.

National Balloon Classic (515-961-8415; www.nationalballoonclassic.com), Indianola. An eight-day hot-air balloon festival with races, rides, and some uniquely shaped balloons.

August: **Iowa State Fair** (515-262-3111; www.iowastatefair.com), State fairgrounds, East 30th Street and East University Avenue, Des Moines. The quintessential state-fair experience, including agricultural events, music, rides, and all the food-on-a-stick you can think of—and then some.

Adel Sweet Corn Festival (515-993-5472; www.partners.adeliowa.org/sweetcorn.page), town square, Adel. All the sweet corn, dipped in vats of butter, you can eat along with a parade and street dance.

Mid-Iowa Antique Power Show (641-752-2147; www.miapa.org), on IA 30, 8 miles west of Marshalltown. Hundreds of antique tractors and other agricultural equipment, plus parades and demonstrations.

Knoxville Nationals (641-842-5431; www.knoxvilleraceway.com), Knoxville Raceway, Knoxville. More than 100 of

SKYGLIDERS WHISK FAIRGOERS ACROSS THE EXPANSIVE FAIRGROUNDS OF THE IOWA STATE FAIR

the best sprint-car racers compete for a cash prize, with events, music, and the "bizarre bazaar" craft show.

September: **Latino Festival** (515-465-4601; www.perryia.org), Pattee Park, Perry. A celebration of this town's Latino immigrants and culture.

Pufferbilly Days (1-800-266-6312; www.booneiowa.com), Boone County Fairgrounds, Boone. Railroad heritage is celebrated the first weekend after Labor Day.

Storytelling Festival (515-733-4214; www.storyfestival.net), throughout Story City. A celebration of the art of storytelling, with guests and workshops.

Octagon Art Festival (515-232-5331; www.octagonarts.org), Main Street, Ames. Local and regional artists share their work during this one-day festival.

Oktemberfest (641-754-9044; www.oktemberfest.com), Main Street, Marshalltown. It has all the festivities a festival could have: chili contests, motorcycle rodeos, 5K runs, and Little Miss Oktemberfest pageants.

Peru Apple Days (515-462-1185; www.madisoncounty.com), East Peru. Farmer Jesse Hiatt discovered the first Red Delicious apple here in 1872. On the third weekend in September, local residents commemorate this discovery with family-friendly events. A descendent of Hiatt's original tree still stands in the orchard north of town.

Latino Heritage Festival (515-279-0715; www.latinoheritagefestival.org), Blank Park Zoo, Des Moines. The largest annual ethnic festival in the state celebrates the culture of Latinos and their influence on life in Iowa with food, entertainment, and exhibits.

October: **World Food Prize** (515-245-3783; www.worldfoodprize.org), Des Moines. Considered the "Nobel Prize of food and agriculture," the $250,000 World Food Prize honors pioneers in the science and policy of ending world hunger and includes the elegant Laureate Award Ceremony and the more casual World Food Festival in the East Village.

The Covered Bridge Festival (515-462-1185; www.madisoncounty.com), Winterset. Francesca slept here! Always the second full weekend in October, the Covered Bridge Festival offers guided tours of the bridges of Madison County plus antiques, crafts, and food.

November and December: **DeVries Dutch Country Light Display**, more than 55,000 twinkling lights decorate the city of Pella.

The Great River Road

2

ALLAMAKEE COUNTY

CLAYTON COUNTY

DUBUQUE COUNTY

JACKSON AND CLINTON COUNTIES

SCOTT COUNTY

MUSCATINE COUNTY

LOUISA AND DES MOINES COUNTIES

LEE COUNTY

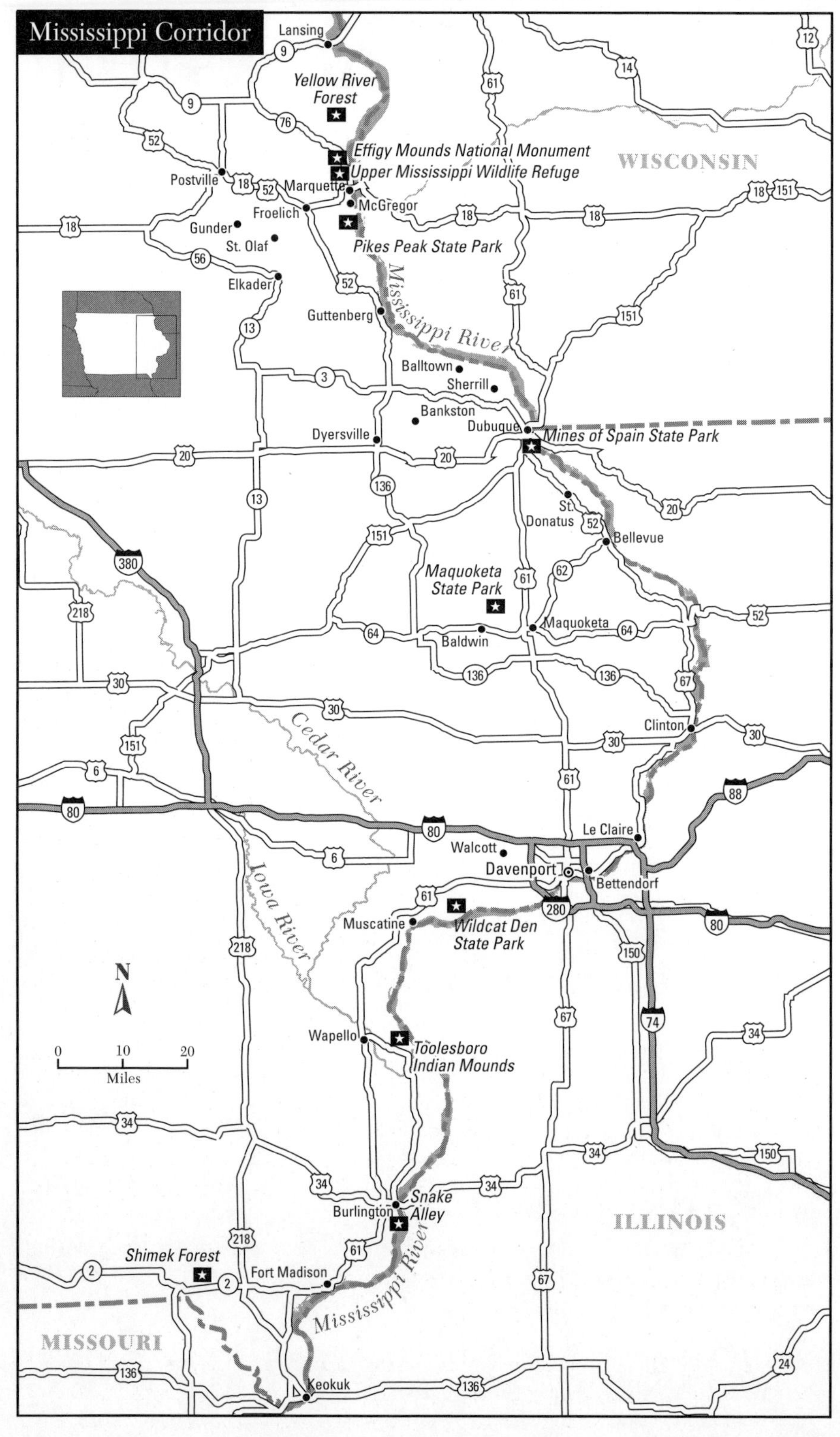
Mississippi Corridor
Lansing
Yellow River Forest
Effigy Mounds National Monument
Upper Mississippi Wildlife Refuge
WISCONSIN
Postville
Marquette
McGregor
Froelich
Gunder
St. Olaf
Pikes Peak State Park
Elkader
Guttenberg
Mississippi River
Balltown
Sherrill
Bankston
Dubuque
Dyersville
Mines of Spain State Park
St. Donatus
Bellevue
Maquoketa State Park
Maquoketa
Baldwin
Clinton
Cedar River
Le Claire
Walcott
Davenport
Bettendorf
Muscatine
Wildcat Den State Park
Iowa River
Wapello
Toolesboro Indian Mounds
N
0 10 20
Miles
Snake Alley
Burlington
ILLINOIS
Shimek Forest
Fort Madison
Mississippi River
MISSOURI
Keokuk

THE GREAT RIVER ROAD: A BRIEF OVERVIEW

The longest river in the United States has had a profound impact on Iowa's geography, history, economy, and culture. Ancient Native American burial mounds, such as the Effigy Mounds and Toolesboro Mounds, bear witness to the importance of the river to the ancient peoples of Iowa. The earliest explorers of the state, Dubuque and Joliet, found their way to the fertile lands of Iowa by way of the Mississippi River, and the earliest permanent settlements in the state were built on its banks. Many buildings that the first settlers constructed still stand, and visitors may find themselves staying in an inn built before the Civil War (Black Horse Inn) or eating in a restaurant that has satisfied diners stretching from Jesse James to Brooke Shields (Brietbach's).

Travelers made their way into the Midwest from New Orleans and St. Louis on steamboats paddling up the river, and with them came their cultural experiences. Mark Twain journeyed through the state and is said to have stayed at the American House Inn in Lansing. The Mississippi moved Dixieland jazz and Delta blues music into the heartland, where it is celebrated today in events such as the Mississippi Valley Blues Festival. The river moved goods and people from back East and Europe into the state. Nowadays huge barges pushed by tugboats transport the bounty of Midwestern grain to the port of New Orleans and from there out to feed the world.

The glaciers that turned the rest of the state into rolling plains bypassed the lands along the Mississippi, leaving behind the steep bluffs and rich forests of the "driftless" area. The Upper Mississippi National Wildlife Refuge is home to thousands of species of animals, birds, and plants unique to the Midwest, and bald eagles make Iowa their home as they fish the waters of the river. Farther downriver, the Mississippi's waters deposited rich sediment from upstream to create fertile fields along its banks.

The river's waters can also cause destruction—as they did most recently during the summers of 1993 and 2008, when, fed by heavy continuous rains, the Mississippi breached levees and flooded the surrounding lands.

Because of their unique position, the 10 counties along the Mississippi (Allamakee, Clayton, Dubuque, Jackson, Clinton, Scott, Muscatine, Louisa, Des Moines, and Lee) have qualities that make them feel different from other parts of Iowa. They are home to river towns rather than country towns, and in some ways they have more similarities with St. Louis or Baton Rouge than they do with cities like Des Moines or Cedar Rapids. Of course, agriculture is important, too, as the world saw when a baseball field was harvested from a cornfield in the Field of Dreams outside of Dyersville. And farmers along the river are taking a fresh look at the land, as at Tabor Farms Vineyard and Winery outside of Bankston, where Iowa's grape-growing and winemaking heritage is being restored, or on the elk and buffalo ranches at Quarry Creek in Fort Madison. The counties' blend of river and rural life, their long and well-preserved history, and their continued importance for commerce and tourism make them fascinating places to visit and explore.

The Great River Road—which has been designated a National Scenic Byway—stretches from Canada to the Gulf of Mexico. It is a 3,000-mile, 10-state network of roads that parallel both sides of the Mississippi. Some 400 miles of the River Road travel through some of the most beautiful scenery in the state of Iowa along a route indicated with scenic byway signs. It is not the fastest way to get from one part of the state to the other, but it is by far one of the most beautiful and fascinating.

This section is organized mainly by county starting in the north, but travelers may want to use a larger city, such as Dubuque in Dubuque County or the Quad Cities in Scott County, as a jumping-off point. And don't be afraid to leave your car. One of the best ways to explore the region is from the water, so several excellent riverboat excursion companies and boat-rental facilities are included in my recommendations.

ALLAMAKEE COUNTY

Allamakee County, in the farthest northeastern corner of Iowa, is probably also the most distant from the rest of the state in terms of geography and lifestyle. The city of Lansing, tucked into the bluffs over the Mississippi, guards the sharpest curve of the river, where the steamboats of the past and the barges of today slow down to make the turn. Many of the buildings along the waterfront and up on the hills are as old as the state itself. North of Lansing, the waterways and bluffs are protected areas, including the Upper Mississippi River National Wildlife and Fish Refuge. Farther downriver, adventure seekers can enjoy the Yellow River and the surrounding state forests and also Effigy Mounds National Monument, a sacred site for the Native Americans who once hunted and fished in the area's rich lands and waters. The agricultural city of Postville (see sidebar) in the southwest part of the county has an especially unique past and present combining people of diverse cultures.

GUIDANCE **Lansing Chamber of Commerce** (563-538-4231; www.lansingiowa.com), PO Box 156 Main Street, Lansing. The chamber is not really set up for visitors, so call or visit their Web site for more information. Lansing is a small community, and everyone knows everyone. (I went for a walk one evening and ran into my innkeeper and the mayor chatting in the street.) Call the chamber ahead of time, and they can set you up.

GETTING THERE *By car:* **IA 76** and **IA 9** cover most of Allamakee County, though visitors may find themselves arriving on **IA 26** from Minnesota, and Postville is on **IA 18** in the southwestern corner of the county.

MEDICAL EMERGENCY Call **911**.

Veterans Memorial Hospital (563-568-3411; www.vmhospital.com), 40 First Street Southeast, Waukon. Emergency department and walk-in clinic available for all patients.

INTERNET ACCESS Wireless Internet is available in a few cafés and hotels in Allamakee County.

✷ To See

Effigy Mounds National Monument (563-873-3491; www.nps.gov/efmo), IA 76, 4 miles north of the village of Marquette. Visitors center and monument open weekdays 8–4:30, weekends 8:30–4:30, extended hours June–Labor Day. Admission: $5 adults. These effigy mounds are one of the most mysterious and amazing relics of ancient Native American life in Iowa. There are 206 known prehistoric mounds in this 2,526-acre park, and 31 were shaped to look like bears and birds. From above, the enormous mounds appear as white outlines against the green of surrounding grass. Guided and self-guided tours are available. On the north side, the 2-mile Fire Point Trail climbs 300 feet to offer overlooks of the mounds. Other rewarding trails include the Third Scenic View Trail (4 miles round-trip) and the Hanging Rock Trail (7 miles round-trip). Hikes start from the visitors center on the south side of the park; the **Marching Bear Group** and the **Compound Mound** are the reward for 4-mile round-trips. The **Fish Farm Mounds**, IA 26, 3 miles south of New Albin, on the north side of the county include a 3-acre prehistoric

POSTVILLE, HOMETOWN TO THE WORLD

On the sign outside of town, Postville claims to be HOMETOWN TO THE WORLD, and its history is diverse for sure. Like other towns in the area, it was settled in the mid-19th century by Scandinavians and Germans who worked in agriculture. Then in the 1980s, a group from the orthodox Jewish movement known as Lubavitchers bought the local meat-processing plant. Agriprocessors became one of the largest producers of kosher meat in the United States, but the cultures of the Hasidic Jews and the native Gentiles clashed on the streets of this tiny town.

More recently, the high-paying jobs at the meatpacking plant attracted Hispanic immigrants, bringing another new culture to Postville—but also trouble. In the spring of 2008, local and federal authorities raided Agriprocessors and arrested many of the workers who were found to be illegal immigrants. Other workers from as far as Somalia and Palau have also arrived to find work at the plant. The waves of diverse immigration can be seen on the streets of Postville, in fading cafés where old-timers drink coffee, in the Latino markets with *quinceanera* dresses and international calling cards, and the kosher grocery. For more details of the town's fascinating story, read University of Iowa professor Stephen Bloom's book *Postville: A Clash of Culture in the Heartland of America.*

The tiny town doesn't offer much for travelers, but for amazing pastrami, try **KCG Market and Restaurant** (563-864-7133), 121 West Green Street, Postville. Open 8–8 daily except Saturday. Calling this place a "restaurant" is a bit of a stretch; a dusty dining room that doubles as an office is where diners can eat their deli sandwiches, sour pickles, and coleslaw. (My friend almost killed himself eating a giant and delicious chocolate babka.) The atmosphere in the grocery is reserved but helpful.

cemetery in a larger wildlife preserve. The 30 conical-shaped mounds were built between 100 B.C. and 650 A.D.

✱ To Do

✪ **Mississippi Explorer Cruises** (1-877-647-7397; www.mississippiexplorer.com), located at the boat dock, where Main Street (IA 9) runs into the river. There are also ports in Dubuque, La Crosse, and Prairie du Chien, Wisconsin, and Galena, Illinois. Call for reservations at the most convenient location. Captain Jack and his crew take visitors out on cruises that are both astonishing and educational in the protected wildlife refuges of the upper Mississippi River. Captain Jack is a master boat captain who has been featured in the Smithsonian National Museum of American History. No mere cruise, the tour offers a look into the unique life of the river's environment, navigation, and people. Visitors can expect to see and learn about the plants and animals that make their home on the Mississippi, from microscopic duckweed to majestic bald eagles that nest on the islands and shores. Both regular and special charter cruises are available; consult their Web site, or call for more information. Cruises cost $19.50–$29.99 for adults and are well worth it.

S&S Houseboat Rentals (563-538-4454; www.ssboatrentals.com), 9900 South Front Street, Lansing. Enjoy the Mississippi as the captain of your own boat. S&S has been renting houseboats and pontoons for over 45 years. The boats are essentially cabins that float—bring food, beverages, and bath linens. Rates depend on the size of the boat and season; call the owners to discuss your vacation needs. Rentals start at $860 for midweek in the spring or fall on the basic 10-passenger Liberty Bell and range up to $3,561 for a week in summer for the 10-passenger *Sumerset,* which has a water slide.

***Maiden Voyage* Tours** (563-586-2123; www.maidenvoyagetours.com), Harpers Ferry. Robert Vavra captains the 49-passenger *Maiden Voyage* out of Harpers Ferry. Open-boarding day trips are available on Sundays June–Oct. from 10:30–2

CAPTAIN JACK LEADS ECO-TOURS INTO THE HEART OF THE RIVER ON HIS MISSISSIPPI EXPLORER CRUISES

THE DRIFTLESS AREA

For anyone who still believes Iowa is flat, a trip northeast is in order. In contrast to the rest of the state, glaciers did not cover this corner, so the area is called the Driftless Area ("drift" refers to the dirt, gravel, and rocks left behind when the glaciers receded). And because it was not compressed by the glaciers, the land along the 3-mile-wide river valley features towering bluffs and massive rolling hills. The area is home to thousands of protected and endangered plants and animals, and there are countless rivers and cold-water trout streams for recreation and fishing, making for one of the most unique landscapes in the state.

The best way to enjoy the region is to drive from **New Albin** to **Lansing** along IA 26. This segment of the "Great River Road" treats drivers and passengers to views of commanding bluffs, several wildlife refuges, the mouth of the Upper Iowa River, and the **National Wildlife and Fishing Refuge** on the upper Mississippi. Another way to get to know the area is from the water. Captain Jack of the **Mississippi Explorer Tours** (see *To Do*) runs charter boats out of Lansing and takes sightseers deep into the backwaters of the river where wildlife from bald eagles to beavers abound.

for $12 adults and $6 children. The boat gets passengers up close and personal with river life and wildlife. Or take a multiday tour. The "Tom Sawyer Adventure" is four days and three nights and includes fishing, log cabins, and campfires. Stops include the **Villa Louis** mansion in Prairie du Chien, Wisconsin, and **Effigy Mounds State Park.** A less literary package includes a weekend cruise with a stay in new, furnished log cabins.

✷ Green Space

✪ **Mount Hosmer City Park** is perched high above the city of Lansing. On clear days, the views extend for 40 miles into three states. Below the park are Black Hawk Bridge and the Upper Mississippi National Wildlife Refuge. The fit can run up the winding road to the park at the top, but for the rest, bring a picnic, and enjoy a peanut butter sandwich while watching for bald eagles. The park has bathroom facilities, a shelter, playground equipment, and a World War I memorial, too.

✪ **Upper Mississippi River National Wildlife & Fish Refuge** (507-452-4232; www.fws.gov/midwest/UpperMississippiRiver), main office 51 East Fourth Street, Winona, Minnesota. The refuge covers 240,000 acres in four states—including the northern half of Iowa's Mississippi—and its river, marshes, flood plains, and grasslands are home to countless species of plants, animals, fish, reptiles, and birds. The refuge is open for a variety of activities. Visitors can boat, fish, swim, hike, hunt, observe wildlife, or go geocaching. Visit their Web site for maps, hunting and fishing regulations, and special events.

Yellow River Forest (319-335-1575; www.iowadnr.gov/forestry/yellow river.html), CR B25, 3 miles west of Harpers Ferry. The Yellow River Forest

THE UPPER MISSISSIPPI NATIONAL WILDLIFE AND FISH REFUGE IS HOME TO COUNTLESS SPECIES OF FLORA AND FAUNA

includes several areas for recreation, among them **Paint Creek,** where there are plenty of hiking, snowmobile, and bridle trails with scenic overlooks. The backpacking trails in the forest were named the best in the state. The Paint Creek area includes campsites for both tent and equestrian camping. Rates: $9 per night in the summer, $6 the rest of the year.

✷ Where to Stay

BED & BREAKFASTS **McGarrity's Inn on Main** (563-538-9262; www.mcgarritysinn.com), 203 Main Street, Lansing. Photographer J. R. McGarrity had a thriving studio in downtown Lansing in 1885. Today guests can stay in his lovingly restored studio just one block from the Mississippi River. His black-and-white portraits and landscapes cover the walls of this modern four-suite inn. Each of the rooms is lovely and comfortable, but Suite 3 is truly exceptional and expansive, with two balconies overlooking the water and Black Hawk Bridge, a jetted tub and glass shower, a complete kitchen, surround sound, and a ridiculously huge bed. A roof deck at the top of a spiral staircase is in the works. Rooms from $85–$170.

Thornton House B&B (563-538-3373; www.thethorntonhouse.com), 371 Diagonal Street, Lansing. Built in 1873, this elegantly appointed home was owned by the Thornton family for over 120 years. Dr. Thornton ran his office out of the home, and throughout the house innkeeper Frank Ebersold has placed thoughtful notes describing the purpose the rooms served in their previous life. The house is beautifully and richly decorated, and the public spaces are comfortable and inviting. There are five guest rooms, and the one on the first floor has the benefit of the wraparound screened-in porch. Breakfast is included and is served buffet style, with a main dish and Frank's famous homemade jam. Thornton Cottage, a quaint two-bedroom house on the river, is also available. Rooms from $82–$165.

Sous le Sapins (mcmellenthin@gmail.com; www.frenchcreek-farmhouse.com), Lansing. This 100-year-old farmhouse is tucked way back in the hills of the **French Creek Wildlife Area,** perched on one of the highest ridges in the region. The neighbors are the milk cows from an organic dairy, and the views of rolling countryside are stupendous. The farmhouse has six bedrooms, two baths, a dining room, kitchen, and living room. The woodwork, floors, staircase, and French and pocket doors are all original; the rooms are bright, airy, and splendidly "shabby chic." Guests are welcome to help themselves to the library and the garden and to grill out back. Accommodations are for the entire house and have a two-day minimum. The proprietor lives in Madison, Wisconsin, so the best way to contact her is via e-mail. The house is deep in the woods; get directions from the proprietor before heading out. Rates for a weekend stay $350, a one-week stay $700.

Murphy's Cove, (563-568-6448; www.lansingiowa.com/murphyscove.htm), 51 North Front Street, Lansing. This brand-new cottage on the riverfront is equipped with three bedrooms and two baths (linens included), screened-in porches, cable television, and a complete kitchen. All that just steps from the river—with views of the barges passing under the bridge—and situated in the middle of the business district. Weekend rates during the summer $380, $190 per night in the off-season, $150 for weeknights; weekly rentals available.

A SIMPLE YET ELEGANT BEDROOM IN THE SOUS LE SAPINS FARMHOUSE IN LANSING

CAMPING **Red Barn Resort & Campground** (563-538-4956), 2609 Main Street (IA 9), Lansing. In this resort just west of Lansing, RVs can pull in and enjoy full hook-ups, a large shower house, a laundry, miniature golf, and a trout stream for fishing. Other amenities include video games, propane, firewood, ice, a pavilion, and basketball court. The resort also offers a bar and grill open daily, featuring very tasty Bloody Marys. Areas for tent camping and rental RVs are available.

Yellow River State Forest See *Green Space*.

✱ Where to Eat

EATING OUT 🍸 **Safehouse Saloon** (563-538-4228), 359 Main Street, Lansing. Open for dinner Tues.–Sat. evenings. On the other side of the authentic bank-vault entrance and through the double-swinging doors is a saloon that will put thirsty cowpokes in mind of the days of Wyatt Earp and the Wild West—though those guys didn't have pizza. The big padded barstools are a recent addition; before, patrons simply bellied up to the bar. There are also deep wooden booths and free popcorn and peanuts. There's plenty of beer on tap and a menu with thin-crust pizzas and appetizers. $–$$

TJ Hunters Pub & Grub (563-538-4544), 377 Main Street, Lansing. Open daily for breakfast, lunch, and dinner; bar stays open until "close." "Grub" is an understatement. The menu is packed with interesting and upscale dishes: rib eye, for example, and lobster tail. At breakfast there are crepes, stuffed French toast, and, hearty oatmeal for the health conscious. The wacky menu wanders down Mexico way, includes enormous $10 "monster burgers," and tops it all off with fancy after-dinner drinks like a Pink Squirrel or Brandy Alexander. $–$$

Milty's (563-538-4585; www.miltys.net), 200 Main Street, Lansing. Open daily for breakfast, lunch, and dinner; the bar stays open until close Tues.–Sun. Milty's has it all on the menu: pizza, burgers, sandwiches, and steaks. Friday night is the seafood buffet, and buckets of either fried chicken or cod are available. Milty's also has apartment-style lodging upstairs for guests who need a place to rest after all that food. $–$$

J-N-J Pizza (563-568-4800; www.jnjpizza.com), 31 West Main Street, Waukon. Open for dinner daily, lunch and dinner Fri. High-quality pizzas are made thick or thin, with lots of sauce or just a little, and covered with plenty of wacky topping options. There's a pizza with BLT toppings, one with nacho cheese, and a so-called tropical pizza with pineapple and sauerkraut. This pizza parlor also has a location in Elkader (563-245-2800), 127 North Main Street, Elkader. $$

Selective Shopping

Horsfall's (563-538-4966), 300 and 360 Main Street, Lansing. Open 9–5 Mon.–Sat. 12–4 Sun. The phrase "you have to see it to believe it" is used with hesitation in this manuscript, but it truly applies to this Main-Street dime store in Lansing. Shoppers come from as far as Cedar Rapids and Minneapolis to rummage through the million-dollar inventory of discounted goods. The store (and, in the summer, the sidewalk) is packed with sunglasses, kites, Chicago Bears throw rugs, Iowa State Cyclone T-shirts, posters, sandals, antiques, dishes, beer koozies, sunscreen, and knickknacks.

Yellow Bird Art (563-538-4350; www.yellowbirdart.com), 201 Main Street, Lansing. Open 10–5 Mon.–Fri. 10–5, 10–4 Sat. If you are not a quilter, you may be ready to learn after visiting this fresh quilt shop in Lansing. This is not your grandmother's quilt shop. Many of the fabrics are vintage or Asian styled, and there are simple patterns for first-time quilters or purse makers. On the walls are beautiful quilts with modern styling, and lessons are available for the newly converted.

CLAYTON COUNTY

Across the water from Prairie du Chien, Wisconsin—and home to some of the cutest little river villages in Iowa—Clayton County offers a truly unique concoction of river and rural life and is full of unique oddities. The town of McGregor, they say, was larger than Chicago before and during the Civil War, and it was an important port for steamboat travel during that era. McGregor was founded as a ferry landing in 1837, and became incorporated as a town in 1857. The settlement grew with the popularity of steamboat travel up the Mississippi. Today, the town is a colorful glimpse into the past. The main street is tucked between two bluffs and passes the Mississippi River beforing continuing north to the little village of Marquette. The Ringling Brothers were born in a house that still stands on the south side of town. In the villages themselves, travelers will find great shops for antiquities and more modern treasures, hotels and B&Bs both historic and quirky, and delicious dining and casual eateries. Clayton County is also the access point to Pikes Peak State Park, a busy marina for boaters, and other exciting outdoor recreation.

GUIDANCE **McGregor-Marquette Chamber of Commerce** (1-800-896-0910; www.mcgreg-marq.org), 146 Main Street, McGregor. Open during normal business hours with a lobby full of brochures and a helpful staff knowledgeable about the county. Maps for the McGregor Historic Walking Tour are available at the office. Information is available on their Web site or via e-mail: mac-marq@alpinecom.net.

GETTING THERE *By car:* Marquette and McGregor are just across the river from Prairie du Chien, Wisconsin, on **US 18. US 52** runs north-south through the county through Monona and Guttenberg, and the county seat of Elkader is at the intersection of **IA 56** and **IA 13.**

MEDICAL EMERGENCY Call **911**.

Central Community Hopsital (563-245-7000; www.centralcommunityhospital.com), 901 Davidson Street Northwest, Elkader. Twenty-four-hour care provided by hospital nurses. Ambulance service available 24 hours a day.

INTERNET ACCESS Nearly all the cafés and overnight accommodations offer free wireless Internet access, as does the town bar.

✷ To See

McGregor Historical Museum (563-873-2221), 254 Main Street, McGregor. Open Memorial Day to mid-Oct., 11–3 Wed.–Sat., 1–4 Sun., or by appointment. The museum offers a look into McGregor's interesting history. Learn about Emma Big Bear Holt, the last known Winnebago Indian who lived in the area, and town founder and local hero Alexander MacGregor. The museum also features the work of Andrew Clemens who, seemingly magically, created elaborate and detailed sand paintings in glass bottles. The **Marquette Depot Museum** (563-873-1200), at 216 Edgar Street, Marquette, open daily May–Oct. 10–4, offers a similar look into that village's past, with a focus on the turning point from steamboat transport to railroad transport. The depot also has a gift shop and tourist information.

Spook Cave & Campground (563-873-2144; www.spookcave.com), 13299 Spook Cave Road, McGregor. Call for hours and schedule. Admission: $10 adults. The cave's name comes from the sound of water and wind early settlers heard coming from the bluff before the mouth of the cave was blasted open, not any ongoing supernatural activities. The guided tour aboard a boat takes around 35 minutes and is a blend of geological, historical, and fanciful information about the cave. The tours are a little corny, but even the bravest heart will get a little nervous when the lights are extinguished and there is total blackness. The area around the cave is a scenic valley with a waterfall, and there is a pleasant, modern campground.

The Village of Froelich (563-536-2841; www.froelichtractor.com), 24397 Froelich Road, McGregor. Open Memorial Day–end of Sept. 11–5 daily except Weds., weekends through Oct. weather permitting. Tiny Froelich, established in the 1870s, was home to John Froelich, who invented the first gasoline-powered tractor. That tractor and the company that built them evolved into the famous John Deere Company. This heritage village contains a general store, warehouse, one-room school, blacksmith shop, railroad depot, and covered bridge. The monument and museum to the inventor who changed farming (we can also thank Mr. Froelich for the air-conditioner, which he also invented) provide plenty of information on the history of farm equipment.

THE GUIDED BOAT TOUR OF SPOOK CAVE IN MCGREGOR IS ONE OF JUST TWO SUCH CAVE TOURS IN THE U.S.

✷ To Do

McGregor Historical Walking Tour (563-873-2186; www.mcgreg-marq.org), McGregor. This walking tour covers approximately 24 square blocks of central McGregor; for a small fee, guidebooks for the walk are available at the chamber of commerce on Main Street and in some local shops. Most of the buildings on the tour post a tartan sign with a number that corresponds with the information in the tour book.

McGregor Marina (563-873-9613), 101 Front Street, foot of Main Street at the Mississippi River, McGregor. Open 7 AM–9 PM daily in-season. Rent a boat from the marina, and enjoy the river from the water. Captain a fishing boat, get some speed in a "runabout," or take a crew out on a pontoon boat. The full-service marina also provides dock space, maintenance, and gas and refreshments at the small waterfront store. Boat rentals, including gas, from $75–$950 plus deposit. On shore, hungry river rats can fill up at **Mr. McGregors Beer and Bratz Garden**, which serves casual breakfast, lunch, and dinner. $

MCGREGOR'S UNIQUE HISTORY

Alexander MacGregor's grandparents came to the United States from Scotland in 1785. The founder himself came to northeast Iowa in 1835 and discovered a land rich in fur-bearing game and embroiled in conflict among four Native American tribes. MacGregor invested in the land west of Prairie du Chien and began a ferry business to shuttle goods and furs across the river.

In 1847 MacGregor plotted the town, built a hotel, and welcomed the steamboat traffic that brought prosperity and population to the town. When the railroads took over transportation from the steamboats, the town of McGregor dwindled. Then the wooden buildings of the city were destroyed in a fire, and replaced with the brick buildings visitors see today.

McGregor has been home to both tragedy and celebrity. Fires and catastrophic floods have crushed both McGregor and its sister village, Marquette. Mark Twain is said to have slept in the **American House Inn**, and Dr. Lucy Hobbs, America's first female dentist, practiced in the same building. The Ringling Brothers launched their famous circus in the backyard of their family home in McGregor. It is just south of the ancient and mysterious Native American site at **Effigy Mounds** (Iowa's only national monument—see *Allamakee County*) and **Pike's Peak**, a state park with lofty views of the Mississippi and home to countless bald eagles.

Today the villages of McGregor and Marquette are working to preserve their unique history in a way that visitors can experience, rather than just see. From the caves dug into the bluffs behind the buildings on Main Street to bonnets and dusters at **River Junction Trading Company**, these communities showcase the vibrancy and history of life on the Big Muddy, the mighty Mississippi.

TAKE A WALKING TOUR OF THE QUAINT, ECLECTIC VILLAGE OF MCGREGOR

Big Foot Canoe Rental (563-539-4272; www.bigfootcanoerental.com), 419 Big Foot Road, Monona. The Yellow River runs through limestone cliffs, meadows, and woods until it finally reaches the Mississippi at the Effigy Mounds; explore it from a canoe, kayak, or tube. Trips can start at **Volney, Sixteen,** or the village of **Ion**; most sections are relatively relaxing and also good for fishing.

Eagles Landing Winery (563-873-2509; www.eagleslandingwinery.com), 127 North Street, Marquette. Open daily 10–5. The Eagles Landing Winery offers special and award-winning wines from the region. It is one of the few wineries in Iowa to offer an ice wine or a port wine. Other wines from unique Iowa grapes include the sparkling Edelweiss and the Frog Hollow Foch. Wine lovers can shop in the tasting room—which is set among the antiques shops of Marquette—and take tours of the winery. The owners also have a bed & breakfast right down the road. (See *Where to Stay: Bed & Breakfasts.*)

Guttenberg Historic Rivertown Driving Tour (www.guttenbergiowa.net). Guttenberg was settled in the mid- to late 1800s by German immigrants, and many of the stone buildings they created remain. The town is located between an impressive bluff and one of the prettiest stretches of the Mississippi River. Directions for both driving and walking tours can be arranged and offer some insight into the history of each building. For example, the **Old Brewery** at 402 South Bluff Street was built in 1850 and used the caves in the hillside for cooling and storing beer.

✷ Green Space

Pikes Peak State Park (563-873-2341; www.exploreiowaparks.com), 15316 Great River Road, McGregor. Open daily during daylight hours. Pikes Peak is the highest bluff on the Mississippi River, and the view from the top is spectacular. Look down from the bluff, and see bald eagles and other birds flying below. Boardwalks take visitors along the bluff and into the valley to the **Bridal Veil** waterfall, which is especially gorgeous in the winter when it freezes into a solid sheet of ice. The park

AT THE NATURAL GAIT CABINS AND CAMPGROUND, HARPERS FERRY, HORSES ARE WELCOME—THOUGH NOT INSIDE THE RUSTIC CABINS

offers 11 miles of hiking trails, picnic areas, and a well-maintained campground. Campsites from $11–$16.

✷ Where to Stay

MOTELS AND CABINS 🐾 **The Natural Gait Cabins and Campground** (563-535-7314; www.thenaturalgait.com),1878 Old Mission Drive, Harpers Ferry. Don't even dream of Mapquesting this address; save the trouble and call ahead for directions. The Natural Gait Resort is located on 400 acres along the Yellow River, but without a bridge, visitors have to drive around the countryside on dirt roads to get to the two main homesteads of cabins and campgrounds. The payoff for the dusty drive are furnished log cabins, a lodge, bunkhouses, and a well-groomed campground in a scenic valley full of the owners' horses and the wildflowers they grow for their other business, the Ion Exchange. The facility can accommodate travelers with horses and pets, and there are miles of hiking and riding trails. Cabins $150, bunkrooms $50, apartment $100, camping $15–$25.

Frontier Motel (563-873-3497; www.thefrontiermotel.com), 101 South First Street, Marquette. This family-owned motel is located across from the river and next to the **Isle of Capri Casino.** The rooms are very clean, the service is friendly, and the beds are new. There is wireless Internet and a heated outdoor pool. Rooms from $45–$95.

BED & BREAKFASTS **McGregor's Landing** (563-873-3150; www.mcgregorslandingbedandbath.com), 111 First Street, McGregor. On a block built to look like the town of McGregor before fire destroyed the wooden buildings, these six rooms are outfitted as a "bed and bath." The comfortable rooms are in the style of the 1850s, with antique fixtures, iron bed frames, and quilts on the bed. Don't worry, this is not the wild west.. Despite appearances, the rooms are modern, with heat, air-conditioning, claw-foot tubs in most rooms, and TVs in some of the rooms. One room is a suite that includes a kitchen and separate bedroom. Each room has an individual entrance. The balconies look out onto the Triangle Park and are in the middle of McGregor shops and restaurants. Rooms from $89–$120.

McGregor Lodging (563-873-3112; www.mcgregorlodging.com), 214½ Main Street, McGregor. Beth and Zip Regan have four unique accommodations for travelers. The Courtyard Studio and the Lost and Found at 214 A Street were once the home and studio for a couple who were famous puppeteers who worked in the area. The rooms—though modern with queen-size beds, kitchenettes, and access to the courtyard—have fun touches from their previous tenants. And above the courtyard on the bluff are the caves that many homes in McGregor once used for storage. They have little doors and porches that make them look like hobbit homes. Other accommodations include a loft on the bluff and the Suite on Main, which both sleep six. Call for rates.

The Old Jail & Firehouse Guest Suite (563-873-2759; www.mcgreg-marq.org/oldjailfirehouse.htm), 212 A Street, McGregor. Visitors don't have to hold up a bank to spend the night in jail in McGregor. Charlene and Richard Palucci renovated the old jailhouse and adjacent fire station, originally built in 1874, into a studio apartment that sleeps up to five people. The ceilings still show signs of their former clientele: the planks are lined with iron and bolted and riveted in place. But this accommodation is no hard time as the studio offers air-conditioning, a kitchen and private bath, and television. Call for rates.

The American House Inn (563-873-3364; www.americanhouseinn.com), 116 Main Street, McGregor. Innkeepers Bill and Patricia Eckhardt continue the tradition of the American House Inn, established in 1854, with attention to both history and comfort. Guests can stay downstairs in the three-room Stagecoach Stop Suite, once both a stagecoach office and saloon, which sleeps six. The entire second floor makes up the Steamboat Landing Suite, which has expansive views of the river and three bedrooms sleeping up to eight guests. Mark Twain is thought to have slept in this upstairs suite on his single steamboat journey to Iowa. Call for rates.

Little Switzerland Inn (563-873-2057; www.littleswitzerlandinn.com), 126 Main Street, McGregor. This bed & breakfast is built in an 1862 building that once served as the office for the *North Iowa Times.* The balcony over the sidewalk is original and looks out over the Mississippi River. Each of the four rooms is unique: the Chalet has one queen bed and two twin beds in a loft and a Jacuzzi tub; the Rob Roy Suite offers a balcony; and Sadie's Log

CAVES IN THE CLIFFS ABOVE THE MCGREGOR LODGING COURTYARD ARE A REMINDER OF THE CITY'S PAST

Cabin next door includes one queen and three twin beds, a Jacuzzi, and a fireplace. Rooms are available to accommodate up to six people. Rooms for two people with breakfast from $85–$175.

The Landing—a Riverfront Inn (563-252-1615; www.thelanding615.com), 703 South River Park Drive, Guttenberg. This 1850s limestone building was a factory where river clamshells were turned into "pearl" buttons until the 1950s. Today it is a modern inn with river views and a great location in Guttenberg's park. Each of the 10 guest rooms has limestone walls, exposed beams, and folksy quilts. There are four suites with views of the river and five with private balconies. Rooms from $39–$149.

Elkader Jail House Inn (563-245-1159; www.elkaderjailhouseinn.com), 601 East Bridge Street, Elkader. This stone inn was originally built as a county jail in 1870 and held prisoners through 2006. Today's guests won't need bail money, just a toothbrush and an overnight bag to experience a night in the slammer. The renovation of the building left the guest rooms and common areas with plenty of hardwood floors and light. They are uncluttered and full of amenities. Rooms from $100–$115.

Eagles Landing Bed & Breakfast (563-873-2509; (www.eagleslandingwinery.com/eagleslanding/), 82 North Street, Marquette. Just down the road from their Eagles Landing Winery and sitting on the bank of the Mississippi, Connie and Roger Halvorson built this award-winning B&B that has two suites, a three-bedroom family suite, and a two-bedroom winery suite, all with private baths and an in-room fridge. Amenities include a hot tub on the balcony, complimentary bottles of wine in each room, and a four-course breakfast. Rooms from $85–$150.

✷ Where To Eat

DINING OUT Y **Old Man River Restaurant & Brewery** (563-873-1999; www.oldmanriverbrewery.com), 123 A Street, McGregor. Open for lunch and dinner Mon.–Sun. Built in a historic steamboat building on the main street in McGregor, this microbrewery produces German and American-style beers on site. The restaurant offers a diverse slew of options for diners, from a Thai salad to a rib-eye Philly sandwich. At dinner surf-and-turf specialties reign, including crab cakes, coconut shrimp, and excellent cuts of beef and chicken as well as salads and pasta. The onion rings are thick and hand breaded, and the portions are only manageable if you've got someone to share them with. Patio seating is always available in the screened-in and weatherproof deck. $$

Schera's (563-245-1992; www.scheras.com), 107 South Main Street, Elkader. Open Wed.–Sat. for lunch and dinner, brunch Sun. 10–2 summer only. The story behind Schera's is almost as interesting as the food. Brian, an Iowan, and Frederique, a French-Algerian, met in Boston in 2001. While traveling, Frederique noticed the name of the town Elkader, which is named for the greatest Algerian hero, Emir Adb El Qadir. The pair ended up falling in love with the town, buying a landmark restaurant, and moving to Elkader, where they opened a restaurant named after the heroine of *A Thousand and One Arabian Nights.* Now they serve Algerian and American cuisine on the bank of the Turkey River. Samosas, za-atar, and couscous are served side by side with cheddar nuggets, steaks, and salmon. $$

EATING OUT **Riverview Restaurant** (563-873-9667), 102 US BUS 18, McGregor. Open daily for breakfast, lunch, and dinner. This hometown café is casual, comfortable, and a little bit funky. There are hamburgers, both beef and bison, in regular size and a daunting half-pound size, along with pork fritters, patty melts, and hot ham and cheese. Breakfast offers a long list of options. Everything is cheap and delicious. $

✪ **The Irish Shanti** (563-864-9289; www.thegunderburger.com), 17455 Gunder Road, Elgin. Open daily for lunch, dinner, and bar hours. The address says Elgin, but the Irish Shanti is actually in the teeny-tiny town of Gunder, population 27. A great big burger put this little town on the map, though. The "Gunderburger," a massive one-and-a-half pounder, is slow cooked, tender, and delicious and ensures that this beloved restaurant goes through 100 pounds of ground beef a day. The restaurant also offers up a fantastic Reuben and American fries with cheese and onions. The bar also has a great selection of draft and bottled beer, with a focus on the beers of the United Kingdom. $

Johnson's Restaurant (563-245-2371; www.johnsonsrestaurantelkader.com), 916 High Street, Elkader. Open daily for breakfast, lunch, and dinner. Locals call Johnson's a "supper club," but it is more like a community center. Breakfast is served all day long. Lunch is served buffet style, and a salad bar goes along with the steaks, burgers, sandwiches, and homemade pie. The restaurant also offers guesthouse accommodations. $–$$

COFFEE AND MARKETS **McGregor Coffee Roasters** (563-873-2233; www.mcgregorcoffeeroasters.com), 211 Main Street, McGregor. Open 8–6 Mon.–Fri., 7–6 Sat., 8–2 Sun., until 10 on Fridays when live entertainment is scheduled. This coffee shop right in the middle of the main drag offers weary shoppers freshly roasted coffee, espresso drinks, and smoothies, along with sandwiches and light lunches. The cashew chicken salad sandwich is a favorite. Take some freshly roasted beans home, or hang out on the sofas or on the patio with a cup of java and watch the sidewalk traffic drift by.

McGregor's Top Shelf (563-873-1717), 221 Main Street, McGregor. Open 9–6 Mon.–Thurs., 9–7 Fri.–Sat., and 10–2 Sun. An upscale market with a focus on high-quality meats and cheeses as well as a small but well-selected offering of wines, including some local favorites. Most are reasonably priced at around $10. You'll find the wine in the basement along with liquor and mixing ingredients. Upstairs among the cheeses are the delicious curds from across the river. They are best at room temperature, when they squeak in the teeth. Above the market is a two-bedroom apartment accommodation.

Treats Etc. (563-245-2242; www.treatsetc.net), 110 West Bridge Street, Elkader. Open 7–5 Mon.–Sat. More than a coffee shop and casual lunch spot, this café gives back to the community. The lunch menu includes sandwiches, soups, and wraps, but call ahead to find out about the special of the day. Along with the coffee and espresso drinks come ice cream and fresh-baked goodies, wireless Internet, and a rotating gallery of artwork. Lunch $$

Pedretti's Bakery (563-245-1280; www.pedrettisbakery.com), 101 North Main Street, Elkader. Open Tue.–Fri. 6–5:15, Sat. 6–4, closed Sun. and Mon. A hometown bakery that whips up fresh cookies, elegant wedding cakes, daily bread, and a heavenly array of homemade doughnuts.

✷ Entertainment

McGregor's Landing Event Center (563-873-3150), 111 First Street, McGregor. Along the Triangle Park,

THE BIGGEST (AND BEST) TENDERLOINS IN IOWA

Iowa may be famous for its corn, but one of the most beloved sandwiches is the pork tenderloin, more often just called a tenderloin. The pork tenderloin starts with a cut of meat that is pounded flat, then breaded, deep fried, and usually served on a hamburger bun. Lots of restaurants also offer grilled tenderloins, without all the breading and frying, and while they are delicious, they are an entirely different beast. Don't confuse a tenderloin with a "pork fritter," which is made of ground pork and, in my opinion, is not as delicious as the traditional cut. Pickles and onions are the customary condiments, but ketchup and mustard also work well, and I enjoy my tenderloins with mayonnaise. Many people also dress their tenderloins like a hamburger with tomatoes and lettuce.

Several establishments in Iowa claim to have both the biggest and the best tenderloin in Iowa, but without a comprehensive survey of every tenderloin contender in the state, it is hard to know. Therefore, I offer you a selection of tenderloins that I found superb. I won't hazard to name the best since there is always, you will find, yet another delicious tenderloin waiting for you just down the road.

That being said, there are some universal qualities for tenderloin excellence. First, the pork should be fresh, never frozen, and ideally they are breaded by hand daily. Tenderloins must hang off the edges of the bun, and in some cases—which will be discussed shortly—several buns wouldn't be enough to contain the loin. The bun is merely a vehicle. While the consistency of the breading varies, the meat inside the breading should be juicy. Some tenderloin connoisseurs believe that the loin can be *too* juicy, but I disagree. Few things are worse than a tenderloin with the consistency and moisture of cardboard.

And, now, without further ado, Lauren R. Rice's Favorite Tenderloins:

THE MASSIVE 1-POUND TENDERLOIN AT THE ST. OLAF TAP PUTS ANYONE'S APPETITE TO THE TEST

The biggest tenderloin in the world (probably) is made at the **St. Olaf Tap** (563-783-7723), 106 South Main Street, St. Olaf. This beast is an almost unfathomable 1 pound. The hamburger bun is comically small—five buns wouldn't be enough to cover the real estate—and looks like a silly little hat on a gigantic head. Not only is this tenderloin huge, it's also quite tasty. It's pounded thin, hand breaded, and crispy.

In my opinion, the best tenderloin in Iowa is made at **D & D's Bar and Grill** in Villisca (see Section 5). Though it has been overlooked by the award committees, I believe this tenderloin is an all-around winner. The pork is bought fresh from a local butcher and hand breaded every day. I promised not to reveal the secret ingredient in the breading—suffice to say it was super-crispy but dense enough to hold its own against the flavorful meat inside.

Clear Lake has two fantastic tenderloins that bear mentioning here. The **Muskie Lounge** (641-829-3850) serves a very juicy tenderloin. One of my friends argued that it is too juicy, but I commend this succulent sandwich not just for moisture content but also for being served up on a garlic-buttered piece of grilled French bread, which is a surprisingly classy addition. The other great tenderloin in Clear Lake comes from **PM Park** (641-357-1991) on the other side of the lake. This massive tenderloin is breaded in the puffy, crispy breading one normally finds only at a fish fry.

The favored tenderloin of most Des Moinesians is a factor not so much of taste but of neighborhood, and the rivalry between friends is as hot as among high-school football fans. My recommended Des Moines tenderloin, because it is my mother's favorite, comes from **Smitty's Tenderloin Shop** (515-287-4742; www.smittystenderloins.com) on the south side of the city. The restaurant is not much to look at—just stools in a rundown café—but they've been making tenderloins since 1952. The loins are Frisbee size but pounded thin enough to create a desirably high breading-to-meat ratio. Today I live in the Beaverdale neighborhood on the northwest side of the city, where **George the Chili King** (515-277-9433) reigns. George's is an old-time drive-in restaurant with a tenderloin—called "the Fatman"—that is served with a piece of ham along with the other fixings.

Just to the north of Iowa City, **Joensy's Bar and Grill** (319-624-2914) claims to have the biggest tenderloin in the state; they thoughtfully serve up a half portion that will still make your eyes pop. Still, Joensy's loins fall short of St. Olaf's king of tenderloins. It lacks the heft, not the girth. They are well seasoned, though, and the bar offers some wacky ice cream drinks like the pink squirrel and golden Cadillac to wash down the pork.

Just south of Audubon, in a bump in the road called Hamlin, is **Darrell's Place** (see Part 5). It was the winner of the 2004 Best Breaded Tenderloin in Iowa contest, and my relatives swear it is the best loin they have ever eaten. This writer gives it points not only for its all-around excellent levels of crispiness and thickness but also for its (relatively) modest size. I managed to eat one in the car while driving.

Tenderloins inspire plenty of devotion, and while I would love to wax poetic about pork, others do a much finer job. For a more detailed and determined discussion of the tenderloins of Iowa, visit Tristan Frank's blog at www.des-loines.blogspot.com. He's eaten tenderloins in 70 counties and really knows his pork.

just off the main street in McGregor, is a row of businesses that re-creates the appearance of the town in the 19th century. Inside that façade of storefronts is an event center whose large period-themed rooms can be rented for parties or special occasions, and on the weekends, Uncle Sam's Saloon—which looks exactly like an Old West saloon should look—offers music, entertainment, and shows. Each year the "Hole in the Sock" Gang re-creates a shoot-out, Mark Twain occasionally comes to town, and there is often music of a more modern persuasion.

Isle of Capri Casino and Hotel (563-873-3531; www.isleofcapricasino.com), US 18, Marquette; open Mon.–Thurs. 9 AM–2 AM, Fri.–Sun. 24-hours a day. Pinkiet, a giant pink elephant, greets gamblers as they cross the skywalk to the blackjack, craps, and poker tables and slot machines on the riverboat casino. The adjoining hotel, built on the bluff, offers 25 rooms, a full buffet, and a showroom for entertainment.

Elkader Opera House (563-245-2098; www.elkaderoperahouse.com), 207 North Main Street, Elkader. This renovated 1903 opera house is one of the premier spots for entertainment in northeast Iowa. Shows include opera, classical music, comedy, and Broadway musicals. Call or visit their Web site for schedules and ticket info.

SHOP IN AN AUTHENTIC 1800S GENERAL STORE: THE RIVER JUNCTION TRADING CO. IN MCGREGOR

✱ Selective Shopping

You can't dock a boat in the McGregor/Marquette area without splashing an antiques store, but there are several unique shops in the area that should not be missed.

River Junction Trading Co. (563-873-2387; www.riverjunction.com), 312 Main Street, McGregor. Walking into the two dry goods stores—one for men and one for women—is literally like walking back in time. These are not similar to general stores in the 1850s; these *are* the general stores of the 1850s. Men can purchase dusters, fitted hats, and mustache wax; women will find bonnets, aprons, and dresses. In here, it is still the 19th century. The period clothes are made by seamstresses in the area and are reasonably priced, and the stores are worth visiting as a retail history lesson.

Paper Moon (563-873-3357), 206 A Street, McGregor. Open 10–5 Mon.–Sat., 12–4 Sun., 10–5 Wed.–Sat.; Jan. 2–Mar. 31, Wed.–Sat. 10–5. The Paper Moon is three floors of funky shopping fun. Start at the top—under the solar panels that heat the building—for strange and eclectic books, with an especially good Iowa section. Then work your way down to the second floor for unique children's clothing, books, and toys. On the first floor is a surprising mix of 1950s-style kitsch, stationary, and gifts.

Rivertown Fine Books (563-873-1111), 148 Main Street, McGregor. Open "most days" 10–5. It doesn't take long to find a literary treasure in this antiquarian bookstore. The shelves are browsable and full of rare and out-of-print editions. The owners also buy books of the same vintage.

DUBUQUE COUNTY

The first permanent settlement in Iowa was in Dubuque County, named after Julien Dubuque who settled there in 1788. The area was opened for settlement in 1833, and the Pope designated the Dioceses of Dubuque in 1837; the city has a strong Catholic culture to this day. Irish and German families came from the East in large numbers. The 1920s were marred by the hatred of the Ku Klux Klan, who burned several crosses and held a 50,000-person rally in 1925. The popularity of the Klan diminished, thankfully, and today Dubuque is experiencing a rebirth. Don't miss the attractions in downtown, including the National River Museum, which is part of the Smithsonian system, or the abundance of charming and historic accomodations. From those beginnings the county became an important hub on the Mississippi River. The city of Dubuque saw the first execution of a prisoner on Iowa's soil before statehood. Dubuque County is home to the oldest restaurant in the state as well as the Field of Dreams Movie Site in Dyersville. In the last decade, Dubuque has gone from being a run-down little factory town to an up-and-coming gem in the state; it has plenty to attract visitors and many historic and charming places for them to stay and eat.

GUIDANCE **Dubuque Area Chamber of Commerce** (563-557-9200; www.dubuquechamber.com), 300 Main Street, Suite 200, Dubuque. Open during normal business hours. The Dubuque Area Chamber of Commerce publishes an excellent visitors guide; available as hard copy or online. The **Iowa Welcome Center** (563-556-4372), 300 Main Street, Suite 100, Dubuque, is open 9–5 daily, though hours vary seasonally, for comprehensive information about the state and the region.

GETTING THERE *By car:* The city of Dubuque is located at the connection between **US 61** and **US 151** on the Mississippi River. Those highways also connect Dubuque to the rest of the county.

MEDICAL CARE Call **911**.

Finley Hospital (563-582-1881; www.finleyhospital.org), 350 North Grandview Avenue, Dubuque. Emergency and trauma care available.

INTERNET ACCESS Most cafés, restaurants, and accommodations provide free wireless Internet access.

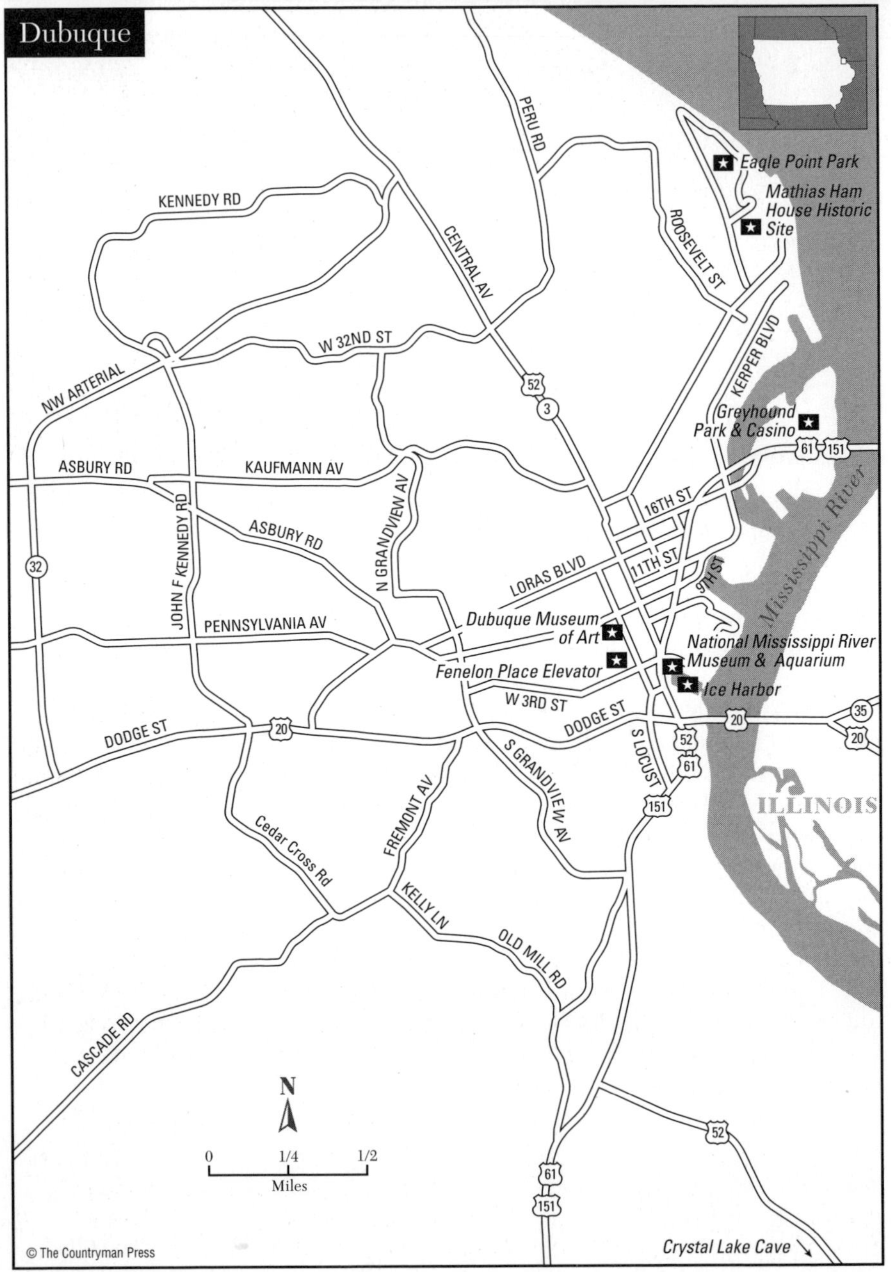

✷ To See

✪ **National Mississippi River Museum & Aquarium** (563-557-9545; www.mississippirivermuseum.com), 350 East Third Street, Dubuque. Open 9–6 daily. Admission: $10.50 adults, $9.50 seniors, $8 youths, $4.50 children; combination tickets available with the **Mathias Ham House Historic Site** and the **Old Jail Museum**. The river museum is actually several facilities in one. The **National**

THE NATIONAL MISSISSIPPI RIVER MUSEUM AND AQUARIUM IN DUBUQUE HAS LOTS TO EXPLORE, BOTH INSIDE AND OUT

Mississippi River Museum & Aquarium studies the complex and fascinating life and culture of the Mississippi River from every perspective, from the murky depths to the people that make their livings on its waters and its shores. The Mississippi shaped and continues to shape life not only in Iowa but across the United States as a thoroughfare for people, goods, and services; a habitat for rich and diverse wildlife; and an inspiration for exploration, art, and culture. Plan to spend at least an afternoon at this museum; there is plenty to see, including the **William Woodward Discovery Center,** which allows visitors to get up close and personal with the creatures in the river's depths such as cownose rays, alligators, river otters, and catfish the size of ponies. In the interactive touch-and-see room, you can touch the pelts of the mammals that live on the river and interact with various aquatic creatures. There are also several wet labs, a towboat simulator, and the wide-screen high-definition Journey Theater. The **National River Hall of Fame** celebrates the explorers, visionaries, and characters of river life. Here, learn about hall-of-fame inductees, including Mark Twain, Louis Armstrong, Diamond Jo Reynolds, and many more. A steamboat invention theater explains how the quintessential vehicle of river travel came to be.

Outside, visitors can tour the **Woodward Wetland** where, even in the city, animals thrive alongside a replica Indian home and log cabin. In the **Pfohl Boatyard** float the towboat *Logsdon,* steamboat artifacts, houseboats, and the steamboat *William H. Black,* a dredging ship the size of a football field. Tour the boat or spend the evening at the "boat and breakfast." Guests dine in the galley and then stay in a stateroom. Call 1-800-226-3369 for arrangements. The museum also includes an exhibit dedicated to traveling to the Mississippi River region, information on the Luxembourger village of St. Donatus (located south of Dubuque), a working boat shop, and a café.

The Old Jail Museum (563-557-9545), 721 Central Avenue, Dubuque. Open 11–4 Wed.–Sat. Admission: $5 adults, $3.50 children; combination tickets available with **National Mississippi River Museum & Aquarium.** The 1857 jail was built in the Egyptian-Revivalist style and includes historical artifacts from Dubuque's history and a basement dungeon. A sound-and-light show tells the story of Patrick O'Connor, the first European settler to be tried and hanged for murder in the Iowa territory in 1834.

Mathias Ham House (563-583-2812), 2241 Lincoln Avenue, Dubuque. Open May 1–Oct. 31 Wed.–Sat. 11–4,; $5 adults, $3.50 children; combination tickets available with the **National River Museum & Aquarium.** Tours led by costumed guides illuminate the history of this 1856 Italianate mansion. Mathias Ham was a lead-mining entrepreneur. Lead was not as shiny as gold, but it was just as lucrative, and his home features the fine American and European furnishings of the wealthy owner. (The mansion is also thought to be haunted by the ghost of a revenge-seeking pirate.) An 1833 log cabin, Iowa's oldest building, is also restored and onsite.

Crystal Lake Cave (563-556-6451; www.crystallakecave.com), 6684 Crystal Lake Drive, Dubuque. Open daily 9–6 in summer, spring and fall hours are shortened, and tours given only on weekends; visit the Web site for full details. Admission: $12 adults, $6 children. The cave was discovered by lead miners in 1868, and lead deposits and other precious gems have been unearthed. This living cave just south of Dubuque is full of natural rock formations that continue to grow and change. The cave is packed with fascinating formations, but the tours lean toward showmanship rather than a thorough discussion of the anatomy of a cave. Many of the formations are named after what they look like rather than what they actually are. Tours last around 45 minutes, and because the cave is always 52 degrees, bring a jacket.

Dubuque Museum of Art (563-557-1851; www.dbqart.com), 701 Locust Street, Dubuque. Open Tues.–Fri. 10–5, Sat.–Sun. 1–4. Free. The highlight of this art museum has to be the fabulous collection of Grant Wood paintings, including *Approaching Storm* and *Iowa Autumn, Indian Creek*, but there are plenty of other works from national, regional, and local artists. The museum features several traveling exhibits throughout the year and provides entertaining and educational programs.

✪ **Field of Dreams Movie Site** (563-875-8404; www.fodmoviesite.com), 28995 Lansing Road, Dyersville. Open daily 9–6 Apr.–Nov. Free. Is this heaven? No, it's Iowa, and the most famous line of the Kevin Costner film is still true: if you build a baseball field in an Iowa cornfield, people will indeed come. Based on the book *Shoeless Joe* by University of Iowa Writer's Workshop graduate W. P. Kinsella, the 1988 film is one of the most beloved film portrayals of Iowa. The movie site, which still very much resembles the film about a down-on-his-luck Iowa farmer, a mysterious writer, and some ghostly ballplayers, is one of the most popular tourist draws in the state. Baseball and movie fans should bring their gloves and bats and hit the field; everyone is welcome to run the bases. While there's no admission fee, there are plenty of souvenirs to buy in the gift shop.

National Farm Toy Museum (563-875-2727; www.nationalfarmtoymuseum.com), 1110 16th Avenue Court Southeast, Dyersville. Open 8–6 daily; closed major holidays. Admission: $5 adults, $4 seniors, $3 children 6–17, under 5 free. Dyersville is the "farm toy capital of the world," so this is the place to find lots of minitractors, combines, barns, and animals. The museum includes bales of toys, along with a life-size John Deere tractor, farm toys throughout history, vintage cast-iron toys, and foreign toys. The toys are not only fun to play with but also offer insight into the intricate details of farming and farm machinery. Some 15,000 farm-toy enthusiasts flood Dyersville every Nov. for *Toy Farmer* magazine's National Farm Toy Show.

The Basilica of St. Francis Xavier (563-875-7325) 104 Third Street Southwest, Dyersville. Open from sunrise to sunset. There are only 52 basilicas—churches with special privileges by the Pope—in the United States, and St. Francis Xavier is one of them. An example of medieval Gothic architecture, the basilica has many unique architectural features—from the pavilion and bell to the ornate sanctuary ceiling to the pipe organ designed to fill the massive space with song and especially to the twin spires 212 feet tall that dominate the landscape. Construction of the basilica began in 1887 and was completed two years later.

THE BASILICA OF ST. FRANCIS XAVIER TOWERS OVER DYERSVILLE

✷ To Do

✪ **Fenelon Place Elevator** (563-582-6496), 512 Fenelon Place, Dubuque. Open daily 8 AM–10 PM Apr.–Nov. Admission: $2 round-trip. The world's shortest and steepest railroad was built by a successful businessman who wanted a convenient way to get from his office at the bottom of the bluff to his lunch at the top; along the way, he would take a little nap. Today, the elevator chugs visitors 296 feet up to the scenic bluff at the top, where the views include the Mississipppi River and even neighboring Illinois and Wisconsin.

Dubuque River Rides (563-583-8093; www.dubuqueriverrides.com), Third Street, Ice Harbor, Dubuque. Tours by appointment. Enjoy Dubuque from the river on *The Spirit of Dubuque,* an authentic paddle-wheel boat, or the *Miss Dubuque,* a modern yacht. Daily sightseeing tours explore the ecology and history of the Mississippi River and the region and include lunch and entertainment, but there are plenty of specialty cruises, including dinner, murder-mystery tours, Mother's Day tours, and fall leaf-peeping tours. From aboard the replica steamboat, passengers are likely to see barges, the Chicago Central Pacific Railroad Bridge, the Shot Tower, the **Julien Dubuque Monument**, and **Eagle Point Park.** Prices for tours range from a $15 "Blues Cruise" to a $75 fireworks tour.

✐ **Grand Harbor Resort & Water Park** (563-690-4000; www.grandharborresort.com), 350 Bell Street, Dubuque. Open Mon. 9 AM–1 PM, Tue. 4 PM–9 PM, Fri. 9 AM–11 PM, Sat. 8 AM–10 PM, Sun. 8 AM–9 PM. Tickets: $12–24 adults, $10–20 children. This themed water park, based on *The Adventures of Huckleberry Finn,*

THE FENELON PLACE ELEVATOR IN DUBUQUE IS THE STEEPEST RAILROAD IN THE WORLD

is 25,000 square feet of moist fun, with water slides, tube rides, a giant dump bucket, a lazy river, giant whirlpool hot tubs, and Huck Finn's tree house. The resort also features a café. The on-site hotel includes 193 rooms and suites (including luxury suites) with views of either the Mississippi or downtown Dubuque. Each features wireless Internet, minifridge, cable television, and access to the fitness center. Rooms from $109–$389.

Dubuque Greyhound Park & Casino (563-582-3647; www.dgpc.com), 1855 Greyhound Park, Chaplain Schmitt Island, Dubuque. Open Sun.–Thurs. 8–3, Fri.–Sat. 24-hours with dog racing May–Oct. and simulcast in the winter. Gamblers can watch and wager on live greyhound racing inside or out at this modern new casino and dog track. All the conveniences of a casino await, from valet parking outside to slot machines, table games, and live poker inside—plus free soft drinks. Dining and lodging are also available.

Mississippi Riverwalk, Port of Dubuque, Dubuque. This stretch of the **Heritage Trail**, which runs from the Mississippi to Dyersville, meanders along the river past **Diamond Jo's Casino**, the **Grand Harbor Resort**, and the **River's Edge Plaza,** an outdoor pavilion. From the promenade, steps lead down to the water. The walk offers great views of the river, the bridges, and downtown Dubuque, taking strollers by the **Shot Tower** at East Fourth Street. The tower is a memorial to the early ammunition industry in the area during the Civil War, where molten lead was dropped from the top of the tower through screens and into a cooling water bath at the bottom, thus forming perfect lead shot.

Park Farm Winery (563-557-3727; www.parkfarmwinery.com), 15159 Thielen Road, Bankston. Open Mon.–Thurs. 10–6, Sun. 12–5, additional hours in summer. A chateau sits on a hill above a valley and rows of green vines. Inside this transporting spot is a winery with handcrafted, award-winning wines made from native Iowa grapes such as La Crosse and Foch. Visitors can buy a bottle or a glass and soak in the views from the back deck.

SKIING **Sundown Mountain** (563-556-6676; www.sundownmtn.com), 16991 Asbury Road, Dubuque. Opening day–mid-Dec. Mon.–Fri. 10–9, Sat. 9–9, Sun. 9–6; mid-Dec.–end of season Sun.–Thurs. 9–9, Fri.–Sat. 9–10, and Fri. 9–noon midwinter. Sundown Mountain has long been one of Iowa's favorite skiing areas. The park includes 20 trails, 7 chairlifts, and 475-foot drops. The park can produce up to 100 percent of its own snow, so the skiing and snowboarding is always weather ready.

JULIEN DUBUQUE MONUMENT AND THE MINES OF SPAIN

Julien Dubuque is given credit for being the first white settler on Iowa soil. He arrived in 1788, and in 1796 the governor of Spain gave him a grant to work the land and mine the lead in the area. Though Dubuque befriended the Meskwaki Indians (he married the chief's daughter), he was thought to be a bit of a trickster. To impress tribe members with his power, he claimed he could light the river on fire. Upstream, a friend poured a slick of oil into the water and when it passed the Indian camp, at Catfish Creek, Dubuque tossed a torch onto the oil and set the water aflame. Meskwakis worked for and with Dubuque in the lead mines, but he suffered from some financial troubles and died in 1810.

Today, the **Julien Dubuque Monument** (563-556-0620; www.exploreiowaparks.com; 8991 Bellevue Heights, Dubuque), built in 1897, sits atop Dubuque's original grave. The limestone tower is perched high on a bluff with a panorama of the city, river, and the rest of the park.

ADMIRE THE VIEWS FROM THE MONUMENT TO JULIEN DUBUQUE, THOUGHT TO BE IOWA'S FIRST WHITE SETTLER

Trails for hiking and cross-country skiing fill the park and offer views of winding logging roads, limestone bluffs, forests, and prairies. The **Horseshoe Bluff** is a thick layer of Ordovician dolomite rock that was exposed in a horseshoe shaped quarry and is a unique geological feature of the area. The park, which is open year-round, can also be used for picnicking, limited hunting, and canoeing.

✷ Green Space

Eagle Point Park (563-589-4263), 2601 Shiras Avenue, Dubuque. Eagle Point, named for the winged inhabitants on the river below, is 164 acres of gorgeous views of the mighty Mississippi and the states beyond. The views alone make it a must-see spot in the Dubuque area, but this city park is also complete with picnic tables, grills, restrooms, tennis courts, playground equipment, and viewing tours.

The park is a little tricky to find for out-of-towners, so don't be afraid to stop and ask a local for directions.

Heritage Trail (563-556-6745; www.dubuquecounty.com), running from Dubuque to Dyersville. A $2 day-use pass can be purchased at area sporting stores or at self-registration stations trailside. The 26-mile trail is composed of compacted limestone for bicycling in the summer and is available for cross-country skiing and snowmobiling in the winter. Formerly a railroad line, the trail runs through a valley, past mining towns, across woodlands, through limestone bluffs, and past river outlooks, but there are no steep climbs. The trail connects with the Mississippi Riverwalk.

✷ Where to Stay

HOTELS AND RESORTS **Hotel Julien** (563-556-4200; www.julieninn.com), 200 Main Street, Dubuque. The Hotel Julien, formerly the Julien Inn, is the next chapter in 150 years of elegant accommodations in the Dubuque area. The hotel recently underwent an extensive, multimillion-dollar renovation and reopened in the autumn of 2008. Rooms from $45–$145.

Grand Harbor Resort See *To Do.*

BED & BREAKFASTS AND INNS Dubuque and the surrounding communities are a hotbed of historic, and fabulously comfortable accommodations. It would be a shame to visit the area and not stay in one of these charming and luxurious establishments.

✪ **The Hancock House** (563-557-8989; www.thehancockhouse.com), 1105 Grove Terrace, Dubuque. High above Dubuque in the West 11th Historic District is a Queen Anne mansion that blends amazing views, romantic accommodations, and friendly special features. The 1891 house was home to Charles T. Hancock, a prominent business leader. Each of the rooms offers a private bath; the suites have whirlpool tubs. (The Dollhouse Room makes lady guests feel like princesses: the tub is in the third-floor turret.) The public rooms are richly furnished and comfortable. In the pantry guests will find complimentary beverages and amazing fresh-baked cookies. The wraparound front porch with swing is a relaxing place to while away a warm afternoon. Rooms from $80–$175.

The Richards House (563-557-1492; www.therichardshouse.com), 1492 Locust Street, Dubuque. Built by the same architect as the **Hancock House**, the Richards House appears much as it did when the original family resided in it, with features including more than 80 stained-glass windows and embossed Victorian wallpaper. The seven guest rooms are furnished with antiques, and TVs and phones are concealed to retain the home's historic feel. Many of the rooms have working fireplaces that make the house especially cozy in the winter. Rooms from $45–$115.

The Mandolin Inn (563-556-0069; www.mandolininn.com), 199 Loras Boulevard, Dubuque. Named for the luminous Tiffany stained-glass window of a girl with a mandolin, this 1908 Edwardian mansion is a work of art. The dining room is lined with an original mural painted in Europe just for the room, along with leaded windows and antiques. Two suites feature verandas overlooking the garden and the bluff, and a water feature on the side of the home meanders under the wheelchair-accessibility ramp. Gourmet breakfast, central air-conditioning, and two adorable cats make this showcase home a relaxing place to stay. Rooms from $85–$150.

The Redstone Inn & Suites (563-582-1894; www.theredstoneinn.com), 504 Bluff Street, Dubuque. When he was 17 and traveling north on the river to St. Paul, a stray bullet hit A. A. Cooper in the toe and forced him off a steamboat to seek medical attention in Dubuque. In his new hometown, he found success as a blacksmith and as the owner of the Cooper Wagon Works. Cooper's business acumen and luck brought him the wealth to build the red-stone mansion in 1894. Today the mansion he built from his industry is a 14-room inn. The rooms feature private baths, gorgeous antique beds and period furnishings, and modern conveniences like Internet access. Rooms from $75–$195.

Quiet Walker Lodge (1-800-388-0942; www.quietwalkerlodge.com), 16432 Paradise Valley Road, Durango. This log-cabin inn should be mentioned because it is so determinedly packed with romantic features. Tucked away in the quiet countryside, the seven themed suites have large garden tubs; two of the suites even contain an in-room floor-to-ceiling waterfall with pond that can be turned on and off. The themes range from the Secret Garden suite to the Scandinavian Northern Lights suite. Homemade breakfasts are served in either the main lodge or a continental breakfast basket left outside the guest's door. Rooms from $125–$225.

✷ Where to Eat

DINING OUT 🍸 **Pepper Sprout** (563-556-2167; www.peppersprout.com), 378 Main Street, Dubuque. Open Tues.–Sat. for dinner and bar time. Kim Wolff, chef and owner of the Pepper Sprout, takes Midwestern cuisine to the next level. His version includes fresh, seasonal ingredients, careful preparation, and an often-rotating menu. Along with plenty of seafood choices, such as cedar-plank salmon and spicy Hawaiian prawns, comes plenty of beef. The "manly man" steak is an enormous T-bone with blue cheese butter, and there are bison tenderloina, and grilled lamb chops. The wine list is as extennsive and eclectic as the menu, and save room for homemade desserts. $$–$$$

Mario's Italian Restaurant (563-556-9424; www.mariosdubuque.com) 1298 Main Street, Dubuque. Open Mon.–Sat. for lunch and dinner and bar time. Tonio "Mario" Bertollini brings the flavors of his youth on a farm in Pescara, Italy, to this much-adored local Italian restaurant. Nightly specials include Pork Chop á la Mario and Linguine Carbonara, but the menu is full of fun and takes on the classics such as Manicotti á la Abruzzese, handmade crepes filled with ricotta and spinach, and the hearty Fettuccine á la Lumberjack. There's also plenty of tender veal, seafood, pizza, and sandwiches $$.

🍸 **L May's** (563-556-0505; www.lmayeatery.com), 1072 Main Street, Dubuque. Open for dinner Thurs.–Sun. 4–close. Fusion cuisine, flat-bread pizza, and they're open Sunday nights. It's easy to let a dinner of flatbread pizza, salads, steaks, and pasta drift into a relaxing evening with a glass of wine at this super-friendly and unique restaurant and bar. $$

Sweeny's Supper Club (563-552-1101), 11777 IA 52 North, Dubuque. Open for dinner Tues.–Sat. Located just north of Dubuque on highway 52, Sweeny's specializes in American cuisine in the classic white-linen-tablecloth, supper-club style. Meats are smoked outside in the wood oven, the dishes are well prepared, and the service is thoughtful. $$

BLACK HORSE INN

High on a ridge above the Mississippi River Valley and just 10 miles north of downtown Dubuque, some of the most historic and unique accommodations in the state of Iowa can be found at the **Black Horse Inn** (563-552-1800; www.blackhorse-inn.com; 5259 South Mound Road, Sherrill). The B&B is the newest role for the Sherrill Mount House, built in 1856, thereby predating the Civil War. The three-story building was constructed of native limestone quarried 2 miles from the site and carted up the hillside to the prominent spot on the top and at the center of the little village. The walls at the base are 4 feet thick and rise up to the cupola at the top.

In its long life, the inn has served as a hotel, dance hall, doctor's office, hospital, and apartments, and throughout it all has always played a role in the life of northeast Iowa. Jesse James, they say, spent a night at the inn. The Black Horse is rich with local history and color, which the innkeeper is happy to share.

Innkeeper Mark Meier resurrected the building from decrepitude and abandonment. When he found it, it was suffering from crumbling stone walls and water damage; he restored it to its current splendor and filled it with unique furniture and art from his adventures and world travels. The Black Horse is no stuffy historical museum turned bed & breakfast. From the handcrafted European headboards to Gus, the mounted buffalo over the fireplace, to the mystery clock, the inn feels equally historic and eclectic. Outside a Monet-style garden blooms in vivid colors all summer long.

Today guests can enjoy this special place in five comfortable suites—ranging in price from $60 to $90—each with special touches, and the inn has all sorts of modern amenities: an elevator to the third floor, wireless

Star Restaurant & Ultra Lounge (563-556-4800; www.dbqstar.com), 600 Star Brewery Drive, Suite 200, Dubuque. Open daily for dinner, no lunch on Sundays, and the bar stays open late on the weekends. This ultra-trendy restaurant presides over the riverfront in the Star Brewery building. The food is upscale fusion—think white-chicken nachos, Asian beef noodles, and cheesecake lollipops. The bar, the **Ultra Lounge**, is chic and prides itself on concocting sexy martinis. The overall feel is ultramodern and urbane. $$–$$$

EATING OUT ✪ **Café Manna Java** (563-588-3105), 269 Main Street, Dubuque. Open daily for breakfast, lunch, and early dinner. The food in this café is so delicious, it elicits feelings of ecstasy. It is absolute taste-bud bliss. With so many choices (there are no fewer than 10 specialty pizzas and 14 gourmet sandwiches), it's hard to believe every morsel could be so tasty, but by using natural, high-quality ingredients, wood-fired ovens, European cooking styles, and care, the lunches, pastries, pizzas, breads, and even coffee are outstanding. My prosciutto, pesto, and montcharet pizza

PREDATING THE CIVIL WAR, THE BLACK HORSE INN IS SAID TO HAVE WELCOMED THE OUTLAW JESSE JAMES

Internet access, king-size beds, and a hot tub on the back patio.

Meier welcomes arriving guests with a happy-hour beverage, and in addition to made-to-order breakfasts, guests can make special arrangements to enjoy the innkeeper's special schnitzel or roast beef. (Be sure to try a pastry from Meier's sister's bakery.) The commercial kitchen can create delicious meals for parties with up to 40 people. Meier also hosts such events as a local wine festival and Oktoberfest.

made me do a double take. Seriously, you need to eat here. Call me. I'll drive. \$–\$\$

Bricktown Brewery & The Blackwater Grill (563-582-0608; www.bricktowndubuque.com), 299 Main Street, Dubuque. Open daily for lunch and dinner. More than 25 varieties of beer are brewed on site at this big local brewery. The selection seems to change monthly, so the brews are fresh, tasty, and unique. The on-site restaurant offers the usual brewery food—burgers, sandwiches, appetizers—but it is well prepared, and the big corner windows look out on the heart of Dubuque's Main Street. \$\$

Dollar Dish (563-556-2375), 1099 University Avenue, Dubuque. Open daily for breakfast, lunch, and dinner. How the restaurant can manage is unclear, but the poor college students at Loras and Clarke must see this "everything's a dollar" restaurant as manna from heaven. The food is homemade and folksy—smothered mashed potatoes, mom's goulash, green-bean casserole, cookies, ice cream—and the portions are not teeny-tiny, but the menu is a scream because everything is, literally, a dollar. Bring a five-spot and eat like a king. The restaurant also offers free wireless and is a pretty and attractive place to hang out. \$

Jack's Chicken Palace (563-588-2003), 1107 University Avenue, Dubuque. Open Tues.–Sun. for lunch and dinner. The fryer reigns at this down-home chicken joint and deli. The smell of delicious—and diet-smashing, artery-clogging—fried chicken wafts out over of the sidewalk, but if you can bring yourself to eat something else on the menu, you'll find pork fritters (see "Tenderloins" in the previous section), fried pike, shrimp, cheeseburgers, and sides. $

Shot Tower Inn (563-556-1061) 390 Locust Street, Dubuque. Open daily for lunch and dinner. Named after the lead-shot tower, this restaurant is known for its pizza. It is thick, cheesy, and delicious. Pastas, chicken, and salads are also on the menu. It's dark inside, but there is a beer-garden patio on the roof. $$

Salsa's Mexican Restaurant (563-588-2880), 1091 Main Street, Dubuque. Open daily for lunch and dinner. Salsa's is a step above most Mexican restaurants, and its chimichangas, burritos, and taco salads are fresh and plentiful. The dining room has wood floors, big windows, and exposed brick, and it feels almost trendy. $–$$

✪ **Breitbach's Country Dining** (563-552-2220), 563 Balltown Road, Balltown. Open daily for breakfast, lunch, and dinner. High above the Mississippi in the little village of Balltown sits the oldest continuous restaurant and bar in the state of Iowa. The Breitbach family have owned and operated the restaurant since 1850, serving up buffet-style country food and drinks to both Jesse James and Brooke Shields. On Christmas Eve in 2007, a fire broke out in the historic building and it burned to the ground, but the owners rebuilt, and a new restaurant complete with beer garden is open for operation. The food is folksy and delicious, with an outstanding tenderloin on the menu. Walk off a little bit of the meal by strolling north on Balltown Road a half block to one of the best overlooks of the Mississippi River. $

Country Junction Restaurant (563-875-7055; www.countryjunctionrestaurant.com), junction IA 20 and 136 (exit 294), Dyersville. Open Mon.–Thurs. 7–9, Fri.–Sat. 7–9:30, Sun. 9–9 for breakfast, lunch, and dinner. This homestyle restaurant is famous for cooking country classics like Grandma: from scratch and with love. The favorites from the farm include roast beef, chicken, ham steak, and all the fixings: coleslaw, applesauce, and cottage cheese plus, of course, lots and lots of pie. $–$$

COFFEE **Monks** (563-585-0919) 373 Bluff Street, Dubuque. Open daily for coffee and into the evening for wine and beer. This funky little coffee shop in the heart of the Bluff Street shopping district offers espresso drinks, wine, and beer. It's a comfortable place to hang out, with cushy chairs, live music, and wireless Internet. There are tables and chairs on the front porch, which is lovely in the evenings in summer. $

Jitterz Coffee & Café (563-557-3838), 1073 Main Street, Dubuque. Open Mon.–Sat. This locally owned coffee shop aims to please. It is a cozy, friendly, and easy place to grab a cup of java on a busy day or to hang out on a slow one. The coffee drinks are excellent, and they also offer light lunches and snacks. $

Groovy Grounds (563-875-6251), 211 First Avenue East, Dyersville. Open Mon.–Weds. and Fri. 6:30–4, Thurs. 6:30–8, Sat. 6:30–2. It is as much fun to look at this coffee shop as it is to eat there. The goal is to "serve up creativity," and creativity comes in the form of decadent ice cream drinks, salads, wraps, and paninis, along with big comfy chairs, local photography on the walls, and a gift and scrapbooking shop upstairs. Wireless Internet is available, as well. $

Drinking Establishments

The Busted Lift (563-584-9712; www.180main.com), 180 Main Street, Dubuque. Open nightly until 2 AM. The exposed stone walls and wooden beams, not to mention the candlelight, gift this Irish pub with old-fashioned charm. The fun starts with the great selection of beers on tap, a shuffleboard table, live music, and karaoke. Upstairs, at **180 Main**, is a casual restaurant serving burgers, sandwiches, and salads for lunch and seafood and pasta dishes for dinner. Imagine Tuscan seafood pasta with crabmeat, scallops, and shrimp in a spicy oil-based sauce. Open Mon.–Sat for lunch and dinner. $–$$

Paul's Big Game Tavern (563-556-9944), 176 Locust Street, Dubuque. Open afternoons and evenings daily. As bars go, Paul's is a bit on the divey side, but it has two things going for it. One, it has great, cheap burgers. They come highly recommended. Two, it is packed with taxidermy. Above the bar, encased in glass, is a polar bear skin. There are also four kinds of bighorn sheep, two grizzly bears, and lots of other critters. Next to each is the name of the animal and when it was killed (most in the 1960s), and though their faces are locked in a perpetual snarl, after a couple beers it's almost as if they're smiling at you. $

Isabella's at the Ryan House (563-585-2049; www.isabellasbar.com), 1375 Locust Street, Dubuque. Open Tues.–Sun. 4–close. Isabella's is in the basement of the 1873 Victorian mansion built by meat-packing magnate William "Hog" Ryan, but don't be intimidated by all the Old-World splendor. Isabella's is a friendly and never-fussy joint, with a huge list of beers from around the world as well as wine by the glass and cocktails. There's a happy hour every afternoon and often live music. $$

The Palace (563-875-2284), 149 First Avenue East, Dyersville. Open daily for breakfast, lunch, dinner, and bar hours. Belly up to an antique backed bar at the Palace. It's over 100 years old and a working piece of history. The ornate wooden bar has huge mirrors that reflect a bygone era. Ask the bartender to see a special binder with pictures from the bar throughout its long history. The food is bar standard, such as the enormous and tasty Palace Burger, but they've been in business for long enough that they know what they're doing. $

Entertainment

Five Flags Center & Theater (563-589-4254; www.fiveflagscenter.com), Fourth and Main Streets, Dubuque.

A TAXIDERMY ZOO KEEPS DINERS AND DRINKERS COMPANY AT PAUL'S BIG GAME TAVERN IN DUBUQUE

The Five Flags Center plays host to a variety of entertainment options, from intimate space productions in the Fly-by-Night Theater to Dubuque Thunderbirds Hockey. The historic building is home to the Dubuque Symphony Orchestra, ballet, Broadway productions, concerts, and assorted sporting events. Call the box office, or check their Web site for schedules and ticket information.

Grand Opera House (563-588-4356; www.thegrandoperahouse.com), 135 West Eighth Street, Dubuque. Dubuque's oldest theater, built in 1890 and recently restored, is home to community theater in addition to musicals, plays, ballets, and other special events. Call or check their Web site for schedules and ticket information.

THE FIVE FLAGS CENTER & THEATER IN DUBUQUE IS A HUB FOR ARTS AND ENTERTAINMENT

✷ Selective Shopping

Sweet Memories (563-556-0445), 454 West Fourth Street, Dubuque. Open daily 10–5 in-season, call for off-season hours. After a ride on the **Fenelon Place Elevator** (see *To Do*), stop in for ice cream, homemade fudge, bonbons, and other assorted sugary goodies. The café tables outside are great for people watching.

Calico Bean Market (563-557-8159; www.calicobeanmarket.com), 392 Bluff Street, Dubuque. Open Mon.–Sat. 10–5, Sun. 11–4, extended summer hours. A tiny shop packed with both tasty and good-for-you foods. Buy bulk goods, homemade peanut butter, and caramels made by the nuns of a local abbey.

Evers Toy Store (1-800-962-9481; www.everstoystore.com), 204 First Avenue East, Dyersville. Open Mon.–Fri. 8:30–5, Sat. 8–4. Classic and unique American toys fill this fun store. Think tiny farm animals and implements of all varieties. There are model tractors, puzzles, games, and lots of other entertaining—and sometimes educational—toys.

JACKSON AND CLINTON COUNTIES

Jackson and Clinton Counties are at the center of Iowa's Great River Road, and they mark the transition from the steep, wooded bluffs of the north to the lower rolling hills and wetlands of the south. Jackson County was formed in 1837 and named for President Jackson. The city of Maquoketa in Jackson County is an often-missed Iowa treasure, but a visit rewards travelers with caves, world-class art, unique history, and small-town charm. Clinton dates back to 1835 when settlers moved into the area and didn't have more than a few houses and stores until the Chicago, Iowa, Nebraska Railroad announced it would cross the river near Clinton in 1855. Clinton became a lumber town, and between 1880 and 1890 boasted 13 millionaires--more than anywhere else in the nation. Clinton's boon faded with the forests that produced its wealth. Today this sleepy river community is known as one of Iowa's great places.

GUIDANCE **Maquoketa Area Chamber of Commerce** (563-652-4602; www.maquoketaia.com), 117 South Main, Maquoketa. The city launched a new Web site that serves as a portal for information on Maquoketa, its local businesses, and its attractions. E-mail works best for extended information.

Clinton Iowa Convention & Visitors Bureau (563-242-5702; www.clintoniowatourism.com), 721 South Second Street, Clinton. Office staffed during the week, but phone calls and e-mails work best. Clinton's tourism Web site includes fairly comprehensive city information along with some information on local attractions, restaurants, and shopping.

GETTING THERE *By car:* **US 61** runs north-south through both counties, and Clinton County is bisected east-west by **US 30.**

MEDICAL EMERGENCY Call **911**.

Mercy Medical Center (563-244-5555; www.mercyclinton.com), 1410 North Fourth Street, Clinton. Emergency services available.

INTERNET ACCESS/PUBLIC LIBRARY **Maquoketa Public Library** (563-652-3874; www.maquoketa.lib.ia.us), 126 South Second Street, Maquoketa. Open Mon., Tues., and Thurs. 10–8; Wed. and Fri. 10–6; and Sat. 9–4 in winter, 9–3 in summer. Public computers available for research and Internet use.

THE FACES OF MAQUOKETA LINE THE WALLS AND FLOORS OF THE OLD CITY HALL GALLERY

✷ To See

Old City Hall Gallery (563-652-3405; www.oldcityhallgallery.com), 121 South Olive Street, Maquoketa. Art is alive and well in Maquoketa. Typically open 11–5 daily, but call to be sure. Free—unless you buy some art. In the 1901 Old City Hall building, artists Rose Frantzen and Charles Morris display their art and the work of other locals. Frantzen, a Maquoketa native, studied art in Chicago and on the East Coast and traveled extensively before returning home to showcase her astounding and beautiful work in her gallery. Her luscious paintings—many with allegorical themes—often include gilding, stained glass, and mosaic, and the result is other-worldly. Frantzen also completed a project called Faces of Maquoketa, in which she painted the portraits of 100 local residents of all ages whose faces line the gallery.

Frantzen and Morris hope to cultivate an artists' colony in Maquoketa, attracting other artists to the empty storefronts on the main street and leading drawing classes on Tuesday nights for locals. Learn more about the work of **Maquoketa Art Experience** at www.maquoketa-arts.org.

Hurstville Interpretive Center (563-652-3783; www.jacksoncountyiowa.com), 18670 63rd Street, Maquoketa. Open Mon.–Fri. 9–4, Sat. and Sun. 12–5 Apr.–Oct., and Sat. and Sun. 12–4 Nov.–Mar. The center is named after the Hurstville Lime Kilns, relics of a bygone era when a massive lime-producing factory was located on the site. All that remains are wood-fired limestone kilns. Visitors can learn about the kilns, local history, and ecology, or take a naturalist-led hike.

Clinton County Historical Society Museum (563-242-1201), 601 South First Street, Clinton. Open Wed. 1–3, Sat.–Sun. 1:30–4:30, and by appointment. This county museum is housed in an 1858 steamboat-commission house between the river and the downtown. Horse-drawn wagons and trucks were once loaded with wood and goods; today the space includes a research library, displays of historic rooms—such as a dentist and doctor's office—along with teapots, a railroad display from the Chicago Northwestern Railroad line, farm equipment and tools, and displays on some of such famous Clinton residents as author Marcus Childs and actress Lillian Russell.

✷ To Do

Tabor Home Vineyard & Winery (563-673-3131; www.taborwines.com), 3570 67th Street, Baldwin. Open Jan.–May 11–5 Thurs.–Mon, June–Dec. 11–6 daily. Tabor Home led the reemergence of Iowa wines from obscurity. Paul Tabor, the manager and winemaker, determinedly produces some of the best wines in the state and also supports the unique heritage and quality of Iowa wines. The farm, set on rolling countryside, has been in the family for more than 100 years. Rows of vines grow among fields of corn. Sample the wines in the tasting room, take a tour of the winery, and then enjoy a picnic at the big red barn.

✷ Green Space

✪ **Maquoketa Caves State Park** (563-652-5833; www.iowadnr.gov), 10970 98th Street, Maquoketa. The caves at Maquoketa make this one of Iowa's most popular and unique state parks, and truly, it doesn't feel like "Iowa." Six miles of trails wind through a little valley that features 11 caves, a natural bridge 50 feet above Raccoon Creek, the 17-ton balanced rock, and restored prairie land. The scope of the 1,100-foot **Dancehall Cave** is indicated in its name, and spelunkers will love **Ice Cave,** which stays air-conditioning cool on muggy summer afternoons. (Dancehall Cave is easily accessible with paved walkways and a lighting system, but others require a flashlight and some crawling.) **Dugout Cave** stretches deep into the limestone bluffs and is not for the faint-of-heart or the claustrophobic. The park also features an interpretive center where visitors can learn about the lives of the Native Americans who lived in this region—and see some of the relics that they left behind—along with local flora and fauna. The modern campground is accessible for both RVs and tent campers and includes a modern shower house. Campsites from $11–$16.

THE VINEYARD AND HISTORIC BARN AT TABOR HOME VINEYARD AND WINERY, BALDWIN

THE STATIONS OF THE CROSS IN THE CHURCHYARD OF ST. DONATUS CATHOLIC CHURCH IN THE LUXEMBOURGIAN VILLAGE OF ST. DONATUS

ST. DONATUS: LUXEMBOURG IN IOWA

For the longest time, St. Donatus was referred to as a "Historic French Village," when in actuality it was from Luxembourg that settlers to the area emigrated. The misconception comes from the original name of the area, *Tete Des Morts* or "Heads of Death," which was given to the place when a French explorer came across a Native American massacre in the 1600s. And to add to the confusion, St. Donatus was a third-century African bishop in Carthage.

Bellevue State Park (563-872-4019; www.exploreiowaparks.com), 24668 IA 52, Bellevue. Comprising 770 acres of scenic bluffs and timber along the Mississippi River, the park is full of hiking trails perfect for picnicking, watching wildlife, or simply taking in life along the river. Some trails lead visitors to Indian burial grounds and through restored prairie lands. The park has a nature center and the **Bellevue Butterfly Garden** (open daily during daylight hours), which attracts 60 species of butterflies. Camping is available at 46 RV and tent sites in the park's modern campground.

Bickelhaupt Arboretum (563-242-4771; www.bickarb.org), 340 South 14th Street, Clinton. Open daily dawn to dusk. Free. Fourteen acres of trees, shrubs, and perennial and annual flowers create an outdoor museum and classroom for regional plant life—the group of garden conifers is one of the top collections in the country. The arboretum is more than 30 years old, and many of the plants are reaching maturity. The visitors center has a meeting room and horticulture library. Group and self-guided tours are available.

The first settler, John Noel, arrived in the area in 1838, and he was followed by other Luxembourger families through the middle part of the 1800s. Eighteen of the stone structures built by these settlers are still standing in St. Donatus, and the entire valley has a European feel. The tiny town has fewer than 200 residents.

Contact the **Luxembourg Society of Iowa** (563-773-2767) for a pamphlet that describes the history of the significant buildings in the village. Be sure to see **St. Donatus Catholic Church** on the hill. The village's first church was a log cabin, and the current church was built in 1907. Inside are the **Shrines of Our Lady of Luxembourg**. Behind the church and past the graveyard, with some stones dating back to the time of the earliest settlers, is a hill with the **Outdoor Way of the Cross**. It was built in 1861 and includes 14 brick alcoves containing lithographs of the walk of Jesus Christ to crucifixion. The trail winds its way to the top of the hill to the **Pieta Chapel,** which was built in 1885 and is modeled after the Chapel du Bildchen in Vianden, Luxembourg.

While in the village, stop in at **Kalmes Restaurant** (563-773-2480; IA 52), which is open daily for breakfast, lunch, and dinner. The restaurant traces its roots back to 1840, when the owner's great-grandparents emigrated from Luxembourg. Kraut sausage, or trippen, is a house specialty, but there is something for everyone on the menu. The burgers are outstanding, and there are also steaks, sandwiches, pizza, and a seafood buffet on Friday night.

And, if that's not enough Luxembourg fun, spend the night across the street at 101 North Main Street at the **Gehlen House Bed & Breakfast** (563-773-8200; www.gehlenhouse.com). The inn is over 150 years old and was built by Peter Gehlen, from the Luxembourg village of Olm. There are seven comfortable rooms and suites, some with fancy bathtubs, in this historic white-stone inn.

✷ Where to Stay

HOTELS **Decker Hotel and Restaurant** (563-652-6654; www.deckerhotel.us), 128 North Main, Maquoketa. This 1875 Italianate hotel has been restored to reflect its origins while offering modern conveniences. The 12 guest rooms and 5 suites are furnished with antiques but also have private bathrooms, television, and wireless Internet access. The hotel restaurant (open for lunch and dinner Tues.–Sun.; $$) is comfortable, and the menu includes such Midwestern favorites as chicken-fried steak along with some very special seafood dishes. The lounge in the basement is a comfortable, neighborhood bar with big-screen televisions. Rooms from $60–$130.

Riverview Hotel and Restaurant (563-872-4142), 100 South Riverview Street, Bellevue. This independent hotel has 11 inexpensive and basic rooms above the restaurant of the same name. The location is convenient for enjoying the river and the shops along Bellevue's riverfront. The dining downstairs is on a par with the accommodations: an inexpensive and serviceable option for breakfast, lunch, and dinner. Rooms from $35–$60.

BED & BREAKFASTS **Squiers Manor Bed and Breakfast** (563-652-6961; www.squiersmanor.com), 418 West Pleasant, Maquoketa. This 1882 Queen Anne mansion is an anchor of Maquoketa's historic district and takes guests back to Victorian elegance. Each of the eight rooms is special, reminding their occupants of the charmed life of the Squiers family that lived here in splendor. The suites are the real treasures. The high-ceilinged Ballroom Suite on the third floor includes an enormous and romantic bathtub under a cozy eave. A selection of desserts and beverages are served around the table in the evening, and for breakfast innkeeper Kathy Banowetz always creates something tasty, but her specialty is an amazing quiche. Rooms from $80–$195.

Mont Rest Inn (877-872-4220; www.montrest.com), 300 Spring Street, Bellevue. Bellevue's "castle" was built in 1893 for Seth Lluellyn Baker, a wealthy businessman. The inn includes nine romantic and luxurious rooms and suites: each offers a fireplace, whirlpool bathtub, and cable television, along with such treats as imported chocolates, flowers, and free beverages. Provisions can be made for canoe trips on the Maquoketa River, golfing, and massage. The innkeepers also operate the **Moon River Cabins,** which sleep three to four and include kitchenettes, air-conditioning, cable television, and docking privileges. Inn rooms (including breakfast) from $149–$199, cabins from $125–$175.

CAMPING **Rock Creek Marina and Campground** (563-259-1876; www.clintoncountyiowa.com/conservation/RockCreek.htm), 3942 291st Street, Camanche. Located on the Great River Road on the backwaters of the Mississippi, this marina offers full marina services and boat rentals. Guests can enjoy the rich fishing and public hunting in the area. The campground accommodates both RVs and tent campers, and small cabins with air-conditioning, a microwave, and refrigerator are available. Campsites $10 primitive, $15 electric; cabins from $25–$40, weekly rates available. Guests should bring their own linens and tableware.

Maquoketa State Park See *To Do.*

✱ Where to Eat

DINING OUT **Potter's Mill Restaurant** (563-872-3838; www.pottersmill.net), 300 Potters Drive, Bellevue. Open daily for lunch, dinner, and Sun. brunch. Built in 1845, Potter's Mill is Iowa's oldest gristmill and was selling flour to customers all over the Midwest before Iowa was officially a state. Today diners can enjoy high-end home cooking in the historic mill on the banks of the Mississippi. Chef Chad Myers prepares lovely and filling dishes such as Alfredo lasagna and meat loaf along with steaks, sandwiches, and salads. $$

Potter's Mill also offers bed-and-breakfast rooms in the inn. Each of the four rooms is comfortable and has high ceilings with exposed beams. Several rooms have views of the Mississippi and whirlpool tubs. Rooms from $95–175.

Hillside Stables Restaurant (563-687-2479; www.hillsidestables-ia.com), 1412 North IA 67, Sabula. Open for dinner Tues.–Sat. and lunch and dinner Sun. This German restaurant is at the center of the stables, and horses graze on the green fields just outside the door. The food inside is classic German American cuisine (schnitzel, goulash, sauerbraten) along with steaks, chicken breasts, and pork loin. The restaurant also offers a large selection of German and domestic wines and beers. $$

Rastrelli's (563-242-7441; www.rastrellis.com), 238 Main Avenue, Clinton. Open daily for lunch and dinner. Clinton's longest established restaurant was born in 1939, when the Rastrelli family settled in the area. The Italian cuisine goes back to the restaurant's immigrant roots, but there is much more to the menu than traditional pasta. Look for carefully cut steaks, fish, and fowl. Pizza and sandwiches are also available. The restaurant is full service and offers delivery to hotels, takeout, two banquet facilities, a swanky bar, and brunch on Sun. Lunch $$, Dinner $$–$$$.

EATING OUT ✪ **Bluff Lake Restaurant** (563-652-3272), 9343 95th Avenue, Maquoketa. Open Thurs.–Sun. for dinner. Hungry diners come from far and wide for the catfish, chicken, and shrimp "fries" at the Bluff Lake. The restaurant is tucked away in a hollow, and there is often a wait—enjoyed with beer—but all those diners can't be wrong. The "fries" are the real treasure and will fill even the most ambitious eater, but the menu also includes fish, steaks, and chicken dishes. $–$$

Cazador's (563-652-4597), 100 North Main, Maquoketa. Open daily for lunch and dinner. This authentic Mexican restaurant is a local favorite for the fresh and tasty dishes, the plentiful cheese, and the ridiculously large portions. The menu is huge, but it's hard to go wrong; the white-cheese sauce, fajitas, and bacon-wrapped shrimp are all yummy and will leave plenty for leftovers.

Patrick's Steakhouse and Brewery (563-243-5539; www.patrickssteakhouse.com), 132 Sixth Avenue South, Clinton. Open Mon.–Sat. for lunch, and dinner. The steaks are certified Angus beef, the chicken is cooked on a rotisserie, and the grill is wood fired. The menu is edgy pub food with the likes of beer-battered onion rings, Creole crab cakes, and jambalaya among the burgers, steaks, and fried delights. There are plenty of choices for beer, both on tap and in imported bottles, and the restaurant—located in Clinton's historic paper company—is full of 42-inch plasma-screen televisions for watching your favorite teams. $$

Espresso, Cigars & More (563-242-0197), 2007 North Second Street, Clinton. Open daily for lunch and dinner. This crowded little coffee and cigar shop doesn't look like much—the tablecloths and dishes are plastic, and computers line one of the walls. It's the kind of place where they sell international calling cards. But look past the decor to the authentic Cuban food on the menu. Tostadas, plantains, fried yucca, and the classic Cuban sandwich are all available—and quite good. The espresso and café con leche are intense and sweet, just as they ought to be. The proprietors also sell cigars made from Cuban-seed tobacco. $

✷ Entertainment

61 Drive In Theater (563-674-4367; www.maquoketa.com/61drivein), 1228 IA 61, Delmar. Box office opens at 6:30, movies show at 8:30 through the summer. One of the few drive-in theaters left in Iowa, the 61 shows two first-run films per night and hearkens back to an almost-forgotten American style of going to the movies. The movie's soundtrack is projected with a low-power radio transmitter, so patrons listen on portable radios or car radios. Tickets: $6.50 adults, $3.50 children.

Clinton Area Showboat Theater (563-242-6760), Riverview Park,

Clinton. Tickets: $18 adults, $12 per student, $9 children. A professional theater on "Iowa's East Coast" produces several plays and musicals throughout the year in a showboat parked on the Mississippi River. The boat was built in 1935 as a two-deck tug to push barges up and down the Ohio River; eventually, the boat was given to the state of West Virginia, where it was converted to a showboat. The city of Clinton purchased it in 1966 at a public auction, and nowadays the boat and the theater produced on its decks are some of the city's signature attractions.

✷ Selective Shopping

The Book Worm (563-872-4802; www.bellevuebookworm.com), 110 South Riverview, Bellevue. Open Mon.–Sat. 10–5, Sun. 11–4, limited hours in winter. The slogan "books and things" hardly covers the variety in this river-town bookstore. The selection of books is wide and well chosen and covers fiction, nonfiction, popular, and children's genres, but there is also a great selection of local and Iowa history and travel books. On top of the books are antiques, country decorations, and rocks, along with sundry cards and gifts.

Banowetz Antique Mall (563-652-2359; www.banowetzantiques.com), 122 McKinsey Drive, Maquoketa. Open Mon.–Sat. 9–5, Sun. 10–5. With over 150 dealers and covering 50,000 square feet, this gigantic antiques mall is full of treasures while being comfortably "shopable." The mall features furniture pieces large and small, architectural antiques, artwork, lamps, dishes, quilts, jewelry, and even some clothing and shoes. Owner Virl Banowetz is a charmer and knows his stuff, so be sure to say hello and ask for help.

SCOTT COUNTY

Scott County is home to the Quad Cities: Davenport and Bettendorf on the Iowa side and Moline and Rock Island on the Illinois side. European settlement in the area dates to 1832 when Chief Keokuk gave Marguerite LeClarie, wife of Antione LeClaire and granddaughter of a Sac Indian chief, a large track of land. Keokuk required the LeClaire house be built on the exact location where the treaty that ended the Black Hawk war was signed. The Rock Island Railroad built the first bridge connecting Davenport and Rock Island in 1856, and during the Civil War Davenport became a military headquarters. Today, as always, the Quad Cities are manufactoring towns. The Mississippi River brings waterborne traffic, and busy I-80 brings road traffic, making the area an important hub for eastern Iowa. The John Deere Company was founded in the region, and the factory brings both prosperity and tractor groupies to the area.

GUIDANCE **Quad Cities Convention and Visitors Bureau** (563-322-3911; www.visitquadcities.com). Great Web site for extensive Quad City information. **Union Station Visitor Center** (309-227-0937), 102 South Harrison Street, Davenport. Open Mon.–Fri. 9–5, Sat. June–Aug. 10–4. Information and bike rentals are available here.

Mississippi Valley Welcome Center (563-322-3911; www.iowawelcomecenter .com), 900 Eagle Ridge Road, Le Claire. Open Apr.–Sept. 8:30–8, Oct.–Mar. 8:30–4:30. Located in a big house high on the bluff, this visitors center has more than brochures. Enjoy a scenic overlook, gift shop, art gallery, and historical displays. Wireless Internet available.

GETTING THERE *By air:* **Quad Cities International Airport** (309-764-9621; www.qcairport.com), 2200 69th Avenue. Moline is about 60 miles from Iowa City and offers connections to major airports in the region.

By car: The Quad Cities are located between **I-80** and **I-280**.

MEDICAL CARE **Genesis Health System** (563-421-1000; www.genesishealth .com), 1227 East Rusholme Street, Davenport.

GETTING AROUND Like most cities in Iowa, car travel is almost essential in the Quad Cities. Some areas are great for walking, yet visitors need a car or a dedication to bus schedules to get around. However, the Quad Cities do offer a unique

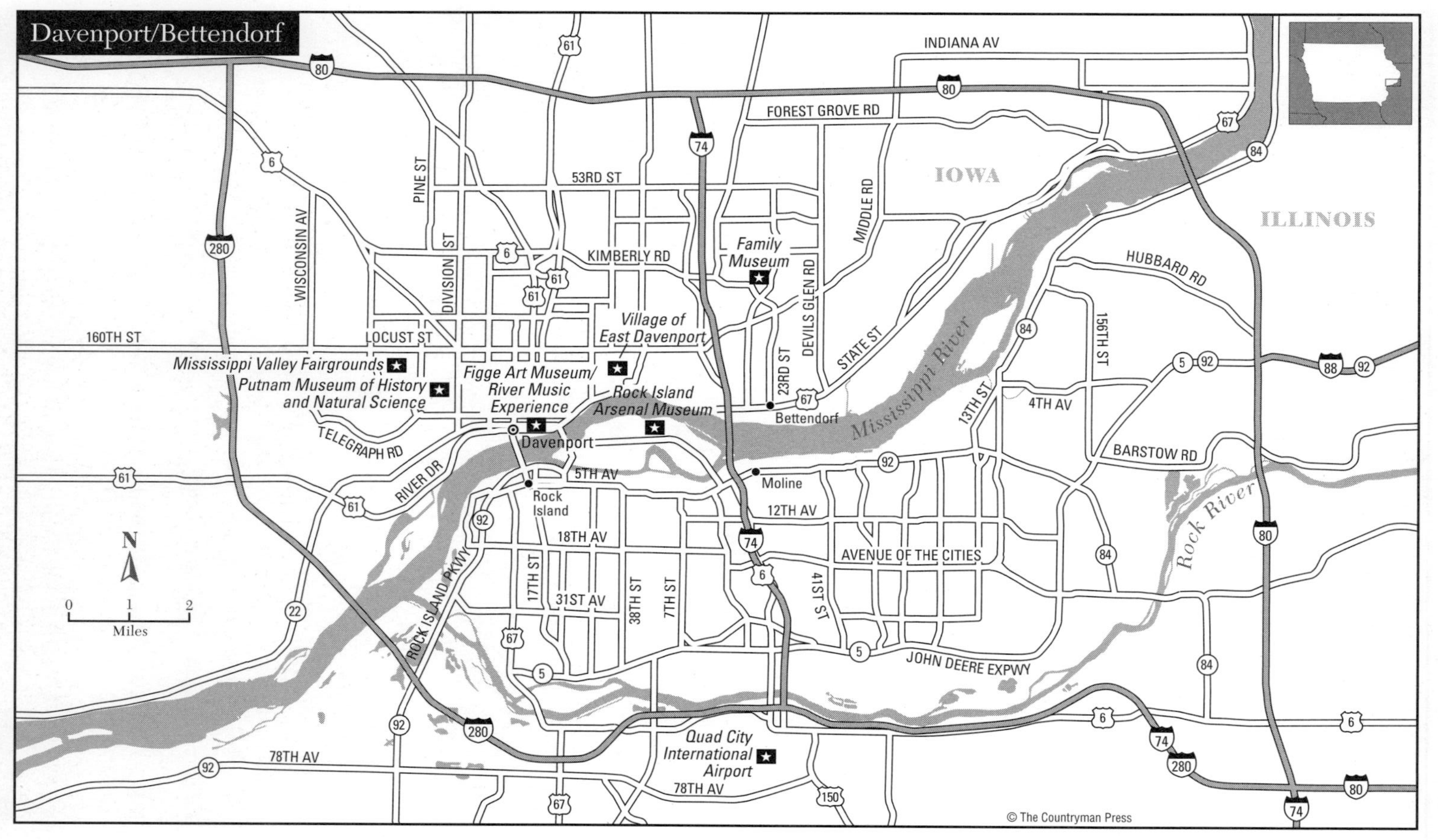

Davenport/Bettendorf
IOWA
ILLINOIS
Mississippi River
Rock River
INDIANA AV
FOREST GROVE RD
53RD ST
KIMBERLY RD
PINE ST
DIVISION ST
WISCONSIN AV
160TH ST
LOCUST ST
MIDDLE RD
DEVILS GLEN RD
23RD ST
STATE ST
HUBBARD RD
156TH ST
13TH ST
4TH AV
BARSTOW RD
TELEGRAPH RD
RIVER DR
5TH AV
12TH AV
18TH AV
17TH ST
31ST AV
38TH ST
7TH ST
41ST ST
AVENUE OF THE CITIES
JOHN DEERE EXPWY
ROCK ISLAND PKWY
78TH AV
Family Museum
Village of East Davenport
Mississippi Valley Fairgrounds
Putnam Museum of History and Natural Science
Figge Art Museum/ River Music Experience
Rock Island Arsenal Museum
Quad City International Airport
Davenport
Bettendorf
Moline
Rock Island
N
0
1
2
Miles
© The Countryman Press

form of public transportation. The **Channel Cat Water Taxi** (309-788-3360; www.qcmetrolink.com), which docks at the Village of East Davenport and the Isle of Capri Casino, ferries passengers among two docks in Iowa and three in Illinois. Riders can hop on and off at any spot all day long, and bikes are welcome.

INTERNET ACCESS Most cafés, restaurants, and hotels offer free wireless.

✷ To See

✪ **Figge Art Museum** (563-326-7804; www.figgeartmuseum.org), 225 West Second Street, Davenport. Open Tues.–Sat. 10–5, Thurs. 10–9, Sun. 12–5. Admission: $7 adults, $6 per senior, $4 children. In a dramatic glass structure overlooking the Mississippi River, the Figge Art museum is as beautiful outside as it is inside. The "winter garden" is a vast, open-air staircase that walks visitors between the floors as they gaze at the splendor of the river. The art is world-class, with a focus on Haitian, Mexican, Colonial, and American art. The Haitian gallery and the Mexican shrine offer rich and vibrant insight into those cultures. Several Grant Wood pieces, including his self-portrait, are on display in a special gallery, and the Figge always offers unique and fascinating traveling exhibitions. Activities are available for children and families, and the museum has both a café and a gift shop.

Buffalo Bill Museum (563-289-5580; www.buffalobillmuseumleclaire.com), 199 North Front Street, LeClaire. Open year-round Mon.–Sat. 9–5, Sun. 12–5. Admission: $5 adults, $1 children. The legendary "Buffalo Bill" Cody was born near LeClaire in 1846. He would go on to become a cowboy, Pony Express rider, scout, marksman, and international star and showman in his own Wild West extravaganzas. The museum is full of artifacts from Cody's life and displays and information on life in Iowa during the period when he lived there. Visitors learn about riverboat pilots, Sauk and Fox Indians, and pioneer life, and they can also step aboard the *Lone Star Steamer*, a wood-hulled sternwheeler. Another Cody site is the **Buffalo Bill Cody Homestead**, (563-225-2981), 28050 230th Avenue, Princeton; open daily Apr.–Oct. by appointment. The stone home was built in 1847 by Cody's father, and the homestead includes a stagecoach and a live buffalo.

✐ **Putnam Museum of History and Natural Science** (563-324-1933; www.putnam.org), 1717 West 12th Street, Davenport; open Mon.–Sat. 10–5, Sun. 12–5. Call or visit their Web site for ticket prices as they vary per exhibit. With a special

THIS MODERN-GLASS STRUCTURE HOUSES THE FIGGE ART MUSEUM IN DAVENPORT

focus on life on the Mississippi River, the Putnam offers budding scientists of all ages the chance to get some hands-on learning experience with the environment and chronicle of the river. Other permanent exhibits illuminate Iowa's history, geography, and traditions as well as Egyptian and Asian cultures, mammals, and the history of the planet. There are always interesting traveling exhibits, too, plus lots of special events and workshops for children. The Putnam is also home to an **IMAX** theater, which offers a nice balance between larger-than-life educational films, such as the film on the Mississippi River or life under the sea in 3-D, and blockbuster entertainment fun.

Iowa 80 Truckstop (563-284-6961; www.iowa80truckstop.com), 755 West Iowa 80 Road, I-80 Exit 284, Walcott. Open 24 hours daily. The "World's Largest Truck Stop" is just over the Mississippi River in Walcott. The 200-acre facility offers fuel, food, truck washes, a trucking museum, restaurants, and even a dentist. The truck stop is also home to a truckers' jamboree each summer.

✪ **River Music Experience** (563-326-1333; www.rivermusicexperience.org), 131 West Second Street, Davenport. Open Mon.–Sat.; call or visit their Web site for show schedules and ticketing. The Mississippi River inspired musicians up and down its shores and brought the blues and jazz up from the Delta to the rest of the country. Visitors can learn about Quad City musical icons—the most famous being Jazz Age cornetist Bix Beiderbecke—see a scale model of the SS *Capitol* that piped people and music up the river, and tap into the audio files and databases for in-depth information on American music. The "experience" also includes the **Redstone Room**, a 250-seat music venue for local, regional, and visiting musicians. The experience continues at **Mojo's**, a coffee shop and Internet café that serves hot java and light snacks to budding rockers and their fans.

Bucktown Center for the Arts (309-737-2066; www.bucktownarts.com), 225 East Second Street, Davenport. Open Wed.–Sat. 11–6. In one warehouse art lovers will find 17 working studios and galleries. Artisans working in media as varied as oil painting to custom-made clothing create and sell their artwork in their individual workspaces. Wander from studio to studio, see the artists at work, and shop for arts and crafts. Bucktown is also the home of the **Midcoast Fine Arts** project and the **Midwest Writing Center.**

Rock Island Arsenal, though technically in Illinois, is a must for Quad City visitors. It is composed of several different facilities. The **Mississippi River Visitor Center** (309-794-5338; www.missriver.org; open 9–5 daily, western tip of Arsenal Island) lets visitors get up close to the boats that pass through the lock-and-dam system. In building 60 on the same island is the **Rock Island Arsenal Museum** (309-782-5021; www.riamwr.com/museum.htm; open 10–4 Tues.–Sun.) is dedicated to the history of the arsenal and the island. Plenty of military and small arms are on display—it's an arsenal, after all. Also check out the **Colonel Davenport Historic Home** (309-786-7336; www.davenporthouse.org) on the north shore of Arsenal Island at Hilman Street, Rock Island. Open 12–4 Thurs.–Sun. early May–late Oct. Admission: $5 adults, $3 children, $10 per family. Colonel George Davenport's 1833 Federal-style mansion is now a museum. The colonel came to the area to create an army fort, and he developed a prosperous fur trade in the area.

German-American Heritage Center (563-322-8844; www.gahc.org), 712 West Second Street, Davenport. Open 1–4 Tues.–Sun. and by appointment; small admission fee. The German immigrants to the Mississippi region had a profound impact on the culture and settlement on the state of Iowa. Learn about their experiences at this museum and interactive community center.

✷ To Do

River Cruises (815-777-1660; www.riverboattwilight.com), foot of Wisconsin Street, Le Claire; boats leave at 8:30 AM Sun., Tues., and Thurs. through the summer months; $305 per person. Float 166 miles north to Dubuque and back on this overnight cruise that comes complete with meals, lodging, and entertainment.

FROM HERMITS TO HAIR SALONS: THE VILLAGE OF EAST DAVENPORT

In the 1840s the area that is now East Davenport was known as "Stubbs' Eddy," named for James R. Stubbs, a hermit who lived in a cave in a mound near the river. At that time the Upper Rapids stretched 18 miles and were thought to be the longest chain of river rapids in the world. Today they are controlled by the lock-and-dam system.

The village was founded in 1851 and served as a logging town before the Civil War. Many historic buildings and original structures remain, and in 1980 the Village of East Davenport Historic District was put on the National Registry of Historic Places. (For more information on the area visit the Village of East Davenport Web site: www.villageofeastdavenport.com.)

Nowadays the village is home to more lattés than logjams, and visitors delight in the charming streets, historic architecture, and adorable shops and restaurants offered by this quaint little city-within-the-city. Grab a cup of coffee from **Java Station Espresso Café** (563-326-0969; 1018 Mound Street), and browse the shops and galleries. Be sure to stop in at the **Isabel Bloom Gallery** (563-324-5135; 1109 Mound Street) to see the sculptures of one of the Quad Cities' most beloved artists. Bloom studied under Grant Wood, and her unique, blue-tinged sculptures (concrete finished to look like weathered bronze) are loved for their simplicity and joy. Also don't miss **The Soap Box** (563-322-4096; www.thesoap-box.com; 2033 East 11th Street), which has been selling fine soap and bath products in the village for 25 years.

Afternoon snacks are at their best at **Lagomarcino's** (563-324-6137; www.lagomarcinos.com; 2132 East 11th Street). The confectionery was founded by Angelo Lagomarcino, an immigrant from northern Italy, in 1908 and has remained a family business since the turn of the 20th century. Their specialty is homemade hot-fudge sauce, which comes to the table in its own pitcher to be poured on according to the taste of the lucky devil eating the sundae. For something more substantial, try the **11th Street Bar & Grill** (563-322-9047), 2108 E 11th Street for a famous unbreaded (aka grilled) tenderloin and hand-cut French fries.

Now isn't that nicer than a cave dwelling?

Along the way, guests can promenade on the decks of the classic Mark Twain-style steamboat, enjoy onboard entertainment and activities, or simply gaze out at the wonders of the mighty river. Guests stay overnight in Dubuque at the **Grand Harbor Resort** (see *To Do* in the Dubuque County section) and have plenty of time to see the city.

Family Museum (563-344-4106; www.familymuseum.org), 2900 Learning Campus Drive, Bettendorf. Open Memorial Day–Labor Day Mon.–Sat. 9–5, Sun. 12–5; winter hours Mon.–Thurs. 9–8, Fri.–Sat. 9–5, Sun. 12–5; call for admission pricing. This museum built for children lets them learn about nature and science through hands-on exhibits. Children can touch a tornado, play with musical instruments, create a garden, or run around at the playground. The museum also hosts traveling exhibits and a pretty fun gift shop.

Michael's Fun World (563-386-3826; www.michaelsfunworld.com), 354 West 76th Street, Davenport; admission varies by activity. Open Mon.–Sat. 12–10 and Sun. 12–8 in summer; shorter hours in winter. If the kids aren't worn out by the museums, burn some energy playing trampoline basketball, rock climbing, or hitting the indoor batting cages. Miniature golf, go-carts, a jungle zone, and laser tag should provide enough high-adrenaline excitement to wear out even the most determined young traveler.

Isle of Capri Casino and Hotel (563-441-7000; www.isleofcapricasinos.com), 1777 Isle Parkway, Bettendorf. Open 24 hours a day. A towering skywalk takes visitors from the hotel on the bluff to high-stakes slots, table games, and poker in the boat on the river. Several restaurants ranging from fine dining to deli are on site.

✷ Green Space

Vander Veer Botanical Park (563-326-7818; www.cityofdavenportiowa.com), 215 West Central Park Avenue, Davenport. Open 10–4 Tues.–Sun. This botanical garden was first built in 1885 and showcases a nationally recognized rose garden, a hosta glade, and Old World-style gardens near the stone fountain. The park is a lovely spot for plant enthusiasts and casual strollers.

✷ Where to Stay

HOTELS **Abbey Hotel** (563-355-0291; www.theabbeyhotel.com), 1401 Central Avenue, Bettendorf. The Carmelite nuns who once lived cloistered in this abbey may have taken vows of poverty and chastity, but the guests certainly won't feel that way in this now-luxurious 19-room hotel. The award-winning rooms are gorgeous and offer secular guests king- and queen-size beds, marble bathrooms, wireless Internet access, free breakfast and airport shuttle, and an evening honor bar. Most of the rooms have Mississippi River views from the abbey's perch high on the bluff. Rooms from $104–$169.

The Lodge (563-359-7141; www.lodgehotel.com), I-74 and Spruce Hills Drive, Bettendorf. The freshly renovated guest rooms are uniquely appointed and include expanded cable and access to the fitness room plus an indoor pool, a whirlpool, and saunas. The restaurant at the lodge serves breakfast, lunch, and dinner and an excellent Sunday brunch. Rooms from $69–$179.

BED & BREAKFASTS **Beiderbecke Inn** (563-323-0047; www.bbonline

.com/ia/beiderbecke), 532 West Seventh Street, Davenport. The Beiderbecke mansion, built in 1880 in Stick-style architecture, is something out of a fairy tale, complete with a tower, a turret, balconies, and magnificent hickory doors. The home is furnished with antiques and stately beds. Rooms (including breakfast) from $85–$105.

Fulton's Landing Guest House (563-322-4069; www.fultonslanding.com), 1206 East River Drive, Davenport. This Italianate mansion sits high on a bluff above the Quad Cities. A large gable offers great views and a comfortable place to relax, and the four rooms are almost decadent with period wallpapers and furnishings. Rooms (including breakfast) from $90–$140.

✷ Where to Eat

DINING OUT **The Faithful Pilot Café** (563-289-4156; www.faithfulpilot.com), 117 North Cody Road, LeClaire. Open daily for dinner; Sun. brunch and dinner during summer months. This elegant little café brings locally grown produce, meats, eggs, and herbs to the table with seasonal menus and thoughtful preparation. The food may be local, but the scope is worldly with dishes such as tuna carpaccio and shrimp satay and an impressive and globally minded wine list. $$–$$$

Trattoria Tiramisu (563-323-2787; www. trattoriatiramisu.com), 1804 State Street, Bettendorf. Open for lunch Mon.–Fri., dinner Mon.–Sat. Authentic Italian cuisine served in the traditional style of appetizer, salad, pasta (a long list!), and meat courses. The menu is updated often, and there is always a daily special. $$–$$$

EATING OUT 🍸 **Front Street Brewery** (563-322-3483), 208 East River Drive, Davenport. Open daily for lunch and dinner. In a tiny brick building facing the river, this brewery produces fine handcrafted beers. Drink a pint at the cozy brick bar, or buy a growler and take it home. Excellent pub food is available in the restaurant and is designed to complement the beer—fresh, soft pretzels are served warm as are big pork chop and steak sandwiches and burgers. Deli sandwiches are on the lighter side, and hearty entrées, such as ahi tuna and bangers and mash, are available in the evenings. $$

✪ **Iowa Machine Shed** (563-391-2427; www.machineshed.com), 7250 Northwest Boulevard, Davenport. Open daily for breakfast, lunch, and dinner. In 1978 the Whalen family opened the first Iowa Machine Shed on the outskirts of Davenport. Since then the restaurant—which celebrates the food and lifestyle of the humble Iowa farmer—has become a small, Midwestern chain, but it's still as close to eating on a farm as most people get. The waiters wear overalls and John Deere hats, the ice water comes in Mason jars, and the portions are big enough to feed a famished farmhand. Bring a friend along and split a meal, but be sure to try the baked potato soup. $–$$

Bier Stube Bar & Grill (563-323-2174; www.bier-stube.com), 2228 East 11th Street, Davenport. Open daily for lunch, dinner, and bar. Anyone can be a little German, especially after sampling the huge selection of German beer, wine, and food. Along with the requisite burgers and appetizers come bratwursts, sausages, and other fine German delights. $$

Mo Brady's Restaurant (563-445-0684), 4830 North Brady Street, Davenport. Open daily for dinner. Mo Brady's is famous for serving a fresh-baked cinnamon roll with all of the varied entrées. Why a breakfast pastry with dinner? The story is unclear, but who are we to question a cinnamon roll alongside hand-cut steaks, seafood, BBQ, and sandwiches. The menu is enormous, so there is something for everyone plus a full bar. $$

Exotic Thai (563-344-0909), 2303 East 53rd Street, Davenport. Open daily for lunch and dinner. Exotic Thai serves up the flavors of the Far East to devoted diners from all over eastern Iowa. The food is authentic, the curries are delicious, and the service is friendly. $$

✷ Entertainment

Adler Theatre (563-326-8500; www.adlertheatre.com), 136 East Third Street, Davenport. Call or visit their Web site for schedules and ticket pricing. The home of the Quad City Symphony is this Art Deco masterpiece built in the 1930s. Today it is a venue for entertainment that ranges from alternative music to stand-up comedy to ballet.

Putnam Museum of History and Natural Science/IMAX. See *To See*.

River Music Experience. See *To See*.

MUSCATINE COUNTY

The river turns west at Davenport and runs into the little town of Muscatine, in Muscatine County. This river city was once the "Pearl Button Capital of the World," when it turned Mississippi clamshells into the closures for countless shirts and jackets through the last century. The city went through several names before it settled on Muscatine. It was known as Bloomington (that was changed due to confusion with mail service) and Casey's Woodpile. Before the Civil War, Muscatine had a large population of African Americans, fugitive slaves escaping the south. Samuel Clemens (later known as Mark Twain) worked for the Muscatine Journal (the paper still exists today), and he recorded memories of his years there in his book Life on the Mississippi. Muscatine isn't big, but there are several nice restaurants and places to stay, especially in the Pearl Plaza, a historic button factory turned into a hub for shopping, eating, and entertainment.

GUIDANCE **Muscatine Convention and Visitors Bureau** (1-800-257-3275; www.meetmuscatine.com), 319 East Second Street, Muscatine. Open during regular business hours. Visit the Web site for a free visitors guide and map or stop by for personal guidance.

GETTING THERE *By car:* **US 61** is the main thoroughfare through the county and runs parallel to the river.

MEDICAL EMERGENCY Call **911**.

Unity Healthcare Hospital (563-264-9100; www.unityiowa.org), 1518 Mulberry Avenue, Muscatine. Emergency care and short-stay units can assist visitors.

INTERNET ACCESS/PUBLIC LIBRARY **Musser Public Library** (563-263-3065; www.musserpubliclibrary.org), 304 Iowa Avenue, Muscatine. Open 10–9 Mon.–Thurs., 10–5 Fri. and Sat., 1–5 Sun. Computers with Internet are available but in high demand so there is often a waiting list.

* To See

Muscatine History and Industry Center (563-263-1052; www.muscatinehistory.com), 117 West Second Street, Muscatine. Open 10–4 Tues.–Sat. Muscatine didn't need oysters to create 1.5 billion pearl buttons a year, just Mississippi River clams. Learn about this industry, unique to the Mississippi River area, through

FOUNTAINS SPLASH IN MUSCATINE'S RIVERFRONT PARK

hands-on exhibits. Visitors can also check out historical artifacts from other industries and aspects of Muscatine County life in this downtown storefront museum.

Muscatine Art Center (563-263-8282; www.muscatineartcenter.org), 1314 Mulberry Avenue, Muscatine. Open Tues., Wed., Fri. 10–5, Thurs. 10–7, Sat.–Sun. 1–5. Free. For a small river town, Muscatine has a fun and surprising art center in the restored 1908 mansion of Laura Musser, a prominent daughter of Muscatine. Alongside national traveling exhibits are both fine and decorative arts. A few of the features include paintings by Grant Wood, Georgia O'Keeffe, and Edgar Degas. Furniture, textiles, glass, and children's toys round out this small but charming collection.

* Green Space

Wildcat Den State Park (563-263-4337; www.iowadnr.com), 1884 Wildcat Den Road, Muscatine. The trails at Wildcat Den take hikers through the fabulous limestone features known as **Steamboat Rock,** the **Devil's Punch Bowl,** and **Fat Man's Squeeze,** over picturesque bluffs and rock outcroppings, and along views of the river and the countryside. Visitors can also learn about the **Pine Creek Grist Mill** (563-263-4337; www.pinecreekgristmill.com), a restored 1848 mill with intact machinery and millstones, which is located at the state park and is on the National Register of Historic Places. The park is also home to the **Melpine Schoolhouse.** Visitors can picnic around the park or at the two shelters and camp at one of 28 campsites served with a primitive restroom facility.

* Where to Stay

BED & BREAKFASTS **Strawberry Farm B&B** (563-262-8688; www.strawberryfarmbandb.com), 3402 Tipton Road, Muscatine. The three guest rooms in this 1850s Victorian farmhouse are done in an antiques and country-inspired theme but remain crisp, clean, and delightful. A full breakfast is served, either in the communal dining room or delivered to individual rooms, and guests are encouraged to relax in the quiet of the countryside (though technically still within city limits), read a book on the porch, or loll in one of the claw-foot bathtubs. Rooms from $90–$110.

Pines on the Prairie (563-299-0144; www.pinesontheprairie.com), 2196 Union Avenue, Wilton. Just a short drive from the Quad Cities and Muscatine, Pines on the Prairie is a lovely rural getaway, complete with barnyard animals and a big friendly dog to welcome visitors to this idyllic farmhouse in the countryside run by kindly innkeepers. The two guest rooms are clean, comfortable, and very relaxed. The upstairs suite sleeps up to six, and the Prairie Room has a king-size bed, quilts, and a private bathroom. Both accommodations have snacks, a fridge, and a microwave. Be sure to take a stroll on the "prairie trail" across the road. Rooms (including breakfast) from $85–$125.

The Muskie Motel (563-263-2601; www.muskiemotel.com), 1620 Park Avenue, Muscatine. The 35 rooms of this independent motel have all the basic essentials: air-conditioning, fridges, cable television (including HBO), and free ice, and the rates are budget friendly. Rooms from $35–$55.

✱ Where to Eat

DINING OUT 🍸 **The Button Factory Woodfire Grille** (563-264-8590; www.buttonfactoryrestaurant.com), 215 West Mississippi Drive, Muscatine. Open daily for lunch and dinner. Housed in the refurbished Hawkeye Button Factory, this classy-casual restaurant offers plenty of patio seating for diners who want to enjoy a meal next to the mighty Mississippi. The menu is mostly American-with-a-twist fare, with a special focus on steaks cooked over a wood fire, unique sandwiches, and desserts. Sunday brunch is buffet style, the wine list is long and geographically diverse, and the bar is large and lively. $$

EATING OUT **Tantra Thai Bistro** (563-263-2345), 101 West Mississippi Drive, Muscatine. Open daily for lunch and dinner. Probably the most adventurous restaurant in little Muscatine, Tantra cooks up both classic Thai and specialty dishes, from curry to spicy-basil noodles. Spiciness is added to order, so everyone's tastes—from super mild to raging-Thai hot—can be satisfied. Wash your meal down with imported Thai teas and beers. The restaurant, in the old Hotel Muscatine, is hip and modern, with wooden floors, Buddha statues, and the vibrant colors of South Asia. $–$$

Port City Underground (563-263-4743), 208 West Second Street, Muscatine. Open for lunch Tues.–Fri. and dinner Tues.–Sat. In the lower level of the Pearl Plaza, this Italian restaurant manages to be casual and romantic. The service is fast and friendly and dishes up classic favorites: pizza, pasta, and sandwiches. There are few surprises on the menu, but it is hard to go wrong. Wine, beer, and cocktails are available with plenty of options. $–$$

🍸 **Mami's Authentic Mexican Restaurant** (563-262-5505), 201 West Second Street, Muscatine. Open Mon.–Sat. for lunch and dinner with nightclub hours on the weekends. All the customary dishes done in an authentic style are available at this downtown favorite. In the evenings the restaurant does double duty as a sports bar and nightclub for margarita-fueled fun. $

Clamshell Diner (563-263-7999), 115 West Mississippi Drive, Muscatine. Open Mon.–Sat. for breakfast, lunch, and dinner. One of the few remaining historic "Valentine Diners" (a diner that seats between 8 and 10 people and can be run by just two employees) in the state, the Clamshell is still serving up burgers, hot dogs, fries, and milkshakes. $

COFFEE AND TREATS **The Wilton Candy Kitchen** (563-732-2278), 310

Cedar Street, Wilton. Open Mon.–Sat. 7:30–5, Sun. 7:30–12 and 2–5, and by appointment. George and Thelma Nopoulos welcome ice-cream lovers into the world's oldest continuous ice-cream parlor, tracing its history back to 1867 in a building dating from 1856. The current proprietary dynasty began after Gus George Nopolous arrived in the United States from Greece in 1907 and started an ice-cream tradition in the parlor that has lasted for seven generations and counting. The candy kitchen is full of Old-World touches: walnut booths, leaded-glass lamp-shades, and delicious homemade ice cream. Light sandwiches are also available, but the sweet stuff is the real treat. $

Green's Tea and Coffee (563-263-5043), 208 West Second Street, Suite 8, Muscatine. Open Mon. 7–4, Tues.–Fri. 7–6, Sat. 8–4. Located on the main floor of the Pearl Plaza, Green's Tea is more than a coffee shop—it is an experience in delicious food. The special sandwiches include fresh tastes along the lines of a swanky roast-beef sandwich, a rosemary chicken salad, and a "VEG" with hummus, carrots, and peppers. The desserts are naughty and the coffee and tea come by the cup or in bulk. $

Sweet Temptations (563-263-2169; www.sweettemptationscreations.com), 208 West Second Street, Muscatine. Open Mon.–Wed. 10–6, Thurs.–Sat. 10–9. Consider this locally owned shop when in the market for a place to spoil your dinner. There are 31 flavors of fresh, hand-dipped ice cream, gelato, fudge, and fine chocolates. The shop also specializes in bygone vintage favorites such as Beeman's gum, Double Bubble, and pop rocks.

✷ Drinking Establishments

The Pearl Martini Bar (563-263-2207), 101 West Mississippi Drive, Muscatine. Closed Sun. A treasure in the old Hotel Muscatine, this martini bar can shake up more than 50 martinis. The atmosphere is Rat Pack chic with original marble, wood, and light fixtures from the 1918 hotel, plus wireless Internet access as a modern convenience. A light menu of panini sandwiches and appetizers goes well with all the vodka and gin, but cocktails, imported beer, and wine are also available.

✷ Selective Shopping

Crazy Girl Yarn Shop (563-263-9276; www.crazygirlyarnshop.com), 208 West Second Street, Muscatine. Open Mon.–Sat. 10–5, Sun. 1–4. This is the yarn store for people who don't yet know how to knit. The shop sells upscale yarns in a rainbow of colors and textures and also offers free knitting classes. Beginning knitters can learn how to create that argyle sweater for Grandpa in less than 15 minutes. Located in the Pearl Plaza, Crazy Girl is very welcoming and a fun place to hang out.

LOUISA AND DES MOINES COUNTIES

While Lewis and Clark were exploring the Missouri, Lt. Zebulon Pike worked his way up the Mississippi, at the request of President Thomas Jefferson. In 1837 Burlington became a territorial capital of the Wisconsin territory, and later the first capital of the Iowa territory. The streets of the hilly river city are cobbled, including its most famous thoroughfare, the "crookedest alley in the world," that slithers up the steep hills into the tony neighborhoods above, but the rest of the city and the county also have their charms. The state's nickname, Hawkeye, came from a Burlington newspaper, and the city was important both as a port for steamboats and a hub for railroads. With nearly constant views of the river and a balance of the historical (Toolesboro Mounds), the natural (Flaming Prairie), and the entertaining (Catfish Bend Casino), these counties have just enough for a very fun day or a relaxing weekend.

GUIDANCE **Greater Burlington Partnership** (319-752-6365; www.growburlington.com), 610 North Fourth Street, Suite 200, Burlington. Open during normal business hours. Contact for a visitors guide and information on attractions, dining, lodging, and the like.

GETTING THERE *By car:* **US 61** runs north-south through both Louisa and Des Moines Counties. The city of Burlington is at the crossroads of **US 61** and **US 34.**

MEDICAL EMERGENCY Call **911**.
Great River Health Systems (319-768-1000; www.greatrivermedical.org), 1221 South Gear Avenue, West Burlington. Emergency-care services available.

INTERNET ACCESS **Burlington Public Library** (319-753-1647; www.burlington.lib.ia.us), 210 Court Street, Burlington. Open Labor Day–Memorial Day Mon.–Thurs. 9–9, Fri.–Sat. 9–5, Memorial Day–Labor Day Mon.–Thurs. 9–8, Fri.–Sat. 9–5. This modern library on the bluff has 30 computers and wireless Internet throughout the building, along with information on Burlington, genealogy, and historical materials. The library has a great story-time room, a coffee shop, and a gift shop, too.

SNAKE ALLEY, THE "CROOKEDEST ALLEY IN THE WORLD," IN BURLINGTON

✷ To See

✪ **Snake Alley** is located between Washington and Columbia streets on Sixth Street, Burlington. The town's most famous tourist attraction is the "crookedest alley in the world"—according to Ripley's Believe It or Not the curves are even sharper than world-famous Lombard Street in San Francisco. The brick alley was built in 1894 as an experiment in street design. The hope was that the winding street, like a switchback on a mountain trail, would make the steep climb easier for horses and wagons. The alley climbs 58.3 feet with five half-curves and two quarter-curves. Walk up the historic road to see the homes in the historic district at the top of the hill, or if you are feeling very athletic, sign up for the annual Snake Alley Criterium.

At the top of Snake Alley is the **Phelps House Museum** (512 Columbia Street). Open Sat.–Sun. May–Oct.; call for hours and tour information. Nine rooms of this 1851 Victorian home display antique furnishings and medical artifacts from the years when the building housed the first Protestant hospital in town. The homes in the Heritage Hill National Historic District, between High and North Streets, and Central and North Third Streets, were built as status symbols between the 1870s and the 1900s by the prominent German families who settled in the area. Late Victorian, Greek, Gothic, Italian Villa, Queen Anne, and Georgian styles are all featured in the nearly 160 homes in the area.

Port of Burlington Welcome Center (319-752-8731; www.growburlington.com), 400 North Front Street, Burlington. Open 9–6 daily. The welcome center, located in the historic 1928 Burlington Municipal Docks, is a great place to start a visit to Burlington. Not only is it full of useful tourist information, but it is right on the river with beautiful views of the bridge. Visitors can find souvenirs, videos, and information for self-guided tours.

Wildlife Lakes Elks Farm (319-752-4659; www.wildlifelakes.com), 13852 Washington Road, West Burlington. No set hours. Visitors are always welcome, but call ahead to be safe. Check out the day-to-day operations of a working elk ranch. The picturesque lakes and ponds attract Canada geese and other wildlife.

Toolesboro Indian Mounds (319-523-8381; www.lccb.org), 6568 Toolesboro Road, Toolesboro. Open Memorial Day–Labor Day 12–4 daily, 12–4 weekends remainder of the year. Two burial mounds built by the woodland Hopewell Native Americans remain in this small park and are some of the best-preserved mounds in the state. Learn more about the culture of the ancient people of Iowa, see Oneota cultural artifacts in the visitors center, and enjoy a picnic area and small prairie reconstruction.

Lovers Leap Bridge (www.cjiowa.com), south of Oak Street, the bridge that connects Third and Fourth Streets in Columbus Junction. The swinging bridge was constructed in 1886 of barrel staves and wire, but stilts were added. The shaky construction was condemned in 1902. A new 160-foot swinging bridge was built, but it broke in 1920. The bridge as it stands today was built in 1922 and reaches 262 feet; new planks and cables were added in 1954, but it's not the construction so much as the swing that makes this bridge so unique. The bridge—named after a legend of an Indian maiden tossing herself into the crevasse after her lover died in battle—swings and sways and is not for those inclined to motion sickness.

✻ To Do

Catfish Bend Casino (1-800-372-2946; www.catfishbendcasino.com) and **Fun City** (877-543-2386; www.onefuncity.com), 3001 Winegaard Drive, Burlington. Open Mon.–Thurs. 8 AM–3 AM, Fri.–Sun. 24 hours. Gamers can play thousands of slot machines, video poker, and table games at this new 24,000-square-foot casino. Children and less financially daring thrill-seekers can enjoy Fun City, an entire municipality dedicated to good times that includes an indoor/outdoor water park, a 10,000-square-foot arcade, a 3-D virtual roller coaster, laser tag, bowling, electric go-karts, billiards, and indoor golfing along with restaurants and bars. Kids of all ages can scream down the 19 water slides, relax in the lazy river, or shoot each other with water cannons before hitting the less aquatic adventures inside this complex. Admission and hours vary per activity; water park $6–$10, laser tag arena $5.

Burlington Bees Baseball (319-754-5705; www.gobees.com), 2712 Mt. Pleasant Street, Burlington. The Bees are a farm team for the Kansas City Royals and the only professional sports team in southeast Iowa. The ballgames are intimate and lively, and there are nightly promotions. Visit their Web site, or call for ticketing information during baseball season.

✻ Green Space

Starr's Cave Nature Center & Preserve (319-753-5808; www.dmcconservation.com), 11627 Starr's Cave Road, Burlington. Open daylight hours. Tucked into a neighborhood on the north side of the city, this preserve includes three caves, limestone bluffs, and prairie remnants in a picturesque wooded valley. The Nature Center offers insight into the endangered plant species and native wildlife along with historical displays, activities, and education programs.

Mosquito Park, at the corner of North Third and Franklin Streets, Burlington. This park at the top of a bluff is named for its tiny size, not for any especially pesky inhabitants. The views of the river are spectacular, and there is just enough room to relax.

Geode State Park (319-392-4601), 12 miles west of Burlington on US 34. Geodes, the state rock of Iowa, form when a sparkling quartz center lines the cavity of a limestone rock. These special rocks can only be found in this corner of the United States, and several Keokuk geodes are on display at the campground of this state park. In addition to the unique geology, the park also includes a small lake for swimming and fishing, a modern campground, and hiking and cross-country skiing trails.

✷ Where to Stay

The Burlington area has several national chain hotels and motels. Many visitors find themselves staying at the casino, but the region has a few smaller and more special accommodations, as well.

HOTELS AND MOTELS **The Hotel Wapello** (319-532-2341), 227 North Main Street, Wapello. This historic hotel looks and feels like a step into the past. The nine inexpensive guest rooms are charming in their old-fashioned, folksy way. The hotel is clean, comfortable, and air-conditioned—and not a mass-market chain. Rooms from $35–$55.

BED & BREAKFASTS

Squirrel's Nest Bed & Breakfast (319-752-8382; www.artysquirrel.com), 500 North Street, Burlington. The Squirrel's Nest refers to the third-floor penthouse suite with huge windows, a balcony, a queen-size bed and a queen-size futon, kitchenette, and a whirlpool tub. The home is comfortable and cute, but visitors find themselves falling in love with the romantic view. Another smaller room, the Bear's Den, is also available. Breakfast is continental, and innkeeper Inez Metzger is a helpful resource for her city. Rooms from $75–$125.

Mississippi Manor Bed & Breakfast Inn (319-753-2218; www.mississippimanor.com), 809 North Fourth Street, Burlington. This Italianate home was built in 1877 by a lumber baron and is one of Burlington's historic architectural gems. In 1991 the home was renovated to include three suites with private baths, wood-burning fireplaces, and air-conditioning. Rooms (including breakfast) from $75–$95.

TAKE IN THE VIEW WHILE DINING AT THE DRAKE IN BURLINGTON

CAMPING **Flaming Prairie Park** (319-523-8381; www.naturallylouisa county.com), 14624 CR X61, Muscatine. This little park highlights the unique environment of the Mississippi's wondrous wetlands. The 24 campsites are modern and spacious, with plenty of room for trailers and boats. Wildlife lovers and fishers have easy access to the river, which is just over a levee. Campsites from $10–$15.

✷ Where to Eat

DINING OUT **The Drake on the Riverfront** (319-754-1036; www.the drakerestaurant.com), 106 Washington Street, Burlington. Open Mon.–Sat. for lunch and dinner. The Drake has an excellent patio for dining outside on fine days, and the menu is unique and well prepared. Enjoy big cuts of beef cooked over a wood fire, BBQ cooked in a pit, or farm-raised elk, buffalo, or steak while savoring views of the Mississippi River. The game is raised locally. Many visitors don't know that buffalo is a tasty and lean alternative to beef. Diners can also find specialty pizzas, Italian entrées, seafood, and salads. $$

EATING OUT **7th Inning Stretch** (319-754-5341), 304 North Third Street, Burlington. Open for lunch Mon.–Sat. All-beef hot dogs are served in an authentic Chicago style in this downtown lunch joint that celebrates the Cubs. Sub sandwiches, gyros, BBQ, and wraps are tasty and fresh and draw in downtown workers of all types. $

COFFEE **Diggers Rest Coffeehouse & Roaster** (319-758-6067), 314 Jefferson, Burlington. Open daily for breakfast and lunch. This downtown coffee shop specializes in freshly roasted coffee and light sandwiches for lunch. The picture windows look out onto one of Burlington's main streets, and the service is friendly. $

LEE COUNTY

In the southeast corner of Iowa, Lee County was the site of Fort Madison, built at the critical junction of the Des Moines River and the Mississippi River. The county was also across the river from Nauvoo, Illinois, the historic Mormon settlement from where the Mormons, fleeing persecution, set off on their epic trip westward. Today Lee County sits on Lake Cooper, created by Lock and Dam No. 19 on the Mississippi, and is home to the historic cities of Fort Madison and Keokuk.

GUIDANCE

Fort Madison Area Convention & Visitors Bureau (319-372-5472; www.visitfortmadison.com), 709 Ninth Street, Fort Madison. Open during regular business hours. Information about the area available online or by phone.

GETTING THERE *By car:* **US 218/IA 27** and **US 61** run north-south through the county.

MEDICAL EMERGENCY Call **911**.

Keokuk Area Hospital (319-524-7150; www.keokukhealthsystems.org), 1600 Morgan Street, Keokuk. Emergency-medicine services available on a walk-in basis.

✷ To See

Old Fort Madison (319-372-6318; www.oldfortmadison.com), Riverview Park, Fort Madison. Open May and Sept. Sat.–Sun. 9:30–5, June–Aug. Wed.–Sun. 9:30–5. Admission: $5 adults, $2.50 children. Fort Madison was one of the earliest settlements in the territory that would become the state of Iowa. The fort was built in 1808–1809 under the leadership of Lieutenant Alpha Kingsley to protect the government trading posts and secure the area for American exploration of the Louisiana Purchase. But when hostilities with Native Americans increased in 1813, the soldiers, under the cover of darkness, dug a tunnel and slipped downstream in boats, setting fire to the fort as they left. While the original fort no longer exists, a huge wooden re-creation stands on the shores of the Mississippi. Inside, guides in authentic costumes illustrate the life and work of the soldiers and their families at the fort with hands-on demonstrations.

TRAIN ENTHUSIASTS LOVE FORT MADISON—ESPECIALLY THE TOWN'S OLD SANTA FE DEPOT HISTORICAL COMPLEX

Old Santa Fe Depot Historical Complex (319-372-7661), Avenue H and Ninth Street, Fort Madison. Open May–Sept.; call ahead for hours or to make an appointment. Train enthusiasts love Fort Madison. One of the reasons is the Old Santa Fe Depot, which was built in 1909 in the Mission-Revival style. Today it is a museum dedicated to northern Lee County history. It includes information on the railroads, firefighting, the Schaeffer Fountain Pen local history, and the early settlement of the county. Visitors can step on a Santa Fe Railroad caboose, as well. Just upriver from the historical complex is the **Santa Fe Swing Span Bridge** at the foot of Second Street, Fort Madison. It is the longest double-decker swing-span bridge in the world; built in 1927, it stretches 525 feet.

Fort Madison Area Arts Association (319-372-3996; www.easterniowa tourism.org), 804 10th Street, Fort Madison. Open Mon.–Sat.; call for hours as they vary. The arts association is located in the old Burlington Northern depot. The gallery features local and regional artists in the media of paint, drawing, photography, pottery, and sculpture. Aspiring artists can take classes in ceramic glazing. There are also kids' classes, art workshops, and local art for sale.

***George M. Verity* River Museum** (319-524-4765; www.geomverity.org), Victory Park, Keokuk. Open daily 9–5 Memorial Day–Labor Day. Admission: $4 adults, $3 seniors, $2 children. Located in the riverfront park, this paddleboat was built in 1927 in Dubuque for the U.S. Government, providing transportation and moving goods from St. Louis to St. Paul. After it was retired in 1960, it was donated to the city of Keokuk. Today visitors can see the inner workings of a paddleboat along with information on river life on this walk-aboard museum.

Samuel F. Miller House and Museum (319-524-5599), 318 North Fifth Street, Keokuk. Open Memorial Day–Labor Day 1–4 Fri.–Sun.; $2 per person. Built in 1859, this home was owned by Samuel F. Miller, a U.S. Supreme Court justice appointed by Abraham Lincoln. The Federal-style home includes 19th-century furnishings, an early dentist's office, Native American artifacts, and information on the dam and powerhouse.

✷ To Do

Faeth Farmstead and Orchard Historical District (319-372-1307; www.faethorchards.com), 2469 IA 2, Fort Madison. Retail store open daily 9–5; call for apple-picking hours in-season. The Faeth Farm has been in the same family for over 150 years and is also one of the oldest orchards in the state of Iowa. The barn dates back to 1883, and visitors can see both modern and vintage orchard operations, cider making, and heritage varieties of apples.

Putt Around (319-372-3335), 203 First Street, Fort Madison. Open daily in-season 10–10. Enjoy mini-golf and ice cream in the shadow of the Fort Madison State Penitentiary. If that doesn't sound appealing, remember that the prison, originally built in 1839, looks like a castle on the hillside, and several of the buildings are in the National Historic Register. Lockdowns aside, this putt-putt course is well maintained and exciting, with water features and animal sculptures to dodge and, well, putt around. There are batting cages, too.

Hillside Go-Carts (319-372-2122), 2201 IA 61, Fort Madison. Open daily in-season; call ahead for rates and hours. Speed demons can zip around this curvy (and, yes, hillside) outdoor go-cart track.

✷ Green Space

Fort Madison has several very nice city parks, each with different features.

Riverview Park, at Fifth Street and Avenue H, includes the **Old Fort Madison**, views of the **Santa Fe Swing Bridge**, **Engine 2913,** and access to **Lake Cooper.** Lake Cooper, which is maintained by the Lee County Conservation Board (319-463-7673), offers 30,000 acres of excellent fishing and is home to national fishing contests.

Central Park, at Ninth Street and Avenue H, hosts concerts every Sunday evening in summer. The local town band plays in the gazebo, and the park features a modern limestone fountain.

THE MISSISSIPPI WIDENS AND SLOWS INTO A FERTILE LAKE AT FORT MADISON

On the other side of the historic district is **Old Settler's Park**, at Fourth Street and Avenue E, which is shady, lined with Victorian homes, and has playground equipment for kids.

Rodeo Park (319-372-7700), at CR X32, north of town, is the most exciting park in the city. It is home to the **Fort Madison Tri-State Rodeo** every September, a famous and significant event in the rodeo world that packs the city with visitors. The park also offers walking trails, disk golf, picnicking, and primitive camping.

✷ Where to Stay

HOTELS **Kingsley Inn** (319-372-7074; www.kingsleyinn.com), 707 Avenue H, Fort Madison. The elegant 18 rooms and suites of the Kingsley Inn have all the charm of the 19th century with all the amenities of today. Each room is uniquely decorated, and the suites include whirlpool tubs, queen-size beds, and fireplaces. The inn also has a large atrium and common area for guests to enjoy, featuring sofas, a piano, televisions, and around-the-globe artifacts from the owner's collections. Many of the rooms have river views, and each comes with cable TV and DVD players. Breakfast is served in an elegant dining room on the second floor or in the very nice restaurant on site. Rooms from $100–$185.

BED & BREAKFASTS **The Manor** (319-372-7994; www.themanorbedandbreakfast.com), 804 Avenue F, Fort Madison. Ric Roxlau's 1880s brick Victorian home is a real treasure. Two upstairs guest rooms are beautifully decorated and comfortable. The sunny front room has a king-size bed and tons of windows; the back room showcases a handmade and elaborately decorated dollhouse. A ground-floor suite has a private entrance and a sitting room. Outside is an in-ground swimming pool. But the best part of the house is the breakfast room, a screened-in patio completely covered with ivy. Free wireless is accessible throughout the house. Roxlau is a determined and capable ambassador for his city. He knows everyone, and if you ask him nicely, maybe he will take you for a spin in his Chrysler convertible to show off the best views and secret treasures of Fort Madison and the surrounding area. Rooms (including breakfast) from $75–$115.

The Victoria Bed & Breakfast & Studios (319-372-6842; www.victoriabedandbreakfastinnandstudios.com), 422 Avenue F, Fort Madison. This 1850s Georgian-style home is located on the lovely Old Settlers Park on the shady east side of town. The B&B is elegant, with four-poster beds, antiques, and plenty of art. (The innkeeper is an artist who also sponsors art workshops.) Rooms (including breakfast) from $65–$95.

QUIET ELEGANCE ABOUNDS AT THE MANOR B&B IN FORT MADISON

The Grande Anne (319-524-6310; www.bbonline.com/ia/grandanne), 816 Grand Avenue, Keokuk. This gorgeous 22-room mansion is perched high above the Mississippi. Built in 1897, the home is elaborate inside and out with five guest suites—each with a fireplace—formal gardens, original woodwork, and antiques. Wireless Internet available. Rooms (including gourmet breakfast and evening dessert) from $119–$159.

Pelican Peg's Bed & Breakfast (319-463-5955; www.pelicanpegs.com), 3046 Koehler, Montrose. Pelican Peg's offers the best access to the Mississippi: the river is right outside the front door. The single suite has a king-size bed and two twin beds, with a private bathroom, private deck, satellite television, air-conditioning, and a continental breakfast. Guests are welcome to use the kitchen and boat dock, and pontoon boat rides on the river are available. Room $60.

✷ Where to Eat

DINING OUT **Alpha's on the Riverfront** (319-372-3779; www.kingsleyinn.com), 707 Avenue H, Fort Madison. Open daily for lunch and dinner and Sunday brunch. Located in the **Kingsley Inn**, and on the riverfront with views of the historic fort and Mississippi River, Alpha's is a surprisingly elegant restaurant in little Fort Madison. The two dining rooms are comfortable, and the food is outstanding. The well-prepared steaks are of the highest quality and delicious as are the seafood, salads, and sandwiches. Alpha's offers a tempting array of desserts, nightly specials, and a full bar. The waitstaff is upbeat, friendly, and hardworking. $$

Kumar's (319-372-1411; www.kumarsdining.com), 5001 Avenue O, Fort Madison. Open Tues.–Sun. for lunch and dinner. Nationally recognized chef Kumar Wickramasingha honed his cooking skills in his home country of Sri Lanka and in restaurants around the Midwest. With this restaurant located in the Iowan Inn & Suites, his experience and commitment to quality help to elevate the Fort Madison dining scene beyond that of most Iowa towns. The menu is full of traditional favorites: juicy steaks, rosemary chicken, and pesto ravioli, but a few Sri Lankan dishes and flavors sneak in with dishes like the mild curry and the chicken kabob wrap. Reservations are recommended. $$

EATING OUT ✪ **Ivy Bake Shoppe & Café** (319-372-9939), 622 Seventh Street, Fort Madison. Open daily for breakfast, lunch, and special events. The Ivy Bake Shoppe started out as a collective of women creating delicious baked goods and selling them out of the basement of what is now The Manor B&B. The pastries, scones, cakes, and cookies were so fresh and yummy, they expanded to a gorgeous storefront on the main street in Fort Madison. The building was once a men's clothing store, and many of the fixtures remain to make this a charming place to enjoy coffee, breakfast, or lunch.

Captain Kirk's Marina (319-372-6477), 902 Fourth Street, Fort Madison. Open daily for breakfast, lunch, dinner, and bar time. Boaters can smell the BBQ from the water at this "relentlessly casual" restaurant and bar on the Mississippi River in Fort Madison's riverfront park. There is a patio with views of the swinging bridge plus live music. The food is tasty and comfortable, with plenty of burgers, sandwiches, and a Saturday night BBQ rib special.

The Wild Whisk Bistro (319-372-1711; www.wildwhisk.com), 807

Avenue G, Fort Madison. Open Mon.–Wed., Fri. and Sat. for breakfast and lunch; dinner the last Sat. of the month. This bistro/bakery/coffee bar on the main street in Fort Madison whips up tasty breakfasts such as croissant French toast and Greek omelets. For lunch, sandwiches and salads are tasty and inventive, and there are always gourmet coffee, espresso beverages, and freshly baked goodies. $

Fort Sandwich Shop (319-372-1949), 801 Avenue H, Fort Madison. Open daily for lunch and dinner. From the road, the sign on this sandwich joint looks like it reads "Eat the Fort," and you may find some truth in that when you get a glimpse of the size of the 2-pound hamburgers they serve up. $

Parthenon (319-372-7755), 715 Eighth Street, Fort Madison. Open daily for lunch and dinner. An American-style pizza and steak house with a Greek name, this comfortable and casual local joint also offers gyros, tenderloin sandwiches, and a buffet. $–$$

The Cellar (319-524-4040), 29 South 2nd Street, Keokuk. Open Mon.–Sat. for lunch and dinner; live music Saturday nights. This restaurant and bar offers visitors to Keokuk food and entertainment while looking out over the river and Victory Park. The dishes are mainly bar staples—burgers, fries, salads, and the like—and the atmosphere is friendly and fun. $

✷ Drinking Establishments

Lost Duck Brewery (319-372-8255; www.lostduckbrewing.com), 723 Avenue H, Fort Madison. Open Wed.–Sun. for dinner and bar hours. The brew house where the award-winning beers are produced is on the second floor, but the drinking happens by the warm wooden bar on the first floor with views of the Mississippi River beyond. The beers are exceptional, and the brewery also produces handcrafted root beer and grape and cherry sodas. Watch out for the Oatmeal Stout. It is thick, rich, and a little dangerous. Growlers available for those who'd like to take the duck home. The menu includes upscale pub-style food that complements the beers: bratwursts, fried pickles, and elk and bison burgers. $$

Meier's Den (319-372-9463), 801 Avenue G, Fort Madison. Open nightly. Sample and sip local wines in a gorgeous and warm bar. Located on

DELICIOUS BREWS AND GORGEOUS VIEWS AT THE LOST DUCK BREWERY, FORT MADISON

the first floor of the impressive red-brick Lee County Bank building, Meier's Den is all hardwood floors, antique bars, and leather couches. The wines come from both Iowa wineries and other states. $$

✷ Entertainment

The Grand Theatre (319-524-1026; www.keokukgrandtheatre.org), 26 North Sixth Street, Keokuk. The "new" theater was built on the grounds of the Keokuk Opera House, which entertained locals from 1880 to 1923, when it was destroyed by a fire. Today the Grand Theatre is owned by the city and is used as a municipal performing-arts center. Call ahead for performance and ticket information and for guided tours.

✷ Selective Shopping

Pendemonium (319-372-0881; www.pendemonium.com), 619 Avenue G, Fort Madison. Open 10–6 Mon.–Fri., 10–4 Sat., but call ahead to make sure the shop is open since the owners are frequently traveling to pen shows. It is fitting that in a town that was home to the Schaeffer Fountain Pen Company, another excellent pen company is doing business. Vintage, antique, and unique pens from around the world are bought and sold in this unique specialty shop.

Quarry Creek Elk & Buffalo Company (319-372-8966; www.quarrycreek.com), 1866 303rd Avenue, Fort Madison. Call or visit their Web site for shop hours. Both buffalo and elk meat are tasty, nutritious, and extremely low in fat. Buy some elk steaks or buffalo burgers from this locally owned farm where the animals are well loved and cared for.

Under the Sun (319-372-2828), 739 Avenue G, Fort Madison. Open Mon.–Sat. 10–6. Like the name implies, they've got it all in this gift shop that began as a bath and body store, and has grown into china, candles, holiday decorations, and local and gourmet food products.

✷ Special Events

January: **Bald Eagle Appreciation Days** (319-524-5599) riverfront park, Keokuk. A large number of bald eagles make their winter home on the river near Keokuk. This event, sponsored by the Lee County Conservation Board, celebrates the majestic birds of prey.

April: **Civil War Reenactment** (319-524-5599), Rand Park, Keokuk. Includes a ladies' tea and fashion show, military ball, breakfast with the troops, two battles, and a memorial service.

May: **Annual Snake Alley Criterium** (319-752-0015; www.snakealley.com/criterium), Burlington. A weekend of bicycling events includes the 80-mile Burlington Road Race and a race up twisty Snake Alley.

June: **Burlington Steamboat Days** (319-754-4334; www.steamboatdays.com), Memorial Auditorium and the Port of Burlington building, Burlington. A music festival featuring rock, country, pop, R&B, big bands, jazz, and oldies on outdoor stages, complete with fireworks, parades, and a midway.

America's River Festival, (1-800-798-8844) Port of Dubuque, Dubuque. A three-day festival that celebrates life on the Mississippi.

Dubuque Catfish Festival, (563-583-8535) near the river, Dubuque. A catfish tournament and fish fry along with carnival rides, live entertainment, and concessions.

Strawberry Festival (563-933-4417; www.strawberrypt.com), Strawberry Point. An annual summer fest of BBQ cook-offs, mud runs, and music, all topped off with a free scoop of vanilla ice cream with strawberries on top.

July: **Bix Beiderbecke Memorial Jazz Festival** (563-324-7170; www.bixsociety.org), LeClaire Park, Quad Cities. A celebration of the Quad Cities' beloved native cornet player and America's jazz heritage.

Mississippi Valley Blues Festival (563-322-5837; www.mvbs.org), LeClaire Park, Davenport. During this weekend-long event, national and regional blues musicians celebrate the music that traveled up the Mississippi.

Clinton Riverboat Days (1-800-395-7277; www.riverboatdays.org), Riverview Park, Clinton. A small-town festival with carnival rides, mud volleyball, bingo, and awesome '70s bands like Blue Öyster Cult.

Truckers Jamboree (563-284-6961; www.iowa80truckstop.com), Iowa 80 Truck Stop, Walcott. A celebration of trucks, trucking, and truckers at the World's Largest Truck Stop.

Bix 7 Run (563-383-2489; www.bix7.com), Brady Street, Davenport. An annual 7-mile race up Brady Street named for Davenport's cornet-playing favorite son.

July–August: **Mississippi Valley Fair** (563-326-5338; www.mvfair.com), Mississippi Valley Fairgrounds, Davenport. A bistate county fair with foods, music, agricultural events, and much more.

August: **Rollin' on the River Blues Festival** (319-524-5599), Victory Park, Keokuk. Two nights of national and regional blues music on the Mississippi.

Great River Tug Fest (563-289-3946; www.tugfest.com), LeClaire, Iowa, and Port Byron, Illinois. Teams from Iowa and Illinois compete in a yearly river-spanning tug-of-war contest, accompanied by BBQ, a road race, and a parade.

Celtic Highland Games (309-794-0449; www.celtichighlandgames.org), Mississippi Valley Fairgrounds, Davenport. Kilts requested but not required during this daylong festival of Celtic heritage. Strength is tested during the caber toss, hammer throw, and stone throw, and there is a heavy dose of bag piping and dancing to boot.

September: **Fort Madison Tri-State Rodeo** (1-800-369-3211), Rodeo Park, Fort Madison. A rodeo that fills Fort Madison with countless rodeo fans who watch the champs ride, rope, and cling to those bulls for dear life. The rodeo weekend is a giant festival, and accommodations book up years in advance.

Northeast Iowa

3

CLEAR LAKE AND THE MASON CITY AREA

MITCHELL, FLOYD, AND CHICKASAW COUNTIES

WINNESHIEK, HOWARD, AND FAYETTE COUNTIES

CEDAR FALLS AND THE WATERLOO AREA

FRANKLIN, HARDIN, BUTLER, AND GRUNDY COUNTIES

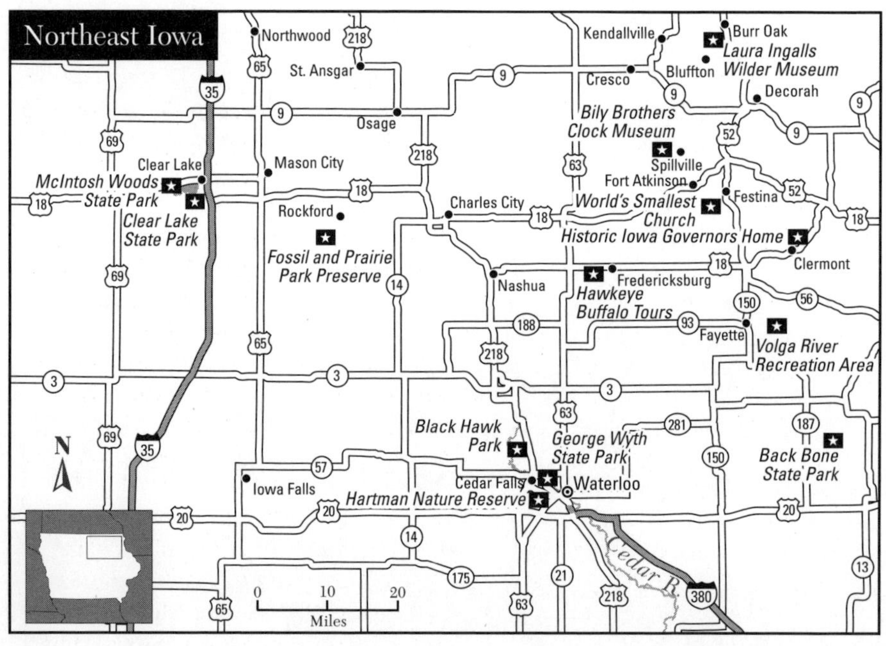
Northeast Iowa
Northwood
St. Ansgar
Osage
Mason City
Clear Lake
McIntosh Woods State Park
Clear Lake State Park
Rockford
Fossil and Prairie Park Preserve
Charles City
Nashua
Kendallville
Burr Oak
Laura Ingalls Wilder Museum
Bluffton
Cresco
Decorah
Bily Brothers Clock Museum
Spillville
Fort Atkinson
Festina
World's Smallest Church
Historic Iowa Governors Home
Clermont
Fredericksburg
Hawkeye Buffalo Tours
Fayette
Volga River Recreation Area
Black Hawk Park
George Wyth State Park
Back Bone State Park
Cedar Falls
Waterloo
Hartman Nature Reserve
Iowa Falls
Cedar R.
N
0
10
20
Miles

NORTHEAST IOWA: A BRIEF OVERVIEW

The land of northeastern Iowa includes deep and cool glacial lakes for sailing, wild rivers for canoeing, and trout streams for fishing. The region's charm is its connections to these waterways. Clear Lake, whose deep waters are spring fed, is seven miles long and two miles wide. Stories of the beautiful lake in the north brought settlers Joseph Hewitt and James Dickirson to the Clear Lake region in 1851. They defied harsh weather and warring Native Americans to build a thriving town. Clear Lake is still the stately, lakeside resort community that once drew vacationers escaping the steaming metropolises of Minneapolis–St. Paul and Chicago at the turn of the 20th century. Clear Lake is not as wild as the resorts at Okoboji. The lake front, the downtown, and the restaurants are cheerful, but sedate. Mason City—Meredith Willson's "River City" from *The Music Man*—showed its wealth as the economic capital of the north with a neighborhood of homes designed by Frank Lloyd Wright and his students.

The communities of Iowa Falls, Cedar Falls, and Charles City were all important spots on the Iowa and Cedar Rivers for the Native Americans who inhabited the plains and for settlers and merchants as they made their way deep into the prairie. Today they are quaint river communities with thriving main streets, shady avenues, and families going about their business. Today, Cedar Falls is home to Iowa's third largest public university, the University of Northern Iowa. The campus is on the western side of Cedar Falls, and is covered in rolling hills and elegant buildings. Closer to Waterloo, visitors will find a cozy main street with shops, restaurants and nightlife. Though it is not far, Waterloo feels much different from Cedar Falls. Waterloo used its important position on the river to build an industrial center.

Cedar Falls and Waterloo make up the largest metropolitan area in the northeast part of the state, and are hubs for cultural and historic attractions. Beyond the city limits, visitors will find well-preserved natural resources for camping, hiking, and boating. Decorah, in the far northeast, is tucked into the rolling hills of the Upper Iowa River—one of the wildest rivers in the state—and adventurers and nature lovers come for miles to paddle its waters, fish its streams, and hike in deep woods and bluffs. Decorah is home to Luther College, a small liberal arts school, and the Scandinavian roots of the area cannot be missed. Travelers will find Norwegian heritage in the Vesterheim Museum, in the shops along Water street, and in the lively Scandinavian festival held each summer. For a small town, cuisine, culture, and elegant accommodation are plentiful.

CLEAR LAKE AND THE MASON CITY AREA

Clear Lake is thought of as either the first or the last of the ten thousand great lakes of Minnesota, depending on the direction from which one is coming. The deep waters were formed by ancient glaciers, and sitting on one of the highest ridges in the state, Clear Lake offers sailors a consistent breeze year-round. This quiet lakefront community has long drawn vacationers from as far as Chicago and Minneapolis for its fun on both the water and the quaint main street. Even in the height of summer, the town is a little sleepy, but there are plenty of opportunities for boating and fishing, dining and shopping, and just relaxing. The town is also known for the historic Surf Ballroom, a living shrine to rock-and-roll legend Buddy Holly, who played his final show there before his untimely death.

The earliest inhabitants of northern Iowa were the Winnebago and Sioux, but white trappers and farmers quickly settled the area around Clear Lake and Mason City. Nathan Boone, the son of Daniel Boone and the person for whom the county and town of Boone were named, is thought to have visited the area in 1832. The 20th century saw the cement industry thrive as limestone and clay deposits were discovered and harvested. Today Mason City is known as one of the musical capitals of Iowa. Home of Meredith Willson, playwright and composer of *The Music Man,* Mason City celebrates marching bands each year in an annual festival.

GUIDANCE **Clear Lake Area Chamber of Commerce** (641-357-2159; www.clearlakeiowa.com), 205 Main Avenue, Clear Lake. Open weekdays 9–5. Call ahead or stop in at the lakefront office for lots of information about Clear Lake and Mason City.

Mason City Convention and Visitors Bureau (641-422-1663; www.masoncitytourism.com), 25 West State Street, Mason City. Open weekdays 9–5. Visit their Web site, e-mail, call ahead, or stop in at the downtown office for maps and information on area attractions.

GETTING THERE *By car:* Clear Lake and Mason City straddle **I-35** near the Minnesota border.

MEDICAL EMERGENCY Dial **911**.

Mercy Medical Center of North Iowa (641-422-7000; www.mercynorthiowa

.com), 1000 Fourth Street Southwest, Mason City. Comprehensive 24-hour emergency care.

✷ To See

✪ **Surf Ballroom and Museum** (641-357-6151; www.surfballroom.com), 460 North Shore Drive, Clear Lake. Open 8–4 Mon.–Fri. Call or contact their Web site for box office information; $5 suggested donation for self-guided tours. On February 9, 1959, Buddy Holly, Ritchie Valens, and J. P. Richardson, "The Big Bopper," played at the Surf Ballroom in Clear Lake on their Winter Dance Party Tour. After the show, they took off in their small chartered plane for their next gig in Moorhead, Minnesota, but they never made it. The plane crashed into a frozen field just 5 miles from Mason City. Today, fans still make the trek to the farm at Gull Avenue and 315th Street in Mason City to see the spot where the plane went down. (The current owner asks that visitors stay outside the fence line and not trample the crops.) But a Holly tour isn't complete without a visit to the Surf. This classic American ballroom is no history museum. Big bands, rockers, and many other regional and national acts continue to play the venue and pay tribute to the day the music died.

Clear Lake Art Center (641-357-1998; www.clearlakeartscenter.org), 17 South Fourth Street, Clear Lake. Open 11–5 Tues.–Fri., 11–4 Sat., 1–4 Sun. in spring and fall, 10–2 Tues.–Fri. in winter, but call ahead for hours as the center is staffed by volunteers. See the work of regional artists in the rotating exhibits of the Hanson Gallery, and shop for local and regional art in the sales gallery. Art classes and workshops are available for children and adults as are seminars and theater events. The gift shop offers art and supplies, cards, and Clear Lake merchandise.

Iowa Trolley Park (641-357-7433; www.iowatrolleypark.org), 3429 Main Avenue, Clear Lake. Open Memorial Day–Labor Day, 10–4 Sat.–Sun. and by appointment. Admission: $4 handcar rides, $6 speeder rides, but free admission to the depot and exhibits. Visitors provide their own speed on a handcar at this interactive railroading museum. Pumping the handles up and down takes riders around a ½-mile circular track near a 1910 train depot. Exhibits and photos of steam locomotives and railroad history are also on display.

Clear Lake Fire Museum (641-357-2613), 112 North Sixth Street, Clear Lake. Open 1–4 Sat.–Sun. Memorial Day–Labor Day and by appointment. Admission: free but donations welcome. See what life was like in a 1900s fire station, complete with a still-working vintage 1924 Ahrens-Fox fire truck and a hand-pulled hose car. Other antiques include a fire bell, extinguishers, photographs, and brass poles for sliding down.

Charles H. MacNider Museum (641-421-3666; www.macnider.org), 303 Second Street Southeast, Mason City. Open 9–9 Tues., Thurs.; 9–5 Wed., Fri., Sat.; 1–5 Sun. Admission: free. A large portion of the museum is dedicated to the work of Bil Baird, a famous master puppeteer and Mason City local perhaps best remembered for creating the "Lonely Goatherd" marionettes in the film *The Sound of Music*. The museum also features a fine collection of American art from the 19th and 20th centuries, with examples of local and regional artists. The museum also offers a rotating exhibit, educational programs, and an art library. Guided tours are free and available by request.

THE FRANK LLOYD WRIGHT–DESIGNED STOCKMAN HOUSE IN MASON CITY IS AT THE CENTER OF A NEIGHBORHOOD CREATED IN WRIGHT'S STYLE BY HIS STUDENTS

✪ **Frank Lloyd Wright Stockman House** (641-421-3666; www.stockmanhouse.org), 530 First Street Northeast, Mason City. Open June–Aug., 10–5 Thurs.–Sat., 1–5 Sun.; Sept.–Oct., 10–5 Sat., 1–5 Sun.; last tour at 4:30. Admission: $5 adults, $1 children. The Stockman House was the first building designed by Wright in Iowa; it is also the only middle-class home in his Prairie School period. The 1908 home, with an open floor plan centered around a fireplace, has been restored and is furnished with Arts-and-Crafts pieces. Wright's influence extends beyond the doors of the home. Across the street and around the Rock Crest and Rock Glen neighborhood are homes designed by Wright's students: William Drummond, Curtis Besinger, Francis Barry Byrne, and Walter Burley Griffin. (Wright also designed the City National Bank Building and the Park Inn Hotel—his only hotel—both of which are undergoing restoration.)

Meredith Willson Boyhood Home and **The Music Man Square** (641-424-2852; www.themusicmansquare.org), 308 South Pennsylvania Avenue, Mason City. Open 1–5 Tues.–Sun. Admission: $4 adults, $2 children for the house; $5 adults, $2.50 children for self-guided tours of the museum. They may have trouble in River City, but Mason City, the boyhood home of Meredith Willson, has no trouble celebrating its native son. Visitors can tour the 1895 Queen Anne house that is filled with family and musical treasures and period furnishings. In Music Man Square, visitors can see the 1912 "River City" streetscape; in the museum, they can learn about Willson's life and work and shop for souvenirs and ice cream in the storefront displays.

Kinney Pioneer Museum (641-423-1258), IA 122 West at airport, Mason City. Open May–Sept., 1–5 Tues.–Sun. Admission: $2.50 adults. The museum showcases a little bit of everything related to Mason City history: See a 1906 Model N Ford and one of the Colby cars made in Mason City between 1911 and 1914. Check out a horse-drawn dairy wagon, a 1912 blacksmith shop, a schoolhouse, a radio station, and an antique farm. Large displays are dedicated to vintage dolls and toys and "music man" Meredith Willson.

Diamond Jo Casino (641-323-7777; www.diamondjocasino.com), 777 Diamond Jo Lane, Northwood, I-35 Exit 214. Open 8 AM–3 PM Mon.–Thurs., 24 hours

Fri.–Sun. This casino at the top of Iowa just keeps growing. Look for a wooden water tower with a neon sign to find more than 500 casino games, a restaurant, and entertainment.

Worth Brewing Co. (641-324-9899; www.worthbrewing.com), 826 Central Avenue, Northwood. Open 5–11 Mon., Wed., Fri., and 12–11 Sat. Sample high-quality craft beers at Worth Brewing, whose locally produced beers, inventive and full of flavor, not only taste better than many traditional beers but also create a link to the past and build community. The brewery is housed in the old gas-and-power building in the historic district of Northwood. Tours are provided when convenient, and the taproom is a great place to relax and enjoy a wide range of styles of beer.

✷ To Do

Lady of the Lake (641-357-2243; www.cruiseclearlake.com), on the seawall in downtown Clear Lake. Open daily June–Aug. and weekends May and Sept.; call for departure times. Tickets: $12 adults, $6 children. Cruise across Clear Lake on this two-level sternwheeler riverboat. The enclosed main salon has a dance floor and stage for a small band. The upper deck is open, with tables and chairs. Music is piped throughout the boat, and drinks are available at the bar. Special cruises, such as the Taste of Clear Lake, Ghost Story, and Pirate Party Cruise, run throughout the summer. Narrated tours and private charters are available.

Fort Custer Maze (641-357-6102; www.fortcustermaze.com), 2501 Main Avenue, Clear Lake. Open Memorial Day–Labor Day, 9:30–8 Mon.–Sat., 10–7 Sun.; May and Sept., 10–7 Sat. and 10–6 Sun. Admission: $6 adults, $4 children. Built like a western fort and with over 2 miles of trails, the Fort Custer Maze is a challenge all summer long. Designs change weekly. Wind through walls built with 250,000 feet of lumber to find eight stamps. The maze includes a central lookout tower and four block towers. It was designed by a renowned maze designer from England, but the helpful "maze patrol" can offer assistance for those who lose their way.

Clear Lake Boat Rentals (641-357-5571; www.clearlakeboats.com), 15296 Raney Drive (PM Park Marina) or 1604 South Shore Drive, Clear Lake. Open daily in-season. Call for reservations. Rentals start at $90 per hour. Rent ski boats, a pontoon boat with a water slide, or three-passenger Yamaha wave runners for a few hours or a week. Safety equipment is included with all rentals, and ski equipment or tubes are included with ski boats.

Clear Lake Yacht Club (641-357-800; www.clycliowa.com), 103 Main Avenue, Clear Lake. Open daily in the summer; hours vary. The waters are deep, and the wind is brisk on Clear Lake, which makes it perfect for sailing. Novice sailors can earn their stripes on a variety of boats at the local yacht club's sailing school. Most classes run for several weeks, but private lessons are available.

Hiking and Biking Trails of Mason City. The **River City Greenbelt Trail** (641-421-3673) runs from Coolidge Avenue through the **Winnebago Trail** (641-423-3673) to the **Lime Creek Nature Center**. These trails lead through urban and rural landscapes to the limestone bluffs above Lime Creek. The **Trolley Trail** (641-423-5309) runs between Mason City and Clear Lake parallel to CR B-35. The trail—the old trolley line between the sister cities—is mostly flat and runs through farmland.

✷ Green Space

McIntosh Woods State Park (641-829-3847; www.exploreiowaparks.com), 1200 East Lake Street, Ventura. Free for day use. Open during daylight hours; later for people staying at the campground. One of the best public sand beaches in Iowa is on a small peninsula of land at this state park on the northwest side of Clear Lake. The park also includes a modern boat ramp and areas for fishing and picnicking. A shower house, restroom, and playground are available in the campground. Campers can spend the night in 49 sites, most with electricity. Or rent one of the yurts–16-foot-diameter round tents with bunk beds, a futon, and a table and chairs–instead of a cabin. Rates: $11–$16 per night for camping.

Central Gardens of North Iowa (641-357-0700; www.central-gardens.org), 800 Second Avenue North, Clear Lake. Open daylight hours Apr.–Dec. Admission: free. Twenty-two themed gardens make up this nearly 3-acre public garden. Walk across bridges and over brick paths through twenty-two thousand flowers and plants. Unique plantings include a pond garden, an Indian Summer garden, and an ornamental-grass garden with kinetic wind sculptures.

Lime Creek Nature Center (641-423-5309; www.co.cerro-gordo.ia.us/conservation_naturecenter.cfm), 3501 Lime Creek Road, IA 69 North, Mason City. Open 7:30–4 Mon.–Fri., 9–5 Sat., 1–5 Sun.; closes at 4 Nov.–Apr. The nature center, on a bluff above the Winnebago River, focuses on the wildlife of northern Iowa. Mounted displays and aquariums provide visual and interactive displays for children and adults. Outside, the 450 acres of parkland include many of Iowa's native landscapes: forests, ponds, and grasslands. Multiuse trails loop through the park. Two primitive hike-in campgrounds are on the grounds as are the ruins of the Lime Creek Brewery.

✷ Where to Stay

COTTAGES, MOTELS, AND HOTELS **Clear Lake Cottages** (641-357-5780; www.clearlakecottages.com), 200 South Shore Drive, Clear Lake. Eight individually decorated and fully furnished cottages are located within a block of the city boat launch, public dock, and sand beach. The cottages have either two or three bedrooms plus a bathroom; some of the cottages have decks and lake views. Rentals available year-round. Cottages from $60–$140; weekly rates also available.

Hilltop Motel (641-357-2127; www.hilltopclearlake.com), 10 Allen's Alley, Clear Lake. Across the street from the Surf Ballroom, this inexpensive hotel offers uniquely decorated rooms—some with kitchenettes—an outdoor pool, and BBQ grills. Guests can walk to the lake and downtown. Rooms from $45–$75.

Silver Boot Motel (641-357-5550), 1214 South Shore Drive, Clear Lake. The Silver Boot is an older, low-slung motel, but the rooms are clean and inexpensive and across the street from the lake. Internet access available. Rooms from $40–$100.

Hanford Inn (641-424-9494; www.hanfordinn.com), IA 122 West, Mason City. The inn offers 72 guest rooms with cable television and Internet access, a heated indoor pool, a game room, and an on-site lounge and restaurant. Rooms from $49–$140.

BED & BREAKFASTS AND RENTAL HOMES **Larch Pine Inn** (641-357-0345; www.larchpineinn

.com), 401 North Third Street, Clear Lake. The four suites in this 1875 Victorian home are richly decorated with wallpaper, antiques, and quilts. Guests can relax on the wraparound screened-in porch or in the formal parlor. The carriage-house suite offers apartment-style accommodations with a king-size bed and a deck. Rooms (including breakfast) from $100–$150.
Blessings on Main (641-357-0341; www.blessingonmain.com), 1204 Main Avenue, Clear Lake. An 1883 Victorian home with two guest rooms decorated with country furnishings, claw-foot tubs, and antiques. A full breakfast is served in the formal dining room, and guests can walk to most of Clear Lake's attractions. Rooms from $85–$105.

Pyramid House (515-771-3647), 1102 North Shore Drive. One house stands out among the bungalows and lake houses on the shore. Drive by this address even if you don't need a place to stay in Clear Lake. The pyramid house looks exactly like it sounds. This modern, 5,500-square-foot house with five bedrooms, two and a half baths, lake views, fireplace, surround sound, and modern kitchen is available to rent, completely furnished. Weekly summer rental $1,750.

Decker House (641-423-4700; www.masoncityia.com/deckerhouse), 119 Second Southeast, Mason City. The columned white house just east of downtown was the 1890s home of Mason City's meatpacking magnate, Jacob Decker. Today it is a big, airy bed & breakfast featuring six antiques-filled guest rooms with private baths and a third-floor suite with whirlpool tub. Downstairs, the Sour Grapes bistro offers elegant lunches daily and special-occasion dinners for groups. Rooms (including breakfast) from $85–$150.

CAMPING **Clear Lake State Park** (641-357-4212; www.exploreiowaparks.com), 2730 South Lakeview Drive, Clear Lake. With 176 sites, most with electric hook-ups, the campground at Clear Lake is one of the most popular in the state. Campers can swim at the 900-foot sandy beach, picnic, and fish.
McIntosh Woods State Park See *Green Space.*

✷ Where to Eat

DINING OUT **GeJo's By the Lake** (641-357-8288), 12 North Third Street, Clear Lake. Open daily for lunch and dinner in-season. A favorite place for locals and vacationers seeking casual fine dining. On warm summer evenings, tables are set up in the crowded front yard of this family home turned restaurant, and diners are treated to the sight of the square and the lake beyond. The food is delicious and distinctive, with flavorful pizzas, chicken dishes, and steaks. Wine, beer, and cocktails are served, but the wait can be long on busy weekend evenings. $$–$$$
✪ **Northwestern Steakhouse** (641-423-5075; www.northwesternsteakhouse.com), 304 16th Street Northwest, Mason City. Open daily for dinner. Some of the best steaks in the state of Iowa are served in this humble family-owned restaurant in Mason City. Established more than 80 years ago to serve the workers of Mason City's cement plants, the Northwestern Steakhouse serves Greek-style steaks. That means gorgeous, hand-cut pieces of beef are served tender, hot, and lusciously sauced in seasoned butter and olive oil. On the side, be sure to have the pasta, which is served in the same butter sauce, and the traditional Greek salad. The menu also includes lamb chops, chicken, fish, and prime rib on weekends. The restaurant is always

busy, but the wait for a table is eased in the bar upstairs. $$–$$$

Prime N' Wine (641-424-8153; www.primenwine.com), 3000 Fourth Street Northwest, Mason City. Open for lunch Mon.–Fri., dinner daily, and Sun. brunch. This expansive and dim steakhouse offers fine steaks, poultry, and seafood along with a selection of Mediterranean, Asian (salads and egg rolls), and Cajun cuisine. $$–$$$

EATING OUT **Muskie Lounge** (641-829-3850), 704 East Lake Street, Ventura. Open for lunch in the summer season. The Muskie Lounge has a lot of "no's" on the menu: no credit cards, no seating for more than eight, no reservations, no free refills, no cigars, and no naughty children. But despite the negative attitude, the Muskie is a great place to eat. It's the only eat-on-the-lake restaurant, for one, and a downed giant log turned into a snarling muskie greets diners outside. The menu includes delicious sandwiches and burgers and dangerous cocktails. The fried tenderloin is outstanding. $$

PM Park (641-357-1991), 15297 Raney Drive, Clear Lake. Open daily for breakfast, lunch, and dinner in the summer season. PM Parks were named and run by a branch of the fraternal organization Independent Order of Odd Fellows called the Patriarch's Militant. At one time virtually every state in the country had at least one PM Park, which served underprivileged children as summer camps. This park, which opened in 1914, is one of the few remaining PM Parks in the U.S. Located just across from an island that used to be the home of a casino and racetrack, today, the island is overgrown and deserted and receives only an occasional visit from paddlers. PM Park offers a full-service restaurant, inexpensive lodging upstairs, and a tiki bar. Diners can enjoy their drinks and burgers on the lawn looking out on the water. The menu is mainly basic burgers, fish and chips, eggs, and pancakes, but there are two special items on the menu: a 2-pound hamburger, the finishing of which will earn the very full diner a free T-shirt, and an outstanding, battered tenderloin sandwich. $–$$

A GIANT MUSKIE DEVOURS A TIPSY PATRON OUTSIDE THE MUSKIE LOUNGE IN VENTURA

Azzolina's Hole in the Wall (641-357-1740), 425 Main Avenue, Clear Lake. Open for lunch Tues.–Fri., dinner Fri.–Sun. Great pizza and homemade Italian food are served in a slightly rundown, aptly named joint. Traditional mostaccioli and ravioli are served with garlic bread and pasta, and all the usual toppings are available for the pizza. $$

Backyard Deli (641-357-2234), 300 Main Avenue, Clear Lake. Open daily for breakfast and lunch in summer, breakfast and lunch Mon.–Sat. in winter. Eat in or takeout salads, deli and grilled sandwiches, burgers, and soups. It'd be hard not to find a pleasing sandwich because they range from a classic club to Ragin' Cajun burgers. The fried chips are homemade, and there is a small list of breakfast foods. $–$$

Papa's American Café (641-424-1593), 2960 Fourth Street Southwest, Mason City. Open daily for lunch and dinner. This café is both a diner and a sports bar. The menu offers BBQ, pasta, sandwiches, burgers, steaks, Mexican food, and pizza. The full-service bar can blend up some margaritas or mudslides, and there is a small selection of bottled beer and wine by the glass. $$

Chandler's Grill (641-421-1525; www.chandlersgrill.com), 3229 Fourth Street, Southwest, Mason City. Open for lunch and dinner daily. Steaks, salads, and a wide array of sandwiches are served in this locally owned, family-friendly restaurant. Several days of the week serve up all-you-can-eat specials, and on the weekend, there is prime rib. $$

COFFEE AND TREATS **Cookies Etc.** (641-357-1060; www.cookies-etc.com), 217 Main Avenue, Clear Lake. Open daily 7:30 AM–9:30 PM in summer, 8–4 in winter. Stop in for chewy, fresh, and delicious chocolate chip, oatmeal raisin, and monster cookies. The "Etc." refers to ice cream and other goodies.

Cabin Coffee Company (641-357-6500), 303 Main Avenue, Clear Lake. Open for breakfast and lunch. Delicious coffee is sold by the cup or by the pound along with espresso beverages and smoothies. Light sandwiches, soups, and pastries are served throughout the day in this log-cabin coffee shop. $

✪ **Birdsall's Ice Cream** (641-423-5365), 518 North Federal Avenue, Mason City. Open daily. Birdsall's has been dishing up handmade ice cream for more than 50 years. The butter pecan is amazing as are the traditional chocolate and strawberry. The high-school students that work in the classic red-and-white parlor must maintain a C or better average—so you know you're in good hands. $

BIRDSALL'S HAS BEEN DISHING OUT HOMEMADE ICE CREAM IN MASON CITY FOR MORE THAN 50 YEARS

✷ Drinking Establishments

Elly's Lake Front Tap (641-357-9589), 12 South Shore Drive, Clear Lake. Open . . . well, it's hard to say, so stop by or give a call. Tucked into the basement of a little brick house near the city beach and dock is this tiny dive bar. Locals meet for beer and good times under the Buddy Holly Memorial Guitar.

✷ Selective Shopping

Lyla's Boutique (641-357-1461), 314 Main Avenue, Clear Lake. Open 10–5 Mon.–Sat. year-round, and 10–3 Sun. in summer. In the afternoon the gals behind the counter pop open bottles of champagne for the ladies shopping for unique and dressy outfits, shoes, and accessories.

Lakeside Cyclery (641-357-4660), 5435 South Shore Drive, Clear Lake. Open 9–6 Mon.–Fri., 9–5 Sat. Stop in for a new Raleigh bike or cycle accessories to cruise the shores of Clear Lake, or bring in your older model for service and repairs.

Collector's Wonderland (641-357-0182), 403 Main Avenue, Clear Lake. Open 10–5 Mon.–Sat. There are six antiques shops in downtown Clear Lake, each with a unique take on antiquities. Collector's Wonderland is fun for the range of treasures: from baseball cards to old movie-projection screens.

Back Alley Wine (641-357-7075), 12 North Third Street B, Clear Lake. Open 11–5:30 Tues.–Fri., 12–5 Sat. Tucked away off the main streets is a quaint wine shop with over six hundred bottles of local and imported wines, beers, and accessories. This little wine shop often hosts tastings and special events in the evenings in-season.

MITCHELL, FLOYD, AND CHICKASAW COUNTIES

Charles City, in Floyd County, is a colorful community on the Cedar River. The town was known for its picturesque swinging bridge, a suspension bridge built in 1906 to connect the neighborhoods on the north side of town to the Chautauqua celebrations in Lion's Field. Sadly, the bridge, on the National Register of Historic Places and much-loved by the community, was destroyed during the five-hundred-year flood of the summer of 2008. While the landmark is being restored, visitors can still find plenty to admire in Charles City—a quiet, classic American town with a cheerful main street, world-class art, and a historic art-deco cinema.

Up the road in Mitchell County are the communities of Osage and St. Ansgar. St. Ansgar's claim to fame is a historic Lutheran church, and the town's white deer mascot, whose postmortem residence is a glassed-in gazebo in the center of town. The main streets of both communities are peppered with adorable places to eat and shop.

Chickasaw County traces its history back to the Viking conquerors who some historians believe discovered North American before Christopher Columbus. Norwegian American residents of the county think that some mysterious runes carved on glacial erratics and ancient Viking throne chairs are indicators that the raiders explored the Midwest. Another remnant of past Iowa residents is the buffalo herd at Hawkeye Buffalo Tours. Visitors can feed and touch the animals that once dominated the plains.

GUIDANCE **Charles City Area Chamber of Commerce** (641-228-4234; www.charlescitychamber.com), 401 North Main Street, Charles City. Open during business hours. The Charles City Chamber of Commerce works hard to attract travelers and to show them a good time. Call ahead or stop by the office to learn everything there is to know about the town.

GETTING THERE *By car:* Charles City is located at the junction of **IA 27** and **IA 18**. State highways and county roads link the cities and towns.

MEDICAL EMERGENCY Call **911**.

Floyd County Medical Center (641-228-6830; www.fcmc.us.com), 800 Eleventh Street, Charles City. Emergency and trauma center open 24-hours a day seven days a week.

ARTISTIC CHARLES CITY

For a small town, Charles City has a lot of art. Start with a walk along the Cedar River to see a collection dedicated to "art that you can sit on." The sculpture benches are modern and eclectic and add to the beauty of the riverscape. For more information and a walking-tour map, contact **Community Development,** at 641-228-2335 or visit their Web site: www.charlescitychamber.com.

While on the river, stop in at the public library (106 Milwaukee Mall) to see works by the Old Masters in the **Mooney Collection.** This fine collection of paintings, engravings, woodcuts, and more was donated to the city by photographer Arthur Mooney, a Charles City native, in 1941. The works include pieces by Rembrandt, Picasso, Matisse, Dali, and Iowa native Grant Wood. For more information, call 641-257-6319. The library is open Mon.–Thurs. 10–8, 10–5 Fri., 1–5 Sat. and Sun. Memorial Day–Labor Day.

Finally, head north to the **Charles City Arts Center** at 301 North Jackson Street. This gallery of local and regional art is housed in the 1904 Carnegie Library building and is the epicenter for artistic endeavors in the area. Classes, events, and studio space are offered to old and young alike. Phone 641-228-6284, or visit www.charlescityarts.com for more information. Open Wed.–Thurs. 1–7, Fri.–Sat. 1–5, and by appointment. Free.

WHIMSICAL SCULPTURES LINE THE CEDAR RIVER IN CHARLES CITY

✷ To See

Floyd County Historical Society Museum (641-228-6284; www.floydcountymuseum.org), 500 Gilbert Street, Charles City. Open 9–4:30 Mon.–Fri. year-round, 1–4 Sat. May–Sept., and 1–4 Sun. June–Aug. Admission: $4 adults, $2 children. Of all the county museums, Floyd County's is one of the best. Its 110,000 artifacts tell the story of life on the plains of Iowa. The former laboratories of Dr. Salsbury, a prominent local citizen, are on the National Registry of Historic Places and now provide a home for the museum. Artifacts in the museum include historic tractors and agricultural implements. Tractor buffs can see a Hart-Parr tractor along with the original manual. The museum shows visitors a turn-of-the-20th-century drugstore, a one-room schoolhouse, and a cabin dating back to 1853.

Carrie Lane Chapman Catt Girlhood Home and Museum (641-228-3336; www.catt.org), 2379 Timber, Charles City. Open Memorial Day–Labor Day 10–4 Mon.–Sat., 1–5 Sun., and by appointment. Free but donations welcomed. Carrie Chapman Catt was a principal of the women's suffrage movement who led the National American Woman Suffrage Association and the League of Women Voters to help ratify the 19th Amendment to the Constitution. Raised in rural northeast Iowa, Catt worked hard to educate herself and attended what is now Iowa State University. Her girlhood home, a brick dwelling built in 1865, now serves to tell the story of both Catt and the women's struggle for equality in the last century in addition to depicting what life was like on the prairie frontier.

Mitchell County Museum (641-732-5957), North Sixth and Mechanic, Osage. Open Memorial Day–Labor Day 1–4 weekends and by appointment. Housed in the historic Cedar Valley Seminary built in 1873, the antiquities of Mitchell County include vintage clothing, Civil War artifacts, a 1900s doctor's office, and American Indian artifacts.

Mitchell County Historical Society Cedar Valley Memories (641-732-1269), 18791 IA 9, Osage. Open Memorial Day–Labor Day 1–4 Sat.–Sun. Fans of antique machinery will adore the five still-functioning antique steam tractors—a Reeves 40-140, a 1913 Case model 110, a 1910 Phoenix caterpillar log hauler, a 1922 32-hp Advance-Rumley, and an 1878 Blumentritt two-cylinder—plus Iowa's first gasoline-powered car. Next door is the **Mitchell County Nature Center** (641-732-5204; www.osage.net/~mccb), 18793 IA 9, Osage, showcasing wildlife specimens, bird feeding, and a habitat for trumpeter swans. Open 9–4 Tues.–Fri., 1–4 Sun. Free.

Historic Homes Tour (641-228-2335; www.charlescitychamber.com), west of Main Street and north of the Cedar River, downtown Charles City. Stop by the Community Development office at 401 North Main Street for a self-guided audio-narrated version of the tour. The historic homes of Charles City were built in the late 1800s and the early 1900s. The oldest on the tour dates to 1855 and is one of the first 10 houses to be built in the area. That log cabin has been built into the northwest corner of the existing home. Other highlights include the **Charles Theatre** and a white limestone home built from local quarries in 1863.

✪ **White Deer of St. Ansgar** (641-713-4921; www.stansgar.org), White Deer Park, Fourth and Mitchell Streets, St. Ansgar. In 1980 a white fawn was born near St. Ansgar. The albino white-tailed deer never left the area and gave birth to 15 fawns before dying of illness in 1988. Locals found her body, mounted her, and built her a glassed-in gazebo for admiration. Just down the street is the **St. Ansgar Heritage Museum** (641-713-2776), 126 West Fourth Street, St. Ansgar. Open 10–4 Wed.–Fri. Apr.–Oct. and by appointment. The museum displays rotating exhibits of local interest; guided tours are available and include a look at the First Lutheran Church, a stone church still in operation after one hundred years.

Little Brown Church (641-435-2027; www.littlebrownchurch.org), 2730 Cheyenne Avenue, CR 346, Nashua. Open 7–dusk daily, worship 10:15 Sun. The song "The Church in the Wildwood," composed by William Pitts in 1857, popularized this quaint church tucked away in the woods. It was built as a frontier church in 1855. Today it is known mainly as a location for weddings—more than 72,300 of them to date—and the pastoral beauty of the surrounding parkland. Tours last an hour and include the history of the building, wedding stories, singing, and prayers.

Viking Sites of Chickasaw County (1-877-200-1099) and **Viking Throne Chairs**, Elma Park, CR B17 and V18, Elma. For some scholars and northeast Iowa locals, the question of who discovered the landmass of North America is clear: Vikings. Several purported Viking sites of ancient and weathered stones with runes of the Viking alphabet have been discovered around Chickasaw County. St. Peter's Stone is thought to be the largest of these relics. Many of the sites are in fields and require some hiking, so contact the county for maps and guided tours, or visit the city park in little Elma to see two throne chairs. These wooden seats were thought be carved by Vikings who made their way deep into North America in ancient times, although many people remain skeptical of that claim.

Carnegie Cultural Center (641-394-2354; www.carnegieculturalcenter.com), 7 North Water Avenue, New Hampton. Open June–Aug. 1–7 Wed.–Fri., 10–4 Sat., 1–4 Sun.; Sept.–May 1–7 Thurs., 10–4 Sat., 1–4 Sun. Free. The permanent exhibitions at the center feature the Natvig Brothers Circus, the Billy J's Clown Circus, Doc Tunnell & Co. Eyeglasses, and a popular railroad room. Each exhibit, along with rotating displays and programs, highlights a unique aspect of Iowa's cultural heritage.

Brown Opera Block Stage Paintings (641-985-2273), 307 Woodland Avenue, Riceville, in the city library. Open 10–6 Mon.–Fri., 10–1 Sat. Free. A complete set of five opera backdrop scenes have been restored through a collaboration with the National Endowment for the Arts, and they are some of the finest in the Midwest.

✷ To Do

✐ **Fossil and Prairie Park Preserve and Center** (641-456-3490; www.fossilcenter.com), 1227 215th Street, Rockford. Open sunrise–sunset daily; nature center open 1–4 daily Memorial Day–Labor Day, 1–4 weekends May, Sept.–Oct. Free. Along the Winnebago River is a 400-acre park with valleys for fossil hunting. Visitors can collect Devonian fossils from the limestone and shale quarry. No tools are needed to find the corals, crinoids, brachiopods, clams, and gastropods, remnants of an ancient sea that covered Iowa millions of years ago. There is no fee for collecting fossils as long as they are not used for commercial purposes. The park also includes native prairie land, beehive kilns, and an interpretive nature center.

Charley Western Recreation Trail (641-228-2335; www.charlescitychamber.com), Charles City. The Charley Western Trail circles the city and connects with the **Riverside Trail.** Walkers and bikers will pass the Wildwood Park and Golf

Course, the Municipal Pool, the library, and downtown on this 5-mile loop. The trail once ran over the Cedar River Suspension Bridge, but, sadly the historic bridge was destroyed during the flooding of the summer of 2008. Contact the chamber of commerce for a trail map.

All Iowa Lawn Tennis Club (www.alliowalawntennisclub.com), 2667 240th Street, Charles City. Open Memorial Day–Sept. 10–8 and by appointment; e-mail visit@alliowalawntennisclub.com, or write for reservations. Mark Kuhn always dreamed of building a grass tennis court after hearing broadcasts of the competition at Wimbledon on a shortwave radio. The courts, which resemble Wimbledon's Centre Court, opened in 2003 and are sometimes known as the "court of dreams." Make a reservation and experience a bit of the magic.

Wildwood Park & Golf Course (641-257-6322), 1 Wildwood Road, Charles City. Call for green fees and hours. Dating back to 1912, this park and golf course housed a POW camp for German soldiers during World War II. The stone bridges in the park were built by prisoners, and the clubhouse was used as a barracks. Today visitors can play 9-holes on the course. Golfers can also play at the **Cedar Ridge Golf Course** (641-228-6465), 2147 Underwood Avenue, Charles City, an 18-hole, par-72 course. Call for hours and green fees.

Hawkeye Buffalo Tours (563-237-5318; www.hawkeyebuffalo.com), 3034 Pembroke Avenue, Fredericksburg. Tours available during daylight hours year-round; reservations recommended. Admission: $6 adults, $3 students. Before riding out to the buffalo herd, visitors learn about these bovines—technically, American bison—and participate in a Lakota Sioux smudge feather ritual. Then tour goers are driven out to the herd in a wagon to hand-feed sweet corn to the 80 majestic beasts. Tours last around an hour. The farm also includes llamas, mustangs, and two adorable burros. Back at the ranch, skulls, hides, pottery, and jewelry are on display and buffalo meat and jerky are for sale. Hunters can participate in historic and exciting two-day hunts on foot that honor the Native American tradition. Hunters spend the night on the ranch, and after the hunt, they take home the trophy head, hide, skull, and meat.

Comet Bowl See *Where to Eat: Eating Out*.

* Green Space

Lylah's Marsh (563-547-3634), Lylah's Road, northwest of Elma. Open during daylight hours. See one of Iowa's native landscapes, which is full of rich flora and fauna. There are opportunities for hiking, picnicking, and primitive camping.

Spring Park (641-732-3709; www.osage.net), 3540 Spring Park Road, Osage. Open during daylight hours. The artesian well has long drawn people to this city park to make a wish and drink from the cool water. The park also offers hiking, camping, and a playground.

* Where to Stay

MOTELS AND INNS **Hometown Inn** (641-228-4820; www.hometowninn.com), 1001 South Grand Avenue, Charles City. A small, independent motel with 18 individually decorated rooms, cable television, continental breakfast, and Internet access. Rooms from $50–$75.

THE YOUNGEST RESIDENT OF THE HAWKEYE BUFFALO RANCH WITH HIS MOTHER

WHERE THE BUFFALO ROAM: A PERSONAL ADVENTURE

On a hot and sunny July morning, after spending the previous night in a dairy barn (albeit an exceptionally comfortable and friendly one), I drove to Fredericksburg to get up close to a herd of buffalo.

Hawkeye Buffalo Ranch is a heritage farm, meaning it has been worked by one family for more than 150 years. Dan McFarland's family settled it in 1854. Huge chickens pecked around the yard, which was in bloom with wild hollyhocks. When I had made arrangements for the visit, McFarland warned me about his grandkids. He wasn't lying. Three children were just finishing breakfast when I arrived, and they were giddy about visiting Grandpa. Dan McFarland is an old soul, with the cowboy build and weather-beaten face of a man who has always worked the land. McFarland showed me into his front room. An enormous buffalo head looked on. We talked about his business, about taxidermy (a favorite subject of mine), about the winter buffalo hunts, and about how he got into the business.

Before visitors get to meet the buffalo, they get a brief tutorial in buffalo history and lore in a room full of mounted creatures large and small, fossils, and Native American artifacts. Before anyone goes out to see the herd, McFarland does a Sioux smudge ceremony that pays respects to the spirits. His oldest grandson stood at his side, ready to help. The air fills with the rich, herbal smell of burning sage while McFarland wafts the smoke over each person with an eagle feather.

Then, spirits cleansed, McFarland pulled up the pickup truck. When the rancher has a larger group, he takes them out in a wagon, but the bed of the

Southgate Inn (641-394-4145; www.newhamptoniowa.com/southgateinn2), 2199 McCloud Avenue, New Hampton. This big, friendly independent motel offers the basic accommodations: queen beds, microwaves and refrigerators, on-site laundry facilities, and free continental breakfast in the morning. Internet access is available. Rooms from $39–63.

BED & BREAKFASTS **Sherman House** (641-228-3826), 800 Gilbert Street, Charles City. This 1888 home pickup worked fine for us, and I climbed into the back and perched on a bench with his grandkids and wife. The buffalo herd lives in a pasture across the road. We first drove up to the resident llamas—looking exotic and out of place in this Iowa field—who perked their heads up as we passed. The pasture is also home to two comical burros, rescued mustangs, and a retired jumping horse. The llamas were skittish and the mustangs too aloof to approach the truck; but the burros marched right up, demanding corn and ear scratching. We stopped to oblige.

The buffalo herd was farther out in the pasture. We couldn't see them from the road, but as we bumped along the path and through a gate, they came into view, dotting the green field like so many chocolate-colored boulders. They knew what the truck meant, and they graciously ambled over to where McFarland stopped. Buffalo are wild animals, and I was under strict instructions not to try to pet them, but McFarland and the family know their herd, and they pointed out an older cow, tamer than the rest, who wouldn't mind a scratch. Suddenly we were surrounded. Massive shaggy heads leaned over the sides of the truck, mouths open and drooling, ready to be hand-fed "buffalo candy"—whole ears of sweet corn. We plugged the ears right into their mouths, and they chomped and groaned noisily.

The biggest and the strongest bulls made their way to the truck, while the cows and the calves milled around on the outskirts. Soon we were hand-feeding the head bull, Tonka, who towered over the rest of the herd. It wasn't his sheer size but his presence that made him breathtaking, yet despite his dominance, we fed him corn as if he were a big, slobbery dog. The grandkids tossed some ears far out into the field so the weaker bulls and cows could get a taste, and McFarland drove a little deeper into the herd so we could glimpse a newborn calf, who darted behind his mother for cover.

The buffalo soon lost interest in us and began migrating toward the marsh. We turned the truck back toward the road. One of the children asked his grandpa if he could stop and play on the rocks, and soon I was scampering around on glacial boulders with the kids while McFarland and his wife looked on. "Come on, Lauren, climb over here!" the kids yelled for me. And as often happens in Iowa, I went from being a tourist to a guest to part of the family.

features lots of luxuries and a great view. The wraparound porch looks out over downtown Charles City and the Cedar River. Inside are four guest rooms and one suite with whirlpool tubs, fireplaces, flat-screen televisions, and wireless Internet. Rooms (including breakfast) from $110–$165.

Walnut Manor (641-732-4532; www.thewalnutmanor.com), 628 Walnut Street, Osage. Three comfortable rooms with private bathrooms and a sweet dog named Nutmeg greet guests. The inn offers an enclosed swimming pool with a diving board and whirlpool and a large shady deck. Rooms (including breakfast) from $90–$100; cash or check only.

The Barrett House (641-732-1982; www.thebarretthouse.com), 830 Main Street, Osage. Romantic suites and family-friendly suites—complete with whirlpool tubs and king-size beds—are both offered in a gorgeous historic home in downtown Osage. Rooms (including breakfast) from $80–$160.

Blue Belle Inn (641-713-3113; www.bluebelleinn.com), 513 West Fourth Street, St. Ansgar. Innkeeper and gourmet cook Sherrie Hansen charms her guests with eight whimsical rooms and delectable lunches. Each room has an intriguing name, from On the Banks of Plum Creek to Sherwood Forest, and the rooms are charming and comfortable with king- and queen-size beds, whirlpool tubs, fireplaces, and skylights. Lunch is served to the public Mon.–Sat. and dinner Fri.–Sat., but reservations are required. The menus are also themed, from Swiss Chalet to Midsummer Night's Dream Cuisine. $$–$$$ Rooms (including breakfast) from $70–$200.

The Dairy Barn (641-394-6302; www.thedairybarn.com), 1436 210th Street, Ionia. Innkeepers Don and Gerrie Etter raised and milked dairy cows on their farm outside of Ionia for years before converting the red barn into a bed & breakfast. The eight simple rooms are named after beloved cows. There is plenty of public space, and the family's horses and chickens live in the quiet barnyard. Rooms (including supper and breakfast) $86–$125.

Farmhouse B&B and Winery (563-237-5969; www.thefarmhousebb.com), 2866 207th Street, Fredericksburg. The rooms in this bed & breakfast on a working Iowa farm are a blend of country chic and modern convenience. Rooms offer queen-size beds; some have whirlpool tubs and views. A hearty breakfast is served in the morning along with homemade cookies, and guests are encouraged to enjoy the farm (they can help out if they wish) or just relax with a glass of the house wine. Rooms from $70–$150.

CAMPING **R Campground** (641-257-0549; www.rcampground.com), 1908 Clark Street, Charles City. A full-service campground with electric and water sites for RV campers, spaces for tent campers, and a shower building. Recreation includes a beach, biking and canoeing along or on the Cedar River, pedal boats for the lake, and volleyball. There is also a 3-acre pond for swimming and sunbathing. Laundry facilities, groceries, and firewood are available on-site. RV sites from $15–$20, tent sites $10, canoes $25 a day; pedal boats $5 per hour.

✱ Where to Eat

DINING OUT **Reminisce** (641-713-3112), 410 West Fourth Street, St. Ansgar. Open for brunch and lunch 9:30–4 Mon.–Sat. Dine on elegant lunches in this unique tearoom. A daily selection of quiche, sandwiches, salads, and desserts are offered, along with fresh coffee and tea. After lunch, shop for antiques, vintage clothing, and gifts in this charming spot. $$

The Pub at the Pinicon (641-394-4430), 2205 South Linn Avenue, New Hampton. Open for dinner Mon.–Sat. In a spacious bar or elegant dining room, the hungry can find classic American cooking: surf and turf, walleye, and enormous Iowa chops. The restaurant also serves pastas, pot pies, dinner salads, and steaks. $$–$$$

Blue Belle Inn See *Where To Stay: Bed & Breakfasts*.

EATING OUT **Comet Bowl** (641-228-2115; www.cometbowl.com), 1100 South Grand Avenue, Charles City. Open for lunch and dinner Mon.–Sat. and dinner Sun. The bowling alley is a popular lunch spot for locals who enjoy daily specials and home-style classics like pork, hot beef sandwiches, and mashed potatoes. There is also a full-service pizza menu complete with delivery. $–$$

Y **Retlaw's Riverside Bar and Grill** (641-228-5387), 101 North Jackson Street, Charles City. Open daily for lunch, dinner, and bar time. All the menu items including pizza can be delivered, but with a riverside view and a Tiki bar on the deck, why not stop in? The food is bar basics: burgers, fried appetizers, and pizza, and there's often a wait, but the friendly atmosphere keeps things fun. $–$$

Uptown Café (641-228-2801), 223 North Main Street, Charles City. Open daily for breakfast, lunch, and dinner. The Uptown is a classic American diner with a counter, stools, and delicious pie for dessert. Breakfast delivers all the favorites: eggs, pancakes, and the like. Try a plate lunch of whatever the cook is inclined to dish up, or stick with a menu of burgers and sandwiches. $–$$

Y **Teluwut Grille House & Pub** (641-832-3300), 627 Main Street, Osage. Open daily for lunch and dinner. This place may be in the middle of land-locked Iowa, but the menu here includes coconut shrimp, citrus grilled mahimahi, Cajun catfish, and plenty of other seafood. An enormous 1-pound steak, burgers, pastas, and dinner-size salads are also served in this friendly neighborhood bar and grill. $$

Paradise Pizza (641-713-2434), 202 West Fourth Street, St. Ansgar. Open for lunch and dinner Mon.–Sat., dinner Sun. Come in off Ansgar's main drag and enter the tropics. This unique pizza joint has tropical landscapes on the walls and a faux thatched roof covering a restaurant with pizza, sandwiches, fried chicken, and ice cream. $

Fourth Street Coffee Co. & Deli (641-736-2100), 230 West Fourth Street, St. Ansgar. Open Mon.–Sat. for breakfast, lunch, and dinner. This coffee bar offers fresh deli sandwiches, breakfast sandwiches, panini, soups, and salads. It is brightly painted, friendly, and a speedy place to grab lunch. $

COFFEE AND MARKETS **Aromas Coffee Bar** (641-228-4773), 105 North Main Street, Charles City. Open daily 7–6 (most days). A comfortable coffeehouse in a renovated storefront with freshly roasted beans, plenty of tables and comfortable chairs, and occasional music and entertainment in the evenings. Free wireless Internet. Cash or check only.

Charles City Downtown Farmers Market is held Wednesday afternoons from 3:30–6 and Saturday mornings 9–12 May–Oct. in Central Park, Charles City. The market includes several vendors offering fresh, locally grown produce, baked goods, and Iowa products.

Turtle Creek Trading Co. (641-713-2023; www.turtlecreektradingcompany.com), 319 West Fourth Street, St. Ansgar. Open 8–5 Mon.–Sat. Mosey to the back of the shop and find fresh coffee, espresso, and pastries. Then browse for country gifts and decorations and scrapbooking materials. Travelers with more time can take writing classes and paint their own pottery.

✷ Entertainment

✪ **Charles Theatre** (641-228-3821), 409 North Main Street, Charles City.

THE STUNNING ART-DECO CHARLES THEATER IN CHARLES CITY HAS BEEN AN ENTERTAINMENT VENUE SINCE THE 1930S

Shows nightly at 7 PM. Catch first-run movies for just $2! The ornate art-deco theater is the crown jewel of Main Street. Originally built in the 1930s, this theater has been renovated and is now run completely through the work of volunteers. It is also the home of the Stony Point Players, a community-theater troupe.

Watts Theatre (1-800-509-2887; www.wattsthreatre.com), 714 Main Street, Osage. Open daily. Tickets: $4.50 adults, $3.50 children, plus matinee prices. In 1950 the Watts family opened this art-deco theater with a showing of *Dancing in the Dark.* It was restored in 1994 and is still a family-run theater with low prices, family movies, and delicious popcorn. The local bank sponsors a free film on the last Thursday of every month. Call or visit their Web site for show information.

✷ Selective Shopping

✪ **Thymeless Treasures** (641-713-4318), 108 South Washington Street, St. Ansgar. Open 9:30–5 Mon.–Sat. The dwelling that houses this gift and home-decor shop is so ornately furnished and adorned with the merchandise for sale that it is a delight for the eyes—and for dedicated shoppers. A soda fountain in the back offers ice cream and other refreshments as well as a selection of Iowa wines for sale.

Picket Fence Antiques (641-736-4438), 244 West Fourth Street, St. Ansgar. Open 10–5 Tues.–Sat. A downtown storefront packed with antiques, furniture, linens, jewelry, and much more. It's busy inside the two-level store, but it makes for great browsing.

WINNESHIEK, HOWARD, AND FAYETTE COUNTIES

The far-northeastern corner of the state is sometimes referred to as "wild Iowa," for its natural beauty and outdoor adventure opportunities. The Upper Iowa River is a favorite of paddlers, hikers, and fishers. It runs through the center of Decorah in Winneshiek County before turning toward the Mississippi River, and the hills and bluffs around Decorah—the base camp for launching trips in the area—are filled with canoe and kayak outfitters, cabins both rustic and luxurious, and campgrounds. After conquering the river, visitors can enjoy the urbane, if not urban, joys of downtown Decorah. An area once hotly contested by Native American tribes, it was later settled by Scandinavian immigrants, whose presence is still obvious in Decorah. Luther College, to the west of town, is a small liberal-arts school established by Norwegian émigrés in 1861. The Vesterheim Norwegian American Museum is the oldest and largest museum in the United States dedicated to a single immigrant population, and the Nordic Fest draws thousands of Scandinavians and the people who love them to the city. Decorah offers the finest dining options in the region, and the Hotel Winneshiek has to be one of the most beautiful, historic hotels in the state. Just south of Decorah is the Czech settlement of Spillville, which is home of the Bily Clock Museum. The clocks may well be the most recommended tourist attraction in Iowa and must be seen to be believed.

Cresco is the Howard County seat and the boyhood home of Nobel Peace Prize–winner Dr. Norman Borlaug.

THE HISTORIC HOTEL WINNESHIEK IN DECORAH

The cheery small city celebrates the doctor—who led the Green Revolution in Latin America, the Middle East, and Asia—with a statue and a harvest festival.

Fayette County stretches over rich farmland and rolling hills. Clermont, "the brick city," was built both economically and physically with bricks manufactured locally from the clay deposits in the area. From 1850s to the 1940s, bricks of all kinds were made in Clermont. Many of the buildings in town are made from local brick. Montauk, the historic brick governor's home, looks down over the river valley. The county is also home to Fayette, a town so tiny that it has a university (Upper Iowa) but no high school.

GUIDANCE **Decorah Area Chamber of Commerce** (563-382-3990; www.decoraharea.com), 507 West Water Street, Decorah. Visitors center lobby open Mon.–Sat. 10–6. The Decorah Chamber's Web site is especially helpful not only for visiting the city but also for the surrounding countryside. The office—located downtown and close to area attractions—is full of information, a helpful staff, and souvenirs.

Cresco Welcome Center and Chamber of Commerce (563-547-3434; www.crescochamber.com), 101 Second Avenue Southwest, Cresco. Open Mon.–Fri. 9–5. This center can offer resources for visitors to Cresco and the surrounding area, but it has an added attraction for those who stop by. The **Iowa Wrestling Hall of Fame** is located inside and offers information on the athletes, coaches, and officials who make wrestling Iowa's favorite sport.

GETTING THERE *By car:* Decorah is at the junction of US 52 and IA 9, not far from the Minnesota border to the north and the Mississippi River to the east.

MEDICAL EMERGENCY Dial **911**.

Winneshiek Medical Center (563-382-9671; www.winnmedical.org), 901 Montgomery Street, Decorah. State-of-the-art trauma and emergency center serves walk-in patients with medical emergencies from catastrophes to minor injuries 24 hours a day.

INTERNET ACCESS/PUBLIC LIBRARY Because Decorah is a college town, expect to find plenty of free wireless Internet access at cafés, restaurants, and hotels.

Decorah Public Library (563-382-3717; www.decorah.lib.ia.us/), 202 Winnebago Street, Decorah. Open Mon.–Thurs. 10–8, Fri. and Sat. 10–5, Sun. 1–4. The library has 20 computers available to the public, all with high-speed Internet. Free wireless Internet is available throughout the building.

✷ To See

✪ **Seed Savers Exchange** (563-382-5990; www.seedsavers.org), 3076 North Winneshiek Road, Decorah. Visitors center open Apr.–Dec., weekdays 9–5, weekends 10–5; office open year-round weekdays 9–5. Admission: $1 per person suggested donation. In 1975 Diane Ott-Whealy and Kent Whealy began a garden to preserve the favorite flowers and tomatoes Diane's grandfather had brought with him when he emigrated from Bavaria. Since then, the farm has been seeking out the seeds of

A LEGACY OF HEIRLOOM PLANTS AND ANIMALS IS HARVESTED AT SEED SAVERS EXCHANGE, DECORAH

rare vegetables, fruits, and flowers in the hopes of preserving biodiversity and our agricultural heritage. Visitors will be surprised to see purple carrots, green zebra tomatoes, and blue potatoes. The farm is also home to 50 White Park cattle, a rare breed that roamed England before the Roman invasion. Visitors can tour the gardens and orchards, hike the trails around the farm, or shop for seeds and books in the visitors center. Dedicated farmers can join the exchange and begin buying and selling seeds with other farmers committed to rare and traditional plants or participate in gardening workshops. Yearly events include December sleigh rides, an annual convention, and a fall harvest celebration each October.

Vesterheim Norwegian American Museum (563-382-9681; www.vesterheim.org), 523 West Water Street, Decorah. Open May–Oct. 31 9–5 daily; Nov. 1–Apr. 10–4 Tues.–Sun.; $7 adults, $5 students. Tours of the outdoor buildings are scheduled throughout the day during the summer. Founded in 1877 to preserve and celebrate the rich heritage of Norwegians in the United States, the Vesterheim Museum is one of the country's most comprehensive immigrant museums. *Vesterheim* means "western home," and the museum tells the story of how and why Norwegian immigrants came to America. Don't miss the small sailboat *Tradewind,* which brought two intrepid Norwegian men across the rough Atlantic. The museum features several replica homes, a

ARTIFACTS AT THE VESTERHEIM NORWEGIAN-AMERICAN MUSEUM TELL THE STORY OF NORWEGIAN IMMIGRANT LIFE IN THE U.S.

TWO CZECH BROTHERS, LONG IOWA WINTERS, AND CLOCKS

In 1913 Frank and Joseph Bily took over a clock-building project from their neighbor, who had ordered a kit to construct a clock but couldn't finish it. The Bily brothers took it home, finished the carving, and got it to tick. From then on, the brothers occupied themselves during the long winters in northeast Iowa carving clocks. Not just any clocks but the most elaborate and awe-inspiring clocks ever seen.

The brothers started out using clock-building kits but soon moved on to designing their own. They ordered and carved various types of wood, from native beech to exotic tropical woods, and constructed 42 clocks so detailed and gorgeous that visitors have been clamoring to see them ever since. Most are standing clocks, and they have themes such as "The History of the United States," "The Parade of Nations," and "The History of Travel." Though their clocks were worldly, the brothers never traveled more than 35 miles from their home.

The clocks made the bachelor brothers famous in their own time. Visitors started showing up to see the clocks, but the stoical Czech brothers weren't interested in making money, so their sister started charging visitors a nickel to walk through the house to see the timepieces. The brothers never cashed in the change, and jars of coins were found hidden in the floorboards of their home. In 1928, during the height of the depression, Henry Ford offered the

HEADSTONES OF SPILLVILLE'S EARLY CZECH SETTLERS FILL THE GRAVEYARD OF ST. WENCESLAS CHURCH

THE ELABORATE CRAFTSMANSHIP OF THE BILY CLOCKS—AS SEEN IN SPILLVILLE'S BILY CLOCK MUSEUM—WERE INSPIRED BY LONG IOWA WINTERS

brothers $1 million for their "Pioneer Clock," but they refused. In fact, they never sold a single clock and even considered burning them when they died. Fortunately they donated them to the city instead, under the condition that they would never be sold or divided.

Today the clocks reside at the **Bily Clock Museum,** where visitors can see and hear the clocks ticking and ringing and chiming, plus the tools the brothers used and a miniature carving of the **Little Brown Church** at Nashua. The museum is housed in the home where **Antonin Dvorak,** the famous Czech composer, spent the summer of 1893 in the green valley of the Turkey River. He walked in the park, played the organ at the local church, and wrote his famous American *Quartet* while in the little Czech community. Information and artifacts about Dvorak are on the upper floor of the clock museum. Visitors can also walk up the street to see **St. Wenceslas Church**, which was built in 1860 and where Dvorak played the organ.

✪ **Bily Clock Museum** (563-562-3569; www.bilyclocks.org), 323 Main Street, Spillville. Open May–Oct., daily 9–5; Apr., daily 10–4; Mar. and Nov. weekends; closed Dec.–Feb.; hours are subject to change. The last tour starts one hour before closing. Admission: $5 adults, $3 children.

fishing boat, an altar from a Norwegian seaman's church, and artwork. Crafts such as rosemaling (Norwegian flower painting), carving, knife making, quilting, and textiles are on display, as are fascinating changing exhibits. The museum complex incorporates 16 historic buildings, including a farmstead and church outside the city. The museum also offers lots of activities for children throughout the exhibits, and classes, workshops, and travel are also available. Folk-art supplies are for sale at an adjoining store, and the museum gift shop sells books, sweaters, jewelry, and folk art.

Burr Oak and Laura Ingalls Wilder Museum (563-735-5916; www.lauraingallswilder.us), 3603 236th Avenue, Burr Oak. Tours Memorial Day–Labor Day, 9–5 Mon.–Sat. and 12–4 Sun., Sept.–Oct. 10–4 Mon.–Sat. and 12–4 Sun. Admission: $7 adults, $5 children, or $25 families. In 1875 the Ingalls family was farming along Plum Creek when the worst grasshopper plague in history struck. Friends had recently purchased a hotel in Burr Oak and asked the Ingalls to come and help manage the place. But living in Iowa wasn't easy for the Ingalls. The work was hard and life at a country hotel was rough, which is why some scholars believe Ingalls never wrote about her time in the state. After only one year, the family moved back to Minnesota and then eventually farther west. The museum, which has been furnished with period items, is the only childhood home of the author that remains on its original site. Tours begin in the visitors center in the historic bank building.

Porter House Museum (563-382-8465; www.porterhousemuseum.com), 401 West Broadway, Decorah. Open June–Aug. 10–4 daily, May and Sept. 1–4 weekends or by appointment. Admission: $4 adults, $3 students and seniors. The Porter House shows off the collections of naturalist and artist Bert Porter. Outside, the home is surrounded by a unique rock wall studded with minerals, and hidden water beasts such as a giant tortoise, a whale, and sea monsters. Inside the Italianate mansion are original furnishings, Porter's extensive collection of butterflies and insects, Indian relics, and rocks as well as his artwork.

THE ONLY REMAINING GIRLHOOD HOME OF FAMED WRITER LAURA INGALLS WILDER IS THE HOTEL IN BURR OAK

StoryPeople (563-382-8060; www.storypeople.com), 110 Winnebago Decorah. Brian Andreas, the creator of StoryPeople, and other artists in studio here use several different kinds of media in their art. They are best known for colorful prints, sculptures made from recycled wood, paintings, and electronic art. Each piece is hand-stamped with amusing sayings, stories, and wisdom. Check out the studio and buy some art to take home.

A WALL STUDDED WITH SEMIPRECIOUS STONES AND MINERALS SURROUNDS THE PORTER HOUSE MUSEUM IN DECORAH

Fort Atkinson (563-425-4161), IA 24, Fort Atkinson. The fort was established in 1842 to enforce the Treaty of 1830, which moved the Winnebago Indians out of Wisconsin and into the area. The fort—comprising 24 buildings and a stockade wall—was later abandoned and sold to settlers, though the state bought the land in 1921 and reconstructed the fort. Today visitors can see the replica fort and the museum—which is located in one of the barracks—and spend time in the surrounding parkland. Although the fort was never attacked, and nothing really exciting happened there, it is an excellent example of the kind of garrison that helped to settle the state. A festival in September celebrates life in Iowa in the 1840s.

The World's Smallest Church or **St. Anthony of Padua Chapel** (319-382-3990), Little Church Road, Festina. Open daily during daylight hours. Free. Johann Gaertner built the church in 1885 to keep a promise his mother made to the Virgin Mary: if her son survived the war in Napoleon's Army, she would build a church. Gaertner's mother died, but he eventually honored her promise when he was 92. With his children he built a stone chapel that is only 14 by 20 feet and seats but eight people.

A STATUE OF DR. NORMAN BORLAUG CELEBRATES THE NOBEL PRIZE WINNER'S LEGACY

Norman Borlaug Statue, Heritage Train, and Historic Log Cabin (563-547-3434; www.crescochamber.com), Beadle Park, Cresco. In 1970 Dr. Norman Borlaug—who grew up on a farm outside of Cresco—was awarded the Nobel Peace Prize. His

agricultural innovations, known as the "Green Revolution," are credited for saving over a billion people from starvation in Mexico, India, Pakistan, China, and several other countries. Also the recipient of a Congressional Gold Medal and the Presidential Medal of Freedom, Borlaug established the World Food Prize, an annual prize, much like the Nobel, that awards scientists, politicians, and others for their work toward ending world hunger. Cresco pays tribute to its favorite son with a statue in the town's central park. Cresco is also home to the Normal Borlaug Heritage Foundation (www.normanborlaug.org), which seeks to turn Borlaug's boyhood home into a National Historical Monument. Also in the park is a restored 101A/Model FP7 diesel electronic locomotive, the first model sold to the Milwaukee Road railroad line. For tours of the restored train, contact the chamber. Finally, a visit to the park would not be complete without checking out the log cabin, occupied between 1854 and 1964. It is original except for the roof and the downstairs floor.

Bronze Statues of Cresco (563-547-3434; www.crescochamber.com), 101 Second Avenue Southwest, Cresco. Throughout the city of Cresco are 20 bronze statues of children having fun. The money to create the statues was donated by the citizens to beautify and add a dash of merriment to the city's landscape.

Montauk (563-423-7173; www.iowahistory.org/sites), US 18 East, 26223 Harding Road, Clermont. Open Memorial Day–Oct. 12–4 daily. Free. Montauk, named after a lighthouse on Long Island, was home to Iowa's 12th governor, William Larrabee. Both he and his wife were originally from Connecticut and had connections to the sea. The 1874 brick mansion was in the Larrabee family for more than one hundred years, and the original furnishings and artwork remained with the home. Larrabee and his family loved to collect and create art, and there are several special pieces, including the statues of great generals on the front lawn. Larrabee was a successful businessman, but he was also interested in agriculture and introduced the Brown Swiss dairy cow to the region. The tour is detailed and interesting and concludes on the back porch with lemonade.

MONTAUK, THE MANSION OWNED BY IOWA'S SEVENTH GOVERNOR, GRACES A HILL ABOVE CLERMONT

Hruska's Canoe & Kayak Livery (563-547-4566; www.bluffcountry.com/hruska's.htm), 3233 347th Street, Kendallville. Call ahead for hours and reservations. The Upper Iowa River is the most beloved river in the state for canoeing and kayaking. At the heart of "wild Iowa" is Hruska's, which offers canoe and kayak rental and two river-access points and campgrounds for boaters. Hruska's can help floaters plan their trips from a few hours to a few days. Try routes starting in Lime Springs and ending in Decorah. Canoes are $30 per day, kayaks $20–$25 a day, and tubes are $6 per day. Hruska's can provide trailers for boaters with their own crafts and offers a 20 percent discount for those who wish to transport their watercraft themselves. Hruska's runs two campgrounds, one at Kendallville and one at Bluffton. Both have sites for tents and RV campers. The Kendallville campground has electricity, showers, and recreation, while the Bluffton site is primitive. Campsites from $7–$12 per night.

Randy's Bluffton Store and Campground (563-735-5738; www.bluffcountry.com/randy.htm), 2619 West Ravine Road, Decorah. Call ahead for hours and reservations; store open daily in-season. Canoes and shuttle service available on the Upper Iowa River. Floaters can stop on their way down the river at this store for carry-out lunches, cold beverages—adult and otherwise—and ice. Or rent a canoe for $18–$25 a day or a kayak for $15–$20 a day with shuttle service. Campsites with electricity are available for both tents and RVs for $12–$18 per night. Modern showers and a playground are on hand at the campground. The last weekend in July brings the popular Light Up the Bluffs country-music festival.

Decorah Bicycles (563-382-8209; www.decorahbicycles.com), 101 College Drive, Decorah. Open 10–6 Mon.–Fri., 9–5 Sat., 12–4 Sun. Between sales and service plus bikes, cross-country skis, skates, and hockey equipment for rent—and plenty of tips and guidance for enjoying outdoor recreation around Decorah—this cycle shop is a full-service outfitter. They also retail bags, child carriers, hockey skates, soccer shoes, and a wide range of accessories.

River & Trail Outfitters (563-382-6552; www.canoedecorah.com), 212 Pulpit Rock Road, Decorah. Call ahead for hours and reservations. Luke and Sue Cote offer comprehensive outfitting services. They rent bikes and helmets and provide trail maps, plus they offer one-person, two-person, and sit-upon kayaks and aluminum canoes. Boat rental includes shuttle service and ranges from $25–$30 per day. They can help plan trips, too.

Chimney Rock Canoe Rental & Campground (563-735-5786; www.chimneyrocks.com), 3312 Chimney Rock Road, Cresco. Open Apr.–Nov. 7 AM–10 PM daily; Dec. 1–Mar. 31 by appointment. This full-service canoe livery offers canoes and kayaks for trips along one of Iowa's most beautiful rivers, the Upper Iowa River. The river in this area has towering limestone bluffs, excellent fishing in trout streams, and lots of wildlife. A shuttle service is free to pick-up and drop-off sites, and the folks at Chimney Rock are happy to help with trip planning. There's also a full-service campground with shelters, a shower house, a recreation room, and a swimming area as well as firewood, ice, and bait for sale. Canoes $25–$30 per day, kayaks $25 per day, tubes $6 per day, cabins $60–$75, tent sites $12 per night, electrical camp sites $15 per night.

Full Circle Corn Maze (563-547-5900; www.fullcirclegallery.net) 1.5 miles west of Cresco on IA 9. Open Aug. 1–Oct. 31 during daylight hours. Admission: $7 adults, $5 children. Open during daylight hours. Visitors wind through two routes and 14 acres of corn at this maze, punching numbers at various checkpoints as they wander. With a focus on green living, the maze uses solar lights and the owners ask visitors to bring recyclable items to get a discount on their tickets. "Corn cops" stationed in the maze check on visitors and keep them safe. A concession stand is on site.

Maize Maze (563-423-5927), just east outside of Elgin; follow the signs. Open July–Oct. during daylight hours, weekends and groups by appointment, call for hours. Admission: $6 adults, $4 children under 12. This corn maze is sponsored by the "Take A Kid Outdoors" organization and was designed by Upper Iowa University Professor John Siblik. When the corn gets as high as an elephant's eye, it can make for a challenging and entertaining maze of maize. Corn mazes are unique because the pattern can be changed every growing season. Enjoy this one mid-July through the end of October, when spooks haunt the maze.

Skip-a-Way RV Park & Campground (563-423-7338; www.skipawayresort.com), 3825 Harding Road, Clermont. Open May–mid-Oct. Call ahead for hours, rates, and reservations. The best way to enjoy the scenic and beginner-friendly Turkey River is on an inner tube. Skip-a-Way has tube and canoe rentals for relaxing floats. Rent crafts just east of the city park on US 18. Shuttle service is available. This full-service camping resort also offers sites for both RVs and tents, a rental log cabin, an 18-acre fishing lake, a restaurant and bar called the Quarry Lodge, wagon rides, a playground, movies, and games.

Hub City Brewing Company (319-283-7369; www.hubcitybrewingcompany.com) 11352 40th Street, Stanley. Open for tasting Tues.–Sat. 10–5 (but someone is usually around on Mondays if you knock loudly). With bragging rights as "the largest microbrewery in Stanley, Iowa," Hub City has made a name for itself across northeast Iowa for selling microbrews by the bottle. The oatmeal stout is a must try, and a six-pack is a steal at around $8. Tastings and group tours of the brewery are available, as is a gift shop.

✱ Green Space

Around Decorah there are several excellent parks. Some offer glimpses into the wilderness of "wild Iowa" and others reflect more laid-back pursuits. Start with **Phelps Park** off Park Drive on the southwest side of town. The 56-acre park is at the top of the bluff with a historic rock-and-wood lookout over the valley below. The park includes shelters, playgrounds, restrooms, and grills. **Dunnings Spring Park** and **Ice Cave Hill,** on Ice Cave Road on the north side of town, have a scenic waterfall and stream, lots of trails for hiking, biking, and skiing, and grills for cooking. Across the road is **Palisades Park**, which offers more great trails and scenic overlooks. Contact the **Decorah Parks and Recreation Office** (563-382-4158; www.decorahia.org), City Hall, 400 Claiborne Drive, for more information and maps.

Prairie Farmer Recreational Trail (563-534-7145; www.winneshiekcounty.org/winncon), 2546 Lake Meyer Road, Fort Atkinson. Open during daylight hours. This 20-mile trail runs from Calmar to Cresco on a converted Milwaukee Railroad line that dates back to 1866. Hikers, bikers, and cross-country skiers enjoy spectacular views of prairie grasses, flowers, woodlands, and farmland.

A UNIQUE STONE WALKWAY MEANDERS ALONG THE BLUFF IN DECORAH'S PHELPS PARK

Trout Run Trail (563-382-2023; www.decoraharea.com/troutruntrail), 507 West Water Street, Decorah. Open during daylight hours. A 12-mile paved trail for walking, biking, and cross-country skiing that passes over the Trout Run creek and through the countryside around the city. Contact the city for maps and trailhead information.

Volga River Recreation Area (563-425-4161), 10225 Ivy Road, Fayette. The Volga River runs through the 5,000-acre park, and with it come the fish—smallmouth bass, rock bass, and catfish—as well as songbirds, wild turkey, and deer. The recreation area includes scenic limestone bluffs, rolling hills, woodlands, farmland, and **Frog Hollow Lake.** Several trails for hiking, biking, and horses wind through the area. A primitive campground is available as of this writing, but plans for a modern campground are in the works.

✷ Where to Stay

HOTELS AND MOTELS **Hotel Winneshiek** (563-382-4164; www.hotelwinn.com), 104 East Water Street, Decorah. The Hotel Winneshiek is a turn-of-the-20th-century hotel in downtown Decorah that has just completed a $14 million restoration-and-renovation project. Though small with just 31 rooms and suites, the hotel has big-city luxury, starting with the octagonal three-story lobby under a stained-glass skylight. The rooms are comfortable, complete with fluffy towels, coffeemakers, and other niceties. The old opera house

THE VAULTED LOBBY OF THE HOTEL WINNESHIEK SPEAKS TO THE GRANDEUR OF DECORAH'S HISTORY

adjoins the hotel and is used for concerts and special events, and the hotel offers a luxury day spa. The hotel restaurant, **Albert's Lounge**, serves up high-end BBQ along with soups, salads, and sandwiches. Open daily for dinner, $$. Rooms from $99–$300.

Bluffs Inn & Resort (563-382-8600; www.bluffs-inn.com), 1101 IA 9 West, Decorah. The inn is located on the outskirts of town and looks a little shabby, but recent renovations make this an inexpensive and comfortable place to stay, especially for families. In addition to the usual hotel rooms with a king or one or two queen-size beds, Bluffs cans also offer larger suites and three-bedroom accommodations for larger parties. The resort also has an indoor pool and walking track, exercise facilities, high-speed Internet, and free continental breakfast. Rooms from $59–$79.

Old Hospital Lodge (563-546-7847; www.oldhospitallodge.com), 3484 Highlandville Road, Highlandville. The four units in this historic former country hospital all have two queen-size beds, private bathrooms, full kitchens, air-conditioning, and cable TV. The lodge is near some of the best trout fishing streams in the state; many are stocked weekly. Rooms start at $50.

Cresco Motel (563-547-2240; www.crescomotel.com), 620 Second Avenue Southeast, Cresco. A motel with clean rooms, cable television, wireless Internet, and small-town hospitality. Rooms from $40–$100.

BED & BREAKFASTS, INNS, AND APARTMENTS 🐾 **Palisades Inn** (563-387-7110), 2566 Ice Cave Road, Decorah. In the heart of Palisades Park, this apartment-style suite offers comfortable and contemporary accommodations. The suite offers a full kitchen and full bath, queen-size bed and pullout sofa, and a private deck. The suite is modern, bright, and cheery and in spring looks out on a field full of wildflowers and summer. Below the home is access to the Upper Iowa River along with hiking and biking trails. Two more rooms with double beds are available inside the home. Two friendly dogs live at the house, and visitors are welcome to bring their

GUESTS AT THE PALISADES INN IN DECORAH CAN ENJOY PALISADES PARK

own pups along. Studio $100 per night, $60 for rooms in the house.

Leytze's Corner (563-382-5856) 704 West Water Street, Decorah. In a former life (the 1890s), this English Tudor–style inn was a church. It was converted into a private home in 1922 and completely renovated in 2008. The three unique rooms are located on the second floor, each featuring interesting antique furnishings and a television. A kitchenette and living room are available for guests to use, and one of the bathrooms is bedecked with vintage Barbra Streisand albums. No breakfast is provided, but the rooms are just steps from downtown coffee shops and restaurants. Rooms from $65–$90.

Dug Road Inn (563-382-9355; www.dugroadinn.com), 601 West Main Street, Decorah. Nestled into a hill just a block from the main drag, the Dug Road Inn is worth a visit for the front porch alone. It is broad and shady with ceiling fans, perfect for wiling away summer afternoons. The three upstairs guest rooms are elegantly decorated, and breakfast is served in the dining room of this restored Italianate home. The B&B is conveniently located near the new walking and biking trail that circumnavigates the city. Rooms from $78–$100.

The Loft on Water Street (563-380-9189; www.agoraarts.com/loft) 106 East Water Street, Decorah. A large apartment right in the middle of Decorah's downtown offers two bedrooms, a full kitchen, living room, cable television, and Internet access. The apartment is totally chic with contemporary design and 500-thread-count sheets on queen-size beds. Guests can use the two car-garage, washer and dryer, and two entryways. The loft offers great accommodations for groups or parties like baby showers and girls-get-together weekends. Rent the apartment for $195 a night, with a two-night minimum, or $900 per week.

B&B on Broadway (563-382-1420; www.bandbonbroadway.com), 305 West Broadway, Decorah. The rooms at this B&B are designed for royalty, and after a night in the Royal Suite—which is tucked into the turret of this historic home—guests will feel ready for either a joust or a browse of the shops. Each of the five guest rooms is distinctive, with hand-carved beds and relaxing private bathrooms. Rooms from $70–$165; packages available.

Taylor-Made (563-562-3958; www.taylormadebandb.com), 330 Main Street, Spillville. Just across the street from the **Bily Clock Museum**, this bed & breakfast offers quaint country accommodations. The quilts and the bread are homemade and the breakfast is home cooked. There are five bedrooms in the Victorian-style home and two private cabins in the backyard. Rooms from $69–$95.

CABINS **Whispering Pines Cabin** (563-380-2285; www.whisperingpinesdecorah.com), 1824 Canoe Ridge Road, Decorah. This spacious log cabin amid pine trees is just a few miles north of downtown Decorah. It is complete with a fireplace, full kitchen, whirlpool tub, heat and air-conditioning, and satellite television. The first floor offers a queen bed and a pullout sofa, and the unfinished basement has several other beds and a foosball table. $125 per night, $100 each additional night.

The Roundhouse Retreat (563-382-2194; www.theroundhouseretreat.com), 2884 Bluffton Road, Decorah. For truly unique accommodations in the hills above Decorah, try a geodesic dome. This guesthouse offers a fully equipped kitchen, expansive living and dining rooms, two full bathrooms, and

THE APPROPRIATELY NAMED ROUNDHOUSE RETREAT IN DECORAH

four bedrooms that can sleep up to 16 people. A loft above the living room has queen-size and bunk beds for additional sleeping options. The recreation room includes a foosball table, pool table, and television with VCR and DVD (but no cable). Outside is a deck with a view, a grill, and a fire ring. Rent the home for $150 a night or $600 a week.

Bear Creek Cabins (563-546-7722; www.bearcreekcabinsia.com), 3497 Highlandville Road, Highlandville. Three gorgeous pine log cabins in the wild and picturesque Bear Creek area include lofts, Amish-made beds, fireplaces, decks, whirlpool tubs, full kitchens, and modern bathrooms. A general store and campground are also in the valley with both electric and primitive campsites, a trout stream, groceries, and tackle. Hunting and fishing guides are available for hire, and the trout streams do not freeze. Cabins from $85–$265, depending on size and season.

CAMPING **Hutchinson Family Farm Campground** (563-382-3054; www.hutchff.com), 2299 Scenic River Road, Decorah. Outdoor recreation abounds on this working beef cattle and quarter horse farm. The campground includes both primitive and horse-camping sites. Also available is an Amish-built cabin that's completely furnished and sleeps up to eight people. Visitors who'd rather not rough it can stay inside the farmhouse in two bedrooms, complete with continental breakfast. Farm tours, rugged riding trails, canoe and kayak rental, and boat shuttling are all available on site. Primitive camping $10 per night, electric hook-up camping $15 night, cabin $75–$100 per night, bed & breakfast $50 per night; hot showers $2 per person; kayaks and canoes $15–$25 per day including paddles and life jackets, but shuttle fees vary, depending on location.

Pine Creek Cabins and Campground (563-546-7912; www.visitiowa.org/pinecreekcabins.htm), Old Spruce Drive, Decorah. Six modern cabins and a full-service campground await visitors just north of Decorah. The cabins can sleep 5 to 16 people, and the campground is completely modern with water and electric sites, showers, a laundry room, and a picnic shelter. Sites offer great views of the river valley. Cabins $110–$140, tent sites $15, RV sites $18. No credit cards; cash or check only.

Pulpit Rock Campground (563-382-9551; www.decorahia.org/pr/pr.asp?id=prpulpit_rock&level=10), 505 Pulpit Rock Road, Decorah. Open Apr. 1–Nov. 1. With access to the Upper Iowa and a great trout stream (Twin Springs), Pulpit Rock is a campground in the middle of the action. Gravel and grass sites are available, with 15 pull-through RV sites with electricity. Modern showers and a playground are on site. Campsites from $12–14.

Gouldsburg Park, 5 miles north of Hawkeye on CR W14. This family campground is tucked between the Turkey River and Crane Creek. Children play in the shallow waters or on the playground equipment. Boaters enjoy canoeing or inner-tubing along the waterways. The campground is small but modern, with a shower house, electricity, and a shelter house. Campsites $12.

Hruska's Canoe & Kayak Livery See *To Do*.

Randy's Bluffton Store and Campground See *To Do*.

Skip-a-Way Resort Skip-a-Way RV Park & Campground See *To Do*.

Volga River State Recreation Area. See *Green Space*.

✷ Where to Eat

DINING OUT Ÿ **La Rana** (563-382-3067), 120 Washington, Decorah. Open for lunch, dinner, and bar time. Dine on the flavors of the world in this intimate bistro near Water Street. The cuisine—prepared from fresh, local ingredients—ranges from duck comfit to blackened catfish with radicchio. The ingredients are often simple, but the results are extraordinary, such as a tapas plate with exotic olives and salted cashews or a beet salad. The waitstaff is knowledgeable and charming. The bar is a friendly place to enjoy a fine selection of wine, beer, and liquor. $$–$$$

Ÿ **Rubaiyat** (563-382-9463; www.rubaiyatrestaurant.com), 117 West Water Street, Decorah. Open for dinner Wed.–Sat. and brunch Sun. Reservations recommended. This large, modern downtown restaurant and bar offers a seasonal menu with local ingredients. Everything from Cornish hen to capon pot pie is homemade, but the real treasure is the 200-bottle wine list. The bar is a hip place to hang out and look beautiful. Brunch $$–$$$, Dinner $$$.

Dayton House (563-382-9683), 516 West Water Street, Decorah. Open for lunch and dinner Wed.–Sat., brunch Sun. Located in the Vesterheim Museum complex, the Dayton House serves both locally grown foods and dishes from around the world. The menu changes often, but look for such delights as a jerked shrimp lollipop and a stacked tomato salad with mozzarella and basil. Lamb chops and Korean BBQ are also popular. $$–$$$

EATING OUT **T-Bocks Sports Bar & Grill** (563-382-5970; www.tbocks.com), 206 West Water Street, Decorah. Open for breakfast, lunch, dinner, and bar time Mon.–Sat. T Bocks is more than just a sports bar. They've got the best burgers in northeast Iowa, and health-conscious diners can get them made with lean, all natural grass-fed beef. Breakfast is served all day—they've got great blueberry pancakes—and the daily lunch specials are homemade. In the evenings, the crowd is mostly Luther College students. $–$$

Mabe's Pizza (563-382-4297), 110 East Water Street, Decorah. Open for lunch and dinner Mon.–Sat. Mabe's is a downtown Decorah icon. The pizza is college friendly: a thin, crispy crust with lots of cheese and toppings. The menu also includes salads, pastas, and sandwiches. Delivery is available to a limited area. $$

The Train Station (563-562-3082), 202 North Maryville, Calmar. Open daily for lunch and dinner. Just a pretty drive south of Decorah is a great place to grab a "flash" burger. Calmar's history was built on the trains that ran through the area, and the restaurant is near what is now the Prairie Farmer Trail. This is a family-style restaurant with daily specials and hearty country fare. $–$$

Burl's (563-387-0167) 1101½ Montgomery Street, Decorah. Open daily for breakfast and lunch. A casual local breakfast joint: the food is hearty, and the pies and bread are homemade. Look for daily lunch specials. $

Sabor Latino #2 (563-382-3485), 421 West Water Street, Decorah. Open daily for lunch and dinner. In a downtown brick building, diners can find authentic Mexican cooking. All the favorites are available—enchiladas, fajitas, and tacos—along with Mexican beer and margaritas. The food is not only authentic, the portions are generous and the prices low. $

Brick City Bar and Grill (563-423-2224), 321 Mill Street, Clermont. Open Tues.–Sun. for lunch, dinner, and bar, and Sun. brunch. This spacious bar and grill is clean and inviting with polished wooden floors, a spacious open bar, leather sofas, and a fireplace. The options for eating are more extensive than most places. The menu includes prime rib, cod, and bacon-wrapped scallops as well as steaks, sandwiches, wraps, and pastas. $$

Barrel Drive-In (563-422-5197) IA 18 & CR 56, West Union. Open daily in-season. A classic American drive-in restaurant, serving broasted chicken, milk shakes, corn dogs, and cheeseburgers. Root beer is available by the gallon, quart, or float. $

COFFEE AND TREATS **Hart's Tea & Tarts** (563-382-3795; www.hartsteaandtarts.com), 113 West Water Street, Decorah. Open 9–5 Mon.–Sat., 11–3 for lunch (reservations recommended), 11–5 for tea and pastries. Elegant lunches of chicken salad on croissants, pear triangles on homemade bread, and lovely soups and salads are just some of the delicacies on the lunch menu. Or stop in for tea and pastries after lunch or browse the shop to take home select teas, tea-making accessories, fine chocolates, and gifts. The shop, in downtown Decorah, is as lovely as the food. Lunch $$.

✪ **Sugar Bowl Ice Cream Company** (563-382-1242; www.sugarbowlicecream.com), 410 West Water Street, Decorah. Open daily. Eat an ice-cream treat upstairs in this bright, white ice-cream parlor with a classic 1950s soda fountain, and enjoy views of downtown. There are plenty of special flavors, and the ice cream is all hand-dipped and fresh. $

Ede's Gourmet (563-382-9600; www.edesgourmet.com), 521 West Water Street, Decorah. Open 11–6 Mon.–Sat. Both a gourmet grocery store and a deli, Ede's serves some of the best sandwiches in Decorah, along with fancy breads, cheese, meats, and oils. They also offer "take-away" meals that are fully prepared and ready to be heated and eaten. This cute shop is a great place to stop for picnic sandwiches for the canoe or an evening meal for the cabin. $$

Magpie Coffeehouse (563-387-0593; www.magpiecoffehouse.com), 118 Winnebago, Decorah. Open 7 AM–10

PM Mon.–Sat. The coffee at Magpie is outstanding; it's hand-roasted in micro-batches, and they know how to brew a very tasty cup. The shop also offers light meals of funky sandwiches, pastries, and treats. There is wireless Internet access, and on sunny afternoons the tables out front are the perfect place to watch street traffic. $

Dough & Joe (563-547-2811), 114 North Elm Street, Cresco. Open Tues.–Sat. 7–5. This full-service bakery serves locals and travelers alike the fresh-baked favorites they crave, including doughnuts, cookies, pastries, muffins, bread, and cakes. This coffee shop is also a nice place to hang out, and enjoy a full range of brewed coffee, espresso drinks, and other piping-hot beverages. $

MARKETS **Oneota Community Food Co-op** (563-382-4666; www.oneotacoop.com), 415 West Water Street, Decorah. Open Mon.–Sat. 8:30–8:30, Sun. 10–7. This friendly neighborhood co-op is open to the public and has some of the best sandwiches in town. Try a southwestern turkey club or a grilled peanut butter and jelly. The deli also serves a hot-lunch line with creative and comforting favorites, breakfast burritos, soups, and salads. The ingredients are fresh, local, and organic. There is a complete grocery with produce, frozen foods, wine and beer, and gifts. Tables are available for diners at the front of the store by the window, or food can be prepared to go.

Farmer's Market 563-547-3434; www.crescochamber.com), between Balk Park and Fareway Grocery Store on First Avenue Southwest, Cresco. Open 2–5:50 Tues. and Fri. May 1–Oct. 30. Local farmers bring fresh fruits, vegetables, meats, and baked goods to the streets of Cresco twice a week.

Drinking Establishments

Kleve's Pub (563-547-2516), 110 North Elm Street, Cresco. Open Mon.–Sat. afternoons and evenings. This is a welcoming neighborhood pub where visitors can meet friends or make them. Sports are on the television, and there's a pool table and jukebox.

Tap't Out (563-422-6089), 122 South Vine, West Union. Open daily 10–close. Small-town bars have to play a lot of roles. The Tap't Out plays them well. During the day diners can enjoy casual bar food, Mexican, pizza, sandwiches, and steaks while stock-car races and professional and college sports play on the TVs. In the evening patrons come to drink beer, play with the jukebox, and generally have a good time. $–$$

Entertainment

Cresco Theatre (563-547-4292; www.crescotheatre.com), 115 Second Avenue West, Cresco. Shows nightly at 7:30; $3 adults, $2 children. The Cresco Opera House was built in 1914 at an opportune time. While vaudeville and live performances were still in vogue, motion pictures were also on

THE FRIENDLY NEIGHBORHOOD ONEONTA COMMUNITY FOOD CO-OP IN DECORAH OFFERS SOME OF THE BEST SANDWICHES IN TOWN

the rise. The builders, with some foresight, built the theater with both floodlights for the stage and a projection booth and large balconies for the films. Today, the citizens of Cresco use their theater for movies shown nightly unless there is an engagement with a theater group or other program.

✷ Selective Shopping

Decorah Chick Hatchery (563-382-4103; www.decorahhatchery.com), 406 West Water Street, Decorah. Open Mon.–Sat. 10–5. If this shop were anywhere but Iowa, the sound of chicks peeping would be piped in for ambiance, but this is Iowa, and the peeping inside this T-shirt shop and hatchery comes from real-live chickens. The working hatchery has been in business since 1923 and recently began selling clothing and footwear for the outdoor-inclined shopper, along with fly-fishing equipment, birdseed, and shirts suggesting that the wearer is a "quality chick."

Bookends & Beans (563-382-0110; www.bookendsbeans.com), 309 East Water Street, Decorah. Open 7–6 Mon.–Fri., 8–4 Sat. Half of the red-brick home that houses the shop is devoted to four thousand well-chosen titles, from bestsellers to classics. The other half is for the coffee—four fresh brews daily, plus hot and iced espresso drinks. Bring a laptop, and use the free wireless, or kick back in one of the comfy leather chairs.

YOU PROBABLY WON'T BE CHICKEN SHOPPING DURING YOUR STAY IN IOWA, BUT YOU CAN ALSO PICK UP T-SHIRTS AND OUTDOOR APPAREL AT THE DECORAH CHICK HATCHERY

Vanberia (563-382-4892; www.vanberiadecorah.com), 217 West Water Street, Decorah. Open 9–5 Mon.–Sat., 9–8 Thurs. Crafts and gifts from all the Scandinavian countries: needlework, pottery, knives and utensils, jewelry, and much more.

Ace Kitchen Place (563-382-3544; www.acekitchenplace.com), 106 East Water Street, Decorah. Open 9–6 Mon.–Fri., 9–8 Thurs., 9–5 Sat., and 12–4 Sun. If the many Scandinavians and lutefisk in Decorah inspire you to spend more time cooking, stop in this high-end kitchen shop for books, gadgets, linens, and ingredients.

Craft's at Bluffton (563-735-5533; www.craftsatbluffton.com), 2572 Village Road, Decorah. Call for hours. The Norton family breeds and raises Jacob sheep on their farm outside Decorah. Visitors can see the award-winning sheep and purchase wool and yarn for spinning, weaving, and knitting.

The Art Gallery and Home Accents (563-423-2213; www.theartgalleryandhomeaccents.com), 301 Mill Street, Clermont. Open Tues.–Sat. 10–6. All the nice little things a shopper could desire are available in the heart of Clermont. The Art Gallery offers art and crafts from 80 local and regional artists, but they specialize in photography of the area's beauty spots. They also sell paintings, hand-blown glass, pottery, and sculpture. But there is more than art; the gallery also sells gourmet coffee beans, Iowa wines, and home decor.

CEDAR FALLS AND THE WATERLOO AREA

Situated on the banks of the Cedar River, Waterloo is one of the most historic cities in Iowa. George and Mary Hanna settled on the east bank in 1845. They were soon joined by the Virden and the Mullan families, and by 1851 the settlement was on its way to becoming a city, named after the site in Belgium where Napoleon met defeat at the hands of a coalition of European powers. The Iowa Waterloo's history is dominated by waves of settlement, the railroad, industries, and its important location on the river. Travelers should visit Fourth Street in downtown Waterloo for an abundance of dining options.

Its neighboring city, Cedar Falls, is the home of the University of Northern Iowa. Once the Iowa State Teaching College and now the smallest of the three state universities, UNI is a hub for cultural and artistic events. The city's Main Street is a quaint district for dining, shopping, and nightlife, and the best place to stay is in the heart of the action at the Historic Black Hawk Hotel.

The counties around the bustling metropolitan area are dotted with sites such as Wartburg College in Waverly; Cedar Rock, a Frank Lloyd Wright house near Quasqueton; and Backbone State Park, the oldest park in the state system. With its towering dolomite cliffs, Civilian Conservation Corps buildings, and wooded hiking trails, it is considered the "Yellowstone of Iowa."

Visitors should note that, in the summer of 2008, heavy rainstorms caused epic flooding in eastern Iowa. The "500-Year Flood" affected downtown Waterloo, and several of the museums, attractions, and businesses listed in this book, such as the Dan Gable International Wrestling Institute and Museum, were affected. Visitors are advised to call ahead or visit Web sites to confirm the location and hours of these establishments.

GUIDANCE **Waterloo Convention & Visitors Bureau** (319-233-8350; www.waterloocvb.com), 313 East Fifth Street, Waterloo. Open Mon.–Fri. 8–5. The office for the WCVB is located downtown, and just a block from the restaurant district on Fourth Street. The friendly staff is happy to make personalized suggestions for places to visit and eat.

Cedar Falls Tourism and Visitors Bureau (319-268-4266; www.cedarfalls tourism.org), 6510 Hudson Road, Cedar Falls. Open Mon.–Fri. 9–5, Sat. 9–4, Sun.

12–4. Brochures available at an antique-gas-station kiosk near the Ice House Museum.

GETTING THERE *By car:* Three major roads intersect in Cedar Falls/Waterloo. **I-380** runs between the metro through Cedar Rapids to **I-80** at Iowa City. **US 20** runs east-west through the state and connects with **I-35. US 218** runs north to Charles City.

MEDICAL EMERGENCY Dial **911**.

Allen Hospital (319-235-3941; www.allenhospital.org), 1824 Logan Avenue, Waterloo. Emergency services 24 hours a day, urgent care services 8 AM–8 PM daily.

INTERNET ACCESS/PUBLIC LIBRARY **Cedar Falls Public Library** (319-273-8643; www.cedarfallspubliclibrary.org), 524 Main Street, Cedar Falls. Open 9–9 Mon.–Thurs., 9–5 Fri. and Sat., 1–5 Sun. in winter. Computer resources and wireless Internet access available.

✱ To See

Waterloo Center for the Arts (319-291-4490; www.waterloocenterforthearts.org), 225 Commercial Street. Call or visit their Web site for hours and events. Free. This local art center both maintains an extensive permanent collection and offers a dizzying array of visiting exhibitions each year. Visitors can stroll through the six main galleries and see the work of student and emerging artists in the West Gallery. The museum focuses its main collections on Midwest art from such masters as Marvin Cone and Grant Wood, Haitian and Caribbean folk art, and American decorative arts of clay, metal, fiber, glass, and wood. Classes, workshops, lectures, and performing arts are also offered here. The center is surrounded by a sculpture garden and plaza. The center is also home to the Phelps Youth Pavilion (www.phelpsyouthpavilion.org), an art center for children with engaging and interactive exhibits such as "Grant's Farm," where kids learn about the life and work of Grant Wood, and a "Construction Zone," with a focus on architecture and history. Kids can also create their own masterpieces in the youth studio, where admission is $5 per person.

Hearst Center for the Arts (319-273-8641; www.ci.cedar-falls.ia.us/human_leisure/hearst_center), 304 West Seerley Boulevard, Cedar Falls. Open 8 AM–9 PM Tues. and Thurs., 8–5 Wed. and Fri., and 1–4 Sat. and Sun. Free. The permanent collection at the center includes hundreds of works from local and regional artists and a woodland sculpture garden with ever-changing sculptures by Iowa artists among a rich garden of blooming plants. The center also offers musical performances, special events, classes, and art workshops for all ages.

Dan Gable International Wrestling Institute and Museum (319-233-0745; www.wrestlingmuseum.org), 303 Jefferson Street, Waterloo. Temporarily closed but scheduled to reopen in its original location. Call ahead or visit their Web site for information and fees. Iowans love wrestling, and no wrestler is more beloved than Olympic champion Dan Gable. The mission of the museum is to preserve the history of "Mankind's Oldest Sport." To that end, the museum includes artwork depicting the first Olympics in Greece and Abe Lincoln as a wrestler as well as collegiate history, Dan Gable artifacts, film clips, a Greco-Roman pavilion, and a "teaching center" wrestling gym. It's not all Greco-Roman, though. The pro wing includes a ring for visitors to finally try out their favorite Hulk Hogan moves on friends and family members.

Ice House Museum (319-266-5149; www.cfhistory.org), 303 Franklin Street, Cedar Falls. Open 2–4:30 Wed., Sat., and Sun. May–Oct. The round brick building next to the Cedar River was once used as the headquarters for the massive operation of harvesting and storing blocks of river ice. Hugh Smith built the ice house in 1921 after the old wooden ice house was destroyed by fire. The brick structure is 100 feet in diameter with 30-foot-high tile walls and could hold up to 8,000 tons of ice. The museum uses artifacts and artwork to illustrate how people got their ice cubes before the invention of the freezer. Blocks of ice were sawed from the river, packed in straw, and stored for use all summer long. The museum also features a kitchen icebox with an outdoor delivery door, along with other artifacts from the early part of the 1900s. Also on the site at the park are the **Behrens-Rapp Station, Visitor Information Center**, and a furnished **Little Red Schoolhouse Museum**.

Victorian Home and Carriage House Museum (319-266-5149; www.cfhistory.org), 308 West Third Street, Cedar Falls. Open 10–4 Tues.–Sat., 1–4 Sun. The 1863 home of Azel Barnum sits in grandeur in the quiet and lovely neighborhood adjacent to downtown. Built in the Italianate style with a cupola, the home is furnished with pieces that date back to the 1880s. The historical-society office is in a modern building constructed to resemble a 19th-century carriage house and includes area historical information along with the model-train collection of William J. Lenoir, who constructed O-scale steam locomotives from scratch with hand lettering, seats, lights, and passengers eating dinner in an observation car.

George Wyth House (319-266-5149; www.cedarfallshistorical.org), 303 Franklin Street, Cedar Falls. Tours by advance appointment only. Built with intricate woodwork in 1907 at the height of the Arts-and-Crafts movement, the interior highlights the art-deco fashion of the day. The rooms are furnished with artifacts true to the style, and educational displays offer insight into both the decor and the Wyth family.

Grout Museum District (www.groutmuseumdistrict.org), Waterloo. Open 9–5 Tues.–Sat. Visit their Web site for the various admission fees. With four sites along three blocks near downtown Waterloo, the Grout Museums pack a lot of history and culture into one area. The **Bluedorn Science Imagination** (319-233-8708), 322 Washington Street, is a three-floor hands-on laboratory for children to explore science, with demonstrations on Saturdays. The **Grout Museum of History and Science** (319-243-6357), 503 South Street, is filled with artifacts and exhibits that illustrate the culture and natural history of the Cedar Valley region with both permanent and rotating exhibits and planetarium shows throughout the day on Saturday. **Rensselaer Russell House Museum** (319-233-0262), 520 West Third Street, is listed on the National Register of Historic Places and is one of Iowa's finest examples of Italianate architecture. Inside is a glimpse at life during Waterloo's Victorian period. The newest museum is the **Sullivan Brothers Iowa Veterans Museum,** a state-of-the-art facility that opened in November 2008.

UNI Museums (319-273-2188; www.uni.edu/museum), 3219 Hudson Road, Cedar Falls. Open 9–4:30 Mon.–Fri., 1–4 Sat. **Marshall Center School** open 2–4

Fri.–Sat. and by appointment. Free. For travelers who would like to get in all of their historical, cultural, and natural-history learning as efficiently as possible, the UNI museum is a great option. It's pretty small, but inside is a collection of wild beasts and birds (stuffed, of course), fascinating fossils and shells, Native American artifacts, anthropology, and geology. One exhibit highlights the history of the university, which started as the Iowa State Teachers College. A large gallery features special and traveling exhibits that offer more insight into special topics. Up the road, visitors can get a peek at a one-room schoolhouse. It is located on campus and furnished to represent the period when local students studied there, but it has a few features that set it apart from other sites of this kind: double doors, a telephone, and even wallpaper.

Silos and Smokestacks National Heritage Area (319-234-4567; www.silosandsmokestacks.org), 209 West Fifth Street, Waterloo. Iowa doesn't have any national parks, but it does have a system of farms, museums, and public areas that offer visitors a special glimpse into the unique agricultural and industrial history of the state and of the Midwest as a whole. Think of it as a park that is dotted

THE SULLIVAN BROTHERS

In 1942, the five Sullivan brothers of Waterloo joined the U.S. Navy under the condition that they be allowed to fight the war effort together. George is recorded as saying "Well, I guess our minds are made up, aren't they, fellows? And when we go in, we want to go in together. And if the worst comes to the worst, why, we'll have all gone down together." George, Francis, Joseph, Madison, and Albert were aboard the USS *Juneau*, a light cruiser, making their way to the South Pacific. On November 13, the ship was one of many involved in the ferocious battle of Guadalcanal. When Japanese submarines torpedoed the *Juneau*, the ship went down, as did four of the brothers. Brother George survived the battle only to be lost at sea while waiting for a rescue boat. One of the myths of the Navy is that after the tragedy of the Sullivan brothers, Congress passed legislation requiring that siblings serving in action be separated, but no such law ever passed. Genevieve Sullivan, their sister, enlisted in the WAVES after learning of her brothers' deaths. She lived to see the end of the war.

In Waterloo there are several sites that acknowledge the sacrifice of the hometown boys. The city's convention center is named for them (Five Sullivan Brothers Convention Center) and displays a mosaic mural in the lobby. The brothers' home at 98 Adams Street is no longer standing, but there is a memorial. The brothers went to school and church at St. Mary's (East Fourth and Parker Streets), and their graves are in the Calvary Cemetery (Fletcher and Fall Avenue, but enter through the gate on Falls Avenue; the gravesite is three-quarters of the way back on the left side). To learn more about the brothers, visit the Sullivan Brothers Iowa Veterans Museum (www.groutmuseumdistrict.org/sullivan/index.cfm), which is part of the Grout Museum throughout the state, this program, affiliated with the National Park Service, is headquartered in Waterloo and includes dairy farms, vineyards, tractor plants, and 1800s furniture makers. Stop by the office, or visit their Web site for more information as you plan your trip through the area.

Iowa Band Museum (319-466-4308), 203 Main Street, Cedar Falls. Open 2–4 Wed. and Sun. June–July and by appointment. The Cedar Falls Municipal Band has been entertaining locals since 1891. The museum—located in the historic band hall—displays the history and memorabilia of the band. After learning about the band's history, hear them play Tuesday nights in June and July in Overman Park.

African American Historical and Cultural Museum (319-433-1234; http://ci.coe.uni.edu/facstaff/zeitz/museum/index.html), 320 East Fourth Street, Waterloo. Open by appointment only. At the site of the future museum stands a boxcar that holds many of the artifacts that the museum will contain. It is an appropriate symbol because the boxcar was the principal means of transportation for African Americans migrating to the Midwest from the south to work for the Illinois Central Railroad. Boxcars also served as the first homes for African American laborers in the area.

A STATUE OF A SAILOR COMMEMORATES THE FIVE SULLIVAN BROTHERS WHO WERE LOST AT SEA IN WORLD WAR II

District (see *To See*). The museum lets visitors walk in the steps of the sailors and soldiers. Dog tags issued at the door give personal information at stations throughout the museum. There are combat-era communication stations, touch screens, and the "Voices of the Veterans" Theater and the Sullivan Brothers family home. The memorial on the grounds honors combat veterans and includes a statue, bell carillon, artifacts, and flowering crabapple tree.

A GIANT CLAMSHELL IS ONE OF THE MANY ODDITIES TO BE FOUND IN THE UNI MUSEUM IN CEDAR FALLS

UNI Gallery of Art (319-273-3095; www.uni.edu/artdept/gallery), Kamerick Art Building, Hudson Road and West 27th Street, Cedar Falls. Open 9–9 Mon.–Thurs., 9–5 Fri., 12–5 Sat.–Sun. during the academic year and Mon.–Fri. 12:30–4:30 and Sat.–Sun. 12:30–4:30 June–July; guided tours available by appointment. Free. With an extensive permanent collection and a busy schedule of rotating exhibits, this university art gallery offers an in-depth look into the issues and work of contemporary artists. Student artists also display their work here at the end of each semester, and the lectures and opening receptions are free and open to the public.

Cedar Rock: The Walter House (319-934-3572; www.exploreiowaparks.com), 2611 Quasqueton Diagonal Boulevard, Bush Co. Hwy W35, Independence. Open 11–5 Tues.–Sun. May–Oct. with tours departing every half hour. Admission: $3 donation that goes toward maintaining the house. Overlooking the Wapsipinicon River near Quasqueton is Cedar Rock, the Frank Lloyd Wright–designed former home of Lowell Walter and his wife. Wright's touch is evident throughout the house. He designed the furniture, selected the carpets and drapes, and picked out the accessories for the home, which was completed in 1950. Built of concrete, brick, glass, and walnut, it is one of the 10 remaining Wright buildings in the state and characterizes his "Usonian" style. From the sky, the home looks like a tadpole as it stretches 150 feet to the one expansive room in the house: the Garden Room. The house is full of natural light from windows and abundant skylights. It remains in trust, as it was one of Wright's favorite designs.

Wapsipinicon Mill (319-334-4616), 100 First Street West, Independence. Open 12–4 Tues.–Sun. mid-May–mid-Sept.; guided tours available with reservations. Free. Located on the beautiful Wapsipinicon River, this 1867 gristmill is one of the largest in the state and a historic treasure. The museum on the second and third floors celebrates milling and agricultural history.

Manchester State Trout Hatchery (563-927-3276; www.iowadnr.com), 22695 205th Avenue, Manchester. Open daily during daylight hours; guided tours by appointment. Free. Kids can see giant trout, and everyone can learn about the cultivation of the fish and their habitat in Iowa waterways. Trout fishing is also available on site.

✷ To Do

✐ **Lost Island Adventure Park** (319-233-8414; www.thelostisland.com), 225 East Shaulis Road, Waterloo. Open 10:30–6:30 daily June 3–Aug. 28, 6–10 pm Fri., 2–10 Sat., 2–7 Sun., and weekends May–Sept. Tickets: $23 per person for the water park, $6.25 per person for mini-golf and go-karts. Lost Island is a South Pacific wonderland in the middle of the heartland, with massive waterslides, pools, and wet attractions just for kids, this water park is a great place to escape the humid Iowa summers. Some of the water slides are pretty extreme—like the Molokini Crater, in which thrill-seekers ride a four-passenger raft down a 75-foot tunnel into a giant funnel and then are dumped out down a waterfall and into a pool. High, speedy, single-person water slides are also on hand as are a river for floating, a wave pool, and a relaxing lagoon. Food and drink stands dot the park, and there are also mini-golf, go-karts, and an arcade.

✐ **The Falls Aquatic Center** (319-266-8468; www.cedarfalls.com/index.asp?NID=397), 3025 South Main Street, Cedar Falls. Open 12–8:30 Mon.–Sat. and 1–8:30 Sun. May–Aug. Admission: $5 adults and $4 children. This massive Cedar Falls water park includes three "falls" for aquatic adventurers. Kids will love Safari Falls, with zero-depth entry, floating creatures, fountains, slides, and a dump bucket in shallow water. Adventure Falls includes a 196-foot tube slide, a 176-foot raft slide with a 21-foot tower, a lazy river with fountains, rapids, and falls, and 20-foot totem pole that periodically sprays swimmers. Rock Falls offers an eight-lane pool with a lap lane plus water basketball, dump buckets, diving boards, and a shaded area.

✐ **Hansen's Farm Fresh Dairy** (319-939-2187; www.hansendairy.com), 8617 Lincoln Road, Hudson. Tours available by reservation Mon.–Sat. Admission: $3.50 per person walk-through tour, $5 per person hands-on tour. This dairy farm has been operated by the Hansen family since 1861. Today, with 150 purebred Holsteins, the Hansens and their sons produce high-quality milk, cheese curds, cream, ice cream, butter, eggnog, and, alas, ground beef. The milk is produced and processed locally, contains no growth hormones, and is not homogenized. Tours of the farm cover the entire process, from feeding to shipping. With the hands-on tour, visitors can feed a calf, make butter, milk a cow, and get up close and personal with the family of wallabies, which, though not native to Iowa, are extremely cute.

Cedar Valley Recreational Trails (319-233-8650; www.cedartrailspartnership.org), 6510 Hudson Road, Cedar Falls. With over 80 miles of hard-surface trails creating a network around the metro area, Cedar Falls/Waterloo is a great place to bring a bike or some walking shoes. Pass lakes, streams, and woods and also the urban entertainment districts.

Cadillac Lanes (319-234-6888; www.cadillaclanes.net), 650 La Porte Road, Waterloo. Open Mon., Wed., Thurs., Fri., and Sun. 11 AM–close, Tues. and Sat. 8

AM–close. Fifty bowling lanes stretch out into the vanishing distance at this classic American bowling alley. With bumper bowling, night bowling, an arcade, a snack bar, and a pro shop, this is a family friendly place to roll.

Red Carpet Golf Course (319-235-1242; www.redcarpetgolf.com), 1409 Newell Street, Waterloo. Open seasonally; call for hours and tee times. The Red Carpet has the feel of a 1920s country club. The par-72 course has wide, rolling fairways much like the U.S. Open courses, and the clubhouse is a convivial place for a pre- or postgame cocktail.

EQUIPMENT RENTAL

Bikes:

Bike Tech (319-266-5979; www.biketechcf.com), 122 Main Street, Cedar Falls. Open Mon. 10–8, Tues.–Fri. 10–6, Sat. 9–5, closed Sun. Located downtown and close to the area bike trails, these guys are the bike experts. Visit them for sales, service, repairs, rental, and ride recommendations.

Canoe and Kayaks, Cross-Country Skis:

Crawdaddy Outdoors (319-352-3129; www.crawdaddyoutdoors.com), 107 East Bremer Avenue, Waverly. Open Tues., Wed., Fri. 10–6, Thurs. 10–8, Sat. 9–2. Rent canoes and kayaks for trips on the Cedar River and elsewhere from this locally owned, knowledgeable, and friendly outfitter. In addition to boats, the shop stocks other gear for outdoor adventures, from dry bags to sleeping bags to stoves to cross-country skis. The shop also sponsors special events, demo days, and adventure-travel trips.

✷ Green Space

🐾 **Cedar Valley Arboretum & Botanical Gardens** (319-226-4966; www.cedarvalleyarboretum.org), 1927 East Orange Road, Waterloo. Open during daylight hours Apr.–Nov. Free. This is just what a city park ought to be. Besides a plethora of trees, shrubs, and flowers, the garden offers visitors plenty of space to get lost while enjoying the green space. The gardens include both a formal labyrinth and a corn maze, along with two activity lawns, walking trails, display and herb gardens, a learning center, and a children's garden with a dinosaur dig and peek-a-boo forest. Visitors are asked only to clean up after their leashed dogs, to keep their wheels on the road, and to leave the plants intact for future guests. Restrooms are available outside the learning center.

George Wyth State Park (319-232-5505; www.iowadnr.com/parks), 3659 Wyth Road, Waterloo. Open during daylight hours. This state park is made up of a series of lakes along the Cedar River and offers a host of outdoor recreation opportunities. Not only is the area packed with birds and other wildlife, but the park is full of picnic areas, playgrounds, boat launches, and fishing spots. Hiking, paddling, and multiuse trails crisscross the park. Visitors can also swim at the beach or camp in one of two modern campgrounds with full hook-ups.

Hartman Reserve Nature Center (319-277-2187; www.hartmanreserve.org), 657 Reserve Drive, Cedar Falls. Trails open daylight hours daily; interpretive center 8–4:30 Mon.–Fri. On a wooded island near Waterloo, the 300 acres of this park include a bluff overlooking the river valley and the banks of the river, with ponds, prairies, meadows, and upland forests. The park includes several hiking trails, a tree house deck, an observation deck, and an educational facility. The center offers campouts and workshops for kids and Friday-night nature events for adults with topics like "Geocaching and Winery Tour" and "Climb a Wall." The gift shop offers unique nature-themed presents such as maple syrup, bug pencils, arrowhead necklaces, and folding binoculars for spotting the wildlife that call the park home.

Hickory Hills Park (319-342-3350; www.co.black-hawk.ia.us/depts/conservation), 3338 Hickory Hills Road, La Porte City. Open during daylight hours. Located on a *paha*—the Native American word for high ground—this 723-acre public area is both close to the Cedar Falls/Waterloo area and offers an abundance of recreation activities. With basketball, volleyball, disk golf, hiking, fishing, sledding, and ice skating, outdoor athletes can enjoy the wild space. The park also offers camping and picnicking, public hunting, and an archery course. The campground includes sites for 82 RVs, many with full hook-ups, and a large tent campground. Three rustic cabins with electricity and air-conditioning and a cold-water sink are also available, along with four all-season cabins, which are more like houses with space for six, televisions and DVD players, bathrooms with showers, and complete kitchens. Cabins $30–$90 with a two-night minimum preferred. Campsites from $12–$20.

🐾 **Paw Park** (319-273-8624; www.50613.com), Rownd Park, South Main Street at IA 58, Cedar Falls. Open 5 AM–10:30 PM daily. Fee: $2 daily pass, $10 annual pass. Proof of rabies vaccination per dog required. Let the dogs loose at this 3-acre fenced-in dog park. They will enjoy the hilly terrain and the company of other friendly canines. Be sure to bring a leash and a pooper scooper—or at least a plastic bag.

✪ **Backbone State Park** (563-924-2527; www.iowadnr.com/parks), 1347 129th Street, Dundee. Open during daylight hours, except for campers. Backbone is known as the "Yellowstone of Iowa" for its rugged dolomite limestone cliff faces reaching to 80-feet with columns, towers, and flying buttresses. Climbers and rappellers are welcome but must register before hitting the rocks. More than 20 miles of trails loop through the wooded park. Much of the park was developed by the Civilian Conservation Corps, which built the stone lodge, dammed the lake, and is now celebrated in an on-site museum. Boat rental is available on the lake, and there is plenty of room for swimmers and fishers. There are 125 campsites available in two campgrounds along with modern cabins. Cabins $100, campsites $10–$16.

✷ Where to Stay

HOTELS AND MOTELS ✪ **Black Hawk Hotel** (319-277-1161; www.blackhawk-hotel.com), 115 Main Street, Cedar Falls. The historic Black Hawk Hotel in downtown Cedar Falls is the longest operating in the state and offers luxurious accommodations for travelers. Each of the 29 rooms has been modernized to include amenities such as minibars, wireless Internet, and tasteful decor, but the rooms

THE HISTORIC BLACK HAWK HOTEL IN CEDAR FALLS IS THE OLDEST CONTINUOUSLY OPERATING HOTEL IN THE STATE

maintain their grand charm with marble bathrooms and antique furniture. Accommodations range from standard rooms to a deluxe loft with kitchenette. A hip bar and restaurant are both on site, and the staff is extremely helpful, but being a historic hotel it does not have an elevator. Guests who have difficulty with stairs should be sure to request a first-floor room. Rooms from $70–$150.

Trails End Lodge Inne Downtown (319-277-6400), 122 Washington Street, Cedar Falls. Trails End's 15 rooms close to downtown have microwaves, refrigerators, and some kitchenettes. All the fun of downtown Cedar Falls is within walking distance as is the trail system. The "inne" also offers the **Red Stone Guesthouse** at 113 Main Street, a one-bedroom, fully furnished suite with an attached garage.

University Inn (319-277-1412; www.universityinncf.com), 4711 University Avenue, Cedar Falls. The inn doesn't look like much from the busy street, but inside are 50 clean and comfortable rooms with full amenities plus a whirlpool, a sauna, and an exercise room. The inn is close to the attractions of the University of Northern Iowa and Cedar Falls. Rooms from $60–$90.

Midway Inn (319-277-6931), 4117 University Avenue, Cedar Falls. Located on the main thoroughfare of Cedar Falls, this motel offers 78 inexpensive rooms with refrigerators, microwaves, Internet access, and cable television. Coffee is served daily and fresh doughnuts and a continental breakfast are available on weekends. The inn also features an outdoor pool. Rooms from $40–$90.

BED & BREAKFASTS **Carriage House Inn** (319-277-6724; www.cfcarriagehouseinn.com), 3030 Grand Boulevard, Cedar Falls. Tucked away in the woods not far from downtown Cedar Falls is a bed & breakfast with two spacious and elegant suites. The home is filled with antique furnishings, gas fireplaces, and skylights, and the suites each include romantic whirlpool tubs. The Walnut Suite includes a walnut mantelpiece and a Rococo-Revival walnut bed. The Oak Suite is similarly appointed, though with Mission-style furnishings and teal Victorian wallpaper. Both rooms are located in the privacy of the carriage house. Breakfast is fresh and gourmet quality and always includes fresh fruit. Suites (including breakfast) $125.

CAMPING **McFarlane Park** (319-342-3844; www.co.black-hawk.ia.us/depts/conservation), 13619 King Road, La Porte City. This park, just 20 miles south of the metro, offers rolling hills and forests with plenty of wildlife. Wolf Creek and the Cedar River form the north border of the park. The park has a large area owned by the state dedicated to hunting, fishing, and nature studies, but there is a large campground, as well, with sites for RVs and tent campers and a small campground with some amenities. Cabins $90, campsites from $11–$15.

Black Hawk Park (319-266-6813; www.co.black-hawk.ia.us/depts/conservation), 2410 West Lone Tree Road, Cedar Falls. The park's 1,490 acres form a greenbelt along the Cedar River from Cedar Falls to the Washington Union Bridge and include the **Cedar Valley Lakes Trail**. Outdoors people have access to boat ramps, hunting, and an archery range. The park offers several camping options: modern, hook-ups, primitive, and two rustic cabins. Cabins $30 plus $100 deposit, campsites from $11–$20.

Deerwood Park and Campground (319-232-6683), River Forest Road and Gilbert Drive, Evansdale. Located on a curve in the Cedar River, this campground is conveniently close to I-380, but with abundant trees, lawns, and riverfront, the traffic is heard but not seen. The park offers fishing, playgrounds, basketball, disk golf, and boat ramps, and the campground has sites for RVs and tent campers. A shower house and a laundry facility are located in the center of the campground. Campsites from $10–$12.

Hickory Hills Park See *Green Space.*

✱ Where to Eat

DINING OUT **Galleria de Paco** (319-833-7226; www.paco-rosic.com), 622 Commercial Street, Waterloo. Open for dinner daily; reservations required. Finally someone has seen the potential of combining graffiti art and fine dining. Paco Rosic, born in Sarajevo in 1979, escaped his war-torn country and eventually made it to Waterloo, Iowa, where many refuges were settling in the 1990s. Paco's passion was paint—spray paint—and his can art can be seen adorning walls all over the Waterloo/Cedar Falls area, from the **Waterloo City Hall** to the **Bourbon Street Bar**. His finest work has to be the massive (2,000 cans of spray paint) reproduction of Michelangelo's Sistine Chapel on the ceiling above what is now this upscale restaurant. In this atmosphere, far away from Rome, diners will find romantic atmosphere, European fusion cuisine, and world-class wines. Downstairs is a jazz and tapas bar called **The Catacomb** (open evenings Mon.–Sat.), which features spooky cocktails that smoke and tasty little dishes in a relaxed atmosphere. $$$

✪ **Cottonwood Canyon Jamaican Café** (319-277-0730; www.cottonwoodcoffee.biz), 1806 Waterloo Road, Cedar Falls. Open for breakfast, lunch, and dinner daily. Delicious and authentic Jamaican cuisine can be found in Cedar Falls. The taste of the islands includes hot and spicy jerked-, mango-, and curried-chicken dishes along with lamb chops with sweet potatoes, ox-tail stew, curried goat, ginger-coated scallops, and fresh salads. Breakfast and lunch are more traditionally American, with sandwiches, bagels, and egg dishes. $$

Cu (319-274-8888; www.cuandthecellar.com), 320 East Fourth Street, Waterloo. Open Mon.–Fri. for lunch, Mon.–Sat. for dinner. In the warm, dim light of this dining room, the creative entrées and desserts really shine. The hand-cut steaks, catch of the day, poultry, and lamb are surprising and full of flavor. The chef prepares a different kind of bruschetta daily, and the specials highlight seasonal flavors. The wine list is extensive. $$–$$$

Soho Sushi Bar and Deli (319-266-9995; www.barmuda.com), 119 Main Street, Cedar Falls. Open for lunch and dinner Mon.–Sat. California sushi and New York deli delights blend in Middle America at this chic downtown restaurant. The maki rolls, sashimi, and 30 kinds of deli sandwiches are all fresh and homemade. The martini bar next door serves 80 different martinis and a light tapas menu. $$–$$$

🍸 **Bourbon Street** (319-266-5285; www.barmuda.com), 314 Main Street, Cedar Falls. Open for dinner daily. It's all New Orleans inside this fine-dining spot in Cedar Falls; in the center of the dim and romantic dining room is a faux oak tree, and the graffiti art of Paco Rosic dons the walls. The menu includes some bayou specialties such as crawfish étouffée and shrimp Creole, but the menu also features steaks, chicken dishes, and pastas. Upstairs is the **Voodoo Lounge** where revelers can continue their Mardi Gras evening with cocktails? $$–$$$

EATING OUT **Mama Nick's Circle Pizzeria** (319-233-3323), US 218 and West Eighteenth Street, Waterloo. Open Sun., Tues.–Fri. for lunch and dinner, Sat. for dinner. Mama Nick's has been serving classic American pizza in a fun, family-style atmosphere since 1962. They also serve pasta and sandwiches. Look for both lunch and dinner buffets for a taste of everything. $$

Beck's Sports Grill (319-277-2646; www.barmuda.com), 2210 College Street, Cedar Falls. Open daily for lunch, dinner, and bar time. Voted best burgers in the Cedar Falls area, this bar feeds wraps, fried appetizers, soups, and salads to hungry sports fans while they watch the large and plentiful televisions. Their other location, **Beck's Sports Brewery** (319-234-4333), 3295 University Avenue, has a little more space for both parking and microbrewing, with much the same menu. $$

Waffle Stop Grill (319-277-1729), 904 Rainbow Drive, Cedar Falls. Open for breakfast and lunch daily. This beloved local breakfast spot has great waffles, pancakes, and eggs for hearty, early-morning breakfasts and a selection of burgers and sandwiches for lunch. $

Maid Rite (319-277-9748), 116 East Fourth Street, Cedar Falls. Open for breakfast and lunch daily. Home of the famous loose-meat sandwich, the Maid Rite, located downtown just off Main Street, also serves breakfast sandwiches. $

Barn Happy (319-266-0888; www.barnhappy.net), 11310 University Avenue, Cedar Falls. Open for breakfast and lunch Wed.–Sat. Mar.–Dec. If you weren't born in a barn, you can eat in one. The pastries served in this 1925 dairy barn are legendary: don't miss the raspberry coffee cake. Wash them down with a cup of coffee or a smoothie. For lunch the kitchen cooks up delicious homemade soups and sandwiches. Try the crab Louie sandwich or the poppy-seed chicken salad. Take a taste of Iowa home, too, with gift baskets made exclusively with Iowa products: honey, popcorn, granola, and beef sticks. $$

The Pump Haus (319-277-8111; www.thepump-haus.com), 311 Main Street, Cedar Falls. Open for lunch and dinner daily. With an extensive menu of upscale pub grub, this friendly neighborhood bar and grill is a great place to grab a beer, have a sandwich, and watch the game. The menu features the standards: wraps, salads, chicken strips, and burgers. Wireless Internet available. $$

Ruby's Tacos (319-234-5686), 2401 Falls Avenue, Waterloo. Open for lunch and dinner Mon.–Sat. This locally owned Mexican-fusion restaurant focuses on serving the freshest local ingredients. The chicken comes from a family farm, vegan dishes are available, and both the salsa and guacamole are homemade and delicious. $$

The Fainting Goat (319-352-2335), 118 Tenth Street Southwest, Waverly. Open daily for lunch and dinner. This bar and grill, housed in the old sweet-corn canning factory in Waverly, is named for skittish barnyard friends whose genetic heritage includes a proclivity to pass out when startled. The menu may not offer as many startling surprises, but it does feature a wide range of sandwiches from chicken cordon bleu to roast "beast." BBQ ribs, steaks, pasta, and fish are also served. $$

COFFEE, TREATS, AND MARKETS **Cup of Joe** (319-277-1596), 102 Main Street, Cedar Falls. Open early morning to evenings daily.

The coffee they serve up in this funky little shop is as lively as the atmosphere. Try seasonal and themed blends of beans, espresso drinks, smoothies, and artisan tea. Pastries, cakes, and snacks go with the joe in a colorful, retro room outfitted with vinyl sofas and plenty of tables, inside and out, for socializing and studying.

Roots Market (319-266-3801; www.rootsmarket.net), 2021 Main Street, Cedar Falls. Open 9–7 daily. With a large selection of organic and locally sourced produce, dairy, eggs, and honey, and a fantastic deli, this natural-foods market is a full-service grocery store for shoppers looking for a healthier alternative. The market offers a large selection of wine and beer, a bakery, bulk foods, and a health and beauty department.

✪ **Granny Annie's** (319-277-4650), 1724 West 31st Street, Cedar Falls. Open for breakfast and lunch Mon.–Sat. Doughnut lovers will adore this old-fashioned bakery, and clearly they do because by midmorning, most of the breakfast treats are sold out. When the fritters and frosteds are gone, go for cookies, éclairs, and brownies. For a bit of everything, try the kitchen-sink cookies. The bakery also serves home-cooked soups and sandwiches for breakfast and lunch. Meals $

Cottonwood Canyon Gourmet Coffee (319-233-5018; www.cottonwoodcoffee.biz), 218 East Fourth Street, Waterloo. Open 7 AM–7 PM Mon.–Thurs., 8 AM–11 PM Fri.–Sat. With over 22 custom-roasted beans and 52 blends, this is a coffee lover's coffee shop. The focus is on amazing brews from the Caribbean, but these guys import beans from around the world. Stop in for a pick-me-up and an afternoon snack.

✷ Drinking Establishments

The Hub (319-266-2360; www.thehublivemusic.com), 406 Main Street, Cedar Falls. Open daily for bar time and Sat. afternoons for college football. The Hub is the collegiate venue for live music in downtown Cedar Falls. Half the bar is devoted to bands and entertainment; the other half offers big-screen televisions and cocktails for the college crowd. Call or visit their Web site for performance schedule.

Lava Lounge (319-234-5686), 2401 Falls Avenue, Waterloo. Open Mon.–Sat. Attached to **Ruby's Tacos,** the Lava Lounge has a cult following for serving the area's largest selection of imported beer, on tap and in the bottle, along with hand-shaken margaritas and single-malt scotches.

Monica's Spirits and Cigars (319-233-1319), 324 East Fourth Street, Waterloo. Open Mon.–Sat. afternoons and evenings. With a baby grand piano, single-malt scotch, cigars, and martinis, this swanky little downtown club offers big-city nightlife without the pretension.

Toads Bar and Grill (319-266-3507; www.toadsbarandgrill.com), 204 Main Street, Cedar Falls. Open daily for lunch, dinner, and bar time. There are plenty of ways to play at this local sports bar—sports on 21 televisions, shuffleboard, darts, a pool table, and foosball. The restaurant serves appetizers, pizza, salads, and great chicken wings. $$

✷ Entertainment

Waterloo-Cedar Falls Symphony (319-273-3373; www.wcfsymphony.org), Gallagher-Bluedorn Theater, UNI Campus, 8201 Dakota Avenue, Cedar Falls. This regionally well-respected symphony produces a series of concerts throughout the year that range from the classic to the surprising. As most symphonies do, they produce a holiday pops concert and perform Mozart and Brahms, but music lovers will also be surprised with events such as The Wizard of Oz and performances from world-renowned guest artists. Call or visit their Web site for schedule and ticket information.

National Cattle Congress (319-234-7515; www.nationalcattlecongress.com), 257 Ansborough Avenue, Waterloo. Don't let the name fool you. Yes, there are cattle events at this events center—cowboys try to ride 'em during rodeos—but there is also a whole lot more. Throughout the year, the center hosts a range of entertainment from bingo to BMX racing to ballroom dances to concerts. If you really need to see some cattle, a free petting zoo with barnyard animals is open 11–8 Tues.–Sat., 12–5 Sun. May–Sept. Call or visit their Web site for more information

Black Hawk Children's Theatre (319-235-0367; www.wcpbhct.org), 225 Commercial Street, Waterloo. Performances take place at the **Waterloo Center for the Arts** (see *To See*); call or visit their Web site for show schedule and box-office information. With four productions a year based on popular books and fairy tales, the theater focuses on works that promote harmony and are both educational and entertaining.

Gallagher-Bluedorn Performing Arts Center (319-273-7469; www.gbpac.om), University of Northern Iowa Campus, University Avenue, Cedar Falls. Call or visit their Web site for show schedule and box-office information. With over 150 events a year—including such musicians as violinist Itzhak Perlman, touring Broadway shows, and, of course, the Waterloo-Cedar Falls Symphony—this performing-arts space is the main hub of live entertainment in the area.

UNI-Dome (1-877-216-3663; www.uni.edu/unidome), 2501 23rd Street and Hudson Road, Cedar Falls. During the autumn, catch a game of UNI Panthers football under the massive, climate-controlled dome that dominates the Cedar Falls skyline, or visit their Web site for the schedule of state high-school sporting events, track-and-field events, and big-name concerts.

THE UNI-DOME, CEDAR FALLS, IS HOME TO PANTHER SPORTING EVENTS AS WELL AS CONCERTS

Oster Regent Theatre (319-277-5283; www.cedarnet.org/regent), 103 Main Street, Cedar Falls. Box office open 9–4 Mon.–Fri.; call or visit their Web site for performance schedule or to arrange for a tour. The Cedar Falls Community Theatre raised more than $1 million to restore the 500-seat 1910 Cotton Theatre. Today it provides a gorgeous and historic space for theatrical productions, concerts, and other events.

Waterhawks Ski Shows (www.waterhawks.org), Eagle Lake, IA 20 and I-380 Exit 68, Evansdale. Watch daring jumps and speed from the members of Iowa's oldest ski club. Hundred of people attend their Sunday-night shows. Visit their Web site for more information.

✷ Selective Shopping

University Book & Supply (319-266-7581; www.panthersupply.com), 1009 West 23rd Street, Cedar Falls. Open 9–7 Mon.–Thurs., 9–5 Fri., 10–5 Sat., 12–5 Sun. Dress yourself in purple and gold with UNI Panthers' gear from this locally owned bookstore. Along with textbooks and office supplies, the shop has a selection of popular books, games, and home decor.

Indulgence (319-266-6109), 305 Main Street, Cedar Falls. Open 12–10 Mon.–Thurs., 12–12 Fri. and Sat. Lovers of the finer things in life can buy their wine and sample it, too, at this goodie shop. Sit on the sidewalk out front or in the garden in the back with a glass of wine, or buy a bottle to take home along with fine European chocolates, cheeses, and cigars.

World's Window (319-268-1584), 214 Main Street, Cedar Falls. Open 10–5:30 Mon.–Sat. The world comes to Cedar Falls by way of unique, handcrafted gifts from around the world. The **Ten Thousand Villages** project coordinates the sales of local crafts with shops in the United States as a means to help people living in the Third World. The shop sells everything from jewelry to decorative art to stationery. It's shopping for a good cause.

FRANKLIN, HARDIN, BUTLER, AND GRUNDY COUNTIES

The counties between I-3, the north-south thoroughfare through the state, and the metropolitan area of Cedar Falls and Waterloo offer visitors more classic American heartland. Bisected by IA 20, Franklin, Butler, Hardin, and Grundy Counties are full of historical sites, outdoor recreation, and friendly places to stay. Be sure to visit the towns along the Iowa River, such as Iowa Falls and Eldora, for waterborne adventures aboard the *Scenic City Empress* in Iowa Falls or on a lazy tube trip at Rock-n-Row Adventures in Eldora.

GUIDANCE **Iowa Falls Chamber/Main Street** (641-648-5549; www.iowafallschamber.com), 520 Rocksylvania, Iowa Falls. Open during business hours. Call or visit the Web site to learn more about this small but vibrant community.

Eldora Welcome Center and Railroad Museum (641-939-3241; www.eldoraiowa.com), 1215 Park Street, Eldora. Open Memorial Day–Oct. 1 12–4 Sat., 1–5 Sun., and holidays, and by appointment. Step inside this renovated railroad depot to learn about area attractions and see a collection of railroad memorabilia. Outside the warmer-weather landscape is full of wildflowers and prairie grasses.

Franklin County Convention & Visitors Bureau (641-456-5668; www.franklincountycvb.com), 5 First Street Southwest, Hampton. Open during business hours. Learn about the attractions of Franklin County, conveniently located east of I-35. Web site or phone calls are best for information.

GETTING THERE *By car:* **US 20** and **US 65** run through or near most of the towns in this part of the state.

MEDICAL EMERGENCY Dial **911**.

✱ To See

Pat Clark Art Collection (641-648-4611; www.patclarkart.org), Carnegie-Ellsworth Building, Iowa Falls. Open 9–12 and 1–4 Mon.–Fri. and by appointment. Free. A collection of 270 works of art, including oil paintings, watercolors, ink drawings, and sculptures by nationally and internationally renowned artists. Named for its local benefactress, the collection is full of diverse works from many different cultures. The images depicted in the works range from the landscapes around Iowa Falls to a portrait of Mother and Child by an artist from Kazakhstan.

The Hemken Collection (515-689-1047; www.the-hemken-collection.org), 202 Main Street, Williams. Open 1–5 Wed. and Fri. May–Oct. and by appointment. Admission: $5. The private collection of the Hemken family is on display in a building originally designed as a showroom for carriages. The collection originated with the late Daryl Hemken, whose interest in cars began in 1958, and it now includes rare convertibles from the 1940s. All the cars in the collection were chosen for a unique feature such as a fresh-air heater or twin ignition. Most of the 100 cars are in their original condition.

Ackley Heritage Center (641-847-2201; www.ackleyheritagecenter.com), 208 State Street, Ackley. Open 1:30–4:30 Mon.–Fri. and by appointment. Free. At the heart of this historical center is a working corner drugstore with soda fountain. The menu is true to the era, with Green Rivers, a carbonated lime soda-fountain drink, and malted milk shakes. While enjoying a treat, visitors can see displays and artifacts from the city and the surrounding area. The Ackley Historical Society is creating an attraction called the *Settlement on the Prairie* that includes an 1870s house, a country schoolhouse, a windmill, and a restored prairie; it is currently open by appointment.

Hardin County Historical House (641-939-5137; www.hardincountyonline.com), 1601 Washington, Eldora. Open May–Oct. 1–4 second Sun. of the month and by appointment. Free. Inside this large Victorian home from 1891, the story of Hardin County and Eldora is told via antiques, collectibles, and a research library. Ask about visits to the **Hardin County Farm Museum** (641-393-7107; www.eldoraiowa.com/farmmuseum.asp), 203 North Washington Street, Eldora. It is just up the road but is open only during special events and by appointment. The 12-acre agricultural museum includes antique farm equipment and a country schoolhouse.

Little Valley Church (641-775-3457), 513 Early Street, Bristow. Open by appointment. There is no shortage of tiny churches in Iowa, as you've already determined. This contender, which is in Bob and Edee Ressler's backyard, measures just 6 by 8 feet and is only 10 feet tall, not including the steeple. Constructed in Allison in 1972, it seats four adults and includes an altar.

✵ To Do

✪ **Scenic City Empress Boat Club** (641-648-9517; www.iafalls.com), 1113 Union Street, Iowa Falls. Public cruises May–mid-Oct. at 2 PM Sat.–Sun. Tickets: $5 adults, $2 children. Cruise the gorgeous Iowa River on the *Empress*, passing limestone bluffs, city parks, and the swinging bridge. The narrated tour provides a historical perspective of this river town. Guests can bring their own food and drinks for the 90-minute tour.

✪ **Rock-n-Row Adventures** (641-858-5516; www.rock-n-row-adventures.com), 23539 First Street, IA 175, Eldora. Rentals: $20 per tube, $30 per kayak, $40 per canoe. Open daily from Memorial Day to mid-September, with floats leaving three times a day. Call for hours and reservations as they vary with the season and the weather. Enjoy a rocking float down the Iowa River. This is no sedate paddle; this is a party float. Floaters can soak up the sun, coolers in tow, on 3–4 hour floats.

Two-person canoes and kayaks are also available to rent. Stay and play at the headquarters, which offers camping (for tubers only), sand and mud volleyball, concessions, inside and outside showers, a beer garden, movies and live music, and mini-golf. Adult beverages welcome.

Eagle City Winery (641-648-3669; www.eaglecitywinery.com), 28536 160th Street, Iowa Falls. Open 10–5 Tues.–Sun. The wines at Eagle City are inspired by the tiny village whose name the winery bears. The tasting room and winery are in an old sawmill, and many of the fruits and grapes that make the wine are grown in the vineyard. The winery specializes in both California-style wines, like Chardonnay, and Iowa-style wines, such as Concord and Riesling. Though the vineyard is small, producing only 1,000 gallons a year, many of the wines have won state and local competitions.

Highway 3 Raceway (319-267-9999; www.highway3raceway.com), north of IA 3 at Main Street, Allison. Dirt-track racing is a popular sport. Locals warn that "you better like getting dirt in your drank" when the stock cars and figure-eight racers get going. This ½-mile, semibanked track is open all summer long. Call or visit their Web site for schedules and tickets.

Ridge Stone Golf Club See *Dining Out*.

✱ Green Space

Prairie Bridges Park (641-485-1623; www.hardincountyonline.com/prairiebridges), just north of IA 20 and CR S-56, Ackley. Open during daylight hours. Prairie Bridges is a gem of a county park. It offers miles of wide hiking trails, 12 acres of restored prairie grass, pretty little streams crossed by bridges, and ponds for fishing, swimming, and boating. The park is dotted with glacial erratics—boulders weighing from 1 to 5 tons that were left behind as the glaciers receded. Camping is also available at the park, with plenty of sites for both RV and tent camping. Campsites from $7–$14.

Pine Lake State Park (641-858-5832; www.iowadnr.com/parks), 22620 CR S-56, Eldora. Open during daylight hours. The smell of pine, rare in most of the state, fills the air around the aptly named Pine Lake. The 585-acre park features an upper and a lower lake—50 and 69 acres, respectively—that are surrounded by 250-year-old white pines white birches, 10 miles of developed hiking trails, and wildlife. A beach is located at the lower lake, and fishers can find bass, crappie, and catfish. The Iowa River runs past the lower lake and offers excellent opportunities for catching channel catfish and smallmouth bass. The park is a great place to picnic, and a bike trail network connects Pine Lake with **George Wyth Park** in Cedar Falls. Camping for both RVs and tents are available at 124 sites. The park also rents cabins built by the Civilian Conservation Corps. They have appliances and electricity, but campers will need to bring their own dishes, utensils, and linens. Cabins $75, campsites from $11–$16.

✱ Where to Stay

MOTELS Most of the small cities have chain motels or inexpensive, locally owned motels, especially along I-35.

Boondocks USA Motel (515-854-2201), I-35 at exit 144, Williams. There really is a Boondocks USA, and weary travelers on I-35 can stay there. But be warned: just like Billy Joe Royal sang, people might put you down because that's the side of town you'll be staying in. Even if the motel doesn't exactly "fit her society," it does have cheap rates and a restaurant. Rooms from $38–$42.

BED & BREAKFASTS **River's Bend** (641-648-2828; www.iafalls.com/riversbendbandb.htm), 635 Park Avenue, Iowa Falls. The columns over the portico and in the foyer accentuate the feel of this 1900s Greek-Revival building. An evening dessert and yummy candlelight breakfast fill guests up while they pass their hours in Iowa Falls. The antiques-decorated rooms overlook the Iowa River, and comforts such as terrycloth robes and high-speed wireless are provided. Rooms from $79–$129.

Bed and Breakfast of Cabin Cove (641-648-9571; www.bbcabincove.com), 820 Indiana Avenue, Iowa Falls. Go to sleep in peace, and wake up to birds chirping at this two-bedroom private cabin on the Iowa River offering such amenities as a gas fireplace, central air-conditioning, and a full breakfast. Guests get a free ride on the *Scenic City Empress* and have a private boat dock to call their own. Cabin for two $125.

Country Heritage (641-456-4036; www.countryheritagebb.com), 1034 IA 3, Hampton. Innkeeper Lacey Borcherding's family built this 1920 colonial farmhouse. Since then, the quiet location has served families and visitors alike. Three comfortable guest rooms are simply decorated and comfortable, and the bridal suite on the third floor offers added privacy and an in-room whirlpool tub for romantic evenings. Some rooms have fireplaces and private balconies. Special rates are available for families. Rooms (including breakfast) from $65–$90.

The Parsonage in Hampton (641-456-4998; www.theparsonageinhampton.com), 420 Central Avenue East, Hampton. For quiet, relaxing evenings, it is hard to beat spending the night at a parsonage. This comfortable Arts-and-Crafts home is no historic throwback, either; Pastor Jan Ekstedt and his wife, Elaine, welcome visitors with two guest rooms named for their daughters. Only one room is rented at a time, so the bathroom is private. The parsonage offers the comforts of home, including breakfast, for $89.

CAMPING **Beeds Lake State Park** (641-456-2047; www.iowadnr.com/parks), 1422 165th Street, Hampton. Nearly 100 electrical sites and 44 primitive sites make up this popular campground, which offers access to lake activities such as fishing, swimming at the sandy beach, and "no-wake boating." Campsites from $10–$16.

Pine Lake State Park See *Green Space*.

Prairie Bridges Park See *Green Space*.

✱ Where to Eat

DINING OUT **Ridge Stone Golf Club** (641-892-8040; www.ridgestonegolfclub.com), 7 Brickyard Road, Sheffield. Open for dinner Tues.–Sat. Dine in country-club style on shrimp scampi, hand-cut steaks, and juicy chicken dishes; hearty cuts of prime rib are served on the weekends. Although the food is good, the atmosphere is a bit drab. $$–$$$

EATING OUT **Princess Grill & Pizzeria** (641-648-9602), 607 Washington Avenue, Iowa Falls. Open for lunch and dinner Mon.–Sat. The Princess is restaurant royalty. Open since 1915, this old-fashioned pizza restaurant and soda fountain serves top-notch pies, sandwiches, and treats in a lovely old building. Look for enormous portions of fried appetizers and a wide range of choices of sandwiches—everything from Reubens to gyros. The floors are stone, and the friendly waitstaff know an order is up when the antique elevator dings. Cash only. $–$$

Camp David (641-648-3221), 119 Main Street, Iowa Falls. Open for lunch and dinner Mon.–Sat., Sun. brunch. Enjoy delicious food and an even more delicious view when the weather permits: the deck lets visitors enjoy dining over the Iowa River. This American-style restaurant serves tasty classics, burgers, steaks, sandwiches, and lots more. The BBQ chicken is not to be missed. $$

Peppercorn Pantry Tea Room (319-347-2797), 911 Parriott Street, Aplington. Open Tues.–Sat. 9–5. Wake up with a cup of tea and a muffin, or dine on a small menu of light lunches in this tearoom filled with flowers, Iowa wines, and antiques. In the afternoon don't miss a piece of the Angel Cream Coconut Cake with a cup of coffee—it is indeed heavenly. Lunch $$.

Ackley Heritage Center See *To See.*

✱ Entertainment

Metropolitan Theatre (641-648-3605), 515 Washington Avenue, Iowa Falls. Call for show times and ticket information. Built in the popular Italianate style, this former opera house once brought big-city theater productions to little Iowa Falls. Today this two-screen movie house still lets visitors get a glimpse of what it would've been like to see *Faust* or Shakespeare.

✱ Selective Shopping

The Wood Cellar (641-456-5510), 8 First Street Northwest, Hampton. Open 9:30–5 Mon.–Fri., 9:30–4 Sat. Shop for one-of-a-kind handcrafted wood furniture with a historical feel, dishes, linens, gourmet foods, home decorations, and gifts.

The Kaleidoscope (641-456-2787; www.ourfocusisyou.com), 112 First Avenue Northwest, Hampton. Open 12–6 Mon.–Tues., 11–7 Wed.–Thurs., 11–5 Fri., 12–4 Sat. Browse a thoughtful selection of children and grown-ups books at this independent bookstore. They've also got an excellent selection of local-interest books.

✱ Special Events

February: **50s in February** (641-357-6151; www.surfballroom.com) Clear Lake. Locals mark the tragic deaths of Buddy Holly, "the Big Bopper" (J. P. Richardson), and Ritchie Valens, at the Surf Ballroom with music and costumes.

March: **Maple Syrup Festival** (319-277-2187), Hartman Reserve Nature Center, Cedar Falls. See how real maple syrup is made, from collecting the sap to pouring it over pancakes, at this annual event.

Waverly Horse Sale (319-352-2804; www.waverlysales.com), Waverly Sales Barn, Waverly. Premium horses and equipment go up for auction at this event that draws horse enthusiasts from around the country and the world. The sale also takes place in October.

May: **North Iowa Band Festival** (641-422-1663; www.visitmasoncity iowa.com/), Mason City. Celebrate with no fewer than 76 trombones in a large celebration of marching bands, parades, food, and music.

My Waterloo Days Festival (319-233-8431; www.mywaterloodays.org), throughout Waterloo. A citywide festival, with parades, fireworks, musical entertainment, a 5K run/walk, bike races, dragon boats, and children's activities.

June: **Laura Days** (563-735-5916; www.lauraingallswilder.us), Burr Oak. A two-day festival centered on Laura Ingalls Wilder, with tours, a Little Miss Laura contest, 5k run, pioneer demonstrations, food, games, and parades.

June–July: **River Bend Rally** 641-648-5549; www.iowafallschamber.com), Iowa Falls. A classic small-town festival that includes music, entertainment, crafts, and food in downtown Iowa Falls.

Sturgis Falls Celebration and Cedar Basin Jazz Festival (319-268-4266; www.sturgisfalls.org), Cedar Falls. With over 20 bands, a parade, a street fair, and lots of delicious food, this is the area's not-to-miss party.

Bosnian Fest (1-800-728-8431), throughout Waterloo. Celebrate Waterloo's rich Bosnian immigrant population with an international dance tournament, karate tournament, and soccer tournament.

Howard County Fair (www.mhcfair.com), Howard County Fairgrounds, Cresco. Billed as the "Mighty Howard County Fair"—and thought to be the most progressive county fair in the state—this fair offers entertainment that includes music, rodeo, stock cars, rides, food, and games.

July: **Nordic Fest** (1-800-382-3378; www.nordicfest.com), Decorah. A weekend of lefsa and lutefisk: thousands of visitors are *velkommen* with music, parades, traditional Scandinavian costumes, and, of course, food.

Bicycles, Blues and BBQ Festival (1-800-285-5338; www.bicyclebluesbbq.com), Clear Lake. BBQ and beer kick off this three-day festival of food, bike rides for all skill levels, and great music. Sunday-morning races for the United States Cycling Federation bring an end to the fest.

Fourth of July (641-357-2159; www.clearlakeiowa.com), Clear Lake. This lake city knows how to celebrate the Fourth: parades, rides, food, and music, and fireworks over the water.

August: **Battle of Vicksburg** (641-424-3519; www.civilwariowa.org), East Park, Mason City. See a historical reenactment of this Civil War battle. Take a tour of the camp, see a wound and nurses' clinic, and attend a military dress ball.

North Iowa Fair (641-423-3811; www.northiowafair.org), Mason City. Agricultural events, music, food, and entertainment at this large county fair.

Art-A-Fest (641-228-6284), outside the Charles City Art Center, 301 North Jackson Street, Charles City. More than 40 artists gather to display and sell art, along with food and entertainment.

Power Show (641-732-1269) Mitchell County Historical Society Cedar Valley Memories, Osage. See five functioning antique steam engines and much more at this early-August festival.

Little Brown Church in the Vale Wedding Reunion (641-435-2027; www.littlebrownchurch.org), Nashua. Celebrate with the thousands of couples from all over the world who have been married in the historic church. There's an ice-cream social, and all are welcome.

Norman Borlaug Harvest Fest (563-547-3434), various locations throughout Cresco. This relatively new festival celebrates the Nobel Prize winner with music, athletic events, quilt auctions, food vendors, and a parade.

Southeast Iowa 4

CEDAR RAPIDS AREA

IOWA AND POWESHIEK COUNTIES

IOWA CITY AREA

FAIRFIELD, MOUNT PLEASANT, AND THE VILLAGES OF VAN BUREN COUNTY

OTTUMWA AND THE LAKE RATHBUN AREA

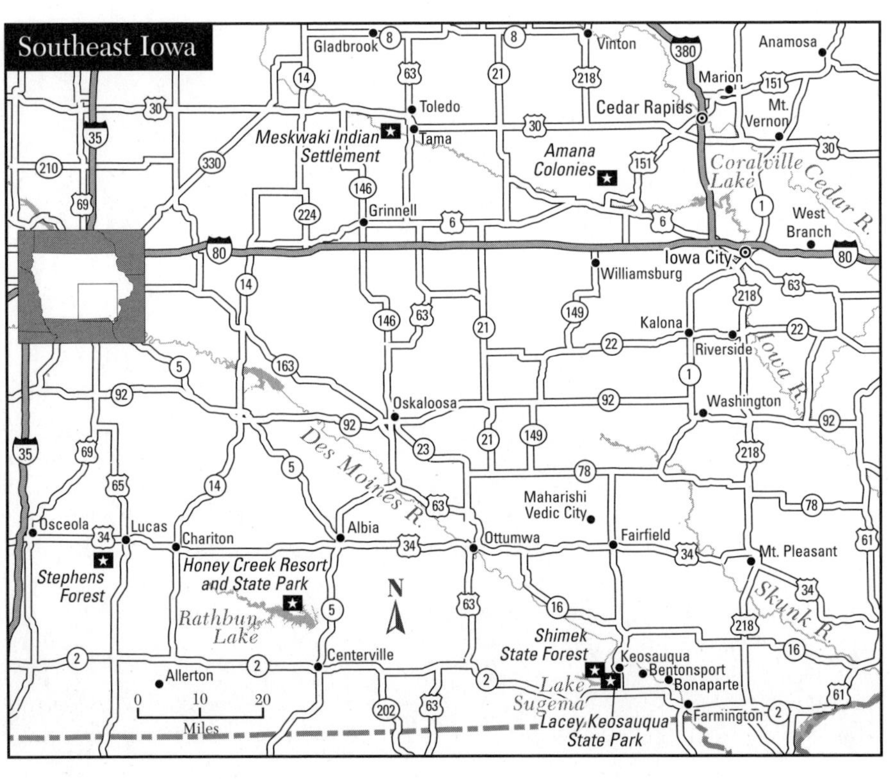
Southeast Iowa
Gladbrook
Vinton
Anamosa
Marion
Mt. Vernon
Cedar Rapids
Toledo
Tama
Meskwaki Indian Settlement
Amana Colonies
Coralville Lake
Cedar R.
West Branch
Grinnell
Iowa City
Williamsburg
Kalona
Riverside
Iowa R.
Washington
Oskaloosa
Des Moines R.
Maharishi Vedic City
Fairfield
Mt. Pleasant
Skunk R.
Osceola
Lucas
Chariton
Albia
Ottumwa
Stephens Forest
Honey Creek Resort and State Park
Rathbun Lake
Centerville
Allerton
Shimek State Forest
Keosauqua
Bentonsport
Bonaparte
Lake Sugema
Lacey Keosauqua State Park
Farmington
N
0 10 20
Miles

SOUTHEAST IOWA: A BRIEF OVERVIEW

Nowhere else in Iowa will travelers find such an astounding range of attractions as southeastern Iowa. In this region is the state's most cosmopolitan city, Iowa City, where big-city entertainment and fine dining fit effortlessly in a literate and progressive college town, home of the University of Iowa. Students mingle with townies, high-end boutiques sit next to cheap sandwich shops, and there are plenty of casual spots to grab a drink and watch the Hawkeyes. At the heart of campus is the Old Capital, the first state capital of the state of Iowa, now a college building and museum. Plum Grove, the private home of Iowa's first governor is another interesting historical site in the area. One county away, around the community of Kalona, more than a thousand Amish and Mennonite families continue to live life in a traditional way, and the back roads are traveled with as many horse and buggies as automobiles. Visitors will find shops, filled with handmade furniture and antiques, bakeries, and some eclectic restaurants tucked away in the rolling fields.

The Villages of Van Buren County along the lower Des Moines River grew and prospered in the era of the steamboat and still have the feel of river-town life at the turn of the 20th century. The Des Moines River brought people and goods into the heart of the state, until it was deemed to shallow for navigation. Today, the villages feature steamboat Gothic architecture, historic buildings, natural resources, and an abundance of shops with views of the peaceful river. The Amana Colonies in Iowa County were established as utopian religious communities in the 1800s by German settlers. The colonies are probably the best-known attractions in Iowa. Their quaint Old World-looking streets are full of shops and family-style restaurants, but outlet shopping and a small water park also attract visitors to Iowa Colony. Just down the road in Tama and Toledo, the Meskwaki Indians, resisting resettlement in the West, established their own community when they purchased a tract of land from the state.

In the 20th century, a group of Transcendental Meditationists transformed the landscape and the destiny of the town of Fairfield and have also since established Vedic City, a town entirely designed and organized along the laws and teachings of the ancient Sanskrit *Vedas.* Cities like Cedar Rapids and Ottumwa built themselves by bringing industry to rural Iowa, and yet the region is also known for the pastoral splendor depicted in the works of Grant Wood. His paintings come to life in Stone City and at the *American Gothic* House in Eldora. On the shores of one of Iowa's largest manmade lakes, Rathbun, looking firmly toward the future, is the state's first luxury eco-resort at Honey Creek. All of these wonders are tucked into the rolling hills, fertile fields, and sleepy small towns just waiting to be explored.

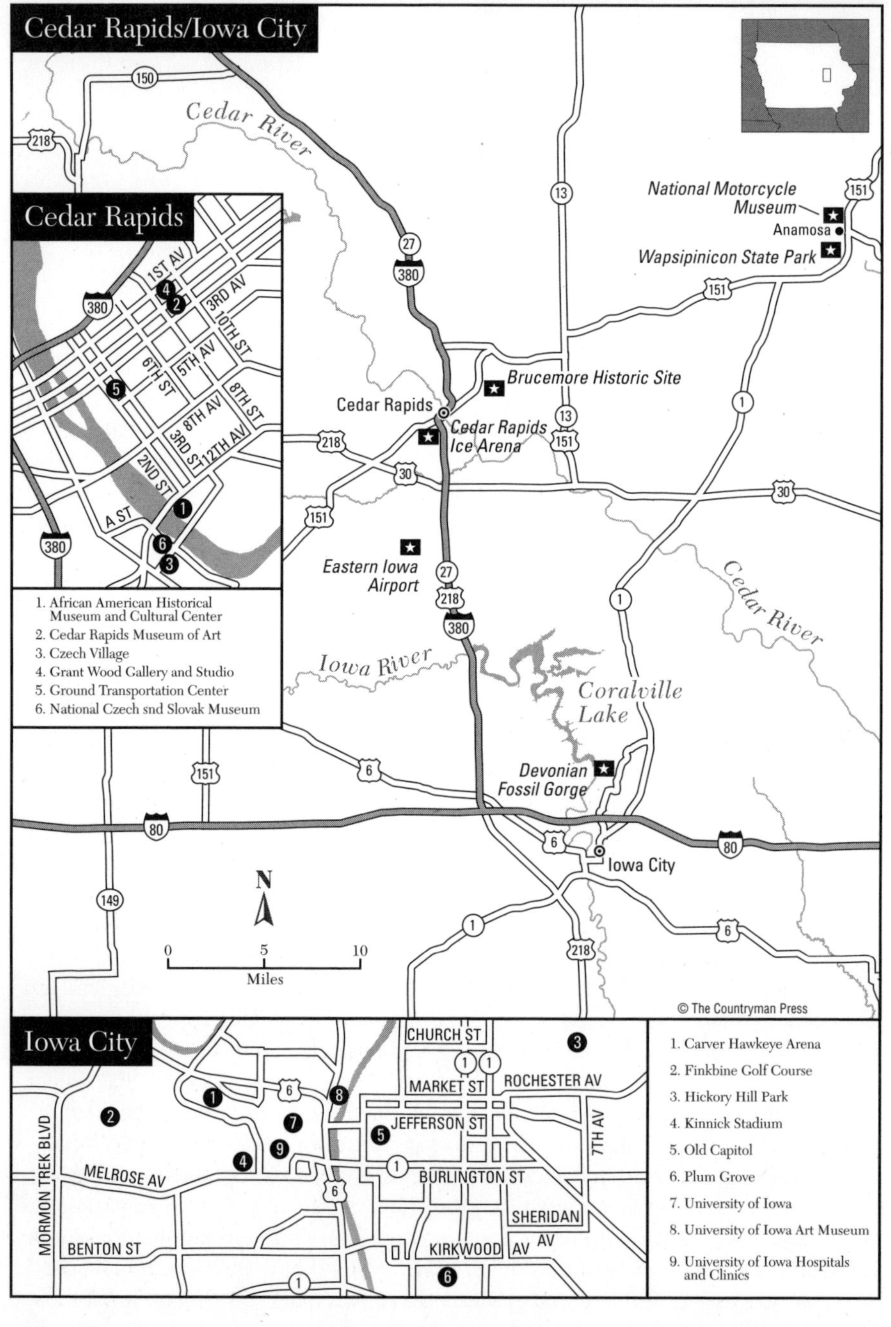

Cedar Rapids/Iowa City
Cedar River
National Motorcycle Museum
Anamosa
Wapsipinicon State Park
Brucemore Historic Site
Cedar Rapids
Cedar Rapids Ice Arena
Eastern Iowa Airport
Iowa River
Coralville Lake
Devonian Fossil Gorge
Iowa City
N
0
5
10
Miles
© The Countryman Press
Cedar Rapids
1ST AV
3RD AV
10TH ST
5TH AV
6TH ST
8TH AV
8TH ST
3RD ST
12TH AV
2ND ST
A ST
1. African American Historical Museum and Cultural Center
2. Cedar Rapids Museum of Art
3. Czech Village
4. Grant Wood Gallery and Studio
5. Ground Transportation Center
6. National Czech snd Slovak Museum
Iowa City
CHURCH ST
MARKET ST
ROCHESTER AV
JEFFERSON ST
7TH AV
MORMON TREK BLVD
MELROSE AV
BURLINGTON ST
SHERIDAN AV
BENTON ST
KIRKWOOD AV
1. Carver Hawkeye Arena
2. Finkbine Golf Course
3. Hickory Hill Park
4. Kinnick Stadium
5. Old Capitol
6. Plum Grove
7. University of Iowa
8. University of Iowa Art Museum
9. University of Iowa Hospitals and Clinics

CEDAR RAPIDS AREA

Cedar Rapids, the "City of Five Seasons," is Iowa's second-largest city. Built on the Cedar River, it is one of the few cities in the world (Paris is another) that houses its government offices on an island in the river. Cedar Rapids was first established in 1838 and grew into an industrial center when the Sinclair meatpacking company was founded in 1871. Mr. Sinclair's money built the fabulous home of Brucemore, although the meatpacking magnate died in an accident and never saw the mansion completed.

In the 1860s the growing industries in Cedar Rapids attracted Czech and Slovak immigrants, who built social institutions like the Bohemian Dance Hall. In the late 1800s and early 1900s, African Americans emigrated to the state to work in the coal industry but soon migrated to urban centers, like Cedar Rapids, when mining declined. The people of Cedar Rapids share a strong identity with these groups still. Visitors can learn more by visiting the wonderful National Czech and Slovak Museum and the African American Heritage Museum.

Cedar Rapids today is home to many large companies such as General Mills, Cargill, Rockwell Collins, and Quaker Oats, whose factory sometimes inspires visitors and locals alike to refer Cedar Rapids as the "city of five smells." The city is also home to Coe College and Mount Mercy College, while Cornell College is in neighboring Mount Vernon. Like much of eastern Iowa, Cedar Rapids fell victim to the catastrophic flooding of 2008, and many of its thriving cultural and historical areas were greatly damaged.

Directly to the east of Cedar Rapids and Linn County are Jones and Cedar Counties. On a farm outside of Anamosa, the great American artist Grant Wood was born and raised. His work was inspired by the rolling hills and the stalwart rural characters of the region, and visitors can explore many of the places where Wood lived and worked, including his colony in Stone City and his studio in Cedar Rapids. Many of his works are on display at museums and galleries through the area. Iowa's only president, Herbert Hoover, was born in West Branch, where his presidential library and the tiny house he was born in are located.

To the west of Cedar Rapids are Benton and Tama counties. The Meskwaki Indians, bucking government authority, refused to leave the area, and instead they bought and settled on land in Tama County; others returned after resettlement in the West and joined the community. Their cultural heritage endures in an annual powwow, and today the Meskwaki entice visitors to the Meskwaki Casino and Resort.

MAY'S ISLAND IN THE CEDAR RIVER IS THE MUNICIPAL CENTER FOR CEDAR RAPIDS

GUIDANCE **Cedar Rapids Convention and Visitors Bureau** (319-398-5009; www.cedar-rapids.com), 119 First Avenue Southeast, Cedar Rapids. Open during business hours. Flood location in the Lindale Mall. Call or visit their Web site for community information and flood updates.

Jones County Tourism Association (319-462-4101; www.jonescountytourism.com), 120 East Main Street, Suite C, Anamosa. Open during business hours. Call or visit their Web site for information on Grant Wood, Anamosa, Monticello, and other communities in the county.

Main Street West Branch (319-643-7100; www.mainstreetwestbranch.org), 109 North Downey Street, West Branch. Open during business hours. Learn more about the restaurants, shops, and attractions in historic West Branch.

Mount Vernon–Lisbon Marketing and Tourism Association (319-210-9935; www.visitmvl.com), 311 First Street Northwest, Mount Vernon. Visitors center staffed during business hours. For more information on the towns of Mount Vernon, Lisbon, Palisades-Kepler State Park, and Cornell College, call or visit the Web site.

GETTING THERE *By Air:* **Eastern Iowa Airport** (319-362-8336; www.eiairport.org), 2121 Arthur Collins Parkway Southwest, Cedar Rapids, offering connecting flights to major airports.

By car: **I-380** runs north from **I-80** just west of Iowa City and continues on to Waterloo and Cedar Falls. **US 30,** the old Lincoln Highway, runs east-west through Cedar Rapids, and **US 151** leads north to Anamosa and Dubuque and south to the Amana Colonies. Mount Vernon is just 10 miles south and east of Cedar Rapids on **US 30**.

GETTING AROUND *By Bus and Taxi:* **Ground Transportation Center** (319-286-5573), 200 Fourth Avenue Southeast, Cedar Rapids. This hub includes the headquarters for local and interstate buses and cab companies.

MEDICAL EMERGENCY Dial **911**.

St. Luke's Hospital (319-369-7211; www.stlukescr.org), 1026 A Avenue Northeast, Cedar Rapids. St. Luke's emergency room serves patients with both major and minor injuries. The ER has an area designated for less serious injuries and usually gets patients home within an hour.

✳ To See

Anamosa Penitentiary Museum (319-462-2386; www.asphistory.com/museum), North High Street, Anamosa. Open May–Oct. 12–4 Fri.–Sun. and by appointment (museum hours seem to fluctuate, so call ahead). Admission: $2.50 adults. The Anamosa State Penitentiary, known as the White Palace of the West, is an impressive stone complex constructed in 1872. The prison is Iowa's largest correctional facility, and it has been home to such inmates as the notorious John Wayne Gacy, who served 18 months here before being relocated to Illinois. While in Anamosa, Gacy was a model prisoner who sang in the choir and organized for the Jaycees. Another strange inmate was Wesley Elkins, an 11-year-old sentenced to life in a maximum-security prison after he murdered his parents in 1989, although he was paroled after serving 12 years. The first prison movie, *Penitentiary,* was shot here in 1935. Today, visitors can learn about the history of the prison and prison life. Housed in the old cheese factory, the museum has a replica cell, a prison guards' exhibit, a diorama of prisoners pounding rocks, and prison crafts on display. Visitors can also buy souvenirs and prison-made crafts.

National Motorcycle Museum (319-462-3925; www.nationalmcmuseum.org), 200 East Main Street, Anamosa. Open Apr.–Oct., 9–5 Mon.–Sat., 10–4 Sun.; Nov.–Mar., 9–5 Mon.–Fri., 10–4 Sat., 11–4 Sun.; closed Sun. in Jan. Admission: $7 adults. Out front, motorcycles are always lined up in their angled glory while their riders tour the two-level shrine to America's favorite two-wheeled machine. More than two hundred rare and vintage bikes illustrate the history of the motorcycle,

THE NATIONAL MOTORCYCLE MUSEUM, ANAMOSA, IS A SHRINE TO AMERICA'S FAVORITE TWO-WHEELED MACHINE

TAKE A BREAK DURING YOUR GRANT WOOD TOUR AT THE GENERAL STORE IN STONE CITY, PERHAPS THE MOST BEAUTIFUL SPOT IN THE WORLD TO ENJOY A BURGER AND A BEER

IOWA CORNFIELD, 1941: A GRANT WOOD TOUR

If the rolling hills, bountiful fields, and hard-working Iowans of Jones County seem strangely familiar, don't be alarmed. These scenes and many other landscapes of the state inspired the work of Iowa artist Grant Wood (1891–1942). Wood was born on a farm outside of Anamosa. As a child he showed both a talent for art and a love for rural life. Wood's father died when Grant was just 10, and his mother moved the family to Cedar Rapids, where his talents continued to develop. After serving in the military and traveling through Europe, Wood realized the best muse for his art was in his own backyard. Wood's work, which became popular during the Great Depression, spoke to people. They felt it was easier to understand than most modern art and people loved the fairy tale–like beauty of the American landscape.

Start your Grant Wood tour on the **Grant Wood Scenic Byway**. Begin in the town of Bellevue on the Mississippi River and follow the signs through the rolling hills, fields, and communities of Springbrook, Maquoketa, Wyoming, and Anamosa. Stop in at the **Grant Wood Art Gallery** (319-462-4267; www.grantwoodartgallery.org; 124 East Main Street, Anamosa; open

Apr.–Dec. 10–4 Mon.–Sat., 1–4 Sun.; Jan.–Mar. 1–4 daily). Art lovers will find historical photos of the artist and his colony as well as books, posters, and gifts. The gallery is also an information center, with a friendly staff of local volunteers.

Then visit the **Antioch School** (319-480-0221; IA 64, 3 miles east of Anamosa; open May–Oct. 1–4 Sun. and by appointment). The schoolhouse Wood attended from first to fourth grades has been restored to that period and adjoins a gallery featuring local artists. Wood is buried in Anamosa's **Riverside Cemetery**, but don't look for him at the Wood family plot. He hated the gaudy lion statue, so he is buried nearby with his mother's side of the family.

Just 4 miles west of Anamosa is the little town of Stone City on the Wapsipinicon River (just call it the "Wapsie"). Stone City, tucked deep in the river valley and depicted in a painting by the same name, is still known for the limestone blocks quarried here. During the summers of 1932 and 1933, Wood established the Stone City Art Colony at the limestone mansion of Green Estate. Many of the artists who attended, such as Isabel Bloom, went on to have successful careers, although the colony was eventually abandoned.

While visiting Stone City, don't miss lunch at the **General Store Pub** (319-462-4399; CR X28; open Thurs. for dinner, Fri.–Sun. for lunch and dinner). In the basement of the 1890s limestone building is a cozy bar and grill, with excellent burgers, sandwiches, and pizza. It is a perfect day trip for bikers, both motorcyclists and bicyclists, and everyone else. When the weather allows, be sure to get a table on the two-tiered deck over the Wapsie. From this writer's experience, it is hard to beat an early-fall afternoon spent here, when the leaves in the valley are just beginning to yellow, kayakers are paddling up the river, a tenderloin sandwich and a cold beer sit on the table, and the Iowa Hawkeyes are winning. No wonder Wood's paintings are so lovely.

Next, drive on to Cedar Rapids. Wood did much of his professional work at his **Studio** at 5 Turner Alley (call 319-366-7503; or visit www.crma.org for hours and admission). The studio, now part of the **Cedar Rapids Museum of Art,** has been restored. Visitors are treated to a guided tour of the home and studio. The **CRMA** is home to the largest collection of Grant Wood's works. Learn more about other important locations in Wood's life and the location of many pieces of his art through the "Grant Wood's Trail," a map on the museum's Web site. Grant Wood is not only Iowa's most famous artist but also Iowa's best ambassador. His interest in the land inspired the Regionalist movement in the United States, which illustrated the beauty and romance of the Midwest and showed Iowans and the world at large this lovely state.

from its early days as little more than a gas-powered bicycle to the hardcore hogs and sleek racing beauties we know today. The museum is home to the original bike of Captain America (a.k.a. Peter Fonda) from the 1969 movie *Easy Rider,* Steve McQueen's 1947 Indian Chief, and Evel Knievel's 1972 Harley-Davidson XR750. Even visitors who've never ridden a chopper will be impressed by this collection of bikes, trophies, toys, helmets, engines, and paintings.

Herbert Hoover Presidential Library and **Museum and National Historic Site** (319-643-5301; www.hoover.archives.gov), 210 Parkside Drive, West Branch. Open 9–5 daily, closed major holidays. Admission: $6 adults, $3 seniors, children under 16 free. The permanent exhibits in the presidential library illustrate the life of Hoover, who was born in small-town Iowa and died in the Waldorf Towers in New York City. Along the way he lived in Oregon, China, and, of course, Washington DC, working as a mining engineer, humanitarian, statesman, and, after leaving the presidency, author of numerous books. The presidential library tells the story of his sometimes glorious, sometimes troubled career through videos, displays, artifacts, and documents. Adjacent to the library is the museum and national historic site, which includes the tiny two-room home that Hoover was born in, Jesse Hoover's blacksmith shop, and other buildings from the period. A self-guided walking tour takes visitors through the buildings, and helpful staff and demonstrations offer more in-depth information along the way.

Grant Wood Gallery (563-886-6266), Tipton Public Library, 206 Cedar Street, IA 38, Tipton. Open 10–8 Mon.–Thurs., 1–6 Fri., 10–1 Sat.; free. This Carnegie Library from 1903 houses a number of Grant Wood pieces, including oil paintings, charcoal sketches, as well as letters signed by the artist. Other regional painters such as Marvin Cone are represented in this free public collection.

Cedar Rapids Museum of Art (319-366-7503; www.crma.org), 410 Third Avenue Southeast, Cedar Rapids. The museum sustained flooding in 2008 but was open at the time of publication. Call or visit their Web site for current hours and

HERBERT HOOVER'S LIFE IS CELEBRATED IN HIS PRESIDENTIAL LIBRARY AND HISTORIC SITE IN WEST BRANCH, INCLUDING THE TINY TWO-ROOM CABIN WHERE HE WAS BORN

BRUCEMORE. LIONS, GERMAN SHEPHERDS, AND BEARS

When Caroline Sinclair dreamed of Brucemore, she dreamed the grandest home west of Chicago. The 21-room mansion with a great hall, grand staircase, 8 modern bathrooms, and 14 fireplaces was completed in 1886. It had the first carriage porch in Iowa and, true to Cedar Rapids's industrial history, it was built with meat-packing money and was further glorified in the hands of cereal tycoon George Bruce Douglas and his family. The Douglas family improved the house a great deal, adding butternut paneling, a mural depicting images from Wagner's *Ring of the Nibelung* operas, and adding an enormous pipe organ. The home, now a part of the National Trust for Historic Preservation, is being restored to the period of the Douglas family (1907–1937).

While that is all fine and good, what makes Brucemore stand out from all the other grand historic mansions in Iowa are the wacky additions of the last family who inhabited it. Margaret and Howard Hall were a fun-loving modern couple; he was president of the Iowa Steel and Iron Works and established the Iowa Manufacturing Company. The Halls liked to party. Howard installed a Tahiti Room in the basement, complete with a feature to create rain falling on the tin roof. He also built the "grizzly bar" in his basement, featuring a bearskin rug. The Halls were friends with a Hollywood lion trainer and were given two lion cubs, descendants of the MGM lion, who romped around the extensive grounds. Both were named Leo. The Halls also had a series of German shepherds, all named King. Needless to say, the pet cemetery on the mansion grounds is well worth a visit.

Joking aside, the grounds around Brucemore are breathtaking. Stroll around the property on your own, or pick up a self-guided tour map and take in the sites. The grounds include a formal garden, an alfalfa field grown for the horses, an orchard and playhouse, and a bindery and squash court.

Brucemore (319-362-7375; www.brucemore.org) is located at 2160 Linden Drive Southeast, Cedar Rapids. Tours Feb.–Dec., 10–3 Tues.–Sat., 12–3 Sun.; exhibits year-round 9–5 Mon.–Sat., 12–4 Sun. Admission: $7 per person.

BRUCEMORE: A CEDAR RAPIDS MANSION FILLED WITH ANTIQUES AND INTERESTING SURPRISES

THE 500-YEAR FLOOD

People in the Midwest described the catastrophic floods of the summer of 1993 as the "100-Year Flood," believing that natural disasters of such magnitude could only happen once a century. Yet in the summer of 2008, after a long and extremely snowy winter, heavy rains doused Iowa beginning in early June. After two weeks the rivers were swollen, and levees began to buckle. Rivers from the Des Moines to the Mississippi flooded the cities and fields situated on their banks.

The flood is considered the Hurricane Katrina of the Midwest, with the cities of Cedar Rapids and Iowa City being some of the hardest hit. Downtown Cedar Rapids, on the Cedar River, received more damage than anyone could have anticipated. Mays Island—home to City Hall, the Linn County Court House, and the county jail—was overrun with water; those municipal buildings were flooded up to the second floor, as were downtown buildings to both the north and south of the river. Nearly four thousand homes were inundated, and of the 70 square miles of the city, more than 10 square miles were under water. The **National Czech and Slovak Museum, African American Museum and Cultural Center,** the **Cedar Rapids Public Library,** and the **Cedar Rapids Art Museum** all sustained serious damage from the floods. The neighborhoods around the **Czech Village** and **New Bohemia** were devastated.

In Iowa City water flowed over the emergency spillway at Coralville Lake and deluged several parts of the city and Coralville. As citizens were warned to evacuate the 500-year-floodplain, volunteers moved the collections of the **University of Iowa** library to higher ground. The university's library, student union, art museum, student housing, and **Hancher Auditorium** all sustained flooding.

Countless other cities, small towns, and rural areas suffered greatly from the flooding, and the estimated costs rose into the billions. While many of the businesses, attractions, cultural institutions, and citizens are already on the road to recovery at the time of publication, many continue to struggle. To the traveler, some of the effects of this flooding will be obvious, others will not. I've tried to indicate places that were particularly damaged and included establishments that have reopened or plan on reopening, but because of the uncertainly that follows natural disasters, I recommend visitors call ahead or visit the individual Web sites before planning a visit—and consider donating to the **Red Cross** (www.redcross.org) or to the nonprofit clearinghouse **Save Iowa** (www.saveiowa.org). Iowans are a plucky, hardworking, and resourceful bunch, so I know they will be back on their feet and dry land soon.

admission. View the world's largest collection of Grant Wood's work, which is housed at this museum along with his studio, which is located a couple of blocks away at 5 Turner Alley. Be sure to stop at the **Grant Wood Studio and Visitor Center** (319-366-7503; www.grantwoodstudio.org), open 12–4 Fri.–Sat. Visitors can see where Wood lived and did much of his work, along with classic images of Iowa such as *Woman with Plant,* a portrait of Wood's mother. Other collections include the work of Regionalist painter Marvin Cone, Roman art, prints, and contemporary American art. The museum also hosts a wide variety of rotating exhibits, including a large exhibit of photographs from the floods of 2008.

✪ **National Czech and Slovak Museum** (319-362-8500; www.ncsml.org), 30 16th Avenue Southwest. Admission: $7 adults, $6 seniors, $2 children. Postflood location in the Lindale Mall. Call and visit their Web site for current location, schedule, and admission. Northeast Iowa is rich in the heritage of the Czech and Slovak immigrants who settled in the region. The story of the Czech and Slovak people in Europe, in the United States, and their culture is told through permanent and changing exhibits. The museum also hosts a variety of rotating exhibits that probe into more specific subjects pertinent to the Czech and Slovak people, such as life under Communism.

Czech Village (319-364-0001; czechvillageiowa.com/), 76 16th Avenue Southwest, Cedar Rapids. Open 10–5 Mon.–Sat. Free. The village was completely flooded in 2008, though at the time of publication, restoration was underway. Step out of Iowa and into the motherland on the streets of the Czech Village near the National Czech and Slovak Museum. The street that makes up the Czech village is lined with buildings, bakeries, and shops that create an Old World atmosphere. Many of the establishments are operating businesses that visitors can patronize.

African American Historical Museum and Cultural Center of Iowa (319-862-2101; www.blackiowa.org), 55 12th Avenue Southeast. Mon.–Sat. 10–4. Admission: $4 adults, $2.50 children. (The museum sustained flooding but reopened in January 2009.) Since York, a slave on the Lewis and Clark expedition, explored Iowa, the history of African Americans in the state has been an interesting one. With permanent and rotating exhibits and outreach, the museum explores the slave ships, Underground Railroad stops, and industry that brought African Americans to the state. Learn about Buxton, the coal-mining city with a large population of African Americans, among other special topics.

Iowa Masonic Library and Museum (316-365-1438; www.gl-iowa.org), 813 First Avenue Southeast, Cedar Rapids. Open 8–12 and 1–5 Mon.–Fri., and Sat. by appointment. Free. The brilliantly white grand lodge is an impressive structure and houses an equally impressive collection of books in the library, which is open to the public. The ambitious collection includes one of only two remaining copies of *Johnson's Dictionary,* compiled in 1755. The museum includes Masonic artifacts along with displays of Native American artifacts, pioneer and military displays, and art. One tabletop is a mosaic composed of 37,373 pieces of wood.

Carl and Mary Koehler History Center (319-362-1501; www.historycenter.org), 615 First Avenue Southeast, Cedar Rapids. Free admission but voluntary donation requested. Open 10–4 Tues., Thurs., Sat. Learn about the history of the Cedar Rapids region though permanent and rotating exhibits on such special topics as Mays Island, the Chautauqua movement, and the people and places of Linn

County throughout history. Permanent collections include Native American history, archeology, and industrial history.

Duffy's Collectible Cars (319-364-7000; www.duffys.com), 250 Classic Car Court Southwest, Cedar Rapids. Open 8:30–5 Mon.–Fri., 8:30–4:40 Sat. Duffy's was one of the first of the collector-car dealers in the United States. In the showroom are 75 fully restored vehicles, all of which are for sale, dating from the 1930s through the 1970s. Period antiques such as a phone booth, neon signs, and wall murals are also on display.

Cornell College (319-895-4215; www.cornellcollege.edu), Mount Vernon. It is hard to find a place lovelier than Mount Vernon, home to Cornell College. The entire facility is one of two college campuses that are wholly listed on the National Register of Historic Places. The brick buildings on the hill look down across grassy lawns and stately oak trees. Besides being a particular beauty spot, Cornell is a unique liberal-arts college that offers a one-course-at-a-time academic calendar. Walk the grounds alone, or call to arrange for a tour.

Lisbon History Center (319-455-2714), 102 East Main Street, Lisbon. Open 10–2 Sat. Free. Civil War buffs will thrill at the collection of Mountain Howitzer cannons; it's the largest in the nation. Besides the big guns, the museum offers a collection of artifacts and memorabilia, historical documents, and a genealogical research library.

✪ **Matchstick Marvels** (641-473-2410; www.matchstickmarvels.com), 319 Second Street, Gladbrook. Open Apr.–Nov. 1–5 daily, by appointment only Dec.–Mar.; $3 adults, $1 children. Blame the long Iowa winters. Perhaps all the cold and snow on the plains drive men to pursuits of crafts both ambitious and odd, but like the **Bily Brothers** in Spillville (see Part 3, "Decorah"), Pat Caton began tinkering in his woodshop in the 1970s and never looked back. His medium? Matchsticks—three million of them glued and shaped into models of such scale and detail as to be absolutely astonishing. Consider, for example, the grandest work in the museum, a

THE U.S. CAPITOL AS RENDERED AT MATCHSTICK MARVELS IN GLADBROOK

model of the U.S. Capitol, made of 500,000 matchsticks that stretches some 12 feet long and 4 feet high. Or the model of the *Cutty Sark*, whose sails are even made from matchsticks, or the USS *Iowa* battleship made from 137,000 matchsticks. Other models include Hogwarts Castle from the *Harry Potter* series and the Iowa governor's mansion, Terrace Hill. The models are so popular, they have been purchased by an art museum in Spain and Ripley's Believe It Or Not.

The Winding Stairs (319-478-2346; www.traer.com/visit), Second Street, Traer. E. E. Taylor founded the Traer *Star-Clipper* newspaper when he was just 16; the newspaper's office was small, though, so to give himself a little extra space, in 1894, he had the Burlington Iron Works construct a 23-step, 2,000-pound winding iron staircase to the second floor. When the sidewalks were widened in 1916, Taylor simply added a catwalk to the stairs so they would reach the new curb. The stairs were damaged and repaired, sold and repurchased, and finally placed on the National Registry of Historic Places. Today the building is owned by the Traer Historical Society, and travelers may want to "wind up" in Traer during the Winding Stairs Festival, held every August.

Lincoln Highway Bridge (641-484-6661; www.tamatoledo.com), Fifth Street just off US 30, Tama. The Lincoln Highway, today's US 30, was the first transcontinental highway in the United States. The only remaining bridge of this roadway, which dates back to 1915, is in Tama. The vertical concrete joists holding up the bridge spell out "Lincoln Highway."

Tama County Historical Museum (641-484-6767), 200 North Broadway, Toledo. Open 1–4:30 Tues.–Sat. Feb.–mid-Dec. Free. The county historical museum is housed in the 1870s jailhouse and is well worth a visit. Tama's history is unique as it has the only Native American settlement in the state, and the museum is full of artifacts from the tribe and the pioneer settlers. On the grounds is a preserved 1800s Bohemian cabin.

✷ To Do

Wallace Winery (319-643-3000; www.wallacewine.com), 5305 Herbert Hoover Highway Northeast, West Branch. Open daily, but call or visit their Web site for hours and events. Dr. Ed Wallace knows wine country, and when he moved to Iowa in 1992, he had a vision for producing top-notch wines with grapes cultivated for their cold-weather hardiness. Using Midwestern grapes, the winery produced European-style wines that pair well with a variety of foods. The tasting room is an airy, wood-filled space set in the heart of the rolling vineyard.

Bloomsbury Farm (319-446-7667; www.bloomsburyfarm.com), 3260 69th Street, Atkins. Open Sept.–Oct. 9–6 Mon.–Sat., 12–5 Sun., and by appointment. Admission: $9 per person weekends, $7 weekdays. A combination farm and amusement park, kids can find all sorts of "agritainment." Visit in late autumn for corn mazes, a haunted barn, and the largest pumpkin patch in the region. Barnyard buddies, including fainting goats, are around for petting, along with hayrack rides, pedal cars, and various cannons for shooting pumpkins and corn cobs. The farm has café and snack-counter refreshments.

Ushers Ferry Historic Village (319-286-5763; www.ufhv.org), 5925 Seminole Valley Trail Northeast, Cedar Rapids. Open daily June–Aug., weekends May–Oct. Admission: $4 adults, $2 children. Walk through history in a turn-of-the-20th-century village. Take a self-guided tour in the role of a member of the Usher family dressed up in period clothing. Visitors don't just see the village of a town hall, ice-cream shop, and smokehouse, they experience it as the villagers once did. The village also produces a number of special events each season, such as spooky, Halloween-time performances of the works of Edgar Allen Poe and candlelight tours during the holidays.

Science Station and IMAX Dome Theatre (319-363-4629; www.sciencestation.org), 427 First Street SE, Cedar Rapids. Call for hours and admission as they were still being revised after the flood of 2008. The science center is a not-for-profit institution, built in a historic 1917 fire station; the poles remain on the main floor. The center offers more than 100 exhibits, many of them interactive and imaginative. Exhibits designed for children explore dinosaurs, physics, and environmental sciences. The IMAX theater shows educational films on its massive dome and seats 170 people.

Cedar Rapids Ice Arena (319-398-0100; www.cricearena.com), 1100 Rockford Road Southwest, Cedar Rapids. Public skating from 1:30–5 Mon.–Tues., 1:30–4:45 Wed., 1:30–5 Thurs.–Fri., and 6:45–8:45 Thurs. evenings, 7–9 Fri. evenings, 2–5 and 7–9 Sat., 2–4 Sun. Public skating and skate rental are available at the local ice arena, home of the Cedar Rapids Rough Riders hockey team.

Planet X Fun Center (319-294-2237; www.planetxfuncenter.com), 200 Collins Road Northeast, Cedar Rapids. Open 11–10 Mon.–Thurs., 11–12 Sat.–Sun., 12–9 Sun. Prices vary by activity, but range from $2.75–$7 per person. With an epic indoor miniature-golf course, rock-climbing wall, laser tag, and bumper cars, this facility is way more than an arcade, though the video games, space bikes, and batting cages are all here, too. A full-service food counter dishes up snacks, so hungry astro warriors can continue vanquishing those pesky aliens.

THE MESKWAKI PEOPLE

A tribe of Algonquian origin sometimes known as the Fox, the Meskwaki were living in the area of the Louisiana Purchase and fought against the French in the "Fox Wars" from 1701–1742. The French, fed up with the resistance, ordered the tribe's complete extermination, but they allied with the Sauk in 1735 to fend off Europeans and other tribes. After the Black Hawk War of 1832, both tribes were relocated to a reservation in Kansas. Many Meskwaki later returned to Iowa, where others had remained. In 1857 the tribe purchased 80 acres in Tama County from the state; due to their private ownership of the land, they lived outside the jurisdiction of federal rule, with more independence than tribes on other reservations. Today, the federal government has jurisdiction over the settlement, and the Meskwaki tribe continues to thrive in central Iowa. On the only Native American settlement in the state, they built a massive resort and casino as a source of income. The Meskwaki are proud that with perseverance they outlasted the French monarchy that once sought their demise.

Sutliff Cider Company (319-455-4093; www.sutliffcider.com), 382 Sutliff Road, Lisbon. Call to arrange a tour and tasting. Locally grown apples are pressed and fermented in oak barrels in two historic farm buildings. Near the unincorporated town of Sutliff, this hard-cider company is a lovely, off-the-beaten-path spot to try an alternative to beer and wine.

Meskwaki Resort and Casino (641-484-2108; www.meskwaki.com), open 24 hours a day. The Meskwaki were the only Native American tribe to remain in the state and not go to a reservation. They bargained with the newly created state of Iowa to form a settlement in Tama County, and as many other tribes have done, they opened a casino. It features a 500-seat bingo hall, reel and video slot machines, live Keno, poker, and table games along with the live entertainment. Also on site are a 400-room hotel, a campground, and a variety of dining options available in the casino complex.

John Ernest Vineyard and Winery (641-484-8048; www.johnernestvineyard.com), 3291 N Avenue, Tama. Open May–Aug. 11–6 daily, Sep.–Apr. 11–6 Tues.–Sun. On a beautiful vineyard in Tama County, this winery creates both a selection of native Iowa wines and California-style varieties. Bottles are very reasonably priced. Stop in for a tasting, or see their Web site for special events and live music throughout the summer.

✷ Green Space

Wapsipinicon State Park (319-462-2761; www.iowadnr.com/parks), 21301 CR E34, Anamosa. Open during daylight hours. Located along the river, called the "Wapsie" by locals, the park is known for rocky bluffs, crevices, and caves. The bowl-shaped Horse Thief Cave was once thought to shelter a pair of criminals who used it for a campsite. The Ice Cave remains cool year-round. The park is a great place for picnics, and it is crisscrossed with a network of multiuse and bicycle trails. The river is famous for catfish, spring crappies, bullheads, and smallmouth bass, especially near the mouth of Dutch Creek. The park also includes a nine-hole golf course run by the **Wapsipinicon Country Club** (319-462-3930). Camping is available at 26 shady sites; 14 have electrical hook-ups. Campsites from $11–$16.

Indian Creek Nature Center (319-362-0664; www.indiancreeknaturecenter.org), 6665 Otis Road Southeast, Cedar Rapids. Open 9–4 weekdays, 11–4 Sat., trails open during daylight hours. At the heart of this 240-acre nature preserve is an interpretive center in a restored 1930s dairy barn. Exhibits in the barn provide insight into the wildlife outside, with natural habitats, a beehive, and an observation tower. Trails take visitors through restored prairie lands, oak and hickory savannas, floodplains, and wetlands. A Vermont-style maple-sugar house, butterfly garden, and a frog pond make for excellent picnicking backdrops.

Wickiup Hill Outdoor Learning Center (319-892-6485; www.linncountyparks.com), 10260 Morris Hills Road, Toddville. Open 9–12 Wed., 1–4 Thurs.–Fri. and Sun., 10–4 Sat. See a full-size replica of a wickiup and a Native American family in this 10,000-square-foot learning center. In the Hall of Habitats, visitors can learn about Iowa's diverse ecosystems, and then step outside to see them from a network of trails, natural habitats, and a bird-watching area.

Ellis Park (319-286-5760), 2000 Ellis Boulevard Northwest, Cedar Rapids. Open during daylight hours. More than 400 acres of parkland along the Cedar River includes everything from a formal Shakespeare Garden, with specific plantings from his writings, to sand volleyball courts to an 18-hole golf course and a boathouse harbor. The park also has boat ramps, water-skiing facilities, baseball diamonds, tennis courts, and a pool.

Palisades-Kepler State Park (319-895-6039; www.iowadnr.com/parks), 700 Kepler Drive, Mount Vernon. Open during daylight hours. Some of the best hiking in the state—more than 6 miles' worth, in fact—can be done in this 840-acre park just east of Mount Vernon. The park, along the Cedar River, offers great fishing and boating; and a modern campground that has 44 campsites, 26 with electricity, four rental cabins, and a bath-and-shower facility. It also features the **Palisades-Dows Observatory** (www.cedar-astronomers.org/paldows), located on the south side of the park. The observatory houses several permanently mounted telescopes used by regional scientists to explore the heavens. Visitors are welcome to see the learning center and attend monthly Public Observing Nights. Visit their Web site for more information. Cabins $50, campsites from $11–$16.

✷ Where to Stay

HOTELS AND MOTELS There are many hotels and motels in the Linn County area offering a range of accommodations and fitting every price range, but there are few independent establishments. Additionally, many of the high-rise chain hotels in downtown Cedar Rapids experienced flooding in the summer of 2008, though all planned on reopening.

Aspen Inn (319-363-9999; www.aspeninncr.com), 3233 Southridge Drive Southwest, Cedar Rapids. Close to I-380, this convenient hotel offers guests laundry facilities, wireless Internet, refrigerators, and microwaves in every room, along with a free continental breakfast and an indoor pool. Rooms from $35–$125.

Mount Vernon Motel (319-895-4039; www.mountvernonmotel.com), 353 US 30 West, Mount Vernon. This small roadside motel has 14 basic rooms with queen beds and cable television. Microwaves and refrigerators are available by request. Rooms from $40–$80.

The Blue Inn (319-465-6116), 250 North Main Street, US 151, Monticello. This small-town motel offers 27 spacious and individually decorated rooms, some with large whirlpool tubs. The motel offers Internet, an indoor pool, a 24-hour fitness facility, and a fun restaurant and bar on site. A free continental breakfast is served in the morning. Campers are welcome to pitch their tents out back. Rooms from $49–$99.

Designer Inn and Suites (641-484-5678; www.designerinnandsuites.com), 403 US 30 West, Toledo. Don't be fooled by the outside of this generic-looking side-of-the-highway hotel. Inside, lovers dive into romantic splendor in seven theme rooms. Live out prehistoric-man fantasies in the Crystal Cave, or shiver into the hot tub in the Northern Lights. Other fantasy rooms are the Heart's Delight, with heart-shaped bed and whirlpool tub; the Arabian Nights room; the Rain Forest room; the Roman Retreat; and Aces Wild, a Las Vegas room. The hotel also offers more traditional rooms with cable television, an indoor pool, and a free hot breakfast. Fantasy rooms from $110–$220, regular rooms from $60–$70.

BED & BREAKFASTS **Historic Lincoln Hotel** (563-941-7563; www.lincolnhoteliowa.com), 408 Main

Street, Lowden. Stay in one of five guest rooms in this historic and award-winning hotel. Built in 1915 to house workers on the Pacific and Northwestern Railroads, the hotel is both relaxing and elegant. Room (including breakfast) from $80–$100.

The Inn Springville (319-854-7097; www.innspringville.com), 258 Broadway, Springville. Two peaceful guest rooms await visitors in a historic two-story brick building. The suite features three rooms with a king-size bed and a whirlpool tub. Rooms (including breakfast) from $65–$105.

Grant Wood Country Bed & Breakfast (www.grantwoodcountry bedandbreakfast.com), 13982 Rock Road, Monticello. Doug and Micaela Monk created a two-room suite—bedroom, private lounge, and full bathroom plus an 8-foot by 30-foot second-story deck—on the second floor of their home located on a country farm outside Monticello in art-inspiring countryside. Stroll through the orchard, visit the dairy farm across the street, or just relax on the front porch. In the evening unwind with refreshments and the comforts of a sleigh bed in your room. Breakfasts are both hearty and healthy. Room $80.

Belmont Hill Victorian (319-366-1343; www.belmonthill.com), 1525 Cherokee Drive Northwest, Cedar Rapids. The three guest rooms in this 1890s Victorian home have been renovated to comfortable elegance. They are richly appointed but not stuffy, and each includes a private bathroom. The grounds are lovely, as are the gourmet breakfasts. Wireless Internet is available. Rooms from $95–$145.

Victorian Lace (319-377-5138; www.victorian-lace-iowa.com), 300 East Main Street, Marion. The summer kitchen of this turn-of-the-20th-century Victorian house was converted into the delightful private Summer Kitchen Suite, which is filled with antiques, quilts, and a whirlpool tub for two. A second suite, the charmingly decorated Tree-Top Holiday Suite, is on the third floor of the house and also offers a whirlpool tub for two as well as a fabulous view of downtown Cedar Rapids. In-season, guests can use the heated swimming pool and enjoy romantic treats such as chocolates, sparkling wine, and dessert. Rooms (including breakfast) from $70–160.

Brackett House (319-895-4425; www.cornellcollege.edu/brackett-house), 418 Second Street Southwest, Mount Vernon. Guests can stay on the Cornell College campus in an 1877 home with four guest rooms with private baths. Depending on room size, from two to six guests can be accommodated in each. The house offers wireless Internet, cable television, and a continental breakfast. Rooms from $65–$80.

Lion and Lamb (319-472-5086; www.lionlamb.com), 913 Second Avenue, Vinton. This truly unique bed & breakfast is housed in a decadent 1892 Victorian "painted lady" home, which features seven fireplaces with ornate mantles, pocket doors, stained-glass windows, and an oak-paneled great hall. The six guest rooms are appropriate for the house's period without being over the top. The B&B is known for mystery dinners and weekends. Room (including breakfast) range from $65–$175.

CAMPING **Wapsipinicon State Park** (319-462-2761; www.iowadnr.com/parks), 21301 CR E34, Anamosa. The park has 26 sites, about half with electrical hook-ups and a modern shower facility. Campsites from $11–$16. See *Green Space.*

Palisades-Kepler State Park See *Green Space.*

✱ Where to Eat

DINING OUT **Daly Creek Winery and Bistro** (319-462-2525; www.dalycreekwinery.com), 106 North Ford Street, Anamosa. Open for lunch and dinner Tues.–Sat., lunch Sun. in summer. Tasting room and gift shop open 11– Tues.–Sat. and 11–3 Sun. Nestled in the quiet streets of downtown Anamosa is a winery creating both California- and Iowa-style wines, so wine lovers can find a Cabernet Sauvignon and a "Penitentiary Red," named for the local prison. Browse the gift shop while sampling; then head into the adjoining bistro for casual fine dining. The chef creates dishes with Iowa beef, chicken, and pasta, along with rich appetizers and desserts. Everything from pizza to baked tilapia is on the menu. In-season take a bottle of the wine outside to an ivy-strewn garden for a relaxing afternoon drink. $$–$$$

Champagne's Supper Club (319-643-5511; www.cajunfoodandspices.com), 313 East Main Street, West Branch. Open for lunch and dinner Wed.–Sat., lunch buffet Sun. Savor the flavors of the bayou in this Cajun restaurant. With massive seafood platters, classic Louisiana cuisine, and authentic po'boys, Champagne's is a spicy alternative to most Iowa restaurants. The menu also includes more standard middle-America fare of steaks, chicken, and salads. $$–$$$

Winifred's (319-364-6125; www.winifredsrestaurant.com), 3847 First Avenue Southeast, Cedar Rapids. Open for dinner Mon.–Sat. Soft candlelight and mirrored walls make a meal at Winifred's a romantic dining experience. The restaurant has offered Cedar Rapids high-quality American cuisine for 22 years. The menu includes chef-prepared steaks, seafood, and elegant dinner salads. $$$

Ced-Rel Supper Club (319-446-7300; www.cedrelsupperclub.com), 11909 16th Avenue Southwest, US 30 West, Cedar Rapids. Open for dinner Tues.–Sat. This classic American steakhouse is an institution in Cedar Rapids. They've been serving up delicious cuts of beef, ribs, and chicken for years. The menu ranges from elegant mussels in white wine sauce to down-home fried chicken livers, and everything is prepared with care. $$$.

🍸 **Blend** (319-366-3364; www.blendcr.com), 221 Second Avenue Southeast, Cedar Rapids. Open for lunch and dinner Mon.–Sat. This upscale American-fusion restaurant serves an innovative and artistic array of dishes. The restaurant includes a large lounge for enjoying the cocktail hour and wine-tasting dinners drawing on the interesting wine list. Lunch $$, Dinner $$–$$$.

Daniel Arthur's (319-362-9340; www.danielarthurs.net), 821 Third Avenue Southeast, Cedar Rapids. Open for lunch Mon.–Fri. and dinner Mon.–Sat. This upscale yet intimate restaurant is located in a late-19th-century mansion. With two lounges, outdoor seating, and three fireplaces, the staff works to create a dining "experience" rather than just an evening out. The menu is nothing but class, from the excellent cuts of beef tenderloin to the seafood flown in from both coasts. Vegetarian options change nightly, and the Caesar salad for two is prepared at table. The wine list is varied and reasonably priced. $$$

🍸 **Vino's Restaurant** and **R. G. Books Lounge** (319-363-7550; www.vinosristorante.com), 3611 First Street Southeast, Cedar Rapids. Open for dinner Mon.–Sat. While much of the menu in this elegant restaurant is Italian—fettuccine, chickens Napoli and Marsala—the seafood entrées really shine: the crab, avocado, and smoked-salmon Napoleon; the seafood salad with avocado and mango; and the bouillabaisse are almost too beautiful to eat. The adjoining bar serves martinis and other fancy cocktails in a classy, book-lined lounge. $$–$$$

✪ **Lincoln Café** (319-895-4041; www.foodisimportant.com), 117 First Street Northwest, Mount Vernon. Open for lunch and dinner Mon.–Sat., brunch Sun. The Lincoln Café is simply one of the best restaurants in Iowa. The menu—which changes both according to what is in season and according to the chef's whims—features eclectic, innovative, and delicious dishes. Perhaps the coca-rubbed elk with rock shrimp-butternut ceviche or the grilled Niman Ranch pork tenderloins with vanilla fingerling potatoes will suit your fancy. The café does not have a liquor license, but they do run a wine bar just down the street, so diners can BYO, and the small corkage fee is waived entirely when the bottles come from their bar. Brunch is served à la carte with such choices as eggs, challah French toast, and biscuits and gravy. The restaurant fills up quickly, and they don't take reservations, but diners are welcome to wait in the restaurant's wine bar down the street. The dress code is casual. $$$

EATING OUT **General Store Pub** (319-462-4399), CR X28, Stone City. Open for dinner Thurs., for lunch and dinner Fri.–Sun. (For details, see the Grant Wood sidebar in *To See*.) $

Betty's Hometown Café (319-462-6199), 300 West Main Street, Anamosa. Open early for breakfast, lunch, and dinner Tues.–Fri. and breakfast and lunch on Sat. Betty's is a cozy little diner with two personalities. The dining room in the front is open and filled with antiques, but farther back in the restaurant, diners can enjoy their strawberry croissant French toast and breakfast burritos in a room that looks like a Victorian parlor. This is a super-friendly, family-run restaurant with great home-cooked food, daily hot specials for breakfast and lunch, and some fancier entrées for dinner, such as raspberry-basil chicken and salmon patties. $$

Knuckleheads (319-462-2724), 205 West Main Street, Anamosa. Open daily for lunch, dinner, and bar time. After a visit to the National Motorcycle Museum, it's only natural to head to the local biker bar. Here it is, and it *is* a biker bar. Don't give the guys at the pool table the stink eye while drinking beers and eating burgers, tenderloins, and fried appetizers. $

Herb N' Lou's (319-643-7373), 105 North Downey, West Branch. Open daily for lunch and dinner. Housed in a historic building, this pizzeria dishes up tasty pies—like the impressive "Herb Heaper"—and spirits in a friendly atmosphere. $$

Zio Johno's (319-362-9667; www.ziojohnos.net), 1125 First Avenue Southeast, Cedar Rapids. Open daily for lunch and dinner. "Uncle" Johno opened his spaghetti house across the street from Coe College in 1984 with the humble goal of creating a delicious and inexpensive Italian restaurant. The business grew from the little shop on First Avenue to a small chain of locations around Cedar Rapids and Iowa City. All the food is made fresh daily, and the spaghetti and meatballs is both inexpensive and outstanding, but the best part of the meal is the bread—garlicky, buttery, and just slightly sweet. Eat in or dine out in the original restaurant, or try one of the scrubbed-up locations around the region. $

Y **The Lighthouse Inn** (319-362-3467; www.crlighthouseinn.com), 6905 Mount Vernon Road Southeast, Cedar

Rapids. Open for dinner Tues.–Sat. Established in 1912 as a roadside inn between Cedar Rapids and Iowa City, the Lighthouse became a place for Chicago gangsters to hide out during Prohibition. Both Al Capone and John Dillinger were rumored to have eaten at the inn. Today, less-notorious diners can enjoy the old-school American-style food: steaks, chicken, shrimp, and pasta dishes. The menu features both prime rib and breaded "salsa cheese." On the weekends hear live jazz in the adjoining bar. $$–$$$

Vernon Inn a.k.a. **The Greek Place** (319-366-7817), 2663 Mount Vernon Road Southeast, Cedar Rapids. Open for lunch Mon.–Fri., dinner daily. The Vernon Inn is a Cedar Rapids cult favorite. Sample traditional Greek dishes like moussaka, gyros, and dolmathes as well as American-style steak, chicken, and seafood dishes. Outside seating is available, and the atmosphere could be described as casual fine dining. $$

Dublin City Pub (319-247-7180), 315 Second Avenue Southeast, Cedar Rapids. Open daily for dinner and bar hours. Relax with a beer in this Irish pub. The dining is casual pub fare (burgers, chicken, sandwiches, and the like) well done and reasonably priced. The crowd is friendly and varied. In the afternoon young professionals relax after work, but as the evening wears on, the crowd gets younger and livelier. $$

Starlite Room (319-362-4759), 3300 First Avenue Northeast, Cedar Rapids. Open daily for lunch and dinner. The Starlite Room is the kind of dive people either love or hate. There are bar flies, mega-touch machines, and televisions playing sports. The Starlite is known for its burgers (the Super-Burger, the Six-Dollar-Burger, and the Whopper), greasy tenderloins, and French fries—basically, food that goes great with beer. That being said, it is a Cedar Rapids institution with a following. $

Croissant Du Jour (319-363-7767; www.croissantdujour.biz), 3531 Mount Vernon Road Southeast, Cedar Rapids. Bakery open 6:30–4 Mon.–Sat., Lunch served 11–2. Light French-style sandwiches, quiches, salads, and soups are served for lunch. "Le Vegetarian" sandwich is particularly good: cold grilled eggplant, zucchini, squash, and brie with a vinaigrette. French pastries and cheesecakes can be ordered à la carte the rest of the day. $–$$

Zoey's Pizzeria (319-377-2840; www.zoeyspizza.com), 690 10th Street, Marion. Open for lunch Mon.–Sat., dinner daily. People can't help but rave about this locally owned pizza joint. The only complaint most locals have is how crowded the place gets, but that is only a testament to the delicious pies. The taco pizza is exceptional, but put any of the fresh toppings in the deep-dish Chicago crust for pure pizza bliss. The New York–style thin crust is also exceptional. $$

Baxa's Store and Tavern (319-624-2204; www.sutliffbridge.com), 5546 130th Street Northeast, Lisbon. Open daily for lunch and dinner. Enjoy views of the river from the one-hundred-year-old Sutliff Bridge, an iron bridge constructed at the local ferry site. Then stop in at Baxa's for a burger and a beer. Visitors can pin a signed dollar bill to the ceiling to add to the growing fortune (last estimate, about $3,500).

Skillet Café and Bakery (319-895-8540; www.skilletcafe.net), 101 East First Street, Mount Vernon. Open for breakfast and lunch Mon.–Sat., and dinner Thurs. Fran and Cherie serve up made-to-order pastas, sandwiches, salads, and side dishes at this owner-operated café in downtown Mount

Vernon. What started out as a breakfast spot quickly grew into offering lunches. Daily specials are hearty and fresh and can be enjoyed in the restored dining room with exposed brick, original tin ceilings, and wooden floors or outside on the back deck. $–$$

Bluegrass Café (641-484-3040; www.bluegrasscafetama.com), 200 West Third Street, Tama. Open for breakfast and lunch Tues.–Sat., and dinner when bands are scheduled to play. This friendly neighborhood restaurant is dedicated to preserving and promoting bluegrass music in Iowa. Lunch and band-night dinners are served buffet-style and feature home cooking. Bands play most Saturday nights. $–$$

COFFEE, TREATS, AND MARKETS

Witte's End Coffee House (319-573-2277), 630 Tenth Street, Marion. Open 7–2 Mon.–Sat. Enjoy exceptional espresso drinks in a cozy Italian-style café in downtown Marion. In a bright, historic building full of art, books, and the warmth of a fireplace, the talented baristas prepare fresh coffee, tea, smoothies, and more. The pastries are delicious, as well.

Tatyanna's Kitchen (319-551-3553), 224 First Street West, Mount Vernon. Open 7–3 Mon.–Fri., lunch served 11–2. Fresh-baked international pastries, cookies, and cakes are served all day in this quaint Russian-style bakery. They also serve lunch; stop in for soups, salads, and sandwiches. Lunch $$

Big Creek Market (319-895-8393; www.mybigcreekmarket.com), 100 First Street Southwest, Mount Vernon. Open Mon. 8–5, Tues., Wed., Fri. 9–5, Thurs. 9–7, Sat. 9–5, Sun. 12–4. Shop for natural and organic foods, local produce, and dairy products, or grab an afternoon pick-me-up of gourmet coffee and baked goods. Healthy lunches and sandwiches are also available.

Fuel (319-895-8429), 103 First Street Northeast, Mount Vernon. Open 7–5 Tues.–Sat. and 8–4 Sun. A funky, independent coffee shop that features craft-roasted beans, espresso beverages, and delicious baked goods. Wireless Internet is available, and the coffee shop shares space with **Nest**, a unique shop of art, antiques, and gifts.

Anamosa Dairy Barn (319-462-2553), 204 West Main Street, Anamosa. Open 11–5 Mon.–Thurs., 11–10 Fri.–Sat., 11–4 Sun. Stop in this simple downtown ice-cream shop and lunch counter for frozen treats, burgers, hot dogs, and more. $

✷ Drinking Establishments

Hot Shots (319-462-9913), 101 East Main Street, Anamosa. Open daily for bar hours; breakfast served at last call Friday nights. Done in a decor of black and bright-orange flames, Hot Shots is a new neighborhood bar with a biker attitude. The shots in the name are the alcoholic kind, not the billiards kind, and they are strong.

✷ Entertainment

MUSIC, THEATER, AND FILM

Hardacre Theater (563-886-2455), 112 East Fifth Street, Tipton. This classic small-town movie theater has been showing first-run films since it opened in 1917. Today it also hosts the **Hardacre Film Festival** every August. There's usually just one showing a night. Call for showtime and admission.

Legion Arts and CSPS (319-364-1580; www.legionarts.org), 1103 Third Street Southeast, Cedar Rapids. Open 11–6 Wed.–Sun. Located in the landmark building near downtown Cedar

Rapids, Legion Arts is a nonprofit arts organization. With a blend of visual arts, music, theater, and film, CSPS is a combination gallery, museum, studio, and performance venue with the goal of supporting young artists, cutting-edge arts, and community development.

Cedar Rapids Symphony Orchestra (319-366-8203; www.crsymphony.org), Paramount Theatre, 123 Third Avenue Southeast, Cedar Rapids. Call or visit their Web site for schedule and box office information. The area's first municipal symphony started in 1921 with 48 volunteer musicians. Today the orchestra performs classical music and the popular "Follies" events.

Theatre Cedar Rapids (316-366-8591; www.theatrecr.org), Iowa Theatre Building, 102 Third Street Southeast, Cedar Rapids. Call or visit their Web site for schedule and box office information. See one of the longest-running community-theater groups in Iowa perform popular shows and musicals.

Bijou Movie Theater (319-895-6165; www.bijouonline.com), 123 Second Street Southwest, Mount Vernon. Call or visit the Web site for movie schedule. Tickets are just $4, and the snacks are very inexpensive! The single screen of this independent movie theater shows an eclectic variety of films about 4–6 weeks after their release nationwide. Before each show a staff member introduces the film and announces the coming attractions.

SPORTS EVENTS **Cedar Rapids Kernels** (319-363-3887; www.kernals.com), Veterans Memorial Stadium, 950 Rockford Road Southwest, Cedar Rapids. Call or visit the Web site for game schedule and ticket information. Watch minor-league baseball at the Dale and Thomas Popcorn Field. Lucky baseball fans can watch the game from the "home-run hot tub" in left field.

Cedar Rapids Rough Riders Hockey Team (319-247-0340; www.roughridershockey.com), 1100 Rockford Road Southwest, Cedar Rapids. Season runs Sept.–Apr. Box office and store open 9–5 Mon.–Fri. This junior-league, USHL Tier One team offers a busy hockey season for up-and-coming players.

Hawkeye Downs Speedway (319-365-8656; www.hawkeyedownsspeedway.com), 4400 Sixth Street Southwest, Cedar Rapids. Call or visit their Web site for schedule and box office information. With ½-mile and ¼-mile paved tracks, Hawkeye attracts race fans from all over the Midwest for auto racing, go-kart racing, and bingo.

✷ Selective Shopping

Herbert Hoover Eastern National Bookstore (319-643-5301; www.nps.gov/heho), 201 Parkside Drive. Open 9–5 daily. Shop for Hoover memorabilia along with books and souvenirs in this not-for-profit bookstore that supports national parks.

Cats 'N Dogs Antiques (319-643-5505), 103 North Downey, West Branch. Open 9–5 Mon.–Sat. Shop for furniture, lighting, and country Americana among the handpicked selection in this downtown shop.

Campbell Steele Gallery (319-373-9211; www.campbellsteele.com), 1064 Seventh Avenue, Marion. Open Thurs.–Sat. 10–6; all other times by appointment—just give them a day's notice. A constantly fresh look at fine art from regional, national, and international artists in a range of venues welcomes travelers to admire the work and shop.

BIKERS AND BISCOTTI: ANAMOSA

Anamosa is a city with dual personalities. As with many small towns, Main Street is lined with antiques shops. There is a casual yet elegant winery and bistro in the heart of town, and the café is as friendly and warm as a neighbor's kitchen. Jazz music is piped from unseen speakers on the street, but competing with the jazz music is the rumble and throb of the hundreds of motorcycles that cruise the streets every day. Bikers and their leather-wearing babes visit the **National Motorcycle Museum** and **J&P Cycles** Harley-Davidson showroom, and patronize the many rough-and-tumble biker bars. The city claims world-renowned artist Grant Wood as its native son, but one of the major tourist attractions is the museum in the state penitentiary. It can be a travel-book cliché, but in Anamosa there really is something for everyone.

Czech Feather and Down Co. (319-364-0952; www.czechfeatherdownco.com), 72 16th Avenue Southeast, Cedar Rapids. Open 9:30–5 Mon.–Fri., 10–3:30 Sat. Shop for handcrafted feather beds, comforters, and pillows made in a fine European tradition, and stay warm on those cold Iowa nights.

Iowa Popcorn Company (319-377-7551), 720 10th Street, Marion. Take home corn in its tastiest forms—popped and flavored with caramel, cheese, butter, and almonds and pecans—plus other treats and gifts.

Liberty Iron Works (319-895-9353; www.l-i-w.com/), 117 First Avenue Northwest, Mount Vernon. Open 9–5 Tues.–Fri., 10–4 Sat., and by appointment. Don't be surprised to see a giant iron T. Rex outside the gallery of sculptor Dale J. Merrill. He specializes in large-scale works in iron. If the dinosaurs are too big for your living room, he also creates furniture and garden pieces.

Art from the Farm (641-328-4159; www.artfromthefarm.com), 103 East High Street, Toledo. Open 9:30–4 Mon.–Fri. and weekends by chance. "When the flag is flying, we're here," Vicki Ferriss says of her studio. Inside she crafts sculptures and garden art out of used barbed wire.

IOWA AND POWESHIEK COUNTIES

Iowa County is known for the Amana Colonies, Iowa's best-known tourist attraction. The colonies are seven villages with a touch of Old-World-German flavor. They were established by a utopian community called True Inspirationalists who lived a modest and communal life. The streets of the villages are lined with shops whose names end in the word *haus* and are filled with homemade products hearkening back to a simpler time. The colonies are also known for restaurants serving big, family-style home-cooked meals. Many wineries and Iowa's oldest brewery call the colonies home, as well. To the south of the Amana Colonies are the Tanger Factory Outlets, a modern, discount name-brand shopping complex.

Horace Greeley offered Josiah B. Grinnell the immortal advice, "Go West, young man." The young man did, eventually settling in Iowa. Grinnell's legacy lives on in a beautiful small town and a prestigious liberal-arts college that both bear his name. Since then Grinnell College has educated some of America's finest, including jazz musician Herbie Hancock.

GUIDANCE **Amana Colonies Visitors Center** (1-800-579-2294; www.amanacolonies.com), 622 46th Avenue, Amana. Open 9–5 Mon.–Sat., 11–5 Sun. The visitors center is located in a restored corn crib. Inside are travel information on the colonies and the surrounding area, wireless Internet, and public restrooms.

Grinnell Convention and Visitors Bureau (641-236-6555; www.grinnellchamber.org), 833 Fourth Avenue, Grinnell. Open during business hours. Call or visit the Web site to learn more about this small but diverse community.

GETTING THERE *By car:* **I-80** runs east-west through Iowa and Poweshiek Counties making easy access to the attractions of the region. The Amana Colonies are on a loop near **US 6,** and the region is close to Cedar Rapids and Iowa City.

MEDICAL EMERGENCY Call **911**.

Grinnell Regional Medical Center (641-236-7511; www.grmc.us), 210 Fourth Avenue, Grinnell. Twenty-four hour emergency care available.

INTERNET ACCESS The city of Grinnell is full of coffee shops with free wireless Internet access. Rest stops along **I-80** also offer free wireless Internet.

✱ To See

Amana Arts Guild Gallery (319-622-3678; www.amanaartsguild.com), 1210 G Street, High Amana. Open May–Sept. 10:30–4:30 Mon., Wed.–Sat.; 11–4 Sun.; and Oct. weekends. Free. A gallery and workshop space housed in a former church building connects the arts and crafts of the past with the artisans of today. Visitors can see a variety of arts created in the colonies in the traditional way, from blacksmith work to delicate lace, from sculptures carved from gourds to rag dolls. Along with quilts, pottery, needlework, and woodwork are fine arts such as paintings, etchings, and prints. The gallery also offers a busy season of workshops for locals and a large sales shop.

Amana Heritage Museum (319-622-3567; www.amanaheritage.org), 4310 220th Trail, Amana. Open Apr.–Oct. 10–5 Mon.–Sat., 12–4 Sun.; year-round 10–5 Sat. Admission: $7 adults, children free; admission to all the heritage sites can be combined for $8 per person. Through exhibits in three buildings, travelers can explore the unique heritage of the Amana Colonies. Often confused with the Amish people, who also settled in the region, the people of Amana lived a communal and highly religious lifestyle. Special exhibits illustrate how the Amana colonists dealt with a changing world. The combination of video presentations and actual artifacts illustrates how they lived and thrived in this system of devoted life. The Amana Heritage Society also runs several other museums and heritage spots, including the church, kitchen, general store, and agricultural site.

Amana Community Church Museum (319-622-3567; www.amanaheritage.org), 4210 V Street, Homestead. Open June–Sept. 10–5 Mon.–Sat. Admission: $4 adults, children free; admission to all the heritage sites and museum can be combined for $8. The people of the Amana colonies were a deeply spiritual people and worshipped as a community in their churches. Docents explain the beliefs and practices of the church.

Communal Kitchen and Cooper Shop Museum (319-622-3567; www.amanaheritage.org), 1003 26th Avenue, Middle Amana. Open June–Sept. 10–5 Mon.–Sat. Admission: $4 adults, children free; admission to all the heritage sites and museum can be combined for $8. One of the unique features of early life in the Amana colonies was the cooking. Rather than families' preparing meals individually, the colonists built communal kitchens in which food was prepared and shared among the entire settlement. The kitchen museum showcases the cooking and dining rooms as they were when the communal system came to an end in 1932. Across the way is the shop where the barrels were made.

Homestead Store Museum (319-622-3567; www.amanaheritage.org), 4430 V Street, Homestead. Open June–Sept. 10–5 Mon.–Sat.; $4 adults, children free, admission to all the heritage sites and museum can be combined for $8. The colonists built the town of Homestead to link their communities throughout the valley with the railroads that brought commerce and travel to Iowa. Exhibits demonstrate the role of commerce in a community that was based on the principle of sharing.

Communal Agriculture Museum (319-622-3567; www.amanaheritage.org), 505 P Street, South Amana. Open 10–5 Sat. May–Sept. Admission: $4 adults, children free; admission to all the heritage sites and museum can be combined for $8. The Amana colonists practiced a unique form of communal agriculture. Displays in this restored 1860 barn include authentic tools, artifacts, and photographs.

IDENTITY CRISIS: NO, THE AMANA COLONIES ARE NOT AMISH

Travelers won't see any buggies on the streets of Homestead, or men in old-fashioned wool clothes and big black hats working the fields around Middle Amana. It is a common misconception, even among Iowans, that the Amana Colonies—an old-fashioned community of seven villages—were settled by the Amish. Not true. While there are many Amish and Mennonite settlements in the region—Kalona, for example, has a large population of Amish families—the Amana Colonies were settled by a quite different group.

In the 19th century a German carpenter declared himself a prophet and, as prophets are wont to do, established a following called the True Inspirationalists. In 1842 he immigrated to Buffalo, New York, with four of his followers in the hopes of establishing a utopian community. In 1843 some 800 more people followed him from the Old World, bringing millworks and factory equipment with them from Germany and creating the Ebenezer Society.

The True Inspirationalists were a conservative group. They spoke only in German, avoided idle conversation, and believed in plain clothes and homes. Soon, though, the city of Buffalo and its libertine morality began to encroach on the borders of Ebenezer. Before their beliefs could be tainted, the Inspirationalists moved.

In 1855 the TIs purchased 26,000 acres in the Iowa River Valley. They packed up their mills and factories once again and settled in Iowa. Amana, which means "believe faithfully," was the settlement's first village.

The Amana colonists led a communal life. Families had their own homes but ate in communal kitchens. Labor was assigned by the church elders, and if the society needed a worker with specialized training—a dentist, perhaps—the elders chose an individual to be sent out to receive education. Colonists were buried not with their families but according to when they died.

The colony, with its socialist principles, was successful until the Great Depression. The combined forces of economic setbacks and the push for more individual freedom changed the fundamental principles of the colonies. In 1932 the members voted to become capitalists. The colonies became a corporation, and the members were given stocks according to their age and status in the community.

Nowadays the Amana Colonies are one of Iowa's most popular and longest-lasting tourist attractions. Visitors stroll the streets reminiscent of the Old World, eat delicious home-style German-American cuisine, and browse the shops for homemade jams, wines, lace, and fine furniture. The colonies do an excellent job of capitalizing on their communal history to attract and delight visitors today.

High Amana General Store (319-622-3232; www.amanaheritage.org), 1308 G Street, High Amana. Open Apr.–Oct. 10–5 Mon.–Sat., 12–5 Sun.; Nov.–Dec. 10–5 Sat. Free. Located halfway between the shop and the museum, the village store appears much as it did one hundred years ago. It was established in 1857 and has remained virtually the same since then, with the tin ceiling, wooden floors, and display cases still intact. The shelves are stocked with historic novelty items, such as Beeman's gum and Amana jam and jellies, along with toys, books, soaps, and gifts.

Amana Woolen Mill (319-622-3432; www.amanawoolenmill.com), 800 48th Avenue, Amana. Open May–Oct. 8–6 Mon.–Sat., 11–5 Sun.; Nov.–Apr. 9–5 Mon.–Sat., 12–5 Sun. Free. Traditionally, woolen goods produced in the mill provided for the communities needs and were also sold to outsiders. The looms run during the week. Take a self-guided tour through Iowa's only operating woolen mill. Then shop the collection of blankets, sweaters, and gifts. The mill shop also sells substandard woolen goods, so as long as mismatched mittens are not a problem for you, the deals are great.

Pioneer Heritage Museum (319-642-7018), 675 East South Street, Marengo. Open June–mid-Sept. 1–4 Thurs.–Sat. or by appointment. Free. In a museum complex spanning half a city block, visitors can learn about the life of the early settlers through the buildings they lived and worked in: an 1861 log house, an 1856 cabin, a 1930s filling station, and a Rock Island Railroad depot.

Faulconer Gallery (641-269-4660; www.grinnell.edu/faulconergallery), Bucksbaum Center for the Arts, Grinnell College, Grinnell. Open June–Aug. 11–5 daily, 11–8 Thurs.; Sept.–May 12–5 Sun.–Wed., 10–8 Thurs.–Sat; guided tours by appointment. With more than 7,000 square feet of exhibition space, this gallery designed by architect Cesar Pelli is at the heart of the fine-arts building on the Grinnell Campus. The gallery showcases rotating exhibits of cutting-edge contemporary art and has a fine permanent collection, as well. Student art is also on display.

Louis Sullivan Jewel Box Bank (641-236-1626; www.grinnelliowa.gov/Sullivan Bank), Fourth Avenue and Broad Street, Grinnell. Open 9–5 Mon.–Fri., 10–4 Sat., 1–4 Sun. Louis Sullivan, father of the skyscraper and student of the Prairie School, designed the "jewel box" bank in Grinnell. The bank features an ornate portal over the front door, stained glass, and sleek lines. (Other similarly bejeweled banks can be seen across the Midwest.) The bank is open for public viewing. Grinnell is also home to another building inspired by Frank Lloyd Wright, the **Ricker House**, designed by Walter Burley Griffin, which can be viewed in an online tour at: web.grinnell.edu/faulconergallery/rickerhouse/virtual_tour.

Grinnell Historical Museum (641-236-3732; www.grinnellmuseum.org), 1125 Broad Street, Grinnell. Open Sept.–May Sat.–Sun. 2–4, June–Aug. 2–4 Tues.–Sun. Free; not wheelchair accessible. Docent-led tours take visitors through the house and discuss life in the early 20th century. The home is filled with period furniture, antiques, and memorabilia.

Brooklyn, Community of Flags (641-522-5300; www.brooklyniowa.com), 138 Jackson Street, Brooklyn. Brooklyn's claim to fame is that it is bedecked with flags, from the Old Glory in the state park to the nations-of-the-world flags lining Jackson Street. But besides the flags, there is not much to see in Brooklyn.

✱ To Do

Amana Colonies Heritage Trail (www.amanacolonies.com); the driving tour links the seven Amana Colonies along US 151, US 6, and IA 220. Signs lead the way and guide visitors to the sights of each colony. The trail winds through the picturesque Iowa River Valley and crosses the Millrace Canal built by the colonists. Drivers will see agricultural landscapes, Amana farms, prairie, and wetlands. A CD titled *The Amana Colonies by Car: An Audio Driving Tour* can be purchased at the visitors center and many of the local shops; it offers an entertaining narrative with history and music to go along with the drive.

Amana Colonies Golf Club (1-800-383-3636; www.amanagolfcourse.com), 451 27th Avenue, Amana. The course is a championship 18-hole course that is open to the public. The course designers embraced the lovely natural landscape of rolling hills, white oak stands, and streams and ponds. Five tee sets are available for all skill levels. Lessons and a driving range are available. The clubhouse offers dining, and on-course overnight accommodations are available.

Wasserbahn Waterpark (319-668-1175; www.wasserbahn.com), Holiday Inn, I-80 at exit 225, Amana. Open 9–9 Mon.–Thurs., 8–10 Fri.–Sat., 8–9 Sun. Admission: $16 adults, $10 children. It is hard to imagine how the modest settlers of the Amana colony would have reacted to a water park. They believed unnecessary chit-chat would lead to sinfulness, and yet their hardy, pioneer spirit inspired all of this roadside aquatic fun. With two massive waterslides, a 160-gallon dump bucket, a rope climb, geysers, waterfalls, and vortex pools, this hotel waterpark could be the perfect reward for kids who were forced to spend a day patiently shopping for antiques.

Grinnell Recreational Trail (641-236-6311; www.imaginegrinnell.com), runs on 6 miles of hard surface from the town of Grinnell to **Rock Creek State Park** in Jasper County (see Part 1). The trail, which starts at 11th Street and Sunset, makes for a great day trip for bicyclists to the park's beaches and fishing spots.

BREWERIES AND WINERIES The Amana Colonies have several options for travelers who want to taste the fermented fruits of Iowa's fields. Several wineries and wine shops line the streets of the colonies, and Iowa's oldest microbrewery, **Millstream,** is located in Amana. For many years the syrupy-sweet fruit blends (boysenberry, strawberry, dandelion) of Amana have defined the taste of Iowa wines. Recently there has been a resurgence of grape growing and winemaking in the state, with vintners producing clean, crisp California-style wines, and the palate for Iowa wines has become more sophisticated. At the same time the wineries around the Amana Colonies continue to hold the torch for these unique and ever-popular styles.

✪ **Millstream Brewing Co.** (319-622-3672; www.millstreambrewing.com), Amana. The hours for this brewery change every month, so it's best to visit the Web site or call ahead; in June they are open Mon.–Wed. 9–5, Thurs. 9–6, Sun. 9–6. Millstream is Iowa's oldest microbrewery. In a quaint clapboard building, it creates a fine selection of brews, from a traditional German pilsner to a special "Maifest" brew. The brewery offers samples and sells beer by the glass and growler to be enjoyed in the beer garden or taken home. They produce an assortment of nonalcoholic drinks, as well, such as Old Time Root Beer and a tasty Black Cherry soda. Millstream also hosts the popular Festival of Iowa Beers every summer.

SAMPLE THE BREWS IN THE TASTING ROOM AT THE MILLSTREAM BREWING CO. IN AMANA

Ackerman Winery (319-622-3379; www.ackermanwinery.com), 4406 220th Trail, Amana. Open 9–5 Mon.–Sat., 10–5 Sun. The Ackermans opened their winery in 1956 selling homemade grape and rhubarb wines. Since then, this winery—the oldest in Iowa—has produced wines from a variety of fruits, including apricot, blueberry, and cherry among others. They also produce a small variety of grape wines like Riesling and Merlot. The winery offers a self-guided tour, tastings, and gifts and accessories.

Ehrle Brothers Winery and Alma's Washhouse (319-622-3241), 4105 V Street, Homestead. Open daily 9–6 in summer, limited hours in winter. Named for one of the colony's original wineries, the Ehrle Brothers offer a variety of fruit and grape wines in their shop along with pottery items. Sample the wine, and browse a selection of gifts and accessories. They also offer their wine in a crock jug that is perfect for hoedowns.

Collectively Iowa (319-622-3698; www.collectivelyiowa.com), 4515 F Street, Amana. Open Mon.–Sat. 9–6, Sun. 11–5. Step into either the "wine gallery" or the "coffee studio" to experience a new way of sampling both products. With a collection of wines from around the state, insight into the winemaking process, tastings of diverse grape and fruit varieties, and occasionally, meeting the winemakers themselves, the gallery is a clearinghouse for this up-and-coming industry. In the coffee studio, sample custom-roasted coffee, learn about and sample different styles, and shop for coffee that is matched to individual tastes.

Fireside Winery (319-662-4222; www.firesidewinery.com), 1755 P Avenue, Marengo. Open 10–6 Wed., Thurs., Sat.; 10–9 Fri.; 12–5 Sun. With a vineyard packed with native Iowa grapes, Fireside creates award-winning wines in varieties to suit every taste and a beauty spot in which to enjoy them. Both the patio and lawn feature fire rings.

✱ Where to Stay

HOTELS AND MOTELS Die Heimat Country Inn (319-622-3937; www.dheimat.com), 4430 V Street, Amana. This small motel is located in the old stagecoach stop that also served as an inn for travelers in the 1850s; later it served as a communal kitchen for the colonists. Eighteen quaint country accommodations await visitors, with canopy beds, quilts, and antique furniture. With the room comes a buffet-style breakfast of toast, eggs, coffee, and more. Rooms from $60–$90.

Zuber's Homestead Hotel (316-622-3911; www.zubershomesteadhotel.com), 2206 44th Avenue, Homestead. Each of the 15 guest rooms in this historic hotel are decorated in a tasteful prairie theme. Accommodations range from standard rooms to deluxe suites, and all include modern conveniences such as flat-screen televisions and wireless Internet, which, along with breakfast, complement the Old-World charm. Rooms from $84–$115.

Heritage Inn Amana Colonies Hotel and Suites (319-668-2700; www.heritageinnamanacolonies.com), I-80 at exit 225, 2185 U Avenue, Amana Colonies. Located near the restaurants and shops of the Amana Colonies, these 61 basic motel rooms and suites offer accommodations with an indoor pool and cable television. Rooms from $55–$150.

Amana Colonies Guest House Motel (319-622-3599), 4712 220th Trail, Amana. This comfortable motel near the attractions of Amana offers accommodations with air-conditioning and cable television. Rooms from $45–$75.

BED & BREAKFASTS Carriage House (641-236-7520), 1133 Broad Street, Grinnell. This award-winning bed & breakfast offers six beautiful guest rooms in a stunning Victorian home. The house includes a front porch and fireplaces in the common rooms, and the breakfast is homemade and excellent. Rooms from $60–$80.

Marsh House (641-236-0132), 833 East Street, Grinnell. This 1892 Victorian home underwent an extensive restoration that highlighted the beautiful interior and architectural features. Three guest rooms offer down bedding, robes, and complimentary beverages. A full breakfast is served. Rooms from $60–$85.

English Valley (641-623-3663; www.englishvalleybnb.com), 4459 135th Street, Montezuma. Set in the picturesque splendor of the English River Valley, a 1930s barn offers two guest rooms and three suites that range from the rustic bunkroom to the modern and elegant master suite. The breakfasts are hearty and gracious. Trail and corral rides are also available on their friendly horses. Rooms from $75–$125.

Annie's Garden Guest House (319-622-6854; www.timeandtides.com), 716 46th Avenue, Amana. The three guest rooms in this 1893 B&B are cozy retreats from the outside world. Beds are covered in down comforters and canopies, and the rooms are filled with light. A large common space offers guests the opportunity to relax in front of the television or the fire. Rooms (including breakfast) $85.

Rawson's Bed & Breakfast (319-622-6035; www.iowacity.com/amanas/rawson/), 4424 V Street, Homestead. Within this charming brick home is an award-winning B&B with seven guest rooms. The accommodations range from comfortable queen-size bedrooms to suites with fireplaces and whirlpool tubs. The inn also offers guests an in-ground swimming pool, cable television, and a full breakfast. Rooms from $69–$119.

Village Guest Suites (319-622-6690; www.villageguestsuite.com), 4312 F Street, Amana. For travelers who need a little more space, this restored 1865 Amana home offers three suites—one mini, two large. The amenities include continental breakfast and custom floral arrangements. Guests also enjoy the back porch and beautiful grounds. Rooms from $55–$90.

CAMPING **Amana Colonies RV Park** (319-622-7616; www.amanarv park.com), 39 38th Avenue, Amana. Open mid-Apr.–Nov. Located between Amana and Middle Amana, this 60-acre RV park plays host to a fleet of recreational vehicles. Some 450 sites are available with electricity and water, showers, free wireless Internet, a store, and a laundry facility. Pets welcome. Campsites from $12–$28.

✷ Where to Eat

DINING OUT **Colony Inn Restaurant** (319-622-3030;), 741 47th Avenue, Amana. Open daily for breakfast, lunch, and dinner. Since 1935, when the restaurant was built to serve locals and workers, the Colony Inn has been dishing out big, family-style meals. These meals are traditional Iowa and German dishes—schnitzels, fried chicken, and the like—but the real treat here is the breakfast. The pancakes are thin, crispy, and sizzling with butter. Try them rolled up with the homemade strawberry jam, alongside amazing English muffin toast, thick cuts of sausage, and unending bacon. $$

Ox Yoke Inn (319-622-3441; www .oxyokeinn.com), 4420 220th Trail, Amana. Open for breakfast, lunch, and dinner Mon.–Sat, brunch Sun. Sample all of the flavors of the Midwestern table: ham, roast beef, fried chicken, potatoes, cole slaw, and, of course, pie at this comfortable family restaurant. All the meals are hearty, generous, and delicious, if not diet friendly. The restaurant also has a location on I-80 (1-877-668-1443) at exit 225, for travelers who don't have time to drive into the heart of the colonies. $$

The Ronneburg Restaurant (319-622-3641; www.ronneburgrestaurant .com), 4408 220th Trail, Amana. Open for breakfast, lunch, and dinner. The Ronneburg serves its American and German dishes out of one of the Amana Colonies' original kitchens. Try the sauerbraten and Wiener schnitzel for a taste of the old country. The restaurant serves family style but also offers smaller, lighter portions for less-ambitious eaters. $$

P.H.A.T. Daddy's (319-642-7332; www.phat-daddys.com), 1185 Court Avenue, Marengo. Open for dinner Tues.–Sat., brunch Sun. A name like Phat Daddy's calls to mind soul food, not elegant cuts of beef tenderloin and Chilean sea bass, but despite the cognitive dissonance—or perhaps

EATING FAMILY STYLE

Dining in the Amana Colonies is a bit different from elsewhere in the state. At many restaurants, food is served family style. Instead of individuals ordering their own dishes, everyone shares communal platters and bowls: take what you want, pass the rest around the table, and when the platters are empty, the waitstaff brings more. Most restaurants offer a traditional plate-style service, as well, but to truly take in the spirit of the colonies—and a lot of stick-to-the-ribs home cooking—be prepared to pass the potatoes.

because of it—the food at this funky eatery is the bomb. In the lounge, called Phool's Gold, drinkers will find martinis, ice-cream drinks, and live music. $$–$$$

EATING OUT **Amana Stone Hearth Bakery** (319-622-7640; www.amanabakeries.com), 4522 220th Trail, Amana. Open daily for breakfast and lunch. Enjoy sandwiches made with fresh bread, pastries, pies, and soups in this casual restaurant. Summertime, enjoy ice cream on the outdoor patio. $–$$

Y **Depot Crossing Restaurant** (641-236-6886; www.depotcrossingrestaurant.com), 1014 Third Avenue, Grinnell. Open for lunch and dinner Mon.–Fri., dinner Sat. Located in the historic Grinnell train depot, this relatively new restaurant offers high-quality down-home cooking. The menu ranges from homemade onion rings to a chicken cordon bleu sandwich to spinach salad with bacon dressing, along with steaks, burgers, seafood specials, and vegetarian choices. To drink there is an array of imported, domestic, and craft beers. $$

West Side Family Restaurant (641-236-5939; www.westsidefamilyrestaurant.com), 229 West Sixth Avenue, Grinnell. Open for breakfast and lunch Mon.–Sun., breakfast, lunch, and dinner Tues.–Sat. This Grinnell tradition serves great hot sandwiches, such as hot turkey and a fantastic tenderloin, plus breakfast all day and slow-cooked prime rib on the weekends. $$

Comeback Café (641-236-0176), 804 Commercial Street, Grinnell. Open daily for breakfast and lunch. Located in the restored warehouse district, this casual café offers light lunches of sandwiches, salads, and wraps plus great coffee drinks. $–$$

Jimbo's Pizza (641-236-7849; www.grinnellpizza.com), 908 Main Street, Grinnell. Open daily for dinner. No college town is complete without a pizza joint, and this one dishes up great New York–style thin-crust pizzas nightly. The specials include unique toppings such as ricotta cheese and Buffalo chicken. Jimbo's also operates the **No Name Deli** (641-236-7849), which specializes in sandwiches and nachos during the afternoon at 829 Broad Street.

COFFEE AND TREATS **Hahn's Bakery** (319-622-3439), 2510 J Avenue, Middle Amana. Open 7–until sold out Apr.–Oct. Tues.–Sat.; Nov., Dec., and Mar. Wed. and Sat. Homemade bread and pastries are baked in one of the colonies' original hearth ovens. The wholesome breads and goodies sell out fast, so try this shop early for a morning treat. When the goods are gone, the shop closes.

The Chocolate Haus (319-622-3025; www.chocolatehaus.com), 4521 220th Trail, Amana. Open 10–5 Mon.–Sat., 11–5 Sun. The smell of chocolate pours out the door of this candy and coffee shop. Visitors can watch through a viewing glass as candy is made the old-fashioned way, sip gourmet coffee and smoothies, and take home cheesecake and candies.

Java Lounge (319-668-2263; www.iowajavalounge.com), 523 Court Street, Williamsburg. Open 6:30–4 Mon.–Fri., 7:30–2 Sat. The coffeehouse is just like a very nice living room—except instead of hogging the remote, your hosts serve up fresh coffee, tasty espresso drinks, and pastries and light lunches.

Saint's Rest Coffee House (641-236-6014), 919 Broad Street, Grinnell. Open 6:30–8 Mon.–Thurs., 6:30–5 Fri. and Sat., 9–5 Sun. This comfortable coffee shop is a nice place to relax and recaffeinate. It serves appetizing beverages and delicious cinnamon rolls and shares seating with an adjoining deli.

Grinnell Coffee Company (641-236-0710), 915 Main Street, Grinnell. Open 7–6 Mon.–Fri., 8–6 Sat., 9–5 Sun. The coffee is freshly roasted, and light lunches and snacks of sandwiches and pastries are offered throughout the day. The coffee comes directly from farmers in Peru. Free wireless Internet access is available.

✷ Entertainment

Old Creamery Theatre Company (319-622-6034; www.oldcreamery.com), 39 38th Avenue, Amana. Call or visit their Web site for box office information. The Old Creamery Theatre Company is one of the oldest and the best professional theaters in the state. With a wide array of professional actors and a hectic schedule of plays, musicals, and seasonal events, there is always something entertaining happening in Amana.

✷ Selective Shopping

The Amana Colonies blend their unique cultural heritage with an abundance of shopping. Some of the historical sites are working stores, and many of the stores incorporate historical artifacts and practices into their shops. Even the restaurants are not excluded. Like that authentic strawberry jam on your toast? Here's a jar to take home. Think of it as "shoppertainment." All the colonies are packed with antiques stores, toy stores, galleries, wine shops, and specialty shops; most, it seems, with *haus* or *shoppe* tacked onto the name. There are too many to list here, but they are easy to find and enjoyable to browse. Iowa County is also famous for the Tanger Outlets at the Williamsburg exit, just west of the colonies, which offers an entirely different shopping experience.

Henry's Village Market (319-622-3931), 4125 V Street, Homestead. Open Mon., Wed.–Fri. 10–6, Sat. 9–6, Sun. 9–4, closed Tues. Shop an abundance of Amana and European products from chocolates and pastries to locally made cheese and bratwurst.

Amana Meat Shop and Smokehouse (1-800-373-6328; www.amanameatshop.com), 4513 F Street, Amana. Open Mon.–Fri. 10–5, Sat. 9–5, Sun. 10–4. The smokehouse in the Village of Amana opened in 1855. Since then it has been producing quality meats: ham, bacon, steaks, and sausage. (Tip: Don't say no to a sample of the smoked ham.) Visitors can also shop for cheese, jam, and other specialty foods.

West Amana Wood Shop (319-622-3315), 618 Eighth Avenue, West Amana. Open 9–4:30 Mon.–Sat. Standing 11 feet tall and weighing in at 670 pounds, the world's largest walnut rocking chair is located in this woodshop and gallery. Climb aboard for some front-porch sitting of epic portions; then browse the shop for unique wooden gifts and furniture.

Lehm Books and Gifts (319-622-6447; www.lehmbooksandgifts.com), 4536 220th Trail, Amana. Open daily 10–5. This bookstore offers a large selection of books about the colonies and Iowa, along with children's and cookbooks, gifts, figurines, and much more.

Tanger Outlets (319-668-2885; www.tangeroutlet.com), Williamsburg. Open 9–9 Mon.–Sat., 10–6 Sun. With more than 50 stores and merchandise direct from the manufacturers, Tanger Outlets is a popular destination for savvy shoppers. The outdoor mall includes a diverse range of name-brand stores from Calvin Klein to Nike, along with casual franchise dining and a public bathroom.

IOWA CITY AREA

On July 4, 1838, Congress gave Iowa territorial status, with Robert Lucas serving as the first territorial governor. He selected Iowa City as the territorial capital due to its then-central location plus its proximity to the Iowa River. The gold-domed limestone building now known as the Old Capitol was designed by John Francis Rague and today stands at the heart of the University of Iowa campus. Lucas served out his term as governor and then built a modest brick home on a farm called Plum Grove that was then outside the city. In 1844 politicians held the state's constitutional convention in Iowa City, but President James K. Polk did not admit Iowa into the union as the 29th state until 1846. The capital was eventually relocated to Des Moines in 1876, but Iowa City had already established itself as an important hub.

Iowa City's claim to fame is the University of Iowa, the state's largest academic institution that is home to both the Big Ten Iowa Hawkeyes and the world-renowned University of Iowa Hospitals and Clinics. The university was established in 1855 with 124 students in attendance; today its colleges instruct more than 30,000 thousand students. Among the points of pride is the Iowa Writer's Workshop, considered by many the best creative-writing program in the country, which draws famous and up-and-coming authors to its classrooms.

The diversity of the university fostered a worldly atmosphere and lively arts scene in the city. Downtown Iowa City—centered around the meandering pedestrian mall, or "Ped Mall"—is full of ethnic restaurants, fine dining, high-end shopping, and world-class art. The town is also the best place in Iowa—and one of the best places in the Midwest—to hear a variety of live music. Of course, there are also all sorts of college-town good times in the many bars and nightclubs in the area.

Just south and east of Iowa City is one of the largest communities of Amish people in the state, where road signs warn drivers to WATCH FOR HORSE-DRAWN VEHICLES. The Amish are a modest, private people who value their traditions. Because they believe that technology, including things like electricity, divides families and communities, they avoid the trappings of modern society. They use windmills to pump water, wood-burning stoves for heat, horses and buggies to get around, and farm with horse-drawn equipment. The Amish are an active part of the Kalona community, and the quality of their cooking and produce is known and respected throughout the Midwest. In the city of Kalona, visitors will find both the heritage and traditions of the Amish and elegant restaurants and lots of antiques and furniture shops.

GUIDANCE **Iowa City/Coralville Area Convention and Visitors Bureau** (319-337-6592; www.iowacitycoralville.org), 900 First Avenue, Coralville. Open during business hours. Call or visit their Web site for information on the city, day trips in the region, and maps.

Kalona Area Chamber of Commerce (319-656-2660; www.kalonachamber.com), 514 B Avenue, Kalona. Open during business hours. Visit the Kalona Chamber Web site for an up-to-date travel guide and links to the many attractions of Amish Country. The barns around Washington County are decorated with 8-by-8-foot quilt blocks of the traditional folk art. For more information, visit www.barnquiltsiowa.com.

Riverside Area Community Club (319-648-5475; www.trekfest.com). Call or visit their Web site to learn about the future birthplace of Captain James T. Kirk, the casino and resort, and area restaurants.

GETTING THERE *By Car:* Iowa City is conveniently located on **I-80,** 110 miles from Des Moines and 60 miles from the Quad Cities.

By Air: Most travelers fly into Cedar Rapids, 30 miles north of Iowa City, through the **Eastern Iowa Airport** (319-362-8336; www.eiairport.org), 2121 Arthur Collins Parkway Southwest, Cedar Rapids, which offers connecting flights to major airports.

Quad Cities International Airport (309-764-9621; www.qcairport.com), 2200 69th Avenue. Moline is about 60 miles from Iowa City and offers connections to major airports in the region.

GETTING AROUND *By Bus:* The **Cambus** (319-335-8633; www.uiowa.edu/cambus) is the University's free bus service, which runs throughout the day and night around campus. The **Iowa City Transit** runs buses around the city during the day Mon.–Sat.

MEDICAL EMERGENCY Call **911**.

University of Iowa Hospitals and Clinics (319-384-8442; www.uihealthcare.com), 200 Hawkins Drive, Iowa City. Consistently ranked one of the best hospitals in America, the University of Iowa hospital is an academic and research facility that attracts some of the best health-care professionals in the world. Emergency and walk-in clinics.

INTERNET ACCESS/PUBLIC LIBRARY Most coffee shops, bookstores, restaurants, and lodging offer free wireless Internet access.

Iowa City Public Library (319-356-5200; www.icpl.org), 123 South Linn Street, Iowa City. Open 10–9 Mon.–Thurs., 10–6 Fri.–Sat., 1–5 Sun. Wireless Internet access and public computers are available in this gorgeous modern library in downtown Iowa City.

✷ To See

Old Capitol Museum 319-335-0548; www.uiowa.edu/~oldcap) 21 Old Capitol Pentacrest, Iowa City. Open 10–3 Tues., Wed., Fri., 10–5 Thurs. and Sat., 1–5 Sun. Free. In the center of the University of Iowa Campus is the old capitol building,

THE "OLD CAPITOL" OF IOWA IS NOW AT THE HEART OF THE UNIVERSITY OF IOWA, IOWA CITY

limestone topped with a gleaming gold dome. Take a tour through the building, which has been restored to reflect the period when it served as Iowa's first state building. The galleries include permanent and rotating exhibits on Iowa's culture and history.

University of Iowa Museum of Natural History (319-335-0480; www.uiowa.edu.edu/nathist), Clinton and Jefferson Streets, Iowa City. Open Aug.–May 10–3 Tues., Wed., Fri., 10–5 Thurs. and Sat., 1–5 Sun.; June–July 10–5 Tues.–Sat., 1–5 Sun. Free. "Mammal Hall" is an old-school natural-history museum with glass cases full of the university's collection of mounted animals, from the least weasel to the whale—or at least its bones. The Hageboeck Hall of Birds includes more than 1,000 specimens. Other exhibits celebrate Iowa's geological, cultural, and ecological history. Look out especially for the mysterious and fascinating giant sloth; a model in Mammal Hall offers information about the Giant Sloth excavation project, taking place near Shenandoah to extract the bones of the very sleepy elephant-sized ancient creature.

Plum Grove Historic Home (319-351-5738; www.iowahistory.org/sites), 1030 Carroll Street, Iowa City. Open Memorial Day–Oct. 31, 1–5 Wed.–Sun. This seven-room redbrick Greek revival was built by Iowa's first territorial governor, Robert Lucas, and his wife, Friendly. Their home has been restored to the period of 1844–1853 with antique furnishings.

✪ **MacBride Raptor Center** (319-398-5495; www.recserv.uiowa.edu/programs/raptor), CR F28, Coralville Lake. Open Apr.–Oct. 6 AM–8 PM daily, Nov.–Mar. 9 AM–6 PM daily; guided tours available. Free. The MacBride Raptor Center was designed to preserve Iowa's birds of prey through rescue and rehabilitation. A large "flight cage" allows the majestic birds to fly in a controlled area before they are released back into the wild. Some birds cannot be released due to permanent disability. The public is welcome to visit these birds, learn about their habitats, and also enjoy the hiking and cross-country skiing area around the center.

University of Iowa Museum of Art (319-335-1727; www.uiowa.edu/uima), 150 North Riverside Drive, Iowa City. Open 12–5 Wed., Sat., Sun., 12–9 Thurs.–Fri. Free. The art museum experienced dramatic flooding in 2008. Please call or visit the Web site to find relocated exhibits and learn about the planned reopening. Luckily, the famous Jackson Pollack *Mural*, which the artist created for Peggy Guggenheim, was spared damage during the flooding. The museum's permanent collection of more than twelve thousand pieces includes a great deal of interesting contemporary art, print work, ceramics, and metal, along with a comprehensive and globally renowned selection of art from African cultures. The museum also features traveling exhibitions from national artists.

Iowa Children's Museum (319-625-6255; www.theicm.org), Coral Ridge Mall, Coralville. 10–6 Tues.–Thurs., Fri.–Sat. 10–8, 11–6 Sun. Admission: $6 per person. With 28,000 square feet of interactive exhibits for children, visitors should plan to spend an entire afternoon at this museum. The exhibits are hands-on and educational. Children can romp through a mini-village and try out the roles of grown-ups in the City Works hospital, pizza parlor, and post office. They can also learn about construction, interact with dinosaurs, and enter a puppet kingdom. An education gift and toy store is on site.

University of Iowa Athletics Hall of Fame and Museum (319-384-1031; www.hawkeyesports.com), 2425 Prairie Meadow Drive, Iowa City. Open 11–6 Mon.–Fri., 10–6 Sat., 12–5 Sun. Admission: $4 adults. Hawkeye fans can interact with exhibits and see video clips from more than one hundred years of athletic excellence. The crown jewel of the museum is Nile Kinnick's 1939 Heisman Trophy. Other exhibits celebrate the Big Ten traditions of Iowa softball, baseball, wrestling, swimming, and more. To learn more about Hawkeye sporting events, visit their Web site.

Antique Car Museum of Iowa (319-354-3310; www.antiquecarmuseumofiowa.org), 860 Quarry Road, Coralville. Open 10–5 Tues.–Sat., 1–5 Sun. Admission: $2 suggested donation. More than 65 antique and vintage cars that date from the 1890s to the 1990s are on display. The museum also features a replica Skelly gas station and a model-train exhibit. The displays on models and technology rotate often and are especially insightful for car enthusiasts.

Kalona Historical Village (319-656-2519), Kalona. Open Apr.–Nov.1, 9–4 Mon.–Sat.; Nov. 2–Mar. 31, 11–3 Mon.–Sat. Admission: $7 adults for full tour, $4 adults for inside-only tour. In the heart of Amish country, at the old train depot, is this historical village that lets tourists walk through buildings the way they once were. The buildings include the 1842 Snyder log house with a rope bed and cast-iron stove, a loom house, a washhouse, an Amish "grandpa" house, a country store, a post office, and a unique "straw college." In Miller's buggy barn, the vehicles built on the main floor were then hoisted upstairs for a paint job. The museums feature displays on Amish textile making and rocks and minerals, a Mennonite museum, and early mechanical equipment such as a telephone switchboard and newspaper office.

Dumont's Museum of Dreamworld Collectibles (641-622-2592; www.dumontmuseum.com), 20545 255th Street, Sigourney. Open May–Oct. 10–5 Sat.–Sun. or by appointment. Admission: $8 per person. It all started with an innocent Roy Rogers collection, but soon Lyle and Helen Dumont were collecting everything: restored tractors, Barbie dolls and memorabilia, horse-drawn equipment, dishes, model trains, and lots more. The museum is a testament to the quirky passions of Iowans, and the 24,000-square-foot "museum" preserves their collections for future generations. What future generations will do with the vast, sundry effects is unclear.

✷ To Do

Devonian Fossil Gorge and **Coralville Lake** (319-338-3543; www.coralvillelake.org), 3.5 miles north of I-80 at exit 244 on Dubuque Street, Iowa City. Open during daylight hours. Coralville Lake is named for the fossils deposited in the area by the ancient seas that once covered the land. In 1993 high floodwater created a gorge below the Coralville Reservoir and exposed fossil deposits in the limestone created 375 million years ago. Signs and a detailed brochure found at the lake's visitors center offer more insight into this fascinating geological history. Coralville Lake also offers 8,400 acres of land and lake for recreation: hiking, fishing, boating, and camping.

Coral Ridge Ice Arena (319-354-7870; www.coralridgeice.com), 1451 Coral Ridge Avenue, Coralville. Open daily, but call or visit the Web site for a schedule. Tickets: $6 per person, $2 for rental skates. Inside Coral Ridge Mall is an NHL-size indoor ice-skating rink. It hosts public skating, hockey leagues, broomball, skating lessons, and Rock'n'Skate parties. Ice-skate rental is available.

Robert A. Lee Community Recreation Center (319-356-5100; www.icgov.org), 220 South Gilbert Street, Iowa City. Open 6 AM–10 PM Mon.–Sat., 1 PM–9 PM Sun.; hours vary for some activities, so call or check their Web site. Iowa City's downtown recreation center offers free access to a lap swimming pool, gymnasium, game room, racquetball courts ($3.50 per courts), weight rooms, potter's studio, and darkroom. Anyone can use the community exercise facility, and equipment is available for check out.

Finkbine Golf Course (319-335-9246; www.finkbine.com), 1400 Melrose Avenue, Iowa City. Open 7 AM–sunset Apr.–Dec.; call for tee times. Operated by the University of Iowa Athletics Department, Finkbine, a gorgeous collegiate course, was home to the 1991–1993 PGA Nike Tour Hawkeye Open and is listed in *Golf Digest*'s "Places to Play." The 18-hole championship course ranges over rolling green hills, through wooded areas, and past a 6-acre lake.

Riverside Casino and Golf Resort (1-877-677-3456; www.riversidecasinoandresort.com), 3184 IA 22, Riverside. Open 24 hours daily. This resort brings the complete Las Vegas experience to rural Iowa. More than a thousand slot machines, 14 poker tables, black jack, craps, and roulette are among the gambling options. Hungry gamblers can choose from four restaurants ranging from fast food to fine dining or relax in the salon and spa. The event center attracts live shows and entertainment; the resort also includes a golf course and 200-room hotel.

Amish By-Ways Tour (319-656-2660; www.kalonaiowa.org), 514 B Avenue, Kalona. Open Apr. 15–Oct. 31; tours at 11 and 1 Mon.–Sat. Tickets: $12 adults, $6 children. See more than just the buggy on the road. This van tour offers an in-depth look into Amish life. Guides take travelers through back roads to see Amish homes, schools, farms, and gardens. Tour stops include Amish farmer's markets, cheese factories, and country stores.

BIKE RENTAL **Bike Library** (www.bikelibrary.org), 100 East College Street, Iowa City. Open 10–1 Sat. and by chance. Volunteer mechanics accept donated bikes in good running order, fix them up, and then check them out just like a library. Their goal is to get more people on bikes. Prospective cyclists fill out a checkout form, pay a deposit, and get the bike for up to six months along with helmets and safety equipment. All kinds of bikes are available for both kids and adults. The library also sponsors a bikers' breakfast on the first Friday of each month from 7:30–9:30, and they rent out bench space and tools for $5 per hour on Saturday afternoons. Pick up a bike while in Iowa City and enjoy the area's bike trails, freedom from downtown parking woes, and hipster street cred. Bikes are "checked out" for a deposit of anywhere from $10–$80.

World of Bikes (319-351-8337; www.worldofbikes.com), 723 South Gilbert Street, Iowa City. Open Apr.–Sept. 10–7 Mon.–Fri., 10–5 Sat., 12–4 Sun. Rentals $20–$50 per day. Road bikes, mountain bikes, hybrids, and tandem bikes, along with helmets, can be rented at this independently owned bike shop. The store also offers bike and accessory sales, service, and repair.

✱ Green Space

City Park (319-356-5100; www.icgov.org), Park Road, Iowa City. Just north of downtown Iowa City and the arts campus, City Park hugs a curve in the Iowa River. The park extends from a wooded bluff down to the water's edge and includes playgrounds for every interest. The park's Carnival Rides, open 12–8 during the summer, include a carousel, a small-scale train, and kiddie rides. The park also includes an off-leash dog park and skate park on the other side of the river. Boat ramps, picnic areas, and ball fields fill the rest of the park. A replica of Shakespeare's Globe Theater hosts an annual festival in the Bard's honor, and the **Iowa Women's Music Festival** fills the trees with music and dancing each summer.

Hickory Hill Park (319-356-5100; www.icgov.org), Davenport and Seventh Streets, Iowa City. Open during daylight hours. Hickory Hill Park is a wooded haven in the heart of the city. Countless undeveloped trails cross the park for hikers, cross-country skiers, and dog walkers. The heavily wooded hills, cascading overlooks, and babbling streams make the park a great place to reconnect with nature.

Lake MacBride State Park (319-624-2200; www.iowadnr.com/parks), 3525 IA 382 Northeast, Solon. Open during daylight hours. Before the Iowa River flows into Iowa City, it first passes through Lake MacBride. The lake, circled with deeply forested hills, offers fishing, sailing, camping, and swimming. Visitors can rent canoes, kayaks, and paddleboats in the summer as well as the Civilian Conservation Corps–built stone lodge. Multiuse trails meander through the park and run from the entrance to the nearby city of Solon. The park has two campgrounds, one modern and one primitive. (See also *Where To Stay: Campgrounds.*) The park also borders on **Coralville Lake,** a large, man-made reservoir that offers boating, swimming, and fishing, as well.

F. W. Kent Park (319-645-2315; www.johnson-county.com/conservation), US 6, 3 miles west of Tiffin. Open during daylight hours. The "gem" of the Johnson County park system is this park featuring a large lake that both fishers and swimmers enjoy. Around the lake are picnic areas and shelters, multiuse trails, and a modern campground. (See *Where To Stay: Campgrounds.*) Campsites from $10–$15.

✱ Where to Stay

HOTELS AND MOTELS

hotelVetro (319-337-4058; www.hotelvetro.com), 201 South Linn Street, Iowa City. The hotelVetro is a ridiculously chic place to stay during a visit to Iowa City. Located in the Plaza Tower—a 14-story high rise that features fine dining, luxury shopping, and upscale housing—the hotel rises up above the downtown Ped Mall. The 56 studios are spacious, modern, and full of slick decor and ultramodern architecture and furnishings. Each room has plasma televisions and high-speed Internet access, along with kitchenettes, oversized bathrooms, and fine linens. Rooms from $140–$300.

Iowa House Hotel (319-335-3513; www.iowahousehotel.com), 121 Iowa Memorial Union, Iowa City. With 96 rooms on the second and third floors of the student union, and right in the center of campus, guests will find the comfort of queen-size beds, river views, and free parking. The hotel offers also offers suites, complimentary breakfast, a workshop facility, and Internet access. Rooms from $80–$190.

Alexis Park Inn & Suites (319-337-8665; www.alexisparkinn.com), 1165 South Riverside Drive, Iowa City. The Alexis Park Inn styles its 30 suites in an aviation theme. The rooms are more like apartments and include full kitchens (some have whirlpool tubs); they come with a full breakfast delivered to the door. Outside, the hotel has an in-ground pool. Rooms from $50–200.

Pull'r Inn Motel (319-656-3611; www.pullrinn.com), 110 E Avenue, IA 1 & IA 22, Kalona. The 29 rooms at this motel offer free wireless Internet, kids stay for free, cable television, and free continental breakfast. Rooms from $60–$67.

Hawkeye Motel (319-653-7510; www.hawkeyemotel.com), 1320 West Madison, Washington. The furnishings of the 22 accommodations call to mind 1970s rec rooms, but the spacious single, double, and triple rooms of this inexpensive motel are both clean and well appointed. Internet access available. Rooms from $42–$53.

Riverside Casino and Golf Resort See *To Do*.

BED & BREAKFASTS **The Golden Haug** (319-354-4284; www.goldenhaug.com), 517 East Washington Street, Iowa City. Located upstairs from the city's premier vegetarian restaurant is a bed & breakfast that honors the swine. The six guest rooms are homey and a little whimsical, decorated with porcine themes and flowery wallpapers. The Haug offers visitors two other styles of accommodations. At the inn next door, the rooms are spacious and elegant with king-size beds and whirlpool tubs. The guesthouse offers more modest rooms designed for a homelike stay of a week or more. All of the rooms include a delicious breakfast, and Haug is just a short walk from downtown Iowa City, the New Pioneer Co-op, and the lovely historic neighborhoods. There are 15 rooms in all. Rooms (including breakfast) from $100–$175.

Brown Street Inn (319-338-0435; www.brownstreetinn.com), 430 Brown Street, Iowa City. The Brown Street is as lovely as a *Better Homes and Gardens* magazine spread. The 1913 Gambrel cottage–style mansion is located on beautiful and historic Brown Street. Inside are five guest rooms and one suite, each with complete amenities, simple luxuries, and lots of light. Common areas such as the library and the front porch are welcoming. During weekday mornings an expanded continental breakfast is served, and a computer and Internet access are available to travelers. Rooms from $85–$165.

Smith's Bed & Breakfast (319-338-1316; smithsbandb.home.mchsi.com/smith_bb/Welcome.html), 314 Brown Street, Iowa City. Mark Smith is a professional massage therapist. He practices out of his 1890s home and extends the gift of relaxation to his guests with both his services and his comfortable guest rooms. The three rooms are understated yet lovely, and the home is bright and airy. Rooms (including breakfast) from $45–$75.

The Mission House (319-358-2854; www.missionhousebedandbreakfast.com), 228 Brown Street, Iowa City. The Mission-style home, built in 1908, is flavored with a taste of the Southwest. The three guest rooms are attractively decorated, and the deep front porch is a divine place to unwind. Rooms (including breakfast) from $65–$100.

The Carriage House (319-656-3824; www.carriagehousebb.net), 1140 Larch Avenue, Kalona. Dan and Edie Kemp built their carriage-house suite on their Kalona farm. Deep in Amish and Mennonite country, the rural setting is both peaceful and romantic. The two bedrooms have private bathrooms, and one has a Murphy bed. Breakfast is served in the carriage house's dining room, and guests are asked to pay between $80 and $150 for their stay—whatever they believe it was worth.

Columns & Chocolate (319-656-2992; www.columnsandchocolate.com), 212 Fourth Street, Kalona. With two huge suites and two adorable rooms above a tearoom and lunch spot, Columns & Chocolates has all the required equipment for romance—even if only romancing oneself. The columns at the front door welcome guests, and one of the suites is in the spacious turret. The suites include antique furniture, whirlpool tubs, and full baths. The tearoom offers elegant lunches, coffee and tea, and a general mercantile daily. Room (including breakfast) from $75–$125.

CAMPING **Devonian Fossil Gorge** and **Coralville Lake** (319-338-3543; www.coralvillelake.org), 3.5 miles north of I-80, exit 244 on Dubuque Street, Iowa City. More than 500 electric and nonelectric sites for tents and RVs. Campsites from $10–$22. (See also *To Do.*)

Lake MacBride State Park (319-624-2200; www.iowadnr.com/parks), 3525 IA 382 Northeast, Solon. State-run campground with both electric and primitive campsites. Campsites from $11–$16.(See also *Green Space.*)

F. W. Kent Park (319-645-2315; www.johnson-county.com/conservation), US 6, 3 miles west of Tiffin. This park offers 38 electric sites and 48 primitive sites with modern shower facility. Campsites from $10–$15. (See also *Green Space.*)

✷ Where to Eat

DINING OUT **One Twenty Six** (319-887-1909; www.onetwentysix.net), 126 East Washington Street, Iowa City. Open for lunch and dinner daily. This downtown bistro serves some of the most delicious food in the area. The menu rotates often and focuses on local, seasonal, and organic cuisine. Look for a French-Iowan fusion such as grilled natural rib eye with blue cheese and sautéed vegetables or applewood smoked Iowa Berkshire pork chops; the dishes are as beautiful to behold as the restaurant is warm and intimate. In the summer, score a bistro table out front. The wine list is long and varied, and there's a four-course prix fixe meal on Monday nights. $$$

Y **Atlas** (319-341-7700; www.atlasiowacity.com), 127 Iowa Avenue, Iowa City. Open for lunch, dinner, and bar time daily. True to its name, the Atlas serves food that tends to be worldly, though many of the ingredients are local. Exceptional daily specials are a treat, but the classic Atlas wraps—like the Buffalo chicken wrap—salads, and desserts are always winners. During warm weather, sidewalk seating is available, and the downstairs Atlas bar is a chic den for upscale cocktails and beer. $$–$$$

Y **The Sanctuary** (319-351-5692; www.sanctuarypub.com), 405 South Gilbert Street, Iowa City. Open for dinner Mon.–Sat. Dine on sophisticated and eclectic dishes such as coq au vin, short ribs, and Argentine sirloin, all prepared with care and seasonal ingredients. The menu changes often but always features European-style cuisine, sandwiches, and elegant salads. The dining room is warmly lit and wood paneled with a fireplace in the center. The adjoining bar is a comfortable and relaxing place to hang out and dabble in the lengthy selection of draft and imported beers and wines. $$–$$$

Red Avocado (319-351-6088; www.theredavocado.com), 521 East Washington Street, Iowa City. Open for lunch Tues.–Fri., dinner Tues.–Sat., brunch Sun. Discover just how delicious and inventive all-organic vegan cuisine can be at this locally owned restaurant. The menu ranges from vegetable peanut satay to a quesadilla made with tofu cheese; all the dishes use absolutely no animal products. The flours are whole grain, and the bread is baked on site; the ingredients are locally sourced and artisan quality; even the cleaning materials are nontoxic. All the drinks (espresso, tea, and juices) are made to order. Meals can be tailored to fit gluten-free, sugar-free, low-salt, and hypoallergenic diets. $$–$$$

Givanni's Italian Café (319-338-5967; www.givannis.net), 109 East College Street, Iowa City. Open for dinner nightly. Givanni's is an upscale and hip Italian restaurant. The menu is filled with high-end pasta dishes such as handmade sweet potato ravioli and rich lasagna. The chef features new specials every other week, inspired by Italian, American, and vegetarian cuisine, but of course, steak, seafood, and chicken dishes are also on the menu, along with a good wine list. $$–$$$

Linn Street Café (319-337-7370; www.linnstreetcafe.com), 121 North Linn Street, Iowa City. Open for lunch Mon.–Fri., dinner Mon.–Sat. The inspirations for the dishes at this elegant bistro come from as far as Asia and as near as the local farmer's market. Try Idaho trout pâté, a citrus marinated pork tenderloin, or pan-seared prawns. Lunch brings more casual sandwiches and salads. Daily specials and an excellent wine list round out this fine-dining experience. Lunch $$, Dinner $$$.

Tuscan Moon Grill on Fifth (319-656-3315; www.tuscan-moon.com), 203 Fifth Street, Kalona. Open for lunch and dinner Wed.–Sat. With several dining rooms and a lush garden patio in the back of the town's old hotel, the Tuscan Moon is a high-end grill for intimate dinners. The menu has an Italian soul but a global scope. Dishes range from yellowfin sashimi to New Orleans gumbo with shrimp and sausage. The steaks are hand cut and served with either a potato or garlic risotto. The bar offers a wide range of beers and liquors, and daily specials pair rotating entrées with wines. $$

The Fireside Grill Steakhouse and Martini Bar (319-656-3001; www.thefiresidegrill.com), 111 Fifth Street,

Kalona. Open for lunch and dinner Tues.–Sat., brunch Sun. The bistro cuisine—mopped BBQ platters and jerked pork steaks—is fun, and diners can build their own Angus burgers with cheese and toppings. The menu also includes panini and deli sandwiches and a wide range of à la carte sides. The martini bar mixes up a variety of alcoholic delights. $$

EATING OUT 🍸 **The Mill Restaurant** (319-351-9529; www.icmill.com), 120 East Burlington Street, Iowa City. Open for lunch, dinner, and bar time. The Mill has been an Iowa City institution for great music and food since 1962. Up front, enjoy the delicious pizza and sandwiches, and Italian-style dinner entrées such as chicken Marsala and their famous spaghetti. In back, excellent local and regional bands play almost nightly, and the beer flows to make a convivial atmosphere. $$

✪ **Hamburg Inn No. 2** (319-337-5512; www.hamburginn.com), 214 North Linn Street, Iowa City. Open for breakfast, lunch, and dinner daily. Joe Panther and his brother opened the first Hamburg Inn in Iowa City in the 1930s. Eventually the Panther brothers opened three Hamburg Inns, along with several other restaurants. No. 2 is the only remaining location, an iconic 1950s diner. Presidents Reagan and Clinton ate here, and various journalists have profiled the institution, but go for the legend, not the food. The greasy omelets, burgers, and clam baskets are great for nursing a hangover but don't offer much in terms of nutrition or flavor. $

Masala (319-338-6199), 9 South Dubuque Street, Iowa City. Open daily for lunch and dinner. For classic vegetarian Indian cuisine, nothing beats Masala. The lunch buffet is inexpensive and offers a taste of everything, and their evening meals are delicious and filling. The mali kofta, a vegetable dumpling served in a savory sauce, and the naan flatbread are rich and comforting. The dining room is a little rinky-dink, but the food makes up for it. $–$$

The Wedge (319-351-9400; www.thewedgepizzeria.com), 136 South Dubuque Street, Iowa City. Open daily for breakfast, lunch, and dinner, and late Thurs.–Sat. The Wedge is one of the two great pizza joints in Iowa City. They are known for exotic ingredients, lots of vegetables, high-quality sauces, and delicious crusts. Strange and special pies include jerked chicken, Rajun Cajun, and Thai veggie, but they also do the basics—pepperoni and cheese—very well. At the downtown location diners will find the same kind of deliciousness during the day with pizza by the slice, frittatas and French toast, fancy salads, and sandwiches. For delivery or takeout pizzas, call the location at 517 South Riverside Drive (319-337-6677). The Wedge is a little more expensive than most college-town pizza but well worth the extra for the quality. $$

Falbo's (319-337-9090; www.falbobros.com), 457 South Gilbert, Iowa City. The pizza won't come in 30 minutes or less as those chain places promise, but the stuffed pizza by the Falbo brothers is worth the wait. Like Chicago-style stuffed pizza but loaded with cheese and toppings, it is baked slowly in special ovens. One slice is a meal, two are naughty, three are life threatening. Carry out or delivery only. $$

Lou Henri (319-351-3637), 630 Iowa Avenue, Iowa City. Open for breakfast, lunch, and dinner daily. Lou Henri is a sunny, neighborhood breakfast joint with a hippie disposition. The food is tasty and healthy: whole-grain breads, omelets and huevos rancheros, and banana-bread French toast. Everything is an excellent choice, and there are lots of vegetarian options. The staff is friendly, but the kitchen is usually pretty slow, so plan on a long, leisurely breakfast. Cash only. $–$$

🍸 **Quinton's Bar and Deli** (319-354-7074), 215 East Washington Street, Iowa City. Open daily for lunch, dinner, and bar time. The first Quinton's opened in Lawrence, Kansas, in 1991. Since then, the popular lunch spot and bar has become a college-town chain. Famous for bread-bowl sandwiches, exceptional specialty sandwiches, and home of the "tall girl" glass of beer, the Quinton's in Iowa City also offers a small but wonderful sidewalk patio from where to eat, drink, and watch the foot traffic go by. Try the beef-and-brie sandwich or the stuffed baked potatoes. $$

The Cottage (319-351-0052; www.thecottagebakerycafe.com), 230 East Benton Street, Iowa City. Open 6:30–5:30 Mon.–Fri., 6:30–2 Sun. Serving delicious hot breakfasts, light and fast lunches, and a huge array of fresh-baked breads, cakes, and other desserts, along with tea, juice, and coffee, the Cottage is the perfect spot for a light but delicious meal. $$

Joensy's (319-624-2914), 101 West Main Street, Solon. Open daily for lunch, dinner, and bar hours. The bar in Solon claims to have the biggest and best pork tenderloin in the state of Iowa, and while it *is* massive, this writer's investigations find the claim is not exactly true. Regardless, the tenderloin at Joensy's is thin, crispy, and generous—to say the least; a half order is plenty. The bar also serves up burgers and fries, but this is definitely a neighborhood dive, and travelers who are sticklers for atmosphere and hygiene may want to dine elsewhere.

Icehouse Bar and Grill (319-648-2565), 70 West First Street, Riverside. Open for lunch, dinner, and bar time Tues.–Sat., lunch and dinner Sun. This two-story bar and grill honors the historic ice harvesters on the English River and draws a crowd of motorcyclists and NASCAR fans for hearty sandwiches, heavyweight burgers, appetizers, and beer. $$

COFFEE AND TREATS ✪ **Java House** (319-341-0012; www.thejavahouse.com), 211½ East Washington Street, Iowa City. Open Mon.–Sat. 6:30 AM–12:30 AM, Sun. 7 AM–12 AM. The truly exceptional coffee here is brewed one cup at a time. It takes a little longer to wait for the water to drip through the hand-roasted beans, but the result is a cup of coffee so fresh and flavorful, it will spoil you for any other coffee shop. The Java House also serves a full range of espresso drinks made in the classic style, with some designed for more intense academic pursuits: the "depth charge" is a cup of coffee with a shot of espresso in it, and the "all-nighter" is a latte with five shots of espresso. Pastries and desserts are served. Free wireless is available. The Java House has seven other locations around town, too.

The Tobacco Bowl (319-338-5885), 111 South Dubuque Street, Iowa City. Open 7 AM–midnight Mon.–Sat., 10–10 Sun. In a state where tobacco consumption in public places has been banned, outlaws and hipsters still gather at this coffee and retail-tobacco shop. The air is redolent with the sweet smell of flavored tobaccos and rich espresso coffees, and the shop has both a 500-cigar humidor and free wireless Internet access.

Bread Garden Bakery and Café (319-354-4246), 224 South Clinton Street, Iowa City. Open daily for breakfast, lunch, and dinner. Under the glass counters at the Bread Garden is a fantastic spread of baked goodies. The macaroons are chewy and covered in chocolate, the cookies are scrumptious, and they sell their decadent cakes whole or by the slice. Loaves of freshly baked bread are for sale, as well. The café also serves up delicious soups and sandwiches every day, plus coffee and espresso and fresh-squeezed juices. Lunch $$.

Kalona Bakery (319-656-20131 www.kalonabakery.com), 209 Fifth Street, Kalona. Open for breakfast and lunch Mon.–Fri. Before settling down to a snack of homemade pastries, watch the bakers as they create pastas. The bakery also specializes in homemade bread, pie, cakes, traditional Czech kolaches, and cinnamon rolls. On weekends the grill offers burgers and sandwiches for lunch. Locally produced foods and gifts are for sale. Lunch $.

MARKETS ✪ **New Pioneer Food Co-op** (319-338-9441, 319-358-5513; www.newpi.com), 22 South Van Buren Street, Iowa City; open 7 AM–11 PM daily; and 1101 Second Street, Coralville; open 7 AM–10 PM daily. The New Pioneer Food Co-op, which first opened its doors in the 1970s, is probably the best example of what a market should be. The member-owned co-op is also open to the public, and it brings to Iowa City the best of organic and locally raised produce, meat, and dairy. It offers a full line of natural foods, many sold by bulk, and natural health and beauty products. The bread and pastries are baked fresh daily in the Coralville location, and the deli sandwiches and prepared foods are outstanding. Both locations offer full coffee bars, wine and beer, and frozen foods. The co-ops are beautiful, welcoming places to shop, stop for a cup of coffee, or grab a healthy lunch.

John's Grocery (319-337-2183; www.johnsgrocery.com), 401 East Market Street, Iowa City. Open 7:30 AM–midnight Mon.–Thurs., 7:30 AM–2 AM Fri.–Sat., 9 AM–midnight Sun. If there ever is a nuclear holocaust, and humans are forced to seek shelter underground, you'll find this writer in the basement of "Dirty John's." The teeny-tiny grocery store is housed in an 1848 brick building and specializes in beverages alcoholic: more than 450 varieties of beer, over 1,500 bottles of wine, and a huge selection of liquor. Alongside the hooch is a great deli and a full-service, though small, selection of groceries.

Iowa City Farmers Market (319-356-5110; www.icgov.org), Chauncey Swan parking garage, between Washington and College Streets, Iowa City. Open 7:30–11:30 Sat. and 5:30–7:30 Wed. Iowa Citizens love their farmer's markets, so much so that the city had to enforce a strict start-time rule. The ritual goes like this: patrons scope out the stalls before the market opens, then jostle, money ready, into position to get their hands on the pumpkin bread or kale bunches most to their liking. The tension rises. When the whistle blows, all hell breaks loose in a flurry of transactions to rival the New York Stock Exchange. Thankfully, the pace slows down considerably after the first heady moments.

✷ Drinking Establishments

Old Capital Brew Works (319-337-3422; www.oldcapitalbrewworks.com), 525 South Gilbert Street, Iowa City. Open daily for lunch, dinner, and bar time. The brewery in Iowa City was established in 2004 and since then has created craft brews for the college community. Each season brings a new offering that is interesting, refreshing, and brewed with care. A pub menu of burgers, sandwiches, and pizza is served throughout the day, and there are daily specials on beer. Meals $$.

Dublin Underground (319-337-7660), 5 South Dubuque Street, Iowa City. Open afternoons and evenings daily. Step downstairs into a bar that feels like a real Irish pub. The Dublin is a comfortable, friendly bar with Irish beer, a big fish tank behind the counter, and plenty of booths for relaxing with friends, old and new.

Joe's Place (319-338-6717; www.joesplaceic.com), 115 Iowa Avenue, Iowa City. Open 10 AM–2 AM Mon.–Fri., 11 AM–2 AM Sat. and Sun. Joe's has been an institution in Iowa City since 1934. The crowd is a diverse mix of locals, professionals, and students, and the bar is always busy and fun. A recent renovation cleaned the joint up a bit and added a beer garden.

The Deadwood (319-351-9417; www.deadwoodic.com), 6 South Dubuque Street, Iowa City. Open 9 AM–2 AM daily. The Deadwood calls itself an institute for higher learning, and it has long been a favorite for students of the school of drinking. Nicer than a dive bar but certainly not swanky, the Deadwood is sort of like drinking in a buddy's basement—if your buddy likes pinball and has a mounted dolphin on the wall.

Martini's (319-351-5536), 127½ East College Street, Iowa City. Open 5 PM–2 AM Mon.–Sat. Martini's offers a litany of the titular cocktail, plus a good selection of domestic and imported beers, and both a cigar and a tapas menu. In the early evening the bar is chic and relaxed, but it can get boisterous when the undergraduate set rolls in.

Fox Head Tavern (319-351-9824), 402 East Market Street, Iowa City. Open afternoons and evenings daily. A legendary hangout for the writers of the famed Iowa Writers' Workshop, the Fox Head is a highly literate dive bar, with cheap drinks and a friendly atmosphere that has benefited greatly from the statewide smoking ban.

✷ Entertainment

MUSIC AND THEATER **Hancher Auditorium** (319-335-1160; www.hancher.uiowa.edu) 231 Hancher Auditorium, Iowa City. The magnificent Hancher Auditorium—host to fine music, theater, and entertainment—was badly damaged during the flooding of 2008. The University plans to reopen the venue early in 2010. Many events are still scheduled, although at different locations. Check their Web site for details.

Englert Theatre (319-688-2653; www.englert.org), 221 East Washington Street, Iowa City. Call or visit their Web site for box office information. Originally built in 1912 and once a cinema, the Englert went through a $5 million renovation. Today it is a premier venue for live music, touring comedians, author readings, and artists.

Riverside Theatre (319-338-7672; www.riversidetheatre.org), 213 North Gilbert Street, Iowa City. Call or visit their Web site for box office information. Iowa City's sole resident professional theater troupe produces contemporary and classical plays and the annual Shakespeare Festival.

Picador (319-354-4788; www.thepicador.com), 330 East Washington Street, Iowa City. Call or visit the Web site for show schedule and ticket information. The Picador features local, regional, and national indie rock bands. A bit on the divey side, it is a den of music-loving hipsters and punks.

SPORTS EVENTS **Hawkeye Sports** (1-800-424-2957; www.hawkeyesports

.com), UI Athletics Ticket Office, 402 Carver-Hawkeye Arena, Iowa City. Sales window open 9–4 Mon.–Fri. with extended hours for walk-up sales. Throughout the year, the University of Iowa Hawkeyes compete with teams from across the Big Ten. In the fall, take in a tailgate all morning, and then cheer on the football team at **Kinnick Stadium**. In the winter, see exciting men's and women's basketball at **Carver Hawkeye Arena**. In the spring and summer, try to catch fantastic track and field events, baseball, softball, tennis, soccer, and golf, among other sports. Check their Web site for schedules.

✷ Selective Shopping

Downtown Iowa City is packed with distinctive shops that range from high-end clothing and accessories to Nag Champa incense and Frisbee golf disks to Iowa Hawkeye apparel. Included are a few shops not to miss, but be sure to schedule plenty of time for browsing into any trip to the area.

✪ **Prairie Lights** (319-337-2681; www.prairielights.com), 15 South Dubuque Street, Iowa City. Open 9–9 Mon.–Sat., 9–6 Sun. Prairie Lights is the best bookstore in the state and possibly the entire universe. Paul Ingram, the book buyer, is an absolute font of knowledge about the printed word. His recommendations are legendary, and the entire staff is helpful and approachable. The bookstore is packed with intelligent and unique selections in every category; there are always great deals on the bargain tables. The basement is a whimsical children's bookshop, and the **Java House** has a location upstairs. In the evening there is always a great reading event, either by the world-famous University of Iowa Writer's Workshop or a nationally recognized author. Do not miss this paragon of independent booksellers: Prairie Lights is absolute bookstore nirvana.

Iowa Artisans Gallery (319-351-8686; www.iowa-artisans-gallery.com), 207 East Washington Street, Iowa City. Open 10–6 Mon.–Wed., 10–7 Thurs.–Fri., 10–5:30 Sat., 12–4 Sun. The works of more than two hundred artists are on display in this downtown gallery and art shop. The artist-owned and -operated gallery showcases the work of local and regional artists whose media range from handcrafted jewelry to photography to woodcarving. The contemporary crafts—including Sticks furniture, paintings, and glass—must be seen to be believed.

Vortex (319-337-3434; www.vortexgifts.com), 211 East Washington Street, Iowa City. Open 10–7 Mon.–Thurs., 10–8 Fri.–Sat., 12–5 Sun. This downtown shop is a favorite for a quirky and sundry selection of gifts: designer jewelry, books, cards, patron-saint magnets, crystals, and candles.

Iowa Book (319-337-4188; www.iowabook.com), 8 South Clinton Street, Iowa City. Open 9 AM–8 PM Mon.–Fri., 10–6 Sat., 12–5 Sun. Across from the Old Capitol, Hawk fans can find 15,000 square feet devoted to those who bleed black and gold. Hawkeye apparel ranges from the classic hoodie to upscale embroidered polo shirts. The place to find all required University of Iowa textbooks, Iowa Book is also a full-service bookstore plus they have office supplies and gifts.

Dulcinea (319-339-9468; www.dulcineala.com), 2 South Dubuque Street, Iowa City. Open 10–5:30 Mon.–Sat., 12–5 Sun. This warm and welcoming corner store invites women of all ages to shop for unique casual and formal apparel, accessories, and shoes.

The Soap Opera (319-354-1123; www.soapoperaiowacity.com), 119 East

College Street, Iowa City. Open 10–8 Mon.–Fri., 10–7 Sat., 11–6 Sun. For 25 years this Ped Mall shop has sold the best bath and beauty products in the state. For soaps, hair-care products, men's shaving brushes, candles, and more, visit this charming store.

The Den (319-339-4500; www.hawkeyeden.com), 123 East Washington Street, Iowa City. Open Mon.–Sat. 8 AM–10 PM, Sun. 10 AM–9 PM. Home of the "buy one, get two free" T-shirt deal on Iowa Hawkeyes merchandise, and the legendary 50-cent fountain pops, the Den is like a fueling station for undergraduates. Stop in for apparel, music and DVDs, incense, snacks, and more.

Pet Central Station (319-351-4453; www.petcentralstation.org), 114 South Clinton Street, Iowa City. Open Mon.–Sat. 10–6, Sun. 11–5. Most travelers don't plan on bringing home a pet from a trip to Iowa City, but this locally owned store offers up-close encounters with adorable rescued dogs and cats in need of good permanent homes and is OK with visitors petting the merchandise.

Kalona General Store (319-656-3535), 121 Fifth Street, Kalona. Open 9–5 Mon.–Sat. The general store markets Amish products, souvenirs and apparel, and general merchandise.

Kalona Furniture Co. (319-656-2700), 210 Fifth Street, Kalona. Open 10–5 Mon.–Sat. One of the best souvenirs of a trip to Iowa has to be a piece of handmade Amish furniture—although it can be hard to fit in a suitcase. High quality, long-lasting wooden dining room sets, armoires, and bed frames fill the store along with more portable gifts, baskets, and candles.

Kalona Antique Company (319-656-4489; www.kctc.net/kac), Fourth Street and C Avenue, Kalona. Open 9–5 Mon.–Sat. Step inside an antique church in downtown Kalona and shop reasonably priced antiques, glassware, quilts, and primitives stacked up to the steeple.

FAIRFIELD, MOUNT PLEASANT, AND THE VILLAGES OF VAN BUREN COUNTY

Mount Pleasant in Henry County and Fairfield in Jefferson County are cities similar in size and history, yet they offer two distinct perspectives on the future. Mount Pleasant, home to Iowa Wesleyan College, was once considered the Athens of Iowa. As with many small towns, it is a quiet, retiring place, perhaps best known for the Old Threshers Reunion, a celebration of antique farming machines and railroads.

On the other hand, Fairfield, to the west in Jefferson County, experienced the economic decline that many Midwestern cities felt during the farm crisis. Then the destiny of the town took an odd turn. A group teaching Transcendental Meditation bought the failed Parsons College, reopened it as a school for meditation, Eastern philosophy, and wellness, and attracted followers and artists from around the world (see sidebar). Today Fairfield is full of young people, exotic restaurants, and art. Both communities are charming, but rarely does a traveler go so far in so few miles.

Van Buren County, to the south, was once the gateway to the interior of the state as steamboats traveled up the Des Moines River from its mouth at the Mississippi. Towns such as Farmington, Keosauqua, Bentonsport, and Bonaparte grew rich as they welcomed travelers and goods, but when the federal government declared the Des Moines unfit for river travel, and railroads changed the way people moved goods, Van Buren County slipped into obscurity. Today the villages still have the air of river towns like those found along the Mississippi. The Hotel Manning in Keosauqua and the Steamboat Gothic House in Bentonsport reflect the unique architectural designs inspired by the boats. The villages are sleepy and quaint and offer an abundance of outdoor recreation activities, from canoeing to hunting.

GUIDANCE **Fairfield Convention and Visitors Bureau** (641-385-2460; www.travelfairfieldiowa.com), 200 North Main, Fairfield. The Fairfield CVB's Web site features a great guide to the local art and restaurant scene. Also visit the site for more information on Fairfield and Vedic City.

Henry County Convention and Visitors Bureau (319-385-2460; www.henrycountytourism.org), 101 South Jefferson, Mount Pleasant. Visit their Web site, or stop by the office during business hours for information on the county and attractions.

The Villages of Van Buren (1-800-868-7822; www.villagesofvanburen.com), 902 Fourth Street, Keosauqua. The villages of Van Buren County are served by one tourist organization. Learn more about each of these historic places by visiting their Web site or calling during business hours.

GETTING THERE *By car:* Mount Pleasant is at the junction of **US 218** and **US 34**. Fairfield is just to the west on **US 34**, and the Villages of Van Buren are located on **IA 1** and **IA 2**.

By train: The Mount Pleasant **Amtrak** station (www.amtrak.com), 418 North Adams Street, is served by the *California Zephyr.* The station is open Mon.–Fri. 10:30–6:15, Sat.–Sun. 10:30–11:30 and 5:30–6:30; ticket office closed on weekends. No checked-baggage service.

MEDICAL EMERGENCY Call **911**.

Henry County Health Center (319-385-3141; www.hchc.org), 407 South White Street, Mount Pleasant. Emergency services provided 24 hours a day.

Jefferson County Hospital (641-472-4111; www.jchospital.org), 400 Highland Street, Fairfield. Emergency department is staffed 24 hours a day at this regional hospital.

✷ To See

Icon: Iowa Contemporary Arts (641-469-6252; www.icon-art.org), 58 North Main Street, Fairfield. Open 12–4 Tues.–Sat. This nonprofit art gallery on the main square is an anchor of Fairfield's artist colony. The gallery not only displays the work of artists from around the region but also offers lectures, workshops, chamber music, and video nights. Art installations range from paintings to large-scale sculptures. The gallery is open to the public, but visit their Web site for special events. The first Friday of every month is Fairfield's First Fridays Art Walk (www.fairfieldartwalk.com), when galleries open up for an evening gallery hop, entertainment, and food. More than 500 artists and 40 galleries strut their stuff around the main square.

ART ABOUNDS IN FAIRFIELD AT ICON, WHICH SHOWCASES WORKS BY LOCAL AND NATIONAL ARTISTS

Midwest Old Threshers Heritage Museums (319-385-8937; www.oldthreshers.org), 405 East Threshers Road, Mount Pleasant. Open Memorial Day–Labor Day 8–4:30 Mon.–Fri., 9–4:30 Sat.–Sun.; Labor Day–Memorial Day 8–4:30 Mon.–Fri. Admission: $5 per person. For travelers who can't make it to Mount Pleasant for the Old Threshers Reunion every September, these museums offer some consolation. See steam traction engines, antique tractors, and all sorts of agricultural implements, along with exhibits on Native Americans and women during Iowa's pioneer days. The **Theatre Museum of**

A STEAMBOAT GOTHIC–STYLE HOUSE IS A REMINDER OF THE PAST IN THE BENTONSPORT NATIONAL HISTORIC DISTRICT

Repertoire Americana is on the same grounds, and open Memorial Day–Labor Day 10–4 Tues.–Sun. or by appointment. Admission: $5. Inside is a collection of memorabilia from American entertainment, including stage drops, scripts, and musical scores from the 1850s. A trolley runs through the museum complex and is available for groups by request.

Swedish American Museum (319-254-2317), 107 James Avenue, Swedesburg. Open 9–4, closed Wed. and Sun. Free. In 1845 a group of immigrants formed the first Swedish settlement in the Midwest. Through Scandinavian-style hard work, they turned the wetlands into productive farmland. This local museum, marked with a huge red Swedish horse on the highway, tells the story of Swedish heritage through artifacts and documents. Learn about family and social life, farming and business, and major events. Tours are free, and Swedish meals are available for groups.

Bentonsport National Historic District (319-592-3579; www.bentonsport.com), CR J40, Bentonsport, Van Buren County. Bentonsport, established in 1839, was once an important port of call for steamers on the Des Moines River. One of the first paper mills was located in the town, as was a lock-and-dam system built in the 1800s. When transportation shifted away from boats and toward railroads, Bentonsport's significance declined. In recent years, though, Bentonsport's charm—not as a center of commerce but as a site of historical importance—has drawn both investment and tourists. The quaint community is now a hub of specialty shops and historic buildings on the riverfront. Visitors can walk across the 1882 iron bridge, see a Steamboat Gothic–style house, walk through the rose garden, and stay in an inn built by Mormons who passed through the area en route to settling in Utah.

* To Do

Van Buren County Water Trail (www.desmoinesriver.org) starts in Selma and ends in Farmington. The mighty Des Moines River was once the main thoroughfare for goods and settlers into the heart of the state as steamships traveled up

THE TOWER OF INVINCIBILITY IN THE TRANSCENDENTAL MEDITATIONIST COMMUNITY OF VEDIC CITY

FAIRFIELD AND VEDIC CITY

The main square of Fairfield looks much like other small-town squares. There are grand buildings dating back to the early part of the last century, small grocery shops, clothing stores, and restaurants, and people all going about their business. But there is something a little different about Fairfield. Lively, exotic music echoes in the alleyways, and more people than usual seem to have accents.

The town, much like other small Midwest communities, was struggling after the farm crisis. Parsons College had closed its doors, and young people were fleeing to big cities and other states. Then in 1974 the Maharishi Mahesh Yogi, founder of the Transcendental Meditation (TM) movement,

from the Mississippi to Des Moines. Today the villages along the lower Des Moines reflect some of the same river-town characteristics of the cities on the Mississippi, and one of the best ways to see these places is from the water. Along the water trail's 41 miles are various rest stops and access points every 5 to 8 miles. The river is very gentle, with no rapids except at the old dam at Bonaparte. Learn more about the trail at their Web site, and use caution and common sense on the river.

Troublesome Creek Float Trips (319-293-6424; www.troublesome-creek.com), 108 Main, Keosauqua. Call to schedule a float. Trips from May–Oct. depending on weather; $30 per day per canoe. Arrange a float trip down the Des Moines River or a fishing trip on peaceful Lake Seguma. Outfitters will meet groups at the launch site, provide life jackets and safety information, and lead fun trips down the scenic river. The company also offers two rustic cabins ($65–$85 per night) and an outfitting store with live bait and hunting and camping supplies.

Rent a Horse! (319-878-3596), IA 2, Farmington. Open daily but rather catch as catch can, so call for reservations. $25 per ride with refreshments provided. Just outside the village of Farmington is the **Shimek Forest.** Ride the forest trails on horseback. The owners of this facility, the Westercamps, match horses to riders, and all skill levels are welcome.

bought the college located just north of Fairfield. It started as the Maharishi International University, today known as the **Maharishi University of Management**, or MUM (641-472-1110; www.mum.edu; IA 1, Vedic City). At the center of campus is the Golden Dome of Pure Knowledge, where students practice Yogic Flying, a yoga method that proponents say significantly alters EEG waves.

In 2001 the followers of TM incorporated their own town: Vedic City, which is based on the principles of Maharishi Sthapatya Veda. All buildings face east, only organic foods are served, and the official language is Sanskrit. MUM and Vedic City attracted faculty, students, and others who wanted to be near the vibe from around the country and around the world. With them came a global perspective—and money. Soon restaurants serving foreign food began to crop up, and artists began to set up studios. Diners in both Vedic City and Fairfield can find all sorts of worldly options: Indian, Thai, French, Italian, and American. It is impossible to miss a health-food store. There is always entertainment at the event center, and the community abounds with art and theater. On the first Friday of every month, the streets fill with art, music, and food as locals celebrate art with an **Art Walk**. The town now blends the followers of the New Age TM movement, artists, and the salt-of-the-earth Iowans who have always lived in Fairfield, and the blend is certainly unique and completely magical. Anyone can drive around the campus and Vedic City, but check the Web site for visitors' weekends.

✷ Green Space

Lacey Keosauqua State Park (319-293-3502; www.iowadnr.com/parks), just south of Keosauqua on IA 1, Van Buren County. Nineteen Native American burial mounds overlook the Des Moines River in the northwest corner of this park, and visitors can visit these important archaeological sites. Beyond its historical importance, the park is one of the largest and loveliest in the state. Hiking trails wind through the gorges and cliffs of the river valley, which is packed with wildlife. The 30-acre lake offers beach swimming and limited boating. Visitors can also camp in 113 campsites, 45 with electrical hook-ups, or in one of the 6 modern family cabins. Cabins $50, campsites from $11–$16.

Lake Sugema (1-877-293-3224; www.iowadnr.com/fish), south of Keosauqua on IA 1, Van Buren County. Open during daylight hours. Fish the waters of this 574-acre lake, and hope to catch largemouth bass, bluegill, black crappie, channel catfish, and walleye. The manmade lake was designed to have special underwater habitats for these species. The lake is surrounded by 3,600 acres of aboveground habitat for Iowa wildlife from wild turkeys to bald eagles.

Oakland Mills (319-986-5067; www.henrycountyconservation.com), 2591 Nature Center Drive, Mount Pleasant. This 100-acre park on the Skunk River features a nature center and outdoor classroom, a historic wagon bridge, and the hydroelectric dam and plant built in the 1920s. Trails wind through the park for hiking. Bald eagles and other wildlife and fish inhabit the park. The park has two cabins (with bathrooms and kitchenettes) and primitive and electric hook-up campsites (with shower building) available. Cabins from $50–$75, campsites from $8–$12.

Lake Geode State Park (319-392-4601; www.iowadnr.com/parks), 3249 Racine Avenue, Danville. Named for the state rock that has brilliant crystals hidden in its cavity, this state park features the beauty of the manmade lake for fishing, swimming, and boating. It is nearly 200 acres and is known for largemouth bass. The park also offers excellent opportunities for hiking, mountain biking, picnicking and camping. The campground includes 186 sites, about half with electric hook-ups, and shower buildings. Campsites from $11–$16.

* Where to Stay

HOTELS AND MOTELS **Landmark Inn** (641-472-4152; www.fairfieldlandmarkinn.com), 115 North Main, Fairfield. Eleven charming and understated historic rooms await visitors just off the main square. The rooms and lobby underwent extensive restoration and include Internet access. Rooms from $44–$59.

Brazelton Hotel and Suites (319-385-0571; www.hotel.brazelton.com), 1200 East Baker Street, Mount Pleasant. The 60 rooms in this hotel cover all the bases for travelers. They've got everything from themed suites to basic two-bed rooms. A large complimentary continental breakfast is served daily, and the hotel includes an indoor pool and hot tub. Rooms from $60–$125.

Rukmapura Park Hotel (641-469-1919; www.rukmapura.com), 1702 Rukmapura Park, Vedic City. The Rukmapura is fashioned after a European country inn, with pine and spruce finishes, marble fireplaces and baths, full kitchens in suites, an indoor hot tub, and a sauna. The park around the hotel is 250 acres of rolling hills for ambling and reflecting. Free breakfast and Internet access available. Rooms from $110–$150.

The Raj (641-472-9580; www.theraj.com), 1734 Jasmine Avenue, Vedic City. The Raj Ayur-Veda Health Center in Vedic City is a health spa that offers more than mud dips and four-hand massage with herbalized oil. To heal a wide variety of illnesses and create deep relaxation, the Raj uses the most comprehensive system of natural wellness and offers visitors spiritual succor. Rooms from $88–$240, depending on service.

Bonaparte Inn (319-592-3823; www.bonaparteinn.com), 802 First Street, Bonaparte. In 1889 Isaiah Meek built a three-and-a-half-story building to house the family pant-making business. By 1896 the factory was cranking out thirty thousand pairs of pants a year. In 1909 the pants factory and the mill were sold to the Fairfield Glove Company, which operated from 1920 to 1999. The factory was renovated and is now a gorgeous inn with views of the Des Moines River. The nine rooms and four suites are incredibly spacious and include wireless Internet and satellite television plus a full breakfast and afternoon refreshments. Visitors can relax in the adjoining garden and watch the river go by. Rooms from $75–$175.

Hotel Manning (319-293-3232; www.thehotelmanning.com), 100 Van Buren Street, Keosauqua. Edwin Manning built this historic hotel as a tribute to the steamboats that had ferried goods

THE LOBBY OF THE HOTEL MANNING LOOKS MUCH THE WAY IT DID WHEN IT WAS BUILT IN 1899

to his mercantile store. The style is Steamboat Gothic, with ornate balconies and cupola on the roof. The hotel opened in 1899, and much of the interior looks as it did more than one hundred years ago. The lobby has 14-foot ceilings, pine woodwork, and antique fixtures that include a Vose rosewood grand piano and a grandfather clock. (The hotel saw "grand" days; the poet T. S. Eliot stayed there in 1919.) Upstairs, the 16 rooms will remind visitors of the bygone days seen today only in Westerns. The rooms are furnished with antiques, and the suites offer views of the river. The hotel serves a Sunday buffet from mid-May to mid-Oct. Guests who prefer more modern accommodations can stay at the **Riverview Inn** with television and wireless Internet access. A modern and inexpensive motel is also on the property. Hotel rooms from $69–$149, inn rooms from $47–$58, motel rooms from $42–$47.

BED & BREAKFASTS **The Mainstay Inn** (641-209-3300; www.mainstayfairfield.com), 300 North Main Street, Fairfield. The 1890s inn is adjacent to the **Fairfield Arts and Convention Center** and close to downtown. The three guest rooms are named after composers and are furnished simply and elegantly with queen-size beds. Wireless Internet and cable television available. Guests can also stay at the private cottage next door with three bedrooms The inn is green, using no toxic-chemical cleaning products, and the breakfasts are organic. Rooms from $100–$130.

Seven Roses Inn (641-209-7077), 1208 East Burlington, Fairfield. Each of the four quiet bedrooms features a private bath and luxurious linens. Guests can enjoy the common areas of the library, music room, dining room, and eat-in kitchen. A hot gourmet breakfast made from organic local food is served every morning. Rooms from $75–$140.

✪ **Manson House Inn** (1-800-592-3133; www.mansonhouseinn.com), 21982 Hawk Drive, Bentonsport. This Bentonsport hotel began serving guests in 1846 when it was built by Mormon craftsmen for travelers heading west. The tradition of "a cookie jar in every room," which continues today, was started by Nancy Mason, who bought the hotel with her husband in 1857.

THE MASON HOUSE INN IN BENTONSPORT WAS BUILT IN 1846 TO ACCOMMODATE MORMONS TRAVELING TO UTAH

The brick building has survived the great floods of 1851, 1903, 1905, 1947, 1993, and 2008; served as a hospital for Civil War soldiers; and was a station on the Underground Railroad. Each guest room has antiques, a private bathroom, a historic theme, and its own charm, but perhaps the best accommodation is down the street in the caboose cottage. Guests can stay in this furnished and air-conditioned RS&P caboose with a kitchen and bath, satellite television, and computer hook-ups. A hearty country breakfast is served daily. The inn also hosts quilting retreats, murder-mystery weekends, and ghost-hunting workshops. Rooms from $79–$125.

Pine Ridge Retreat (319-293-3322; www.pineridgeretreat.com), 24120 Lacey Trail, Keosauqua. Near both **Lake Seguma** and **Lacey Keosauqua State Park,** the four cabins at Pine Ridge are excellent accommodations for hunters, fishers, or anyone who loves the outdoors. Stay in the family cabin with queen bunk beds, the bunk house that sleeps 10 adults, or the lodge that sleeps 10 and offers meeting space. All of the cabins have an indoor bathroom, refrigerator, stove, cooktop, and dishes and are available year-round. The general store on-site offers camping supplies, groceries, ice, beverages, tackle, and firewood. Cabins from $65–$110.

Trimble-Parker Guest House (641-664-1555; www.trimble-parker.com), 23981 Otter Trail Drive, Bloomfield. On a historic farm in southern Iowa, this 1914 Craftsman farmhouse offers a quiet retreat for visitors who can choose to walk around the property or just sit on the front-porch swing. Barn tours are available as are a complimentary snack and beverage. The four guest rooms on the second floor share a bath; the first-floor room has a private bath. Room (including breakfast) from $60–$75.

CAMPGROUNDS **Old Threshers Campground** (319-385-8937; www.oldthreshers.com), 405 East Threshers Road, Mount Pleasant. This 60-acre campground offers electrical and water hook-ups year-round along with restrooms and showers. Note that the campground fills up fast during the Old Threshers Reunion in September, so make reservations accordingly. Groceries are available on site. Campsites $15 per night.

Oakland Mills See *Green Space.*

Lake Geode State Park See *Green Space.*

✷ Where to Eat

DINING OUT ✪ **Vivo Restaurant** (641-472- 2766; www.vivofairfield.com), 607 West Broadway, Fairfield. Open daily for dinner. Vivo offers fine dining with an eye toward all-natural and organic ingredients. Offering entrées like blueberry chicken with brie, international flavors like kofta balls, and gnocchi with vegetables, Vivo is both delicious and capable of serving diners with special preferences. $$$

Top of the Rock (641-470-1515; www.topoftherockgrille.com), 113 West Broadway, Fairfield. Open for lunch and dinner 11–9 daily. At dinner, diners can mix and match their surf-and-turf selections from a fine array of aged, Angus beef and seafood. The menu also includes shrimp, chicken, and a small selection of pastas. Lunch brings a wider selection of grilled chicken sandwiches, the signature "walnut burger," and pasta dishes. The bar serves martinis, beer, blended drinks, and a selection of wine by the glass and bottle. Despite the elegant food, there is a comfortable bar, pinball, and a pool table. $$

Petit Paris (641-470-1624; www.petitparisnow.com), 111 North Court Street, Fairfield. Open for lunch and dinner Mon.–Sat., brunch Sun. This quaint French bistro takes diners on a trip to Paris without the jet lag. For lunch try a savory crepe or a casual sandwich. At dinner look for traditional dishes such as coq au vin and ratatouille as well as exquisite desserts. The chef places special emphasis on fresh and natural ingredients, using free range chicken, hormone-free milk, and organic local produce. The wines are, of course, French and thoughtfully chosen. $$; credit cards only accepted for meals over $20.

Iris Restaurant (319-385-2241; www.irisrestaurant.com), 915 West Washington, Mount Pleasant. Open for lunch and dinner Mon.–Sat.; brunch Sun. The Iris is an old-time supper club serving hearty Midwestern fare in buffet-style dining, plus the occasional stint of dinner theater. $$

Bonaparte Retreat Restaurant (319-592-3339), 711 First Street, Bonaparte. Open for lunch and dinner Mon.–Sat. Dine at a national historic site in the village of Bonaparte. Meals include enormous cuts of beef and pork—the rib eye is the specialty—as well as fried chicken and seafood including Alaskan king crab and oysters. All dinners come with the soup of the day, salad, and either a potato dish or pan-fried bread. $$

EATING OUT **Mohan Delights** (641-469-6900; www.mohandelights.com), 101 West Broadway, Fairfield. Open for lunch Mon.–Fri. For light, organic, and all-natural Indian lunches, stop in at this corner restaurant. $–$$

Small Planet Restaurant and Bakery (641-209-9021), 108 North Main, Fairfield. Open for lunch and dinner. This all-organic restaurant offers delicious American dining options. Stop in for burgers and salads for lunch or dinner or coffee in the afternoon. Bread and baked goods are available for take-out. $$

Torino's Pizza and Steakhouse (641-472-9071), 115 West Broadway, Fairfield. Open daily 5 PM–close. For classic American-style cuisine and for pizza made with fresh dough kneaded by hand, stop in at this family restaurant.

There are plenty of toppings for the pies, fried chicken, seafood, steaks, and pasta dishes. Dessert is on the house; free ice cream with every meal. $–$$

El Asadero Restaurant (319-385-3008), 101 West Monroe Street, Mount Pleasant. Open Tues.–Sat. for lunch and dinner. Iowa is full of great Mexican restaurants, but this one takes the usual menu of tacos and enchiladas up a notch with plates of salmon, tilapia, and red snapper. Try the artichoke heart with tomato sauce or the roasted chicken breasts. $–$$

Henny Penny (319-385-1413), 124 North Main Street, Mount Pleasant. Open for breakfast and lunch Mon.–Sat., dinner Fri.–Sat. This sunny, colorful café starts serving breakfast pie and thick French toast bright and early in the morning. During the day, the menu focuses on dishes that Mom used to make: tuna casserole, sandwiches, and soups, and excellent prime rib for weekend dinners. $–$$

Revelations Café (641-472-6733; www.revelationscafe.com), 112 North Main, Fairfield. Open for lunch Mon.–Sat., dinner Fri.–Sat.; hours Mon.–Thurs. 8:30–5, Fri. 8:30–10, Sat. 9 AM–10 PM. At the heart of this coffee shop and used-book store is a wood-fired pizza oven. The tables are sprinkled among the shelves of used books, which make for great browsing over espresso and lattes, sandwiches, and pastries and desserts. The wood floors and Tuscan garden make this café warm and inviting. The coffee is all organic and craft-roasted, and the vegetables and ingredients on the pizzas, sandwiches, and salads are fresh and abundant. $$

COFFEE AND TREATS **The Chocolate Café** (641-209-1999), 55 South Court, Fairfield. 10–5:30 Mon.–Thurs., 9–9:30 Fri.–Sat., 12–5 Sun. It's hard not to love a European chocolate shop with homemade truffles, Dutch-style bonbons, and other delectable, mood-lifting goodies. The chocolate-dipped toffee is to die for, and the menu also offers cheesecake, brownies, extraordinary homemade ice cream, and a complete coffee and espresso bar.

Village Cup and Cakes (319-293-8200; www.villagecupandcakes.com), 202 Main Street, Iowa. Open for breakfast Mon.–Sat., lunch Mon.–Fri. Full breakfasts and lunches are served in this downtown bakery, with tasty and simple soups, salads, and sandwiches. Or forego nutrition, and dig into a big piece of gourmet cake and a latte from the full-service espresso bar. Meals $$.

✷ Entertainment

Fairfield Arts and Convention Center (641-472-2000; www.fairfieldacc.com), 200 North Main Street, Fairfield. Call or visit their Web site for box office information. The theater in Fairfield is exceptionally grand for such a small community. Inside this architecturally lovely building, professional theater companies present off-Broadway works and touring musical acts perform.

✪ **Café Paradiso** (641-472-0856; www.cafeparadiso.net), 607 West Broadway. Open 7:30–5:30 Mon.–Fri., 7:30–5 Sat., 8–5 Sun. Café Paradiso is a world-class espresso bar that has become a hotbed for art-house entertainment. Hear music from around the world while enjoying ultrafresh organic coffee and espresso drinks. Open-mike night is Wednesday, films show the second and fourth Thursday of the month, and there is a brunch on Sunday. But visit their Web site for a complete schedule.

Southeast Iowa Symphony (319-385-6352; www.seis.us), 601 North Main Street, Mount Pleasant. Call or visit the Web site for box-office information. This locally grown symphony group started in 1950 when a group of musicians gathered to play for their own enjoyment. Since then the symphony has grown to represent Burlington, Mount Pleasant, and Ottumwa, with performances in each area. Truly a community symphony, they produce concerts for children, pops concerts, and summer concerts, along with hosting festivals, workshops, and artists-in-residence.

THE MODERN FAIRFIELD ARTS AND CONVENTION CENTER HOSTS THEATER AND MUSICAL EVENTS YEAR-ROUND

✷ Selective Shopping

Dutchman's Store (31-397-2322), 103 Division Street, Cantril. Open 8–6 Mon.–Fri., 8–5 Sat. With bulk foods and candy, homegrown and home-canned foods, a large deli, fresh produce, gifts, and even a fabric department, this store is a model of the classic American general store. Stop in for a sandwich, local jams and jellies, or work boots and shoes.

At Home (641-472-1016; www.athomestoreonline.com), 52 North Main Street, Fairfield. Open Mon.–Fri. 9–5:30, Sat. 9–5, and Sun. 1–4. All the comforts of home await shoppers in this gourmet-cooking and knitting store on the square. Shop for elegant kitchen accessories, baking dishes, books, and gifts in the front, and find a wide selection of fluffy and silky yarns in the upscale knitting studio. The store also offers demonstrations, a small selection of stationary, and gifts for gardeners and children.

Overland (641-472-8480; www.overland.com), 2096 Nutmeg Avenue, Fairfield. Open 9–5 daily. Outside of Fairfield, in a wood-plank, four-story building on an 80-acre llama farm, is the Overland company headquarters. Shearling coats, leather jackets, gloves, handbags, UGG boots and slippers, and warm sheepskin rugs will all keep shoppers warm during long Midwestern winters.

Greef General Store (319-592-3579; www.greefstore.com), Hawk Street, Bentonsport. Open 10–5 daily Apr.–Oct. and 10–5 Sat.–Sun. Nov.–Dec. The Greef General Store is the information headquarters for life in Bentonsport, but it is also an antiques shop for several vendors, offering furniture, china, handmade wool, tools, glassware, and—perhaps most important—homemade fudge.

Iron and Lace (319-592-3222; www.ironandlace.com), corner of Walnut and Hawk Drive, Bentonsport. Open Apr.–Oct. 10–5 daily, Nov.–Dec. 10–5 Sat.–Sun. Tourists don't just shop this gift store. They actually watch the craftspeople, Betty and Bill Printy, create pottery, rugs, and ironwork in their studio and shop. Betty fires unique pottery with the impression of Queen Anne's lace and weaves on five looms, and Bill creates iron art and teaches workshops next door.

OTTUMWA AND THE LAKE RATHBUN AREA

Ottumwa, the county seat of Wapello County, is the city of five bridges. It was originally an important coal mining and meatpacking center for the state. Many of the cities in this area share a history of coal mining, but none embrace it as deeply as the little city of Lucas, which celebrates this past with the John L. Lewis Mining and Labor Museum dedicated to the famous labor leader. Oskaloosa, northwest of Ottumwa, is home of the Quaker William Penn University, and its charming main square offers a nice array of dining and shopping. Just to the southeast of Ottumwa, in the tiny town of Eldora, is the American Gothic House, the backdrop for the famous painting of that name that launched Grant Wood's career.

Lake Rathbun, in Appanoose County, is the site of an enormous state project, the Honey Creek Resort. Owned and operated by the Iowa Department of Natural Resources, the resort, on manmade Lake Rathbun, includes an eco-friendly hotel, luxury cabins, and camping plus a golf course, restaurant, indoor water park, and boat and bike rental. The lake itself offers a wide array of recreation, from swimming to sailing. In the surrounding communities, of which Centerville is the largest, visitors will find fine dining and casual restaurants, shopping, rustic cabins and campgrounds, and family-style entertainment.

GUIDANCE **Lake Rathbun Information Center** (641-647-2464; www.nwk.usace.army.mil/ra/), 20112 CR J5T, Centerville. Open 8–4 Mon.–Fri. Before any adventures on the lake, stop in at the information center. Inside are detailed maps of the lake, dioramas of the wildlife, lake history, and information about the surrounding areas.

Centerville-Rathbun Lake Area Chamber of Commerce (641-437-4102; www.centerville-ia.com), 128 North 12th Street, Centerville. Open during business hours. Centerville is the largest city near Lake Rathbun, and its chamber can answer questions and provide guidance for the entire region.

Getting There

By Car: **I-35** runs north-south through the city of Osceola, and **US 34** and **IA 2** run east-west through the region and connect many of the cities.

By Train: Ottumwa is served by the *California Zephyr* at its downtown **Amtrak** (www.amtrak.com) station at 210 West Main Street. The station is open daily. Osceola, just off I-35, also has an **Amtrak** station at the corner of Main and East Clay Streets but no ticket-office hours.

MEDICAL EMERGENCY Call **911**.

Ottumwa Regional Health Center (641-684-2300; www.orhc.com), 1001 Pennsylvania Avenue, Ottumwa. Emergency medical services available.

✷ To See

Nelson Pioneer Farm Museum (641-672-2989; www.nelsonpioneer.org), 2211 Nelson Lane, Oskaloosa. Open May–Oct. 10–4 Tues.–Sat., 12–5 Sun.; $7 adults, $2 children; guided tours lasting nearly three hours are available by appointment only. The Nelson family traveled to Iowa from Ohio in 1841 in a covered wagon. They purchased their farm near Oskaloosa and in 1852 built a large home from local stone and brick. Visitors can see not only the home but also the historic barn, a replica covered wagon, several buggies and sleighs, the summer kitchen, meat house, and rooms and rooms of other exhibits depicting life in early Iowa. The museum is full of Native American artifacts, antique military equipment, and home furnishings, and there are several buildings that make up a small village: a general store, post office, lumber office, barbershop, and log cabin are all on site. The oddest spot on the farm, though, has to be the cemetery with just two plots: one for Jennie and one for Becky, two white mules. The pair was purchased by Daniel Nelson in 1865, then served in the Civil War pulling artillery guns. Becky lived to 34 and Jennie to 42; both were buried with their heads resting on satin pillows. The property is large, and there is a lot to see, but visitors are treated to an insightful self-guided tour of the property.

TWO CIVIL WAR VETERANS—WHITE MULES NAMED BECKY AND JENNY—ARE BURIED AT THE NELSON PIONEER FARM CEMETERY

✪ **American Gothic House Center** (641-652-3352; www.wapellocounty.org/americangothic/), 300 American Gothic Street, Eldon. Visitors center open May–Sept. 1–4 Sun.–Mon., 10–4 Tues.–Thurs., 10–6 Fri.–Sat.; Oct.–Apr. 10–4 Tues.–Fri., 1–4 Sat.–Mon. (but the house is always visible). Free. Bring a pitchfork and a dour expression to the tiny town of Eldon and pose in front of the home that inspired Grant Wood's *American Gothic.* Don't have your own props with you? No problem. The American Gothic House Center can provide various-size

BRING A PITCHFORK AND RE-CREATE GRANT WOOD'S AMERICAN GOTHIC AT THE ICONIC HOUSE IN ELDON

aprons, overalls, dark jackets, spectacles, even that iconic pitchfork. The home, named after the house's rare Gothic window, is one of the most beloved and notorious images of Iowa. Wood painted the picture of his dentist, Dr. Byron McKeeby, and his sister, Nan Wood Graham, for a competition at the Art Institute of Chicago, for which he won $300. The image has inspired hundreds of parodies, including one from *Hustler* magazine. Visitors can make their own parodies and add them to the permanent collection at the American Gothic House Center. A large collection of parodies approved by Nan Wood Graham are in a collection at the **Figge Art Museum** in Davenport (see Part 2).

Airpower Museum (641-938-2773; www.aaa-apm.org), 22001 Bluegrass Road, Ottumwa. Open 9–5 Mon.–Fri., 10–5 Sat., 1–5 Sun. Free. Explore a 30-acre antique airfield and a wide variety of vintage airplanes. There are 20 in all, some dating back to World War II, along with engines, propellers, photos, and artwork.

Historical and Coal Mining Museum (641-856-8040; www.appanoosehistory.org), 100 West Maple, IA 2, Centerville. Open Memorial Day–Oct. 3–5 Fri., 9–12 Sat., and by appointment. Free but donations appreciated. Housed in the 1903 post office one block off the square, this historical museum includes exhibits on pioneer life and the Mormon Trail, which made its way through the county in 1846 between Nauvoo, Illinois, and Utah. On the lower level is a showcase of coal-mining tools and equipment. Coal mining became big business in the county; by 1934 there were nearly a hundred mines under the prairie. The mines died out in the 1940s and '50s, when the poor-quality coal lost value compared to more competitive seams, but visitors will feel like they are in the depths of this dirty industry that was once an important part of Iowa history. While visiting the museum, make an appointment to visit the **Old Jail and Sheriff's Residence** (641-856-8040), 527 North Main Street, Centerville, which was built in 1872 and is furnished with period artifacts.

World's Largest Town Square (641-437-4102; www.centervilleia.com), 128 North 12th Street, Centerville. The historic square around the Appanoose County

Courthouse includes 119 buildings on the National Register of Historic Places. The streets, with plenty of parking, are hopping with people visiting local restaurants and specialty shops.

John L. Lewis Mining and Labor Museum (641-766-6831; www.coalmininglabormuseum.com), 102 Division Street, Lucas. Open Apr. 15–Oct. 15 9–3 Mon.–Sat. and by appointment. Admission: $2 adults, $1 children. Lucas today has a population of around 300, but at the turn of the 20th century, it was a booming coal-mining town. The mines brought prosperity, railroads, and electricity. Lucas was the first town in Iowa to have electricity to light the mineshafts, which still run under the town. The museum includes photographs, documents, mining tools, and exhibits. The site also includes a retired Burlington Northern caboose in a nearby park, and the "old paymaster's office," a tiny brick building dating back to the 1800s, still stands on the outskirts of town.

Community State Bank (641-766-6131; www.csbindianola.com), 104 Front Street, Lucas. Open 8 AM–10 AM Mon.–Fri., 8 AM–12 PM Sat. The little brick bank in Lucas was one of the few that survived the Great Depression, and survive it did. The family-owned bank stayed within the family until the brothers sold it to Community State Bank under the condition that it remain open. All the old fixtures, safes, and counters are still there, though this place takes "banker's hours" to extremes. The friendly lady who works the bank doesn't mind visitors taking a peek.

The Round Barn (641-872-1536), 1 mile east of Allerton. Open June–Aug. 1–4 Thurs.–Sun. Admission: $3 per person. Round barns are a unique and fascinating part of the Iowa landscape. One of the few remaining is this 1912 structure that features a spiderweb construction and loft. Cows were milked in wedge-shaped stalls. Also on the grounds are an 1869 schoolhouse and an 1887 New York Christian church. An 1897 Queen Anne home is currently being restored for display. All of these structures stand on 93 acres of farm and prairie land.

✷ To Do

The Beach Ottumwa (641-682-7873; www.beachottumwa.com), 101 Church Street, Ottumwa. Admission depends on area and season. Visit their Web site for more information. Open at noon Memorial Day–Labor Day, indoor pools and slides open year-round. The slides at the Beach Ottumwa tower over the riverfront at this enormous water park that includes a wave pool, speed slide, sand volleyball, basketball, and indoor tube slide.

Rathbun Marina (641-724-3212; www.lakerathbunia.com), 13541 Marlin Place, Moravia. This full-service marina offers complete access to Lake Rathbun. Bring your own craft, or rent a pontoon boat for $130–$195 a day (gas not included). Before or after a day on the lake, enjoy a casual meal at the on-site restaurant, and spend the night in the Lakeside Inn or at the on-site campgrounds. Rooms from $75–$145, electric campsites $20 per night.

Southern Hills Winery (641-342-2808; www.southernhillswinery.com), 1400 West Clay Street, Osceola. Open 10–6 Mon.–Sat., 12–5 Sun. Operated by the Iowa Wine Cooperative, this center offers wines from vineyards across southern Iowa along with tastings, tours, and special entertainment events.

Terrible's Lakeside Casino (641-342-9511; www.terribleslakeside.com/), 777 Casino Drive, Osceola. Open 24 hours daily. The name refers to the mustachioed bandito that is the casino's mascot rather than the quality of the casino. With more than 1,000 slot machines and 20 table games, this busy casino has become a major attraction. The casino is right off I-35 but overlooks a lake and offers a buffet, bar, and gift shop. The complex also includes the **Lakeside Hotel** with 60 rooms, an outdoor swimming pool, and Internet access. Rooms from $79–$150.

✷ Green Space

Honey Creek State Park (641-724-3739; www.iowadnr.com/parks), 12194 Honey Creek Place, Moravia. Sometimes called "Iowa's Ocean," Rathbun Lake is a large manmade lake at the heart of Honey Creek State Park. The lake offers great fishing and excellent boat launches, playing host to a fleet of large sailboats and family pontoon boats. Around the lake are thousands of acres of rolling timber, quiet backwaters, and prairie land. The **Woodland Interpretive Trail** teaches hikers about the Native Americans who once inhabited the area, and miles of multiuse trails are enjoyed by hikers and cross-country skiers. Honey Creek has a large modern campground of 149 sites with showers, restrooms, and sites with full hookups, electricity only, and primitive camping. The park also rents three cabins at the campground. Cabins $35, campsites from $11–$16.

GUESTS AND RANGERS RELAX IN THE LOBBY OF THE HOTEL AT THE HONEY CREEK RESORT

Stephens State Forest (641-774-4559; www.iowadnr.com/forestry/stephens.html), south and west of the intersection of US 34 and US 65, near Lucas. Large tracks of Iowa's preserved forests are located just south of Lucas. Over 31 miles of trails cross Stephens State Forest and are open for horseback riders, day hikers, and backpackers. The ponds are stocked with bluegill, bass, and catfish. Primitive and equestrian campgrounds are available, but because the forest is large and still under development, contact the Iowa Department of Natural Resources (DNR) for more information and have a detailed, topographical map. Campsites from $11–$16, additional $3 for equestrian sites.

✷ Where to Stay

HOTELS AND RESORTS

Honey Creek Resort (515-875-4818; www.honeycreekresort.com), Rathbun Lake, Moravia. A massive new resort opened on the shores of the manmade Lake Rathbun. Operated by the state Department of Natural Resources, the resort offers visitors an 18-hole golf course, indoor water park, boat rental, and an outstanding 108-room lodge with cabins. The hotel was built with a North Woods theme and offers majestic views over the lake. An eco-conscious hotel, it was constructed with recycled building materials, energy-efficient heating and cooling, and eco-friendly bath products. The rooms are spacious and gorgeously appointed. Children will love the indoor water park, which includes a zero-depth entry, water slide, and lazy river. Outside, guests can rent pontoon boats, canoes, kayaks, and bicycles to enjoy the lake—both on and around. The hotel also features an elegant restaurant and lounge open daily for breakfast, lunch, and dinner. Both the prime rib and the breakfast are excellent, there is outdoor seating, and the prices are reasonable. Meals $. Rooms from $109–$276.

The Continental Hotel & Restaurant (641-437-1025; www.thecontinental.info), 217 North 13th Street, Centerville. The original hotel on this site burned to the ground in 1892, killing one of the owners—but not before, legend has it, she got all of the guests out of the hotel. The hotel was rebuilt in 1893 and operated until the 1990s, when it fell into disrepair. In 1996 Morgan Cline, with the support of the community, restored the hotel to its former glory, and now gleaming wood and period furnishings beautifully adorn the lobby, the restaurant, and the grand staircases. Today the hotel serves three purposes: residential apartments for seniors, a fine restaurant open to the public, and apartment-style accommodations for visitors to Centerville. Each of the guest rooms has a full kitchen, living room, and separate bedroom. Some rooms have two twin beds, others have queens. The restaurant at the Continental is one of the few finer establishments in the area and is open all day, every day. Lunches are fairly casual, offering grilled cheese, homemade tenderloins, and salads, but dinner brings seafood, pasta, grilled chicken, and steak. The restaurant has a fine bar and outdoor seating in a brick courtyard and on the street. Meals $$. Suites from $75–$95.

Hotel Ottumwa (641-682-8051; www.hotelottumwa.com) 107 East Second Street, Ottumwa. The Hotel Ottumwa opened in 1917 with a gala ball; today visitors can still enjoy accommodations in the heart of the city at this historic hotel. The modern rooms offer Internet access, cable, refrigerators and microwaves, and guest laundry. Luxury suites include kitchenettes and whirlpool tubs, but the best feature of the hotel is the complimentary hot breakfast in the café. Rooms from $53–$125.

BED & BREAKFASTS AND CABINS

One of a Kind (641-437-4540; www.oneofakindbendandbreakfast.net), 314 West State Street, Centerville. The grand three-story brick home was built by a town doctor in 1867 and has been renovated with care, now housing a tearoom, a gift shop, and a B&B. Lunch in the tearoom includes light soups, salads, croissants, and a wide array of homemade desserts. Breakfast and lunch served Mon.–Sat.; dinner by reservation. The gift shop offers an abundance of crafting supplies, country gifts, and candles. Upstairs, five guest rooms (two with a shared bath, three with private baths) decorated with charming antiques are comfortable and precious. Breakfast and lunch $–$$. Room (including breakfast) from $50–$80.

Foxtail Cabins (1-877-736-9824; www.foxtailcabins.com), west of Iconium on CR J18. New fully furnished, Amish-built cabins welcome visitors with Amish-built furniture, full kitchens with dishes and cookware, and full bathrooms. All linens are included, and the cabins are set on a large pond near Lake Rathbun. Front porches beckon with large rocking chairs. Cabins range in size and rent for $60–$190 per night, with a two-night minimum.

🐾 **Whispering Breezes Resort Cabins** (641-897-3417; www.whispering-breezes.com), 1133 250th Street, Melrose. Close to excellent hunting and all the fun of Lake Rathbun are six modern cabins, each with a front porch, full modern kitchen, bathrooms, queen-size beds and sleeper sofas, televisions with DVD players, fire pits, and great views of the lake. Guests can rent gazebos, screen rooms, old-fashioned electric fireplaces, and dog kennels. The cabins are great for hunters, fishers, and people who want to get away from it all. The resort also offers accommodations in three recreational vehicles and a three-bedroom farmhouse. Cabins from $80–$90 per night, RVs $80, farmhouse $125.

Inn of the Six-Toed Cat (641-873-4900; www.6toedcat.com), 200 North Central Avenue, Allerton. A favorite among true B&B lovers in Iowa, this inn is a turn-of-the-20th-century railroad hotel, with nine guest rooms that honor different individuals and institutions, such as William Jennings Bryan and the Chautauqua movement. The inn has two large dining rooms, with seating for up to 54, and their breakfast is legendary. The inn, however, is currently for sale, so call ahead or visit their Web site to ensure accuracy of rates and availability. Rooms (including breakfast) from $75–$130.

CAMPING **Indian Hills Inn and RV Park** (641-932-7181; www.indianhillsinn.com), 100 US 34 East, Albia. There are 58 fully furnished guest rooms in the hotel with an indoor pool, hot tub, sauna, and free high-speed Internet. The RV park offers full hook-up sites with sewer, water, electricity, cable, and high-speed wireless Internet access. Shower houses and laundry facilities are on-site. A restaurant is right across the highway from the inn. Hotel rooms from $48–$120, campsites $20 per night with discounts for longer stays.

Honey Creek State Park (641-724-3739; www.iowadnr.com/parks), 12194 Honey Creek Place, Moravia. Three cabins and 149 campsites (full hook-ups, electric only, and primitive) are available at the modern campground of this state park. Cabins $35, campsites from $11–$16. (See also *Green Space.*)

✱ Where to Eat

DINING OUT **Skean Block Restaurant** (641-932-3141; www.attheblock.com), 11 Benton Avenue East, Albia. Open for lunch and dinner Wed.–Sat. In a gorgeous restored storefront on Albia's historic and pretty square is an elegant restaurant that smells of wood-burning ovens smoking prime rib. Along with a fine selection of steaks are refined chicken and seafood dishes, pasta, and meal-size salads. Pan-seared walleye with scallion-butter cream shares the menu with king-crab legs and flatiron steaks. The menu changes monthly, but the food is always delicious. $$–$$$

Tuscany (641-437-7037), 113 Van Buren Avenue, Centerville. Open daily for breakfast, lunch, and dinner. This main-square café brings together the food and decor of an Italian restaurant with traditional café food. The menu includes meaty, rich pastas but also a variety of sandwiches, including a handmade tenderloin, burgers, steaks, seafood and melts. For breakfast, don't miss the light-as-air Belgian waffle. With fruit and whipped cream, it's more like dessert. $$

Amish Home for a Meal (Lucas County Tourism: 641-774-4059), Amish homes around Lucas County. Call the tourism office for the date and location of the next Amish meal. Visitors are welcomed into an authentic Amish home and get to enjoy a buffet spread of homemade dishes and desserts. Locals know the Amish do the best baking in Iowa, and these meals include plenty of homemade bread, butter, and jelly. Reservations and payment need to be made ahead of time and require 10 or more people for dinner. Meal $15 per person; $25 includes a tour of a woodworking shop, basket-making shop, and grocery store.

EATING OUT **2nd Street Café** (641-682-8051; www.hotelottumwa.com) 107 East Second Street, Ottumwa. Open daily for breakfast, lunch, and dinner. Located in the historic **Hotel Ottumwa** (see *Where to Stay*), this café offers tasty comfort food. The sandwiches, tenderloins, and burgers are fresh, hot, and delicious, and the breakfast is hearty and tastes like Grandma's. In the evening, look for buffet-style dining, steaks, and fried appetizers. $–$$

Canteen Lunch in the Alley (641-682-5320), 112 East Second Street, Ottumwa. Open Mon.–Sat. for lunch. Tucked behind a modern parking garage is an old-fashioned diner that has been serving Ottumwa since the 1920s. Diners sit in booths in a bright white lunchroom and enjoy loose-meat sandwiches and milk shakes. All of the food is delicious, and the service is fast and friendly. $

Mi Ranchito (641-672-9773), 112 First Avenue East, Oskaloosa. Open for lunch and dinner daily. Both levels of this main-square Mexican restaurant are always hopping with diners loving the vast menu of cheesy and delicious south-of-the border dishes. The menu has something for everyone, including tons of seafood options. On Wednesdays the margaritas are only $3, so prepare to fiesta. $–$$

Big Ed's Barbeque (641-660-1625), 104 First Avenue East, Oskaloosa. Open for lunch and dinner Mon.–Sat. The decor is gingham and NASCAR inside this folksy downtown BBQ joint. All the meat is slow smoked over hickory wood, and the specialties are sandwiches piled high with pork, beef, and chicken. The menu also includes delicious ribs and fruit cobblers. $$

Taso's Steakhouse (641-682-0200), 1111 North Quincy Avenue, Suite 111, Ottumwa. Open for lunch and dinner Mon.–Sat. (There is also a Taso's location at 109 High Avenue West in Oskaloosa with the same hours and menu.) This small-town-style

TUCKED AWAY IN AN ALLEY IN OTTUMWA IS THE CANTEEN LUNCH, A CLASSIC AMERICAN LUNCH COUNTER

steakhouse has a little of everything, from flat iron steaks to chicken club sandwiches to a small selection of Mexican dishes. Friday night is the catfish special, and Saturday is prime rib. Buckets of fried chicken are available for takeout. $$

The White Buffalo Restaurant and Lounge (641-932-7181; www.indianhillsinn.com), 100 US 34 East, Albia. Open Mon.–Sat. for breakfast, lunch, and dinner; breakfast and lunch buffet Sun. This big country roadhouse serves up enough variety to please everyone. The menu ranges from make-your-own pizzas to prime rib and seafood. There is a full breakfast menu, a salad bar with soup, and an ice cream dessert bar. Try the nightly specials or prime rib and fish fries on weekends. $–$$

Bluebird Café (641-856-5414), 108 East Jackson, Centerville. Open daily for breakfast and lunch. This little joint on the square puts a funky spin on the traditional diner atmosphere. The walls are painted with bright colors, there are all sorts of doodads and whatnots for diners to admire under the glass counter, and the walls are adorned with blow-up, plastic animal heads. The food is pretty standard—burgers, fish fillets, country-fried steaks, and pancakes—but it's as much fun to hang out here as it is to eat here. $–$$

Williamson Tavern (641-862-3615), 108 South Street, Williamson. Open for lunch and dinner Mon.–Fri.; breakfast, lunch, and dinner Sat.; closed Sun. The Williamson Tavern is a pretty forgotten place—just a country bar and grill. But the trip to this faraway little dive may be worth it because the Williamson Tavern is the home of the Big Papa Burger: a 2-pound hamburger. The burgers are served on extra-large buns to accommodate their dinner-plate-size circumference. They are made fresh and served with a choice of toppings for a pittance of around $7. The menu also includes an assortment of gastronomical odds and ends: tenderloins, fried shrimp and gizzards, mini-burritos, and T-bone steaks. The decor is not much to speak of, but because they are the only outfit in town, they do offer sundries such as shampoo and soap in addition to food and brew. $

L&L European Delight (641-774-2104), 101 Main Street, Chariton. Open for lunch Mon.–Fri., early dinner Thurs.–Fri. (hours change, so call ahead). On the square in little Chariton, deep in rural Iowa, travelers can find homemade, authentic Ukrainian cuisine, and the pelmeni, sauerkraut, and cabbage rolls are an appealing alternative to the steaks and burgers most often found on the road. The restaurant is not much to look at. It's big and shabby with old furniture and '80s Muzak, and there is a major Christian motif. Russian cards, gifts, books, and groceries are for sale, too, but the food is delicious and the service super friendly. $$

Lucas Bottoms Up (641-766-6619), 106 West Front Street, Lucas. Open daily for lunch, dinner, and bar time. The only place to eat in the tiny town of Lucas is a slightly battered pub-and-grub joint on the main street. Don't be put off by the rundown wooden bar or the fountain in the "lobby." The nightly specials offer up hearty buffet-style servings of catfish and prime rib, and during the day look for great homemade tenderloins, burgers, and fried cucumbers. Beers rarely cost more than $2, and the food is a steal, too. $

COFFEE AND TREATS **B & C Mercantile** (641-766-6535), 108 East Front Street, Lucas. Open 10–5 Mon., 4–8 Tues., Thurs., Fri., 10–8 Wed. and Sat. Half of this store is devoted to country gifts: candles, cutesy sayings printed on old barn planks, and knickknacks. The other side is the neighborhood ice-cream parlor with hand-dipped and soft-serve ice cream, light snacks, and soda pop. Sundaes and dipped cones are available but easy to pass up when there is hand-dipped black walnut and pralines and cream on the menu.$

Bizzy's Ice Cream Parlor (641-891-2033), 121 North Main, Chariton. Open 11–7 Mon.–Fri. Stop in for a treat at this old-fashioned ice-cream parlor, the interior of which—the building dates back to the turn of the 20th century—is adorned with the original tin walls and ceilings painted brilliant white. Ice cream, shakes, blended coffees, and root beer on tap. They also serve burgers, tenderloins, and sandwiches and other savory snacks. Meals $.

Smokey Row Coffee (641-676-1600), 109 South Market Street, Oskaloosa. Open daily for breakfast, lunch, and dinner. This crown jewel of the Smokey Row empire—a local coffeehouse chain with shops in Pella and Pleasantville (see Part 1)—is located in a big, open, brick building on the main square. A giant old movie marquee decorates one of the walls, and there are tables, leather chairs, and booths for hanging out, studying, or socializing. Not only does the "Row" offer a full line of coffee and espresso beverages, they also serve frozen drinks and ice cream at their soda counter. The café menu includes hot breakfasts any time, sandwiches, bagels, salads, and tasty soups. Meals $–$$

✷ Drinking Establishments

Y **Tom-Tom Tap** (641-682-8051; www.hotelottumwa.com), 107 East Second Street, Ottumwa. Open daily, serving food from the **2nd Street Café** (see *Eating Out*). The Tom-Tom is the historic bar in the **Hotel Ottumwa**. The bar, with its famous, colorful mural of Indians lighting the ceremonial fire, originally opened in the 1930s. Today the horseshoe-shaped bar is a lively and hip place to hang out in the city of five bridges.

THE HISTORIC MURAL GLOWS BEHIND THE BAR OF THE TOM-TOM TAP IN THE HOTEL OTTUMWA

✱ Entertainment

Sunshine Mine Drive-In (641-856-3402), 18905 Sunshine Road, Centerville. Open daily Memorial Day–Labor Day, weekends only May, Sept., Oct. The Sunshine is one of Iowa's three remaining drive-in movie theaters (the others are in Newton and Maquoketa). This theater is fairly new and family owned. Call for schedule and ticket information.

✪ **Rathbun Country Music Theater** (660-344-2310; www.countrymusictheater.com), 1 mile north of the Rathbun Dam, Moravia. Tickets: $8 adults, $3 children. Every Saturday night from Apr. through Oct. stop in at Iowa's longest-running country-music venue for a night of family entertainment after a long day on the lake. Shows include a house band, comedy, and weekly guests. Call the box office, or visit their Web site for schedules.

A TREASURE OF LITERATURE AWAITS IN THE BOOK VAULT, OSKALOOSA

Frontier Trading Post and **Soda Pop Saloon** (641-774-8225), 25281 US 34, Chariton. Open Apr.–Dec. 9–5 Tues.–Sun. Look for the buffalo over the sign to find a Western store and a venue for family entertainment. During the day, shop for diverse wares that include home decor, gifts, dolls, hand and power tools, and bait and tackle. On Saturday nights the "saloon" opens up for live entertainment, music, and dancing in a nonalcoholic venue. Shows start at 8 PM and cost $5 per person.

✱ Selective Shopping

✪ **Book Vault** (641-676-1777; www.bookvault.org), 105 South Market Street, Oskaloosa. Open 9–7 Mon.–Fri., 9–8 Thurs., 9–5 Sat., 12–4 Sun. It is rare to find a bookstore that is so beautiful that it almost distracts from the written word, but here is one. Housed in a turn-of-the-20th-century bank, with a Grecian storefront, marble counters, and the original safe, this local shop offers three levels of selections under mint-green walls and an ornate ceiling. Deposited in the vault is the Iowa section. The shop also offers cooking demonstrations, a Web database for browsing, leather chairs for reading, and access to the coffee shop next store.

Exline Old County Store & Antique Exchange (641-658-2399; www.exlinecountrystore.com), 102 West Main Street, Exline. Open daily 7 AM–8 PM, serving breakfast, lunch, and dinner. Exline is a tiny coal-mining town of 191 people; at the heart of the town is this country store with 4,000 square feet of antiques, groceries, snacks, books, and crafts. Visitors can also enjoy home-cooked country-style dishes—lunch specials are served every day and cost only $4—or just sit by the potbellied stove or in a rocking chair on the front porch. The store encourages visitors to stop and chat. Join the coffee club for $4; refills are only 25 cents. While you are in town, stop in at the **Exline Hose Co. No. 1 Museum** (641-658-2399), Main Street, Exline. Open Memorial Day–Sept. 30 1–4 Sun. and by appointment. Free. Information is available at the **Country Store**. All meals $.

The Columns (641-437-1178; www.thecolumns.info), 107 East Washington Street, Centerville. Open 10–6 Mon.–Sat., 12–4 Sun. Inside, this gorgeous 1895 architectural gem is a temple to the art of shopping. Shoppers will find antiques, Tiffany-style lamps, jewelry, baskets, throws, kitchen goods, and lots more tucked into the airy rooms and quaint nooks.

Front Street Antiques (515-961-8953), 103 East Front Street, Lucas. Open 10–4 Wed.–Sat. and by appointment. With vintage cans and jars, jewelry, bowls, linens, and lots more, this store is well organized, charming, and an extremely fun place to shop. There are more knickknacks than antiques, but collectors will find plenty of treasures. Dachshund Sallie guards the place, but she is easily bribed with treats.

Piper's Old Fashioned Grocery Store (641-774-2131; www.piperscandy.com), northeast corner of the square, Chariton. Open 8–5:30 Mon.–Fri., 8–5 Sat. This grocery store on the square is as quaint as a Norman Rockwell painting. It wouldn't be surprising to see children in knickerbockers buying the homemade candy from the front counter. The rest of the store is devoted to antiques and collectibles.

✷ Special Events

April: **Spring Draft Horse Sale** (319-656-222; www.kctc.net/ksb), Sales

ARTIFACTS AND GOODIES FROM THE PAST LINE THE WALLS OF FRONT STREET ANTIQUES IN LUCAS

Barn, Kalona. This semiannual sale (there's another in Oct.) draws people from around the country to bid on draft horses, buggies, carriages, carts, and wagons. A draft-horse pull, much like a tractor pull, shows off the skills of the animals.

May: **Iowa Renaissance Festival** (1-800-579-2294; www.iowarenfest.com), Middle Amana Park. A festival of history and magical characters in costume, plus medieval contests and events, entertainment, activities, and food.

✪ **Taste Louisiana Cajun and Zydeco Fest** (1-800-579-2294; www.cajunfest.net), Amana Colonies RV Park and Event Center, Big Amana. The Zydeco fest is one of the truly exceptional celebrations in the state. It is a huge celebration of music, dancing, Cajun and Creole cuisine, demonstrations, and lots of fun.

Maifest (1-800-579-2294; www.festivalsinamana.com/maifest.html), Amana. The traditional spring celebration at the Amana Colonies includes the Taste of the Amana Colonies food fair, Maypole dancing, folk music, and a parade down Main Street. The festival runs concurrently with the Renaissance Festival.

May–Sept.: **Iowa City Friday Night Concert Series** (319-337-7944; www.summerofthearts.org), downtown Iowa City. With the students gone for the summer, Iowa City locals hit the Ped Mall every Friday night for live music and dancing from popular local and regional bands.

June: **Grant Wood Art Festival** (319-462-4879; grantwoodartfestival.anamosachamber.org), Stone City, just west of Anamosa. Grant Wood once said, "I realized that all the really good ideas I'd ever had came to me while milking a cow. So I went back to Iowa." Many other artists agree and compete in an annual juried art festival. Music, workshops, food, and demonstrations complete the event.

American Gothic Days (641-652-3352; www.wapellocounty.org/americangothic/index.htm), American Gothic House, Eldon. Locals celebrate the location of great art with a bike ride, 5K run, and Grant Wood–inspired fun.

TrekFest (319-648-5475; www.trekfest.com), Riverside. Celebrate the birth of Captain James T. Kirk of the USS *Enterprise,* who will be born in Riverside on March 22, 2233. The town has its own model spaceship, and the festival features a beer garden, parades, food, and, of course, lots of Klingons.

Juneteenth (319-862-2101; www.blackiowa.org), African American Historical Museum and Cultural Center, Cedar Rapids. Celebrate the Emancipation Proclamation and the official end of slavery. This holiday was originally commemorated in Galveston, Texas, but has since become a nationwide event. In Cedar Rapids mark the occasion with music, dancing, and food.

Centerville Wine and Fine Arts Festival (641-437-4102; www.centervilleia.com), Courthouse District, Centerville. A day of Iowa wines, gourmet foods, bocce ball tournaments, folklore tent, and jazz in the band shell.

Riverside Theatre Shakespeare Festival (319-338-7672; www.river

AT RIVERSIDE'S ANNUAL TREKFEST, THE STARSHIP RIVERSIDE IS ON DISPLAY IN THE FUTURE BIRTHPLACE OF CAPTAIN JAMES T. KIRK

sidetheatre.org), Iowa City. Every summer, the replica of the Globe Theater in the city park fills with resident professional actors who produce the works of the Bard.

Iowa Arts Festival (319-337-7944; www.summerofthearts.org), downtown Iowa City. More than 100 artists and accompanying vendors and entertainment fill the streets of Iowa City for a celebration of the arts. Look for a children's day with special activities, the global village, and world cuisine from local restaurants.

Midsommar Festival (319-254-2317; www.genevachamber.com/swedishdays.html), Swedesburg. This annual celebration blends the local Swedish heritage with the fun of a traditional Iowa summer festival. Enjoy Swedish food and costumes along with musical entertainment.

June–August: **Saturday Night Free Movie Series** (319-337-7944; www.summerofthearts.org), Pentacrest at MacBride Hall, Iowa City. Bring a blanket and enjoy an evening on the campus green with local songwriters, shorts by Iowa filmmakers, and a feature-length film.

July: **Heritage Days** (319-210-9935; www.visitmvl.com), Mount Vernon. A three-day festival of music, parades, and fireworks in historic downtown Mount Vernon. The Art-in-the-Park Festival coincides in Memorial Park.

✪ **Iowa City Jazz Festival** (319-337-7944; www.summerofthearts.org), downtown Iowa City. Jazz and blues musicians from around the country fill the streets of Iowa City during this nationally acclaimed festival. Three stages entertain the crowds along with food and artist booths.

August: **Sauerkraut Days** (319-210-9935; www.visitmvl.com), Lisbon. This celebration of Lisbon's German heritage includes a carnival, bathtub races, entertainment, and lots of bratwurst and kraut.

Winding Stairs Festival (319-478-2346; www.traer.com/visit), Traer. A traditional Iowa summer festival of parades, talent contests, food, rides, and entertainment under the historic winding stairs.

Meskwaki Powwow (319-484-4678; www.meskiwaki.org), Tama. See traditional dances, costumes, drumming, and other entertainment—and eat plenty of the delicious traditional fry bread.

Festival of Iowa Beers (www.millstreambrewing.com/events.html), Amana. Taste craft beers from local brewers across the state, learn about the brewing process, sample beer-friendly dishes, and dance the night away with live music and entertainment.

Hardacre Film & Cinema Festival (563-886-6350; www.tiptoniowa.us/hardacre), Hardacre Theater, Tipton. A celebration of independent films at the historic Hardacre Theater, with accompanying music and food. This film festival is the first of its kind in the state, welcoming regional and national filmmakers to Tipton.

Haystock (641-437-4102; www.centervilleia.com), Centerville. A party in the middle of a hayfield, with hayrack rides, country music, and concessions.

Landlocked Film Festival (319-337-7944; www.summerofthearts.org), Iowa City. Films and their creators come to Iowa City for a weekend of short and full-length films, including student, animation, and Spanish-language submissions.

Bluesmore (www.lcbs.org), Cedar Rapids. The Linn County Blues Society sponsors this annual event with big-name blues and rock bands on the lawn of the stately Brucemore mansion.

August–September: **John L. Lewis Labor Festival** (641-774-4059; www.lucasco.net/tourism), Lucas. Celebrate Labor Day weekend with a hero of the labor movement, John L. Lewis, a leader of the United Mine Workers of America. The festival includes tours of Lewis's eponymous museum, kids' face painting, a tractor parade and show, and food.

September: **Lincoln Highway Arts Festival** (319-210-9935; www.visitmvl.com), Mount Vernon and Lisbon. Fifty artists line the streets as docent-led trolley rides explore the art and history of these two communities.

Kalona Fall Festival (www.kalonaiowa.org) Kalona Historical Village, Kalona. A two-day festival that celebrates Old World skills such as quilting, spinning, rug weaving, rope making, blacksmithing, and cider pressing. The food is homemade, too; sample chicken with biscuits, apple fritters, and apple butter while strolling through the village.

Midwest Old Threshers Reunion (319-385-8937), Old Threshers Heritage Museum, Mount Pleasant. Each year Mount Pleasant is home to one of the largest steam shows in the country, and thousands of visitors come for steam-power demonstrations, steam-train rides, antiques, food, and country music.

Iowa City Brew Festival (319-337-2183; www.johnsgrocery.com), Iowa City. Breweries from around the world offer tastings of their brews along with door prizes, entertainment, and food. The proceeds go to the American Heart Association.

Pioneer Fall Festival (641-672-2989; www.nelsonpioneer.org), Nelson Pioneer Farm Museum, Oskaloosa. A weekend of pioneer demonstrations from butter churning to rope making, traditional children's games, crafts and antiques shows, and an old-fashioned dinner.

October: **Pumpkin Festival and Weigh Off** (319-462-4879; www.pumpkinfest.anamosachamber.org), Anamosa. Before they become pies and jack-o'-lanterns, the state's biggest pumpkins weigh in at Anamosa's pumpkin festival. The second-largest pumpkin in the world in 2008 was a 1,662-pound beast exhibited here at the fest. Other activities include a parade, carving exhibits, a chili cook-off, and a 5K run.

Oktoberfest (www.festivalsinamana.com), Amana. Located in the historic Festhalle Barn, this traditional German festival is celebrated in style with entertainment, dancing, food, and beverages. Vendors line the streets, and local restaurants open their doors to revelers.

Scenic Drive Festival (1-800-868-7822; www.villagesofvanburen.com), Van Buren County. The journey through Van Buren County, which straddles the lower Des Moines River, is always scenic, but with fall foliage, carnival rides, rib-eye sandwich dinners, and city-wide garage sales, mid-Oct. is a great time to make the trip.

Western Iowa 5

IOWA'S GREAT LAKES: OKOBOJI AND ENVIRONS

NORTHWEST

FORT DODGE AND ENVIRONS

WEST CENTRAL

SOUTH AND WEST

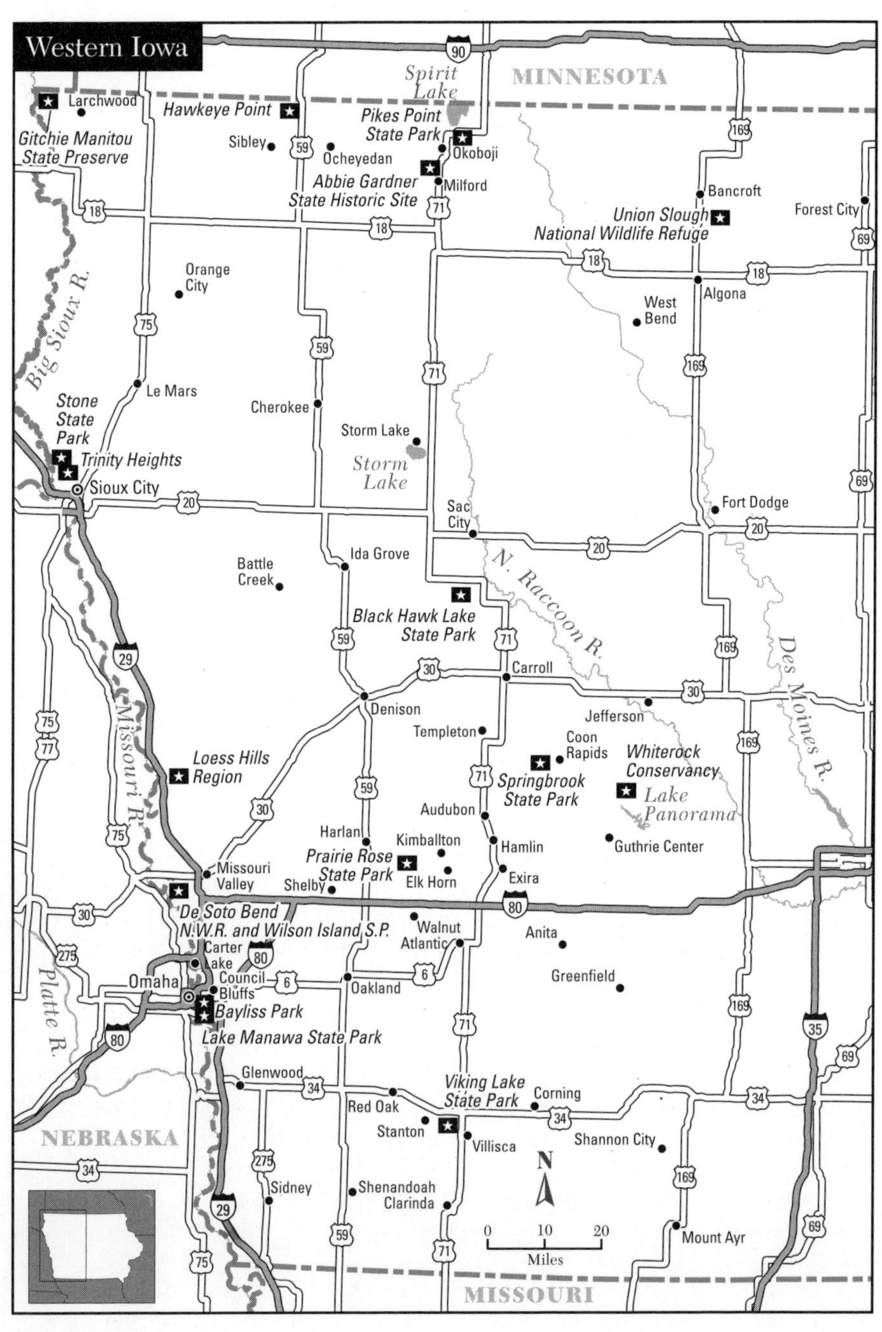
Western Iowa
MINNESOTA
Spirit Lake
Larchwood
Hawkeye Point
Gitchie Manitou State Preserve
Pikes Point State Park
Sibley
Ocheyedan
Okoboji
Abbie Gardner State Historic Site
Milford
Bancroft
Union Slough National Wildlife Refuge
Forest City
Orange City
Algona
West Bend
Big Sioux R.
Le Mars
Cherokee
Stone State Park
Trinity Heights
Sioux City
Storm Lake
Fort Dodge
Sac City
Ida Grove
Battle Creek
N. Raccoon R.
Black Hawk Lake State Park
Carroll
Des Moines R.
Denison
Jefferson
Templeton
Coon Rapids
Whiterock Conservancy
Missouri R.
Loess Hills Region
Springbrook State Park
Lake Panorama
Audubon
Harlan
Kimballton
Hamlin
Guthrie Center
Missouri Valley
Prairie Rose State Park
Elk Horn
Exira
Shelby
De Soto Bend N.W.R. and Wilson Island S.P.
Walnut
Atlantic
Anita
Carter Lake
Omaha
Council Bluffs
Oakland
Greenfield
Platte R.
Bayliss Park
Lake Manawa State Park
Glenwood
Viking Lake State Park
Corning
Red Oak
Stanton
Villisca
Shannon City
NEBRASKA
Sidney
Shenandoah
Clarinda
Mount Ayr
MISSOURI
N
0 10 20
Miles

WESTERN IOWA: A BRIEF OVERVIEW

The western half of Iowa is far away from the rest of the state—not just in miles but in attitude. Residents in the farthest reaches of the region feel closer to their neighbors South Dakota and Nebraska than they do to the capital of Des Moines. Even the weather is different. Situated in the rain shadow of the Rocky Mountains, the land in Iowa's western expanses receives less precipitation than the rest of the state. The farms are vaster, the population is less dense, and driving down some streets in western Iowa feels a bit like driving through the 1950s.

Yet at the same time, western Iowa is home to some of the state's oldest tourist attractions. In this the highest part of the state, lakes carved out by ancient glaciers dot the landscape. On the shores of deep, blue West Lake of Okoboji, Abbie Gardner opened up her family's log cabin to tell the story of the Spirit Lake Massacre in the mid-1800s. The resorts of Okoboji still attract visitors, but for less morbid reasons. Work on the Grotto of Redemption began in the early part of the 20th century, and for almost a hundred years it has drawn visitors to West Bend to the whimsical and awe-inspiring stone shrine. In the southwest, the mystery surrounding a brutal ax murder of a family in their beds still haunts the city of Villisca. And on their trip westward, America's most intrepid travelers, Meriwether Lewis and William Clark, passed through the areas that are now home to Council Bluffs and Sioux City.

The northwest corner is also home to some of the windiest parts of the state, and today investors harness the wind in the air along with the fertile soil on the ground. Silos and barns now share the horizon with massive white wind turbines, whose size are almost beyond comprehension. Among the farms and small towns of western Iowa are the birthplace homes of such beloved celebrities as Johnny Carson, Glenn Miller, Donna Reed, and Andy Williams. Along the spine of the Missouri River, the Loess Hills offer a lush, rolling landscape of fields and timbered valleys amidst a geological formation found in only two places in the world: Iowa and China.

This part is broken into five regions; the first, Iowa's Great Lakes, covers the four counties that surround the lakes of Okoboji. The next region, Northwest, includes Sioux City, Orange City, and Storm Lake as well as Cherokee, Sac City, and Lake View. Fort Dodge and Environs make up the third region. The fourth region—West Central—includes the counties located south of IA 30 and north of

I-80 and covers the Loess Hills, Denison, Carroll, Jefferson, and Lake Panorama. The final region covers the southwest quadrant of the state, including Council Bluffs and bordered by I-80 and I-35. The largest cities in the region are Sioux City, the Council Bluffs–Omaha area, and Fort Dodge, so much of this chapter focuses on those cities and the surrounding areas.

Travelers should expect to cover a lot of ground by car; happily, the highways and county roads are easy to navigate. Every small town in western Iowa, it seems, has a café, an inexpensive motel, and a county museum, but in this section, only the best of these are included.

IOWA'S GREAT LAKES: OKOBOJI AND ENVIRONS

One of Iowa's oldest and most popular vacation destinations is the region of five lakes called Okoboji. These deep, blue lakes were carved by glaciers millions of years ago, and, because of their proximity to the highest part of the state, they feel a breeze year-round.

Native Americans prized the lakes as rich hunting and fishing grounds, and European settlers started building log cabins and busting sod here in the middle 1800s. From the beginning, the lakes have attracted visitors. Abbie Gardner, a pioneer girl who was kidnapped by Native Americans, returned to her family cabin and turned it into a tourist destination for visitors who wanted to see the location of the 1857 Spirit Lake Massacre.

Vacationers began visiting the area before there were roads. Some bought the land surrounding the lakes from local farmers, who sold it for cheap because it was worthless for crops. After building their own cabins and cottages, the vacationers sold parcels of land to their friends, family, and co-workers. These vacation pioneers traveled from the train station to their homes on small steam-powered ferryboats like the *Queen Mary.* Her daughter, the *Queen Mary II,* takes today's sightseers on tours of the West Okoboji Lake.

Okoboji's lakeshores are still crowded with vacationers in the summer. Countless cabins, hotels, campgrounds, and cottages line the lake, and the waters are filled with sailboats, fishermen, swimmers, and scuba divers. In the evenings, the big patios of hot spots on the lake, like the Barefoot Bar and Bracco, fill up with happy revelers imbibing fruity drinks and feeling very nearly tropical.

GUIDANCE **Okoboji Tourism Committee** (712-332-2209; www.vacationokoboji.com) is housed in the **Okoboji Spirit Center** located at 243 West Broadway, Arnolds Park. Open 10–7 Mon.–Sat., 10–5 Sun. in summer, 10–5 Mon.–Fri. in winter. (At the same location as the visitors center is the **Maritime Museum;** see *To See.*) Travel around the lake can be confusing, but the staff is great at giving directions and offering itinerary suggestions.

Getting There

By car: Located at the intersection of **US 71** and **IA 9** near the Minnesota border.

HISTORIC ARNOLD'S PARK AS SEEN FROM THE LAKE AT OKOBOJI

GETTING AROUND *By car:* Driving in the Okoboji area can be a little bewildering. Roads ring the lakes, and the area is made up of a network of small towns.

MEDICAL EMERGENCY Call **911**.

Lakes Regional Hospital (712-336-1230l; www.lakeshealth.org), US 71 South, Spirit Lake. Emergency medicine services.

INTERNET ACCESS Most cafés and many hotels offer free wireless Internet access.

✷ To See

✪ **Maritime Museum** (712-332-2209; www.vacationokoboji.com), 243 West Broadway, Arnolds Park; located in the **Okoboji Spirit Center**. Open 10–7 Mon.–Sat., 10–5 Sun. in summer, 10–5 Mon.–Fri. in winter. Free. Iowa's Great Lakes have a fascinating maritime history, all the more remarkable for it being a landlocked state. The museum is bright, clean, and packed with the crafts and equipment that crossed the lakes' waters as the resort community developed. The museum specializes in rare antique wooden boats and a reproduction of the old "Okoboji Store." A speedboat that crashed and sank in the 1930s and later recovered by a scuba diver is on display. Guided tours are available, but visitors can also just stroll through the museum on their own. A short, somewhat hokey video offers some insight into the history of the lakes.

Abbie Gardner State Historic Site (712-332-7248; www.iowahistory.org), 34 Monument Drive, Arnolds Park. Open Memorial Day weekend–Oct. 1, 12–4 Mon.–Fri, 9–4 Sat.–Sun. Free. This historic site marks the location of the "Spirit Lake Massacre." Dakota warriors, under the leader Inkpaduta, clashed with pioneer families during the long, cold spring of 1857. Thirty-three settlers were killed, and four girls, including Abbie Gardner, were kidnapped and held for ransom. Eventually Gardner purchased her family's cabin and turned it into Iowa's first tourist attraction, where she recounted the story of the massacre in thrilling detail.

Today travelers can see inside the cabin and learn about the massacre in an informative video in the visitors center.

The Higgins Museum (712-332-5859; www.thehigginsmuseum.org), 1507 Sanborn Avenue, Okoboji. Open mid-May–mid-Sept. 11–5:30 Tues.–Sun. Free. In a free-wheeling resort community hell-bent on the pursuit of fun in the sun, it is surprising, to say the least, to find a museum dedicated to the important but oh-so-dull world of banking—and yet, here it is. On display are a large collection of national bank notes, rare sheets of bank notes from the Midwest, and twenty thousand turn-of-the-20th-century Iowa photo postcards.

Iowa Rock 'n Roll Hall of Fame Museum (712-332-6540; www.iowarocknroll.com), 91 Lake Street, Arnolds Park; opposite Arnolds Park amusement park. Open mid-May–mid-Sept. 11–7 Mon.–Thurs., 11–8 Fri. and Sun., 11–9 Sat.; Sept.–May 11–5 Mon.–Fri., and weekends by appointment; $1.00 per person. The permanent displays at this museum, across from the historic Roof Garden, celebrate Iowa's rockers with a reproduction recording studio—including a broadcast booth and recording equipment—and plenty of information, posters, and memorabilia from the museum's inductees.

✷ To Do

✪ **Historic Arnolds Park** (712-332-2183; www.arnoldspark.com) 37 Lake Street, Arnolds Park. Open daily Memorial Day–Labor Day; hours and ticketing vary, but there's no admission to enter the park or beach. The Legend roller coaster is one of the oldest wooden roller coasters in the world. It speeds thrill-seekers through the park with great views of the lake. The park is small and right on the water, so it feels more like Coney Island than Disney World, but the result is quaint and accessible. The park also offers the usual assortment of midway games, concessions, shows, and go-karts, along with a wild, pirate-themed mini-golf park.

THIS SUNKEN WOODEN SPEEDBOAT ON DISPLAY AT THE MARITIME MUSEUM IN ARNOLDS PARK WAS RECOVERED FROM THE LAKE'S DEPTHS

QUEEN II TOURS HIGHLIGHT LAKE OKOBOJI'S HISTORY

✪ ***Queen Mary II* Excursions** (712-332-2183; www.arnoldspark.com), 37 Lake Street, Arnolds Park. Memorial Day–Labor Day; call or visit their Web site for departure information. Tickets: $14 per person. Before roads and cars became the preferred method of travel around the lakes, vacationers would take a train to the shore and then ride a steamboat to their resorts or cabins. The *Queen Mary* ferried hundreds of passengers around the lake before she was retired. Her daughter now takes visitors on 45-minute guided tours of the lake, highlighting the attractions and history of the lake during the excursion. The upper deck is open-air, and refreshments are available for purchase.

Extreme Watersports (712-332-5406; www.extremewatersports.us), Historic Arnolds Park, 37 Lake Street, Arnolds Park. Open daily 10–sunset, but call ahead for reservations. Parasail over the west lake 600 feet above the water; adventurers of all ages can fly, and there is no swimming or even getting wet. The company also offers rentals of Jet Skis, pontoon boats, water skis, inner tubes, wakeboards, paddleboats, and kayaks. Call or visit their Web site for rental rates.

Blue Water Divers (712-332-6370; www.bwdivers.com), Lake Side by Queen's Dock, Arnolds Park. Scuba dive in landlocked Iowa. This full-service dive shop takes visitors to explore the clear, blue depths of the lakes at Okoboji. They offer snorkeling, scuba-dive training, deep-water diving, night diving, and underwater photography. The course schedule is flexible, and classes start at $250. Trained staff can guide boat dives, as well; $40 for one take and $60 for two. They also have a retail shop for scuba gear and offer children's courses.

Okoboji Boat Works (712-332-9904; www.parksmarina.com), 1401 Lakeshore Drive, Okoboji. Located in the historic 1890s boat-building shop on Smith's Bay, this marina rents ski boats, pontoon fishing boats, wave runners, tubes, skis, wakeboards, paddleboats, kayaks, and boat slips. Visitors can also enjoy a swimming beach and a children's playground. The marina is full service and also offers food and beverages plus glass-bottomed boat rides. Call or visit their Web site for rental rates.

Camp Foster YMCA (712-336-3272; www.campfoster.org), 1769 260th Avenue, (CR M56), Spirit Lake. See the Great Lakes of Iowa from horseback. Trail rides can be arranged through this traditional YMCA summer camp, which is situated on East Lake. Call for reservation and rates.

Okoboji Expedition Co. (712-332-9001; www.expeditionco.com), 1021 US 71 South, Okoboji. Open Mon.–Sat. 9–6, Sun. 12–4. A full-service outdoor-recreation shop that offers sales, service, and rentals of high-quality bikes, skis and ski equipment, and kayaks. Guided tours on bike and cross-country skis are also available.

Brooks National Golf Club (712-332-5011; www.brooksgolfclub.com), 1201 Brooks Park Lane, Okoboji. The Brooks National has been serving golfers since 1932, and with three layouts, practice facilities, and private instruction, golfers from beginners to experts will enjoy putting through parkland, prairie, and wetlands preserved in association with the Audubon Cooperative Sanctuary System. Tee times can be reserved up to 30 days in advance on this 27-hole, par 71/72 course. In the evening make a reservation at the **Wileywood Restaurant** (www.diningokoboji.com), for steaks, grilled chops, entrée salads, and signature dishes from east Africa. Lighter fare of sandwiches, soups, and salads are served during the day. $$

Wild Rose Casino and Resort (712-852-3400; www.wildroseresorts.com), 777 Main Street, Emmetsburg. Open 24 hours daily. The Wild Rose Casinos (they also have a location in Clinton) are a step above the typically tacky riverboat casinos. This facility is designed to emulate the architecture and heritage of Emmetsburg without being gaudy. The casino offers table games of all sorts, a golf course, several restaurants, and hotel accommodations. The chic and stylish rooms range from $69–$199.

Arts on Grand (712-262-4307; www.artsongrand.com), 408 Grand Avenue, Spencer. Open 10–5 Mon.–Fri. (10–9 Thurs.), 10–3 Sat. A nonprofit gallery featuring rotating exhibits of works by local artists. During the day, browse the artwork on the gallery floor (all for sale), which ranges from paintings to woodworking. In the evening stop in for poetry readings, films, and special events.

✷ Where to Stay

HOTELS AND MOTELS **The Inn at Okoboji Resort and Conference Center** (712-332-2113; www.bojifun.com), 3301 Lakeshore Drive, Okoboji. With 156 rooms that range from standard accommodations to luxury suites, the inn has something for practically everyone. In operation since 1896, the resort offers a restaurant, bar, coffee bar, golf course, pools, boat rental, and programs for children. Rooms from $95–$395.

Crescent Beach Lodge (1-800-147-1117; www.crescentbeachlodge.com), 1620 Lakeshore Drive, Wahpeton. Open May–Sept. The resort offers 49 renovated, completely equipped rooms, four condos, and a cottage. But the best part is the sand beach. The resort also offers an island playground, mini-golf, tennis courts, and laundry. Accommodations from $50–$250.

Fillenwarth Beach (712-332-5646; www.fillenwarthbeach.com), 87 Lakeshore Drive, Arnolds Park. Fillenwarth is a classic family-beach resort. Nestled under shady trees on West Lake, Fillenwarth offers all types of accommodations—from motel rooms to cottages, from duplexes to apartments—at a wide span of pricing. Daily activities such as boating, water sports, volleyball, and tennis are organized at the park, and there are both indoor and outdoor pools on-site. Accommodations from $70–$970.

Shamrock Inn (712-336-2668), US 71 and CR 9 West, Spirit Lake. The Shamrock is the traditional choice for budget off-lake accommodations in the Okoboji area. The small motel offers 36 rooms with mini-fridges plus an outdoor swimming pool. Rooms (including continental breakfast) from $34–$110.

Wild Rose Casino and Resort See *To Do.*

COTTAGES **Manhattan Beach Resort** (712-337-3481; www.manhattanbeachresort.com), 2714 Manhattan Boulevard, Spirit Lake. The resort at Manhattan Beach is one of the oldest and most historic on West Lake; guests have enjoyed the sand beach and great views of the lake for more than a century. The units are one- to three-bedroom cottages with cable, sofa sleepers, kitchenettes, and outdoor fire pits. Some units can be rented on a daily basis, but most are rented by the week, month, or season. One-bed one-bath rooms are $1,100 per week, two-bed one-bath are $250 per day or $1,600 per week; larger accommodations are available to rent on a per-season basis.

Pick's Lakeshore Resort (712-332-2688), 108 Monument Drive, Arnolds Park. Tucked in the shady trees, just steps from Arnolds Park and the Abbie Gardner cabin, Pick's is a family resort offering great views. They have individually decorated units with kitchenettes, air-conditioning, and cable television. Cabins from $95–$165.

Arnolds Park Classic Cottages (712-332-5320; winter 402-896-3850), 35 Zephyr Drive, Arnolds Park. The 10 cottages are directly across from all of the fun at Historic Arnolds Park. Two- and three-bedroom cottages with air-conditioning, heat, cable television, and stocked kitchens are available at daily or weekly rates. Cottages from $75–$170.

Blue Lake Resort (712-332-2817; www.bluelakeokoboji.com), 113 Monument Drive, Arnolds Park. Situated on West Lake, this resort offers four-bedroom cabins, three-bedroom cottages, or a suite unit with a kitchenette; gas grills and patio fireplaces enhance long summer evenings on the lake. The resort is within walking distance of all the fun of the lakes. Cottages from $75–$265.

BED & BREAKFASTS **Hannah Marie Country Inn** (712-262-1286; www.hannahmarieinn.com), 4070 US 71, Spencer. The romance and elegance of country living await guests at the Hannah Marie. Mary Nichols has run this classic American B&B for more than 20 years. Each of the rooms is elegantly themed and full of such lovely touches as feather beds and whirlpool tubs. Outside, visitors can enjoy the gardens in peace and quiet. Breakfast is amazing and served in courses. Rooms from $50–$75.

Kingman Place Bed and Breakfast (712-336-6865; www.kingmanplace.com), 13710 240th Avenue, Spirit Lake. Open year-round. Guests can relax in this 1870 colonial home on Spirit Lake. Swim or boat from the dock, or relax in private sitting rooms. The three guest rooms offer queen-size feather beds and private bathrooms, and a full breakfast is served by candlelight. Rooms from $109–$149.

The Queen Marie Victorian Bed & Breakfast (712-852-4700; www.nwiowabb.com/newqueen), 707 Harrison Street, Emmetsburg. An 1890s Victorian home that served as a showpiece for its owner, lumber baron J. J. Shaw, the Queen Marie offers six guest rooms and suites decorated with antiques and floral motifs. Room (including breakfast) from $80–$120.

CAMPING **Gull Point State Park** (712-337-3870), 1500 Harpen Street, Wahpeton. Open year-round. Gull Point is a popular state park on the West Lake of Okoboji, with a sandy beach and a boat dock. The lodge dates back to the 1930s and was built by the Civilian Conservation Corps. The campsites are shady and comfortable and range from $11–$16 per night.

Cenla Campground (712-336-2925; www.okobojicamping.com), 1 mile south of IA 9 Junction 3400 US 71, Spirit Lake. Open Apr.–Oct. Many of the 120 sites at this campground are on the lakeshore, and the campground is a complete resort, with television hook-ups, clean restrooms, a heated pool, a dock, and a store on-site. Campsites $20.50 per night.

✷ Where to Eat

DINING OUT ✪ **Kazarelli's at Millers Bay** (712-337-3238), 1127 Lakeside Avenue, Wahpeton. Open for dinner. The classic Italian-American restaurant on the lakes, Kazarelli's serves fresh fish, smoked seafood and chicken, steaks, and decadent pastas. Tues. and Fri. nights bring a fantastic walleye fry, and a retail wine shop is in the works. Takeout is available. $$

Fresh Bistro (712-336-3700), 1621 Hill Avenue, Spirit Lake. Open year-round for breakfast and lunch Mon.–Sat., dinner Thurs.–Sat. This funky little bistro is housed in a sunny storefront on historic Hill Avenue in Spirit Lake. The bistro blends American favorites with international flavors. The menu changes seasonally, but expect unique sandwiches and wraps, burgers, ahi tuna, and elegant salads and pastas. Carry-out service is available, and reservations are recommended, especially during the busy summer season. Breakfast and lunch $$, Dinner $$–$$$.

Y **Bracco** (712-332-7900), 317 240th Avenue, Arnolds Park. Open daily for breakfast, lunch, dinner, and bar time. Settle in under the big umbrellas on the deck at this outdoor bar and grill, and watch the breeze caress the lake while enjoying American/Caribbean/Cajun-style dishes: battered reef fish, fish tacos, flatbread pizzas, nachos, and steaks. A tempting array of frozen, blended daiquiris seem innocent but pack a punch and make for a lively bar scene in the evening. Continental and buffet breakfast served daily. Breakfast $$, Lunch and dinner $$–$$$.

The Prime Rib (712-262-4625), 1205 South Grand Avenue, Spencer. Open for dinner Tues.–Sat. The prime rib at this locally owned restaurant is cooked in a special oven designed to create the juiciest, tastiest beef in the area. The delicious roasted beef sandwiches are hearty, and a select offering of salads and pasta dishes are also on the menu. $$

EATING OUT **O'Farrell Sisters Restaurant** (712-332-7901), 1109 Lakeshore Drive, Okoboji. Open for breakfast and lunch Tues.–Sun. Started by the three O'Farrell sisters and now operated by family members, the sisters' restaurant has been an Okoboji tradition since 1949 for breakfast, pancakes, and homemade pies. $

Bob's in Arnolds Park (712-332-6564), Historic Arnolds Park. Open daily for lunch and dinner. The summer home of the famous Bob Dog: the Historic Arnolds Park venue is owned by the folks at Bob's Drive Inn in LeMars, near Sioux City. Hot dogs, burgers, fries, and ice cream make for casual lakefront lunches; a patio looks out over the water. $

Smokin' Jakes (712-332-5152), 117 West Broadway, Arnolds Park. Open for lunch, dinner, and late-night (or early-morning) breakfast daily 11 AM–3 AM during summer. The meats are hickory-smoked every day, and the sauce goes on the side of the famous baby-back pork ribs. Homemade sandwiches and soups, ice cream, happy-hour specials, and a late-night breakfast menu (11 PM–3 AM) gives diners a tasty alternative at all hours of the day. $–$$

Y **Tweeter's in Okoboji** (712-332-9421; www.tweetersokoboji.com), 127 US 71 South, Okoboji. Open daily for lunch, dinner, and bar time. This sports bar offers an enormous menu, from walleye cheeks to beef nachos. There are melts, skillets, Oscars, chicken wings, and dessert. Or go with the classics: prime rib, sandwiches, steaks, and pasta. The atmosphere is friendly, the big-screen televisions are tuned into sports, and the prices are reasonable. $$

COFFEE, TREATS, AND MARKETS

Muggabeans (712-338-4005; www.muggabeans.com), 1001 Okoboji Avenue, Milford. Open 7–5 Mon.–Sat. Just south of the lake area, this coffee shop in Milford is a comfortable place to get a cup of java and a pastry and plan a day on the Great Lakes.

Hey, Good Cookies! (712-336-4179; www.heygoodcookies.com), 1310A 18th Street, Spirit Lake. Open Mon.–Fri. 7:30–7, Sat. 9–7, Sun. 12–5 year-round. Vacationers don't even have to get out of the car to get a treat—this bakery/ice-cream shop has a drive-through window. Try all seven of the specialty cookies, from triple-chocolate chews to Aunt Bet's original oatmeal, peanut-butter, and chocolate-chip cookies. Hand-dipped ice cream, coffee, soups, and sandwiches are also served through the evenings.

The Okoboji Candy Company (712-332-2315), across from Arnolds Park Amusement Park, Arnolds Park. Open 10–10 daily Memorial Day–Labor Day. This family-owned candy shop has been making their famous black-walnut taffy since 1919. The sticky treat keeps a sweet tooth busy while cruising the boardwalk.

The Market (712-336-2520; www.themarketcoop.com), 1610 Hill Avenue, Spirit Lake. Open Mon.–Fri. 9–6, Sat. 9–3, Sun. 10–3; shorter hours off-season. This brand-new market specializes in natural and organic foods, from produce to meat and dairy. Fresh breads are available on Thurs., and the market offers wine, beer, and all-natural body-care products. In the "global deli," grab a wrap, sandwich, salad, or espresso for a lakeside picnic or a Hill Avenue stroll.

✷ Drinking Establishments

✪ **Barefoot Bar** (712-332-7303; www.parksmarina.com), 1 mile east of US 71 on East Lake. The marina is open year-round, but call ahead for bar hours in the off-season. The bar, in Parks Marina, is the hip place to relax island style after a day on the water. Thirsty vacationers drink fruity tropical blended drinks and listen to live music in this thatched-hut Tiki-themed bar, which creates the illusion of island living in northwestern Iowa.

✷ Entertainment

Okoboji Summer Theatre (712-332-7773; www.stephens.edu/news/stephensevents/okoboji), 2001 US 71 North, Okoboji. Before June 11 write to Okoboji Summer Theatre, Box 341, Spirit Lake, IA 51360 for reservations and tickets. Box office opens after June 11, Mon. 10–5, Tues.–Sat. 10–9, Sun. 1–7. During the short summer season, B.F.A. students from Stephens College in Columbia, Missouri, manage, produce, and star in nine shows that range from comedies to big Broadway-style musicals. The troupe also produces the **Boji Bantam Children's Theater**. Tickets sell out quickly.

Pearson Lakes Arts Center (712-332-7013; www.lakesart.org), 2201 US 71, Okoboji. Open 10–4 Mon.–Sat. (10–9 Thurs.), 12–3 Sun. This art gallery and performance space offers permanent and traveling exhibits of fine arts, presents theatrical events and performances, and sponsors a series of classic and foreign films. The center also hosts a juried art fair, art in the park, and classes and workshops for students of all ages. Call or visit their Web site for ticket and schedule information.

Funny Barn Comedy Club (712-336-4888; www.funnybarn.com), 1605 Hill Avenue, Spirit Lake. National and regional comedy acts perform weekends at this comedy club on Hill Avenue. Pizza, sandwiches, and appetizers are served on the weekends in the on-site restaurant.

✻ Selective Shopping

Hill Avenue Book Co. (712-336-5672), 1711 Hill Avenue, Spirit Lake. Open Mon.–Fri. 9:30–5:30, Sat. 9:30–5, Sun. 12–4.; closed Sundays off-season. Books for everybody on every subject are available in this quaint independent bookstore. The selection is fantastic and well chosen; don't miss the excellent Iowa section, which includes history, travel books, and other titles on the Corn State. Magazines, cards, and gifts are also for sale.

This 'N That Eclectics (712-336-4411), 1618 Hill Avenue, Spirit Lake. Open Mon.–Sat. 9:30–5, call for Sunday hours as they are occasional. This strange shop sells both creative home accents—handmade furniture, Haitian yard art, country arts and crafts—and consignment clothing for the whole family. Leave with a gently used outfit and some trout paperweights.

Okoboji Trading Co. (712-336-9400; www.okobojitradingcompany.com), 2323 165th Street, Spirit Lake. Open Tues.–Sat. 9–6. Shop for treats for a BBQ or to fill a cottage kitchen with fresh fish, gourmet coffee beans, deli sandwiches, prepared foods, and wines.

NORTHWEST

INCLUDING SIOUX CITY, ORANGE CITY, STORM LAKE, CHEROKEE, SAC CITY, AND LAKE VIEW

In 1804 and in 1806 the Corps of Discovery captained by Lewis and Clark traveled through the region that is now where Iowa, Nebraska, and South Dakota meet. The land surrounding Sioux City is known as "Siouxland," and its history was shaped by the Native Americans who roamed the plains, the trappers and settlers who journeyed to the land, and the steamboats that eventually brought goods up the river and to the settlements farther west. Later came railroad and steamboat travel. During the industrial age that followed at the end of the 19th century, Sioux City was the "Chicago of the Great Plains." Wander down Historic Fourth Street to view the freshly renovated buildings, and then be sure to visit the sites dedicated to those intrepid explorers who opened up the West.

Other sites in the region include the highest point in Iowa at a not exactly awe-inspiring 1,670 feet, the Dutch community of Orange City, Storm Lake, Cherokee, Sac City, and the southernmost glacial lake in Iowa, Black Hawk, at Lake View.

SIOUX CITY

Sioux City, dating back to 1857, is the largest metropolitan area in the northwestern corner of the state. It sits on the Missouri River and shares borders with Nebraska and South Dakota. The area was first important to the Great Plains Native Americans, for whom it is named; it later saw fur trappers before the Louisiana Purchase. Lewis and Clark made an unforeseen stop here when one of the crew fell ill and died of appendicitis on the shores of the river that is now named after him. Today many of the attractions of the city are dedicated to their history. The explorers were followed by steamboats bringing settlers and goods from St. Louis, and visitors can learn about the importance of steamboat and railroad travel to the area. Sioux City is also known for the crash of US Airlines flight 232 in 1989, when 111 passengers perished, but 185 were saved by local rescue crews. Recently, the city has seen a resurgence. It hosts a fantastic art museum, a state-of-the-art fitness center, casinos, restaurants, and a lively nightlife scene on Historic Fourth Avenue.

GUIDANCE **Sioux City Tourism Bureau** (712-279-4800; www.siouxcitytourism.com), 801 Fourth Street, Sioux City. Open during business hours. Attraction, dining, lodging, and shopping information for the entire Siouxland region. Call or visit their Web site for tourism information.

Downtown Sioux City (www.downtownsiouxcity.com), for information for the downtown area of the city and Historic Fourth Street, including walking tours, parking, and history. Call or visit their Web site for tourism information.

GETTING THERE *By air:* **Sioux Gateway Airport** (712-279-6165; www.flysux.com), 2403 Aviation Boulevard, Sioux City. Despite the unfortunate airport code of SUX, this modern airport offers connecting and regional flights.

By car: Find Sioux City along the Missouri River on **I-29** and **US 77/US 75.**

MEDICAL EMERGENCY Call **911**.

Mercy Sioux City (712-279-2010; www.mercysiouxcity.com), 801 Fifth Street, Sioux City. This large regional hospital offers emergency medicine and urgent-care services.

INTERNET ACCESS Many cafés, restaurants, and accommodations provide free wireless Internet access.

✷ To See

✪ **Sioux City Art Center** (712-279-6272; www.siouxcityartcenter.org), 225 Nebraska Street, Sioux City. Open 10–5 Tues.–Sat. (10–9 Thurs.), 1–5 Sun. Free. The three-story atrium of this museum offers art lovers nine hundred permanent pieces, including the breathtaking Grant Wood's *Corn Room* mural. The pieces surround the viewer with the golden cornfields of an idealized Iowa landscape. The permanent collection also includes an extensive assemblage of portraits and self-portraits, a rotating exhibit of video art, and student-artist-in-residence works. The museum also hosts traveling exhibits, a gift shop, and interactive programs for both children and adults. The galleries are spacious and thoughtful, and the swift of foot can attempt the labyrinth at the base of the spiral stairs.

Trinity Heights (712-239-8670; www.sctrinityheights.org), 2509 33rd Street, Sioux City. Grounds open 7 AM–6 PM daily, extended hours in summer. Free but donations requested. In a parklike complex, a 33-foot stainless-steel statue of Jesus and a 30-foot statue of the Virgin Mary tower over Sioux City. Walkways and religious tributes abound among manmade streams, ponds, and benches. Inside, stretching 22 feet in length, is a life-size sculpture of the Last Supper.

THE QUEEN OF PEACE RENDERED IN 30 FEET OF STAINLESS STEEL AT TRINITY HEIGHTS, SIOUX CITY

Sioux City Public Museum (712-279-6174; www.siouxcitymuseum.org),

AT THE LEWIS AND CLARK INTERPRETIVE CENTER IN SIOUX CITY, STATUES OF THE FAMED EXPLORERS (AND THEIR DOG) GAZE ACROSS THE MISSOURI RIVER

CAPTAIN LEWIS, CAPTAIN CLARK, AND SERGEANT FLOYD

In 1804 the Corps of Discovery, led by Captain Meriwether Lewis and Captain William Clark, made its way up the Missouri River to explore the lands of the Louisiana Purchase. In August of that year, one of their team, Sergeant Charles Floyd Jr., died of appendicitis. His death was the only casualty of an otherwise-lucky expedition that braved rivers, mountains, and hostile Native Americans

2901 Jackson Street, Sioux City. Open 9–5 Tues.–Sat., 1–5 Sun. Free. Located in the 1893 John Peirce Mansion, the museum explores the history of Sioux City and the surrounding area. The building itself—made of red South Dakota quartzite—is a monument to the unique history of the area. (Peirce attempted to sell the mansion through a nationwide raffle.) Interactive exhibits illustrate the culture of the Lakota Sioux, Winnebago, and Omaha tribes as well as the lives of early settlers with a log cabin and artifacts. Visitors can also learn about the history of the city both inside and out with lectures and walking tours of the historic areas around the city.

Flight 232 Memorial, 100 Larsen Park Road, Sioux City. Open daily. On July 19, 1989, United Flight 232 was en route from Denver to Chicago when an explosion cut off the hydraulic power. Pilot Al Haynes, off-duty captain Dennis Fitch, and the crew kept the plane in the air for 44 minutes until they reached Sioux City. Of as it made its way to the Oregon coast. Today Sioux City remembers the captains and poor Sergeant Floyd.

Start your own personal corps of discovery with a visit to the **Sioux City Lewis & Clark Interpretive Center** (712-224-5242; www.siouxcitylcic.com; 900 Larsen Park Road. Open 9–5 Tues.–Sat. and 12–5 Sun.; free admission). The center, on the banks of the Missouri River, is guarded by a larger-than-life statue of the intrepid captains and their faithful canine friend, Seaman. Inside, explorers will find an elegant interactive museum with talking displays, activities, and a keelboat theater. The center also examines life in the Louisiana Purchase today through rotating exhibits of art, photography, and videos. Then head up the bluff to the **Sergeant Floyd Monument** (712-279-0198; www.siouxcitymuseum.org; 2601 South Lewis Boulevard, open daily year-round), to see the 100-foot white-stone obelisk that marks Sergeant Floyd's burial place. The view over the river valley and city is breathtaking.

Lewis and Clark are also the special focus of the **Sergeant Floyd River Museum and Welcome Center** (712-279-0198; www.siouxcitymuseum.org; 100 Larsen Park Road; open 9–5 daily). Housed in a historic diesel inspection ship that once belonged to the Army Corps of Engineers, the center tells the history of Missouri River Valley transportation with scale-model steamboats and keelboats, photos, artifacts, and dioramas. And, of course, visitors can also learn about the titular sergeant and his leaders.

And just when it seems like there couldn't be any more Lewis and Clark fun, visitors can find their way to the Southern Hills Mall and **Lewis & Clark: An American Adventure** (712-274-0109; www.southernhillsmall.com; IA 20 east to Lakeport Road; open 10–9 Mon.–Sat., 12–6 Sun). Thirty-eight mural scenes depict the dynamic duo's trail, from start to heroic finish.

the 284 passengers and 12 crew, 112 people died. A statue created from a photo taken of Dennis Nielson, an Iowa National Guard rescue worker, carrying a child away from the wreckage serves as a memorial to the tragedy and the heroics of local rescue teams.

✷ To Do

Long Lines Family Recreation Center (712-224-5124; www.sioux-city.org), 401 Gordon Drive, Sioux City. Hours and admission vary by day and activity, so call or visit their Web site for information. The crown jewels of this recreation center are a 53-foot world-class climbing wall and a freestanding boulder for adventurous rock climbers. The facility also includes indoor batting cages, in-line hockey, soccer, basketball, and wrestling.

✱ Green Space

Dorothy Pecaut Nature Center (712-258-0838; www.woodburyparks.com), 4500 Sioux River Road, Sioux City. Open year-round, 9–5 Tues.–Sat., 1–5 Sun.; June–Sept. 1, 9–8 Thurs. The nature center in the heart of **Stone State Park** focuses on the unique geology of the Loess Hills. Hands-on exhibits, history programs, and miles of trails through prairie land and burr-oak forests give visitors an up-close and educational view of the area. Children will love seeing the live reptiles and fish on display plus the butterfly and wildflower gardens. A professional staff produces programs year-round. **Stone State Park** (712-255-4698; www.iowadnr.com/parks; 5001 Talbot Road, Sioux City) offers picnicking, hiking, and camping facilities in a small campground with electrical hook-ups and camping cabins.

✱ Where to Stay

There are few independent hotels, motels, and inns in the Sioux City area, but there are several chain hotels and motels.

Palmer House Motel (712-276-4221; www.palmerhousemotel.net), 3440 Gordon Drive East, Sioux City. A small, clean, family-operated motel with inexpensive rooms, cable, and continental breakfast. Rooms from $30–$55.

✱ Where to Eat

DINING OUT **Luciano's** (712-258-5174), 1019 Fourth Street, Sioux City. Open for dinner Tues.–Sat. The beauty of the space competes with the food in this elegant restaurant. The room is all shiny hardwood, deep booths, and dim lighting, but diners come for the Italian cuisine—seafood fettuccini, ravioli with spicy sausage, and veal Parmesan—along with unique salads and appetizers. Wait for the star corner table at the martini bar, or browse the shelves at the adjoining wine shop. $$–$$$

EATING OUT 🍸 **Rebos** (712-258-0395), 1101 Fourth Street, Sioux City. Open Tues.–Sun. for lunch, dinner, bar time, and Sun. brunch. On Fourth Street, Rebos dishes up fresh and spunky high-end Caribbean, Mexican, and New Mexican cuisine. The specialties include Jamaican jerk chicken, your-choice asadas, and an "evil" blackened-chicken Cajun penne. The sandwiches and wood-fired pizzas are both tasty and refreshingly different, and in the evenings and on the weekends the bar scene is fueled with homemade sangria and vodkas. $$

Green Gables Restaurant (712-258-4246), 1800 Pierce Street, Sioux City. Open daily for lunch and dinner. This family restaurant has been serving Sioux City since 1929. The decor is a little quirky, and the food is American standard (chicken, ribs, hamburgers, and sandwiches), but the service is friendly, the dishes are tasty, and the prices are reasonable. $–$$

Milwaukee Wiener House (712-277-3449), 309 Pearl Street, Sioux City. Open 5 AM–6 PM Mon.–Sun., but call ahead just to be safe. Since 1918 this Sioux City diner has been creating classic "Coney dogs"—small hot dogs served with finely ground meat, onions, and mustard. This Sioux City tradition also offers hamburgers, milk shakes, and soda pop in glass bottles. Credit cards not accepted. $

Sweet Fanny's (712-258-3434), 1024 Fourth Street, Sioux City. Open daily for lunch and dinner. Dine on steaks, chops, wings, and specialties such as beef stroganoff and Greek salad under a decorative motorcycle-and-1940s-army theme. There's a long list of beers in this Fourth Street dining room and pub. $–$$

COFFEE AND MARKETS **Pierce Street Coffee Works** (712-255-1226), 1920 Pierce Street, Sioux City. Open 7–6 Mon.–Fri. and 8–3 Sat.–Sun. Caffeine lovers and laptop rangers couldn't hope for a cuter coffee shop in a funky residential neighborhood just east of downtown. The Coffee Works offers the whole host of bean beverages, including soy lattes and French-press coffee, along with sandwiches, delicious salads, and hummus wraps in a warm, eclectic space with free wireless Internet. Lunch $$.

The Firehouse Market (712-224-3535; www.firehousemarket.com), 1221 Fifth Street, Sioux City. Open 9–6 Mon.–Fri., 9–5 Sat. This market, housed in a historic downtown firehouse, is the heart of the local- and organic-food scene in Sioux City. In the summer months the farmer's market sets up outside, when located inside, produce and products from all over the rich Missouri River Valley can be found in daily specials, regional dairy foods, snacks, baked goods, and health and beauty products.

✷ Drinking Establishments

Buffalo Alice (712-255-4822; www.buffaloalice.com), 1022 Fourth Street, Sioux City. Open daily for lunch, dinner, and bar hours. The walls are covered in vintage signs, the hardwood floors are maple, and the big windows look out on the busy sidewalk, but with a selection of 115 beers, it hardly matters how attractive this pub is. The menus for draft and bottle beer are no light reading, so try homemade pizza, pasta, and chicken wings while making a beverage choice. In the summer, a beer garden opens out back. A lunch buffet is served during the week. $$

✷ Entertainment

Orpheum Theatre (712-279-4850; www.orpheumlive.com), 528 Pierce Street, Sioux City. Events in the restored 1927 Rapp & Rapp theater include symphony concerts, Broadway shows, movies, and conferences. Call or visit their Web site for show schedule and ticket pricing. Tours of the theater are also available.

BUFFALO ALICE IS ONE OF THE MANY RESTAURANTS AND BARS THAT LINE HISTORIC FOURTH STREET IN SIOUX CITY

Tyson Events Center and Gateway Arena (1-800-593-2228; www.tysoncenter.com), 401 Gordon Drive, Sioux City. Call or visit their Web site for hours and ticketing. The arena is the home of the Sioux City Musketeers hockey team and the Bandits indoor football team, along with concerts and conferences.

Promenade Cinema 14 (712-277-8300; www.mainstreettheatres.com), 924 Fourth Street, Sioux City. A multiplex on historic Fourth Street with first-run films and an extensive snack bar.

✷ Selective Shopping

Viva (712-258-8482), 1922 Pierce Street, Sioux City. Open 10–6 Mon.–Sat., Sun. by chance. This kooky shop sells the goods for everyone on a souvenir list. Start by browsing the local products, soaps, Sioux City goodies, and such, but don't miss the funky jewelry, cards, and clothes.

Dowry Costumes & Antiques (712-255-8007; www.dowrycostumes.com), 704 Floyd Boulevard, Sioux City. Open 10–8 Mon., 10–5 Tues.–Sat. Established in 1976 as an antiques and vintage-clothing shop, Dowry's is now one of the largest costume stores in the Midwest, with holiday and period costumes, masks, and makeup for the whole family—along with unique antiques and gifts.

LEMARS, IOWA: ICE CREAM CAPITAL OF THE WORLD

The rich fields of northwest Iowa make for excellent dairy cattle, and since 1913 the Wells family has turned milk into magic. The population of LeMars is only 9,500, but the Wells Dairy freezes and flavors over 120 million gallons of Wells Blue Bunny Ice Cream every year, making it the (self-proclaimed) "ice cream capital of the world."

If you scream and the kids scream, you had better stop for ice cream at the Wells' Dairy **Ice Cream Capital of the World Museum and Visitor Center** (712-546-4090; www.wellsdairy.com; US 75 at exit 118, LeMars; open 10–5 Mon.–Fri., 10–4 Sat., 12–4 Sun. May–Sept., 10–4 Tues.–Sat. Oct.–Apr.; admission: $3 adults, $1 children). The modern, family-friendly museum offers video and interactive computer displays on the history of the dairy, the process of making ice cream, and dairy memorabilia. In one exhibit room guests walk past industrial ice-cream equipment while the heavenly smells of chocolate and cream are pumped into the room. At the end of the tour is a classic American ice-cream parlor and gift shop. Sample the flavors and browse for Wells' Dairy gifts and goodies.

If the ice cream wasn't enough calories, cross the highway and grab lunch or dinner at **Bob's Drive-In**, which has been in business since 1949 and serves the Iowa classic "loose-meats sandwich" ground beef cooked loose, drained of fat, and dressed like a hamburger. Also try "Coney dogs," fries, and malted–milk shakes. The food is inexpensive, but Bob's does not take credit cards.

LeMars is a short drive north and east of Sioux City on US 75.

ORANGE CITY

Orange City is as Dutch as the community of Pella in central Iowa, but it's just a little more out of the way. Tucked up in northwest Iowa between Sioux City and Sioux Falls, South Dakota, this charming, traditional community is worth the drive. Orange City is also home to Northwestern College, a small liberal-arts institution. Iowa's highest elevation is beyond Orange City, near the northwest corner of the state, in Sibley. Visitors will find a few other noteworthy spots in these distant reaches, as well.

GUIDANCE **Dutch Windmill Visitors Center** (712-707-4510; www.orangecityiowa.com), 509 Eighth Street Southeast, CR 10, Orange City. Open 9–4 Mon.–Fri. The Orange City windmill reaches 76 feet, with a 5-ton dome and working blades. Inside the windmill is tourism information for the city and the region as well as Dutch souvenirs.

GETTING THERE *By car:* Cross the northwest corner of the state on **US 60** which runs north-south at a diagonal, or use **IA 9** and **IA 75** to access most of the region.

MEDICAL EMERGENCY Call **911**.

Orange City Hospital (712-737-4984; www.ochealthsystem.org), 1000 Lincoln Circle, Orange City. Emergency medical care services available.

✷ To See

The Old Factory (712-707-4242), 110 Fourth Street Southwest, Orange City. Open 9–5:30 Mon.–Wed. and Fri, 9–7 Thurs., 9–5 Sat. Free. The old wooden-shoe factory is one of the oldest buildings in Orange City and is in the character of the Old World. Demonstrations of shoe carvings are available, and wearable wooden klompen are available for purchase. Imported Dutch delft, lace, antiques, tiles, and food are also for sale.

DUTCH WOODEN SHOES ARE STILL MADE AT THE OLD FACTORY IN ORANGE CITY

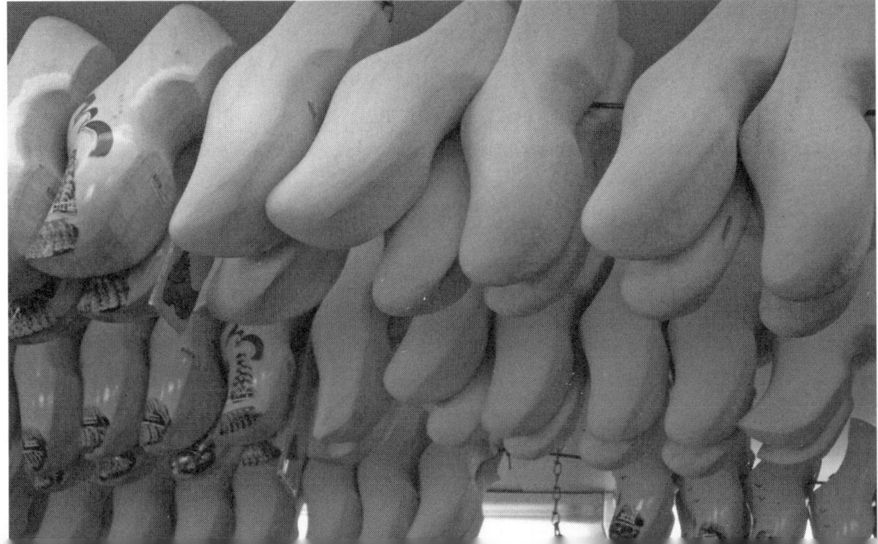

AT 1,670 FEET, HAWKEYE POINT IN SIBLEY IS THE HIGHEST ELEVATION IN IOWA—AND A CORNFIELD

Hawkeye Point, Sterler Farm, IA 60, just north of Sibley. Watch for the road sign. At 1,670 feet, Iowa's highest elevation—the 42nd highest in the United States—is actually located at the end of a feed trough under a silo on the old Sterler family farm. "Highpointers"—people who seek to climb the highest point in each state—and other curious travelers find their way to this distant part of Iowa, but the view from the "top" is not much to write home about. The land around the high point rolls away from it gradually in miles of fields of corn and beans, though the windmills in the distance are awfully picturesque. Still, Hawkeye Point has its charms, even if it is just to say you've been there. The Iowa State Extension bought the farm and runs offices out of the house.

The Ocheyedan Mound (712-754-2523; www.osceolacountyia.com), CR A22, 1 mile south and 1 mile east of Ocheyedan. The mound at Ocheyedan, a glacial kame, was once thought to be the highest point in the state, and it seems like it *should* be the highest point. The mound looms over the much flatter surrounding countryside. It was formed by the same glaciers that dug the deep lakes in the

THE ONE-FINGER SALUTE

Iowans are friendly, that's for sure, and on the gravel roads of rural Iowa, they greet one another in an interesting way. When a driver—usually of a beat-up pickup truck—approaches another car, he will lift his index finger straight up off the steering wheel: the one-finger salute. Occasionally a driver will lift two fingers from his grip, but usually it's just the one. The one-finger salute is just one of the casual, no-nonsense ways Iowans say hello to their neighbors. The one-finger salute does seem to be disappearing as more and more farmers use cell phones in their cars, but don't let that stop you from offering the greeting to passing trucks before they disappear into the distance in a cloud of dust.

area. The park surrounding the mound is small, but there are native grasses, wetlands, and a great view from the top of the easy climb.

✱ Green Space

Windmill Park (712-707-4510; www.octulipfestival.com), Central Avenue and Second Street Northwest, Orange City. Open daylight hours. The park at the center of town is crowded with tulips and fun Dutch touches. The phone and information booths look like windmills, there is a giant wooden shoe, and a pretty little stream runs under bridges and through gardens. The park also has a stage for events and a large playground for children.

Gitchie Manitou State Preserve (515-281-5918; www.iowadnr.com/preserves), CR K10, west of Larchwood. Open daily during daylight hours. Iowa's state preserves are not as developed as its state parks, but they do protect some of the most beautiful landscapes in the state. Gitchie Manitou is a small preserve at the farthest corner of the state. Launch a canoe for a trip down the Big Sioux River, or hike through prairie and timberlands. No Department of Natural Resources staff is on-site, so use caution and common sense.

✱ Where to Stay

BED & BREAKFASTS 🐾 **Aunt Reba's Bed & Breakfast** (712-478-4042; www.auntrebas.com), 2124 IA 9, Larchwood. "Aunt" Reba and her husband, Rich Crawford, welcome guests and their horses to their comfortable country home and ranch in the farthest corner of northwest Iowa. Reba is a horse lover and owns two exotic Peruvian horses, and the ranch is an idyllic spot for both horse and rider. Rootbeer floats welcome guests at the door. Guests can choose either the Honeymoon Suite—a spacious suite that includes a large private bathroom, fireplace, and access to the hot tub on the back patio—or Grandma's Room, which has a queen-size bed, luxurious bath, and patio access. In the summer, fireflies light up the surrounding fields. Breakfast is large, hearty, and lively, with friendly conversation. No credit cards, but checks are OK. Rooms from $60–$85.

✱ Where to Eat

DINING OUT ✪ **Blue Mountain Passport Club** (712-737-3153; www.passportclub.net), 814 Lincoln Place Southeast, Orange City. Open for dinner Tues.–Sat. An evening of fine dining, fine cigars, and fine wine, in the richly furnished and dimly lit halls of the Blue Mountain Passport Club will leave visitors feeling like Ernest Hemingway on a good day. The daily admission for nonmembers is a mere $5—not much, considering the luxury of this semiprivate club. It is adorned with art and artifacts from across the globe: think zebra skins, deep leather seats, and high-end liquor. The menu is as decadent and worldly as the surroundings. The Elephant Room is a thousand-bottle wine cellar with mahogany shelving. $$–$$$. The club also offers a more casual dining experience in the **Smokehouse Grille** (www.smokehousegrile.net), open for lunch and dinner Tues.–Sat., serving BBQ, smoked meats, and sandwiches. $$

EATING OUT **The Hatchery Restaurant and Lounge** (712-737-2889), 121 Third Street Northwest,

Orange City. Open for lunch and dinner Mon.–Sat. This family-style restaurant is located in a historic chicken hatchery. From the 1900s until the 1950s, thousands of chicks were hatched within these walls. Today, the only remnants from this past life are an original wall and tasty chicken dishes. Try one of the many Oscar dishes, roasted steak and chicken with oysters on top, along with burger baskets, Mexican food, and a salad bar. $–$$

TREATS **The Dutch Bakery** (712-737-4360), 221 Central Avenue Northeast, Orange City. Open 7–5:30 Mon.–Fri., 7–5 Sat., closed Sun. No exploration of Dutch culture is complete without a Dutch letter. These flaky, airy, almond-paste-filled lovelies, along with cakes, cookies, and coffee, are sold just off the main square in Orange City. $

STORM LAKE

Storm Lake is Iowa's fourth-largest natural lake. For years the lake struggled with pollution from runoff from nearby farmland, but recent projects have cleaned up the waters and made it an excellent place for boating, fishing, and swimming. King's Pointe Waterpark Resort on the lakeshore is a major draw, featuring both an indoor and an outdoor water park. The lake is surrounded by parks (many with boat access), beaches, and lighthouses, and they are all linked with a network of walking and biking trails. To the north of the lake, the small, very friendly community of Storm Lake is home to Buena Vista University.

GUIDANCE **Storm Lake Visitors Bureau** (712-732-8000; www.stormlake.org), 620 Erie Street, Storm Lake. Open 8–5 Mon.–Fri. Storm Lake is hard at work reinventing the town as a resort community, and the friendly staff at the chamber office is happy to offer all the guidance visitors need. Stop in, or call ahead.

A QUIET MOMENT LAKESIDE IN STORM LAKE

GETTING THERE *By car.* Located at the intersection of **US 71** and **IA 7,** directly south of the Okoboji area and Spencer and east of Cherokee.

MEDICAL EMERGENCY Call **911**.

Buena Vista Regional Medical Center (712-732-4030; www.bvrmc.org), 1525 West Fifth Street, Storm Lake. Emergency services available at this regional hospital.

INTERNET ACCESS/PUBLIC LIBRARY Some restaurants and cafés around Storm Lake offer free wireless Internet access.

Storm Lake Public Library (712-732-8026; www.stormlakepubliclibrary.com), 609 Cayuga Street, Storm Lake. Open Mon.–Wed. 9–7, Thurs. 9–8, Fri. 9–5, Sat. 9–2. Public computers available for Internet use and research.

✷ To See

Living Heritage Tree Museum (712-732-5700; www.stormlakechamber.com), Sunset Park, West Lakeshore Drive, Storm Lake. Always open. Free. In a shady grove on Storm Lake is a living and growing museum dedicated to trees. The trees vary in species from the exotic to the common, and many have links to historical events. The outdoor museum includes a willow said to have descended from a willow tree on Joan of Arc's grave and a tree related to the original apples planted by Johnny Appleseed. A chestnut inspired a Longfellow poem, and its offspring lives in the museum as does a descendant of a tree that was carried to the moon on Apollo 14. The museum is both educational and peaceful—and certainly unique. Tree huggers should also keep their eyes open around town for the sculptures by Jeff Klatt, who chainsaws trees into pelicans, lighthouses, and families of trolls. There are 10 sculptures in Storm City to date. Four are on Lakeshore Drive, and the rest at various locations in town.

✐ **Santa's Castle** (712-732-3780; www.stormlakechamber.com), 200 East Fifth Street, Storm Lake. Open Thanksgiving–Dec. 30, call for hours. Admission: $4 adults, $2.50 children. Packed into a historic Carnegie Library are a hundred restored, animated Christmas characters and a 250-foot toy railroad. The collections come from department-store displays and create a powerful, surreal world of holiday cheer.

Buena Vista County Wind Farm (712-732-3780; www.stormlake.org), west of Storm Lake on CR M27. Open daily year-round. Standing 213 feet tall, the 360 wind turbines on Buffalo Ridge dwarf the surrounding landscape, and their graceful white blades can be seen spinning from miles away. The wind farm is one of the biggest in the world, and the mills produce enough electricity to power more than

TREES OF HISTORIC IMPORTANCE ARE GROWING AT THE LIVING TREE MUSEUM IN STORM LAKE

a 100,000 homes. Self-guided tours are available; contact the chamber of commerce for more information.

Witter Gallery (712-732-3400; www.thewittergallery.org), 609 Cayuga Street, Storm Lake. Open 1–5 Tues.–Fri. (till 6 Thurs.), 10–2 Sat. A rotating series of guest artists showcase their work in this gallery space throughout the year, and it is the permanent home for the art of Ella Witter and Dorothy Skewis, local artists whose vision enabled the creation of the space. The gallery is also home to educational endeavors for both children and adults as well as special events.

✷ To Do

✐ **King's Pointe Waterpark Resort** (712-213-4500; www.kingspointeresort.com), 1520 East Lakeshore Drive. Open year-round; for hours, see their Web site. Admission: $12 indoor park or $14 outdoor park adults, $10 children 4–11, $5 "Land Lovers" (nonswimmers). Patrons get fantastic views of the lake from the top of the outdoor waterslides before jetting down the slides into the plunge pools. The outdoor park offers five slides, including a "splash bowl" slide and a lazy river, along with a lap pool, diving boards, and zero-depth entry pools. The indoor park offers three more waterslides, lily pads, and a water channel. A basketball court and a rock-climbing wall are a dry alternative.

Storm Lake State Marina (712-231-2829; www.iowadnr.com/parks), 207 West Marina, Storm Lake. The first marina to be owned and operated by the Iowa Department of Natural Resources, the $3 million renovation project added 84 boat slips, a lunch counter, gas, a pier, and a beach.

✷ Green Space

Sunrise Park (712-732-3780; www.visitstormlake.com), Sunrise Park Road and East Lakeshore Drive, Storm Lake. Open daylight hours. Sunrise Park is on the eastern edge of the walking and biking trail that connects all the parks on the lakefront. A public boat ramp and docks are available. The park has a large swimming beach and a nine-hole, par-36 golf course at **Sunrise Pointe Golf Course** (712-732-8025) at 1528 East Lakeshore Drive, which is also home to the local campground.

✷ Where to Stay

HOTELS AND MOTELS ✪ **King's Pointe Waterpark Resort** (712-213-4500; www.kingspointeresort.com), 1520 East Lakeshore Drive, Storm Lake. One hundred guestrooms and suites, some with balconies and patios or shore access. All rooms include both wireless and wired Internet access, and suites have microwaves and refrigerators. The rooms are simply and elegantly decorated and are close to the water-park adventures. Rooms from $89–$229.

Lighthouse Inn (712-732-5756; www.lighthouseinniowa.net), 1601 East Lakeshore Drive, Storm Lake. This small inn has 25 rooms, each individually decorated and themed in a charming, folksy way. The inn is steps from both the lake and to the local water park. Rooms from $40–$85.

BED & BREAKFASTS AND HOUSE RENTAL **Metcalf House** (712-732-5576; www.metcalfhouse.com), 226 Geneseo, Storm Lake. A large (25 rooms!) 1909 Queen Anne Victorian-home with original leaded-glass windows and hardwood floors is now a B&B of distinction. The three guest rooms and two suites are decorated with period furnishings and antiques, and there are plenty of common areas, such as the wraparound porch, where visitors can relax. A full breakfast, with homemade bread and muffins, is served daily. Rooms from $66–$150.

Etta's Guest House (712-732-6340; www.ettasguesthouse.com), 5647 105th Avenue, Storm Lake. Rent the entire big white farmhouse on this century-old farm. It features four bedrooms with queen beds, a laundry, a fully equipped kitchen, central air-conditioning, and wireless Internet. Guests have the convenience and privacy of a home away from home. House rental $165 a night.

CAMPING **Sunrise Campgrounds** (712-732-8023), 1001 Sunrise Road, Storm Lake. This full-service campground on the lakeshore has 160 sites for recreational vehicles as well as boating, fishing, and swimming access, and cabin rentals. Wood and ice can be purchased on site, and there is a laundry room, too. Campsites from $14–$21.

✳ Where to Eat

DINING OUT **Martinis Bar and Grill** (712-732-7852), 523 Erie Street, Storm Lake. Open for lunch and dinner Mon.–Sat. A chic bar and grill, with a variety of fancy martinis and lots of sports on the television—and serving up some good food. In true sports-bar fashion, the list of appetizers is lengthy, but there are also steaks, pastas, and a heck of a lot of chicken dishes. The poultry comes with ranch, apple BBQ sauce, Hawaiian-styled, Blackened Cajun-style, and in strip with dip. $$

🍸 **The Regatta Grille** (712-213-5800), 1520 East Lakeshore Drive. Open daily for breakfast, lunch, and dinner. Located in the **King's Pointe Water Park** (see *To Do*), the Regatta Grille is the only lakeside restaurant in Storm Lake. The menu is smaller than most, but steaks, pastas, and desserts are done well. Wood-fire grilled steaks come with Madeira butter, and the fettuccine includes sun-dried tomatoes and spinach. Boat-side takeout and outdoor dining are both available. In the evenings the bar is lively and convivial, and there is a small menu of snacks. $$

EATING OUT **Boz Wellz** (712-732-3616), 507 Erie Street, Storm Lake. Open for lunch and dinner Mon.–Sat. Boz Wellz is a staple in northwest Iowa, and the menu is vast and varied. Italian pasta dishes, pizzas, steaks, Mexican standards, salads, and sandwiches are all there, but the little touches are what make the food: the pizza crust is handmade, the prime rib is slow cooked, and the onion rings are beer battered. $$

Honey Kissed Pizza (712-732-2222), 701 Lake Avenue, Storm Lake. Open for lunch and dinner 9–9 Mon.–Sat. The secret to their delicious pizza is the crust—it is light, chewy, and just slightly sweet—and there is no skimping on the toppings, either, with lots of vegetable options. The best way to sample them all is to go for lunch when there is an excellent buffet, with pizza, salads, pastas, and desserts, but whole pizzas and carryout are also available. Wireless Internet is available, too. $

Little Vientiane (712-213-1999), 805 Flindt Drive, Storm Lake. Open for lunch and dinner daily. A Lao and Thai kitchen right in the middle of the heartland, with exotic favorites: pad thai, spring rolls, and the like. Lunch is served buffet style, and imported beers are available. $

COFFEE **Grand Central Coffee** (712-732-0160), 400 West Fifth Street, Storm Lake. Open daily, with evening hours during the week. This coffee shop is a bit away from downtown but offers drive-thru and walk-up service. Light sandwiches and soups accompany coffee and espresso beverages. $

✱ Drinking Establishments

Boathouse (712-732-1462), 502 Lake Avenue, Storm Lake. Open daily for dinner, lunch on weekends. The Boathouse is a casual sports bar popular with the Buena Vista University crowd. Burgers and fried appetizers make the menu, sports provide the entertainment, and a tiny patio out front offers a front-row people-watching seat. $$

✱ Selective Shopping

Lakeshore Cyclery (712-732-4115), 1523 East Lakeshore Drive, Storm Lake. Open Mon.–Fri. 9–6 (Thurs. 9–8), Sat. 9–4, Sun. 1–4. Tune up the bike before hitting Storm Lake's trail system, or buy a new Schwinn, Raleigh, or Diamondback. A full line of parts and accessories are also for sale, and the employees at this family-owned shop can offer great tips on the best places to ride.

CHEROKEE, SAC CITY, AND LAKE VIEW

The small town of Cherokee sits on a picturesque bend in the Little Sioux River and is home to the oldest planetarium in the state. The historic barns and buildings of Sac County are colorful, painted quilt-block squares, and on the main street of this classic Iowa small town is both a historic Chautauqua building and the world's largest popcorn ball. To the south and east is the town of Lake View, on the shores of Black Hawk Lake, the southernmost glacial lake in Iowa, which offers boating, fishing, and camping.

GUIDANCE Good local resources are pretty slim for this region. Visitors needing more information should look to **Iowa Tourism** at www.traveliowa.com.

GETTING THERE *By car:* The city of Cherokee is at the intersection of **US 59** and **IA 3**; the rest of the area is linked with regional highways and county roads. Travel is pretty simple if you have a good map.

MEDICAL EMERGENCY Call **911**.

See *Storm Lake Medical Emergency* for **Buena Vista Regional Medical Center** (712-732-4030; www.bvrmc.org), 1525 West Fifth Street, Storm Lake. Emergency services available at this regional hospital.

✱ To See

Chautauqua Building (712-662-7383; www.saccountyiowa.com), Chautauqua Park, Park Avenue, Sac City. Open 8–5 Mon.–Fri., 8–8 Sat.–Sun. Memorial Day–Labor Day. The Chautauqua movement of the early and mid-19th century brought lectures, speakers, performances, and art to small-town America. Like circuses brought entertainment, Chautauquas brought education. The octagonal Chautauqua building in Sac City was constructed in 1908 and is the only complete building of its kind in the state. Inside it is full of murals and historical information. The building is in the center of the city park, which also contains a campground and 1850s log cabin.

World's Largest Popcorn Ball and **Sac County Museum** (712-662-7383; www.saccountyiowa.com), 13th and Main Streets, Sac City. Open Memorial Day–Labor Day and holidays 2–4:30 Sat.–Sun. In 2004 some 40 volunteers constructed a 3,100-pound popcorn ball to set a new Guinness world record. That apparently wasn't good enough for the residents of Sac County, for they decided to build a bigger and better ball. In February 2009 some 230 volunteers did just that, constructing a 5,000-pound behemoth. Like its forebear, the new popcorn ball—which is nearly 29 feet in circumference and stands nearly 8 feet 4 inches tall—resides in its own shed at the Sac County Museum. Visitors can see the popcorn ball through a window, even when the museum is not open, and on warm summer days, the sweet smell of sugar wafts out of the shed. The museum houses other artifacts from Sac County history—costumes and farm equipment mainly—a little village in the yard includes buildings as they might have appeared in Sac City's past, but it is hardly ever open.

Barn Quilts of Sac County (www.barnquilts.com), Sac County. The historic barns and corncribs, and even homes, in Sac County are decorated with colorful 8-foot-square painted quilt blocks. While many counties in Iowa have barn quilts, Sac County, with 55, offers more than any other; Sac County also has 19 smaller community quilts near important sites. There is a barn quilt every 5 to 10 miles in Sac County. Learn more about the quilts, and download a map of the 108-mile tour to see all the area quilts.

✪ **Battle Hill Museum of Natural History** (712-365-4414), IA 175 East, Battle Creek. Open 1–5 the first Sun. June–Aug. or by appointment. Free but donations

SOME 55 PAINTED QUILTS DECORATE BARNS AND OTHER STRUCTURES THROUGHOUT SAC COUNTY

encouraged. Crammed into just a few rooms are more than four thousand specimens, including six hundred full-body wildlife mounts, mounted heads, skeletons, skulls, and shells. Most of the animals were Iowa residents—though two moose wandered down from Minnesota. One was killed by a poacher, the other by a semi. While the museum is educational, it is never stuffy or dull. Founder and director Dennis Laughlin provides the tour and the character. This is a man whose response to finding a dead elephant in his front yard was to skin it and boil it down to the bare bones. The dark humor continues in the "petting zoo," where all the animals are dead and reduced to skin, including the Easter bunny, and visitors will find such oddities as a two-faced pig, a two-headed calf, and a basement cave complete with waterfalls and bats (dead, of course).

Sanford Museum & Planetarium (712-225-3922; www.sandfordmuseum.org), 117 East Willow Street, Cherokee. Open 9–5 Mon.–Fri., 12–5 Sat.–Sun. Free. The planetarium in Cherokee was the first of its kind in the state; planetarium shows are given on the last Sunday of each month and explore the seasonal changes of the night sky. The museum also features exhibits on the history of Cherokee, from the fossils of the prehistoric sea to artifacts from pioneers and settlers of the area. Kids can bounce around on moon shoes or pet the pelts of the mammals that inhabit the region.

✷ To Do

Sauk Rail Trail (712-662-4530; www.saccounty.org), 2970 280th Street, Sac City. Open daily 5:30–10:30 year-round. Trail pass: $1 adults, $10 per year. Begin the 33-mile trail under an arch of old bicycles in Lake View and wind through prairies, wetlands, farms, and timberland. Most of the trail is flat, though it does get hillier as it approaches its terminus at **Swan Lake State Park** in Carroll. Contact the **Carroll County Conservation Board** or the **Sac County Conservation Board** for more information.

Lake Black Hawk, Lake View. Black Hawk Lake is named for Chief Black Hawk, and his likeness can be found at the Crescent Beach Campground; the 11-foot statue was constructed under the WPA arts program led by Grant Wood. The rest of the natural spring-fed lake is just as lovely. At 957 acres, it is large enough for boating, fishing, swimming, and picnicking, and 50 percent of the shoreline is open to the public.

The Little Sioux River and the Inkpaduta Canoe Trail (712-225-6709), 629 River Road, Cherokee. The trail is named for the Native American chief involved in the Spirit Lake Massacre (see **Abbie Gardner House**, Okoboji) and runs from Spencer to Smithland. Bring a canoe for three-hour or three-day floats on this gentle prairie stream with great views and fishing.

✷ Where to Stay

HOTELS AND MOTELS **Sac City Motel** (712-662-7109; www.saccitymotel.com), US 20 East at Ash Avenue, Sac City. A friendly small-town motel with basic accommodations. All the rooms have new furniture, cable television, and refrigerators and microwaves. Rooms from $30–$60.

Skyline Motel (712-225-2544; www.cherokeeskyline.com), 768 North Second Street, Cherokee. Basic hotel accommodations, but the rooms are clean, and the rates are reasonable. Wireless Internet and coffee are both free. Rooms from $30–$50.

BED & BREAKFASTS **Hattie Grace** (712-668-2265; www.showcase.netins.net/web/hattiegrace), 317 West Fourth Street, Odebolt. The Hattie Grace bed & breakfast offers four guest rooms in a comfortable renovated home with county decor. A cookie jar, library, and front porch make this an inexpensive and comfortable place to stay. Room (including breakfast) $49.

Prairie Path Bed & Breakfast (712-225-4940; www.nwiowabb.com), 5168 S Avenue, Cherokee. The prairie surrounds the lodge house, log cabin, and log cottage at this retreat in the hills of northwest Iowa. Two suites offer king-size beds, fireplaces, and private bathrooms. Breakfast is served in the sunroom or on the deck. Rooms $65–$110.

CAMPING **Camp Crescent** (712-657-2189; www.lakeview-ia.com), 1109 Third Street, Lake View. Open Apr. 15–Nov. 1. The sandy beach at Camp Crescent is staffed with lifeguards every afternoon in summer. Kids will also enjoy playground equipment and miniature golf. The campground offers 250 reservable campsites, 184 with full hook-ups. A cabin that sleeps four with a kitchenette and air-conditioning (but no water) is available for rent for a minimum two-night stay. Cabin $35 a day, campsites from $11–$20.

Black Hawk State Park (712-657-8712; www.iowadnr.com/parks), 228 South Blossom, Lake View. The campground at the state park offers 129 sites; 89 of those are equipped with electricity. The campground offers swimming, Frisbee golf, volleyball, and playground equipment. The park is close to the **"Stubb" Severson Nature Trail.** The Department of Natural Resources also rents a modern four-bedroom cabin with 1½ bathrooms, heat, and air-conditioning that sleeps 8 to 11 people. It can be rented by the week in summer or for two nights at a time in winter. Cabin $100 per day, campsites from $11–$16.

Riverside Campground (712-662-7593), Chautauqua Park. Next to the historic Chautauqua building, this city campground has 21 full-hook-up campsites with electricity, soft water, and cable television. Primitive sites are also available. Campsites from $10–$16.

✷ Where to Eat

EATING OUT **The Depot** (712-662-4774), 1302 West Main Street, Sac City. Open for dinner daily. This pizza parlor in an old railroad house right across the street from the museum complex is open every day of the year. Stop in for pizza, beer, chicken, and sandwiches. $–$$

The Hub on Fifth (712-662-7898), 119 North Fifth, Sac City. Open for breakfast and lunch Mon.–Fri. This bright, clean coffee shop just off the main street is a great place for a caffeine or snack break. Ice cream, sandwiches, and baked goods go along with fresh coffee and espresso drinks. Black-and-white photography by artist Mark Bassett adorns the walls. $

Gasthaus Bar and Grill (712-225-9908), 214 West Main Street, Cherokee. Open Mon.–Sat. for lunch and dinner. Despite the German name and rathskellerlike decor, the food on the menu at this neighborhood pub is a melting pot of choices. Mexican dishes include both fajitas and also "seven-layer dip," that staple of Midwestern family gatherings. Of course, there are sandwiches, steaks, and burgers made

EVEN THE MUNDANE BUILDINGS IN IDA GROVE ARE CASTLES

IDA GROVE: CITY OF CASTLES

Ida Grove is a small and strange little town, with castles. Yes, castles. But the strangest thing is not that Ida Grove has castles. No, the strangest part is, travelers would hardly know about them. Ida Grove doesn't exactly flaunt the castles, though the chamber of commerce does reference them on its Web site. Many Iowans don't even know about this kooky little town, and the buildings are all private property. Area businessman Byron Godberson, of Midwest

every which way. The popcorn is always free, and on Friday dig into salted-in-the-shell peanuts. $–$$

✷ Selective Shopping

The Book Vine (712-225-2445), 204 West Main, Cherokee. Open 10–5 Mon.–Wed., 10–8 Thurs., 10–6 Fri., 9–5 Sat. and Sun. during winter. The Book Vine is the kind of independent bookstore shoppers would expect to see in a college town; the restored storefront is colorful and full of light, the selection of books is well chosen and complete, and there are great

TRUE TO ITS NAME, THE BOOK VINE IN CHEROKEE OFFERS SHOPPERS BOTH BOOKS AND WINE

Industries, funded the construction of some of buildings in town—the newspaper office, the skating rink, the airport, the ice-cream stand—and left his mark with medieval architecture. Godbersen also owns a half-scale replica of the HMS *Bounty* that sails the waters of Lake La June—again, private property, but visitors can see it from the road. A drive through Ida Grove is a little like an adventure to Arthurian England, only with corn. **Castles and the HMS Bounty** (712-364-3404; www.idagrovechamber.com/castles.html) are at various spots around town, but most are on US 59; also visit the **Ida Grove Skate Palace** (712-364-3430; 201 Oak Grove Drive). Owned and operated by the local American Legion, this skating rink and event center combines all the fun of roller skating with Gothic architecture and a view of Cobb Park. Call ahead for hours, admission, and skate rental fees.

Ida Grove also has a nice local green space at **Moorehead Park** (712-364-3300; 202 Jasper Avenue). Named after Judge John H. Moorehead, who founded the town in 1856, the park is home to the **Stage Coach Inn**, a stop on the Sioux City–Fort Dodge stagecoach route and the town's first hospital and church. Visitors can also see the **Grant Center School**, a one-hundred-year old schoolhouse. Both facilities are furnished with antiques and memorabilia, and Ida Grove schoolchildren still attend class one day a year at the old schoolhouse. The park is a great spot for fishing, hiking, and picnicking. In the winter, Moorehead Parjk makes sledding easy with a rope lift up the hill.

And for a treat, stop in at the **Ida Grove Pharmacy** (712-364-2734; 506 Second Street; open 8–6 Mon.–Fri., 8–4 Sat.), where the American tradition of soda fountains is still alive. Fill prescriptions, shop for household goods, and eat ice cream. They still serve some of the classic treats, such as phosphates and floats, along with light snacks at the counter.

couches for lounging. Coffee and wireless Internet, too. Upstairs is a mezzanine with games and tables, and the owners also sell wines from around the world by the bottle.

The Spice Rack (712-225-0222; www.homemadepizzelles.com), 222 West Main Street, Cherokee. Open 7:30–5:30 Mon.–Thurs. 7:30–4:00 Fri.–Sat. Just walking through the door of this cooking store and bakery is an adventure for the senses; it smells heavenly inside. The historic building is full of the smell of homemade goodies baked and sold fresh daily. Try the famous pizzelles—light, flakey Italian cookies—and shop for kitchen supplies.

FORT DODGE AND ENVIRONS

In 1835 the first U.S. Dragoons—lightly armed cavalry soldiers—made their way up the Des Moines River. The goal was to explore the lands of central Iowa that had been acquired as part of the Louisiana Purchase. In 1850 Brevet Major Samuel Woods and the U.S. infantry scouted the lands where the Des Moines River meets Lizard Creek, which offered good water, timber, and stone. The soldiers at the fort were charged with maintaining peace among the Native Americans and offering protection to the settlers. The town of Fort Dodge quickly followed. It became a hub not just for agriculture but also for mining because gypsum and clay were prominent in the area.

Fort Dodge and its environs offer some of the strangest attractions in Iowa. A replica of the Cardiff Giant resides at the historic Fort Museum in Fort Dodge. In the little city of West Bend you can see one of the largest grottos in the world. The grotto was built from precious stones to honor the Virgin Mary. The town of Britt is home to the annual Hobo Convention every August, when vagabonds and drifters from around the country crown their king and queen.

GUIDANCE **Fort Dodge Convention & Visitors Bureau** (515-573-4282; www.fortdodgecvb.com), 1406 Central Avenue, Fort Dodge. Open during normal business hours. The Web site and publications can provide information on the area, and the staff can answer visitors' questions.

GETTING THERE *By car:* Fort Dodge is directly west of **I-80** on **US 20.** Webster City is in between Fort Dodge and the interstate, and other spots in this section are connected on a simple network of local highways and county roads.

MEDICAL EMERGENCY Call **911**.

Trinity Regional Medical Center (515-573-3101; www.trmc.org), 802 Kenyon Road, Fort Dodge. Emergency services available.

INTERNET ACCESS/PUBLIC LIBRARY **Fort Dodge Public Library** (515-573-8167; www.fortdodgeiowa.org), 424 Central Avenue, Fort Dodge. Open Mon.–Tues. 8:30–8, Wed.–Fri. 8:30–5:30, Sat. 9–5. Public computers with Internet access and free wireless Internet available.

✷ To See

✪ **Fort Museum & Frontier Village** (515-573-4231; www.fortmuseum.com), South Kenyon and Museum Road, Fort Dodge. Open Apr.–Oct. 9–5 Mon.–Sat., 11–5 Sun. Admission: $6 adults, $3 children 6–18. The fort at Fort Dodge was established in 1850 as an infantry post to protect settlers from and enforce boundaries with the Native Americans in the region. As such, the fort museum absolutely abounds in history. Guided tours are available and come highly recommended; there is a lot to see in the fort complex, and the informative guides can point out the special highlights.

The Frontier Village is a complex of several period buildings—among them a modest cabin, a well-appointed cabin, a schoolhouse, a church, a doctor's office—all equipped with artifacts and furniture of the time. Don't miss the carriage collection in the livery, which includes a rare Victorian town carriage, a chuck wagon, buggies, bobsleds, and sleighs. Inside the reconstructed fort, the history continues with Native American and regional artifacts, from period costumes to the gypsum that was mined in the region. The fort is also full of military history, particularly an 1850 log cabin that served as the office of Brevet Major Lewis A. Armistead's office; Armistead led the last wave of Pickett's Charge at Gettysburg in 1863.

One of the strangest sights at the Fort Museum, though, is the **replica Cardiff Giant,** making it a fake of a fake that marks one of the greatest hoaxes of the 19th century. In a complex scam involving a huge hunk of raw gypsum mined in the Fort Dodge area, a traveling cigar maker, and a field in upstate New York, William "Stub" Newell buried a carved "giant," waited a year, and then dug him up, claiming to have discovered a massive prehistoric petrified giant man. He charged 50 cents a head to see the fake, until the scheme was discovered when the giant's sculptor 'fessed up. The "real" fake giant lives in the Farmer's Museum in Cooperstown, New York.

WESTERN IOWA HAS SOME DISTINCT TOURIST ODDITIES—INCLUDING THIS FAKE OF A FAKE (THE CARDIFF GIANT) AT THE FORT MUSEUM IN FORT DODGE, THE "WORLD'S LARGEST POPCORN BALL" IN SAC CITY, AND THE WORLD'S LARGEST CHEETO AT SISTER SARAH'S BAR IN ALGONA

✪ **Blanden Memorial Art Museum** (515-573-2316; www.dodgenet.com/~blanden), 920 Third Avenue South, Fort Dodge. Open 10–5 Tues.–Fri. (10–8:30 Thurs.), 1–5 Sat. and Sun.

Free but donations appreciated. The neoclassical building that houses the art museum was constructed in 1931 and became the first permanent art facility in the state of Iowa. The museum's collection includes works from Chagall, Picasso, Beckmann, and Miro; traveling exhibits of international and regional artists are always featured, as well. The Blanden is also exceptional for creating a culture of community art in the area through programs and outreach.

Oleson Park Zoo (515-955-3258; www.olesonparkzoo.bravehost.com), Oleson Park, 1200 South 17th Street, Fort Dodge. Open May–Labor Day 12:30–3:30. Tues., Thurs., Sat., Sun., weather permitting. Free. In the middle of **Oleson Park** is a community-owned collection of exotic and familiar animals and birds. Visitors can get close to the largest rodent in the world, the 4-foot-long (without a tail!) capybara; a pygmy angora goat; or a sacred ibis from Egypt. The zoo is also home to four varieties of deer, Chinese geese, a miniature horse, and an alpaca from South America. Many of the animals can be seen from the street, but during zoo hours, visitors can enter the barn. The zoo is staffed by volunteers.

Camp Algona P.O.W. Museum (515-395-2267; www.pwcamp.algona.org), Kossuth County Fairgrounds, Fair Street, Algona. Open Sun. Apr.–Dec. 1–4, and by appointment. The city of Algona was home to a large P.O.W. camp during World War II. Lead by Sergeant Eduard Kaib, the 3,200 German soldiers in the camp spent a year constructing a 60-character, half-scale re-creation of the birth of Jesus Christ. The scene includes Jesus, Mary, Joseph, the Wise Men, some 30 sheep, and a stream and small lake. The prisoners spent their own money on plaster and cement. They even built it near the fence so that the townspeople could see it. It

THE WORLD'S LARGEST CHEETO

At **Sister Sarah's Bar** (515-295-7757; 1515 North McCoy Street, Algona), on display in all its glory, is the World's Largest Cheeto. How big is it? About the size of a small potato, the World's Largest Cheeto is some 4 inches long, 5 inches around, and weighing 6/10 of an ounce, but because there is no *Guinness Book of World Records* for Cheetos, another contender could still be out there.

Mike Evans, a Navy petty officer stationed in Pearl Harbor, bought the bag containing the massive Cheeto, and promptly put the nugget up for sale on eBay. Bryan Wilson, an Algona disc jockey, raised $180 to bid on the Cheeto, but the bidding went as high as a million dollars and eBay stopped the auction. Evans finally gave the Cheeto to Algonians with the promise that they would donate the $180 to a food bank. Today, under the care of Tom Straub, the Cheeto lives on a mantel in Sister Sarah's Bar. It is under Plexiglas and sits on a regal purple-velvet pillow on a hand-blown glass pedestal.

Sister Sarah's Bar is a comfortable and classy neighborhood restaurant in Algona. Stop by for lunch and dinner Mon.–Sat. for steaks, chicken dishes, and salads. Cheetos, sadly, are not on the menu. $$

was finished for Christmas 1945, and when they were released in 1946, the townspeople asked if they could keep the scene. Ever since, it has been on display; its permanent home is now at the fairgrounds.

✪ **The Grotto of Redemption** (515-887-2372; www.westbendgrotto.com), 300 North Broadway, West Bend. Grotto and museum open year-round during daylight hours; guided tours May–Oct. and by appointment. Admission: $5 adults, $2.50 children. One of Iowa's earliest tourist destinations, the grotto is the work of Father Paul Dobberstein (1872–1954), who started construction it in 1912. Father Paul arrived in West Bend in 1898, a year after he survived pneumonia, and built the grotto for the Virgin Mary, who he believed saved his life. It is the largest grotto in the world, spanning one city block, and is made of precious stones. Chapels, towers, stairways, and the Stations of the Cross are all constructed from the tiniest gems to a 300-pound Brazilian amethyst. Other precious and semiprecious stones built into the grotto include emeralds, amber, sapphires, jade, jasper, and many others; it even has stalactites and stalagmites. An Italian mosaic, marble statues, and a bird's-eye maple altar adorn the nine sections of the structure. Visitors can learn more about the history of the grotto and see an enormous collection of precious stones in the adjoining museum, then have a snack in the café. Free campsites on the property are also available to visitors, but music and lights stay on until 10:30 PM.

✪ **The Hobo Museum** (641-843-9104; www.hobo.com), 51 South Main Avenue, Britt. Open June–Aug. Mon.–Fri. 9–5 or by appointment. Admission: $1 adults. The town of Britt started courting the annual Hobo Convention in 1896, and since then hobos have been convening in the town to crown their king and queen and

BEGUN IN 1912, THE GROTTO OF REDEMPTION IS ONE OF IOWA'S MOST REMARKABLE ATTRACTIONS

celebrate life on the rails. The Hobo Museum opened in 1991 to preserve the history of the American hobo and it offers a great deal of insight into the differences between a hobo, a tramp, and a bum. There are displays celebrating famous hobos and plenty of historical artifacts. The town is also the location of the hobo cemetery, where hobos want their bodies buried when their life on the road ends. The Hobo Convention is a lot of fun and is held the second weekend in August.

Winnebago Industries Visitor Center (641-585-6936; www.winnebagoind.com), 1045 South Fourth Street, Forest City. Open Apr.–Nov. 1, 8–4:30 Mon.–Fri.; tours 9 AM and 1 PM;, Nov. 1–mid. Dec, tours 1 PM only. Tour the Winnebago factory, and see how the land yachts are constructed. Motor homes combine the building elements of both vehicles and homes, so visitors get to see the cabinet shop and initial road tests. This is the largest motor-home plant in the world, and both current and vintage models are on display. Tours last around 90 minutes.

✷ To Do

Outdoor Adventures (515-571-2300), 214 River Avenue South, Belmond. Trips available daily; call to make arrangements. Rent a kayak, canoe, paddleboat, or tube for adventure on the gorgeous Iowa River or at nearby Moose, Cornelia, or Elm Lakes. Prices include transportation, but "you-haul" trips are also available. Trips can go anywhere from four hours to four days, so make arrangements with the outfitter. Camping is available at the city park in Belmond for boaters who float into town.

✷ Green Space

Dolliver Memorial State Park (515-359-2539; www.iowadnr.com), 2757 Dolliver Park Avenue, Lehigh. From the Copperas Beds—sandstone bluffs standing 100 feet above Prairie Creek—visitors can see petrified logs, sticks, and mineral deposits in the 150-million-year-old formation. **Boneyard Hollows** is a narrow ravine in which early settlers found bison bones. It is possible that Native Americans in the area used the ravine to trap the animals for meat and fur. The campground overlooking the Des Moines River offers 33 sites with electrical hook-ups and modern bathroom facilities; the park has two 1930s-built lodges for day use and two family cabins that sleep four. Boaters and fishermen use the Des Moines River, with a modern boat ramp. Campsites from $11–$16.

Brushy Creek Recreation Area (515-543-8298; www.iowadnr.com/parks), 3175 290th Street, Lehigh. At the heart of one of Iowa's largest recreational areas is the 690-acre lake at Brushy Creek, which is popular for boating, swimming, and fishing. The beach is sandy, and it's a no-wake lake, so speedboats, wake boarding, or waterskiing are not permitted. Some 45 miles of multiuse trails crisscross the area, and there are several comfortable picnic shelters and sites. The area offers equestrian camping at 125 campsites, 50 with electric, with a horse-wash area, shade, and a hitching rail, along with an arena. Sixty-two electric sites, 22 nonelectric sites, and 8 full-water hook-up sites for campers without horses are available at the south campground. Hunting and shooting ranges are also popular. Campsites from $11–$16; equestrian sites are $3 additional, as are water and sewer hook-up sites.

Union Slough National Wildlife Refuge (515-928-2523; www.midwest.fws.gov./unionslough), 1710 360th Street, Titonka. Headquarters open 7:30–4:30

Mon.–Fri.; refuge open daily during daylight hours. Before the land was drained for farming, much of Iowa was covered in wetlands and sloughs. This refuge in the far north of the state offers a glimpse into this natural landscape. An auto-tour route through the refuge offers visitors a chance to see the birds and animals that make the slough their home. The refuge is also open for limited hunting and fishing.

* Where to Stay

HOTELS AND MOTELS 🐾 **Park View Inn & Suites** (515-887-3611; www.parkviewinnandsuites.com), 13 Fourth Street Northeast, West Bend. The pet-friendly Park View Inn offers 36 rooms and suites within walking distance of the Grotto of Redemption. Each of the rooms is clean, includes wireless Internet and a continental breakfast, and comes with access to the indoor pool and whirlpool. Whirlpool, fireplace, and family-size suites are also available. Rooms from $45–$125.

BED & BREAKFASTS AND HOUSE RENTALS **Klemme House B&B** (641-444-4597), 204 Fourth Avenue Southeast, Belmond. Connie Mattison always wanted to live in the Klemme house. The gorgeous hardwood, the breakfast nook, and the spacious rooms called to her as she raised her family in Belmond. Today she welcomes guests to her comfortable home and treats them like family. Friendly cats appreciate petting, and fresh cookies await guests in the three guest rooms. There is an outdoor hot tub on the back deck, and the home is just steps from Belmond's main street. Rooms from $65–$75.

Valkommen House (515-838-2440), 3219 370th Street, Stratford. The streets of the nearby town may be named after Shakespeare, but the area was settled mainly by Swedes. Guests stay in the authentic Swedish farmhouse on the family farm of Carol and Wayne Larson. The house, where

THE VALKOMMEN HOUSE IS A B&B IN AN AUTHENTIC SWEDISH IMMIGRANT HOMESTEAD

Carol's mother was born and grew up, sleeps eight and is quaint and rustic—almost like a cabin but more agricultural. The home is full of history, and be sure to see the cave Carol's grandparents dug when they settled the farm. Rental from $55–$85.

Sisters Inn (515-885-0389; www.sistersinn.net), 310 South Summit Street, Bancroft. Spend a night in peaceful seclusion in this 1954 convent house. Renovated in 2005, the inn offers apartments, suites, and rooms, but a kitchen and living room can also be rented. The apartment and suite have private bathrooms, but the rooms share a large public bathroom. All accommodations are tastefully decorated and comfortable. Rooms from $55–$95.

Hearten B&B (515-295-9445; www.heartenbnb.com), 400 East Nebraska Street, Algona. This bed & breakfast is one of the loveliest and most well tended in the area. The four suites are dressed to the nines with period antiques and furnishings; the South Room Suite even offers a heart-shaped whirlpool tub. This 1913 home of Algona's first surgeon is close to downtown, and accommodations include an excellent breakfast, but this is definitely a showcase, and rumor has it that all guests are required to take off their shoes at the front door. Rooms from $90–$150.

✷ Where to Eat

DINING OUT **Marvin Gardens** (515-955-5333), 809 Central Avenue, Fort Dodge. Open daily for lunch and dinner. The specialty of the house is an eye-popping 12-ounce Iowa pork chop that has been smoked and served with BBQ sauce. All the beef is Iowa grown and aged. The menu also includes a variety of sandwiches, from a French dip to a crab melt on an English muffin. Eight beers are on tap, more in bottles, and a small wine list make this classy downtown restaurant a treat. $$

L. A. Beemer's (515-955-1877), 308 Central Avenue, Fort Dodge. Open for dinner Tues.–Sat. Fresh seasonal cuisine. The menu changes often, but the beef, chicken, and seafood dishes are inspired by the surrounding countryside. Unique and well prepared, though locals complain about "Des Moines prices." $$

Second Street Emporium (515-832-3463; www.secondstreetemporium.com), 615 Second Street, Webster City. Open for lunch and dinner Mon.–Sat. Stop in for casual fine dining at this neighborhood restaurant. The steaks—for which the emporium is famous—are all Angus beef, and there are interesting takes such as a Cajun prime rib, a flat-iron steak, and a carpetbagger with a cheese and burgundy sauce. Diners can also enjoy an evening omelet, shrimp, and plenty of chicken. $$–$$$

EATING OUT **Zakeers** (515-573-7661), 308 Central Avenue, Fort Dodge. Open Mon.–Sat. for breakfast and lunch. *The* neighborhood diner for homemade fried chicken, burgers, eggs, and pancakes. Hang out with the locals for coffee and delicious homemade pie. $

Tea Thyme at Sadies (515-576-2202; www.teathymeatsadies.com), 2021 Sixth Avenue South, Fort Dodge. Open Mon.–Sat. for lunch, and afternoon coffee and dessert; also retail; reservations recommended. Locally owned for over 15 years, this tearoom offers a casual yet upscale approach to lunches. The menu changes daily, but look for bread-bowl soups, inventive salads, and seasonal entrées. In the afternoon stop by for homemade desserts, coffee, and tea, and browse the shop for candies and gifts. $$

✪ **Main Street Pub and Grill** (515-885-0008; www.mainstreetpub.biz), 102 West Ramsey, Bancroft. Open for lunch and dinner daily. The pizza is so good, Algona residents will make the 30-mile round-trip for pickup for take-out. But trust me, it's better to stay and eat it there. The Main Street Pub is a big, comfortable restaurant, with huge windows, wooden floors, and smiles all around. Peanut shells litter the floors, families eat together, and old-timers drink beer at the bar. The food is pretty standard: sandwiches, burgers, pizzas, and steaks, but it is all homemade, with alligator and deep-fried green beans to spice up the menu. $–$$

Sister Sarah's See *Sidebar: The World's Biggest Cheeto.*

✷ Entertainment

Laramar Ballroom (515-576-5550; www.laramarballroom.com), 710 First Avenue North, Fort Dodge. The original armory of Fort Dodge now survives as one of the classiest ballrooms in Iowa. Entertainers such as Buddy Holly, the Everly Brothers, and the Big Bopper played the dancehall. A new renovation will open the space for modern music, entertainment, and events. Call or visit their Web site for show and box office information.

✷ Selective Shopping

Romancing the Home (515-832-5161; www.romancingthehomeonline.com), 707 Second Street, Webster City. Open 10–6 Mon.–Fri., 9–2 Sat. If the spark has gone out of your relationship with your house, spice it up with bed and bath products, wine, gourmet foods, and fragrances. Treat yourself to chocolates, sweets, and a sweatshop-free bathrobe.

WEST CENTRAL

INCLUDING MONONA, HARRISON, CRAWFORD, SHELBY, AUDUBON, CARROLL, GREENE, AND GUTHRIE COUNTIES

The counties along US 30 and north of I-80 include Monona, Harrison, Crawford, Shelby, Greene, Guthrie, Carroll, and Audubon. They stretch from the huge fertile fields of the Raccoon River Valley in the east to the undulating landscape of the Loess Hills along the Nebraska border. Visitors can see historic churches and the remnants of sunken steamboats, taste Prohibition-era whiskey and authentic Danish cuisine, and stay in hotels that date back to the golden era of motoring. And the best part is that all of these attractions are within easy distances from highways and roads.

MONONA AND HARRISON COUNTIES

These counties serve as a gateway to the Loess Hills. Drive past undulating fields, grassy pastures, and deep wooded valleys in these counties along the Missouri River. With a low population density and a high number of scenic vistas, Monona and Harrison Counties make a visitor feel far away from it all. Don't miss the Desoto Wildlife Refuge or the town of Onawa, which offers both the widest main street in America and the birthplace of the Eskimo pie.

GUIDANCE **Harrison County Historical Village and Welcome Center** (712-642-2114; www.harrisoncountyparks.org/welcome), 2931 Monroe Avenue, Missouri Valley. Open 9–5 Mon.-Sat., 12–5 Sun. Admission: $2 adults, 75¢ children for the historical village; welcome center free. The welcome center provides information on the region, especially natural resources.

GETTING THERE *By car:* Monona and Harrison Counties are most easily accessed using **I-29,** which runs along the Missouri River to the west. Local highways cross the region, but a good map is useful as the rolling Loess Hills makes navigation here more challenging than in other parts of the state.

MEDICAL EMERGENCY Call **911**.

ONAWA, BIRTHPLACE OF THE ESKIMO PIE

Onawa's Iowa Avenue is the widest main street in the United States, and its width is impressive, with two lanes of traffic in each direction and lots of room for angular parking on both sides. Northwest Iowa is an ice-cream hotbed—see LeMars, the "ice-cream capital of the world"—and Onawa's other claim to fame, besides its expansive pavement, is as the birthplace of the Eskimo Pie. Christian K. Nelson invented the treat in 1920 to accommodate kids who wanted both candy bars *and* ice cream. Learn more about the treat and local history at the **Monona County Historical Museum** (712-423-2776; 47 12th Street, Onawa; open June–Aug., 1–4:30 Sat. and Sun. and by appointment; free).

✷ To See

The Museum of Religious Arts (712-644-3888; www.mrarts.org) 2697 Niagara Trail, Logan. Open 9–5 Tues.–Sat., 12–5 or by appointment Sun., closed holidays. Admission: $7 adults, $5 children 5–12, but occasionally guests can forgo the fee and make a free-will donation. The centerpiece of this museum of Judeo-Christian artifacts are nine life-size scenes, all in wax, depicting the events of the life of Jesus Christ. The museum also includes religious artifacts, dolls in the costumes of various religious orders, and stained glass, plus a research library and gift shop.

✷ To Do

✪ **DeSoto National Wildlife Refuge** (712-642-4121; www.fws.gov/midwest.desoto), 1434 316th Lane, Missouri Valley. Refuge open a half hour before sunrise to a half hour after sunset, visitors center open daily 9–4:30 except federal holidays. Use fee: $3 per car. The refuge surrounds an oxbow lake, formed when the Missouri River shifted course and left behind a circular channel of water that is a perfect refuge for migrating birds traveling between the Arctic Circle and the Gulf Coast. Visitors can see bald eagles, wild turkeys, waterfowl, raccoons, coyotes, beaver, and muskrat. The visitors center, which is built on the lake, offers panoramic views and engaging interpretive information on the lake and wildlife. The refuge includes several multiuse trails and fishing and boating opportunities.

The other highlight of DeSoto is the site and remains of the steamboat *Bertrand*. The ship went down in 1865, was buried in the Missouri mud, then was lost when the river shifted. The boat was rediscovered in 1968 and the contents—goods intended for the general stores along the Missouri—were unearthed. The hull of the ship remains at the original site, but the museum houses the remarkably well-preserved goods, which include farming equipment, alcohol, dishes, and some clothing—all offering viewers insights into the lives and practices of early settlers in the West.

Sugar Clay Winery and Vineyards (712-628-2020; www.sugarclaywinery.com), 1446 240th Avenue, Thurman. Open 10–6 Thurs.–Sat., 1–5 Sun. This laid-back winery offers great views of the surrounding countryside and handcrafted wines grown from regional grapes. Sample the goods in the tasting room. Then enjoy a bottle with bread and cheese on the deck.

RARE LANDSCAPES: LOESS HILLS

The Loess Hills are a unique geological formation that stretches down the western border of the state. "Loess" is a fine, windblown soil that was deposited in dunes during the last Ice Age. The loess deposits in Iowa formed high rolling hills above the Missouri River. Hills such as these are found only in Iowa and China, and they contain clues to Iowa's prehistoric and Native American past. The soil is both fragile and fertile.

The best way to see the Loess Hills is by car. The **Loess Hills National Scenic Byway** (1-800-429-9297; www.byways.org) is splendid, and the views range from picturesque farmland to wilderness areas. The byway covers paved roads and gravel and includes several "loops" that take drivers deeper into the landscape. The byway passes through many small towns but also includes the metropolitan areas of Council Bluffs and Sioux City.

For more information on the Loess Hills, stop by the **Loess Hills Hospitality Association**) at 119 Oak Street, Moorhead (712-886-5441; www.loess hillstours.com; open Apr. 1–Dec. 24, 9–4:30 Mon.–Sat., 1–4:30 Sun.; Jan. 2–Mar. 31, 1–4 Mon.–Sat. or by appointment). The visitors center offers information on the region in the form of maps, brochures, and a helpful human behind the counter who can answer questions. There is also a gift shop stocked with Iowa products. If you're so inclined, the association offers professionally guided tours: guides will ride along in your car for three hours and point out the historical and geographical points of interest. Tours start at $35 per vehicle and are by appointment only.

THE LOESS HILLS SCENIC BYWAY WINDS THROUGH A PICTURESQUE AND GEOLOGICALLY UNIQUE LANDSCAPE

✱ Green Space

DeSoto National Wildlife Refuge See *To Do*.

✱ Where to Stay

COTTAGES **Hillside Cottages** (712-642-4781; www.hillside-cottages.com), 975 Sunnyside Avenue, Missouri Valley. Outside, it looks like a slightly shabby roadhouse from the golden days of motoring on the historic Lincoln Highway; inside, each remodeled room features a comfortable queen-size bed, a mini-fridge, and a fun theme (think tropical paradise). Guests can enjoy a hot tub, wireless Internet, and hot rolls and coffee in the morning. With rooms at $40 a night (discounts for longer stays), it is both a treasure and a steal.

Loess Hills Hideaway (712-886-5003; www.loesshillshideaway.com) 33774 Plum Avenue, Moorhead. When they say "hideaway," they're not kidding. This pet-friendly cabins-and-campground facility is located way back in a little valley at the end of a long gravel road. The cabins are nestled in the trees, and there are six campsites for either RVs or tents. A modern shower house and laundry are available. Cash or checks only. Cabins start at $60 per night, $360 per week; campsites from $12–$15. A two-bedroom-with-bathroom lodge is also for rent starting at $90 per night to $540 per week.

CAMPING **Wilson Island Sate Recreation Area** (712-642-2069; www.reserveiaparks.com) 32801 Campground Lane, Missouri Valley. Just to the south of the DeSoto National Wildlife Refugee, Wilson Island offers 5 miles of multiuse trails, hunting, and picnicking as well as 135 shady campsites and a camping cabin with electricity but no water. Cabin $25, campsites from $11–$16.

✱ Where to Eat

EATING OUT **Gurney's Restaurant & Pizzeria** (712-642-2580), 229 South Sixth Street, Missouri Valley. Open for dinner Mon.–Sat. 4–10. With steaks, pizza, and a comfortable lounge for drinking, this roadhouse is sure to please most appetites. Pizza is available for takeout, and the menu features the usual sandwiches, burgers, and salads, as well. $

Old Theater Restaurant and Lounge (712-644-3466), 308 East Seventh Avenue, Logan. Open for lunch and dinner Tues.–Sat. 6 AM–2 PM and 5:30 PM–8 PM, bar 8 AM–2 AM. The restaurant area of this main-street tavern is behind of set of swinging doors. Back there or at the bar, diners will find plenty of delicious fried favorites, including a tasty tenderloin and crispy homemade fries. The bar is decorated with promotional Budweiser signs and there are plenty of bar games to enjoy while waiting for your food. $

THE EXTERIOR OF THE HILLSIDE COTTAGES BELIES THE TINY COVES OF WHIMSICAL LUXURY INSIDE

CRAWFORD AND SHELBY COUNTIES

In Crawford County, in the hills above Denison, there was once a sign made of giant white letters—in the style of the famous HOLLYWOOD sign—that read: DENSION. It had been erected to honor the town's favorite daughter, Donna Reed. Today it is still a wonderful life in the city on the hill, which is shady and surrounded by rolling countryside. To the south in Shelby County is Harlan. The area is between Sioux City and Omaha and close to the Loess Hills region in the west.

GUIDANCE **City of Denison** (712-263-3143; www.denisonia.com), 111 North Main, Denison. No real visitor hours as this is the city's main office, but call or visit the city Web site for basic information on attractions, parks, and events.

GETTING THERE *By car:* The city of Denison is located at the convergence of **US 30, IA 141, IA 39,** and **US 59.** It is directly north of **I-80** on **US 59,** which also passes through the town of Harlan in Shelby County.

MEDICAL EMERGENCY Call **911**.

Crawford County Memorial Hospital (712-263-5021; www.ccmhia.com), 2020 First Avenue South, Denison. A small emergency department serves patients throughout the county and provides ambulance services.

INTERNET ACCESS Some cafés and most hotels and bed and breakfasts provide wireless Internet access.

✱ To See

✪ **Donna Reed Center for the Performing Arts** (712-263-3334; www.donnareed.org), Broadway and Main, Denison. Open 10–4 Mon.–Fri., special events, and by appointment. Donna Reed, who starred in both classic films *(It's a Wonderful Life)* and classic TV *(The Donna Reed Show),* was born a humble farm girl in 1921. She left Dension at 17 for Los Angeles, subsequently appearing in 40 feature films and winning a Best Supporting Actress Oscar for *From Here to Eternity.* Denison celebrates its homegrown celebrity in a restored turn-of-the-20th-century theater and soda fountain. What is now the Donna Reed Theater first opened in 1914 as the Deutsche Operahaus Gesselschaft von Denison but was eventually converted to the Ritz Movie Theater, where the budding star fell in love with the silver screen. Donna Reed photos and memorabilia are on display, along with a miniature Bedford Falls; look for the photo of Donna showing her cow at the county fair. Guided tours of the 550-seat theater—which hosts films, theatrical performances, and musical concerts—are available. The theater is also the site of the annual **Donna Reed Performing Arts Festival**, which invites professional performers to share their skills with students from around the state and region.

W. A. McHenry House (712-674-3750; www.denisonia.com/thingstodo.asp), 1428 First Avenue North, Denison. Open Memorial Day–Labor Day 1–4 Thurs. and Sun. Home of the Crawford County Historical Society, the historic McHenry House showcases items of historical interest in a home furnished with original inlaid hardwood floors and period furnishings, but most visitors come to see the Oscar that Donna Reed won for her performance in the 1953 film *From Here to*

Eternity. Apparently the Oscar is kept here rather than at the Donna Reed Center because the McHenry House offers better security for the precious statue.

✷ To Do

Walking Tour of Homes (www.denisonia.com/thingstodo). Visit the city of Denison's Web site to download a copy of a self-guided walking tour of the historic homes on the hill. The homes date from the 1870s to the 1900s and include one of the first "prefab" Sears & Roebuck homes, a Victorian Tudor-style home built by the town dentist, and the gorgeously renovated and richly appointed J. P. Conner home, which is now the **Conner's Corner B&B.**

Majestic Hills Golf Course (712-263-5194; www.majestichillsgolf.com), 2505 Boulders Drive, Denison. The swelling hills south of Denison are some of the loveliest in western Iowa, and set among them is this challenging 18-hole golf course. The 6,417-yard, par-72 course offers four sets of tees and is designed to test golfers at all skill levels. A driving range and new clubhouse, two restaurants, and a conference center are also on-site. Greens fees with cart range from $24–$39, depending on tee time and how many holes you play.

Denison Aquatic Fun Center (712-263-8130; www.denisonia.com), 710 North 16th Street, Dension. Open June–Aug., 1–8 Sun.–Fri., 1–6 Sat.; Sept.–May 3:30–8 Mon.–Fri., 2–6 Sat.–Sun. Admission: $4 adults, $3 children. The aquatic center offers a water adventure for everyone. Swim some laps in the six-lane indoor pool, and then relax in the sauna and hot tub. During summer months, head outside for waterslides, fountains, a sun deck, waterfall, plunge pool, and beach. Then hit the 18-hole miniature-golf course.

✷ Green Space

Yellow Smoke Park (712-263-2070), CR 1, Denison. Named after Chief Yellow Smoke of the Omaha tribe, Yellow Smoke is a small park—just 321 acres—northeast of Denison. Locals use the woodland and 40-acre lake for picnicking, hiking, camping, fishing, and boating. The lake is stocked with bluegill, catfish, crappie, and bass. Both electric and primitive campsites are available. Campsites from $11–$16. Two cabins with sleeping room for six can also be rented for $60 per night.

✷ Where to Stay

HOTELS AND MOTELS **The Historic Park Motel** (712-263-4144; www.theparkmotel.com), 803 Fourth Avenue South, Denison. The Park Motel has long been a fixture in Denison and on the Lincoln Highway. The pale-yellow two-story motel offers visitors a continental breakfast and wireless Internet in 33 interesting rooms and suites. Rooms from $48–$129.

Boulders Inn & Suites (712-263-2200; www.bouldersinndenison.com), 2511 Boulders Drive, Denison. Adjacent to the **Majestic Hills Golf Course** and conference center, this modern hotel has 32 rooms with high-definition television, complimentary breakfast, and a fitness center. The spacious suites offer great views of the surrounding golf course and hillside. Golf packages are also available. Rooms from $89–$159.

Forrest Lodge (712-755-5170), 2004 23rd Street, Harlan. Tucked into a small grove of trees off the highway is this lodge offering 25 rooms with king- and queen-size beds, cable television, free wireless Internet, and free coffee. Whirlpool tub rooms are available. Rooms from $35–$70.

BED & BREAKFASTS ✪ **Conner's Corner Bed & Breakfast** (712-263-8826; www.connerscorner.com), 104 South 15th Street, Denison. The former home of J. P. Conner, businessman and congressman, is a towering brick castle complete with turret just a block from downtown. The 1893 structure is full of breathtaking details like a circular turret seat, inlaid hardwood floors, and stained glass. Each of the five rooms is special. For example, at the top of a spiral staircase is the "Congressman's Chambers," a suite with whirlpool tub, kitchen, and huge windows; but even better is the "Garden Room," which opens onto a pergola and a rich garden beyond. Breakfast is exceedingly elegant, high-speed Internet is available, and the charming innkeepers are bastions of information on the town and region. Rooms from $75–$135.

Glidden House (712-265-2238; www.www.ia-bednbreakfast-inns.com/Gliddenhouse.htm), 2640 Donna Reed Road, Denison. Innkeeper Clarice Glidden is so devoted to welcoming and caring for her guests, she crafted her home around that mission. The Glidden House is a newly built house south of Denison with three guest rooms and one suite, each simple and charmingly decorated. But the best feature of the home by far is the amazing view of western Iowa's rolling hills: the landscape stretches for miles. Clarice is devoted to cooking, so breakfast—served in the kitchen nook or on the back deck—is often surprising and delicious. Rooms from $65–$95.

THE BRICK MANSION OF CONNER'S CORNER, AN ELEGANT B&B IN DENISON

✷ Where to Eat

EATING OUT **Cronk's Café** (712-263-4191), US 30 West, Denison. Open daily for breakfast, lunch, and dinner. Since 1929 Cronk's has been serving weary motorists who've puttered up after an adventure on the historic Lincoln Highway. This locally owned restaurant serves up the basics—steaks, sandwiches, and hearty breakfasts—with a side of Iowa history. $–$$

El Jimador (712-263-2579), 19 South Main Street, Denison. Open daily for lunch and dinner. The unique history of Denison as both a farming and industrial center of western Iowa has brought it the diversity it has today, marked with a large population of immigrants from Mexico and Central America. With immigration comes ethnic food, and El Jimador is one of the best Mexican restaurants in the area. Like most, its menu is large and full of the favorites, but everything—from the fajitas to the margaritas—is done well. $

Somebody's Grille and Bar (712-654-9191), 450 Main Street, Manilla. Open for lunch and dinner Tues.–Sat. In the tiny town of Manilla, this bar and grille is a local favorite not only for the food, which is special, but for its closeness to the community. A pork-chop dish is made with Templeton Rye whiskey. The walls are covered with albums and memorabilia, and it is a comfortable and welcoming place to hang out. $–$$

Wulfy's (712-263-4404), 502 Wolf Street, Deloit. Open for breakfast, lunch, and dinner Mon.–Sat. Wulfy's is a classic small-town bar and restaurant that serves excellent burgers, steaks, and pub food. The owners recently opened a new location in the **Majestic Hills Golf Course** called **Wulfy's Grille** (712-263-4404; www.majestichillsgolf.com), 1215 Donna Reed Road, Denison. Open evenings Mon.–Sat. $$

Joe's on the Square (712-235-5637; www.joesonthesquare.com), 1010 Sixth Street, Harlan. Open for lunch and dinner Tues.–Sat. Fans of Cajun and New Orleans–style food will be happy to find po-boys and Zapps chips on the menu along with gumbo and blackened catfish, but the restaurant also offers a number of grilled dishes and sandwiches, pastas, and well-prepared sandwiches. Joe's is friendly and unique, and people drive into Harlan from surrounding towns for the food and the atmosphere. Lunch specials are available during the week. $$

COFFEE **Hansen Brothers Coffee** (712-755-2883), 919 Seventh Street, Harlan. Open 6:30–5:30 Mon.–Fri., 6:30–3 Sat. Coffee—including espresso beverages and smoothies—is the main draw here, but American-style breakfasts and lunches are also served. The Hansen brothers also sell cigars and bulk coffee in their spacious downtown shop. Meals $$.

✷ Selective Shopping

Reynold's Clothing (712-263-5544; www.reynoldsclothing.com), 1323 Broadway, Denison. Open 8–5:30 Mon.–Fri. (8–9 Thurs.), 8–5 Sat., closed Sun. Reynold Gehlsen opened this men's clothing store in 1972. In a remarkable story of rural renewal, brothers Brett and Troy Gehlsen returned to their hometown of Denison, bought the family store, and continued a tradition of retailing fine men's clothing with a focus on service. The Denison institution also offers casual-lifestyle wear and Carhartt gear.

Audubon and Carroll Counties offer some surprising attractions from the plow-in-the-oak, left behind from the Civil War era to the Garst farm, where one Iowan attempted to create peace during the Cold War. The city of Carroll has some of the best shopping in the region, and Danish culture is alive (and delicious) in Elk Horn.

GUIDANCE **Audubon County Economic Development Corporation** (712-563-2742; www.auduboncounty.com), 800 Market Street, Audubon. Information on the local resources such as hospitals and police, along with some limited tourism information is available through this county agency.

Carroll Chamber of Commerce (712-792-4383; www.carrolliowa.com), 407 West Fifth Street, Carroll. Information on the city of Carroll and the small towns around the county is available through the chamber's Web site.

GETTING THERE *By car:* **US 71** runs north-south through Carroll and Audubon Counties and connects with **I-80** to the south. **US 30** runs through Carroll east-west and connects it with other cities in the region.

MEDICAL EMERGENCY Call **911**.

St. Anthony Regional Hospital and Nursing Home (712-794-5555; www.stanthonyhospital.org), 311 South Clark Street, Carroll. Emergency medical center provides 24-hour access to care and a helipad to connect patients to larger facilities in the state.

INTERNET ACCESS/PUBLIC LIBRARY **Carroll City Public Library** (712-792-3432; www.cityofcarroll.com), 118 East Fifth Street, Carroll. Open 9–8 Mon.–Thurs., 9–6 Fri., 9–5 Sat. in winter, and 9–7 Mon.–Thurs., Fri., and 9–2 Sat. in summer. Public computers and wireless Internet access.

* To See

Hausbarn and Heritage Park (712-655-3131; www.manningia.com), 12196 311th Street, Manning. Open May–Oct. 11–4 Mon.–Sat., 12–4 Sun. Admission: $6 adults, $2 children. *Hausbarn* is German for a house and a barn, also known as a *bauernhaus,* or a farmer's house. Farm families of the Schleswig-Holstein region of Germany would share their homes with the livestock. The hausbarn of Manning was originally built in 1660 in Klein-Offenseth, Germany. It was donated to the town in 1991. Professional thatchers from Germany constructed the roof from reeds that grow near the Baltic Sea. Inside, visitors can learn about the lives of the farm families of Germany and about the heritage of the people who settled the region. Camping is available in shady spots in the adjacent park.

Landmark Tree (712-563-2742; www.aububoncounty.org), Akron Road and 710th Street, Brayton. In 1850 a surveyor jammed his freshly cut walking stick into the ground to mark the line between Aububon and Cass Counties. The cottonwood took root and grew into a healthy tree, which just so happened to be in the middle of one of the dirt roads that cross Iowa every mile, north-south and east-west. Because of local support, the now 100-foot tree slows traffic on the corner, but no one seems to mind. The tree is a bit tricky to find, so don't be afraid to stop and ask for directions.

Plow-in-the-Oak (712-268-2762; www.aububoncounty.org) IA 71, Exira. In the 1860s, they say, Frank Leffingwell unhitched his mules in the field, leaned his plow against a tree, and up and joined the Union Army. Leffingwell is thought to have died in the Civil War or to have traveled out West in search of gold. Either way, the plow was left behind, and a burr oak grew up and around the plow; today, only two corners of the plow are discernible. As the tree grows, the plow becomes less and less visible, so stop by this small city park and see it before it is completely subsumed by the oak.

Nathaniel Hamlin Park and Museum (712-563-2516; www.auduboncounty.com), 1 mile south of Audubon on US 71. Open 1–4 June–Sept. 1 and by appointment. Free. The park complex is named after the first settler to Audubon County and includes a museum with exhibits of local interest, such as corn husking. On the grounds are 18 antique windmills donated by local farmers, a red schoolhouse, and a pair of elk, which were once native to the state of Iowa. The park also includes gorgeous nature trails through native timberland.

The Danish Immigrant Museum (712-764-7001; www.danishmuseum.org), 2212 Washington Street, Elk Horn. Open 9–5 Mon.–Fri., 10–5 Sat., 12–5 Sun. Admission: $5 adults, $2 children. This modern 16,000-square-foot facility is dedicated to the history of Danish settlement in the United States. The museum illustrates with great detail both how and why Danes came to this country, what their life was like here, and how they influenced American culture. Upstairs, the museum features a moving exhibit about the German occupation of Denmark during World War II and the Danish resistance to the Holocaust. A climate-controlled glass storage facility downstairs holds countless artifacts donated to the museum. Outside is the Morning Star Chapel, a tiny church constructed by a Danish immigrant in Waterloo. Visitors can combine the price of their tickets with the **Bedstemor's Hus** (1-800-759-9192; www.dkmuseum.org), open 1–4 May 15–Sept. 15. The restored "grandmother's house" is a Victorian cottage dating to 1908 that reflects the lifestyle of Danish people in the early 20th century.

THIS WORKING MILL—ELK HORN'S VISITORS CENTER—SHOWS THAT DANISH IMMIGRANTS, TOO, BROUGHT A TRADITION OF WINDMILLS WITH THEM TO IOWA

Danish Windmill Museum (712-764-7472; www.danishwindmill.com), 4038 Main Street, Elk Horn. Open

8–7 Mon.–Sat., 10–7 Sun. spring and summer; 9–5 Mon.–Sat., 12–5 Sun. fall and winter. Admission: $2. The Dutch weren't the only immigrants to bring a tradition of windmills with them when they settled in Iowa. An authentic windmill built in Denmark in 1848 welcomes visitors to Elk Horn. Inside, see the mill grind wheat and rye with wind power. The **Viking Hjem**, on the grounds of the museum, is a recreation of a 900 A.D. Viking home with a smithy's shop, a woodworking area, and living space. The museum is also home to a large imported-gifts shop and an Iowa Welcome Center.

The Little Mermaid (712-764-4343; www.metc.net/audubonco/tourism/attraction details.htm), Little Mermaid Park, Main Street, Kimballton. On a rock in a small fountain sits a sculpture of the Little Mermaid, Hans Christian Andersen's aquatic maiden and a symbol of Denmark. This scaled-down version of the statue in the Copenhagen Harbor watches over the village's park, which also includes a miniature Danish farm cottage and a playground.

✷ To Do

Whiterock Conservancy (712-684-2964; www.whiterockconservancy.org), 1390 IA 141, Coon Rapids. During the height of the Cold War, Roswell Garst of Coon Rapids, a farmer famous for having developed hardy strains of hybrid corn, invited Premier Nikita Khrushchev of the U.S.S.R. to visit his family farm. Garst's hope was to share expertise on agriculture and help thaw relations between the two

TEMPLETON RYE, "THE GOOD STUFF"

Prohibition in the 1920s didn't stop the people of Templeton from manufacturing or drinking liquor. They just got sneakier about it. In secret stills in barns and on farms around the town, townspeople produced a smooth and delicious rye whiskey that developed a reputation as "the good stuff." Its fame spread, and legend has it that the rye from Templeton was favored by Al Capone and was at the heart of his bootlegging empire.

After Prohibition ended, the people of Templeton continued to produce the rye in secret. According to rumors, locals can still acquire bottles of the homemade moonshine, which is wildly expensive and oh so delicious; for the rest of us, Templeton Rye is now legal and sold in stores and in bars.

The first bottles of the legal rye whiskey were produced in 2005. Scott Bush, the president of Templeton Rye Spirits, hopes to turn the town into a tourist destination much like Lynchburg, Tennessee, home of Jack Daniel's, but official tours of the distillery are not yet available, and they can't sell bottles. If you are passing through Templeton, call ahead, and they may be able to walk you through the **Templeton Rye** distillery. (712-669-8793; www.templetonrye.com, 209 Third Avenue, Templeton). If not, stop in at **The Still** (712-669-9441) at 107 North Main for a glass of Templeton Rye—neat, of course—or some bar and grill food at the adjoining restaurant. Al Capone would be proud.

countries. During the visit, Khrushchev was reported to have said, "I have seen the way the slaves of capitalism live, and I see they live pretty well. But the slaves of communism live pretty well, too. So let each one of us remain with his own way of life and be friends, living as good neighbors in the world." In 2004 the Whiterock Conservancy was started through generous donations from the Garst family. Named for the white rocks of the Middle Raccoon River Valley, the conservancy works to balance innovative, high-yield, environmentally friendly agriculture with habitat conservation and ecological restoration. The result is a diverse piece of Iowa farmland that welcomes visitors to enjoy hiking, biking, horseback riding, and camping.

Carroll County Historic Church Driving Tour (712-792-4383; www.carroll iowa.com), Carroll Chamber of Commerce, P.O. Box 307, Carroll. Contact the local chamber for a driving-tour guide of the many churches in the county. Most were built in the latter half of the 1800s when settlers turned the open prairie into a state. See imported and Tiffany-style stained glass, a Gothic brick church, and a two-ton church bell that now rings over the town of Templeton. The churches on the tour span the county from Mount Carmel to Maple River, and some are open during the day for visitors and tours.

Danish Countryside Vines and Wines (712-764-2991; www.danishcountryside vinesandwines.com), 1397 280th Street, Exira. Open Tues.–Sat. 10–6, Sun. 1–5 Apr.–Dec. and by appointment. In a renovated European-style barn, the winemakers turn native grapes into fine Iowa wines. Sample the grape and fruit wines in the tasting room, or enjoy a bottle out on the patio. The tour of the winery and vineyard is informative and fun.

✷ Green Space

Swan Lake (712-792-4614; www.carrollcountyconservation.com), 22676 Swan Lake Drive, Carroll. Open 5 AM–10:30 PM daily May–Oct. The park, just 2½ miles east of Carroll, offers multiuse trails for walking, biking, and cross-country skiing. A 115-acre lake for swimming and no-wake boating is stocked with catfish, crappies, bluegills, and largemouth bass. Both paddleboats and canoes are available to rent, as is a one-bedroom cabin that sleeps six and has most of the comforts of home—if your home doesn't have a shower or heat. The **Swan Lake Campground** offers 100 sites for RVs and tent camping, a concession stand with firewood, ice, and snacks. The **Swan Lake Farmstead Museum** offers a glimpse into rural life through agricultural machinery, an old barn with animals, and information on conservation. Cabin rental $55 per night (two-night minimum on weekends), campsites from $10–$15.

✷ Where to Stay

MOTELS **Carrollton Inn** (712-792-5600; www.carrolltoninn.com), 1730 IA 71 North, Carroll. A locally owned hotel with single- and double-queen rooms, free continental breakfast, and an indoor pool. Restaurant, bar, and fitness center all on-site. Some rooms are wired for high-speed Internet. Rooms from $75–$90.

RESORTS **Whiterock Conservancy and Resort** (712-684-2697; www.white rockconservancy.org/accomodations .html), 1390 IA 141, Coon Rapids.

Guests at the resort can chose from a number of different kinds of accommodation, from primitive camping to the elegant Roswell Suite in the 1940s farmhouse. A cottage, carriage house, country house, and rustic cabin are also available for groups of varying sizes. Guests are encouraged to enjoy the conservancy through free recreation, tours, workshops, and lectures (see *To Do*). Rooms from $60–$300.

BED & BREAKFAST **Adams Street Bed & Breakfast** (712-792-5198; www.adamsstreetbandb.com), 726 North Adams Street, Carroll. It would be hard to find a more romantic or luxurious B&B than Adams Street. The 1885 home offers five guest rooms, all with private bathrooms and elegant decorations. The suites are almost too decadent for words with king-size beds covered in rich linens and pillows, deep whirlpool tubs, and fireplaces. At the same time, the home is very comfortable. The solarium is a cozy place to relax with a book, and complimentary beverages and ice cream are available. Breakfast is served in three courses and is outstanding. Rooms from $60–$135.

BREAKFAST AT THE ADAMS HOUSE B&B IN CARROLL IS AS PLEASING TO THE EYE AS IT IS TO THE PALATE

CAMPING **Albert the Bull Park & Campground** (712-563-3355; www.auduboncounty.org), East Division and Stadium Drive, Audubon. The world's largest bull—weighing in at 45 tons of concrete and steel recycled from old windmills—and the symbol of the city of Audubon stands guard at the campground entrance. Behind Albert, the campground has 40 hookup sites, a shelter with a fireplace and electricity, a swimming pool, tennis and volleyball courts, and a playground. Campsites from $10–$17.

Whiterock Conservancy and Resort See *Where to Stay: Resorts* and *To Do.*

✱ Where to Eat

DINING OUT **Danish Inn** (712-764-4251), 4116 Main Street, Elk Horn. Open for lunch and dinner Tues.–Sat., Sun. brunch. This locally owned restaurant is known for its fabulous evening buffets. Diners will find prime rib, roasted ham, sirloin steaks, and chicken dishes. This is no tacky buffet. The food is homemade with fresh ingredients from family recipes, and there are always beloved, though unpronounceable, Danish dishes, such as *frikadeller* (meatballs), *medisterpølse* (sausage), and *rodkall* (red cabbage). On Sundays sample the traditional Danish smorgasbord. $$

John James Audubon Tea Room and Gift Shop (712-563-3319), 329 Washington Street, Audubon. Open for lunch and tea Wed.–Fri. Sip tea or coffee, and choose from five lunch entrées in this elegant tearoom in Audubon's historic downtown. Desserts are made from scratch, so save room for pie. Reservations are recommended. Antiques, collectables, and gifts are for sale. $$

Crossroads Bistro (712-775-5000; www.crossroadsbistro.com), 1012 US 71, Carroll. Open daily for dinner. A fine-dining experience with a focus on Italian dishes and hand-cut steaks. Traditional Italian dishes such as veal Marsala and fettuccine Alfredo are done well as is the gourmet pizza and seafood, $$. Next door is **Coffee World** (712-775-5500; www.carrollcoffeeworld.com), with casual breakfast and lunch offerings in a coffeehouse setting. $

EATING OUT **Darrell's Place** (712-563-3922), 1040 First Street, Hamlin. Open for breakfast, lunch, and dinner Mon.–Sat. Hamlin is the tiniest little town, but it offers an award-winning tenderloin. Darrell's Place is the local restaurant, bar, and community center, and the tenderloin is absolutely classic: fresh, crispy, and just juicy enough. The bar also serves breakfast, burgers, fries, and evening specials. $

Bloomers Bar and Grill (712-792-9101), 1235 Plaza Drive, Carroll. Open for lunch and dinner daily. Tank and Strauto, the proprietors, needed a place to share their love of beer drinking and football watching. In this friendly sports bar, they've added a huge menu that ranges from such sports-bar favorites as onion rings and chicken wings to New York strip steak and seafood. There are plenty of high-definition televisions and a good selection of beers. $$

The Pear Tree Café (712-773-7327), 114 North Main Street, Kimballton. Open for breakfast, lunch, and dinner Mon., Wed.–Sat.; Sun. brunch; closed Tues. A cute small-town café with home cooking, famous for the beef and noodles, great Reubens, and pizzas. Breakfast is served all day. $

* Drinking Establishments

✪ **Little Gussey's**, Maple River. Open Mon.–Sat. 9 AM until close. No, there's no phone number, and there's probably no real address, but travelers who find their way to Maple River can find Little Gussey's. It's *the* bar. Sometimes it's known as the Riverside Tavern—I think. The charm of Little Gussey's, though, is that it *is* so very out of the way, so very forgotten, and, best of all, so very full of taxidermy. No one knows where all the taxidermy came from, but there are small mounted animals all over the place, in addition to the wood-burning stove that was once the only source of heat. Pizza and snacks are served, but this is mainly a tiny village bar that's strange and a lot of fun.

GREENE AND GUTHRIE COUNTIES

Greene County has two seemingly contradictory distinctions. It is so rural that in the entire county there is but one grocery store (in the town of Jefferson), yet it is also home to the only Iowa-owned wind farm in the state. The rest of the attractions of Greene County look toward both the future and the past. In Guthrie County visitors will find the small resort community of Panora with the privately owned Lake Panorama and Springbrook State Park, one of the loveliest in the state and open to all.

GUIDANCE Local resources are slim. For guidance for these areas refer to **Iowa Tourism** (515-242-4795; www.traveliowa.com), 200 East Grand Avenue, Des Moines.

GETTING THERE *By car:* Jefferson in Greene County is directly west of **I-35** on **US 30**. Guthrie County is directly to the south on **IA 25** which connects with **I-35.**

MEDICAL EMERGENCY Call **911**.

Greene County Medical Center (515-386-2114; www.gcmchealth.com), 1000 West Lincoln Way, Jefferson. A small regional hospital with emergency services.

INTERNET ACCESS Public Internet access is pretty slim in this region, but for a comfortable place to check your e-mail, try the coffee shop **Prairie Blue** on the square in Jefferson.

✷ To See

✪ **RVP 1875** (515-975-3083; www.rvp1875.com), 115 South Wilson Avenue, Jefferson. Open 9–5 Tues.–Sat. or by appointment. Robby Pedersen, a master craftsman, builds authentic 1870s wooden furniture in his combination studio, museum, and classroom. Stop by the shop to see the master and apprentices working on beds, chests, and writing desks, using only the tools and techniques that would have been available to them in the 1800s. (Often they even work in the clothing that craftspeople would have worn at the time.) The furniture on display in the shop can be handmade to order, and budding craftspeople can learn about dovetails and using planes during weekend workshops, after which the participants keep the furniture. Pedersen, who has been featured in countless magazines, is a font of information on both Iowa history and furniture making, after working for many years at **Living History Farms** in Des Moines.

Mahanay Bell Tower (515-386-2155; www.jeffersoniowa.com), 220 North Chestnut, Jefferson. Open Memorial Day–Labor Day daily 11–4, weekends in May and Sept., and by appointment; $2 adults, $1 children. Greene County is so small that it only has one grocery store—the Fareway here in the county seat—but looming over the courthouse and crops is a 162-foot bell tower. The 14 bronze bells ring on the quarter hour and play patriotic songs and hymns three times a day. Visitors can take the elevator 12 stories to the top, where the guide will point out every possible feature of Greene County: the birthplace home of George Gallup of Gallup Poll fame, Hardin Hilltop Wind Farm, the highest point in Greene County, and, yes, the grocery store.

Guthrie County Historical Village (641-755-2989; www.panora.org/museum), 206 West South Street, Panora. Open May 1–Oct. 15, 10–4:30 Tues.–Fri., 1–4:30 Sat., and holidays. Admission: $2 adults, $1 children. Walk through history at this 10-building village. See a log cabin, country school, a general store, blacksmith shop, newspaper office, and a depot with caboose. One exhibit hall focuses on the region's coal-mining history, and visitors can even peek in the outhouse.

✷ To Do

Panorama National Resort and Conference Center (641-755-2080; www.lakepanoramanational.com), 5071 Clover Ridge Road, Panora. The 18-hole golf course at Lake Panorama is consistently ranked one of the top 500 by *Golf Digest* magazine and plays host to several tournaments throughout the year. The resort also offers townhouse and motel accommodations that overlook the golf course. A restaurant and lounge is also on-site. Please visit the Web site or call for greens fees, hours of service, menus, and lodging rates.

Guthrie Center Aquatic Center (641-332-2989; www.guthriecenter.com), 206 West State Street, Guthrie Center. Open afternoons and evenings May 24–Labor Day weekend. Admission: $3.50 adults, $3 children. This modern aquatic center includes two slides, a zero-depth entry, a diving board, and concession stand.

✷ Green Space

Springbrook State Park (641-747-3591; www.iowadnr.com/parks), 2437 160th Road, Guthrie Center. Open during daylight hours. The lake at Springbrook State Park isn't the state's largest, but it has to be one of the loveliest. It's tucked back in a valley and surrounded by trees, and the cool water is wonderful for swimming (at the sand beach), fishing, and small-craft boating. A hiking trail circumnavigates the lake, and wildlife is abundant. The campground and picnic areas surround a shady creek; 120 campsites, both electric and primitive, are available through the Department of Natural Resources (DNR) system. Campsites from $11–$16.

✷ Where to Stay

Prairie View Bed & Breakfast (641-755-4356; www.prairieviewbb.com), 2711 IA 44, Guthrie Center. This country home 2 miles west of Panora offers three modern and comfortable guest rooms, each with a private bath and views of the countryside. The innkeepers are science teachers with an interest in ecotourism; only recycled paper products and biodegradable cleaning products are used in the home. Be sure to check out prairie walking trails, and ask about local flora and fauna. Rooms (including breakfast) from $75–$125.

The Lakeside Inn (641-755-4240; www.lakesideinnpanorama.com), 5405 Chimra Road, Panora. Lake Panorama is privately owned, so visitors without generous lake-house-owning friends will need to stay at this local hotel. Each of the 22 suites offers a view of the lake and a balcony and includes a refrigerator, microwave, and coffeemaker. Some of the larger suites also include fireplaces, living rooms, and hot tubs. The inn also offers guests a heated outdoor swimming pool, a hot tub, and cruises of the lake on their 16-passenger pontoon boat. **The Port** is the adjacent restaurant with both casual fine dining and views of the water and a tiki bar during summer months. Open for breakfast, lunch, and dinner Sat. & Sun., dinner only Mon.–Fri. Rooms from $115–$175.

✷ Where to Eat

EATING OUT **Peony Chinese Restaurant** (515-386-3928), 101 East Lincolnway Street, Jefferson. Open for lunch and dinner Mon.–Sat. Everyone in Jefferson, it seems, recommends the Peony Restaurant. The menu doesn't stretch beyond the usual repertoire of lo mein, chow mein, and kung pao chicken, but this is small-town Chinese done well. The food is tasty, well seasoned, and fresh, and the atmosphere is cool and refreshing with beautiful Chinese prints on the wall. Takeout is available. $$

The Howlin' Coyote (641-755-3255), 108 West Main Street, Panora. Open daily but check on Sundays in winter. With smoked meats and BBQ that will have diners howling at the moon, this "pub and grub" serves their pulled pork, chicken, brisket, and ham as sandwiches, in wraps, or on a dinner plate. The "meal deals" are great for takeout. Named after big-game animals, from "the doe," which feeds 3 to 4 to "the grizzly," which feeds 10 to 12, these packages include sides, buns, hushpuppies, and sauce. $–$$

COFFEE **Prairie Blue** (515-386-2299), 114 North Wilson, Jefferson. Open 6:30–3 Mon.–Fri., 6:30–7 Thurs., 7–2 Sat. This big, airy coffee shop offers plenty of visual stimulation for sippers of java and espresso drinks. Check out the art for sale by young local talents. Rugs, paintings, cards, and sculptures are on display. Free wireless Internet is available. You can also enjoy eggs and pancakes for breakfast or wraps, sandwiches, and fancy salads for lunch. $

* Selective Shopping

Junck (515-386-4541; www.junck.biz), 106 East State Street, Jefferson. Open 10–6 Mon.–Fri., 10–2 Sat. Junk from garages, basements, and thrift stores is reincarnated at this locally owned shop. Wind chimes are made from old bicycle frames, old windows are painted into wall art, and power cords become zipper pulls. The gifts are clever, unique, and suited for a green lifestyle.

SOUTH AND WEST

INCLUDING COUNCIL BLUFFS, RED OAK, STANTON, VILLISCA, CLARINDA, SHENANDOAH, WALNUT, ATLANTIC, GREENFIELD, AND ENVIRONS

Just across the Missouri River from the city of Omaha, Council Bluffs is where trails and train lines converged before departure to all points west. Lewis and Clark stopped here to meet with the Missouria and Otoe Indians. Pioneers following the explorers' trail, the Mormon Trail, and the Oregon Trail during the 19th century considered Council Bluffs the last station of civilization before their great western journey. Council Bluffs became a hub for travelers settling the West and building the railroads. The city is packed with historical sights, but for entertainment, dining, and lodging, visitors spend most of their time in Omaha to the west and the three casinos in the city.

East of Council Bluffs are the communities in the Nishnabotna and the Nodaway River Valleys: Clarinda and Shenandoah, the childhood homes of musicians Glenn Miller and the Everly Brothers; Red Oak; and Villisca, which is thought to be haunted by the ghosts of a family murdered in their beds near the turn of the 20th century.

COUNCIL BLUFFS

Council Bluffs presides over the Missouri River just east of Omaha, Nebraska. The town was named in 1804 for the place where the Lewis and Clark expedition met with Native Americans of the region. The city has long been an important crossroads. Settlers and miners stocked up on goods before heading out West to seek their fortune in land or gold. Steamships plied the river bringing goods to the camps of the Dakotas and Montana. Mormons in their great exodus to Iowa stopped along the way in Council Bluffs, and from the hills above the river, General Dodge and Abraham Lincoln dreamed of the great railways that would head West.

Today Council Bluffs celebrates its important role in the settlement of the West. Several museums are dedicated to railroads like the Union Pacific Railroad Museum, and the adventures of Lewis and Clark come alive at the Western Trails

Center. While neither as populous nor as prosperous as its Nebraska neighbor across the river, Council Bluffs has many intriguing and sometimes strange attractions for visitors, whether they are staying for a while or just passing through. History buffs will love a tour of the General Dodge House and the Squirrel Cage Jail, and kids will enjoy splashing around in the fountain and playing with the statues of black squirrels (the city's mascot) at Bayliss Park.

GUIDANCE **Council Bluffs Area Chamber of Commerce** (1-800-228-6878; www.councilbluffsiowa.com) with information on the Council Bluffs area, Nebraska, and Pottawattamie County. While the chamber conducts business hours during the week, the best way to access information is through the Web or by calling.

GETTING THERE *By air:* **Eppley Airfield** (402-661-8017; www.eppleyairfield.com), 4501 Abbott Drive, Omaha, Nebraska. Connecting flights throughout the region and country.

By car: Council Bluffs is at the junction of **I-80** and **I-29**.

MEDICAL EMERGENCY Call **911**.

Mercy Hospital Council Bluffs (712-328-5000; www.alegent.com), 800 Mercy Drive, Council Bluffs. Emergency medical care with locations throughout the region.

INTERNET ACCESS/PUBLIC LIBRARY **Bayliss Park** in the heart of Council Bluffs is an outdoors wireless hotspot for the city of Council Bluffs.

Council Bluffs Public Library (712-323-7553; www.cbpl.lib.ia.us), 400 Willow Avenue, Council Bluffs. Open Mon.–Thurs. 9–9, Fri. and Sat. 9–5, and Sun. 1–5. Public computers with Internet access and free wireless Internet are available at this library along with lots of fun community events.

AN ANGEL MEMORIALIZES RUTH ANNE DODGE AT THE FAIRVIEW CEMETERY IN COUNCIL BLUFFS

✷ To See

Historic General Dodge House (712-322-2406; www.dodgehouse.org), 605 Third Street, Council Bluffs. Open 10–5 Tues.–Sat, 1–5 Sun., closed Jan. and holidays. Tours: $7 adults. General Grenville Mellen Dodge, a Civil War veteran, was one of the greatest railroad builders of all time. It was Dodge who envisioned Council Bluffs as the connection between railroad lines from back East and those from the West, and he convinced Abraham Lincoln of this idea. His house—designed by the architect of the governor's mansion, Terrace Hill, in Des Moines—is a stately Victorian mansion on the bluff. The splendid house—including library, parlor, bedrooms, and ballroom—has been completely restored and is full of Dodge's interesting artifacts, including several French pieces that the Dodge family collected while the general helped build railroads in that country. The tour begins next door at the Beresheim House, 621 Third Street, which was the home of one of General Dodge's business partners and is also on the National Register of Historic Places.

Fairview Cemetery, (712-328-4650; www.rootsweb.ancestry.com/~iapottaw/CemFairviewCB.htm), 308 Lafayette Avenue (at North Second), Council Bluffs; open during daylight hours. Originally called the "Old Burying Grounds," this beautiful cemetery is the final resting place of some of the most prominent early citizens of Council Bluffs. One of the most intriguing gravesites is **the Ruth Anne Dodge Memorial,** which honors the wife of General Dodge. In 1916 Mrs. Dodge began having a recurring dream that a winged angel sailing on the prow of a ship offered Dodge a drink and said, "I bring you both a promise and a blessing." On the third night she drank. She died peacefully the next evening. Her daughters commissioned a bronze sculpture of the angel, complete with overflowing vessel. It is called the "Black Angel" for the tarnished color of the bronze. **Amelia Jenks Bloomer,** suffragette and namesake of the pants, is also buried in Fairview Cemetery. Other residents of the cemetery include Mormon pioneers who traveled and stayed in Council Bluffs on their trek to Utah. Their graves can be found on the east end of the cemetery. Just down the block, from the Black Angel, on Lafayette Avenue is the **Lincoln Monument**. The pylon marks the spot from where General Dodge and Honest Abe surveyed the location for the terminus of the first transcontinental railroad.

Historic Squirrel Cage Jail (712-323-2509; www.thehistoricalsociety.org), 226 Pearl Street, Council Bluffs. Open Apr. 1–Oct. 31 Wed.–Sat. 10–4, Sun. 1–4, or by appointment. Admission: $7 adults, $5 children 6–12. In a clever attempt to keep prisoners from escaping, this county jail was built like a Lazy Susan. Three stories held 10 pie-shaped cells, and the entire cellblock rotated so that one jailer could guard many prisoners. The Victorian-Gothic structure is one of three remaining squirrel-cage jails, but it was decommissioned after it was deemed a fire hazard. Tours offer insight into escape attempts (few were successful) and the ghosts said to haunt the jail.

✷ To Do

Western Historic Trails Center (712-366-4900; www.iowahistory.org), 3434 Richard Downing Avenue, Council Bluffs. Open May 1–Sept. 30, 9–6; Oct. 1–Apr. 30, 9–5; closed Thanksgiving, Christmas, and New Year's Day. Visitors wind their way through a tall-grass prairie to this interpretive center built next to the Missouri River. Inside, interactive displays explain the history of the Lewis and Clark Trail, the Oregon Trail, the Mormon Trail, and the California Trail. What this museum does especially well is show what became of these trails and the role they play in America today. An award-winning video, which is well worth the time, juxtaposes the travelers on the historical trails with the lives of modern travelers heading West. Visitors can explore hiking and biking trails and shop for books in the excellent gift shop. The center is also an Iowa Welcome Center.

ALL POINTS WEST: RAILROADS CONVERGE IN COUNCIL BLUFFS
Council Bluffs celebrates its railroad past with several museums and monuments. The **Golden Spike Monument**, at the corner of South 21st Street and Ninth Avenue, is a 56-foot golden spike at the eastern terminus of the Union Pacific Railroad. The **Union Pacific Railroad Museum** (712-329-8307; www.uprr.com; 200 Pearl Street, Council Bluffs; open Tues.–Sat. 10–4; free) is one of the largest privately owned museums in the country. Located in a 1903 Carnegie Library, the museum showcases photographs, documents, and interactive exhibits that illustrate the role the Union Pacific played in the development of the economy and settlement of the West. The **Railswest Railroad Museum** (712-323-5182; www.thehistoricalsociety.org/depot.htm; 16th Avenue and South Main Street, Council Bluffs; open Memorial Day–Labor Day 10–4, Sun. 1–4, and by appointment; $6 adults, $4 children 6–16) is located in a restored Rock Island Railroad depot. Outside, displays include three engines and railcars. Inside, the museum has an operating HO-gauge model railroad and artifacts.

Lewis and Clark Monument and Scenic Overlook (712-328-4650; www.parksandrec.councilbluffs.gov/historical.asp), 29385 Monument Road, Council Bluffs. Open year-round 8 AM–10 PM. The monument at the top of a bluff overlooking Big Lake Park and the Missouri River Valley was dedicated in 1936 and celebrates the meeting of the Native Americans and the explorers in the region. The park also features a mountain-bike trail, a picnic area, and restrooms.

Mills County Historical Museum, Earth Lodge (712-572-5038), Glenwood Lake Park, 2 Lake Drive, Glenwood. Open May–Sept. 1–4 weekends and by appointment. See an Earth Lodge, and learn about the Native American people who lived in the area between 800 and 1200 A.D. The county museum also includes antique agricultural equipment, a one-room country schoolhouse, a century barn, and a jail.

CASINOS **Harrah's Council Bluffs Casino and Hotel** (712-329-6000; www.harrahs.com), 1 Harrah's Boulevard, Council Bluffs. The casino and hotel complex offers gamblers slot machines and table games, along with flashy dining and entertainment options. The **Stir Concert Cove** (1-888-512-7469; www.stircove.com) features such big-name musical acts as Willie Nelson on a grassy hill outside the casino. The **Horseshoe Casino** (712-323-2500) 1-80/I-29 at exit 1B, another casino in the Harrah's family, offers slot machines, table games, Thoroughbred horse-racing simulcasts, and greyhound racing Tues.–Sat. at 4 PM.

* Green Space

Bayliss Park (www.iowawest.oxblue.com/bayliss), First Avenue and Pearl Street, Council Bluffs. At the center of the Haymarket Square neighborhood, Bayliss Park has been a feature of Council Bluffs life since the land was donated in 1853. The park includes a towering fountain, gazebo, and several larger-than-life black-squirrel statues. (Black squirrels, though rare, live in abundance in Council Bluffs; they are protected by city code and are the city's mascot.) In summer kids can play among the squirrels in the serpentine fountain. The park is also home to **Veteran's Plaza,** a monument designed by artist John Lajba. It honors soldiers from the Civil War to the conflicts in Iraq with a reflection wall, three statues, and a water feature. The park is also a wireless hotspot.

BAYLISS PARK IN COUNCIL BLUFFS IS HOME TO A PASSEL OF RARE BLACK SQUIRRELS—INCLUDING THIS LARGER-THAN-LIFE STATUE OF ONE

Lake Manawa (712-336-0220; www.exploreiowaparks.com), 110 South Shore Drive, Council Bluffs. Open 4 AM–10:30 PM for patrons not staying at the campground. Just 1 mile south of the city, Lake Manawa is an urban park with a view of the skyline of Omaha to the west. The waters of the Missouri shifted in 1881 and created this "oxbow" lake of 660 acres. Recreation is next to the homes and industrial parks around the shore. Several biking, hiking, and walking trails wind around the lake, most notably the **Wabash Trace Trail** and a connecting line to the **Western Historic Trails Center** (see above). There are three boat ramps around the lake, and fishing is popular, as are picnicking and swimming at the supervised beach. Kids can play on the "dream playground" and on Boy Scout Island. The campground, between the lake and a residential neighborhood, offers campers views of the lake from both electric and primitive sites, and there is a modern shower building. Campsites from $11–$16.

IN 1881 THE MISSOURI RIVER SHIFTED, CREATING THE 660-ACRE "OXBOW" LAKE MANAWA, WITH A VIEW OF OMAHA ON THE HORIZON

Carter Lake (www.cityofcarterlake.com) is the only Iowa city located on the west side of the Missouri River. Formed in 1853, the city started on the eastern shore, but in 1877 the river flooded and changed course, leaving the town on the other side. Nebraska and Iowa did legal battle for the 2,000 acres, but in 1892 the Supreme Court awarded the town to Iowa. Today it is surrounded by the city of Omaha, though high-school students cross the river to go to classes in Iowa, and the second "Welcome to Iowa" sign is a bit bewildering. The city's namesake lake offers boating and fishing and other outdoor recreation activities. The **Blue Waters Mini-Golf Course** (712-347-5553; www.bluewatersminigolf.com; 2929 Mabrey Lane, Carter Lake) is an 18-hole championship mini-golf course that will challenge putters no matter which side of the Missouri they call home.

✱ Where to Stay

HOTELS AND INNS **Western Inn** (712-322-4499; www.westerninncb.com), I-80 and Madison Avenue, Council Bluffs. Located just off the interstate, this clapboard inn with 51 freshly remodeled rooms, an indoor pool with a tropical mural, Internet access, and a continental breakfast offers a lot. A juice and coffee bar and warm cookies wait for guests on weekday evenings. Rooms from $48–$70.

Heartland Inn (712-322-8400; www.heartlandinns.com), 1000 Woodbury Avenue, Council Bluffs. This 100 percent smoke-free Iowa chain has accommodations in 18 Iowa cities. The Council Bluffs hotel has 88 rooms with many amenities, including king or queen pillow-top beds, in-room coffee, free high-speed wireless Internet access in every room, and a free breakfast and evening snacks. Rooms from $85–$103.

Harrah's Council Bluffs Casino and Hotel (712-329-6000; www.harrahscouncilbluffs.com) 1 Harrah's Boulevard, Council Buffs. Rooms raging from basic to luxury suites are available at this hotel, which also features a convenient fitness facility and Internet access in every room—and, of course, a casino. Rooms from $59–$299.

BED & BREAKFAST **Castle Unicorn Bed & Breakfast** (712-527-5930; www.castleunicorn.com), Glenwood. Call for directions. Yeah, it really is a castle, with a tower, turrets, garden, and formal gates. Be the king or queen for a weekend at this inn 20 minutes south of Omaha. The two suites include four-poster beds and whirlpool tubs, and the Queen Suite is at the top of the tower. Breakfast is served in the great room, and there are gorgeous views of the Loess Hills. Courtiers (kids or accompanying adults) can stay in the two smaller Duke and Duchess rooms, which share a bathroom. Rooms from $169–$219.

CAMPING **Lake Manawa** (712-336-0220; www.exploreiowaparks.com), 110 South Shore Drive, Council Bluffs. See *Green Space.*Campsites $11–$16.

✱ Where to Eat

The selection of restaurants in Council Bluffs that are not fast food or mass-market chains is slim. Most residents find their way across the river to Omaha for eating and drinking. The casinos each have several restaurants with buffets, casual, and fine dining.

DINING OUT **360 Steakhouse** (712-329-6000; www.harrahscouncilbluffs.com), 2101 South 35th Street, Council Bluffs. Open for dinner nightly. While this steakhouse focuses on choice cuts of beef, the menu also features seafood entreés including Alaskan king crab, swordfish, and scallops. Free-range chicken and BBQ ribs are also on the menu, as is a selection of sides and salads. $$$

Waterfront Grill (1-866-667-3386; www.ameristarcasinos.com), 2200 River Road, Council Bluffs. Open for dinner Tues.–Sat. Named one of the best restaurants in the Omaha area, the grill in the Ameristar Casino features Iowa pork, prime rib, sea scallops, and more. Salads and starters are delightfully out of the ordinary, including a tomato and mozzarella salad and pork empanadas. $$$

EATING OUT **Main Street Café** (712-388-3801) 102 Main Street, Council Bluffs. Open for breakfast, lunch, and dinner Tues.–Sat., and Sun brunch. Casual burgers, sandwiches, and home cooking in a slightly tacky restaurant. Check out the adjoining bakery around the corner on Pearl Street for baked goods. $

Duncan's Café (712-328-3360) 501 Main Street, Council Bluffs. Open for breakfast daily, lunch Mon.–Sat., and dinner Mon.–Fri. This is a bustling diner, especially at breakfast, with brick walls, tall booths, and lots of colorful art. The fare is breakfast basics, sandwiches and burgers, and evening dinner specials. $

✷ Entertainment

Mid-America Center (712-326-2260; www.midamericacenter.com), 1 Arena Way, Council Bluffs. Home of the USHL Lancers and the APFL Blackhawks, the entertainment and convention center offers everything from rodeo and sporting events to concerts and family shows. Contact the box office for schedule and ticket information.

Star Cinema 16 and IMAX (712-256-7827; www.kerasotes.com/Home.aspx) 3220 23rd Avenue, Council Bluffs. This 16-screen complex is a state-of-the-art place to see a movie with an IMAX screen, digital sound, rocking "cuddle seats," and a "Baby Box Office" for parents with small children.

RED OAK, STANTON, VILLISCA, CLARINDA AND SHENANDOAH

The southwesternmost corner of the state can seem very far away, and few visitors find their way to this region. It is not without its charms, though. The cities of Shenandoah and Clarinda offer delightful main streets with a bend. In Villisca, history and horror come together at the Ax Murder House. The region is tucked into low river valleys that are picturesque and peaceful.

GUIDANCE **Clarinda Chamber of Commerce** (712-542-2166; www.clarinda.org), 115 East Main, Clarinda. Open Mon.–Fri. 9–5. The lobby of the chamber office features racks of brochures and a helpful staff to field questions. The Web site doesn't have much to offer for guidance, but e-mail works well: chamber@clarinda.org.

Red Oak Chamber of Commerce (712-623-4821; www.redoakiowa.com), 307 East Reed Street, Red Oak. Open during normal business hours; more information is available on the Web.

GETTING THERE *By car:* These cities and the surrounding counties are on a loop of sorts. Start out from **I-29** on **US 34** going through Glenwood until you reach Red Oak. To the south on **IA 48** is the town of Shenandoah and just east of Shenandoah on **IA 2** is Clarinda. **US 71** goes north-south through Clarinda and passes the town of Villisca. Head east at **US 71** and **US 34** and you will find your way back to Red Oak.

MEDICAL EMERGENCY Call **911**.

Clarinda Regional Health Center (712-542-2176; www.clarindahealth.com), 823 South Seventeenth Street, Clarinda. Emergency medicine is available at this small regional hospital.

MIDWESTERN MURDER MOST FOUL

DARWIN LINN AT THE MOORE HOUSE

The sleepy town of Villisca is home to one of the most brutal unsolved murders in American history. In 1912 eight people—Joe Moore, his wife, their four children, and two overnight guests—were brutally murdered in their beds. The killer crept into the house and used the Moores' own ax. Many believe that a state senator, one Frank F. Jones, was involved, and while two men were tried, no one was ever convicted of the crime.

Today Darwin Linn and his wife, Martha, own the home at 323 East Fourth Street as well as a related museum and give an insightful tour. The tour starts with the "museum," which is sort of a wacky collection of primitive cars and buggies, town artifacts, taxidermy, and very creepy mannequins in period clothing. Then visitors ride through the streets with their guide as he points out significant locations including the homes of Jones and other players in the mystery. A stop at the graveyard follows. The last stop on the tour is the home, which contains a few of the family's belongings. Some scientists and psychics believe that the home is haunted.

The most surprising aspect of the tour is the sensitivity Darwin Linn brings to the tour. This is no hokey spook tour, and, with the exception of a bloody sign on the front of the house, there is no attempt to cheapen the events for profit. Instead, the events are described with intelligence and respect.

Call to book a tour. After-dark "lamplight tours" are also available, and guests with strong nerves can make arrangements to stay overnight in the home or in the barn on the property.

✷ To See

✪ **The Villisca Ax Murder House** and the **Olson-Linn Museum** (712-826-2756; www.villiscaiowa.com), Village Square, 323 East Fourth Street, Villisca. Admission: $10 per person. See the Sidebar: *Midwestern Murder Most Foul*

RESIDENTS OF THE TOWN OF STANTON GET THEIR DRINKING WATER FROM A GIANT COFFEE CUP

Stanton Swedish Heritage and Cultural Center (712-829-2840; www.stantoniowa.com, 410 Hilltop, Stanton. Open Apr.–Nov. Tues.–Sat. 12–4 and by appointment. Admission: $2 adults. True to the town's Swedish roots, all the homes in Stanton are painted white. Rumor has it that if a homeowner paints her or his home any other color, the townspeople will paint it back to white in the middle of the night. Start exploring the city with a tour of the heritage center, which preserves artifacts from the early settlers. The museum offers three floors of videos, photographs, documents, and relics like a telephone switchboard. If you're so inclined, ride down the chute that served as the school's fire escape. Stanton is also home to the world's largest Swedish coffeepot and coffee cup, which serve as the town's water towers. The coffeepot holds 40,000 gallons of water or 640,000 cups of coffee.

Johnny Carson Birthplace (641-322-5229; www.johnnycarsonbirthplace.org), 500 13th Street, Corning. Open Memorial Day–Labor Day 1–4 and by appointment. Free. Johnny Carson, host of *The Tonight Show* for 30 years, was born in little Corning. The Carson family lived all over southeast Iowa before moving to Norfolk, Nebraska. While living in Red Oak, Carson began a correspondence course in ventriloquism, which spurred his interest in magic and performance. The family home is restored with period furnishings and Carson memorabilia.

Glenn Miller Birthplace Home (712-542-2461; www.glennmiller.org), 601 South Glenn Miller Avenue, Clarinda. Open May–Oct. Tues.–Sun. 1–5. Free. Glenn Miller was born March 1, 1904, and his family moved to Colorado in 1908. His birthplace in the family home has been restored to reflect what it may have looked like when Miller lived there. Family photographs, memorabilia, and exhibits on Miller's life and music fill the home.

Goldenrod School (712-542-3073), 1600 South 16th Street, Clarinda. Open May–Oct. Tues.–Sun. 1–4, Nov.–Apr. Tues.–Sun. 2–4, and by appointment. Admission: $2 adults, children under 12 free. In 1901 Jesse Field Shambaugh launched the 4-H movement in a one-room schoolhouse. Focusing on agricultural and domestic skills, the clubs were popular and spread throughout Iowa and other agricultural states. The school is now on the site of the **Nodaway Valley Museum**. The rest of the museum complex includes exhibits dedicated to Glenn Miller, country education, music, and baseball history.

Bricker Botanical Center (712-246-3455; www.shenandoahiowa.net/html/attractions_butterfly.asp), IA 69 and Sheridan Avenue, Shenandoah. Open daily 10–4. Free. Inside this tiny (1,000 square feet) tropical garden, visitors will find exotic beauties of both flora and fauna. Tropical koi fill the ponds, and tropical birds fill the air with song. The floral displays change with the season, and native butterflies flutter around this small greenhouse center. In summer months, the display spreads to the out-of-doors, as do native butterflies.

Greater Shenandoah Historical Museum (712-246-3455; www.simplyshenandoah.com), 800 West Sheridan. Open Mar.–Dec. 1–4 Tues.–Fri. and Sun. and by appointment. Free but donations appreciated. This small-town museum is full of wacky curiosities. Check out the mammoth skull dug up in the local sand pits; see a settlement house from Manti, a Mormon village; and learn about the Everly Brothers, Shenandoah hometown boys. There are all sorts of artifacts from regional history, but the strangest is an X-ray shoe-sizing machine that allowed salespeople and savvy mothers to see through new school shoes to make sure they fit.

Iowa Walk of Fame (712-246-3455; www.shenandoahiowa.net), Sheridan Avenue, Shenandoah. Famous Iowans from Oscar-winning actor Don Ameche to science-teacher-turned-artist Larry Zack are honored on the sidewalks of Shenandoah. Pick up a copy of the *Biographical Information of the People Honored* pamphlet to learn more about each famous Iowan while you walk the main street. It's a little like Hollywood.

✷ To Do

Heritage Hill Tour (712-623-6340; www.redoakiowa.com), starting at First and Coolbaugh. Brochures for this self-guided tour are available at the chamber of commerce. The tour includes the 1890 Montgomery County Courthouse, built of striking red limestone, the city's square park in the business district, and the stately mansions that line the avenues on the hill above town. In summer the gardens are in full bloom, and the scent of night-blooming jasmine fill the streets in the evening. Most of the houses are privately owned and not open to the public, but on the first Sunday in December, some of the holiday-decorated homes are open for tea with the hostesses.

Promenade Tour of Clarinda (712-542-2166; www.clarinda.org), 115 East Main Street, Clarinda. Pick up a pamphlet at the chamber of commerce, and see the sites of this historic small town. The tour starts with the Page County Courthouse, then circles the neighborhoods; it is a short drive or a longish walk. Sites include the **Glenn Miller Museum**, the **Goldenrod School**, and homes with unique histories built at the turn of the 20th century.

✷ Green Space

Nodaway Valley Park (712-542-3864), US 71, 2 miles north of Clarinda. Open daylight hours. With great views of the Nodaway and East Nodaway river valleys, timberland, and open fields, this idyllic hideaway is great for picnicking, hiking, and camping. Fourteen campsites offer electric hook-up, and primitive campsites are also available. Campsites from $10–$15.

✱ Where to Stay

MOTELS **Celebrity Inn** (712-542-5178), 1323 South 16th Street, Clarinda. An independent, family-owned motel offers the basics: clean rooms, free breakfast, and microwaves and refrigerators in rooms. Rooms from $40–$60.

BED & BREAKFASTS AND OTHER ACCOMMODATIONS

Cabin by the Creek (712-623-4757; www.iabedandbreakfast.com/IBBIA/City_Pages/red_oak.htm), 1938 G Avenue, Red Oak. "Cabin" is an understatement for this log home owned by Ron and Carol Keast. The high-ceilinged house is expansive, with two guest rooms that accommodate up to eight. The home is decorated with quilts handmade by Carol Keast's mother. The rooms are cozy, the kitchen is welcoming, and guests get a lot of choices for homemade breakfast. Rooms from $75–$95.

Big Grove Country Inn (712-482-6480; www.biggrove.com), 18807 450th Street, Oakland. There are plenty of pioneer log cabins still standing in Iowa, but there is only one *inside* a B&B. Alexander Frizzell relocated the log cabin—built by Mormons who left it to move to Utah—to its present site in 1860. Guests can stay in the log cabin, which has its own entrance and a stone fireplace, or in two other unique accommodations. The country inn also offers home cooking (a full restaurant is on-site), hayrack rides, antiques, and quiet evenings in the countryside. Rooms (including breakfast) from $55–95.

Colonial White House Bed and Breakfast (712-542-5006; www.colonialwhitehouse.com), 400 North 16th Avenue, Clarinda. In summer this 1906 neo-colonial home is surrounded by gardens filled with thousands of pink flowers and over a hundred different kinds of hostas. Gardeners will enjoy visiting with the innkeepers—both master gardeners—about their hobby. Inside, three guest bedrooms filled with antiques and period furnishings make this a lovely and relaxing place to stay. The bathroom is shared, but fresh robes are provided. Breakfast is served in the formal dining room, and other meals including brunch and high tea are also available by reservation only. Rooms from $65–$99.

Denise's Sweet Retreat (712-246-2295; www.iabedandbreakfast.com), 606½ West Sheridan Avenue, Shenandoah. This apartment-style accommodation includes both a queen-size bed and a fold-out sofa, a kitchen, and sitting room. The suite, above the bakery, is decorated in a Parisian theme and is an elegant alternative to local motels. Apartment $75–$100.

Timberview Bed & Breakfast (1-877-339-2431; www.iabedandbreakfast.com/IBBIA/City_Pages/shannon_city.htm), 2011 Ringgold-Union Street, Shannon City. Innkeeper Ron Simpson's family moved to this farm in southern Iowa in the 1800s and have worked the land ever since. This is an authentic working Iowa

THE 1900 FAMILY FARMHOUSE ON THE TIMBERVIEW FARM IS A B&B

farm. Ron, who loves animals, rides his tough little ponies out of the pasture morning and night to bring in the calves the old-fashioned way. The family farmhouse, with four bedrooms, a full kitchen, dining room, and living room, is rented to just one group at a time, and it feels just like visiting Grandma's house. Room (including breakfast) $65.

CAMPING **Viking Lake State Park** (712-829-2235; www.iowadnr.gov/parks) US 34, 2 miles east of Stanton. A comfortable state park on a big fishing lake offers swimming, boating, and multiuse trails along with 120 sites for RVs and tent camping. Campsites from $11–$16.

✷ Where to Eat

DINING OUT **Firehouse Restaurant** (712-623-3473; www.firehouse1898.com), 310 East Washington, Red Oak. Open for lunch and dinner Mon.–Thurs. 11–8, Fri. 11–9, Sat. 8–9, Sun. 8–7. An 1898 firehouse was given new life when this casual restaurant moved in. The decor is true to its firehouse roots, but the menu offers a New Orleans twist. The owner grew up in the Big Easy, so they serve authentic gumbo and real Leidenheimer's bread for the po' boys in addition to the usual steaks, chops, salads, and sandwiches. Small breakfast selection is served on the weekends. $–$$

Runaway Bay Eatery (712-623-3878; www.runawaybayeatery.com), 204 East Washington, Red Oak. Open for lunch Tues.–Sat. 11:30–2:30, dinner Thurs.–Sat. 5–9. Diners can taste the flavors of the islands in tiny Red Oak. With entrées as exotic as curried goat, jerk chicken, and island fish cakes, Runaway Bay is a spicy and surprising alternative to usual small-town fare. True to island life, the hours are a little flexible, so consider calling ahead. $$

M's Casual Fine Dining (712-246-2401), 504 West Sheridan Avenue, Shenandoah. Open for dinner Tues.–Sat. A dinner spot that is both intimate and fun. The bar and casual front room are lively for happy hour and into the evening. Appetizers and small plates are served. In the main dining room the lighting is dim, and the food is excellent. The shrimp dishes are delicious, and the kitchen staff knows its way around a piece of beef. The bar offers up everything from Budweiser to strawberry daiquiris. $$

EATING OUT ✪ **D&D's Bar and Grill** (712-826-9342) 307 Fourth Street, Villisca. Open for breakfast, lunch, and dinner Mon.–Fri. 9–9, Sat. 6–9. Just down the block from the Olson-Linn museum, D&D's serves sandwiches, baskets, salads, and fries. (For the uninitiated, "baskets" are typically sandwiches or fried chicken strips with French fries served in a small plastic basket, lined with paper.) The menu also includes one of the best—and unsung—tenderloins in Iowa. It is fresh, never frozen, hand-breaded with a secret recipe, and amazingly crispy. There are also daily lunch specials and steak and shrimp dinners. The bar offers bottled beer, but no other alcoholic drinks. $

Viking Lake Restaurant & Concession (712-829-2262), 2780 Viking Lake Road, Stanton. Open for breakfast, lunch, and dinner 7–9 daily in-season. Most concession stands serve basic ice cream and sandwiches alongside the bait-and-tackle business, but before you rent a boat for an afternoon of fishing, get a piece of pie. Julie, the manager, makes every pie from scratch, and in a state of excellent pie, her sour cream and raisin is absolutely outstanding. Get there early because it sells out in hours. The restaurant also offers breakfast before 11, sandwiches and basic dinners: catfish, pork chops, and the like. The dining room is stark but with great views of the lake. After lunch rent a boat and enjoy the water. Fishing boats, canoes, and paddleboats can be had for $10–$30 an hour. $

Y **The Depot** (712-246-4444), 101 Railroad Avenue, Shenandoah. Open Mon.–Sat. for breakfast, lunch, dinner, and bar. Drinks are served through the old ticket window in this historic building. The walls are covered with signs and photos from Shenandoah history. Locals enjoy lively evenings and live music in the convivial bar. Standard café food is served all day. $

The Sanctuary (712-246-5766), 207 South Elm, Shenandoah. Open for breakfast and lunch Mon.–Fri., Sat. brunch. The food is heavenly at the Sanctuary, but it has to be. This café, where the food is fresh, rich, and locally produced, is housed in a retired church. All the food is made from scratch, and the walls are decorated with the work of local artists and craftspeople. $

Vaughn's Café (712-542-3323), 112 East Washington Street, Clarinda. Open for breakfast, lunch, and dinner Tues.–Sun. Vaughn's is a fresh take on traditional café food. Breakfast is served all day and includes hearty portions of biscuits and gravy, French toast, and skillets. The pie is made fresh daily as are the sandwiches and salads. For dinner there are plate specials from fantail shrimp to liver and onions. Takeout is available. $

Susie's Kitchen (712-829-2947), 404 North Broad, Stanton. Open for breakfast and lunch Tues.–Sat. 6–2, Sun. 8–2. If you'd like to have a cup of coffee in the town with the world's largest Swedish coffeepot that also happens to be home to the kindly Swedish lady from the Folgers commercials, then check out this local coffee shop and diner. This is where the old-timers and farmers hang out, coffee still costs a dollar, and you'll find plenty of inexpensive breakfast and lunch fare—but no Swedish meatballs. $

COFFEE AND TREATS **Garrison Coffee House** (712-542-3777), 106 Glenn Miller Avenue, Clarinda. Open early for breakfast and lunch daily. The Garrison Coffee House is a treat for both the eyes and the stomach. Owners Mick and Carolyn Miller renovated their historic downtown building with attention to detail and a desire to bring out the natural beauty of the building. Antique chandeliers from Des Moines adorn the gorgeous tin ceiling. The regular coffee is fantastic as is the iced coffee. Few places in Iowa make it as well. But don't miss sampling the Falk's ice cream. It comes from a local family's recipe and, though now manufactured at a nearby dairy, tastes just like homemade. Bagels, soups, and light sandwiches are also served. Free wireless Internet is available, and there is a small stage for evening special events. $

Denise's Desserts (712-246-2295), 606 West Sheridan Avenue, Shenandoah. Open for coffee and lunch Tues.–Sat. Eat an enormous chicken salad with flavors from the southwest to the Orient, and you will feel justified eating dessert. Under the counter are decorated cookies, brownies, cakes, and other sinful treats to follow up daily soups, sandwiches, coffee, and tea. Lunch $$.

✷ Selective Shopping

Joyce Ellen's on Main and **Joyce Ellen's Too** (712-246-5355), 508 and 514 West Sheridan Avenue, Shenandoah. Open 9:30–5:30 Mon.–Sat., 9:30–8 Thurs., 1–5 Sun. These neighboring shops in the historic Flatiron Building retail elegant home decorations, gifts, jewelry, and antiques.

Ellen's on Main also has an espresso bar for caffeine-supported shopping.

Mae Farmer Boutique (712-246-3305), 608 West Sheridan, Shenandoah. Open 9:30–5:30 Mon.–Sat., 9:30–8 Thurs., 1–5 Sun. Since 1929 this boutique has dressed the ladies of southwest Iowa in style, but that does not mean the styles are out of date. The dress shop sells fashionable, high-end dress-up clothes.

WALNUT, ATLANTIC, GREENFIELD, AND ENVIRONS

Just off I-80 in western Iowa is Walnut City, the antiques city. The streets are lined with antiques shops and cute restaurants. Atlantic, a much larger town east of Walnut offers more dining and lodging options, and throughout the countryside are sites of historic interest for the intrepid driver.

GUIDANCE **Visitors Center** (712-784-2100; www.walnutiowa.org), 607 Highland Street, Walnut. Open Apr. 1–Nov. 30, 10–5 daily; Dec. 1–Mar. 31 Sat.–Sun 10–5. Walk in for brochures and information on Walnut City and the region, and, of course, there are antiques and souvenirs for sale, too.

Atlantic Chamber of Commerce (712-243-3017; www.atlanticiowa.com), Rock Island Depot, 102 Chestnut Street, Atlantic. Open Mon.–Fri. open 9–5. Visit the historic Rock Island depot downtown for friendly advice on the area or pick up an Atlantic business directory. The Web offers some information as well.

GETTING THERE *By car:* Both Atlantic and Greenfield, the major cities in Cass and Adair Counties, are directly south of **I-80.** For Atlantic take **US 71** south and then **IA 83** west. For Greenfield travel directly south on **IA 25. IA 92** runs east-west through the counties. Walnut is just to the west of Atlantic and easily accessed from **I-80**.

MEDICAL EMERGENCY Call **911**.

Cass County Memorial Hospital (712-243-3250; www.casshealth.org), East 10th Street, Atlantic. Cass County is a small regional hospital that can handle minor walk-in emergencies.

INTERNET ACCESS Most cafés and accommodations provide free wireless Internet access.

✱ To See

Hitchcock House (712-769-2323; www.hitchcockhouse.org), 63788 567th Lane, one mine west of Lewis. Open May–Sept. 1–5 Tues.–Sun. Admission: $5 adults, children free. The home, built by Reverend George Hitchcock, was constructed from brown sandstone mined from a local quarry. It was also a stop on the Underground Railroad. In the full basement, a cupboard swings open to reveal a secret room in which fugitive slaves were hidden. Slaves on their way to Canada passed through Iowa and were shielded by a network of northerners who risked arrest:

hiding fugitive slaves was a federal offense. Today the restored home sits in a 65-acre park. It is rather out of the way, but both the home and the grounds are worth the drive. Just down the road is the **Nishnabotna Ferry House** (712-243-1931; www.lewisiowa.com) at 705 Minnesota Street, Lewis. The ferry keeper's home, which is no longer on the riverbank, will eventually be an interpretive center to show the many trails that crossed Cass County, from the stagecoach trails to the Mormon hand-cart trail to the paths that remain from the Gold Rush.

✪ **Dan's Wildlife Creations** (712-249-3917), 417 Chestnut Street, Atlantic. Usually open during the day, but as it is a working taxidermy shop rather than a retail store, the hours vary. Peering out the storefront windows of Dan Mikkelsen's taxidermy shop are the lifelike eyes of some very dead animals. Step inside to see the work of a skilled professional and artist. A wild-boar cape is draped over the sofa, fish leap, and pheasants pick at the ground for eternity. One wall is lined with buck, doe, and elk heads, and because this is Iowa, right in the center is the beautifully mounted head of a local prize-winning steer. Dan's work is geared mainly toward hunters who want to preserve their kills, but the Mikkelsens are very friendly and don't mind when visitors stop in to take a peek.

Carstens 1880 Farmstead (712-544-2638; www.thefarmstead.org), I-80 at exit 34, Shelby. Tours by appointment. Admission: $4 adults, $2 children and seniors. This historic farm is run by a network of volunteers who work to share the life and experiences of Iowa's farmers. The farm still has 80 working acres, period furnishings, machinery, and artifacts from the family. An annual farm show is held there every September.

Henry A. Wallace Country Life Center (641-337-5019; www.henryawallacecenter.com), 2773 29th Street, Greenfield. Open 9–4 Apr.–Oct., self-guided tours available year-round. Free but donations appreciated. Henry A. Wallace served as U.S. vice president, U.S. secretary of agriculture, and U.S secretary of commerce; he also founded the Pioneer Hi-Bred International Company. In 1999 the *Des Moines Register* named him the most influential Iowan of the 20th century. This

"BIG GAME" TAKES ON A NEW MEANING AT DAN'S WILDLIFE CREATIONS IN ATLANTIC

foundation dedicated to his life and works is located on the farm where he was born. The center has an organic-vegetable and community-supported agriculture garden, an orchard, and a restored prairie where visitors can see soil conservation at work. The birthplace home has been restored and includes various exhibits about Wallace's life and his achievements.

Iowa Aviation Museum (641-343-7184; www.flyingmuseum.com), Greenfield Municipal Airport, 2251 Airport Road, Greenfield. Open 10–5 weekdays, 1–5

THE TOWN OF WALNUT IS A DESTINATION FOR ANTIQUES LOVERS, WITH STORE AFTER STORE PACKED FULL OF OLD TREASURES

WALNUT, "IOWA'S ANTIQUE CITY": ANTIQUES SHOP 'TIL YOU DROP

No one would argue that Iowa lacks in antiques stores, ranging from elegant, well organized, and pricey to just-a-step-above-thrift-store funky. And no place in Iowa offers dedicated antiques lovers as many shops as the town of Walnut (www.walnutiowa.org), just off I-80 at exit 46. The main street and side streets are lined with shop after shop just bursting with 1800s wood furniture, farm equipment from across the ages, plates, pistols, primitives, glassware, flatware, jewelry, and all sorts of untold doodads.

Start off a trip to Walnut at the **Welcome Center** (712-784-2100; www.iowasantiquecity.com; 607 Highland Street; open Apr. 1–Nov. 30, 10–5 daily; Dec. 1–Mar. 31 Sat.–Sun 10–5). There visitors will find antiques, of course, but also postcards and gifts, and a friendly staff member to answer questions. Public restrooms are available, too. Then, before hitting the shops, fuel up with coffee weekends year-round with extended Sat. hours in summer; closed holidays. Admission: $3. Home of the **Iowa Aviation Hall of Fame,** the Greenfield airport showcases 15 vintage aircraft along with aviation memorabilia.

Patriotic Rock (www.greenfieldiowa.com), IA 25, 12 miles north of Greenfield. Started as a way to eliminate graffiti on the boulder by the side of the road, painting patriotic rock has become an annual event. Every year a local artist paints a new scene dedicated to the men and women of the Armed Forces.

and a freshly baked pastry at **Robert's Treats and Treasures** (712-784-2253; open 6–4 Tues.–Sat., 6–12 Sun.; 230 Antique City Drive), a full-service bakery with great doughnuts, and, yes, antiques.

Cruise the antiques shops that line the main street. All the shops are open Mon.–Sat. 10–5 and Sun. 12–4. Don't miss **Zimm's Antiques & Accessories** (712-784-3030), 210 Antique City Drive, which is exceptional for eclectic and sundry treasures. In addition to antiques shops, there are several quilting and crafting stores. While strolling the streets, enjoy old fashion murals painted on the town's brick walls. Artist David Weis, sign painter Rick Dophens, and Walnut residents created the signs to preserve the art of sign painting and beautify the city. Some of the murals are related to the city, while others are emblematic of the 1900s. Look for the hidden letters on six of the murals that spell out the name of the town.

When your shopping bags are full and your stomachs are empty, head to **Aunt B's Kitchen** (712-784-3681) at 221 Antique City Drive. Open daily for breakfast, lunch, and early dinners, the busy home-cookin' restaurant offers everything from pizza to burgers to homemade pie for dessert.

Learn about the world that built all of those freshly purchased primitives at the **Walnut Creek Historical Museum** (712-784-3663; open Sat.–Sun. 10–4 in summer; 304 Antique City Drive). The museum tells the history of German settlers and rural life. It's housed in a Masonic lodge, so look for the Masons' symbol in the original tin ceilings. Then walk to 610 Highland Street to see the **Monroe #8 One-Room Country Schoolhouse** (712-784-3663; open Sat. and Sun. in summer). Now a museum, the building has been restored to look as it did in the 1920s.

Over Father's Day weekend every June, some 300 antiques dealers descend on Walnut and hawk their goods to fifty thousand visitors during the **Annual AMVETs Antique Show** (712-784-2100; www.walnutantiqueshow.com/). Aside from booth after booth of every kind of antique imaginable, enjoy lots of good food, as well.

At the end of a long day of treasure hunting, relax on the deck at **Clark's Country Inn Bed and Breakfast** (712-784-3010; www.clarkscountryinn.com; 701 Walnut Street). The 1912 home is decorated with, of course, antiques and offers three guest rooms with king- or queen-size beds, private baths, and a full breakfast. Rooms $70.

✱ Where to Stay

BED & BREAKFASTS **Chestnut Charm** (712-243-5652; www.chestnutcharm.org), 1409 Chestnut Street, Atlantic. Everything about this 1898 Victorian mansion says romance, from the fountains in the courtyard to the red heart-shaped whirlpool tub in the "Heart's Desire Suite." The home offers nine rooms. Suites include king-size beds, claw-foot tubs, a private sauna, and fireplaces. Other rooms offer queen-size beds, fireplaces, and comfortable decor. The home is full of hardwood floors, antiques, and peaceful corners. Breakfast is served in the sunroom. Rooms from $70–$225.

Back Inn Time (641-743-6394; www.backinntimebb.com), 423 Southwest Second Street, Greenfield. Cookies and tea greet guests at the door of this comfortable, family-friendly home. The two guest rooms are cozy, with big, soft beds and just enough antiques to feel quaint. The gardens and the sunroom are treasures during the summer months. Rooms (including breakfast) from $65–$70.

CAMPGROUNDS **Shelby Country Inn and RV Park** (712-544-2766), 15 East Street, Shelby. Just across the highway from the **Carstens 1880 Farmstead**, this independent inn and campground offers accommodations for travelers on I-80. All 125 sites have complete hook-ups, and the facility includes an inn, pizza joint, showers, restrooms, laundry, and a playground. Hotel rooms from $40–$60, RV camping $20.

✱ Where to Eat

DINING OUT **The Redwood Steakhouse** (712-762-3530), 1807 White Pole Road, IA 83 West, Anita. Open for dinner daily. The Redwood has been a fine-dining tradition in Anita for more than 50 years. Iowa pork, chicken, and seafood are on the menu, but carnivores should go for the beef. The steaks are USDA-certified and prepared with care, and the onion rings are homemade and award winning. $$–$$$

SF Martin House (712-243-5589), 419 Poplar Street, Atlantic. One of most elegant places to eat in the town of Atlantic is not a restaurant at all; it's a B&B. The exterior of this 1873 Second-Empire house seems pretty rundown, but don't be frightened off. Inside is one of the most ornately decorated, high-Victorian homes anywhere. The formal dining room, parlor, and front room are decked out in period furniture and art; every corner is a visual treat. Dinner and lunches are provided via special arrangement with the innkeeper and are completely elegant. Three guest rooms are available, but like the outside of the home, they're partially under construction. Reservations required. $$

EATING OUT ❀ **The Farmer's Kitchen** (712-243-2898), 319 Walnut Street, Atlantic. Open for breakfast, lunch, and dinner Mon.–Fri.; breakfast and lunch Sat. The food may be folksy, but it sure is good. Mark Johnson whips up award-winning home cooking. The pies are made daily, the tenderloins are highly ranked, and they do some amazing things with pancakes. Johnson also introduced high-end Kobe beef to the hamburger buns of middle America. The portions are huge—unless, of course, you order the World's Smallest Sundae. $

Spice of Life Delicatessen (712-243-1740), 313 Chestnut Street, Atlantic. Open for breakfast, lunch, dinner Mon.–Fri.; lunch Sat. and Sun. The rich, exotic fragrance of spices for sale in bulk mingles with the smell of fried chicken and fresh sandwiches in this downtown deli. Coffee, ice cream, box lunches, and catering are also available. $–$$

COFFEE **The Brick Coffee House** (641-743-6100; www.thebrickcoffeehouseanddeli.com), 362 Public Square, Greenfield. Open for breakfast and lunch Tues.–Sat. The Brick, on Greenfield's adorable main square, has everything a coffee-shop lover could desire: great java and espresso drinks, light breakfasts, sandwiches, quiches and salads, cookies and pastries, free wireless Internet, tall tables and deep sofas, a flat-screen television, wine, and gifts. Until closing time, there is hardly a need to go anywhere else. $

✷ Special Events

March: **St. Patrick's Day Celebration** (712-852-2283; www.emmetsburg.com), Emmetsburg. Celebrate Ireland's patron saint in Dublin's sister city. The party includes a run around Five Island Lake, a parade, beauty pageants, and a visit from a member of the Irish Parliament.

May: **Tulip Festival** (712-707-4510; www.octulipfestival.com), Orange City. This celebration of Dutch heritage as the tulips bloom around the city includes parades, performances, and Dutch food. There is also a road race, a costume exchange, and activities for children.

Tivoli Fest (712-764-7472; www.elkhorniowa.com), Elk Horn. A traditional Danish celebration with a parade, Viking encampment, music, and fireworks.

Barnes PRCA Rodeo (712-225-6414; www.cherokeeiowachamber.com), Cherokee County Fairgrounds, Cherokee. Sponsored by Bob Barnes, the largest contractor for rodeo livestock in the region, this complete rodeo has been in existence for nearly 50 years.

June: **Glenn Miller Festival** (712-542-2461; www.glennmiller.org), Clarinda. A celebration honoring the famous trombone player and local boy that includes big bands from around the world, lectures, parades, and a scholarship competition.

Midsommers Dag Festival, Stanton. This traditional Swedish festival celebrates the summer solstice—and involves maypole dancing.

Frontier Days (515-573-4231; www.fortmuseum.com), Fort Museum and Frontier Village, Fort Dodge. A festival of music and demonstrations showcasing and celebrating life on the frontier of northwest Iowa in the 1800s.

Donna Reed Festival for Performing Arts (712-263-3334; www.donnareed.org), Donna Reed Theater, Denison. A week-long series of workshops and performances when performing-arts celebrities share their skills with students and families.

Walnut AMVETs Antique Show (712-784-2100; www.iowasantiquecity.com), Walnut. Some 300 antiques dealers sell a huge variety of old goods to fifty thousand visitors.

July: **Star Spangled Spectacular** (712-732-3780; www.stormlakechamber.com), Lakefront Parks, Storm Lake. This huge Independence Day celebration includes boat races, ice-cream socials, musical entertainment, and fireworks over the water that draws 30,000 people to this small lakefront community.

Sidney Championship Rodeo (712-374-2695; www.sidneyrodeo.us), Fairgrounds, Sidney. A competitive professional rodeo takes place every year in the small town of Sidney.

Chautauqua Days (712-662-7383; www.saccountyiowa.com), Chautauqua Park and Main Street, Sac City. A small-town Fourth of July festival, featuring rides, entertainment, and fireworks.

The Lewis & Clark White Catfish Camp Living History Weekend (712-366-4900; www.iowahistory.org),Western Historic Trails Center, Council Bluffs. This weekend of reenactments, presentations, and children's activities celebrates the stopover of the Lewis and Clark expedition in the Council Bluffs area.

August: **The Hobo Convention** (641-843-9104; www.hobo.com), Britt. A celebration of the hobo lifestyle, culminating in the crowning of the Hobo King and Queen in coffee-can crowns.

Ag-Rail Festival (712-276-6432; www.milwaukeerailroadshops.org), Milwaukee Railroad Shops Historic District, Sioux City. This annual festival celebrates the important connection between railroads and agriculture with both antique farming equipment and demonstrations among the buildings in the historic district.

September: **Clay County Fair** (712-262-4740; www.claycountyfair.com), Clay County Fairgrounds, Spencer. The "world's greatest county fair" has an abundance of farm animals, agricultural equipment, carnival rides, musical events, and parades to rival even the Iowa State Fair in size and popularity in northwest Iowa.

Artsplash (712-279-6272; www.siouxcityartcenter.org), Larsen Park, Sioux City. An annual outdoor art festival sponsored by the Sioux City Art Center held every Labor Day weekend.

Carstens 1880s Farmstead Show (712-544-2638; www.thefarmstead.org), I-80 at exit 34, Shelby. Steam-threshing demonstrations, antique-machinery parade, antiques, crafts, and entertainment on a 19th-century farm.

Coca-Cola Days (712-243-3017; www.atlanticiowa.com), Atlantic. A tailgate party, kiddie parade, and swap meet celebrate Atlantic's connection to the town's privately owned Coca-Cola bottling plant.

October: **Iowa State Hand Corn Husking Contest** (712-773-2112), Kimballton. Watch as professional huskers shuck corn by hand, plus a parade of horses and wagons, a Saturday-night banquet, and Sunday-morning Danish breakfast.

November: **Julefest** (712-764-7472; www.elkhorniowa.com), Elk Horn. Kick off the holiday season during the weekend after Thanksgiving with shopping, crafts, food, and antiques.

December: **Sinterklass Day** (712-702-4510; www.orangecityiowa.com), Orange City. The first Saturday of December celebrates the Dutch Santa Claus, Sinterklass, with a tour of decorated homes and entertainment for children.

Santa Lucia Festival, Stanton. The Christmas season opens with the crowning of the queen.

INDEX

A

Abbey Hotel, 148
Abbie Gardner State Historic Site, 312–13
Ace Kitchen Place, 208
Ackerman Winery, 261
Ackley: sights/activities, 225, 226
Ackley Heritage Center, 225
Adams Street Bed & Breakfast, 360
Adel, 87; eating, 90; information, 87; lodging, 89; shopping, 90–91; sights/activities, 88
Adel City Hall, 87
Adel Paddlefest, 97
Adel Public Library, 87
Adel Quilting and Dry Goods, 90–91
Adel Sweet Corn Festival, 22, 97
Adler Theatre, 150
A Dong, 45–46
Adventureland, 39
Adventureland Inn, 43
Aerie Glen, 70
African American Historical and Cultural Museum (Waterloo), 213
African American Historical Museum and Cultural Center of Iowa (Cedar Rapids), 243, 304
Ag-Rail Festival, 384
Ahquabi, Lake, 84
air (aviation) museums, 294, 380–81
airports (airlines): overview, 18. *see also specific airports*
Airpower Museum, 294
A. K. O'Connor's, 49–50
Albert the Bull Park & Campground, 360
Albert's Lounge, 202
Albia: camping, 298; eating, 298, 300
Alexis Park Inn & Suites, 272
Algona, 342–43; lodging, 346
All Iowa Lawn Tennis Club, 26, 185
Allamakee County, 103–9
Allen Hospital, 210
Allerton: lodging, 298
Alma's Washhouse, 261
Alpha's on the Riverfront, 164
Amana, 256; camping, 263; eating, 263–64; entertainment, 265; information, 256; lodging, 262–63; shopping, 265; sights/activities, 257–61
Amana Arts Guild Gallery, 257
Amana Colonies, 256–60; eating family-style, 263; events, 303–6; shopping, 265
Amana Colonies Golf Club, 260
Amana Colonies Guest House Motel, 262
Amana Colonies Heritage Trail, 260
Amana Colonies RV Park, 263
Amana Colonies Visitors Center, 256
Amana Communal Kitchen, 257
Amana Community Church Museum, 257
Amana Heritage Museum, 257
Amana Meat Shop and Smokehouse, 265
Amana Stone Hearth Bakery, 264
Amana Woolen Mill, 259
American Gothic Days, 304
American Gothic House Center, 293–94, 304
American House Inn, 112, 115
American Indians: burial grounds, 138, 156–57. *see also specific tribes*
America's River Festival, 166
Ames, 32, 55–62; eating, 60–61; entertainment, 61–62; events, 95, 98; information, 55; lodging, 59–60; shopping, 62; sights/activities, 56–59; transportation, 55–56
Ames Convention & Visitors Bureau, 55
Ames Downtown Deli, 61
Ames Farmers Market, 61
Ames Public Library, 56
Ames Taxi, 56
Amish, 266, 269, 270, 280, 299
Amish By-Ways Tour, 270
Amish Home for a Meal, 299
Amtrak, 282, 293
AMVETS Antique Show, 381, 383
Anamosa, 235, 255; camping, 249; eating, 250, 251, 253; entertainment, 253; events, 304, 306; information, 236; sights/activities, 237–39, 247
Anamosa Dairy Barn, 253
Anamosa Penitentiary Museum, 237

Anita: eating, 382
Ankeny, 33; eating, 48
Annie's Garden Guest House, 262
Anson, Henry, 63
Antioch School, 239
Antique Car Museum of Iowa, 269
antiques: Bentonsport, 291; Boone, 95; Exline, 302–3; Kalona, 280; Lucas, 303; Maquoketa, 142; Perry, 91; St. Ansgar, 190; Sioux City, 326; Walnut, 380–81, 383; West Branch, 254
Aplington: eating, 228
Apple Tree Inn, 84
Appleberry Farm, 68
apples (orchards), 68, 98, 162, 247, 331
aquarium, 18, 122–23
area code, 18
Arnolds Park: eating, 317–18; information, 311; lodging, 315–16; sights/activities, 312–14
Arnolds Park Classic Cottages, 316
Aromas Coffee Bar, 189
Art from the Farm (Toledo), 255
Art Gallery and Home Accents (Clermont), 208
art museums: overview, 18. *see also specific art museums*
Art on Campus (Ames), 57
Art Walk (Fairfield), 285
Art-A-Fest (Charles City), 229
Arts on Grand (Spencer), 315
Artsplash (Sioux City), 384
Ashworth Park, 40
Asian American Festival, 95
Aspen Inn, 248
At Home Store, 291
Atherton House, 90
Atlantic, 378–83; eating, 382–83; emergencies, 378; events, 384; information, 378; lodging, 382; sights/activities, 379
Atlantic Chamber of Commerce, 378
Atlas Iowa City, 274
Atomic Garage, 52
Attica: eating, 80
attire, 18
Audubon: camping, 360; eating, 360–61; information, 356
Audubon County, 356–61
Audubon County Economic Development Corporation, 356
Aunt B's Kitchen, 381
Aunt Maude's, 60
Aunt Reba's Bed & Breakfast, 329
Azzolina's Hole in the Wall, 179

B

Back Alley Wine, 180
Back Country, 51–52
Back in the Day Lounge, 81
Back Inn Time, 382
Backbone State Park, 217
Backyard Deli (Clear Lake), 179
Bald Eagle Appreciation Days, 166
bald eagles, 74, 78, 106, 113, 166, 286, 349
Baldwin: winery, 137
Bali Satay House, 62
Balltown: eating, 132
Ban Thai, 46
Bancroft: eating, 347; lodging, 346
B & C Mercantile, 300–301
B&B on Broadway, 203
Bankston: winery, 126
Banner Lakes, 84
Banowetz Antique Mall, 142
Barefoot Bar, 318
Barn Happy, 220
Barn Quilts of Sac County, 335
Barnes PRCA Rodeo, 383
Barrel Drive-In, 206
Barrett House, 188
bars: overview, 18–19. *see also specific destinations and bars*
baseball, 39, 157, 254
Basilica of St. Francis Xavier, 125
basketball, 39, 278–79
Battle Hill Museum of Natural History, 335–36
Battle's Barbeque, 60
Baxa's Store and Tavern, 252
Baxter, 68; eating, 71–72; lodging, 69
Baxter Inn, 69
Bayliss Park, 368–69
BBQ, Buggies & Tunes, 96
Beach Ottumwa, 295
Bear Creek Cabins, 204
Beaverdale Books, 52, 54
Beck's Sports Brewery, 220
Beck's Sports Grill, 220
Bed and Breakfast of Cabin Cove, 227
Bedstemor's Hus, 357
Beeds Lake State Park, 227
Behrens-Rapp Station, 211
Beiderbecke Inn, 148–49
Bellevue, 138; eating, 140; lodging, 139–40; shopping, 142
Bellevue Butterfly Garden, 138
Bellevue State Park, 138
Belmond, 344; lodging, 345, 346
Belmont Hill Victorian, 249
Bentonsport, 283; lodging, 287–88; shopping, 291
Bentonsport National Historic District, 283
Bertrand, 349
Bettendorf, 143; eating, 149; lodging, 148; map, 144; sights/activities, 145–48
Betty's Hometown Café, 251
Bickelhaupt Arboretum, 138
Bicycles, Blues and BBQ Festival, 229
bicycling. *See* biking
Bier Stube Bar & Grill, 149
Big Creek Marina, 42
Big Creek Market, 253
Big Creek State Park, 42
Big Ed's Barbeque, 299
Big Foot Canoe Rental, 113
Big Grove Country Inn, 375
Big Sioux River, 329
Big Tomato, 46
Big Treehouse, 64–65, 70
Bijou Movie Theater, 254
Bike Iowa, 41
Bike Library, 271
biking, 19; Ames, 62; Boone, 93–94; Carroll, 359; Cedar Falls, 215, 216–17; Charles City, 184–85; Clear Lake, 180; Dallas County, 88; Danville, 286; Decorah, 199, 201; Des Moines, 41, 42; Eldora, 226; Fort Atkinson, 200; Grinnell, 260; Indianola, 84; Iowa City, 271; Mason

City, 175; Okoboji, 315; Pella, 81; Sac City, 336; Storm Lake, 332, 334; Winterset, 84
Bily Brothers, 194–95, 244–45
Bily Clock Museum, 195
Birdland Marina, 40
Birdsall's Ice Cream, 179
birdwatching, 104, 106, 201, 216, 247, 268, 344–45. *See also* bald eagles
Bistro, The (Story City), 61
Bistro Montage, 45
Bix 7 Run, 167
Bix Beiderbecke Memorial Jazz Festival, 166–67
Bizzy's Ice Cream Parlor, 301
Black Cat Café, 49
Black Hawk Children's Theatre, 222
Black Hawk Hotel, 217–18
Black Hawk Park, 218
Black Hawk State Park, 336, 337
Black Horse Inn, 130–31
Blackwater Grill, 131
Blanden Memorial Art Museum, 341–42
Blank Park Zoo, 37, 98
Blend Restaurant, 250
Blessings on Main, 177
Bloom, Stephen, 25, 104
Bloom (Isabel) Gallery, 147
Bloomer, Amelia Jenks, 367
Bloomers Bar and Grill, 361
Bloomfield: lodging, 288
Bloomsbury Farm, 245
Blue Belle Inn, 188
Blue Horse Enterprises, 85
Blue Inn, 248
Blue Lake Resort, 316
Blue Mountain Passport Club, 329
Blue Water Divers, 314
Blue Waters Mini-Golf Course, 370
Bluebird Café, 300
Bluedorn Science Imagination, 211
Bluegrass Café, 253
Blues on Grand, 51
Bluesmore, 305–6
Bluff Lake Restaurant (Maquoketa), 141
Bluffs Inn & Resort (Decorah), 202
boat cruises, 19; Clear Lake, 175; Des Moines River, 283–84; Dubuque River, 19, 125, 147; Iowa River, 19, 225; Le Claire, 19, 147; Mississippi River, 19, 105–6, 125, 147–48; Okoboji Lake, 19, 314
Boathouse (Storm Lake), 334
boating, 19; Ackley, 226; Arnolds Park, 314; Belmond, 344; Boone, 93–94; Carroll, 359; Cedar Falls, 216; Cherokee, 336; Clear Lake, 175, 176; Council Bluffs, 369–70; Dallas County, 88; Decorah, 199; Des Moines, 40–41; Iowa City, 270; Iowa Falls, 225–26; Kendallville, 199; Knoxville, 77–78; Lehigh, 344; Monona, 113; Moravia, 296; Mount Vernon, 248; Storm Lake, 332; Waterloo, 216. *See also* canoeing and kayaking
Bob Feller Museum, 87–88
Bob's Drive-In, 326
Bob's in Arnolds Park, 317–18
Boji Bantam Children's Theater, 319
Bonaparte, 281; eating, 289; lodging, 286
Bonaparte Inn, 286
Bonaparte Retreat Restaurant, 289
Boneyard Hollows, 344
Book Vault (Oskaloosa), 302
Book Vine (Cherokee), 338–39
Book Worm (Bellevue), 142
Bookends & Beans, 208
books, recommended, 24–25
bookstores, 208; Ames, 62; Bellevue, 142; Cedar Falls, 223; Cherokee, 338–39; Des Moines, 52, 54; Iowa City, 279; McGregor, 120; Oskaloosa, 302; Spirit Lake, 319; Winterset, 86
Boondocks USA Motel, 226–27
Boone, 92; eating, 94–95; emergencies, 92; events, 98; information, 92; shopping, 95; sights/activities, 92–94
Boone, Nathan, 16, 92
Boone & Scenic Valley Railroad, 92–93
Boone Area Convention and Visitors Bureau, 92
Boone County, 92–95
Boone County Fair, 97
Boone County Historical Center, 93
Boone County Hospital, 92
Booneville: eating, 90
Borlaug (Norman) Statue, Heritage Train, and Historic Log Cabin, 197–98
Bos Landen Golf Course, 77
Bosnian Fest, 229
botanical gardens: overview, 19. *see also specific gardens*
Boulders Inn & Suites, 353
Bourbon Street, 219–20
Bowl Full of Blues Festival, 69, 96–97
Boxholm: shopping, 95
Boz Wellz, 333
Bracco Okoboji, 317
Brackett House, 249
Brazelton Hotel and Suites, 286
Bread Garden Bakery and Café, 276–77
Breitbach's Country Dining, 132
Brenton Skating Plaza, 38–39
Brick City Bar and Grill, 206
Brick Coffee House, 383
Bricker Botanical Center, 374
Bricktown Brewery, 131
Bridal Veil Waterfall, 113–14
Bridges of Madison County, 83, 98
Bristow: church, 225
Britt, 340, 343–44; events, 384
Brooklyn, Community of Flags, 259
Brooks National Golf Club, 23, 315
Brown Opera Block Stage Paintings, 184
Brown Street Inn, 272–73
Brown's Woods, 41
Brucemore, 241
Brunnier Art Museum, 57
Brushy Creek Recreation Area, 344
Bryson, Bill, 24, 47
Bucktown Center for the Arts, 146

Buena Vista County Wind Farm, 331–32
Buena Vista Regional Medical Center, 331, 334
Buffalo Alice, 325
Buffalo Bill Cody Homestead, 145
Buffalo Bill Museum, 145
Burlington, 155; eating, 159; emergencies, 155; events, 166; information, 155; lodging, 158; sights/activities, 155–58
Burlington Bees Baseball, 157
Burlington Public Library, 155
Burlington Steamboat Days, 166
Burl's, 206
Burr Oak, 196, 229
business hours, 23–24
Busted Lift, The, 133
Butler County, 224–28
Butler House on Grand, 43
Button Factory Woodfire Grille, 153

C

Cabin by the Creek (Red Oak), 375
Cabin Coffee Company, 179
Cadillac Lanes, 215–16
Café di Scala, 44
Café Manna Java, 130–31
Café Paradiso, 290
Calico Bean Market, 134
California Trail, 367
Calmar: eating, 206
Calvary Wayside Chapel, 76
Camanche: camping, 140
Cambus, 267
Cameo Rose Collection, 91
Camp Algona P.O.W. Museum, 342–43
Camp Crescent, 337
Camp David, 228
Camp Foster YMCA, 314–15
Campbell Steele Gallery, 254
camping, 19–20; Albia, 298; Amana, 263; Anamosa, 247, 249; Audubon, 360; Camanche, 140; Campground, 111; Carroll, 359; Cedar Falls, 218–19; Cedar Rapids, 249; Charles City, 188; Clarinda, 374; Clear Lake, 176, 177; Council Bluffs, 369, 370; Danville, 286; Decorah, 199, 204–5; Des Moines, 43; Eldora, 226; Hampton, 227; Harpers Ferry, 114; Iowa City, 273; Knoxville, 79; La Porte City, 217; Lake View, 337; Lansing, 108; Lehigh, 344; Maquoketa, 137; Missouri Valley, 351; Moravia, 296, 298; Mount Pleasant, 288–89; Mount Vernon, 248; Muscatine, 158–59; Ogden, 94; Pella, 79; Sac City, 337; Shelby, 382; Sioux City, 324; Spirit Lake, 317; Stanton, 376; Storm Lake, 332, 333; Story City, 59–60; Wahpeton, 317; Winterset, 85
Canoe Sport Outfitters (Indianola), 86
canoeing and kayaking: Adel, 97; Boone, 98; Carroll, 359; Cedar Falls, 216; Charles City, 188; Cherokee, 336; Clermont, 200; Decorah, 199, 204; Des Moines, 40; Eldora, 225–26; Indianola, 84, 86; Kendallville, 199; Keosauqua, 284; Larchwood, 329; Monona, 113; overview, 20; Raccoon River, 88; Redfield, 89; Solon, 271; Upper Iowa River, 20, 199; Winterset, 84
Canteen Lunch in the Alley, 299
Cantril: shopping, 291
Captain Kirk's Marina, 164
car museums, 77, 269
car racing, 68, 76–77, 96, 97–98, 254
car travel: traffic, 26. *See also* scenic drives
Cardiff Giant, 341
Carl and Mary Koehler History Center, 243–44
Carnegie Cultural Center, 184
carousels, 40–41, 57–58
Carriage House (Grinnell), 262
Carriage House (Kalona), 273
Carriage House Inn (Cedar Falls), 218
Carrie Lane Chapman Catt Girlhood Home and Museum, 183
Carroll, 348, 356, 359; eating, 361; emergencies, 356; information, 356; lodging, 359–60
Carroll Chamber of Commerce, 356
Carroll City Public Library, 356
Carroll County, 356–61
Carroll County Historic Church Driving Tour, 359
Carrollton Inn, 359
Carson (Johnny) Birthplace, 373
Carstens 1880 Farmstead, 379, 382, 384
Carter Lake, 370
Carver Hawkeye Arena, 279
Casa de Oro, 90
casinos: Bettendorf, 148; Burlington, 157; Council Bluffs, 368; Dubuque, 126; Emmetsburg, 315; Marquette, 120; Meskwaki, 247; Northwood, 174–75; Osceola, 296; Riverside, 270
Cass County Memorial Hospital, 378
Castle Unicorn Bed & Breakfast, 370
Castles and the HMS Bounty, 339
Catfish Bend Casino, 157
Cats 'N Dogs Antiques, 254
Catt (Carrie Lane Chapman) Girlhood Home and Museum, 183
caucuses, 20
Cazador's, 141
Cedar Basin Jazz Festival, 229
Cedar Falls, 209–23; camping, 218–19; eating, 219–21; emergencies, 210; entertainment, 221–23; events, 228, 229; information, 209–10; lodging, 217–18; shopping, 223; sights/activities, 210–17; transportation, 210
Cedar Falls Public Library, 210
Cedar Falls Tourism and Visitors Bureau, 209
Cedar Rapids, 235–55; camping, 249; eating, 250–53; emergencies, 237; entertainment, 253–54; events, 304–6; information, 236; lodging, 248–49; map, 234; shopping, 254–55; sights/activities,

237–48; transportation, 236
Cedar Rapids Convention and Visitors Bureau, 236
Cedar Rapids Ice Arena, 246
Cedar Rapids Kernels, 254
Cedar Rapids Museum of Art, 18, 239, 240, 243
Cedar Rapids Rough Riders Hockey Team, 254
Cedar Rapids Symphony Orchestra, 254
Cedar Ridge Golf Course, 185
Cedar River, 209, 216, 242, 248
Cedar Rock: The Walter House, 214
Cedar Valley Arboretum & Botanical Gardens, 216
Cedar Valley Lakes Trail, 218
Cedar Valley Memories, 183
Cedar Valley Recreational Trails, 215
Ced-Rel Supper Club, 250
Celebrity Inn, 375
Cellar, The (Keokuk), 165
Celtic Highland Games, 167
Cenla Campground, 317
Centerville, 292; eating, 298–300; entertainment, 302; events, 304, 305; information, 292; lodging, 297; shopping, 303; sights/activities, 294–95
Centerville Town Square, 294–95
Centerville Wine and Fine Arts Festival, 304
Centerville-Rathbun Lake Area Chamber of Commerce, 292
Central Community Hopsital, 110
Central Gardens of North Iowa, 176
Central Park, 162
Central State Park Bike Route, 42
Centro Des Moines, 44
Champagne's Supper Club, 250
Chandler's Grill, 179
Channel Cat Water Taxi, 143
Chariton: eating, 300, 301; entertainment, 302; shopping, 303
Charles City, 181, 182; camping, 188; eating, 189; emergencies, 181; entertainment, 189–90; events, 229; information, 181; lodging, 185–87; sights/activities, 182–85
Charles City Area Chamber of Commerce, 181
Charles City Arts Center, 182
Charles City Downtown Farmers Market, 189
Charles City Historic Homes Tour, 183
Charles H. MacNider Museum, 173
Charles Theatre, 183, 189–90
Charley Western Recreation Trail, 184–85
Chautauqua Building, 334–35
Chautauqua Days, 384
Checkerboard Restaurant & Antiques, 80
Cheeto, World's Largest, 342
Cherokee, 334–39; eating, 337–38; events, 383; lodging, 336–37; shopping, 338–39; sights/activities, 336
Chestnut Charm, 382
Chichaqua Valley Recreation Trail, 68
Chickasaw County, 181–90
children, especially for, 20. *see also specific sights and attractions*
Children's Museum (Iowa City), 20, 269
Childs, Marcus, 136
Chimney Rock Canoe Rental & Campground, 199
Chocolate Café, 290
Chocolate Haus, 264
Chocolaterie Stam, 49
Christian Petersen Art Museum, 57
Christopher's Restaurant, 45
Civic Center of Greater Des Moines, 50
Civil War, 16, 229, 244, 369; reenactments, 166, 229
Clamshell Diner, 153
Clarinda, 371–78; eating, 377; emergencies, 372; events, 383; information, 371; lodging, 375; sights/activities, 373–74
Clarinda Chamber of Commerce, 371
Clarinda Promenade Tour, 374
Clarinda Regional Health Center, 372
Clark, William. *See* Lewis and Clark
Clark's Country Inn Bed and Breakfast, 381
Classic Frozen Custard, 49
Clay County State Fair, 22, 384
Clayton County, 110–20
Clear Lake, 172–80; eating, 177–79; emergencies, 172–73; entertainment, 180; events, 228, 229; information, 172; lodging, 176–77; shopping, 180; sights/activities, 173–76; transportation, 172
Clear Lake Area Chamber of Commerce, 172
Clear Lake Art Center, 173
Clear Lake Boat Rentals, 19, 175
Clear Lake Cottages, 176
Clear Lake Fire Museum, 173
Clear Lake State Park, 177
Clear Lake Yacht Club, 175
Clermont, 192; eating, 206; shopping, 208; sights/activities, 198, 200
Clinton: eating, 141; emergencies, 135; entertainment, 141–42; events, 167; information, 135; sights/activities, 136, 138
Clinton Area Showboat Theater, 141–42
Clinton County, 135–42
Clinton County Historical Society Museum, 136
Clinton Iowa Convention & Visitors Bureau, 135
Clinton Riverboat Days, 167
Coca-Cola Days, 384
Cody, William Frederick "Buffalo Bill," 145
Coffee Connection, 81
Coffee Cup Café, 72
coffee shops: overview, 20. *see also specific coffee shops*
Collectively Iowa, 261
Collector's Wonderland, 180
Colonel Davenport Historic Home, 146
Colonial White House Bed and Breakfast, 375

Colony Inn Restaurant, 263
Columns, The (Centerville), 303
Columns & Chocolate, 273
Comeback Café, 264
Comet Bowl, 189
Communal Agriculture Museum (Amana), 257
Conner's Corner Bed & Breakfast, 354
Continental, The (Des Moines), 49
Continental Hotel & Restaurant (Centerville), 297
Cookies Etc., 179
Coon Rapids, 358–60
Cooper, Lake, 162
Cooper Shop Museum, 257
Coral Ridge Ice, 270
Coralville: eating, 277; information, 267; sights/activities, 268–70
Coralville Lake, 268, 270, 271; camping, 273
Cordova Park, 78
Cordova Park Cabins, 79
Cornelia Lake, 344
Cornell College, 244
Corner Sundry (Indianola), 85
Cornerstone Boutique, 81
Cosmopolitan Lounge, 42
costs, average, 21
Cottage, The (Des Moines), 43
Cottage, The (Iowa City), 276
Cottage on Broad (Story City), 60
Cottonwood Canyon Gourmet Coffee (Waterloo), 221
Cottonwood Canyon Jamaican Café (Cedar Falls), 219
Council Bluffs, 365–71; camping, 370; eating, 370–71; emergencies, 366; entertainment, 371; events, 384; information, 366; lodging, 370; sights/activities, 366–70
Council Bluffs Area Chamber of Commerce, 366
Council Bluffs Public Library, 366
counties: overview, 21. *see also specific counties*
Country Connection Bed & Breakfast (Prairie City), 70
Country Heritage Bed and Breakfast (Hampton), 227
Country Junction Restaurant (Dyersville), 132
county museums: overview, 21. *see also specific museums*
Court Avenue Books, 86
covered bridges of Madison County, 83, 98
Craft's at Bluffton, 208
Crawdaddy Outdoors, 216
Crawford County, 352–55
Crawford County Memorial Hospital, 352
Crazy Girl Yarn Shop, 154
Crescent Beach Lodge, 315
Cresco, 191–92; eating, 207; entertainment, 207–8; events, 229; information, 192; lodging, 202; sights/activities, 197–200
Cresco Bronze Statues, 198
Cresco Farmer's Market, 207
Cresco Motel, 202
Cresco Theatre, 207–8
Cresco Welcome Center and Chamber of Commerce, 192
Croissant Du Jour, 252
Cronk's Café, 355
cross-country skiing: Carroll, 359; Cedar Falls, 216; Decorah, 199, 201; Dubuque, 126, 127; Fort Atkinson, 200; Heritage Trail, 126, 128; Iowa City, 271; Moravia, 296; Okoboji, 315
Crossroads Bistro, 361
cruises. *See* boat cruises
Crystal Lake Cave, 124
Cu Restaurant, 219
Cup of Joe, 220–21
Cutler-Donahoe Covered Bridge, 83
cycling. *See* biking
CyRide, 56
Czech Feather and Down Co., 255
Czech Village, 242, 243

D

Dairy Barn, The (Ionia), 188
Dallas Center: eating, 90; lodging, 89
Dallas County, 32, 87–91
Dallas County Fair, 97
Dallas County Hospital, 87
Daly Creek Winery and Bistro, 250
Dan Gable International Wrestling Institute and Museum, 210–11
Dancehall Cave, 137
D&D's Bar and Grill, 119, 376
Daniel Arthur's, 250
Danish Countryside Vines and Wines, 359
Danish Immigrant Museum, 357
Danish Inn, 360
Danish Windmill Museum, 357–58
Dan's Wildlife Creations, 379
Darrell's Place, 119, 361
DART (Des Moines Area Regional Transit Authority), 35
Davenport, 143; eating, 149–50; entertainment, 150; events, 167; information, 143; lodging, 148–49; map, 144; sights/activities, 145–48
Dayton House, 205
De Boerderij Bed & Breakfast, 79
De Soto: lodging, 89
Deadwood, The, 278
Decker Hotel and Restaurant (Maquoketa), 139
Decker House (Mason City), 177
Decorah, 191; camping, 204–5; eating, 205–7; emergencies, 192; events, 229; information, 192; lodging, 201–4; shopping, 208; sights/activities, 192–94, 196–97, 199–201
Decorah Area Chamber of Commerce, 192
Decorah Bicycles, 199
Decorah Chick Hatchery, 208
Decorah Parks and Recreation Office, 200
Decorah Public Library, 192
Deerwood Park and Campground, 218–19
DeKalder, 80
Deloit: eating, 355
Den, The (Iowa City), 280
Denise's Desserts, 377
Denise's Sweet Retreat, 375

Denison, 352, 353; eating, 355; emergencies, 352; events, 383; information, 352; lodging, 353–54; shopping, 355; sights/activities, 352–53
Denison Aquatic Fun Center, 353
Denison Walking Tour of Homes, 353
Depot, The (Sac City), 337
Depot, The (Shenandoah), 377
Depot Crossing Restaurant (Grinnell), 264
Des Moines, 31–54; camping, 43; eating, 43–49; emergencies, 35; entertainment, 49–51; events, 95, 97–98; information, 33; lodging, 42–43; map, 34; perfect day in, 52; shopping, 51–54; sights/activities, 35–42; transportation, 35
Des Moines Art Center, 18, 35–36
Des Moines Arts Festival, 97
Des Moines Botanical Center, 19, 37
Des Moines Buccaneers, 39
Des Moines Central Library, 35
Des Moines Cityview, 35
Des Moines County, 155–59
Des Moines Downtown Farmer's Market, 38
Des Moines Heritage Carousel, 40–41
Des Moines International Airport, 18, 35
Des Moines Metro Opera, 85
Des Moines Playhouse, 50
Des Moines Register, 24, 35
Des Moines River, 16, 31, 40–41, 78, 283–85, 340, 344
Designer Inn and Suites, 248
DeSoto National Wildlife Refuge, 349
Devil's Punch Bowl, 152
Devonian Fossil Gorge, 270, 273
DeVries Dutch Country Light Display, 98
Diamond Jo Casino (Dubuque), 126; (Northwood), 174–75
Die Heimat Country Inn, 262
Diggers Rest Coffeehouse & Roaster, 159
Django Des Moines, 42
DMACC's Bistro, 48
Dodge (General Grenville Mellen) House, 366–67
Dollar Dish, 131
Dolliver Memorial State Park, 344
Don Williams Recreational Area, 94
Donatus, Saint, 138
Donna Reed Center for the Performing Arts, 352
Donna Reed Festival for Performing Arts, 352, 383
Dorothy Pecaut Nature Center, 324
Dos Rios Restaurant, 44
Double Dragon, 49
Dough & Joe, 207
Downtown Farmer's Market (Des Moines), 38
Dowry Costumes & Antiques, 326
Drake Diner, 46
Drake on the Riverfront, 159
Drake Relays, 39, 95
Drake University Athletics, 39
Driftless Area, 106
driving: traffic, 26. *See also* scenic drives
Dublin City Pub, 252
Dublin Underground, 278
Dubuque, 121–34; eating, 129–33; emergencies, 121; entertainment, 133–34; events, 166; information, 121; lodging, 128–29; map, 122; shopping, 134; sights/activities, 122–28; transportation, 121
Dubuque, Julien, 15, 121, 127
Dubuque Area Chamber of Commerce, 121
Dubuque Catfish Festival, 166
Dubuque County, 121–34
Dubuque Greyhound Park & Casino, 126
Dubuque Museum of Art, 124
Dubuque River, 19, 125, 147
Dubuque River Rides, 125
Duffy's Collectible Cars, 244
Dug Road Inn, 203
Dugout Cave, 137
Dulcinea, 279
Dumont's Museum of Dreamworld Collectibles, 269–70
Duncan's Café, 371
Dunnings Spring Park, 200
Durango: lodging, 129
Dutch Bakery (Orange City), 330
Dutch Mill Inn (Pella), 79
Dutch Windmill Visitors Center, 327
Dutchman's Store, 291
Dvorak, Antonin, 195
Dyersville, 121; eating, 132; entertainment, 133; shopping, 134; sights/activities, 124–26, 128

E

Eagle City Winery (Iowa Falls), 226
Eagle Lake, 223
Eagle Point Park, 125, 127–28
eagles. *See* bald eagles
Eagles Landing Bed & Breakfast, 116
Eagles Landing Winery (Marquette), 113
Earlham: eating, 90
East Davenport, 147
East Side Electric Trolley Company, 93
East Village, 33; eating, 46, 48; entertainment, 49; shopping, 53
Eastern Iowa Airport, 18, 236, 267
eating out, 21, 22–23; ethnic restaurants, 21–22. *see also specific destinations and restaurants*
Ede's Gourmet, 206
Edgetowner Motel, 89
Effigy Mounds National Monument, 104–5, 112
Ehrle Brothers Winery, 261
801 Steak and Chop House, 43–44
Eisenhower (Mamie Doud) Birthplace, 93
El Asadero Restaurant, 290
El Bait Shop, 45
El Jimador, 355
Eldon, 293–94, 304
Eldora: information, 224; sights/activities, 225, 226

Eldora Welcome Center and Railroad Museum, 224
11th Street Bar & Grill, 147
Elgin: eating, 117
Elk Horn: eating, 360; events, 383, 384; sights/activities, 357–58
Elk Rock State Park, 78, 79
Elkader: eating, 116, 117; emergencies, 110; entertainment, 120; lodging, 116
Elkader Jail House Inn, 116
Elkader Opera House, 120
Ellis Park, 247–48
Elly's Lake Front Tap, 180
Elm Lake, 344
Elma, 184, 185
Embassy Club, 42
emergencies, 21. *see also specific destinations*
Emmetsburg: events, 383; lodging, 316–17; sights/activities, 315
Empress, 225
Englert Theatre, 278
English Valley B&B, 262
entertainment: overview, 21. *see also specific destinations*
Eppley Airfield, 18, 366
Ericson Public Library, 92
Eskimo Pies, 349
Espresso, Cigars & More, 141
Etta's Guest House, 333
Evansdale: camping, 218–19; events, 223
events: overview, 22, 25. *see also specific events*
Evers Toy Store, 134
Executive Inn Motel, 69
Exira, 357, 359
Exline Hose Co. No. 1 Museum, 303
Exline Old County Store & Antique Exchange, 302–3
Exotic Thai, 150
Extreme Watersports (Arnolds Park), 314

F

factory outlets, 265
Faeth Farmstead, 162
Fainting Goat, 220
Fairfield, 281, 284–85; eating, 289–90; emergencies, 282; entertainment, 290; information, 281; lodging, 286, 287; shopping, 291; sights/activities, 282–86
Fairfield Arts and Convention Center, 290
Fairfield Convention and Visitors Bureau, 281
Fairview Cemetery, 367
Faithful Pilot Café, 149
Falbo's, 275
Falls Aquatic Center, 215
Family Museum (Bettendorf), 20, 148
Farm House Museum (Ames), 57
Farm Toy Store (Boxholm), 95
Farmer's Kitchen (Atlantic), 382
farmer's markets: Ames, 61; Charles City, 189; Cresco, 207; Des Moines, 38; Iowa City, 277
Farmer's Wife (Newton), 73
Farmhouse B&B and Winery (Fredericksburg), 188
Fat Man's Squeeze, 152
Faulconer Gallery, 259
Fayette County, 191–208
Feller (Bob) Museum, 87–88
Fenelon Place Elevator, 125
Festina, 197
Festival of Iowa Beers, 305
festivals: overview, 22, 25. *see also specific festivals*
Field of Dreams Movie Site, 124
50s in February (Clear Lake), 228
Figge Art Museum, 18, 145
Fillenwarth Beach, 315–16
Finkbine Golf Course, 270
Finley Hospital, 121
Firehouse Market (Sioux City), 325
Firehouse Restaurant (Red Oak), 376
Fireside Grill Steakhouse and Martini Bar, 274–75
Fireside Winery, 261
Fisher Community Center, 64
Fisher Impressionist Collection, 64
fishing, 22; Ackley, 226; Anamosa, 247; Carroll, 359; Clear Lake, 176; Council Bluffs, 369–70; Cresco, 199; Danville, 286; Des Moines, 41; Eldora, 226; Fayette, 201; Grinnell, 260; Indianola, 84; Keosauqua, 285; Lehigh, 344; Mount Vernon, 248; Stanton, 376; Waterloo, 216
Fitch House Bed & Breakfast, 85
Five Flags Center & Theater, 133–34
Flaming Prairie Park, 158–59
Fleur Cinema and Theater, 51
Flight 232 Memorial, 322–23
Floyd, Charles, 15, 322–23; Monument, 323
Floyd County, 181–90
Floyd County Historical Society Museum, 183
Floyd County Medical Center, 181
Flying Mango, 45
food: overview, 22–23; pork tenderloin, 118–19. *See also* farmer's markets; *and specific destinations*
football, 222, 278–79
Forest City, 344
Forest Park Museum and Arboretum, 88
Forrest Lodge, 353–54
Fort Atkinson, 197, 200
Fort Custer Maze, 175
Fort Des Moines, 31
Fort Des Moines Hotel, 42
Fort Des Moines Museum, 38
Fort Dodge, 340–47; eating, 346–47; emergencies, 340; entertainment, 347; events, 383; lodging, 345–46; shopping, 347; sights/activities, 341–45
Fort Dodge Convention & Visitors Bureau, 340
Fort Dodge Fort Museum, 341
Fort Dodge Public Library, 340
Fort Madison, 160–66; eating, 164–65; entertainment, 165–66; events, 167; information, 160; lodging, 163; shopping, 166; sights/activities, 160–63
Fort Madison Area Arts Association, 161
Fort Madison Area Convention & Visitors Bureau, 160

Fort Madison Tri-State Rodeo, 163, 167
Fort Museum (Fort Dodge), 341
Fort Sandwich Shop, 165
Fossil and Prairie Park Preserve and Center, 184
Four Seasons Fountain, 56
Fourth of July events, 229, 383, 384
Fourth Street Coffee Co. & Deli, 189
Fox Head Tavern, 278
Fox Indians, 31, 145
Foxtail Cabins, 297–98
Frank Lloyd Wright Stockman House, 174
Franklin County, 224–28
Franklin County Convention & Visitors Bureau, 224
Frantzen, Rose, 135–36
Fredericksburg, 185; lodging, 188
French Creek Wildlife Area, 108
Fresh Bistro, 317
Froelich, 16, 111
Frog Hollow Lake, 201
Front Porch Bed & Breakfast, 70
Front Street Antiques (Lucas), 303
Front Street Brewery (Davenport), 149
Frontier Days (Fort Dodge), 383
Frontier Motel, 114
Frontier Trading Post, 302
Frontier Village (Fort Dodge), 341
Fuel, 253
Full Circle Corn Maze, 199–200
Fulton's Landing Guest House, 149
Fun City, 157
Funny Barn Comedy Club, 319
F. W. Kent Park, 271, 273

G

Gable (Dan) International Wrestling Institute and Museum, 210–11
Gallagher-Bluedorn Performing Arts Center, 222
Galleria de Paco, 219
gambling. *See* casinos
Garden and Galley B&B, 84–85
Garden Barn (Indianola), 86
Gardner, Abbie, 309, 311; State Historic Site, 312–13
Garrison Coffee House, 377
Gasthaus Bar and Grill, 337–38
Gateway Hotel, 59
Gateway Market, 49
Gehlen House Bed & Breakfast, 139
GeJo's By the Lake, 177
General Dodge House, 366–67
General Store Pub, 239, 251
Geode, Lake, 286
Geode State Park, 157–58
George M. Verity River Museum, 161
George the Chili King, 46–47, 119
George Wyth House, 211
George Wyth State Park, 216, 226
German-American Heritage Center, 146–47
Gitchie Manitou State Preserve, 329
Givanni's Italian Café, 274
Gladbrook, 244–45
Gladys Black Bald Eagle Refuge, 78
Glenn Miller Birthplace Home, 373
Glenn Miller Festival, 383
Glenwood, 368; lodging, 370
Glick-Sower House, 65–66
Glidden House, 354
Gold Star Hall, 56
Golden Haug, 272
Golden Spike Monument, 368
Goldenrod School, 373
golf, 23; Amana, 260; Anamosa, 247; Boone, 94; Charles City, 185; Denison, 353; Des Moines, 39; Iowa City, 270; Newton, 68; Okoboji, 315; Panora, 362–63; Pella, 77; Rhodes, 68; Storm Lake, 332; Waterloo, 216
Gong Fu Tea, 48–49
Gouldsburg Park, 205
Grand Central Coffee, 334
Grand Harbor Resort & Water Park, 125–26
Grand Opera House, 134
Grand Theatre, 166
Grande Anne, 164
Granny Annie's, 221
Grant Center School, 339
Grant Wood Art Festival, 304
Grant Wood Art Gallery, 238–39
Grant Wood Country Bed & Breakfast, 249
Grant Wood Scenic Byway, 25, 238–39
Grape Escape Vineyard and Winery, 77
Gray's Lake, 40
Graziano's Brothers Grocery, 49
Great Lakes area, 311–19
Great Plains Sauce & Dough Company, 61
Great River Health Systems, 155
Great River Road, 25, 101–67; map, 100. *see also specific destinations*
Great River Tug Fest, 167
Greater Burlington Partnership, 155
Greater Des Moines Convention and Visitors Bureau, 33
Greater Shenandoah Historical Museum, 374
Greef General Store, 291
Greek Food Festival, 95
Green Gables Restaurant, 324
Greene County, 361–64
Greene County Medical Center, 362
Greenfield, 378; eating, 383; lodging, 382; sights/activities, 379–81
Greenfield Municipal Airport, 380–81
Green's Tea and Coffee, 154
Greenwood Park, 40
Griffin, Walter Burley, 174, 259
Grimes Farm and Conservation Center, 67–68
Grinnell, 256; eating, 264–65; emergencies, 256; information, 256; lodging, 262; sights/activities, 259, 260
Grinnell, Josiah B., 256

Grinnell Coffee Company, 265
Grinnell College, 259
Grinnell Convention and Visitors Bureau, 256
Grinnell Historical Museum, 259
Grinnell Recreational Trail, 260
Grinnell Regional Medical Center, 256
Groovy Grounds, 132–33
Grotto of Redemption, 343
Grout Museum District, 211
Grout Museum of History and Science, 211
Grove Café, 60
Grundy County, 224–28
Gull Point State Park, 317
Gurney's Restaurant & Pizzeria, 351
Guthrie Center, 363; lodging, 363
Guthrie Center Aquatic Center, 363
Guthrie County, 361–64
Guthrie County Historical Village, 362
Guttenberg, 113; lodging, 116
Guttenberg Historic Rivertown Driving Tour, 113

H

Hageboeck Hall of Birds, 268
Hahn's Bakery, 264
Hamburg Inn No. 2, 275
Hamlin: eating, 361
Hampton: camping, 227; information, 224; lodging, 227; shopping, 228
Hancher Auditorium, 242, 278
Hancock House, 128
Hanford Inn, 176
Hanging Rock County Park, 89
Hannah Marie Country Inn, 316
Hansen Brothers Coffee (Harlan), 355
Hansen's Farm Fresh Dairy (Hudson), 215
Hardacre Film & Cinema Festival, 253, 305
Hardacre Theater, 253
Hardin County, 224–28
Hardin County Farm Museum, 225
Hardin County Historical House, 225
Harlan, 352; eating, 355; lodging, 353–54
Harpers Ferry, 105–7; lodging, 114
Harrah's Council Bluffs Casino and Hotel, 368, 370
Harrison County, 348–51
Harrison County Historical Village and Welcome Center, 348
Hartman Reserve Nature Center, 216–17
Hart's Tea & Tarts, 206
Harvest Moon, 90
Harvester Golf Club, 68
Hatchery Restaurant and Lounge, 329–30
Hattie Grace, 337
Hausbarn and Heritage Park, 356
Hawkeye Buffalo Ranch, 186–87
Hawkeye Buffalo Tours, 185
Hawkeye Downs Speedway, 254
Hawkeye Motel, 272
Hawkeye Point, 328
Hawkeye Sports, 278–79
Haystock, 305
Hearst Center for the Arts, 210
Hearten B&B, 346
Heartland Inn, 43, 370
Hemken Collection, 225
Henny Penny, 290
Henry A. Wallace Country Life Center, 379–80
Henry County Convention and Visitors Bureau, 281
Henry County Health Center, 282
Henry's Village Market, 265
Herb N' Lou's, 251
Herbert Hoover Eastern National Bookstore, 254
Herbert Hoover Presidential Library and Museum and National Historic Site, 240
Heritage Hill Tour, 374
Heritage Inn Amana Colonies Hotel and Suites, 262
Heritage Trail, 126, 128
Hey, Good Cookies!, 318
Hickory Hill Park (Iowa City), 271
Hickory Hills Park (La Porte City), 217
Hickory Park BBQ (Ames), 60
Higgins Museum, 313
High Amana General Store, 259
High Life Lounge, 45
Highland Games, 167
Highlandville: lodging, 202, 204
Highway 3 Raceway, 226
hiking, 23; Amana, 260; Burlington, 157; Carroll, 359; Cedar Falls, 215, 216–17; Cedar Rapids, 247–48; Charles City, 184–85; Clarinda, 374; Council Bluffs, 369; Danville, 286; Decorah, 201; Des Moines, 40–42; Dubuque, 127; Fort Atkinson, 200; Grinnell, 260; Harpers Ferry, 106–7; Indianola, 84; Iowa City, 270, 271; Keosauqua, 285; Knoxville, 77–78; Larchwood, 329; Mason City, 175; McGregor, 113–14; Moravia, 296; Muscatine, 152; Newton, 68; Sioux City, 324; Stanton, 376; Storm Lake, 332; Waterloo, 216; Winterset, 84
Hill Avenue Book Co., 319
Hillside Cottages, 351
Hillside Go-Carts, 162
Hillside Stables Restaurant, 140–41
Hilltop Motel, 176
Historic Arnolds Park, 313
Historic General Dodge House, 366–67
historic houses and museums: overview, 23. *see also specific houses and museums*
Historic Lincoln Hotel, 248–49
Historic Park Motel, 353
Historic Squirrel Cage Jail, 367
Historic Tremont Inn on Main, 69, 71
Historical and Coal Mining Museum (Centerville), 294
history museums: overview, 24. *see also specific history museums*
history of Iowa, 15–17
Hitchcock House, 378–79

Hobo Convention, 340, 384
Hobo Museum, 343–44
hockey, 39, 254
Homestead, 258; lodging, 262; shopping, 265; sights/activities, 257, 258, 261
Homestead Store Museum, 257
Hometown Inn, 185
Honey Creek Golf Club, 94
Honey Creek Resort, 296–97
Honey Creek State Park, 296, 298
Honey Kissed Pizza, 333
Hoover, Herbert, 254; Presidential Library and Museum and National Historic Site, 240
Horn's Ferry Bridge, 78
horse racing, 39
horse sales, 228, 303
horseback riding, 284, 314–15
Horseshoe Bluff, 127
Horseshoe Casino, 368
Horsfall's, 109
hospitals, 21. *see also specific destinations*
Hot Shots, 253
Hotel Fort Des Moines, 42
Hotel Julien, 128
Hotel Manning, 286–87
Hotel Memorial Union, 59
Hotel Ottumwa, 297, 299, 301
Hotel Pattee, 89
Hotel Wapello, 158
Hotel Winneshiek, 201–2
hotelVetro, 272
Howard County, 191–208
Howard County Fair, 229
Howell Station Recreation Area, 78, 79
Howlin' Coyote, 363–64
Hoyt Sherman Theater, 50
Hruska's Canoe & Kayak Livery, 199
Hub, The (Cedar Falls), 221
Hub City Brewing Company (Stanley), 200
Hub on Fifth (Sac City), 337
hunting, 24, 41, 106, 140, 204, 217, 218, 284, 344–45
Hurstville Interpretive Center, 136
Hutchinson Family Farm Campground, 204
Hy-Vee Triathlon, 40, 95

I

Ice Cave, 137
Ice Cave Hill, 200
Ice Cream Capital of the World Museum and Visitor Center, 326
ice hockey, 39, 254
Ice House Museum, 211
ice skating, 38–39, 246, 270
Icehouse Bar and Grill, 276
Icon: Iowa Contemporary Arts, 282
Ida Grove, 338–39
Ida Grove Pharmacy, 339
Ida Grove Skate Palace, 339
Independence: sights/activities, 214
Independence Day events, 229, 383, 384
Indian Creek Nature Center, 247
Indian Hills Inn and RV Park, 298
Indianola, 82–86; eating, 85; entertainment, 85; events, 97; information, 82; lodging, 84–85; shopping, 86; sights/activities, 83–84
Indianola Chamber of Commerce, 82
Indianola Public Library, 82
Indulgence, 223
information sources, 23. *see also specific destinations*
Inkpaduta Canoe Trail, 336
Inn at Okoboji Resort and Conference Center, 315
Inn at Strawtown, 78–79
Inn of the Six-Toed Cat, 298
Inn Springville, 249
Insect Zoo, 57
In't Veld Meat Market, 80
Ion, 113
Ionia: lodging, 188
Iowa Arboretum, 94
Iowa Artisans Gallery, 279
Iowa Arts Festival, 305
Iowa Aviation Hall of Fame, 381
Iowa Aviation Museum, 380–81
Iowa Band Museum, 213
Iowa Bike & Fitness, 81
Iowa Book, 279
Iowa Book Festival, 95
Iowa Children's Museum, 20, 269
Iowa Chops, 39
Iowa City, 266–80; camping, 273; eating, 273–77; emergencies, 267; entertainment, 277–79; events, 304–6; information, 267; lodging, 272–73; map, 234; shopping, 279–80; sights/activities, 267–71; transportation, 267
Iowa City Brew Festival, 306
Iowa City City Park, 271
Iowa City Farmers Market, 277
Iowa City Friday Night Concert Series, 304
Iowa City Jazz Festival, 305
Iowa City Public Library, 267
Iowa City Transit, 267
Iowa City/Coralville Area Convention and Visitors Bureau, 267
Iowa Corn Indy 250, 96
Iowa County, 256–65
Iowa Cubs, 39
Iowa 80 Truckstop, 146
Iowa Falls, 224; eating, 227–28; entertainment, 228; events, 229; information, 224; lodging, 227; sights/activities, 224–26
Iowa Falls Chamber/Main Street, 224
Iowa House Bed & Breakfast, 59
Iowa House Hotel, 272
Iowa Machine Shed, 149
Iowa Masonic Library and Museum, 243
Iowa Popcorn Company, 255
Iowa Renaissance Festival, 303
Iowa River, 225–26, 344; boat cruises, 19, 225. *See also* Upper Iowa River
Iowa Rock 'n Roll Hall of Fame Museum, 313
Iowa Sculpture Festival, 96
Iowa Speedway, 68, 96
Iowa State Capitol, 36
Iowa State Center, 62
Iowa State Fair, 22, 96, 97
Iowa State Hand Corn Husking Contest, 384
Iowa State Historical Museum, 24, 36

Iowa State Memorial Union, 56
Iowa State University, 56–57; VEISHEA, 95
Iowa State University Book Store, 62
Iowa Tourism, 23, 25, 334, 361
Iowa Trolley Park, 173
Iowa Veteran's Home, 25, 63
Iowa Walk of Fame, 374
Iowa Wine and Beer Promotion Board, 27
Iowa Women's Music Festival, 271
Iowa Wrestling Hall of Fame, 192
Iowa's Best Burger Café, 72
Iris Restaurant (Mount Pleasant), 289
Iris Tea Room (Boone), 94
Irish Shanti, 117
Iron and Lace, 291
Iron Horse Antique Mall, 95
Isabel Bloom Gallery, 147
Isabella's at the Ryan House, 133
Isle of Capri Casino and Hotel (Bettendorf), 148; (Marquette), 120
Ivans Recreation Area, 79
Ivy Bake Shoppe & Café, 164

J

Jaarsma Bakery, 80–81
Jackie's Kafe and Coffeebar, 90
Jack's Chicken Palace, 132
Jackson County, 135–42
J&P Cycles, 255
Jasper County, 63–73
Jasper County Historical Museum, 66
Jasper Winery, 40
Java House (Iowa City), 20, 276
Java Joes (Des Moines), 48
Java Lounge (Williamsburg), 264
Java Station Espresso Café (East Davenport), 147
Jefferson, 361; eating, 363, 364; emergencies, 362; shopping, 364; sights/activities, 362–63
Jefferson County, 281–91
Jefferson County Hospital, 282
Jester Park, 42, 43
Jimbo's Pizza, 264
Jimmy's Bar-b-Que Pit, 94
Jitterz Coffee & Café, 132
J-N-J Pizza, 109
Joensy's Bar and Grill, 119, 276
Joe's on the Square, 355
Joe's Place, 278
John Deere Company, 111, 143
John Ernest Vineyard and Winery, 247
John James Audubon Tea Room and Gift Shop, 360–61
John L. Lewis Labor Festival, 306
John L. Lewis Mining and Labor Museum, 295
Johnny Carson Birthplace, 373
John's Grocery, 277
Johnson's Restaurant, 117
Jones County Tourism Association, 236
Joyce Ellen's on Main, 377–78
Joyce Ellen's Too, 377–78
Julefest, 384
Julien Dubuque Monument, 125, 127
Junck, 364
Juneteenth, 304

K

Kaleidoscope, The, 228
Kalmes Restaurant, 139
Kalona, 266, 269; eating, 274–75, 277; events, 303, 306; information, 267; lodging, 272, 273; shopping, 280; sights/activities, 269, 270
Kalona Antique Company, 280
Kalona Area Chamber of Commerce, 267
Kalona Bakery, 277
Kalona Fall Festival, 306
Kalona Furniture Co., 280
Kalona General Store, 280
Kalona Historical Village, 269, 306
Kamerick Art Building, 214
Kate Shelley Memorial High Bridge, 93
Kate Shelley Railroad Museum, 93
kayaking. *See* canoeing and kayaking
Kazarelli's at Millers Bay, 317
KCG Market and Restaurant, 104
Kendallville, 199
Keokuk, 160; eating, 165; emergencies, 160; entertainment, 166; events, 166, 167; lodging, 164; sights/activities, 161
Keokuk Area Hospital, 160
Keosauqua, 281; activities, 284; information, 282; lodging, 286–88
Kermis Dutch Summer Festival, 97
Kimballton, 358; eating, 361; events, 384
Kingman Place Bed and Breakfast, 316
King's Pointe Waterpark Resort, 332, 333
Kingsley Inn, 163, 164
Kinney Pioneer Museum, 174
Kinnick Stadium, 279
Kitchen Collage, 52
Klemme House B&B, 345
Kleve's Pub, 207
Klokkenspel, 76
Knoxville, 32, 74; camping, 79; eating, 80–81; information, 74; lodging, 79; sights/activities, 75–78
Knoxville Chamber of Commerce, 74
Knoxville Nationals, 97–98
Knoxville Raceway, 76–77, 97–98
Knuckleheads, 251
Koehler History Center, 243–44
kreativ, ent., 73
Kumar's, 164

L

L. A. Beemer's, 346
L May's Eatery, 129
La Carreta, 94–95
La Corsette Maison Inn, 69–70
La Porte City, 217; camping, 218
La Rana, 205
La Vida Loca Winery, 83–84
Lacey Keosauqua State Park, 285, 288
Lady of the Lake, 19, 175
Lagomarcino's, 147
Lake Ahquabi State Park, 84

Lake Geode State Park, 286
Lake MacBride State Park, 271, 273
Lake Rathbun area, 292–303
Lake Rathbun Information Center, 292
Lake Red Rock, 75, 77–78
Lake Red Rock Campgrounds, 79
Lake View, 334–37; camping, 337
Lakes Regional Hospital, 312
Lakeshore Cyclery (Storm Lake), 334
Lakeside Cyclery (Clear Lake), 180
Lakeside Inn (Panora), 363
Landing, The—A Riverfront Inn, 116
L&L European Delight, 300
Landlocked Film Festival, 305
Landmark Inn, 286
Landmark Tree, 356–57
Lansing, 103, 106; camping, 108; eating, 108–9; information, 103; lodging, 107–8; shopping, 109; sights/activities, 105, 106
Lansing Chamber of Commerce, 103
Laramar Ballroom, 347
Larch Pine Inn, 176–77
Larchwood, 329; lodging, 329
Latino Festival (Perry), 98
Latino Heritage Festival (Des Moines), 98
Laura Days, 229
Laura Ingalls Wilder Museum, 196
Lava Lounge, 221
LeClaire, 145, 147–48; eating, 149
Le Claire River Cruises, 19, 147
Ledges State Park, 42, 94
Lee County, 160–66
Legion Arts and CSPS, 253–54
Lehigh: activities, 344
Lehm Books and Gifts, 265
LeMars, 326
Lewis, John L.: Labor Festival, 306; Mining and Labor Museum, 295
Lewis and Clark, 15, 309, 320, 322–23, 365–68
Lewis & Clark: An American Adventure, 323
Lewis & Clark White Catfish Camp Living History Weekend, 384
Lewis and Clark Monument and Scenic Overlook, 368
Leytze's Corner, 203
Liberty Iron Works, 255
Lift, The (Des Moines), 49
Lighthouse Inn (Cedar Rapids), 252; (Storm Lake), 332
Lillie Mae Chocolate, 72
Lime Creek Nature Center, 175, 176
Lincoln Café, 251
Lincoln Highway, 65
Lincoln Highway Arts Festival, 306
Lincoln Highway Bridge, 245
Lincoln Monument, 367
Linn Street Café, 274
Lion and Lamb, 249
Lisbon: eating, 252; events, 305, 306; sights/activities, 244, 247
Lisbon History Center, 244
Little Bookroom, 62
Little Brown Church, 184, 195, 229
Little Gussey's, 361
Little Mermaid, 358
Little Sioux River, 336
Little Switzerland Inn, 115–16
Little Valley Church, 225
Little Vientiane, 333–34
Living Heritage Tree Museum, 331
Living History Farms, 36–37
L. J. Maasdam Wheel Art, 66
Locust Avenue Tap, 50
Lodge, The (Bettendorf), 148
Loess Hills, 350
Loess Hills Hideaway, 351
Loess Hills National Scenic Byway, 25, 350
Loft on Water Street, 203
Logan, 349; eating, 351
Logsdon, 123
Lone Star Steamer, 145
Long Lines Family Recreation Center, 323
Los Laureles, 46
Lost Duck Brewery, 165
Lost Island Adventure Park, 215
Lou Henri, 275–76
Louis Sullivan Jewel Box Bank, 259
Louisa County, 155–59
Lovers Leap Bridge, 157
Lowden: lodging, 248–49
LT Organic Farm, 90
Lucas, 292; eating, 299–301; events, 306; shopping, 303; sights/activities, 295, 296
Lucas Bottoms Up, 300
Lucas Community State Bank, 295
Luciano's, 324
Luxembourg Society of Iowa, 139
Lylah's Marsh, 185
Lyla's Boutique, 180
Lynnville, 66; lodging, 70

M

Maasdam Wheel Art, 66
Mabe's Pizza, 205–6
MacBride, Lake, 271, 273
MacBride Raptor Center, 268
McFarlane Park, 218
McGarrity's Inn on Main, 107
McGregor, 110, 112; eating, 116–17; entertainment, 117, 120; information, 110; lodging, 114–16; shopping, 120; sights/activities, 110–14
MacGregor, Alexander, 112
McGregor Coffee Roasters, 117
McGregor Historical Museum, 110–11
McGregor Historical Walking Tour, 112
McGregor Lodging, 114–15
McGregor Marina, 112
McGregor-Marquette Chamber of Commerce, 110
McGregor's Landing Bed & Bath, 114
McGregor's Landing Event Center, 117, 120
McGregor's Top Shelf, 117
McHenry House, 352–53
McIntosh Woods State Park, 176
Macksburg Skillet Throw, 97
MacNider Museum, 173
Madison County, 32, 82–86
Madison County Bridges, 83, 98

Madison County Chamber of Commerce, 82
Madison County Courthouse, 83
Madison County Healthcare System, 82
Madison County Historical Complex, 83
Madrid: sights/activities, 93, 94
Mae Farmer Boutique, 378
Magpie Coffeehouse, 206–7
Mahanay Bell Tower, 362
Maharishi University of Management, 285
Maid Rite, 220
Maiden Voyage, 105–6
Maifest, 304
Main Street Café (Council Bluffs), 371
Main Street Cultural District (Ames), 55
Main Street Pub and Grill (Bancroft), 347
Main Street West Branch, 236
Mainstay Inn, 287
Maintenance Shop (Ames), 62
Maize Maze, 200
Majestic Hills Golf Course, 353
Mama Nick's Circle Pizzeria, 220
Mamie Doud Eisenhower Birthplace, 93
Mami's Authentic Mexican Restaurant, 153
Manawa, Lake, 369, 370
Manchester State Trout Hatchery, 215
Mandolin Inn, 128–29
Manhattan Beach Resort, 316
Manilla: eating, 355
Manor, The (Fort Madison), 163
Manson House Inn, 287–88
Maple Syrup Festival, 228
maps, 24; Bettendorf, 144; Davenport, 144; Des Moines, 34; Dubuque, 122; Iowa, 8; Mississippi Corridor, 100; Northeast Iowa, 170; Polk County, 30; Southeast Iowa, 232; Western Iowa, 308
Maquoketa, 135; eating, 141; information, 135; lodging, 139–40; shopping, 142; sights/activities, 135–37
Maquoketa Area Chamber of Commerce, 135
Maquoketa Art Experience, 136
Maquoketa Caves State Park, 25–26, 137
Maquoketa Public Library, 135
Marengo: eating, 263–64; sights/activities, 259, 261
Marion: eating, 252; lodging, 249; shopping, 254–55
Marion County, 32, 74–81
Marion County Development Commission, 74
Mario's Italian Restaurant, 129
Market, The (Spirit Lake), 318
markets. *See* farmer's markets
Marquette: entertainment, 120; lodging, 114, 116; shopping, 120; sights/activities, 104–5, 111, 113
Marquette Depot Museum, 111
Mars Café, 48
Marsh House, 262
Marshall Center School, 211–12
Marshall County, 32, 63–73
Marshall County Historical Society, 65–66
Marshalltown, 32, 63–73; camping, 70–71; eating, 71–72; emergencies, 64; entertainment, 72–73; events, 96–98; information, 63; lodging, 69–70; shopping, 73; sights/activities, 64–69; transportation, 63–64
Marshalltown Convention and Visitors Bureau, 63
Marshalltown Medical & Surgical Center, 64
Marshalltown Public Library, 64
Martini's (Iowa City), 278
Martinis Bar and Grill (Storm Lake), 333
Marvin Gardens, 346
Mary Rose, 91
Masala, 275
Mason City, 172–79; eating, 177–79; emergencies, 172–73; events, 228, 229; information, 172; lodging, 176, 177; sights/activities, 173–76
Mason City Convention and Visitors Bureau, 172
Master Griller's Homestead, 90
Matchstick Marvels, 244–45
Mathias Ham House, 124
Matthew Edel Blacksmith Shop, 66
Maytag Dairy Farms, 66
Maytag Park, 69
mazes, 84, 175, 199–200, 216, 245
medical emergencies, 21. *see also specific destinations*
Meier's Den, 165–66
Melpine Schoolhouse, 152
Melrose: lodging, 298
Mercy Hospital Council Bluffs, 366
Mercy Medical Center (Clinton), 135; (Des Moines), 35
Mercy Medical Center of North Iowa (Mason City), 172–73
Mercy Sioux City, 321
Meskwaki Indians, 127, 233, 235, 246, 247, 305
Meskwaki Powwow, 305
Meskwaki Resort and Casino, 25, 247
Metcalf House, 332–33
Metropolitan Theatre, 228
Mexico Antiguo, 71
Mi Ranchito, 299
Michael's Fun World, 148
Mid-America Center, 371
Midcoast Fine Arts, 146
Mid-Iowa Antique Power Show, 97
Midsommar Festival (Swedesburg), 305
Midsommers Dag Festival (Stanton), 383
Midway Inn, 218
Midwest Old Threshers Heritage Museums, 282–83
Midwest Old Threshers Reunion, 306
Midwest Writing Center, 146
Milford: eating, 318
Mill Restaurant, 275
Miller (Glenn) Birthplace Home, 373
Miller (Samuel F.) House and Museum, 161
Millrace Canal, 260
Mills County Historical

Museum, Earth Lodge, 368
Millstream Brewing Co., 260
Milty's, 109
Milwaukee Wiener House, 324
Minburn: activities, 89; lodging, 89
Miss Dubuque, 125
Mission House (Iowa City), 273
Mississippi Explorer Cruises, 19, 105
Mississippi Manor Bed & Breakfast Inn, 158
Mississippi River, 15, 16, 101–2; America's River Festival, 166; boat cruises, 19, 105–6, 125, 147–48
Mississippi River clams, 151
Mississippi River Corridor, 101–67; map, 100. *see also specific destinations*
Mississippi River Museum & Aquarium, 18, 122–23
Mississippi Riverwalk (Dubuque), 126
Mississippi Valley Blues Festival, 167
Mississippi Valley Fair, 167
Mississippi Valley Welcome Center, 143
Missouri Valley, 349; camping, 351; eating, 351; information, 348; lodging, 351
Mitchell County, 181–90
Mitchell County Historical Society, 183
Mitchell County Museum, 183
Mitchell County Nature Center, 183
Mo Brady's Restaurant, 149–50
Mohan Delights, 289
Molengracht, The, 76
Monarchs Restaurant & Lounge, 80
Monica's Spirits and Cigars, 221
Monks, 132
Monona County, 348–51
Monona County Historical Museum, 349
Monroe #8 One-Room Country Schoolhouse, 381
Mont Rest Inn, 140
Montauk, 198
MonteBello Bed & Breakfast, 59
Montezuma: lodging, 262
Montgomery County Courthouse, 374
Monticello: lodging, 248, 249
Montrose: lodging, 164
Montrose Pharmacy, 85
Mooney Collection, 182
Moorehead Park, 339
Moorhead, 350; lodging, 351
Moose Lake, 344
Moravia: activities, 295–96; camping, 298; entertainment, 302; lodging, 296–97
Mormon Trail, 294, 365, 367
Mormons, 16, 160, 287–88, 365, 367, 375
Mosquito Park, 157
Motorcycle Museum, National, 237, 240
Mount Hosmer City Park, 106
Mount Pleasant, 281–91; camping, 288–89; eating, 289–90; emergencies, 282; entertainment, 291; information, 281; lodging, 286; sights/activities, 282–83, 285–86
Mount Vernon: eating, 251–53; entertainment, 254; events, 305, 306; information, 236; lodging, 248, 249; shopping, 255; sights/activities, 244, 248
Mount Vernon Heritage Days, 305
Mount Vernon Motel, 248
Mount Vernon-Lisbon Marketing and Tourism Association, 236
M's Casual Fine Dining, 376
Muggabeans, 318
Murphy's Cove, 108
Muscatine, 151; camping, 158–59; eating, 153–54; emergencies, 151; entertainment, 154; information, 151; lodging, 152–53; shopping, 154; sights/activities, 151–52
Muscatine Art Center, 151–52
Muscatine Convention and Visitors Bureau, 151
Muscatine County, 151–54
Muscatine History and Industry Center, 151
Museum of Religious Arts, 349
Music Man Square, 174
Muskie Lounge, 119, 178
Muskie Motel, 153
Musser Public Library, 151
must-see symbol, 6, 24
My Waterloo Days Festival, 228–29

N

Nashua, 184, 195, 229
Nathaniel Hamlin Park and Museum, 357
National Balloon Classic, 97
National Balloon Museum, 83
National Cattle Congress, 222
National Czech and Slovak Museum, 243
National Farm Toy Museum, 124–25
National Mississippi River Museum & Aquarium, 18, 122–23
National Motorcycle Museum, 237, 240
National River Hall of Fame, 123
National Sprint Car Hall of Fame and Museum, 77
Native Americans: burial grounds, 138, 156–57. *see also specific tribes*
Natural Gait Cabins and Campground, 114
nature hikes. *See* hiking
Neal Smith National Wildlife Refuge, 67
Neal Smith Trail, 41, 42
Nelson Pioneer Farm Museum, 293, 306
New Albin, 106
New Hampton, 184; eating, 188; lodging, 186
New Pioneer Food Co-op, 277
newspapers, 24, 35
Newton, 63; eating, 72; emergencies, 64; entertainment, 72–73; events, 96–97; information, 63; lodging, 69–70; shopping, 73; sights/activities, 64–69
Newton Convention and Visitors Bureau, 63
Newton Kart Club, 68
Nishnabotna Ferry House, 379
No Name Deli, 264
Nodaway Valley Museum, 373
Nodaway Valley Park, 374

Nordic Fest, 229
Norman Borlaug Harvest Fest, 229
Norman Borlaug Statue, Heritage Train, and Historic Log Cabin, 197–98
North Iowa Band Festival, 228
North Iowa Fair, 229
North Overlook Beach, 78
North Overlook Recreation Area, 79
Northeast Iowa, 171–229; map, 170. *see also specific destinations*
Northwest Iowa, 320–39. *see also specific destinations*
Northwestern Steakhouse, 177–78
Northwood, 174–75

O

Oakland: lodging, 375
Oakland Mills, 285
Ocheyedan Mound, 328–29
Octagon Art Festival, 98
Octagon Center for the Arts, 57
O'Farrell Sisters Restaurant, 317
Ogden: camping, 94
O'Kelly's Steak and Pub, 71–72
Okoboji, 311; eating, 317, 318; entertainment, 318–19; lodging, 315; sights/activities, 313–15
Okoboji Boat Works, 19, 314
Okoboji Candy Company, 318
Okoboji Expedition Co., 315
Okoboji Lake, 311–12, 314–15; boat cruises, 19, 314; scuba diving, 314; water sports, 314
Okoboji Maritime Museum, 312
Okoboji Resort and Conference Center, 315
Okoboji Spirit Center, 311, 312
Okoboji Summer Theatre, 318–19
Okoboji Tourism Committee, 311
Okoboji Trading Co., 319
Oktemberfest, 98
Oktoberfest, 306
Old Brewery (Guttenberg), 113
Old Capital Brew Works, 277–78
Old Capitol Museum (Iowa City), 267–68
Old City Hall Gallery (Maquoketa), 135–36
Old Creamery Theatre Company, 265
Old Factory (Orange City), 327
Old Fort Madison, 16, 160, 162
Old Hospital Lodge (Highlandville), 202
Old Jail & Firehouse Guest Suite (McGregor), 115
Old Jail Museum (Dubuque), 123–24
Old Man River Restaurant & Brewery, 116
Old Mill Riverside Inn (Lynnville), 70
Old Santa Fe Depot Historical Complex, 161
Old Settler's Park (Fort Madison), 163
Old Theater Restaurant and Lounge (Logan), 351
Old Threshers Campground, 288–89
Old Threshers Reunion, 306
Olde Main Brewing Co. and Restaurant, 61–62
Oleson Park, 342
Oleson Park Zoo, 342
Olson-Linn Museum, 372
Onawa, 349
One of a Kind, 297
One Twenty Six, 273
180 Main (Dubuque), 133
one-finger salute, 328
Oneota Community Food Co-op, 207
Orange City, 327–30; eating, 329–30; emergencies, 327; events, 384; information, 327; lodging, 329; sights/activities, 327–29
Orange City Hospital, 327
Orchard Historical District, 162
Oregon Trail, 367
Original Kin Folks Barbeque, 80
Orpheum Theatre, 325
Osage, 181; eating, 189; entertainment, 190; events, 229; lodging, 187–88; sights/activities, 183, 185
Osceola, 295–96
Oskaloosa, 292, 293; eating, 299, 301; events, 306; shopping, 302
Oster Regent Theatre, 223
Ottumwa, 292–303; eating, 299–300; emergencies, 293; entertainment, 301; lodging, 297; sights/activities, 294, 295
Ottumwa Beach, 295
Ottumwa Regional Health Center, 293
Our Lady of Luxembourg Shrines, 139
Outdoor Adventures (Belmond), 344
Overland, 291
Ox Yoke Inn, 263

P

Paint Creek, 107
Palace, The (Dyersville), 133
Palisades Inn, 202–3
Palisades Park, 200
Palisades-Dows Observatory, 248
Palisades-Kepler State Park, 248
Palmer House Motel, 324
Pammel Park, 84
Panora, 361; eating, 363–64; lodging, 363; sights/activities, 362–63
Panorama, Lake, 363
Panorama National Resort and Conference Center, 362–63
Papa's American Café, 179
Paper Moon, 120
Paradise Pizza, 189
parasailing, 314
Park Farm Winery, 126
Park View Inn & Suites, 345
Parsonage in Hampton, 227
Parthenon, 165
Pat Clark Art Collection, 224–25
Patrick's Steakhouse and Brewery, 141
Patriotic Rock, 381
Paul's Big Game Tavern, 133
Paw Park, 217
Pear Tree Café, 361
Pearl Martini Bar, 154
Pearson Lakes Arts Center, 319

Pedretti's Bakery, 117
Pelican Peg's Bed & Breakfast, 164
Pella, 74–81; camping, 79; eating, 80; emergencies, 75; events, 75, 95, 97, 98; information, 74; lodging, 78–79; shopping, 81; sights/activities, 75–78; transportation, 75
Pella Cinema, 81
Pella Convention & Visitors Bureau, 74
Pella Historical Village, 75
Pella Opera House, 81
Pella Regional Health Center, 75
Pendemonium, 166
Penoach Winery, 88
Peony Chinese Restaurant, 363
People's Court, 51
Pepper Sprout, 129
Peppercorn Pantry Tea Room, 228
Perry, 87; eating, 90; emergencies, 87; events, 98; information, 87; lodging, 89; shopping, 91; sights/activities, 88
Perry Bowl, 88
Perry Chamber of Commerce, 87
Peru Apple Days, 98
Pet Central Station, 280
pet-friendly symbol, 7
Petit Paris, 289
Pfohl Boatyard, 123
P.H.A.T. Daddy's, 263–64
Pheasant Run, 85
Phelps House Museum, 156
Phelps Park, 200
Picador, the, 278
Picket Fence Antiques, 190
Pick's Lakeshore Resort, 316
Pierce Street Coffee Works, 325
Pieta Chapel, 139
Pikes Peak State Park, 113–14
Pine Creek Cabins and Campground, 204–5
Pine Creek Grist Mill, 152
Pine Lake State Park, 226
Pine Ridge Retreat, 288
Pines on the Prairie, 152–53
Pioneer Fall Festival (Oskaloosa), 306
Pioneer Heritage Museum (Marengo), 259
Piper's Old Fashioned Grocery Store, 303
Planet X Fun Center, 246
planetariums, 37, 211, 336
Pleasantville: eating, 80; entertainment, 81; information, 74; winery, 77
Pleasantville Tourism Office, 74
Plow-in-the-Oak, 357
Plum Grove Historic Home, 268
PM Park, 119, 178
political caucuses, 20
Polk County, 31–54; map, 30
Popcorn Ball, World's Largest, 335
population of Iowa, 24
pork tenderloin (tenderloin), best, 118–19
Porky's Deli, 85
Port City Underground, 153
Port of Burlington Welcome Center, 156
Porter House Museum, 196
Postville, 104
Potter's Mill Restaurant, 140
Power Show, 229
Poweshiek County, 256–65
Prairie Blue, 364
Prairie Bridges Park, 226
Prairie City, 67; eating, 71; lodging, 70
Prairie Farmer Recreational Trail, 200
Prairie Lights, 279
Prairie Meadows Race Track and Casino, 39
Prairie Moon Winery, 58
Prairie Park, 59
Prairie Path Bed & Breakfast, 337
Prairie View Bed & Breakfast, 363
Prime N' Wine, 178
Prime Rib (Spencer), 317
Princess Grill & Pizzeria, 227–28
Princeton, 145
Principal Park, 39
Promenade Cinema 14, 326
Promenade Tour of Clarinda, 374
Pub at the Pinicon, 188
Pufferbilly Days, 98
Pull'r Inn Motel, 272
Pulpit Rock Campground, 205
Pump Haus, 220
Pumpkin Festival and Weigh Off, 306
Pumpkin Patch, 62
Purviance Farm, 89
Putnam Museum of History and Natural Science, 145–46
Putt Around, 162
Pyramid House, 177

Q

Quad Cities Convention and Visitors Bureau, 143
Quad Cities International Airport, 18, 143, 267
Quarry Creek Elk & Buffalo Company, 166
Queen Marie Victorian Bed & Breakfast, 316–17
Queen Mary II Excursions, 19, 314
Quiet Walker Lodge, 129
quilts, 90–91, 109, 229, 257, 289, 335, 381
Quinton's Bar and Deli, 276

R

R Campground, 188
Raccoon River, 31, 88
Raccoon River Brewing Company, 42
Raccoon River Park, 41
Raccoon River Valley Adventures, 88
Raccoon River Valley Trail, 88
RAGBRAI, 19, 97
railroads, 66, 92–93, 98, 161, 173, 224, 368, 384
Railswest Railroad Museum, 368
Raj Ayur-Veda Health Center, 25, 286
Randy's Bluffton Store and Campground, 199
Rastrelli's, 141
Rathbun Country Music Theater, 302
Rathbun Lake, 292, 295, 296–97
Rathbun Marina, 295
Rawson's Bed & Breakfast, 262
Rebos, 324

Red Avocado, 274
Red Barn Resort & Campground, 108
Red Carpet Golf Course, 216
Red Cross, 242
Red Monk, 50
Red Oak, 371–78; eating, 376; information, 371; lodging, 375
Red Oak Chamber of Commerce, 371
Red Rock Dam, 78
Red Rock Marina, 78
Red Stone Guesthouse, 218
Redfield: activities, 89
Redstone Inn & Suites, 129
Redwood Steakhouse, 382
Reed, Donna, 352–53
Regatta Grille (Storm Lake), 333
Reiman Gardens, 57
Remarkable Rose Floral & Gifts, 72
Reminisce Tearoom, 188
Renaissance Festivals, 39, 303
Rensselaer Russell House Museum, 211
Rent a Horse!, 284
Restaurant at Strawtown, 80
restaurants, 21, 22–23; ethnic, 21–22. *see also specific destinations and restaurants*
Retlaw's Riverside Bar and Grill, 189
Revelations Café, 290
Reynold's Clothing, 355
R. G. Books Lounge, 250–51
Rhodes: golf, 68
Riceville, 184
Richards House, 128
Ricker House, 259
Ridge Stone Golf Club, 227
River & Trail Outfitters (Decorah), 199
River Bend Rally, 229
River City Greenbelt Trail, 175
River Junction Trading Company (McGregor), 112, 120
River Music Experience (Davenport), 146
River's Bend (Iowa Falls), 227
River's Edge Plaza (Dubuque), 126
Riverside: casino, 270; eating, 276
Riverside Area Community Club, 267
Riverside Campground (Sac City), 337
Riverside Casino and Golf Resort, 270
Riverside Cemetery (Anamosa), 239
Riverside Theatre (Iowa City), 278; Shakespeare Festival, 304–5
Rivertown Fine Books (McGregor), 120
Riverview Hotel and Restaurant (Bellevue), 139–40
Riverview Park (Fort Madison), 162
Riverview Restaurant (McGregor), 116–17
Robert A. Lee Community Recreation Center, 270
Robert's Treats and Treasures, 381
Rock Creek Marina and Campground (Camanche), 140
Rock Creek State Park, 71, 260
Rock Island Arsenal, 146
Rock Island Arsenal Museum, 146
Rock 'n Roll Hall of Fame Museum, 313
Rock-n-Row Adventures, 225
Rodeo Park, 163
rodeos, 163, 167, 383
Rollin' on the River Blues Festival, 167
Romancing the Home, 347
Ronneburg Restaurant, 263
Roots Market, 221
Roseman Covered Bridge Shop, 86
Round Barn (Allerton), 295
Roundhouse Retreat, 203–4
Royal Amsterdam Hotel, 79
Royal Mile Bar, 50
Rubaiyat Restaurant, 205
Ruby's Tacos, 220
Rukmapura Park Hotel, 286
Runaway Bay Eatery, 376
Russell, Lillian, 136
Ruth Anne Dodge Memorial, 367
RVP 1875, 362

S

Sabor Latino #2, 206
Sabula: eating, 140–41
Sac City, 334–39; events, 384
Sac City Motel, 336
Sac County Museum, 335
Safehouse Saloon, 108
St. Ansgar, 181; eating, 188, 189; lodging, 188; shopping, 190; sights/activities, 183–84
St. Ansgar Heritage Museum, 184
St. Anthony of Padua Chapel, 197
St. Anthony Regional Hospital and Nursing Home, 356
St. Charles: lodging, 85
St. Donatus, 138–39
St. Donatus Catholic Church, 139
St. Francis Xavier Basilica, 125
St. Luke's Hospital, 237
St. Olaf Tap, 118
St. Patrick's Day Celebration, 383
St. Wenceslas Church, 195
Saint's Rest Coffee House, 264–65
Salisbury House and Gardens, 38
Salsa's Mexican Restaurant, 132
Sam and Gabes, 44
Samuel F. Miller House and Museum, 161
Sanctuary, The (Iowa City), 274; (Shenandoah), 377
S&S Houseboat Rentals, 19, 105
Sanford Museum & Planetarium, 336
Santa Fe Swing Span Bridge, 161
Santa Lucia Festival, 384
Santa's Castle, 331
Saturday Night Free Movie Series (Iowa City), 305
Sauerkraut Days, 305
Sauk Indians, 16, 145
Sauk Rail Trail, 336
Save Iowa, 242
Saylorville Reservoir Area, 41, 43
Scandinavian Days, 95–96
Scenic City Empress, 19, 225
Scenic Drive Festival (Van Buren County), 306
scenic drives, 25; Grant Wood

Scenic Byway, 25, 238–39; Loess Hills National Scenic Byway, 25, 350. *See also* Great River Road
Schaeffer Fountain Pen, 161
Schera's, 116
Scholte House Museum, 75–76
Science Center of Iowa, 20, 37
Science Station and IMAX Dome Theatre, 246
Scott County, 143–50
scuba diving, 314
seasons, 26–27
Second Street Emporium (Webster City), 346
2nd Street Café (Ottumwa), 299
Seed Savers Exchange, 192–93
Seguma, Lake, 284, 288
Sergeant Floyd Monument, 323
Sergeant Floyd River Museum and Welcome Center, 323
Seven Oaks, 93–94
Seven Roses Inn, 287
7th Inning Stretch, 159
SF Martin House, 382
Shady Oaks Campground, 70–71
Shakespeare Festival, 304–5
Shamrock Inn, 316
Shannon City: lodging, 375–76
Sheffield: eating, 227
Shelby: camping, 382; events, 384
Shelby Country Inn and RV Park, 382
Shelby County, 352–55
Shenandoah, 371–78; eating, 376, 377; lodging, 375; shopping, 377–78; sights/activities, 374
Sherman House, 186–87
Shimek Forest, 284
shopping: overview, 25. *see also specific destinations*
Shot Tower, 126
Shot Tower Inn, 132
Shrines of Our Lady of Luxembourg, 139
Sidney Championship Rodeo, 383
Sigourney, 269–70
Silos and Smokestacks National Heritage Area, 212–13
Silver Boot Motel, 176
Simo's Cafistro, 44–45
Sinterklass Day, 384
Sioux City, 320–26; eating, 324–25; emergencies, 321; entertainment, 325–26; events, 384; information, 321; lodging, 324; shopping, 326; sights/activities, 321–24
Sioux City Art Center, 321
Sioux City Lewis & Clark Interpretive Center, 323
Sioux City Public Museum, 321–22
Sioux City Tourism Bureau, 321
Sioux Gateway Airport, 18, 321
Sister Sarah's Bar, 342
Sisters Inn, 346
Sisters of the Heart, 71
61 Drive In Theater, 141
Skean Block Restaurant, 298
Skiff Medical Center, 64
skiing, in Dubuque, 126
Skillet Café and Bakery, 252–53
Skip-a-Way RV Park & Campground, 200
Skunk River, 58, 68, 285–86
Skunk River Cycles, 62
Skyline Motel, 336–37
Sleepy Hollow Sports Park, 39
Small Planet Restaurant and Bakery, 289
Smash, 51
Smith's Bed & Breakfast, 273
Smitty's Tenderloin Shop, 46, 119
Smokey Row Coffee (Oskaloosa), 301; (Pella), 80; (Pleasantville), 80
Smokin' Jakes, 318
smoking, 25
Snake Alley, 155–56
Snake Alley Criterium, 166
Snus Hill Winery, 93
Soap Box, The (East Davenport), 147
Soap Opera (Iowa City), 279–80
Soda Pop Saloon, 302
Soho Sushi Bar and Deli, 219
Solon, 271, 273; eating, 276
Somebody's Grille and Bar, 355
Sous le Sapins, 108
Southeast Iowa, 233–306; map, 232. *see also specific destinations*
Southeast Iowa Symphony, 291
Southern Hills Winery, 295
Southgate Inn, 186
Southwest Iowa, 365–83
special events: overview, 22, 25. *see also specific events*
special-value symbol, 6, 26
spelunking, 25–26, 111, 137, 247
Spencer, 315; eating, 317; lodging, 316
Spice Ames, 60
Spice of Life Delicatessen, 382–83
Spice Rack, 339
Spillville, 191, 194–95; lodging, 203
Spirit Lake, 311; camping, 317; eating, 317, 318; emergencies, 312; entertainment, 319; lodging, 316; shopping, 319; sights/activities, 314–15
Spirit Lake Massacre (1857), 311, 312–13
Spirit of Dubuque, 125
Spook Cave & Campground, 26, 111
Sportsplex West, 88
Spring Draft Horse Sale, 303
Spring Park, 185
Spring Valley, 79
Springbrook State Park, 42, 363
Springville: lodging, 249
Squiers Manor Bed and Breakfast, 140
Squirrel Cage Jail, 367
Squirrel's Nest Bed & Breakfast, 158
Stage Coach Inn, 339
Stage West, 50
Stanley: microbrewery, 200
Stanton, 371–78; camping, 376; eating, 376–77; events, 383, 384
Stanton Memorial Carillon, 56
Stanton Swedish Heritage and Cultural Center, 373
Star Cinema 16 and IMAX, 371
Star Restaurant & Ultra Lounge, 130
Star Spangled Spectacular, 383

Star Trek, 267, 304
Starlite Room, 252
Starr's Cave Nature Center & Preserve, 157
State Capitol, 36
State Center Memorial Rose Garden, 68
State Center Rose Festival, 96
State Historical Museum, 24, 36
state parks: overview, 26. *see also specific state parks*
Steamboat Rock, 152
Stein's, 72
Stephens Auditorium, 62
Stephens State Forest, 296
Stir Concert Cove, 368
Stockman House, 174
Stomping Grounds Café, 61
Stone City, 239; eating, 251; events, 304
Stone State Park, 324
Storm Lake, 330–34; camping, 333; eating, 333–34; emergencies, 331; entertainment, 334; events, 383; lodging, 332–33; shopping, 334; sights/activities, 331–32
Storm Lake Public Library, 331
Storm Lake State Marina, 332
Storm Lake Visitors Bureau, 330
Story, Joseph, 55
Story City, 55–61; camping, 59–60; eating, 60–61; events, 95–96, 98; information, 55; lodging, 59; sights/activities, 57–59
Story City Antique Carousel, 57–58
Story City Greater Chamber of Commerce, 55
Story County, 32, 55–62
StoryPeople, 197
Storytelling Festival, 98
Stratford: lodging, 345–46
Strawberry Farm B&B, 152–53
Strawtown, 78–80
Sturgis Falls Celebration, 229
Sugar Bowl Ice Cream Company, 206
Sugar Clay Winery and Vineyards, 349
Sugema, Lake, 285–86
Suites at Locust, 42
Sullivan, Louis, Jewel Box Bank, 259
Sullivan Brothers, 212–13
Sullivan Brothers Iowa Veterans Museum, 211, 212–13
Sully: eating, 72; lodging, 69
Sully Suites Hotel, 69
Sumerset, 105
Summerset State Park, 84
Summerset Winery, 84
Sundown Mountain, 126
Sunken Gardens, 78
Sunrise Campgrounds, 333
Sunrise Park, 332
Sunrise Pointe Golf Course, 332
Sunshine Mine Drive-In, 302
Surf Ballroom and Museum, 173
Susie's Kitchen, 377
Sutliff Cider Company, 247
Swamp Fox Pub & Grill, 80
Swan Lake, 336, 359
Swan Lake Campground, 359
Swan Lake Farmstead Museum, 359
Swedesburg, 283; events, 305
Swedish American Museum, 283
Swedish festivals, 305, 383
Sweeny's Supper Club, 129
Sweet Corn Festival, 22, 97
Sweet Fanny's, 324–25
Sweet Memories, 134
Sweet Temptations, 154
Swinging Bridge, 58
symbols, key to, 6–7

T

Tabor Home Vineyard & Winery, 137
Tama, 233; eating, 253; events, 305; sights/activities, 245, 247
Tama County Historical Museum, 245
Tanger Outlets, 265
Tantra Thai Bistro, 153
Tap't Out, 207
Taso's Steakhouse, 299–300
Taste Louisiana Cajun & Zydeco Festival, 303
Tasty Tacos, 46
Tatyanna's Kitchen, 253
taxes, 26
Taylor #4 Country School, 66
Taylor-Made Bed & Breakfast, 203
Taylor's Maid-Rite, 71
T-Bocks Sports Bar & Grill, 205
Tea Thyme at Sadies, 346–47
Teluwut Grille House & Pub, 189
Templeton Rye Spirits, 358
Temptations on Main, 61
Ten Thousand Villages, 223
tenderloin (pork tenderloin), best, 118–19
tennis, 26; Charles City, 185
Terrace Hill, 37–38
Terrible's Lakeside Casino, 296
Theatre Cedar Rapids, 254
Theatre Museum of Repertoire Americana, 282–83
Theatrical Shop, 52
13th Street Inn (Marshalltown), 72
This 'N That Eclectics, 319
Thornton House B&B, 107–8
360 Steakhouse, 370–71
Thurman: winery, 349
Thymeless Treasures, 190
Thymes Remembered Tea Room, 90
Tic Toc Restaurant & Flame Lounge, 95
Timberpine Lodge, 89
Timberview Bed & Breakfast, 375–76
time zone, 26
Tipton, 240; entertainment, 253; events, 305
Tipton Public Library, 240
Titonka, 344–45
Tivoli Fest, 383
TJ Hunters Pub & Grub, 109
Toads Bar and Grill, 221
Tobacco Bowl, 276
Toledo: lodging, 248; shopping, 255; sights/activities, 245
Tom-Tom Tap, 301
Tonic, 50
Toolesboro Indian Mounds, 156–57
Top of the Rock, 289
Torino's Pizza and Steakhouse, 289–90
tourist information, 23. *see also specific destinations*
Traer, 245, 305
traffic, 26

Trails End Lodge Inne Downtown, 218
Train Station (Calmar), 206
Trainland U.S.A., 66
Transcendental Meditation (TM), 284–85
Trattoria Tiramisu, 149
Treats Etc., 117
TrekFest, 304
Tremont Grille, 71
Tremont Inn on Main, 69, 71
Trimble-Parker Guest House, 288
Trinity Heights, 321
Trinity Regional Medical Center, 340
Troublesome Creek Float Trips, 284
Trout Run Trail, 201
Truckers Jamboree, 167
Tulip Festival (Orange City), 383
Tulip Time Festival (Pella), 75, 95
Turkey River, 195, 200
Tursi's Latin King, 45
Turtle Creek Trading Co., 189
Tuscan Moon Grill on Fifth, 274
Tuscany, 298–99
Twain, Mark, 101, 112, 115, 123
Tweeter's in Okoboji, 318
Tyson Events Center and Gateway Arena, 326

U

Ulrich's Meat Market, 81
Uncle Nancy's Coffeehouse and Eatery, 72
Under the Sun, 166
Underground Railroad, 16, 243, 288, 378
UNI. *See* University of Northern Iowa
UNI-Dome, 222
Union Pacific Railroad Museum, 368
Union Park, 40–41
Union Slough National Wildlife Refuge, 344–45
Union Station Visitor Center, 143
Unity Healthcare Hospital, 151
University Book & Supply (Cedar Falls), 223
University Inn (Ames), 59
University Inn (Cedar Falls), 218
University of Iowa, 242, 266, 280; museums, 268, 269; sporting events, 278–79
University of Iowa Athletics Hall of Fame and Museum, 269
University of Iowa Hospitals and Clinics, 267
University of Iowa Museum of Art, 269
University of Iowa Museum of Natural History, 268
University of Northern Iowa (UNI), 209, 221–22; museums, 211–12, 214
Upper Iowa River, 171, 191; canoeing and kayaking, 20, 199
Upper Mississippi River National Wildlife & Fish Refuge, 19, 101, 106
Uptown Café (Charles City), 189
Urbandale: eating, 46; lodging, 43; sights/activities, 36–37, 39
Ushers Ferry Historic Village, 245–46

V

Val Air Ballroom, 51
Valkommen House, 345–46
Valle Drive-In Theater, 72–73
Valley Junction, 53
value symbol, 6, 26
Van Buren County, 281–91
Van Buren County Water Trail, 283
Van Hemert's Dutch Oven Bakery and Koffie Huis, 94
Van Meter: sights/activities, 87–88
Vanberia, 208
Vander Veer Botanical Park, 148
Varsity Theatre, 50–51
Vaudeville Mews, 51
Vaughn's Café, 377
Vedic City, 284–85; lodging, 286
VEISHEA, 95
Ventura, 176; eating, 178
Vermeer Mill, 75
Vernon Inn a.k.a. The Greek Place, 252
Vesterheim Norwegian American Museum, 193, 196
Veterans Memorial Hospital, 103
Veteran's Plaza, 369
Victoria Bed & Breakfast & Studios (Fort Madison), 163
Victorian Home and Carriage House Museum (Cedar Falls), 211
Victorian Lace (Marion), 249
Viking Lake Restaurant & Concession, 376–77
Viking Lake State Park, 376
Viking Motel, 59
Viking Sites of Chickasaw County, 184
Viking Throne Chairs, 184
Village Cup and Cakes (Keosauqua), 290
Village Guest Suites (Amana), 263
Village Inn Motel (Des Moines), 43
Village of Froelich, 111
Villisca, 371–78; eating, 376; sights/activities, 372–74
Villisca Ax Murder House, 372
vineyards. *See* wineries
Vino's Restaurant, 250–51
Vinton: lodging, 249
visitor information, 23. *see also specific destinations*
Viva (Sioux City), 326
Vivo Restaurant (Fairfield), 289
Voas Nature Area, 89
Volga River Recreation Area, 201
Volksweg Trail, 78
Vortex Gifts, 279

W

Wabash Trace Trail, 369
Waffle Stop Grill, 220
Wagaman Mill, 66–67
Wahpeton: camping, 317; eating, 317; lodging, 315
Walcott, 146; events, 167
walking trails. *See* hiking
Wallace (Henry A.) Country Life Center, 379–80
Wallace Winery, 245
Wallashuk Recreation Area, 79
Walnut, 378–82; events, 381, 383; shopping, 380–81;

sights/activities, 378–81
Walnut Antique Show, 381, 383
Walnut Creek Historical Museum, 381
Walnut Manor, 187–88
Walter House, 214
W. A. McHenry House, 352–53
Wapello: lodging, 158
Wapello County, 292–303
Wapsipinicon Country Club, 247
Wapsipinicon Mill, 214
Wapsipinicon State Park, 26, 247, 249
Warren County, 82–86
Wasserbahn Waterpark, 260
water parks, 125–26, 215, 260, 295, 332
Water Works Park, 40
Waterfront Grill (Council Bluffs), 371
Waterfront Seafood Market (Des Moines), 44
Waterhawks Ski Shows, 223
Waterloo, 212–13; eating, 219–21; events, 228–29; sights/activities, 211–17
Waterloo Center for the Arts, 210
Waterloo Convention & Visitors Bureau, 209
Waterloo-Cedar Falls Symphony, 221–22
Watson's Grocery Store, 66
Watts Theatre, 190
Waukee, 88; eating, 90
Waukon: eating, 109; emergencies, 103
Waveland Café West, 90
Waverly: activities, 216; eating, 220
Waverly Horse Sale, 228
Wayne, John, birthplace of, 83
weather, 26
Webster City: eating, 346; shopping, 347
Wedge Pizzeria, 275
Welch Avenue Station, 61
Wells Bed & Breakfast, 43
Wells' Dairy, 326
Wells Fargo Arena, 39
West Amana Wood Shop, 265
West Bend, 340, 343; lodging, 345
West Branch, 235; eating, 250, 251; information, 236; shopping, 254; sights/activities, 240, 245
West Central Iowa, 348–64. *see also specific destinations*
West Glen, 53
West Side Family Restaurant, 264
West Union: eating, 206; entertainment, 207
Western Historic Trails Center, 367, 384
Western Inn, 370
Western Iowa, 309–84; map, 308. *see also specific destinations*
Westwood Golf Course, 68
Wheatsfield Co-op, 61
Whispering Breezes Resort Cabins, 298
Whispering Oaks Campground, 59–60
Whispering Pines Cabin, 203
White Buffalo Restaurant and Lounge, 300
White Deer of St. Ansgar, 183–84
White Oak Vineyards, 58–59
Whitebreast Beach, 78
Whitebreast Recreation Area, 79
Whiterock Conservancy and Resort, 358–60
Wickiup Hill Outdoor Learning Center, 247
Wild Rose Casino and Resort, 315
Wild Whisk Bistro, 164–65
Wildcat Den State Park, 152
Wilder, Laura Ingalls: Laura Days, 229; Museum, 196
Wildlife Lakes Elks Farm, 156
Wildwood Park & Golf Course, 185
Wileywood Restaurant, 315
Willard's Fur and Fashions, 73
William H. Black, 123
William Penn University, 292
William Woodward Discovery Center, 123
Williams, 225; lodging, 226–27
Williamsburg: eating, 264; shopping, 265
Williamson Tavern, 300
Willson, Meredith, 172; Boyhood Home, 174
Wilson Island Sate Recreation Area, 351
Wilton: eating, 153–54; lodging, 152–53
Wilton Candy Kitchen, 153–54
Winding Stairs, 245; Festival, 305
Windmill Park (Orange City), 329
windmills, 75, 327, 329, 357–58
wineries, 27; Adel, 88; Amana Colonies, 260–61; Ames, 58–59; Baldwin, 137; Bankston, 126; Cambridge, 58–59; Des Moines, 40; Exira, 359; Indianola, 83–84; Iowa Falls, 226; Madrid, 93; Marquette, 113; Osceola, 295; Pleasantville, 77; Tama, 247; Thurman, 349; West Branch, 245
Winifred's Restaurant, 250
Winnebago Indians, 16, 110–11, 172, 197, 321–22
Winnebago Industries Visitor Center, 344
Winnebago River, 184
Winnebago Trail, 175
Winneshiek County, 191–208
Winneshiek Medical Center, 192
Winterset: camping, 85; eating, 85; emergencies, 82; entertainment, 85; events, 98; information, 82; shopping, 85–86; sights/activities, 83–84
Winterset City Park, 84; campgrounds, 85
Witter Gallery, 332
Witte's End Coffee House, 253
Wood, Grant, 145, 152, 182, 210, 238–39, 321; about, 238–39; American Gothic House Center, 293–94; Art Festival, 304; Art Gallery, 239–40; Cedar Rapids Museum of Art, 239, 240, 243; Dubuque Museum of Art, 124; Studio and Visitor Center, 243
Wood Cellar (Hampton), 228
Woodland Interpretive Trail, 296
Woodward Wetland, 123

Work of Our Hands International Crafts, 81
World Food Prize, 98
World of Bikes, 271
World War I, 38, 106
World War II, 38, 185, 212–13, 342–43, 357
World's Largest Cheeto, 342
World's Largest Popcorn Ball, 335
World's Largest Town Square (Centerville), 294–95
World's Smallest Church (St. Anthony of Padua Chapel), 197
World's Window, 223
Worth Brewing Co., 175
Wrestling Hall of Fame, 192
Wrestling Institute and Museum, Dan Gable International, 210–11
Wright, Frank Lloyd: Cedar Rock: The Walter House, 214; Stockman House, 174
Wulfy's, 355
Wyth (George) House, 211
Wyth State Park, 216, 226

Y

Yellow Bird Art, 109
Yellow River, 103, 113, 114
Yellow River Forest, 106–7
Yellow Smoke Park, 353
Yellow Swan Bed & Breakfast, 89

Z

Zakeers, 346
Zanzibar's Coffee Adventure, 48
Zeno's Pizza, 72
Zimm's Antiques & Accessories, 381
Zio Johno's, 251
Zoey's Pizzeria, 252
zoos, 37, 57, 98, 342
Zuber's Homestead Hotel, 262